THE ROUTLEDGE HANDBOOK OF TOURISM IMPACTS

This handbook explores and critically examines both positive and negative impacts of tourism development focusing on the past, present and future issues, challenges and trends from a multidisciplinary global perspective. Through a comparative approach involving international case studies, this book explores our understanding of tourism impacts and contributes to the theoretical development on relationships between tourism impacts and community support for tourism development.

This handbook focuses on a variety of geographical locations, drawing from the knowledge and expertise of highly regarded academics from around the world. Specifically, it explores the adoption and implementation of various tourism development and impact management approaches in a wide range of global contexts, while identifying their trends, issues and challenges. It addresses strategies relating to innovation, sustainability and social responsibility, and critically reviews the economic, sociocultural, environmental, political and technological impacts of tourism. The text also identifies future trends and issues, as well as exploring the methods used to study tourism impacts.

Conveying the latest thinking and research, this handbook will be a key reference for students, researchers and academics of tourism, as well as development studies, geography, cultural studies, sustainability and business, encouraging dialogue across disciplinary boundaries and areas of study.

Dogan Gursoy is the Taco Bell Distinguished Professor in Hospitality Business Management at Washington State University in the School of Hospitality Business Management, and the editor of the *Journal of Hospitality Marketing & Management*. He is also the recipient of the Changjiang (Yangtze River) Scholar (长江学者) award from the Ministry of Education of the People's Republic of China. The Changjiang (Yangtze River) Scholar award is the highest academic award issued to an individual in higher education by the Ministry of Education of the People's Republic of China. He is also the developer and designer of the Hotel Simulation, a virtual management training game where participants are divided into teams and assigned the task of running 500-room hotels in a competitive virtual marketplace. The Hotel Business Management Training Simulation has been used for both revenue management and hospitality management purposes by several institutions. Dr. Gursoy is recognized as one of the leading researchers in the hospitality and tourism area. His area of research includes sustainability, services management, hospitality and tourism marketing, tourist behavior, travelers' information search behavior, community support for tourism development, cross-cultural studies, consumer behavior, involvement and generational leadership. His research has been published broadly. He has published more than 150 papers in refereed journals. His publications have received more than 13,000 citations to date. His research has also been presented at numerous hospitality and tourism conferences and received numerous research awards. Dr. Gursoy has recently been recognized as one of the top 10 authors in the world in terms of publications in the top six hospitality/tourism journals during the past decade (*Journal of Hospitality & Tourism Research* (2011), 35(3), 381–416).

Robin Nunkoo is an Associate Professor in the Department of Management, University of Mauritius. He is also a Visiting Senior Research Fellow at the University of Johannesburg, South Africa, and an Adjunct Professor at Griffith University, Australia. He holds a Ph.D. from the University of Waterloo, Canada. He is an economist by academic training, specializing in political economy. His current research draws widely from political science and investigates the interplay among citizens' trust (distrust) in government (and institutions), power issues in development, and political support for development and government policies. He also researches on corruption in government, voting behaviors of citizens, and political party affiliations in democratic economies, and is interested in citizens' political support for tourism policies and planning implemented by the government. He has been honored with the Emerging Scholar of Distinction Award 2014 by the International Academy for the Study of Tourism for exceptional contributions to tourism research. He is also the Associate Editor of the *Journal of Hospitality Marketing & Management*, a Resource Editor for *Annals of Tourism Research*, and the Regional Editor (Africa) for the *Journal of China Tourism Research*. He is also an editorial board member of several leading academic journals.

THE ROUTLEDGE HANDBOOK OF TOURISM IMPACTS

Theoretical and Applied Perspectives

Edited by Dogan Gursoy and Robin Nunkoo

LONDON AND NEW YORK

First published 2019
by Routledge
2 Park Square, Milton Park, Abingdon, Oxon OX14 4RN

and by Routledge
605 Third Avenue, New York, NY 10017

First issued in paperback 2022

Routledge is an imprint of the Taylor & Francis Group, an informa business

British Library Cataloguing-in-Publication Data
A catalogue record for this book is available from the British Library

Library of Congress Cataloging-in-Publication Data
Names: Gursoy, Dogan, author. | Nunkoo, Robin, author.
Title: The Routledge handbook of tourism impacts : theoretical and applied perspectives / Dogan Gursoy and Robin Nunkoo.
Description: Abingdon, Oxon ; New York, NY : Routledge, 2019. | Includes bibliographical references and index. |
Identifiers: LCCN 2018058246 (print) | LCCN 2019005569 (ebook) | ISBN 9781351025102 (eBook) | ISBN 9781138494961 (hardback : alk. paper) | ISBN 9781351025102 (ebk.)
Subjects: LCSH: Tourism—Handbooks, manuals, etc. | Tourism—Environmental aspects—Handbooks, manuals, etc. | Tourism—Political aspects—Handbooks, manuals, etc. | Tourism—Social aspects—Handbooks, manuals, etc.
Classification: LCC G155.A1 (ebook) | LCC G155.A1 G87 2019 (print) | DDC 338.4/791—dc23
LC record available at https://lccn.loc.gov/2018058246

ISBN 13: 978-1-138-49496-1 (hbk)
ISBN 13: 978-1-03-240153-9 (pbk)
ISBN 13: 978-1-351-02510-2 (ebk)

DOI: 10.4324/9781351025102

Typeset in Bembo
by Swales & Willis Ltd, Exeter, Devon, UK

CONTENTS

FIGURES

TABLES

CONTRIBUTORS

Syed Zamberi Ahmad holds a Ph.D. from Hull University Business School, UK. Among his research interests are firm evolution and growth strategies, including alliance, market entry and internationalization strategies of SMEs and multinational firms. His research interests also lie in the areas of entrepreneurial management, entrepreneurship education, technology innovation and small- and medium-sized business strategies. He is currently Professor of International Business and Entrepreneurship Management at the College of Business, Abu Dhabi University, United Arab Emirates. Prior to entering academia, he had several years' industrial experience in international banking and treasury with several reputable banks in Malaysia. Dr. Ahmad has served several universities in Malaysia, Yemen and Saudi Arabia.

Edina Ajanovic is a lecturer in the Tourism Faculty and she holds a Ph.D. from Akdeniz University, Tourism Faculty, Turkey. Her main research interests are in the use of ICT in the tourism and hospitality industry and online tourist behavior examined from the sociopsychological perspective.

Orhan Akova is a Full Professor in the Department of Tourism Management at Istanbul University, Turkey. He specializes in tourism studies. His research interests include the sociocultural impacts of tourism, sustainable tourism and management in tourism.

Erdem Aktaş is Research Assistant of Tourism in the Department of Tourism Management, Dokuz Eylul University, Turkey. He obtained his master's degree from Dokuz Eylul University Graduate School of Social Sciences, Department of Business Administration, Division of Management and Organization, in Turkey, in 2010. He is working on his Ph.D. at Dokuz Eylul University Graduate School of Social Science, in the Department of Tourism Management. His research interests include responsible tourism, organizational justice, total quality management and smart technologies.

Nada Al-Sabri earned her bachelor's degree in Electrical Engineering from United Arab Emirates University in Al Ain, in 2001. She also earned the degree of Executive Master in Business Management Administration from Zayed University, United Arab Emirates, in 2009, and completed her Doctorate in Business Administration in 2018, at Abu Dhabi University.

Carlos Alberto Alves is a Professor of the graduate program in Hospitality at Anhembi Morumbi University, Brazil. He holds a Ph.D. in Administration (Marketing) from Nove de Julho University, Brazil, and an M.Sc. in Administration (Business Networks) from Paulista University, Brazil. His research investigates the relationship between hospitality and organizational competitiveness in service companies. He is a member of the Marketing Science Institute and, in Brazil, he is a member of the National Association of Graduate and Research in Administration (ANPAD) and the National Association of Graduate Research and Tourism (ANPTUR).

Sevinç Aslan is a research assistant in the Tourism Management Department at Istanbul University, Turkey. She also has a Ph.D. degree in Tourism Management from Istanbul University. Her research interests include tourism entrepreneurship and small- and medium-sized enterprises.

Ozan Atsiz is a research assistant at Bozok University, Turkey, and a Ph.D. candidate in the Department of Tourism at Istanbul University. His research interests are destination marketing and length of stay.

Solmaz L. Azarmi, a Ph.D. candidate in tourism management, is the Head and Instructor of the Tourism Management Department of Cyprus Science University. Solmaz Azarmi Lafmajani's research area concerns forecasts of solid waste generation by the tourism and hospitality industry, the environmental impact of tourism, water pollution and the reutilization of waste.

Christina Beckmann works closely with small businesses, social enterprises, international development agencies, governments and foundations. In addition to managing AdventureEDU, Christina leads the Adventure Travel Trade Association's research program, prioritizing research needs and developing projects to address them. She has served as an advisor to the National Geographic Center for Sustainable Development and the World Travel and Tourism Council and to start-up technology companies providing services to the adventure travel market. She holds a B.A. in Communication from Cornell University, USA, an M.A. in Communication, Culture and Technology from Georgetown University, USA, and an MBA with a concentration on Entrepreneurship from American University, USA. Originally from Alaska, Christina now lives in San Francisco, California.

Serkan Bertan is an Associate Professor in the Department of Tourism Management, the Faculty of Tourism, Pamukkale University, Turkey. He completed his Ph.D. in the Department of Tourism Management in Dokuz Eylul University, Turkey, in 2006. His research interests are hospitality management, social media marketing, technology and management information systems in tourism.

Edward C. Bolden, III, is the Associate Director of Institutional Research at Case Western Reserve University, USA. He received his Ph.D. in Evaluation and Measurement from Kent State University, USA, where he serves as an adjunct instructor and conducts research with faculty from the Hospitality Management program. His area of research interest is applied statistics and research design, particularly within the field of tourism and hospitality management.

Richard Butler is Emeritus Professor at Strathclyde University, Scotland. A geographer, he has taught in Canada, the UK, Holland and Italy. He has published more than 20 books and

100 papers on tourism. A past president of the International Academy for the Study of Tourism, he was awarded the UNWTO Ulysses medal for excellence in the creation and dissemination of knowledge.

Neil Carr is Professor and Head of Department of Tourism at the University of Otago, New Zealand. In addition, he has been the editor of the *Annals of Leisure Research* since 2013. Neil's research focuses on understanding behavior within tourism and leisure experiences, with a particular emphasis on animals, children and families, and sex. His publications include, among others, *Tourism and Animal Welfare* (with Don Broom; CABI) and *Dogs in the Leisure Experience* (CABI).

Sedat Çelik is Assistant Professor in the Department of Tourism Management, Şırnak University, Turkey. His doctorate was on the quality of the destination. He works in the fields of hotel management and tourism social psychology. He is also a referee for scientific journals.

Zhe Cheng is a doctoral student at the University of Waikato's China–New Zealand Tourism Research Unit, in New Zealand, and is completing his doctoral research on issues relating to place attachment and intergenerational change.

Beykan Çizel is a Dean of Akdeniz University, Tourism Faculty in Antalya, Turkey. His research interests cover the fields of tourist behavior and tourism management, with a focus on a sociopsychological perspective of tourist behavior. He is also Editor-in-Chief of *Advances in Hospitality & Tourism Research Journal*.

Dante Di Matteo is a Postdoctoral Fellow in Applied Economics at Politecnico di Milano (DAStU). He obtained his Ph.D. in Economics and Business in 2016. His major research interests include regional economics, cohesion policies and tourism management studies.

Mithat Zeki Dinçer is a Professor Doctor in the Faculty of Economics at Istanbul University, Turkey. His research interests include economics, tourism economics and sustainable tourism.

Reem Bahaa ElMasry is currently a lecturer in the Department of Hotels and Tourism, College of Management and Technology, Arab Academy for Science, Technology and Maritime Transport, Egypt. She obtained her B.Sc. and M.Sc. from the University of Alexandria, Egypt, and her Ph.D. from the University of Helwan, Egypt. Since 1992, she has been working at the College of Management and Technology. In 2012, she was appointed Head of the Quality Assurance Unit and, in 2013, she was appointed Head of the Hotels and Tourism Department. She shared in the design of the curriculum and the development of courses within the department. She has participated in and attended lots of local, regional and international conferences. She has participated in the organization of, and attended, a number of workshops discussing a variety of topics related to the hotel and tourism industry. She has been part of the college team for the attainment of national and international accreditation for the college and the department. She has published papers in local and international journals and conference proceedings, in addition to supervising M.Sc. students.

Sheereen Fauzel is a Senior Lecturer at the University of Mauritius. Having completed a Ph.D. in International Economics at the University of Mauritius, a master's degree in

Banking and Finance and a bachelor's degree in Economics and Finance, her areas of expertise are international economics, development economics and related areas. She has participated in international conferences and has publications in notable international journals of business, economics and tourism. She is a reviewer for a number of refereed journals, including *Current Issues in Tourism* and *Journal of Hospitality Marketing & Management*, among others.

Ahmet Bülend Göksel is the Rector of Cyprus Science University. Dr. Goksel received his Ph.D. in Marketing from Ege University, Turkey. He has published different books on the topics of strategic public relations management, strategic fair management, basic public relations information and basic marketing information. His research focus is on management and marketing, which are important issues in the current world situation.

Johan Hattingh is Lecturer in Tourism Management in the Department of Tourism and Event Management, Central University of Technology, South Africa.

Mahmoud M. Hewedi is currently Emeritus Professor in the Department of Hotel Studies, Faculty of Tourism and Hotels, Fayoum University, Egypt. He obtained his B.Sc., M.Sc. and Ph.D. from the University of Cairo, Egypt. He is the founder and former Dean (1993–2003) of the Faculty of Tourism and Hotels at Fayoum University. In January 2004, he was appointed the Egyptian Educational Chancellor at the Egyptian Embassy in Tripoli. Through 1980–2003, he supervised several postdoctoral and visiting scholars at University College Cork in Ireland, North East Wales Institute, the University of Salford and Cardiff Metropolitan University in the UK, and the University of Kiel in Germany. Throughout his academic life he has made several short visits to the Universities of Maryland and Kansas State (USA); the University of Bournemouth (UK) and the University of Alberta (Canada). He is the Editor of *The Fayoum Journal of Tourism and Hospitality*, has supervised almost 30 M.Sc. and Ph.D. students, and has published more than 70 articles, internationally and locally, on different aspects of food and dairy sciences and related subjects, including waste management. After he was appointed Dean to establish the Faculty of Tourism and Hotels in 1994, he shifted his research focus towards tourism and hospitality studies, with 30 different publications on education quality, sense of place and travel life cycle. He has participated in and attended tens of local conferences as keynote speaker and some international ones. In 2010, he was granted the Fayoum University Pioneers Award for Social Sciences. He is affiliated to work as peer reviewer and trainer at the National Authority for Quality Assurance Accreditation of Education. Additionally, he was a member of the Supreme Council of Universities Committee for academic promotion for two decades and has published four books in Arabic on tourism, hospitality, and food and beverages.

Onur Icoz is Assistant Professor of Tourism Management in the Department of Travel Management, Faculty of Tourism, Adnan Menderes University, Turkey. He obtained his Ph.D. in Tourism Management from Dokuz Eylul University, Turkey, in 2013. His research interests include marketing in tourism, social media marketing, sport tourism and destination branding.

Orhan Icoz is Professor of Tourism Management in the Department of Tourism Guidance, Faculty of Economics and Business Administration, Yasar University, Turkey. He obtained his

Ph.D. in Tourism Management from Dokuz Eylul University, Turkey, in 1987. His research interests include the economics of travel and tourism, tourism and hospitality marketing, tourism planning and policy.

Grace Kamanga is a lecturer in the Department of Tourism at Mzuzu University, Malawi. She holds a master's degree in Tourism from the University of Otago, New Zealand. She has been a lecturer in the tourism field since 2012. Her research interests are tourism impacts and sustainability, corporate social responsibility and destination management.

Kornélia Kiss, former head of the Research Department of the Hungarian National Tourist Office, is an Associate Professor and Head of the Tourism Department of Corvinus University of Budapest, Hungary. She obtained her Ph.D. in subjective quality of life, and her research interests include well-being and different aspects of consumer behavior in tourism.

Özge Kocabulut completed her master's program in Tourism Management at Akdeniz University, Turkey, in 2015. She has continued her Ph.D. program in Tourism Management at Akdeniz University since 2015. She has several published and submitted papers about niche marketing, consumer behavior, cultural heritage and service quality in the tourism journals and conference proceedings. She works as a research assistant at Pamukkale University, Turkey, in the Tourism Faculty.

Deserè Kokt is Associate Professor of Human Resource Management in the Department of Business Management, Central University of Technology, South Africa.

John Koldowski is a Foreign Expert in Tourism within the School of Tourism at Leshan Normal University in China's Sichuan Province. Previously he was with the College of Innovation at Thammasat University in Thailand, after leaving his position as Deputy CEO of the Pacific Asia Travel Association. John is interested in the changing dynamics of traveler profiles and movements across the Asia Pacific region, as well as the factors that drive those changes.

Ayman Kole studied intensively at the University of Sydney, Australia, completing a B.A. degree with a triple major: English, Performance Studies and Studies in Religion. He also completed an M.A. in English in 2006, at the same university, and wrote the short story "The Mirror," which was the *Phoenix* journal finalist, published by Sydney University Press. He has worked as a writer for various publications and as a lecturer in English, Film and Creative Writing at various universities. He has completed his Ph.D. in History, English and Creative Writing from Charles Stuart University. He is the author of the historical novel *Mark of the Crescent* and writer/editor of academic books. He worked as a lecturer and Head of Department at the American University in Cyprus, the Head of English at Ada Kent University, Cyprus, and is currently the Dean of Students at Cyprus Science University.

Edina Kovács is a Ph.D. student in the Tourism Department of Corvinus University of Budapest, Hungary, and an Assistant Research Fellow in the Tourism Department of Budapest Business School. Her research topic is the relationship between tourism employment and quality of life and well-being in the case of seniors. Her research interests also include the application of findings of behavioral economics in the field of tourism.

Avşar Kurgun is Professor of Tourism in the Department of Tourism Management, Dokuz Eylul University, Turkey. He obtained his Ph.D. in Tourism Management from Dokuz Eylul University, Turkey, in 1999 and became a Professor in 2014. He was the the the Dean of Dokuz Eylül University Reha Midilli Foça Faculty of Tourism. He was the Training Manager and the Quality Management Representative at Sheraton Çeşme Hotel (2000–2001) and served as Vice President and Educational Manager of the athletes' village at the 23rd Universiade Games in İzmir (2004–2005). His research interests include total quality management, organizational behavior, Web 4.0 and smart destinations.

Adjnu Damar Ladkoo is a senior lecturer from the Department of Management, at the University of Mauritius. Her teaching and research interests are in the fields of marketing, communication, sales, negotiation and sustainable tourism development. She has been part of international conferences and published research articles on: guerrilla marketing, consumer buying behaviours, marketing ethics, sustainable tourism development and climate change amongst others. In her research works, she also likes to explore new multi-disciplinary trends and emerging issues in either local or international contexts. As a Ph.D. candidate, her doctoral study is focused on sustainable tourism development and she is keen to continue to contribute to the world of knowledge.

Eric Laws is Visiting Research Fellow at the University of Surrey, UK. He was previously Professor at Siam University, Bangkok. Eric has a Ph.D. from Griffith University and an M.Phil. from the University of Surrey, UK. He is the author or editor of 18 books on tourism management topics, including service quality, marketing, destination impacts, crisis recovery and structural relations in the tourism industry.

Li Linrui completed her master's degree at the University of Waikato, New Zealand, in 2017 and is currently working and exploring the South Island in New Zealand before deciding what she may do next.

Sandra Maria Correia Loureiro (Ph.D.) is a Professor at Instituto Universitário de Lisboa (ISCTE-IUL) Portugal, Business Research Unit (BRU/UNIDE) and SOCIUS. She is the director of Ph.D. program in Tourism Management and the coordinator of the Management Ph.D. specialization of Marketing. Her current research interests include consumer–brand relationships and engagement and tourism marketing issues. Her papers have been published in a variety of peer-reviewed journals that include the *International Journal of Hospitality Management, Journal of Travel & Tourism Marketing, Journal of Retailing, Journal of Service Management, Journal of Cleaner Production, Journal of Brand Management* and *Online Information Review*. Her work has also been presented at respected international conferences such as EMAC, ANZMAC and KAMS-GMC. Sandra serves as a reviewer for several international journals and conferences and has participated in several research projects funded by the EU and Foundation for Science and Technology.

Roseane Barcellos Marques is a Professor of the graduate program in Hospitality at Anhembi Morumbi University, Brazil. She holds a Ph.D. in Public Administration and Government from Fundação Getúlio Vargas and an M.Sc. in Political Economy from the Pontifical Catholic University of São Paulo, both in Brazil. Her most recent work focuses on hospitality studies in thematic discussions such as: "new" economics, social networks in economic sociology, contemporary slave labor, competitiveness in organizations, formal institutions and information, and general systems theory. These are analyzed from the perspective of Brazil's socioeconomic reality or revealed in a fragment of its territory. She is a member of the Regional Council of Economics (CORECON) and the National Association of Graduate Research and Tourism (ANPTUR), in Brazil.

Gábor Michalkó is Professor of Tourism in the Tourism Department of Corvinus University of Budapest, Hungary, and a scientific advisor at the Geographical Institute of MTA. His recent research interests include urban tourism, shopping tourism, and the relationship between tourism and quality of life. He has published eight books and nearly 150 scientific articles.

Gerald Milanzi is a lecturer in the Faculty of Tourism, Hospitality and Management Studies at Mzuzu University in Malawi and is currently a Ph.D. candidate in the Department of Management of the University of Leicester in England. His current research project focuses on exploring ethnic and indigenous entrepreneurship in Malawi.

Karla "Gabbie" Morrison is a master's student in Communication Studies at Ball State University, Indiana, USA

Dan Musinguzi is an Assistant Professor in the Department of Tourism Management of Stenden University of Applied Science, Qatar. He holds a Ph.D. in Tourism Management from the Hong Kong Polytechnic University and a master's degree in Heritage and Cultural Management from the University of the Witwatersrand, South Africa. His research interests include tourism impacts, residents' attitudes to and perceptions of tourism, pro-poor tourism, sustainable tourism, cultural heritage preservation, tourism planning and development, knowledge development in tourism, and others. Dan publishes research in academic journals and conference proceedings and is an active reviewer of research papers for academic journals and conferences.

Perunjodi Naidoo is a Senior Lecturer in the School of Sustainable Development and Tourism, University of Technology, Mauritius. She was awarded a Ph.D. in Tourism in 2014. Her main research areas relate to tourism development and hospitality management. She is particularly interested in tourism development in small island developing states, the well-being of destination communities, enclave tourism, agritourism, tourism in emerging markets, and the tourism experience. She has published in journals such as *Current Issues in Tourism*, *Journal of Destination Management & Marketing*, *Managing Service Quality*, and *International Journal of Quality and Service Sciences*.

Annmarie Nicely is Associate Professor in Hospitality & Tourism, Purdue University, Indiana, USA. She is also lead researcher in the School's Visitor Harassment Research Unit.

Eugenio Njoloma received a Master of Social Science degree in International Studies from Rhodes University, South Africa. He taught Political Studies at the Catholic University of Malawi prior to obtaining a lecturing position in the Department of Governance, Peace and Security Studies at Mzuzu University in Malawi. His research interests embrace the areas of peace and conflict studies and development studies.

Akeem A. Oladipo is an Associate Professor of Material and Environmental Chemistry at Cyprus Science University. Dr. Oladipo gained a Ph.D. in Chemistry from Eastern Mediterranean

University, Cyprus, and is a research chemist with a specialized focus on wastewater treatment using eco-friendly and sustainable treatment techniques. His research interests include the fabrication of high-performance nano fluids, functional materials, controlled drug release, green super capacitors, corrosion inhibition, and solar energy harvesting and biomass conversion.

Avraam Papastathopoulos is currently an Assistant Professor of Management at the University of Abu Dhabi. He has a diversified international experience of 15 years in various positions such as external auditor (Ernst & Young), Manager of Strategic Planning (Svimservice Hellas), Head of Business & Economics Department (Metropolitan College in Athens, Greece) and Deputy Director of Academic Quality (Metropolitan College in Athens, Greece). He teaches various courses including Strategic Management, Business Research Methods, and Strategic Dimensions of Business Functions in the on-campus undergraduate and postgraduate programs. His scientific and research interests mainly focus on strategic management, organizational behavior and tourism studies. Special emphasis is placed on sustainability, corporate social responsibility and green strategies and their impact on innovation, internationalization and business performance of small and medium-sized enterprises. He has published articles in well-known international refereed journals and has been active in presenting papers at international conferences and symposia.

Ivett Pinke-Sziva is an Associate Professor and the leader of the B.A. program in Hospitality and Tourism in the Tourism Department of Corvinus University of Budapest, Hungary. Ivett has a particular interest in research into destination management and competitiveness, as well as health tourism, especially from well-being aspects, and sustainability issues.

Roya Rahimi is a reader in Tourism and Hospitality Management at the University of Wolverhampton, UK. She teaches across the subject areas of tourism, hospitality and events and supervises undergraduate/postgraduate dissertations and Ph.D. students. Her research interests are innovation, big data, customer relationship management, organisational culture, gender equality and tourism higher education. Her work has been published in top-tier journals such as the *Annals of Tourism Research, Journal of Tourism & Hospitality Research, Journal of Travel & Tourism Marketing, International Journal of Contemporary Hospitality Management* and *Anatolia*. Her work has also been presented at various international conferences and appears in book chapters released by Routledge, CABI, Emerald and IGI. Roya is the regional editor (Europe) for the *Journal of Hospitality & Tourism Insights* and also book reviews editor for the *Journal of Hospitality & Tourism Management (JHTM)*. She sits on the editorial board of different leading journals including the *Journal of Hospitality & Tourism Technology, European Management Review, European Journal of Tourism Research, JHTM* and *The International Journal of Tourism Sciences*. Roya is also co-editing a special issue on big data in the tourism and hospitality industry for the *Journal of Hospitality & Tourism Technology*. She received the Valene L. Smith Prize for the best presented paper at the International Conference of Service Quality in Hospitality & Tourism in Isfahan in 2016. In 2017 she was nominated and shortlisted for her outstanding contribution to research in the University of Wolverhampton's Vice Chancellor awards for staff excellence. In 2017 one of her papers, "Impact of Customer Relationship Management on Customer Satisfaction: The Case of a Budget Hotel Chain" became the most-read paper of the year in tourism and hospitality journals published by Taylor & Francis.

Haywantee Rumi Ramkissoon is a Research Professor of Tourism Marketing. She works at Curtin University and Monash University in Australia, and the University of Johannesburg, South Africa and in Europe. She is recognized for her contribution to innovative and ground-breaking tourism research by the International Academy for the Study of Tourism. Dr. Ramkissoon has published widely in reputable journals such as *Tourism Management, Annals of Tourism Research, Journal of Sustainable Tourism, Journal of Travel Research* and *Journal of Hospitality Marketing & Management*, and she sits on the editorial board of several prestigious journals and on international scientific committees. She is the Book Review Editor for *Current Issues in Tourism*, and Research Note Editor for the *Journal of Hospitality Marketing & Management*. She is a reviewer for more than 45 peer-reviewed journals. Dr. Ramkissoon has served as Director of Research (Tourism) and on judging panels of the International Research & Development Grant Councils. She works closely with industry partners and academic institutions and organizations and disseminates her work through conferences, workshops and seminars. She has been a visiting professor and scholar at several reputable international universities and research councils in North America, Asia, Europe, Africa and Australasia, and has been a contributor as keynote speaker, panellist and presenter at national and international academic and industry events.

Prabha Ramseook-Munhurrun is a Senior Lecturer in the School of Sustainable Development and Tourism at the University of Technology, Mauritius. She received her Ph.D. in 2013. Her research interests include customer service experience, destination marketing and management, service quality, consumer behavior, and sustainable development with particular emphasis on sustainable tourism development and sustainable consumption. She has published numerous journal articles and presented several conference papers in these subject areas.

Donald G. Reid is University Professor Emeritus in the School of Environmental Design and Rural Development at the University of Guelph, Canada. Dr. Reid's research focuses on community development and social planning, as well as tourism and leisure planning. Don's work is centered in Canada and Africa. Publications focus on community development, tourism, leisure and the marginalized in society. He has authored four books, numerous book chapters and journal articles, as well as a number of professional reports on these subjects.

João Romão is a Lecturer in Tourism and Regional Economics at Hokkaido University (Japan) and Researcher at the University of Algarve (Portugal), where he obtained his Ph.D. in Tourism. He also holds an M.Sc. in Economics and Management of Science of Technology (University of Lisbon, Portugal) and he has international research experience in environmental studies (Yale University, USA) and spatial economics (Vrije Universiteit Amsterdam, the Netherlands). His research interests and consultancy experience also include aspects related to innovation systems and urban planning. He is a co-chair of the Cluster on Tourism, Leisure and Recreation of the Network on European Communications and Transport Activities Research and a founding member of the Regional Science Academy.

João Ferreira do Rosário, Ph.D., is full-time Marketing Professor-Adjunct at Escola Superior de Comunicação Social (ESCS), Instituto Politécnico de Lisboa, Portugal, coordinator of an ESCS Research Line and member of the Scientific Council. He has a Ph.D. in Management from the Instituto Superior de Economia e Gestão, University of Lisbon, Portugal, and a master's degree from Universidade Católica Portuguesa Business School, Portugal. He is a research fellow at ICML and has published articles in scientific journals, made presentations at conferences and has been a coordinator of European academic projects such as Businet-HedCom, REVE-IP "Business Game" or IP ISTAR-DOT-Erasmus. His research areas are strategic marketing, competition and pricing, marketing analytics and marketing information systems.

Chris Ryan is Professor of Tourism at the University of Waikato, New Zealand. He is director of the Raglan INSTO initiative, editor of *Tourism Management* and has more than 200 refereed journal articles and 14 books to his name.

Eduardo Moraes Sarmento, Ph.D., is a Professor at Lusófona University (ULHT) and a researcher at the same university as well as at CEsA (ISEG – University of Lisbon), both in Portugal. His research interests include various topics such as tourism and sustainability, consumer–brand relationships and engagement and tourism marketing issues. He has written several international papers in a variety of respected peer-reviewed journals. He has been invited to attend several international conferences as an expert. Eduardo is an international reviewer for several international journals and conferences. Finally, he is also an international consultant in the areas of tourism management and sustainability and auditing.

Noel Scott is Professor of Tourism Management in the Sustainability Research Centre of the University of Sunshine Coast. He was previously Deputy Director, Griffith Institute for Tourism, Australia. His research interests include the study of tourism experiences, destination management and marketing, and stakeholder organization. He has had more than 210 academic articles published, and his publications include 13 books. He is on the editorial board of 10 journals and is a member of the International Association of China Tourism Scholars.

Boopen Seetanah is an Associate Professor at the University of Mauritius (UoM), with research interests in tourism and transport economics, international trade and finance, and development economics. He is also currently the Co-Chair of the WTO Chair (UoM) and the Director of Research at the International Center for Sustainable Tourism and Hospitality at the UoM. Boopen has worked as a consultant with the local government and also numerous organizations including the UNEP, UNDP, World Bank, ADB, ILO and RMCE, among others.

Sagar Singh is Senior Researcher and anthropologist with the Centre for Tourism Research & Development, Lucknow, India. He is former editor of the international journal, *Tourism Recreation Research*. Having authored many books on tourism and anthropology, he has also worked as a journalist on leading newspapers and magazines and has written two books of poems.

Vishnee Sowamber is a sustainable development strategist who provides real solutions to issues through multi-stakeholder dialogues and project implementations for Mauritius, Réunion Island, Maldives, China and different stakeholders in South Africa, Europe, US, Asia, among others. She has very strong leadership skills that drive decision-making for strategic reviews, irrespective of the amount of available or unavailable resources (projects such as the Global Reporting Initiative, Integrated Annual Report, the Stock Exchange of Mauritius Sustainability Index, carbon offsetting – the Tread Lightly project – energy efficiency projects, water optimization, waste management, social projects management in collaboration with bodies such as UNDP, various national and international consultants, among others). She has geared projects in line with international sustainability frameworks (Global Reporting Initiative, Montreal Greenhouse Gas Protocol, the UK Department of Environment, Food & Rural Affairs, Hotel Carbon Management Initiative), including sensitization on human rights, social responsibilities and environmental protection.

Wantanee Suntikul, Ph.D., is an educator in the School of Hotel and Tourism Management at the Hong Kong Polytechnic University, Hong Kong. Dr. Wantanee Suntikul's recent books include *Tourism and Political Change*, *Tourism and Political Change* (2nd edition), *Tourism and War* and *Tourism and Religion: Issues and Implications*. She is also Joint Editor-in-Chief of the journal *Tourism, Culture & Communication*. Her other interests include gastronomy and tourism.

Ozlem Tekin is a lecturer in the Tourism and Hotel Management Department of Bandirma Onyedi Eylul University, Turkey. By profession, she is a tourist guide. Tekin's major research interests are technology-based marketing, augmented reality marketing in tourism destinations, touristic product diversification, service quality of tour guides and destination management. Her master's thesis topic was "Within the Scope of Touristic Product Diversification, Ecotourism Routes in Konya," where she researched alternative ecotourism routes with map references and proposed promoting the new routes with destination stakeholders. Her Ph.D. thesis topic was "Usage of Augmented Reality Applications in Destination Marketing – The Case of Travel Agencies." This Ph.D. thesis is one of the foremost pieces of research about augmented reality marketing for tourism in Turkey. Her publications on ecotourism, religious tourism and cultural heritage management have appeared in many conference proceedings, journals and books.

Mary Anne Ramos Tumanan completed her doctoral studies at the China–New Zealand Tourism Research Unit, New Zealand, examining the concepts of place attachment and social change in three rural villages in Anhui Province, China. She lectures at the University of the Philippines and was involved in the Raglan project from 2016 to 2018.

Roozbeh Vaziri is an Assistant Professor of Mechanical Engineering at Cyprus Science University. Dr. Vaziri gained a Ph.D. in Mechanical Engineering from Eastern Mediterranean University, Cyprus. Dr. Vaziri invented the new type of solar air heater with 90% efficiency. Dr. Vaziri's focus of research is on renewable energy, nano technology, environmental issues and sustainable development.

Paige P. Viren is at San Francisco State University and studies consumer behavior and tourism, with a focus on adventure travel and sustainable community-based tourism in rural areas. She has worked closely with the Adventure Travel Trade Association examining adventure industry issues and trends, and in rural communities in eastern North Carolina, working in developing sustainable community-based tourism as an alternative means of diversifying the economy. Over 12 years of travel industry experience provides Dr. Viren with valuable insight into the importance of translating research into practical applications. She was selected as the 2012–2013 Outstanding Faculty Affiliate for the Center for Sustainable Tourism and given the University Scholarship of Engagement award for 2015–2106. Paige holds a B.S. and an M.E. in Recreation and Tourism Studies from Bowling Green State University, USA, and a Ph.D. in Park, Recreation & Tourism Resources from Michigan State University, USA.

Elizabeth Kyoko Wada is a Professor of Hospitality and Competitiveness in Services and coordinates the graduate program in Hospitality (M.Sc. and Ph.D.) at Anhembi Morumbi University, Brazil. Her work focuses on hospitable and hostile relationships and the consequences in a business environment, with impacts on the competitiveness of an organization. She holds a Ph.D. and an M.Sc. in Sciences of Communication, an MBA in Marketing and an undergraduate degree in Tourism and Public Relations. Besides the academic career, she has been a practitioner in the tourism and hotel industries since 1976. She serves as Director of Admin and Finance at the National Association of Research and Graduate Programs, as the VP Finance of the MPI-Brazil Chapter and as a board member of Bourbon Hotels and Resorts.

Nisan Yozukmaz is a Research Assistant in the Department of Tourism Management, Pamukkale University, Turkey. She is continuing her Ph.D. education in the Department of Tourism Management in Mugla Sıtkı Koçman University, Turkey. Her research interests include tourist behavior, tourist psychology, tourism marketing and tourism sociology.

Fisun Yüksel, Ph.D., is Professor of Marketing at the University of Adnan Menderes, Turkey. She completed her Ph.D. at Sheffield Hallam University, UK. She has published in *Tourism Management*, *Journal of Hospitality & Tourism Research*, *Journal of Travel & Tourism Marketing*, *Annals of Tourism Research* and *Journal of Vacation Marketing*. She has co-authored one book and several book chapters. Her research interests include tourism planning, service marketing, destination branding and technology related marketing.

INTRODUCTION TO TOURISM IMPACTS

Robin Nunkoo and Dogan Gursoy

Introduction

Tourism impacts and sustainability

Tourism is a growing contributor to many national economies. The World Travel and Tourism Council (WTTC) estimates that the direct contribution of tourism to GDP was US$2,570.1 bn (3.2% of total GDP) in 2017, and it was forecast to rise by 4.0% in 2018, and by 3.8% per annum from 2018 to 2028, to US$3,890.0 bn (3.6% of total GDP) in 2028. In terms of employment, the industry contributed to 118,454,000 jobs in 2017, representing around 3.8% of total employment. This figure is expected to rise to 4.2% in 2028 (WTTC, 2018). In view of its economic implications, many countries desire an expansion in tourism, a sector that few governments can afford to neglect. At a destination level, tourism is a major contributor to economic development, generates income and foreign exchange, creates new employment opportunities for local people, and helps diversify the local economy (Boley, McGehee, and Hammett, 2017; Latkova and Vogt, 2012; Park, Nunkoo, and Yoon, 2015; Tohmo, 2018; Torre and Scarborough, 2017; Yu, Chancellor, and Cole, 2011). Rural communities experiencing economic decline and hardships have also adopted tourism as a new economic development strategy (Látková and Vogt, 2012; Park et al., 2015; Su, Wall, Wang, and Jin, 2019). The tourism sector has also been considered as a vehicle for preserving the environment, culture, and heritage of the host destination. In view of the economic, environmental, and sociocultural implications of tourism development, residents often consider the sector as a way of strengthening the local economy and improving their quality of life (Andriotis and Vaughan, 2003; Eusébio, Vieira, and Lima, 2018; Gursoy, Ouyang, Nunkoo, and Wei, 2018; Hao, Long, and Kleckley, 2011; Nunkoo and Gursoy, 2012; Nunkoo and Ramkissoon, 2011a, 2011b, 2012).

However, development of tourism is also accompanied by several economic, social, cultural, and environmental costs that affect the lives of local residents (Andereck and Nyaupane, 2011; Liu, Sheldon, and Var, 1987; Long, Perdue, and Allen, 1990; Perdue, Long, and Allen, 1987; Postma and Schmuecker, 2017; Ward and Berno, 2011). The tourism sector has been found to disturb, disrupt, and destroy local communities and bring changes that negatively affect residents' daily lives (Látková and Vogt, 2012; Nunkoo and Ramkissoon, 2010a, 2010b; Nunkoo, Smith, and Ramkissoon, 2013; Postma and Schmuecker, 2017; Stronza Gordillo, 2008). The negative consequences of tourism development have led to growing concerns for the conservation and preservation of natural resources, human well-being, and the long-term economic prosperity of host communities (Haralambopoulos and Pizam, 1996; Healy, 1994; Nunkoo and Smith, 2013; Saarinen, 2006). If the negative impacts of tourism are not managed, the local population can easily turn to open hostility toward the sector's development, eventually contributing to the destination's decline (Harrill, 2004). Residents' negative perceptions toward tourism development also affect tourist satisfaction and the image of a destination (Millar, Collins, and Jones, 2017; Prayag, Hassibi, and Nunkoo, 2018).

The majority of studies on the impacts of tourism are grounded in the principles of sustainable tourism, which emanates from the concept of sustainable development (Lo, King, and Mackenzie, 2017; Nunkoo and Gursoy, 2016). The latter concept was made popular following the publication of the book *Report of the World Commission on Environment and Development: Our Common Future* (Brundtland, 1987). Generally, definitions of sustainable development focus on two aspects. The first component of the definition relates to the meaning of development and the conditions necessary for sustainability (Miltin, 1992), where development implies a process which raises people's standard of living (Bartelmus, 1986). Dudley (1993) argues that development is not only about increasing wealth but also means changes in behavior, aspirations, and the ways in which people perceive the world around them. Development, therefore, not only is concerned with institutional and economic changes but also involves broader concerns such as the quality of life of the receiving communities (Pearce, Moscardo, and Ross, 1996).

The second component of sustainable development takes a futuristic perspective of development. In this respect, Brundtland (1987, p. 42) defines sustainable development as "Development which meets the needs of the present generation without compromising the ability of future generations to meet their own needs." This definition gives rise to some important points which need to be considered when applying the concept of sustainable development (Tosun, 2001). First, the concept of sustainable development is to be considered as a long-term strategy. Second, it focuses on an inter- and intragenerational balance of welfare. Finally, it is a relevant term which applies to any countries, regardless of the type of development taking place, the level of development, and the sociocultural and political conditions.

Following the popularization of the sustainable development concept during the 1980s, and given the resulting negative impacts of tourism, sustainable development as a growth paradigm has gained much popularity in tourism studies and has diffused into different aspects of the industry and its related practices (Bramwell, Higham, Lane, and Miller, 2017; Hunter, 1997; Ruhanen, Weiler, Moyle, and McLennan, 2015; Tosun, 2001). These have led several destinations to adopt sustainable development practices in the process of tourism development. Sustainable tourism development should, therefore, be seen as an adaptive paradigm, borrowed from the parental concept of sustainable development (Tosun, 2001). The objectives of sustainable tourism development should contribute to the overall aims and objectives of the parental concept of sustainable development (Hunter, 1997; Tosun, 2001). Butler (1993, p. 29) provides a very comprehensive and useful definition of sustainable tourism development. He argues that:

> sustainable development in the context of tourism could be taken as: tourism which is developed and maintained in an area (community, environment) in such a manner and at such a scale that it remains viable over an indefinite period of time and does not degrade the environment (human and physical) in which it exists to such a degree that it prohibits the successful development and well-being of other activities and processes.

Butler's (1993) definition focuses on the importance of maintaining and improving a community's well-being as well as promoting a healthy environment in the process of tourism development. The definition also suggests a link between the human and physical environment. Mbaiwa (2005) also notes the link between economic, social, and ecological sustainability and argues that these components are interrelated in the sense that impacts on one are likely to affect all others. The goals of monitoring tourism impacts are to decrease the frequency of unexpected changes, to moderate the unforeseen or undesired consequences of planned or ineluctable changes, and to facilitate sustainable planning aiming at the moderation of (or compensation against) the unavoidable negative impacts of tourism (Meredith, 1991).

Dimensions of tourism impacts: a triple bottom line approach

The triple bottom line approach to sustainability has largely influenced studies on tourism impacts. Impact studies emerged in the 1960s with much emphasis on economic growth, measured in terms of the gross national product, employment rate and the multiplier effect, and the positive effects of tourism (Keogh, 1989; Mathieson and Wall, 1982; Pizam, 1978). Keogh (1989) noted that this phase was characterized by optimism. During the 1970s, more attention was given to the sociocultural consequences of tourism development (Bryden, 1973; de Kadt, 1979; Turner and Ash, 1975; Young, 1973) as, in addition to the economic consequences of tourism, the industry has also been challenged for bringing about social, cultural, and environmental destruction (Ko and Stewart, 2002; Pino et al., 2018). This resulted in a period of pessimism, and the impacts of tourism were generally viewed negatively (Ap and Crompton, 1998). The environmental impacts of tourism also attracted the attention of scholars during the 1980s (Butler, 1980). Following the popularization of the sustainable development concept, the 1980s and 1990s saw the emergence of a more balanced perspective where both the negative and positive impacts of tourism are studied and evaluated (Ap and Crompton, 1998).

Economic impacts of tourism

Tourism is often viewed as playing a major role in economic growth (Andereck, Valentine, Knopf, and Vogt, 2005; Bakhsh, Potwarka, Nunkoo, and Sunnassee, 2018; Roudi, Arasli, and Akadiri, 2018; Paramati, Alam, and Chen, 2017; Walpole and Goodwin, 2000). Studies on the economic impact of tourism tend to focus on the benefits that accrue to a destination area (Ap and Crompton, 1998; Nunkoo and Ramkissoon, 2009). Many studies reveal that the economic impacts of tourism are the most valued elements for the host community (Akis, Peristianis, and Warner, 1996; Husbands, 1989; Liu et al., 1987; Ritchie, 1988; Sheldon and Var, 1984). Tourism is considered a means to increase employment opportunities for the local people (Andereck et al., 2005; Andriotis, 2005; Belisle and Hoy, 1980; Dyer, Gursoy, Sharma, and Carter, 2007; Gu and Ryan, 2008; Gursoy, Jurowski, and Uysal, 2002; Liu and Var, 1986; Milman and Pizam, 1988; Ross, 1992; Rothman, 1978; Sheldon and Var, 1984; Tosun, 2002; Tyrrell and Spaulding, 1984; Vargas-Sanchez, Plaza-Mejia, and Porras-Bueno, 2009), improve the local economy (Gursoy and Rutherford, 2004; Perdue et al., 1990; Tyrrell and Spaulding, 1984), contribute to income and standard of living (Belisle and Hoy, 1980; Liu and Var, 1986; Milman and Pizam, 1988; Pizam, 1978), bring in new businesses and improve investment opportunities (Dyer et al., 2007; Kwan and McCartney, 2005; Köseoglu, Yazici, and Okumus, 2018; Sethna and Richmond, 1978; Zhang, Ma, and Qu, 2018), increase tax revenue (Andereck et al., 2005; Brougham and Butler, 1981; Dyer et al., 2007; Kwan and McCartney, 2005; Milman and Pizam, 1988; Rothman, 1978; Tyrrell and Spaulding, 1984), bring in additional business for the host population and small businesses (Davis, Allen, and Cosenza, 1988; Murphy, 1983), improve opportunities for shopping (Liu and Var, 1986; Tovar and Lockwood, 2008), improve transport infrastructure (Belisle and Hoy, 1980), improve public utilities (Rothman, 1978; Sethna and Richmond, 1978; Tovar and Lockwood, 2008), and increase availability for recreation and entertainment (Nepal, 2008; Tovar and Lockwood, 2008).

Although many studies reveal that residents tend to view economic impacts positively (Andereck et al., 2005; Gursoy et al., 2002; Jurowski, Uysal, and Williams, 1997; Lankford, 1994; McCool and Martin, 1994; Nunkoo, 2015; Nunkoo, Gursoy, and Juwaheer, 2010; Nunkoo and Smith, 2014; Ross, 1992; Tosun, 2002), the perceived negative economic impacts of tourism are also well documented in the literature. Tourism is believed to create negative impacts on occupational distribution by sector and the community's traditional employment pattern (Haralambopoulos and Pizam, 1996; Nunkoo and Ramkissoon, 2010c). Tourism has also been found to contribute to increases in the cost of living (Kwan and McCartney, 2005; Liu and Var, 1986; Nunkoo and So, 2016; Perdue et al., 1990; Ross, 1992), increases in the price of land and housing (Belisle and Hoy, 1980; Brougham and Butler, 1981; Husbands, 1989; Liu et al., 1987; Pizam, 1978; Ross, 1992; Tovar and Lockwood, 2008), increases in the price and shortages of goods (Belisle and Hoy, 1980; Brougham and Butler, 1981; Husbands, 1989; Jackson and Inbakaran, 2006; Pizam, 1978; Ramkissoon and Nunkoo, 2011), and lack of economic diversification (Jackson and Inbakaran, 2006).

Sociocultural impacts of tourism

The social and cultural impacts of tourism are defined as "the ways in which tourism is contributing to changes in value system, individual behavior, family relationships, collective lifestyles, moral conduct, creative expressions, traditional ceremonies and community structures" (Pizam and Milman, 1984, p. 11). Many researchers have also examined the host attitudes toward the social and cultural impacts of tourism development, and such studies have revealed contradictory results (Gursoy and Rutherford, 2004; Nunkoo and Ramkissoon, 2007, 2010d). The most diverse set of impacts that have been revealed in the literature relate to a destination's social and cultural well-being (Ap and Crompton, 1998). Tourism has been found to increase recreational facilities and opportunities (Belisle and Hoy, 1980; Dyer et al., 2007; Liu et al., 1987; Liu and Var, 1986; Liu et al., 1987; Milman and Pizam, 1988; Pizam, 1978; Ross, 1992; Sheldon and Var, 1984), enrich community fabrics and cultural values, heighten community self-esteem (Andereck et al., 2005; Oviedo-Garcia, Castellanos-Verdugo, and Martin-Ruiz, 2008; Stronza and Gordillo, 2008), improve the quality of life of the residents (Baloglu, Busser, and Cain, 2018; Milman and Pizam, 1988; Perdue et al., 1990; Pizam, 1978; Tovar and Lockwood, 2008), create new opportunities and instigate social change (Harrison, 1992), create flexible working patterns and new opportunities for females (Crompton and Sanderson, 1990), improve quality of fire protection (Milman and Pizam, 1988; Pizam, 1978), and improve the quality of security, such as police protection (Pizam, 1978).

Other studies report that residents tend to view the social and cultural impacts of tourism negatively (Ap and Crompton, 1993; Doğan, 1989; Johnson, Snepenger, and Akis, 1994; Jurowski et al., 1997; Liu et al., 1987; Nunkoo and Ramkissoon, 2016; Perdue et al., 1987; Pizam, 1978; Prentice, 1993; Tosun, 2002). Tourism has been found to lead to increased prostitution in the destination area (Belisle and Hoy, 1980; Green, 2005; Liu and Var, 1986; Liu et al., 1987; Nunkoo and Ramkissoon, 2007, 2010a), increased traffic congestion and crowding (Andereck et al., 2005; Dyer et al., 2007; Nunkoo and Ramkissoon, 2007), increased smuggling (Belisle and Hoy, 1980; Milman and Pizam, 1988), heightened tension and an increase in crime rates (Andereck et al., 2005; Rothman, 1978), and psychological tension (Andereck et al., 2005). Green (2005) further notes that tourism has caused displacement and relocation of the host population and disruption to community cohesion and lifestyles. Many studies which investigate the relationship between negative social impacts of tourism and host attitudes reveal a negative relationship between negative social impact and attitudes toward tourism development (Belisle and Hoy, 1980; Gursoy et al., 2002; Lankford, 1994; Liu et al., 1987; Long et al., 1990; Milman and Pizam, 1988; Pizam and Pokela, 1985; Rothman, 1978; Tosun, 2002).

Residents also perceive tourism as having cultural impacts on a destination and its host community (Dyer et al., 2007; Nunkoo Gursoy, 2017). Tourism has been found to create demand for local arts (Dyer et al., 2007), contribute to the renaissance of traditional arts through tourists' expenditure on crafts and souvenirs (de Kadt, 1979), increase pride and preserve cultural identity (Besculides, Lee, and McCormick, 2002; Liu and Var, 1986), promote cultural exchange (Belisle and Hoy, 1980; Besculides et al., 2002; Broughman and Butler, 1981; Dyer et al., 2007; Liu et al., 1987; Liu and Var, 1986; Sheldon and Var, 1984), encourage development of cultural activities (Dyer et al., 2007), improve the understanding and image of different cultures (Besculides et al., 2002; Han, Nguyen, Song, Lee, and Chua, 2018; Liu et al., 1987; Liu and Var, 1986; Milman and Pizam, 1988; Sheldon and Var, 1984), and increase locals' knowledge of their own culture (Jackson and Inbakaran, 2006).

The literature also suggests that tourism results in several negative cultural impacts on the host residents and the destination (Andereck et al., 2005; Gursoy and Rutherford, 2004; Tosun, 2002). Haralambopoulos and Pizam (1996) argue that tourism leads to the deterioration and commercialization of nonmaterial forms of culture. Other negative cultural impacts of tourism cited include the creation of a phony folk culture (Brougham and Butler, 1981) and cultural commercialization (Cohen, 1988), where a destination's culture becomes a commodity for financial transactions (Cooper, Fletcher, Gilbert, Shepherd, and Wanhill, 1998), loss of residents' identity (Rosenow and Pulsipher, 1979), and decline in traditions (Doğan, 1989). Sharpley (1994) further notes that a long term cultural effect of tourism on the host population is that the latter may start adopting the values and norms of the tourists, making the community culturally dependent on the tourist-generating country.

The environmental impacts of tourism are also well documented in the literature. Even though tourism is sometimes perceived as being a clean industry, it can also lead to severe environmental damages (Andereck et al., 2005; Chan, Okumus, and Chan, 2017; Cicerali, Kaya Cicerali, and Saldamlı, 2017). Evidence suggests that the host community has both positive and negative perceptions of the physical and environmental impacts of tourism (Liu and Var, 1986; Liu et al., 1987). On the positive side, tourism can provide the financial resources necessary to restore and maintain historic buildings and enhance the environment, as well as preserving the rural characteristics and natural beauty of a place (Nepal, 2008) and the vernacular architectural forms (Page, 1995). Tourism has also led to the preservation and conservation of historic buildings and monuments (Cohen, 1984; Liu et al., 1987; Mathieson and Wall, 1982; McCool and Martin, 1992; Oviedo-Garcia et al., 2008; Sethna and Richmond, 1978; Sheldon and Var, 1984; Yoon, Gursoy, and Chen, 2001), improvement in an area's appearance (Perdue et al., 1990), preservation of an area's natural environment (Belisle and Hoy, 1980; Liu and Var, 1986; Liu et al., 1987; Mathieson and Wall, 1982; Pérez and Nadal, 2005; Sethna and Richmond, 1978). Tourism has also been considered as a reason for wildlife protection (Page et al., 2002). In Antarctica, the industry has led to increased resistance to degradation of wildlife and natural habitat. Doswell (1997) further argues that tourism has drawn attention to issues related to biodiversity and human impact on the environment.

On the negative side, tourism development in many communities has led to environmental damage. Tourism has led to an increase in pollution and litter (Caneday and Zeiger, 1991; Dyer et al., 2007; Green, 2005; Rothman, 1978; Pizam, 1978; Upchurch and Teivane, 2000; Yoon et al., 2001); destruction of cultural and historical resources (Nepal, 2008; Yoon et al., 2001); overcrowding (Andereck et al., 2005; Brougham and Butler, 1981; Jackson and Inbakaran, 2006; Liu and Var. 1986; Pizam, 1978; Rothman, 1978; Teye, Sonmez, and Sirakaya, 2002; Var, Kendall, and Tarakcioglu, 1985); destruction of wetlands, soil and beach erosion, and deforestation (Andereck, 1995); increase in traffic congestion (Andereck et al., 2005; Brougham and Butler, 1981; Caneday and Zeiger, 1991; Liu and Var, 1986; Liu et al., 1987; Perdue et al., 1990; Rothman, 1978; Sheldon and Var, 1984; Tyrrell and Spaulding, 1984; Var et al., 1985); and unplanned urban developments in some regions (Oviedo-Garcia et al., 2008). Page et al. (2001) further argue that tourism has resulted in inappropriate development in regions such as the Mediterranean, where coastal strips have been covered by urban sprawl to cater for the mass tourism market. Gossling (2002) also discusses the environmental impact resulting from tourism development on a global level and argues that tourism has led to changes in land cover and land use, energy use, and exchange and dispersion of diseases. He further notes that, although tourism may increase environmental knowledge, it might not necessarily lead to positive changes in attitudes, awareness, and environmental behavior. For instance, he argues that tourism may contribute to the idea that humans are separated from nature, a notion which may be detrimental to sustainable development.

Theoretical underpinnings

Early studies on the impacts of tourism were atheoretical, and, as a result, it was unclear why residents perceived and responded to tourism impacts as they did, and under what conditions they reacted to the impacts of the industry (Ap, 1990, 1992; Husbands, 1989; Liu and Var, 1986). In an attempt to address these shortcomings and provide a better theoretical explanation of the impacts of tourism, researchers started making use of a number of theoretical frameworks to guide their research. Some of these theories include social exchange theory (SET; Ap, 1992; Nunkoo et al., 2010), tourist area life cycle (Butler, 1980), irridex model (Doxey, 1975), intrinsic/extrinsic framework (Faulkner and Tideswell, 1997), identity theory (Nunkoo and Gursoy, 2012; Nunkoo et al., 2010), social representation theory (Fredline and Faulkner, 2000, 2001), growth machine theory (Martin, 1999), and theory of planned behavior/theory of reasoned action (Delamere, 2001; Lepp, 2007; Nunkoo and Ramkissoon, 2010c; Ramkissoon and Nunkoo, 2011; Zhang, Inbakaran, and Jackson, 2006).

Social exchange theory

Although each theory has contributed in its own way to this area of investigation, SET has been the most widely utilized in explaining residents' support for tourism and has made significant theoretical contributions to this field of study (Gursoy, Chi, and Dyer, 2010; Lee, Kang, Long, and Reisinger, 2010; Nunkoo and Ramkissoon, 2011a). The popularity of SET can be attributed to the fact that the theory recognizes the heterogeneous nature of a host community where different groups of individuals exhibit different levels of support for tourism, depending on their perceptions of the benefits and costs arising from the sector's development. Originally developed in sociology to explain social interactions, SET has been found to be one of the most applicable and relevant theories in explaining community support for tourism development (Andereck et al., 2005). Emerson (1981) noted that social exchange involves a minimum of two persons, each of whom provides some benefits to the other, and is contingent upon rewards from the other. A few seminal studies that have contributed to the development of SET worth mentioning include that of Homans (1958), Thibaut and Kelley (1959), Emerson (1962), and Blau (1964). Homans (1958) placed emphasis on social behavior in the exchange process. Thibaut and Kelley (1959) discussed how actors in an exchange relationship weigh the benefits of the exchange relation. Emerson's (1962) work related to the concept of power between the actors in an exchange relationship, and Blau (1964) emphasized social interaction as an exchange process.

SET is based on the premise that human behavior or social interaction is an exchange of activity, tangible and intangible, particularly of rewards and costs (Homans, 1961). It analyzes how the structure of rewards and costs in a relationship affects patterns of interaction (Molm, 1991). SET considers exchange as the basis of human behavior (Homans, 1961). Actors in an exchange process are dependent on one another for outcomes they value. They behave in a way that increases outcomes they positively value and decreases outcomes they negatively value, and, if the benefits from the exchange exceed the costs, actors engage in recurring exchanges over time (Cook, Molm, and Yamagishi, 1993). SET posits that all individuals' decisions to engage in an interaction process are based on the use of a subjective cost–benefit analysis and the comparison of alternatives. Individuals engage in an exchange process once they have judged the rewards and the costs, and they will enter relationships in which they can maximize benefits and minimize costs. Actors will engage in an exchange if the resulting rewards are of value to them and the perceived costs do not exceed the perceived benefits (Ap, 1992). Interactions are likely to continue only if both parties feel that they are benefitting more from the exchange than they are giving up.

Social exchanges differ from economic ones in several fundamental ways. Whereas benefits involved in economic exchanges are formal and often contractual, such benefits and their exact nature are rarely negotiated in social exchanges (Blau, 1964). Exchange of benefits is a voluntary action and entails unspecified future obligations (Konovsky and Pugh, 1994; Whitener, Brodt, Korsgaard, and Werner, 1998). Benefits do not occur on a calculated or quid pro quo basis (Konovsky and Pugh, 1994). There is also no guarantee that there will be a reciprocation of benefits. Thus, social exchanges involve uncertainty, particularly in the early stages of the relationship (Whitener et al., 1998). As in economic exchanges, in social exchanges there exists an expectation of some future returns for contributions between the exchange partners, although the exact nature of the returns is not known or negotiated in social exchanges (Blau, 1964). Social exchanges are also characterized by long-term fairness, in contrast to the short-term fairness that underpins economic exchanges (Konovsky and Pugh, 1994). According to SET, social exchange involves benefits with economic and/or social outcomes (Cropanzano and Mitchell, 2005; Emerson, 1976; Lambe, Wittmann, and Spekman, 2001). Whitener et al. (1998) noted that exchanges without any objective utility may have a significant impact on the social dimension of the relationship.

From a tourism perspective, Sutton (1967) argued that the encounter between the host community and the guests "may provide either an opportunity for rewarding and satisfying exchanges, or it may stimulate and reinforce impulses to exploitation on the part of the host" (p. 221). Supporting his assertion, a number of studies (e.g., Gursoy and Rutherford, 2004; Gursoy et al., 2010; Nunkoo and Gursoy, 2012; Nunkoo and Ramkissoon, 2010a, 2010b, 2011a, 2011b; Yoon, Gursoy, and Chen, 2001) found that the economic, social, and environmental impacts resulting from the host–tourism exchange process affect residents' support for tourism development. The findings of these studies suggest that the value attributed to the elements of the exchange influences the way in which residents of a destination perceive tourism and determines the level of community acceptance of tourism development. "The way that residents perceive the economic, sociocultural and environmental elements of exchange affects the manner in which they react to tourism" (Andriotis and Vaughan, 2003, p. 173). Such reactions are manifested in residents' support for or opposition to tourism development. The findings of existing studies suggest that, in a host–tourism context, the elements in an exchange process include not only economic benefits and costs, but also social, cultural, and environmental ones.

Butler's (1980) tourist area life cycle

Another popular model among researchers studying the impacts of tourism is the tourist area life cycle (TALC; Butler, 1980). The model allows researchers to study the historical evolution and future development of tourist destinations (Rodriguez, Parra-Lopez, and Yanez-Estevez, 2008). Butler (1980) argues that destinations progress through six different stages: exploration, involvement, development, consolidation, stagnation, and then decline or rejuvenation. Though the focus of this stage-related model is on the evolution of destinations over time, the model also incorporates the dynamics between destination development and impacts of tourism as part of wider development issues. According to the model, in the exploration stage, the destination is characterized by small levels of visitation by tourists looking for an exotic destination. This is followed by the involvement stage where new services and facilities begin to develop, and these are mostly provided by the local people. During the third stage, development becomes more intense and starts impacting on the lives of the local community. During the consolidation phase, tourist numbers continue to rise, even though the growth rate is slower. At this stage, the economy becomes largely reliant on tourism (Sheldon and Abenoja, 2001) and is dominated by major chains and franchises (Tooman, 1997). During the stagnation stage, the carrying capacity of many resources and factors of production is reached, resulting in further negative environmental, social, cultural, and economic impacts. During the final stage, destinations either experience decline or rejuvenate, depending on the adopted tourism policies. Horn and Simmons (2002) note that, as the destination passes through the first four stages, the number of visitors increases, and the visitors change from being largely adaptive and independent to being less adaptive and more dependent on the local residents for meeting their needs (Cohen, 1972; Smith, 1989). From the perspective of the model, the increase in tourist numbers which destinations experience in their evolutionary process leads to negative residents' attitudes toward tourism development (Horn and Simmons, 2002). Thus, communities in mature tourist destinations tend to exhibit diminished capacity to accommodate tourists, resulting in negative responses from the local residents (Sheldon and Abenoja, 2001).

Doxey's (1975) irridex model

Doxey (1975) provides a four-stage framework, the irridex model, to study community responses to the impacts of tourism development. During the euphoria stage, there is little tourism development, and the residents welcome the new visitors to their community. As the destination develops, the residents start taking notice of the increasing number of tourists, leading to the apathy phase. During this stage, some residents start taking advantage of tourism development and begin to establish commercial relationships with the industry, while others start viewing the industry as an agent of social, cultural, economic, and environmental changes in their community and its environment. During this stage, the presence of tourists is no longer considered as a novelty in the destination, and the enthusiastic attitudes that residents held during the early stage begin to fade out. The next stage, the annoyance stage, is characterized by more intense development where residents start getting irritated as a result of tourism, leading to negative attitudes toward the industry. The final stage is characterized by openly expressed antagonism by the residents over tourism development. The community no longer welcomes visitors and starts displaying behaviors ranging from indifference to hostility. According to Fridgen (1991), not only does the profile of visitors change during this stage, but the community starts developing negative stereotypes about the industry and tourists themselves. The destination no longer appeals to those travelers looking for an exclusive or niche product, and, depending on the product development and tourism policies adopted, the place declines or rejuvenates. Doxey (1975) further argues that the community residents' irritation is influenced by the degree of incompatibility between them and the visitors.

Though both TALC and the irridex are powerful models for explaining changing attitudes as tourism development becomes more intense and they have been supported by several studies (e.g., de Kadt, 1979; Pizam, 1978; Upchurch and Teivane, 2000), their limitations have also been well recognized by researchers. Both models are considered to be too simplistic to be able to provide a comprehensive understanding of community attitudes to tourism (Akis et al., 1996). Both TALC and irridex postulate that intensified tourism development is accompanied by negative residents' attitudes toward the industry (Lawton, 2005). However, studies such as those by King, Pizam, and Milman (1993) and Dowling (1993) reveal that, in spite of high levels of tourism development and increases in tourist numbers, residents were still positive about the tourism industry. Similar findings have been revealed by the study by Dyer et al. (2007) of the Sunshine Coast, Australia. Results indicate that, even though the destination has well-developed tourist facilities, residents still consider the economic and cultural benefits of tourism to be important. The study by Hernandez, Cohen, and Garcia (1996) confirms that attitudes were not positive even in the development phase of tourism. These findings suggest that, even when a destination is characterized by a high level of tourism development, residents' attitudes can still be positive, and negative attitudes can also be experienced during early phases of tourism development. These findings contradict Butler's (1980) TALC and Doxey's (1975) irridex model.

The theories have also been criticized as they cannot explain the variations in attitudes to tourism among residents within a host community (Zhang et al., 2006). The theories assume a degree of homogeneity and unidirectionality among residents, when, in fact, the host community has been found to be heterogeneous in nature (Faulkner and Tideswell, 1997). Lankford and Howard (1994, p. 135) argue that models such as Doxey's (1975) irridex model "ignore the complexity of factors that can influence, either positively or negatively, residents' attitudes towards tourism." Several studies (e.g., Ap and Crompton 1993; Brougham and Butler, 1981; Faulkner and Tideswell, 1997; Husbands, 1989) note the heterogeneous nature of the host communities and the variety of responses to tourism development that may exist.

Faulkner and Tideswell's (1997) intrinsic/extrinsic framework

From the above perspective, the intrinsic and extrinsic framework devised by Faulkner and Tideswell (1997) becomes useful as it takes into account the extrinsic and intrinsic factors influencing attitudes to tourism. The extrinsic dimension:

> refers to the characteristics of the location with respect to its role as a tourist destination – including the nature and stage of tourism development in the area and reflecting, this, the level of tourist activity and the types of tourists involved.
>
> *(Faulkner and Tideswell 1997, p. 6)*

The extrinsic component of the model comprises macro-level factors such as the characteristics of the destination and stage in the life cycle, seasonality of tourism, and pattern of activity (Andriotis and Vaughan, 2003; Belisle and Hoy, 1980; Fredline and Faulkner, 2000), ratio of hosts to guests (Butler, 1980; Doxey, 1975), type and form of tourism (Gursoy et al., 2002; Ritchie, 1988), and the proportion of domestic and international tourism (Garland, 1984; Moore, Cushman, and Simmons, 1995). Within the extrinsic dimensions, one of the major factors that has been found to influence residents' attitudes toward tourism in the literature is the degree or stage of the host destination's development (Andriotis and Vaughan, 2003). These factors are implied in Butler's (1980) TALC and Doxey's (1975) irridex model.

The intrinsic dimension "refers to the characteristics of members of the host community that affect variations in the impacts of tourism within the community" (Fredline and Faulkner, 2000, p. 6). The intrinsic dimension comprises factors such the characteristics of the host population. These include employment with the industry (Akis et al., 1996; Lankford, 1994; Mansfeld, 1992; Pizam, 1978; Snaith and Haley, 1999; Tyrrell and Spaulding, 1984), involvement in tourism (Ap, 1992; Milman and Pizam, 1988, Pizam, 1978), spatial factors (Belisle and Hoy, 1980; Harrill and Potts, 2003; Jurowski and Gursoy, 2004; Korça, 1998; Mansfeld, 1992; Pearce, 1980), length of residence (Allen, Long, Perdue, and Kieselbach, 1988; Lankford, 1994; McCool and Martin, 1994), and old timers and newcomers (Allen et al., 1988; Beyers and Nelson, 2000; Liu and Var, 1986). The intrinsic dimension thus recognizes the fact that residents are not homogeneous in their attitudes toward tourism.

Structure of the handbook

This handbook is informed by the debates on sustainable development and tourism impact and is structured as follows: Part I of the volume investigates the dynamics of tourism impacts. In the opening chapter, Donald Reid discusses the role of tourism planning in managing tourism impacts. Donald sets out the foundation of tourism planning and alerts readers to the challenges planners encounter when developing tourism. His chapter delves further into explaining the role of tourism planning in mitigating the negative impacts of tourism and promoting the positive ones. In Chapter 2, Perunjodi Naidoo and Prabha Ramseook-Munhurrun discuss the impacts of tourism on quality of life of destination communities and expose readers to the various ways in which tourism influences residents' quality of life. Sandra Maria Correia Loureiro, Eduardo Moraes Sarmento, and João Ferreira do Rosário present an overview of tourism impacts in Lisbon in Chapter 3. The contributors also provide a number of policy implications for managing tourism impacts and conclude with an agenda for future research. In Chapter 4, Chris Ryan, Zhe Chen, Li Linrui, and Mary Anne Ramos Tumanan describe the work of the International Network of Sustainable Tourism Observatories (INSTO), a program organized under the auspices of the United Nation World Tourism Organization (UNWTO). The chapter indicates the framework of the Sustainable Development Goals established by the United Nations within which the INSTO initiative is nested. It then specifically describes the way the program can contribute to planning.

In Chapter 5, Neil Carr furthers the debates by delving into the impacts of tourism on animals, which he considers an overlooked dimension in the literature. The discussion explores the myriad, positive and negative, ways in which tourists and the tourism industry impact, both directly and indirectly, the lives and well-being of all animals. It is situated within the realization that animals are sentient beings and that, as a result, humans have obligations to them, given their relative power over nonhuman animals. Elephants in Thailand provide an example of the complex issues surrounding how tourism impacts wildlife. Such is the argument that Eric Laws,

Noel Scott, and John Koldowski formulate in Chapter 6. The chapter explains how structural changes in regulations in Thailand result in abuses and misuses of the elephants, in part owing to lack of appropriate regulations for elephant welfare. This chapter presents a concise history of the development of elephant tourism in Thailand and identifies current issues in their display and interaction with visitors.

Part II of the volume deals with the economic impacts of tourism. In Chapter 8, Orhan Icoz and Onur Icoz lay the theoretical underpinnings by reviewing the various positive and negative economic impacts of tourism on destinations and their communities. Using a dynamic vector error correction model, catering for dynamic, endogeneity, and causality issues, Sheereen Fauzel investigates the link between tourism development and income inequality in Mauritius in Chapter 9. The results show that tourism expansion has contributed toward reducing inequality in both the short run and long run. Furthermore, the results also confirm the presence of uni-causality and in the tourism-inequality model. In Chapter 9, Deserè Kokt and Johan Hattingh provide an overview of local economic development in the context of southern Africa, focusing on the development and challenges of local economic development, the rise of rural tourism and its impact on communities, as well as community-based tourism and route tourism as ways in which communities can benefit from government and private partnerships and tourism. Paige P. Viren and Christina Beckmann trace the economic impacts of adventure tourism in Chapter 10. This chapter provides two case studies comparing adventure and mass tourism economic impacts in the Caribbean and Jordan using the results of comprehensive analysis conducted by a USAID-funded team.

Chapter 11 by João Romão investigates the long-term economic impacts of tourism. Using concepts derived from economic geography, the chapter focuses on the analysis of methodologies to assess the economic importance of tourism (including immaterial and non-market tourism resources) and to evaluate its economic impacts (both positive and negative) on regional economic structures, specialization patterns, and long-term processes of economic growth. In Chapter 12, Sevinç Aslan and Mİthat Zeki Dinçer discuss the effects of small and medium enterprises (SMEs) on destinations. The chapter discusses the foundation for understanding SMEs in tourism and their importance and effects on destinations. Annmarie Nicely and Karla "Gabbie" Morrison look at the economic impacts of visitor harassment in Chapter 13. The discussion draws on some of the latest research on the topic to provide an overview of the practice, its economic impact on destinations, and actions tourism leaders may take to either reduce or overcome the phenomenon. In Chapter 14, Gerald Milanzi highlights the prominent socioeconomic role of women in the rural communities in the realms of tourism as an entrepreneurship propellant. Through the study, sociocultural embedded factors are identified as the main challenges that obscure women's contribution in the society, despite women being the integral financial providers in their families. Boopen Seetanah draws our attention to the role of tourism in poverty reduction in Mauritius in Chapter 15. Employing dynamic time series analysis, the study's findings suggest that tourism development is negatively associated with the level of poverty in Mauritius (pro-poor), although it exhibits a relatively lower impact compared with other classical factors in the aggregate poverty model.

Part III of the volume focuses on the sociocultural impacts of tourism development. The opening discussion (Chapter 16) by Ozlem Tekin and Roya Rahimi focuses on the changes tourism causes in the cultural values and beliefs of societies in the long term. Furthering this debate in Chapter 17, Edina Kovács, Kornélia Kiss, Ivett Pinke-Sziva, and Gábor Michalkó critically review the literature on well-being and tourism development with a particular focus on senior people. The chapter assesses whether the involvement of seniors in tourism – either on the demand side as travelers or on the supply side as service providers – has any (and to what extent) positive effects on their well-being. In Chapter 18, Sedat Çelik looks at the sociopsychological effects of tourism through an evaluation of the tourist–local people interaction within the context of Allport's intergroup contact theory. In Chapter 19, Orhan Akova and Ozan Atsiz investigate the sociocultural impacts of tourism development on heritage sites, outlining both the positive and negative consequences of tourism for cultural heritage. Grace Kamanga and Eugenio Njoloma delve further into the socioeconomic implications of tourism in Nkhata Bay District, Malawi, in Chapter 20. Contrary to the prevailing trend, it has emerged that tourism has contributed to infrastructure development as well as to employment and business opportunities for a significant segment of the people of the district. Nonetheless, the absence of meaningful corporate social responsibility initiatives and the industry's role in shifting cultural attitudes are the most highlighted repercussions.

Part IV of this volume focuses on the environment consequences of tourism development. This section draws on various cases to demonstrate the positive and negative environmental impacts of tourism. In the opening chapter of this part (Chapter 21), Özge Kocabulut, Nisan Yozukmaz, and Serkan Bertan review the theoretical underpinning of environmental impact studies. Mahmoud M. Hewedi, and Reem Elmasry further this conceptualization in Chapter 22. The contributors argue that unplanned or uncontrollable tourism activities pose possible threats to the environment. The consequences include, but are not limited to, all types of pollution and damage to vegetation cover that severely endangers biodiversity distribution, causes loss of natural habitats, and even badly affects local culture and heritage. In Chapter 23, Solmaz L. Azarmi, Roozbeh Vaziri, Ayman Kole, Akeem A. Oladipo, and Ahmet Bulend Goksel introduce readers to the various types of environmental pollution generated by tourism activities; special focus is directed toward physical impacts from tourist activities, solid waste generation, and air and water pollution. Also, the causal relationship between climate change indicators, natural resource depletion, and tourism activities is discussed. The chapter outlines the key sources of solid wastes and water pollution from various tourism sectors and highlights their direct impact on the environment.

Adjnu Damar Ladkoo investigates the challenges small island economies face with respect to climate change in Chapter 24. Adjnu argues that, although it is important to understand who or what is causing climate change, there is a pressing need to sensitize all stakeholders of the tourism industry, namely the primary ones, who are the tourists themselves. This would permit them to contribute to both adaption and mitigation as response strategies to climate change and its impacts. The need to consider tourism as a tool for positive environmental change is emphasized by Vishnee Sowamber and Haywantee Ramkissoon in Chapter 25. This chapter explores how a tourism operator has implemented a robust environmental initiative to align with the Paris Agreement and local environmental policies. The contributors use as a case study the approach of a major hotel group in Mauritius, LUX* Resorts and Hotels, comprising 10 hotels within the destinations of Mauritius, Réunion Island, the Maldives, China, and Turkey. The chapter examines how the hotel group has implemented "Tread Lightly by LUX*" for environmental protection in its hotels and resorts.

Part V of the handbook deals with the political impacts of tourism development. In the opening chapter (Chapter 26) of this section, Richard Butler and Wantanee Suntikul develop a framework to place the political impacts of tourism in a theoretical context, particularly in relation to the other impacts and the level of politics at which such impacts take place. This chapter also examines what changes in political systems and approaches have been influenced and caused by tourism, using examples from specific countries and regions, including Cuba, Egypt, Turkey, China, the United States, and the United Kingdom. In Chapter 27, Dante Di Matteo investigates tourism performances, government effectiveness, and local growth using the Italian cultural heritage perspective. Findings reveal that an increased level of government effectiveness and improvements in tourism coverage across the territory would result in significant economic growth on a provincial scale. Among other findings, through testing for year-round and no-seasonal periods, the results appear not to be affected by seasonality; however, as frequently occurs in mature destinations, it looks as though accommodation overcapacity produces negative effects on growth. Furthering the debate on the political dimensions of tourism development, in Chapter 28, Roseane Barcellos Marques, Carlos Alberto Alves, and Elizabeth Kyoko Wada discuss the impacts of corruption in the construction of the infrastructure related to the 2014 FIFA World Cup and the 2016 Olympic Games in Brazil.

Part VI of this volume deals with the impact of technology on tourism development. In the opening chapter of this section (Chapter 29), Beykan Çizel and Edina Ajanovic elaborate on the technological drivers on which smart tourism attributes have been developed. The contributors further draw on the extant literature to demonstrate how the different tourism stakeholders are affected by smart tourism technologies and their applications. In Chapter 30, Sagar Singh explains how technology has been the single most important factor in development of fast transport in tourism, which, although it has shortened many-days journeys into a matter of hours, has paradoxically increased the distance between the host and the guest. His chapter analyzes these paradoxes and the greatest impact that technology will have, through artificial intelligence, which is fast making inroads in developed countries, including through controversial self-driving cars and robots that threaten to rob people of jobs in tourism. In Chapter 31, Erdem Aktaş and Avşar Kurgun examine the impact of smart tourism ecosystems on tourism destinations. The contributors argue that the use of smart technologies provides the digital restructuring of tourist attractions. In addition, international smart technology-based projects such as citySDK and Cordis are accelerating the development of smart tourism destinations. Fisun Yüksel discusses the application of ICT in the tourism industry and the role it plays in digital marketing in Chapter 32. The chapter compares digital marketing with traditional marketing in the competing environment. The first part of the chapter presents the role of ICT and how it relates to Industry 4.0. The second part explores the role of service provision, digital marketing, and how they are affected by the latest revolution to gain competitive advantage in the context of strategic thinking. Information technology is being utilized in order to obtain a cutting edge in different areas of the tourism industry such as accommodation, transportation, and attractions.

The final part of the handbook presents some of the methods used to study tourism impacts. Edward C. Bolden, III, critically reviews the different statistical techniques and applications used to study tourism impacts in Chapter 33. This chapter serves to provide a brief background of research types and statistical approaches that are commonly used in the literature assessing tourism impacts. Nada Al-Sabri, Avraam Papastathopoulos, and Syed Zamberi Ahmad utilize the social exchange theory and the social identity theory to examine residents' perception of the social and cultural impacts of tourism in Chapter 34. Their study examines the moderating effect of gender and nationality on the relationship between residents' perception of the impacts of tourism and their support for tourism development in the United Arab Emirates. In Chapter 35, Dan Musinguzi examines the application of social exchange theory in the tourism impact studies published by the *Annals of Tourism Research, Journal of Travel Research*, and *Tourism Management*. In doing so, the study assesses the extent to which power between tourism actors (the central tenet of social exchange theory) has been incorporated into the tourism impact research published between 1990 and 2014.

References

Akis, S., Peristianis N., and Warner, J. 1996. Residents' attitudes to tourism development: The case of Cyprus. *Tourism Management*, *17*(7), 481–494.

Allen, L.R., Long, P., Perdue, R.R., and Kieselbach, S. 1988. The impact of tourism development on residents' perceptions of community life. *Journal of Travel Research*, *27*(1), 16–21.

Andereck, K.L. 1995. Environmental consequences of tourism: A review of recent research. *Environmental Consequences Of Tourism: A Review of Recent Research*, (INT-323), 77–81.

Andereck, K.L., and Nyaupane, G.P. 2011. Exploring the nature of tourism and quality of life perceptions among residents. *Journal of Travel Research*, *50*(3), 248–260.

Andereck, K.L., Valentine, K.M., Knopf, R.C., and Vogt, C.A. 2005. Residents' perceptions of community tourism impacts. *Annals Of Tourism Research*, *32*(4), 1056–1076.

Andriotis, K. 2005. Community groups' perceptions of and preferences for tourism development: Evidence from Crete. *Journal of Hospitality & Tourism Research*, *29*(1), 67–90.

Andriotis, K., and Vaughan, R.D. 2003. Urban residents' attitudes toward tourism development: The case of Crete. *Journal of Travel Research*, *42*(2), 172–185.

Ap, J. 1990. Residents' perception research on the social impacts of tourism. *Annals of Tourism Research*, *17*, 610–616.

Ap, J. 1992. Residents' perceptions on tourism impacts. *Annals of Tourism Research*, *19*, 665–690.

Ap, J., and Crompton, J.L. 1993. Residents' strategies for responding to tourism impacts. *Journal of Travel Research*, *32*(1), 47–50.

Ap, J., and Crompton, J. 1998. Developing and testing a tourism impact scale. *Journal of Travel Research*, *37*, 120–130.

Bakhsh, J., Potwarka, L.R., Nunkoo, R., and Sunnassee, V. 2018. Residents' support for the Olympic Games: Single host-city versus multiple host-city bid arrangements. *Journal of Hospitality Marketing & Management*, *27*(5), 544–560.

Baloglu, S., Busser, J., and Cain, L. 2018. Impact of experience on emotional well-being and loyalty. *Journal of Hospitality Marketing & Management*. https://doi.org/10.1080/19368623.2019.1527269

Bartelmus, P. 1986. *Environment and Development* (p. 18). London: Allen & Unwin.

Belisle, F.J., and Hoy, D.R. 1980. The perceived impact of tourism by residents: A case study in Santa Maria, Columbia. *Annals of Tourism Research*, *7*(1), 83–101.

Besculides, A., Lee, A.M., and McCormick, P.J. 2002. Residents' perceptions of the cultural benefits of tourism. *Annals of Tourism Research*, *29*(2), 303–319.

Beyers, W.B., and Nelson, P.B. 2000. Service industries and employment growth in the nonmetro South: A geographical perspective. *Southern Rural Sociology*, *15*, 139–169.

Blau, P. 1964. *Exchange and Power in Social Life*. New York: Wiley.

Boley, B.B., McGehee, N.G., and Hammett, A.T. 2017. Importance-performance analysis (IPA) of sustainable tourism initiatives: The resident perspective. *Tourism Management*, *58*, 66–77.

Bramwell, B., Higham, J., Lane, B., and Miller, G. 2017. Twenty-five years of sustainable tourism and the *Journal of Sustainable Tourism*: Looking back and moving forward. *Journal of Sustainable Tourism*, *25*, 1–9.

Brougham, J.E., and Butler, R.W. 1981. A segmentation analysis of residents attitudes to the social impact of tourism. *Annals of Tourism Research*, *8*(4), 569–590.

Brundtland, G.H. 1987. *Report of the World Commission on Environment and Development: Our Common Future*. Oxford: Oxford University Press.

Bryden, J. 1973. *Tourism and Development: A Case Study of The Commonwealth Caribbean*. Cambridge: Cambridge University Press.

Butler, R.W. 1980. The concept of a tourist area life cycle of evolution: Implications for management of resources. *Canadian Geographer*, *24*(1), 5–12.

Butler, R.W. 1993. Tourism: An evolutionary perspective. In J.G. Nelson, R. Butler, and G. Wall, Eds., *Tourism & Sustainable Development: Monitoring, Planning & Managing* (pp. 26–43). Waterloo, ON: Heritage Resources Centre, University Of Waterloo.

Caneday, L., and Zeiger, J. 1991. The social, economic and environmental cost of tourism to a growing community. *Journal of Travel Research*, *30*, 45–48.

Chan, E.S., Okumus, F., and Chan, W. 2017. The applications of environmental technologies in hotels. *Journal of Hospitality Marketing & Management*, *26*(1), 23–47.

Cicerali, E.E., Kaya Cicerali, L., and Saldamlı, A., 2017. Linking psycho-environmental comfort factors to tourist satisfaction levels: Application of a psychology theory to tourism research. *Journal of Hospitality Marketing & Management*, *26*(7), 717–734.

Cohen, E. 1972. Toward a sociology of international tourism. *Social Research, 39*(1), 164–182.

Cohen, E. 1984. The sociology of tourism: Approaches, issues, and findings. *Annual Review of Sociology, 10*(1), 373–392.

Cohen, E. 1988. Authenticity and commoditization in tourism. *Annals of Tourism Research, 15*(3), 371–386.

Cook, K.S., Molm, L.D., and Yamagishi, T. 1993. Exchange relations and exchange networks: Recent developments in social exchange theory. In J. Berger and M. Zelditch (Eds.), *Theoretical Research Programs: Studies in the Growth of Theory* (296–322). Stanford: CA: Stanford University Press.

Cooper, C., Fletcher, J., Gilbert, D., Shepherd, R., and Wanhill, S. 1998. *Tourism Principles and Practice*, 2nd ed. Harlow, UK: Longman.

Crompton, R., and Sanderson, K. 1990. *Gendered Jobs and Social Change*. Routledge.

Cropanzano, R., and Mitchell, M.S. 2005. Social exchange theory: An interdisciplinary review. *Journal of Management, 31*(6), 874–900.

Davis, D., Allen, J., and Cosenza, R.M. 1988. Segmenting local residents by their attitudes, interests and opinions toward tourism. *Journal of Travel Research, 27*(2), 2–8.

De Kadt, E. 1979. *Tourism: Passport to Development? Perspectives on the Social and Cultural Effects of Tourism in Developing Countries*. New York: Oxford University Press.

Delamere, T.A. 2001. Development of a scale to measure resident attitudes toward the social impacts of community festivals, part II: Verification of the scale. *Event Management, 7*(1), 25e38.

Doğan, H.Z. 1989. Forms of adjustment: Sociocultural impacts of tourism. *Annals of Tourism Research, 16*(2), 216–236.

Doswell, R. 1997. *Tourism: How Effective Management Makes the Difference*. London: Butterworth-Heinemann.

Dowling, R. 1993. An environmentally-based planning model for regional tourism development. *Journal of Sustainable Tourism, 1*(1), 17–37.

Doxey, G.V. 1975. *A Causation Theory of Visitor–Residents Irritants, Methodology and Research Inferences*. The Travel Research Association Conference No.6, Ttra, 195–198.

Dudley, E. 1993. *The Critical Villager: Beyond Community Participation*. London: Routledge.

Dyer, P., Gursoy, D., Sharma, B., and Carter, J. 2007. Structural modeling of resident perceptions of tourism and associated development on the Sunshine Coast, Australia. *Tourism Management, 28*(2), 409–422.

Emerson, R.M. 1962. Power-dependence relations. *American Sociological Review, 27*(1), 31–41.

Emerson, R.M. 1976. Social exchange theory. *Annual Review of Sociology, 2*(1), 335–362.

Emerson, R.M. 1981. *Social Exchange Theory. Social Psychology: Sociological Perspectives*. New York: Basic Books.

Eusébio, C., Vieira, A.L., and Lima, S. 2018. Place attachment, host–tourist interactions, and residents' attitudes towards tourism development: The case of Boa Vista Island in Cape Verde. *Journal of Sustainable Tourism, 26*(6), 890–909.

Faulkner, B., and Tideswell. C. 1997. A framework for monitoring community impacts of tourism. *Journal of Sustainable Tourism, 5*(1), 3–28.

Fredline, E., and Faulkner, B. 2000. Host community reactions: A cluster analysis. *Annals of Tourism Research, 27*(3), 763–784.

Fredline, E., and Faulkner, B. 2001. Residents' reactions to the staging of major motorsport events within their communities: A cluster analysis. *Event Management, 7*(2), 103–114.

Fridgen, J.D. 1991. Dimensions of tourism, the Educational Institute of the American Hotel & Motel Association. *Tourism & Hospitality Research, 5*(3), 235–253.

Garland, R. 1984. *New Zealand Hosts and Guests – A Study on the Social Impact of Tourism*. Palmerston North, NZ: Market Research Centre, Massey University.

Gossling, S. 2002. Global environmental consequences of tourism. *Global Environmental Change, 12*, 283–302.

Green, R. 2005. Community perceptions of environmental and social change and tourism development on the island of Koh Samui, Thailand. *Journal of Environmental Psychology, 25*(1), 37–56.

Gu, H., and Ryan, C. 2008. Place attachment, identity and community impacts of tourism – The case of a Beijing hutong. *Tourism Management, 29*(4), 637–647.

Gursoy, D., Chi, C.G., and Dyer, P. 2010. Locals' attitudes toward mass and alternative tourism: The case of Sunshine Coast, Australia. *Journal of Travel Research, 49*(3), 381–394.

Gursoy, D., Jurowski, C., and Uysal, M. 2002. Resident attitudes: A structural modeling approach. *Annals of Tourism Research, 29*, 79–105.

Gursoy, D., Ouyang, Z., Nunkoo, R., and Wei, W. 2018. Residents' impact perceptions of and attitudes towards tourism development: A meta-analysis. *Journal of Hospitality Marketing & Management*, 1–28. DOI: 10.1080/19368623.2018.1516589

Gursoy, D., and Rutherford, D. 2004. Host attitudes toward tourism: An improved structural modeling approach. *Annals of Tourism Research, 31*(3), 495–516.

Han, H., Nguyen, H.N., Song, H., Lee, S., and Chua, B.L. 2018. Impact of functional/cognitive and emotional advertisements on image and repurchase intention. *Journal of Hospitality Marketing & Management*, 1–26. https://doi.org/10.1080/19368623.2019.1531803

Hao, H., Long, P., and Kleckley, J. 2011. Factors predicting homeowners' attitudes toward tourism: A case of a coastal resort community. *Journal of Travel Research, 50*(6), 627–640.

Haralambopoulos, N., and Pizam, A. 1996. Perceived impacts of tourism: The case of Samos. *Annals of Tourism Research, 23*(3), 503–526.

Harrill, R. 2004. Residents' attitudes toward tourism development: A literature review with implications for planning. *Journal of Planning Literature, 18*(3), 251–266.

Harrill, R., and Potts, T.D. 2003. Tourism planning in historic districts: Attitudes toward tourism development in Charleston. *Journal of American Planning Association, 69*(3), 233–244.

Harrison, D. 1992. *Tourism and the Less Developed Countries*. London: Belhaven.

Healy, R.G. 1994. Tourist merchandise'as a means of generating local benefits from ecotourism. *Journal of Sustainable Tourism, 2*(3), 137–151.

Hernandez, S.A., Cohen, J., and Garcia, H.L. 1996. Residents' attitudes towards an instant resort enclave. *Annals of Tourism Research, 23*(4), 755–779.

Homans, G.C. 1958. Social behavior as exchange. *American Journal of Sociology, 63*(6), 597–606.

Homans, G.C. 1961. *Human Behavior: Its Elementary Forms*. New York: Brace & World.

Horn, C., and Simmons, D. 2002. Community adaptation to tourism: Comparisons between Rotorua and Kaikoura, New Zealand. *Tourism Management, 23*(2), 133–143.

Hunter, C. 1997. Sustainable tourism as an adaptive paradigm. *Annals of Tourism Research, 24*(4), 850–867.

Husbands, W. 1989. Social statue and perception of tourism in Zambia. *Annals of Tourism Research, 16*, 237–255.

Jackson, M.S., and Inbarakan, R.J. 2006. Evaluating residents' attitudes and intentions to act toward tourism development in regional Victoria, Australia. *International Journal of Tourism Research, 8*, 355–366.

Johnson, J., Snepenger, D., and Akis, S. 1994. Residents' perception of tourism development. *Annals of Tourism Research, 21*(3), 629–642.

Jurowski, C., and Gursoy, D. 2004. Distance effects on residents' attitudes toward tourism. *Annals of Tourism Research, 31*(2), 296–312.

Jurowski, C., Uysal, M., and Williams, D.R. 1997. A theoretical analysis of host reactions to tourism. *Journal of Travel Research, 36*(2), 3–11.

Keogh, B. 1989. Social impacts. In G. Wall, Ed., *Outdoor Recreation in Canada* (223–275). Toronto: John Wiley:

King, B., Pizam, A., and Milman, A. 1993. Social impacts of tourism: Host perceptions. *Annals of Tourism Research, 20*, 650–665.

Ko, D.W., and Stewart, W.P. 2002. A structural model of residents' attitude for tourism development. *Tourism Management, 23*, 521–530.

Konovsky, M.A., and Pugh, S.D. 1994. Citizenship behavior and social exchange. *Academy of Management Journal, 37*(3), 656–669.

Korça, P. 1998. Resident perceptions of tourism in a resort town. *Leisure Sciences, 20*(3), 193–212.

Köseoglu, M.A., Yazici, S., and Okumus, F. 2018. Barriers to the implementation of strategic decisions: Evidence from hotels in a developing country. *Journal of Hospitality Marketing & Management, 27*(5), 514–543.

Kwan, F.V.C., and McCartney, G. 2005. Mapping resident perceptions of gaming impacts. *Journal of Travel Research, 44*, 177–187.

Lambe, C.J., Wittmann, C.M., and Spekman, R.E. 2001. Social exchange theory and research on business-to-business relational exchange. *Journal of Business-to-Business Marketing, 8*(3), 1–36.

Lankford, S.V. 1994. Attitudes and perceptions toward tourism and rural regional development. *Journal of Travel Research, 32*(2), 35–43.

Lankford, S.V., and Howard, D.R. 1994. Developing a tourism impact attitude scale. *Annals of Tourism Research, 21*, 121–139.

Látková, P., and Vogt, C.A. 2012. Residents' attitudes toward existing and future tourism development in rural communities. *Journal of Travel Research, 51*(1), 50–67.

Lawton, L.J. 2005. Resident perceptions of tourist attractions on the Gold Coast of Australia. *Journal of Travel Research, 44*, 188–200.

Lee, C.K., Kang, S.K., Long, P., and Reisinger, Y. 2010. Residents' perceptions of casino impacts: A comparative study. *Tourism Management*, *31*(2), 189–201.

Lepp, A. 2007. Residents' attitudes towards tourism in Bigodi village, Uganda. *Tourism Management*, *28*(3), 876–885.

Liu, J.C., Sheldon, P.J., and Var, T. 1987. Resident perception of the environmental impacts of tourism. *Annals of Tourism Research*, *14*(1), 17–37.

Liu, J., and Var, T. 1986. Residential attitudes toward tourism impact in Hawaii. *Annals of Tourism Research*, *13*, 193–214.

Lo, A., King, B., and Mackenzie, M. 2017. Restaurant customers' attitude toward sustainability and nutritional menu labels. *Journal of Hospitality Marketing & Management*, *26*(8), 846–867.

Long, P.T., Perdue, R.R., and Allen, L. 1990. Rural resident tourism perceptions and attitudes by community level. *Journal of Travel Research*, *28*(3), 3–9.

Mansfeld, Y. 1992. "Industrial landscapes" as positive settings for tourism development. *Geo Journal*, *28*, 457–463.

Martin, B.S. 1999. The efficacy of growth machine theory in explaining resident perceptions of community tourism development. *Tourism Analysis*, *4*(1), 47–55.

Mathieson, A., and Wall, G. 1982. *Tourism: Economic, Physical and Social Impacts*. London: Longman.

Mbaiwa, J.E. 2005. Enclave tourism and its socio-economic impacts in the Okavango Delta, Botswana. *Tourism Management*, *26*(2), 157–172.

McCool, S., and Martin, S. 1994. Community attachment and attitudes toward tourism development. *Journal of Travel Research*, *32*(3), 29–34.

Meredith, T. 1991. Environmental impact assessment and monitoring. In B. Mitchell, Ed., *Resource Management and Development* (pp. 224–245). Oxford: Oxford University Press.

Millar, M., Collins, M.D., and Jones, D.L. 2017. Exploring the relationship between destination image, aggressive street behavior, and tourist safety. *Journal of Hospitality Marketing & Management*, *26*(7), 735–751.

Milman, A., and Pizam, A. 1988. Social impacts of tourism on central Florida. *Annals of Tourism Research*, *15*(2), 191–204.

Miltin, D. 1992. Sustainable development: A guide to the literature. *Environment & Urbanization*, *4*(1), 111–124.

Molm, L.D. 1991. Affect and social exchange: Satisfaction in power-dependence relations. *American Sociological Review*, *56*(4), 475–493.

Moore, K., Cushman, G., and Simmons, D. 1995. Behavioral conceptualization of tourism and leisure. *Annals of Tourism Research*, *22*(1), 67–85.

Murphy, P.E. 1983. Tourism as a community industry – An ecological model of tourism development. *Tourism Management*, *4*(3), 180–193.

Nepal, S. 2008. Residents' attitudes to tourism in central British Columbia, Canada. *Tourism Geographies*, *10*, 42–65.

Nunkoo, R. 2015. Tourism development and trust in local government. *Tourism Management*, *46*, 623–634.

Nunkoo, R., and Gursoy, D. 2012. Residents' support for tourism: An identity perspective. *Annals of Tourism Research*, *39*(1), 243–268.

Nunkoo, R., and Gursoy, D. 2016. Rethinking the role of power and trust in tourism planning. *Journal of Hospitality Marketing & Management*, *25*(4), 512–522.

Nunkoo, R., and Gursoy, D. 2017. Political trust and residents' support for alternative and mass tourism: An improved structural model. *Tourism Geographies*, *19*(3), 318–339.

Nunkoo, R., Gursoy, D., and Juwaheer, T.D. 2010. Island residents' identities and their support for tourism: An integration of two theories. *Journal of Sustainable Tourism*, *18*(5), 675–693.

Nunkoo, R., and Ramkissoon, H. 2007. Residents' perceptions of the socio-cultural impact of tourism in Mauritius. *Anatolia*, *18*(1), 138–145.

Nunkoo, R., and Ramkissoon, H. 2009. Applying the means–end chain theory and the laddering technique to the study of host attitudes to tourism. *Journal of Sustainable Tourism*, *17*(3), 337–355.

Nunkoo, R., and Ramkissoon, H. 2010a. Small island urban tourism: A residents' perspective. *Current Issues in Tourism*, *13*(1), 37–60.

Nunkoo, R., and Ramkissoon, H. 2010b. Modeling community support for a proposed integrated resort project. *Journal of Sustainable Tourism*, *18*(2), 257–277.

Nunkoo, R., and Ramkissoon, H. 2010c. Gendered theory of planned behaviour and residents' support for tourism. *Current Issues in Tourism*, *13*(6), 525–540.

Nunkoo, R., and Ramkissoon, H. 2010d. Community perceptions of tourism in small island states: A conceptual framework. *Journal of Policy Research in Tourism, Leisure & Events, 2*(1), 51–65.

Nunkoo, R., and Ramkissoon, H. 2011a. Residents' satisfaction with community attributes and support for tourism. *Journal of Hospitality & Tourism Research, 35*(2), 171–190.

Nunkoo, R., and Ramkissoon, H. 2011b. Developing a community support model for tourism. *Annals of Tourism Research, 38*(3), 964–988.

Nunkoo, R., and Ramkissoon, H. 2012. Power, trust, social exchange and community support. *Annals of Tourism Research, 39*(2), 997–1023.

Nunkoo, R., and Ramkissoon, H. 2016. Stakeholders' views of enclave tourism: A grounded theory approach. *Journal of Hospitality & Tourism Research, 40*(5), 557–558.

Nunkoo, R., and Smith, S.L.J. 2013. Political economy of tourism: Trust in government actors, political support, and their determinants. *Tourism Management, 36*, 120–132.

Nunkoo, R., and Smith, S.L.J. 2014. Trust, tourism development, and planning. In R. Nunkoo and S.L.J. Smith, Eds., *Trust, Tourism Development and Planning* (pp. 15–22). Abingdon, UK: Routledge.

Nunkoo, R., Smith, S.L.J., and Ramkissoon, H. 2013. Residents' attitudes to tourism: A longitudinal study of 140 articles from 1984 to 2010. *Journal of Sustainable Tourism, 21*(1), 5–25.

Nunkoo, R., and So, K.K.F. 2016. Residents' support for tourism: Testing alternative structural models. *Journal of Travel Research, 55*(7), 847–861.

Oviedo-Garcia, M.A., Castellanos-Verdugo, M., and Martin-Ruiz, D. 2008. Gaining residents' support for tourism and planning. *International Journal of Tourism Research, 10*(2), 95–109.

Page, S.J. 1995. *Urban Tourism*. Routledge.

Paramati, S.R., Alam, M.S., and Chen, C.F. 2017. The effects of tourism on economic growth and CO_2 emissions: A comparison between developed and developing economies. *Journal of Travel Research, 56*(6), 712–724.

Park, D.B., Nunkoo, R., and Yoon, Y.S. 2015. Rural residents' attitudes to tourism and the moderating effects of social capital. *Tourism Geographies, 17*(1), 112–133.

Pearce II, J.A. 1980. Host community acceptance of foreign tourists: Strategic considerations. *Annals of Tourism Research, 7*(2), 224–233.

Pearce, P.L., Moscardo, G., and Ross, G.F. 1996. *Tourism Community Relationships*. Oxford: Pergamon Press.

Perdue, R.R., Long, P.T., and Allen, L. 1987. Rural resident tourism perceptions and attitudes. *Annals of Tourism Research, 14*(3), 420–429.

Perdue, R.R., Long, P.T., and Allen, L. 1990. Resident support for tourism development. *Annals of Tourism Research, 17*(4), 586–599.

Pérez, E.A., and Nadal, J.R. 2005. Host community perceptions: A cluster analysis. *Annals of Tourism Research, 32*(4), 925–941.

Pino, G., Peluso, A.M., Del Vecchio, P., Ndou, V., Passiante, G., and Guido, G. 2018. A methodological framework to assess social media strategies of event and destination management organizations. *Journal of Hospitality Marketing & Management, 28*(2), 189–216.

Pizam, A. 1978. Tourism's impacts: The social costs of the destination community as perceived by its residents. *Journal of Travel Research, 16*(4), 8–12.

Pizam, A., and Milman, A. 1984. The social impacts of tourism. *Industry & Environment, 7*(1), 11–14.

Pizam, A., and Pokela, J. 1985. The perceived impact of casino gambling on a community. *Annals of Tourism Research, 12*(2), 147–165.

Postma, A., and Schmuecker, D. 2017. Understanding and overcoming negative impacts of tourism in city destinations: Conceptual model and strategic framework. *Journal of Tourism Futures, 3*(2), 144–156.

Prayag, G., Hassibi, S., and Nunkoo, R. 2018. A systematic review of consumer satisfaction studies in hospitality journals: Conceptual development, research approaches and future prospects. *Journal of Hospitality Marketing & Management, 28*(1), 51–80.

Prentice, R. 1993. Community-driven tourism planning and residents' preferences. *Tourism Management, 14*(3), 218–227.

Ramkissoon, H., and Nunkoo, R. 2011. City image and perceived tourism impact: Evidence from Port Louis, Mauritius. *International Journal of Hospitality & Tourism Administration, 12*(2), 123–143.

Ritchie, J.B. 1988. Consensus policy formulation in tourism: Measuring resident views via survey research. *Tourism Management, 9*(3), 199–212.

Rodriguez, J., Parra-Lopez, E., and Yanez-Estevez, V. 2008. The sustainability of island destinations: Tourism area life cycle and teleological perspectives. The case of Tenerife. *Tourism Management, 29*, 53–65.

Rosenow, J.E., and Pulsipher, G.L. 1979. *Tourism the Good, the Bad, and the Ugly.* Lincoln, NE: Media Productions & Marketing.

Ross, G.F. 1992. Resident perceptions of the impact of tourism on an Australian city. *Journal of Travel Research*, 30(3), 13–17.

Rothman, R.A. 1978. Residents and transients: Community reaction to seasonal visitors. *Journal of Travel Research*, 16(3), 8–13.

Roudi, S., Arasli, H., and Akadiri, S.S. 2018. New insights into an old issue – Examining the influence of tourism on economic growth: Evidence from selected small island developing states. *Current Issues in Tourism*, 1–21. https://doi.org/10.1080/13683500.2018.1431207

Ruhanen, L., Weiler, B., Moyle, B.D., and McLennan, C.L.J. 2015. Trends and patterns in sustainable tourism research: A 25-year bibliometric analysis. *Journal of Sustainable Tourism*, 23(4), 517–535.

Saarinen, J. 2006. Traditions of sustainability in tourism studies. *Annals of Tourism Research*, 33(4), 1121–1140.

Sethna, R.J., and Richmond, B.O. 1978. US Virgin Islanders' perception of tourism. *Journal of Travel Research*, 17(1), 30–31.

Sharpley, R. 1994. *Tourism, Tourists and Society.* Huntingdon, UK: ELM.

Sheldon, P.J., and Abenoja, T. 2001. Resident attitudes in a mature destination: The case of Waikiki. *Tourism Management*, 22(5), 435–443.

Sheldon, P.J., & Var, T. 1984. Resident attitudes to tourism in North Wales. *Tourism Management*, 5(1), 40–47.

Smith, V.L. 1989. Eskimo tourism: Micro-models and marginal men. In V.L. Smith (Ed.), *Hosts and Guests* (2nd ed., pp. 55–83). Philadelphia: University of Pennsylvania Press.

Snaith, T., and Haley, A. 1999. Residents' opinions of tourism development in the historic city of York, England. *Tourism Management*, 20(5), 595–603.

Stronza, A., and Gordillo, J. 2008. Community views of ecotourism. *Annals of Tourism Research*, 35(2), 448–468.

Su, M.M., Wall, G., Wang, Y., and Jin, M. 2019. Livelihood sustainability in a rural tourism destination – Hetu Town, Anhui Province, China. *Tourism Management*, 71, 272–281.

Sutton, W. 1967. Travel and understanding: Notes on the social structure of tourism. *International Journal of Comparative Sociology*, 8(2), 21 8–223

Teye, V., Sonmez, S.F., and Sirakaya, E. 2002. Residents' attitudes toward tourism development. *Annals of Tourism Research*, 29(3), 668–688.

Thibaut, J.W., and Kelley, H. 1959. *The Social Psychology of Groups.* New York: Wiley.

Tohmo, T. 2018. The economic impact of tourism in central Finland: A regional input–output study. *Tourism Review*, 73(4), 521–547.

Tooman, A.L. 1997. Applications of the life-cycle model in tourism. *Annals of Tourism Research*, 24(1), 214–234.

Torre, A., and Scarborough, H. 2017. Reconsidering the estimation of the economic impact of cultural tourism. *Tourism Management*, 59, 621–629.

Tosun, C. 2001. Challenges of sustainable tourism development in the developing world: The case of Turkey. *Tourism Management*, 22, 289–303.

Tosun, C. 2002. Host perceptions of impacts: A comparative analysis. *Annals of Tourism Research*, 29(1), 231–253.

Tovar, C., and Lockwood, M. 2008. Social impacts of tourism: An Australian regional case study. *International Journal of Tourism Research*, 10, 365–378.

Turner, L.W, and Ash, J. 1975. *The Golden Hordes: International Tourism and the Pleasure Periphery.* London: Constable.

Tyrrell, T., and Spaulding, I. 1984. A survey of attitudes toward tourism growth in Rhode Island. *Hospitality Education & Research Journal*, 8(2), 22–33.

Upchurch, R.S., and Teivane, U. 2000. Resident perceptions of tourism development in Riga, Latvia. *Tourism Management*, 21(5), 499–507.

Var, T., Kendall, K., and Tarakcioglu, E. 1985. Residents attitudes toward tourists in a Turkish resort town. *Annals of Tourism Research*, 12(4), 652–658.

Vargas-Sanchez, A., Plaza-Mejia, M., and Porras-Bueno, N. 2009. Understanding residents' attitudes toward the development of industrial tourism in a former mining community. *Journal of Travel Research*, 47, 373–387.

Walpole, M.J., and Goodwin, H.J. 2000. Local economic impacts of dragon tourism in Indonesia. *Annals of Tourism Research*, 27(3), 559–576.

Ward, C., and Berno, T. 2011. Beyond social exchange theory: Attitudes toward tourists. *Annals of Tourism Research*, *38*(4), 1556–1569.

Whitener, E.M., Brodt, S.E., Korsgaard, M.A., and Werner, J.M. 1998. Managers as initiators of trust: An exchange relationship framework for understanding managerial trustworthy behavior. *Academy of Management Review*, *23*(3), 513–530.

WTTC. 2018. Travel and tourism economic impact 2018. Available from www.wttc.org/-/media/files/reports/economic-impact-research/regions-2018/world2018.pdf

Yoon, Y., Gursoy, D., and Chen, J.S. 2001. Validating a tourism development theory with structural equation modeling. *Tourism Management*, *22*, 363–372.

Young, G. 1973. *Tourism: Blessing or Blight?* Harmondsworth, UK: Penguin.

Yu, C.P., Chancellor, H.C., and Cole, S.T. 2011. Measuring residents' attitudes toward sustainable tourism: A reexamination of the sustainable tourism attitude scale. *Journal of Travel Research*, *50*(1), 57–63.

Zhang, J., Inbakaran, R.J., and Jackson, M.S. 2006. Understanding community attitudes towards tourism and host – Guest interaction in the urban–rural border region. *Tourism Geographies*, *8*(2), 182–204.

Zhang, Y., Ma, E., and Qu, H. 2018. Transaction cost and resources based views on hotels' outsourcing mechanism: An empirical study in China. *Journal of Hospitality Marketing & Management*, *27*(5), 583–600.

PART I

Tourism impacts

1

TOURISM PLANNING AND TOURISM IMPACTS

Donald G. Reid

Introduction

This chapter sets out the foundations of planning and alerts the reader to the common pitfalls that the proponents of tourism encounter when planning for tourism development, particularly at the local and community levels. To accomplish this goal, I will review, to a limited but sufficient extent, the major negative impacts tourism development often generates today and the positive outcomes through planning that are possible in the future. Although this entire text deals with impacts, both positive and negative, there are some specific issues that impinge directly on the planning process. This chapter views planning in the context of a complex and fast-changing society. For these reasons, it will stress the human interactions in, and the community educational value of, planning. This type of planning is commonly referred to as 'transactional planning.' Simply put, transactional planning, as the name implies, stresses inclusiveness and the processes of human interaction in the plan activity, rather than focusing solely on the tangible outputs produced by it. It is thought that, by emphasizing the planning process, the appropriate outputs will follow naturally. Additionally, and perhaps just as important as the outputs of the plan, is the education of those involved in its construction. Transactional planning is community-centered and places great value on the dialogue among the participants in the exercise, and on the issues most pertinent to them. The chapter will draw on previous work by this author, mainly from *Tourism, Globalization and Development: Responsible Tourism Planning* (2003) and *Social Policy and Planning for the 21st Century: In Search of the Next Great Social Transformation*, (2017).

Tourism planners often make the mistake of believing their activities are largely benign and that they are engaging a typical, undistinctive social, ecological, and cultural environment and need only concentrate on the primary task at hand, which is setting out an attractive project that will accomplish the goals of their client. This is an erroneous notion. Communities are dynamic and ever-changing assemblies of unique people. They possess a deep and rich collective history that constrains and sets the stage for future development. To ignore these unique features is to place the success of the potential tourism project in peril. The importance of the planning agent and their project proponent becoming intimately involved with, and developing a high level of understanding of, the community in its totality cannot be stressed enough. They must come to understand it deeply and not superficially as a tourist might. Primary in this task is the realization that the project is just as much about the community in which it will be eventually located as it is about accomplishing the goals of the primary client.

Preplanning considerations

There are specific fundamental conditions that must be present in the community in order for a sound and successful planning process to be conducted that will result in a plan that can be embraced by all interested parties. I have laid out these conditions in what I have termed the 'preplanning phase' (see Figure 1.1).

If each of these items is attended to prior to engagement in the actual planning of the project, the community's capacity to participate in the planning process with knowledge and confidence will be greatly enhanced. This confidence will allow the participants to create and review a proposed project without fear of being asked to approve something they truly do not understand and which may not be in their best interests. People will naturally oppose something they either do not truly comprehend or fear because of a lack of information. Planners often lack faith in the community's organizational capacity to analyze and utilize technical information in a sophisticated decision-making process. To overcome these fundamental issues, preplanning activity may be necessary.

Building the *community's capacity* to engage fully in the process will increase the probability of success in designing a mutually beneficial tourism project that the community feels speaks to their needs as well as to the aspirations of the project proponent. Building capacity in the community not only to undertake a planning exercise, perhaps in partnership with the project's proponent, but also to build the community's expertise in planning generally, is a positive benefit to the community beyond the specific project in question. For the project to succeed in the long term, some of the required skills for ensuring the sustainability of the project can be built during the preplanning phase. This not only assists the community but might also produce an increased payoff for the tourism industry as well.

Understanding the *context* in which tourism development occurs is critically important to the success of any project. There are several fundamental areas to highlight when considering

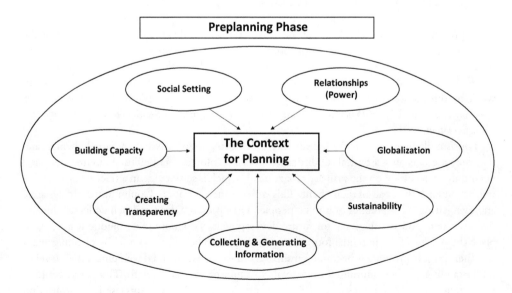

Figure 1.1 Preplanning phase

the setting in which tourism gets played out. The first is the complexity of the *social setting* beyond those aspects critical to, or influenced by, tourism, which often goes unrecognized and unaccounted for when considering tourism development. It is critically important to appreciate and acknowledge the unique history of the social relations in the area undertaking a tourism development plan, particularly as it relates to previous experiences in the locale. The proposal of a potential tourism project will be injected into a social, cultural, and political history, and not simply into a pristine context.

Any new proposal will be viewed and treated in the historical context of the community. It is likely that many projects, be they of a tourism nature or otherwise, will have preceded the present tourism project under consideration. How these projects were organized and carried out will have given local residents some idea about how decisions of this type get made, and, in many cases, past experiences will not necessarily provide a positive blueprint. Historically, input from local citizens may have been ignored, not necessarily out of malice but simply because the proponents of plans have not felt these individuals could add anything of benefit to the discussion. Often, community members have been viewed as being an impediment to getting the project approved and launched in a timely fashion. This occurs when the benefits of the project are simply meant to enrich the proponent of the project or the politicians of a state or community and not necessarily the local inhabitants of the area. It is this type of development that gives rise to the populist politics that seem to be gathering momentum across the globe. Participation by citizens in the plan is often seen as a statutory hurdle that needs to be accomplished as quickly as possible and not as an integral part of the development process. This type of approach will only give rise to community resistance to the project at the development stage and likely in the long term as well. Unfortunately, for most people, a negative planning process has been the norm in tourism development and not the exception, and so communities are naturally skeptical of planning in general.

The area with which I am most familiar is the Amboseli region in Kenya. Originally, the Amboseli National Park was constructed as a game preserve for European colonialists. Following independence, the Kenyan government turned it into a national park. Little, if any, consultation with the local Masai was undertaken at that time, and so the grazing and water needs of the locals were not taken into consideration, which resulted in a long-festering problem. Needless to say, the Masai eventually erupted and threatened to shoot the large animals that provided the main attraction to the tourists who visited the area. Eventually, the Kenya Wildlife Service, under the direction of a progressive director, launched an inclusive process that resulted in an agreement between the tourism sector and the local communities surrounding the park. This agreement has not settled the problem completely, but it has gone a substantial distance in providing some benefits to the locals from the tourism in the park. Transactive planning at the beginning of the project would have gone a considerable distance in averting the problem in the first place, but unfortunately that course was not in keeping with the ideology of colonialism. Although this is just one example of the types of difficulties that are inevitable unless the planning process is constructed on a solid and transactive basis, many similar to this one will be experienced in the future. Although colonialism throughout the world has been greatly reduced, we still plan on a top–down basis too often.

To avoid such negative impacts as described above, the proponents of a project, be they corporations or governments, must lay out how decisions affecting the project will be made, and the entire process must be seen to be *transparent* by all who will be affected by the outcome of those decisions. This transparency will also include providing details of the project, including a realistic assessment of the positive and negative benefits to the community. It must incorporate the feelings and concerns of the local people and not simply dismiss them as being obstructionist.

Often, information is not shared by the proponent of the project for so-called proprietary reasons. Given that the lives of the locals will be affected considerably by any project that may materialize from the plan, there is no justification for not divulging proprietary information that directly affects community life. Often, tourism industry officials feel that local people should not have equal weight in the decision-making process because they do not have any capital at risk in the scheme. Although they may not have capital in the venture, they do have their everyday lives at risk of being severely disrupted, which is equal in value to any capital that a company may have in the project.

The tourism project does not occur in a static environment but in a very complex set of community relationships that affects the totality of community life. As Appadurai tells us,

> [T]his is a world of flows. It is also, of course, a world of structures, organizations, and other stable forms of social life. By this I mean that the paths or vectors taken by these kinds of things have different speeds, axes, points of origin and termination, and varied relationships to institutional structures in different regions, nations or societies.
>
> *(Appadurai, 2001, p. 14)*

Tourism planners need to take these realities into account when conceptualizing and planning a tourism project. In fact, they must be guided by them. The individuals, groups, ideologies, and social classes that make up a community are not homogeneous but extremely variable. We should not speak of community as if it were a single entity, but rather as multidimensional and ever changing. Community alliances often shift form depending on the issue at hand. Some community groups may align with other groups on some issues but be opposing forces on other proposals. A community is made up of many groups with diverse agendas, and they do not always speak with a single voice.

Critical to this discussion is the identification of the *power relationships* and conflicting interests that permeate tourism planning and the community generally. The power relationships that inevitably arise during the planning stage of development have the potential to create a process that strives for a win–win condition for all the parties involved, or a winner-takes-all approach. Naturally, the former is preferred over the latter.

Large-scale tourism is often a multi-jurisdictional matter. Much of the capital and infrastructure required for development is supplied by multinational corporations located in affluent countries, whereas the project is often situated in unique, natural, and sensitive, environments. Tourism development by outside forces often intrudes into traditional cultures and fragile environments, frequently set in far-flung and sometimes exotic and fragile locations. Tourism's technical expertise frequently comes from outside the destination country and is supplied by outsiders who may not possess sufficient knowledge of the culture into which they are embedding their projects. Tourism can easily disturb the sense of place in the destination site, creating diverse types of impacts, both positive and negative. The notion of distance in cultural patterns between the 'industry and its clients' and the 'tourism destination' (host–guest) and how planning can help smooth out this difference will be analyzed and addressed further on in this chapter. But make no mistake, cultural differences can have a profound and long-lasting effect on tourism projects and the communities in which they reside.

It is important to understand who is fundamentally in charge of the planning process and driving the proposed tourism development project. In many cases, it is the industry that initiates and controls the development, in the sense that the outside agent offers a significant project that will increase the economic flows to the community from outside. But, it is also likely to attract substantial numbers of people to the area, which has the potential to disrupt community life.

The tourism agent may correspondingly entice the state to make decisions on their behalf that may not always be in the best interest of local people by promising a significant increase in foreign currency for an often-distressed national budget. That is not to say that the national or local authority are not the final decision-makers, but it must be recognized that the industry has great influence and can shape the outcome of the plan. More often than not, the industry creates the vision for the project and then attempts to persuade the nation or community of its appropriateness and value to the local area. Much of the data collection on such subjects as environmental assessment, cost–benefit analysis, and social impact analysis is completed by the proponent of the project, and not always with the input or comprehension of the local community. And, when it does solicit input from the community, it is not always clear if those they are engaging in the dialogue legitimately represent who they say they represent.

Tourism corporations have considerable resources that they can apply to research and subsequent lobbying. They also contain or can retain expertise that can put together a persuasive case in favor of the project, while ignoring facts that do not necessarily support their arguments. On the other hand, the community is likely to have fewer resources and less sophistication to put toward such an exercise. This is one of the main reasons why building capacity in the community, so it can be actively and constructively engaged in the planning project, is so necessary. It will be important to structure a planning process that considers what may be an imbalance in expertise and resources and adequately represents all points of view. Coming at the project from different points of view with equal strength will allow for the data to be interpreted in many ways. Although data collection and analysis may be ideologically neutral, interpretation is not. There is room for debate about what that data mean to differing perspectives. It may be necessary for the decision-making body to provide funding to community groups so that they can constructively participate in the totality of the panning process, but particularly as it relates to research analysis and interpretation.

Sustainability is also a major question to be addressed in tourism development planning. The issue of 'sustainability' as it pertains to tourism development requires definition. The question of exactly what is being sustained needs to be clearly identified. Is it the tourism product that is the emphasis of attention for sustainability or is it the environment, both social and ecological, that provides the focus for sustainability? Naturally these different vantage points for defining sustainability take the project down different paths, and so the question of what is being sustained is of critical importance at the outset. Those not associated with the tourism industry are likely to view development from the sustainability of the community, environment, and their traditional social structure perspective. For obvious reasons, the tourism industry is interested in the sustainability of their product and the financial payoff that goes with that investment. It is critically important that both points of view be found in the plan, without the product being watered down so that it loses its uniqueness and value to both groups.

All too often the tourism sector, mainly the hotel and resort industry, sees itself as the attraction, when in actuality it is reliant on a unique natural or cultural feature that is the main pull for visitors. Many of these natural and cultural features are not under the jurisdiction of the proponent of the project, and so, quite rightly, the industry does not feel responsible for them. That said, most industry executives understand that, without the cultural or natural feature, their raison d'être does not exist. So, although it may not always be top of mind, they realize they have an interest in, but not necessarily control of, sustaining the natural or cultural feature on which their operation relies. It follows, therefore, that it is in the industry's interest to cooperate in the sustainability of the features around which it builds its operations. Traditional cultures and natural features that people want to visit are finite and in short supply, and the industry cannot continue to spoil them without doing itself harm over the long term.

As suggested in Figure 1.1, those residing in the jurisdiction in which the tourism project is targeted must have absolute *trust* in the planning process. This trust is built by paying attention to the items raised above and by the planning agent acting in a forthright manner with all partners in the process.

When considering the context of tourism planning in the international context, one must contemplate the phenomenon of *globalization*. The global nature of tourism makes it inevitable that dissimilar cultures and interests will collide, and all points of view must be fully comprehended by the planning process and accounted for in the eventual plan. Additionally, global climate change is also on top of mind these days, and the tourism industry is a prolific contributor to this increasing problem. As a consequence, the industry needs to be fully engaged in resolving this problem.

The globalization phenomenon has come under attack in recent times, and tourism is one of the biggest players in the globalizing movement. In fact, tourism has been one of the drivers of economic globalization. And, as we see from the rise of isolationism in many countries, including Britain's exit from the European Union (Brexit) and Donald Trump's populist movement in the USA, globalization of the economy is under severe attack because it has served the mainstream population poorly, or is perceived to have done so. Appadurai suggests that,

> Global capital in its contemporary form is characterized by strategies of predatory mobility (across both time and space) that have vastly compromised the capacities of actors in single locations even to understand, much less to anticipate or resist, these strategies.
>
> *(Appadurai, 2001, p. 31)*

Although Appadurai is speaking generally about globalization, it is not difficult to see how his concern applies directly to tourism development, given that vast amounts of tourism's income winds up in the coffers of multinational companies located in the developed world.

Globalization of the world's economy was constructed on the pretext that the future could only get better if sovereign countries looked beyond their borders for economic growth. It was felt by most nations that all societies would do better financially if tariff barriers were kept to a minimum and all nations engaged in the world economy rather than focusing solely inward. This liberal-democratic view promised a win–win for all countries and citizens involved. The globalization of the economy has not served the mainstream population well, however, and globalists are now fending off severe attempts to roll globalization back. Huyssen argues that, "[S]ince the 1980s, it seems, the focus has shifted from the present futures to present pasts" (Huyssen, 2001, p. 73). This is to suggest that, from the end of World War II to the early to mid 1980s, people looked outward and forward to a brighter future than they had experienced before and during the war. There was a certain optimism that pervaded the industrial West, particularly as leaders talked about expanding the economy beyond national borders, which, hopefully, would bring increased prosperity to all. This has been far from what has happened. Some have benefitted greatly from the globalization of capital, but many more have not. Since the 1980s, people have looked at the past with nostalgia, believing that things were better for them then than they are at present. The populist movement that is evolving out of what some might argue (Reid, 2017) is a failed economic globalization should cause the tourism industry to step back and analyze its practices from the perspective of globalization, from the bottom up, rather than the top–down model which is how it has been constructed and practiced up to the present day.

That said, the tradition of humankind is to continue past and present practices even when confronted by unequivocal evidence that these approaches and ideologies are no longer working but are detrimental to the advancement of humanity, or even to maintaining the status quo. When this point in human development is reached, Bende asks the question,

> [W]hy was nothing done in time? Were the economic and policy elites unaware of the profound disruption that economic and technological change were causing working men and women? What prevented them from taking steps necessary to prevent a global social crisis?
>
> *(Bende, 2001, p. 109)*

This is a perplexing question and one that needs to be addressed by the tourism industry. In fact, this question may represent a turning point for the tourism industry if it can supply a suitable answer. Can the industry consider the needs of all society and the ecosystem in their new developments? Can tourism planning projects incorporate considerations regarding the health of communities and the environment in addition to the corporation's bottom line? These are outstanding questions that may find answers in the near future as the new generation of tourism entrepreneurs and planners construct their projects in light of the new world conditions. And, as Huyssen reminds us, "the past cannot give us what the future has failed to deliver" (Huyssen, 2001, p. 96). Given Huyssen's pithy realization, globalization must be reconstructed and made to work for the mainstream as well as for the wealthy. A new type of internationalism that is built from the bottom up can provide the long-anticipated results of globalization for mainstream people throughout the world. It is the position of this text that the tourism industry will need to embrace the bottom–up approach to development or be swallowed up by it. Given that reality, the transactional planning process advocated in this chapter will provide for a strong focus on citizen involvement in planning and decision-making.

The planning framework

Flowing from the discussion on the importance of preplanning considerations is the introduction of the framework for planning. The planning framework identifies the steps involved in the process. Also, the planning framework sets out the parameters by which the process is constrained and unfolds. Essentially, the framework contains the agreed-upon ground rules under which the plan is carried out. This allows all interested parties to understand what constitutes the process for decision-making and at what stage the process is at any given point in time during its implementation. The framework mediates the aspirations of the project's proponents through the culture, values, and norms of the locale for which the plan is intended. Often, the success of the project is determined at this stage of the process, long before a plan or project emerges. There are several components (see Figure 1.2) of the typical planning framework including: project vision creation (which encompasses how tourism fits into the overall economic development policy of the jurisdiction in question); setting goals and objectives for tourism development; establishing realistic and strategic actions to accomplish these goals and objectives; undertaking and completing environmental, social, and economic impact assessments for the proposed actions; identifying and negotiating responsibilities for plan implementation, including identifying those responsible for implementing the program; and, perhaps most importantly, creating a strategy for involving strategic partners and local community citizens in plan creation and decision-making. These vital issues and processes constitute the main features of the classical planning process.

Unlike the past and present, however, these activities must be undertaken within an ideology that is future-looking and accepts the fact that tourism plans need to be constructed on the new reality that was laid out earlier in this chapter and addressed the realities of the fatally flawed globalization project. No longer does the traditional planning process fit this new reality. Although the steps in the planning process continue to be valid and provide a substantive path for planning, the mindset in which they are implemented must be reset to fit the present social and environmental conditions as described throughout this chapter. As Bende asserts,

> [W]hen the horizon of meaning shrinks, when the process of knowledge disintegrates, and when the passage of time would seem to have changed directions, modern man [*sic*] seeks refuge within a shell of ignorance and denial. To break this shell is what is required of us today.
>
> *(Bende, 2001, p. 109)*

The shrinkage, as Bende describes it, is what we are witnessing today as many of the major countries throughout the world are in a social–political swing to isolationism and populism. Unlike recent history when planning occurred in an atmosphere of progressive liberalism, the new reality is that of protectionist isolationism. This is all to say that the way we have done business in the past will not necessarily be the way we do business in the future, and this applies to tourism planning as well as other industries. Consequently, although the tourism planning process may continue to utilize the classical framework as presented in Figure 1.2, it will need to arrange the playing field so that it is more inclusive and demonstrate clearly the benefits of tourism development to the mainstream population in the locale in which it is projected to function. No longer can citizen participation in the planning process be treated as a marketing and sales initiative. Tourism planning will be required to treat the mainstream population and their representatives as equal partners in the process. This may include providing these groups with funding in order for them to carry out their own research and impact assessments with regard to the plan.

The planning and research process as it relates to tourism development

Involving local people in the planning process is complicated but necessary to ensure the success of the tourism planning project. And, remember, what constitutes success must be clearly defined by all interested parties at the outset of the project. A great deal of thought must be given to establishing the appropriate framework for citizen involvement. What citizen involvement does not mean is to view local residents and groups as obstacles to what the plan's proponent wants to achieve and the process to be construed as a sales and marketing event with the goal of winning the citizens over to the proponent's point of view. Citizen involvement is clearly not intended to be a marketing program by the proponent of the project. It is meant to be an intensive exploration of the aspirations of the citizens in the target locale and of how the proposed project may help a community reach those aspirations. Tourism planning must become more cooperative between the industry and the community, not adversarial. So, as David Graeber suggests, "It is much easier, in the face-to-face community, to figure out what most members of that community want to do, than to figure out how to convince those who do not go along with it" (Graeber, 2004, p. 89).

There is a fine line between providing appropriate public engagement in plan creation and decision-making and giving a veto to citizens or a particular group of citizens in the planning process. One of the questions that must be addressed before any project or plan is commenced involves what weight should be given to the voices of the various players in the community system. This question can be answered in the preplanning exercise as described above. But, let there be no mistake, giving a project veto to any single group in the process is not what is being advocated here.

Consensus is often portrayed as the essence of what is desirable in these types of projects. Although this goal may be theoretically laudable, it is not necessarily feasible in practice. Achieving consensus at all costs can result in a plan that gets so watered down that it inspires no one. What is required, however, is to outline in general terms what percentage of the community and its various groups needs to show support for the plan for it to proceed. In addition, people need to feel that they have been listened to, even if their desires do not appear in the final plan. Being listened to does not mean that the plan incorporates the desires of any one citizen or group of citizens, but that their position was put on the table and thoroughly and honestly vetted, if not necessarily adopted in the plan. If proposals are not accepted, the rationale for their modification or rejection must be clearly stated and understood by all.

The basis on which planning proceeds

People with special interests, such as tourism proponents, plan from a conceptual reality of the world that may be significantly different than other participants who may have an interest in the plan and its outcome. The tourism industry plans from the point of view of cost–benefit analysis, profit maximization, and potential return on capital. Government officials examine the project from a developmental point of view and are particularly concerned with the project's ability to inject foreign capital into the system or, in the case of in-country development, the injection of new, outside money into the region or community economy. They are also interested in creating jobs for their citizens. The interests of members of the community might very well be concentrated on maintaining their sense of place and enhancing their environment, both ecologically and socially. Mbembe uses the term modalities to describe these focused interests of each group. He concludes, "[T]hese modalities depend on histories and local cultures, on the interplay of interests whose determinants do not all lead in the same direction" (Mbembe, 2001, p. 33). The basic goals of each group in the system may not harmonize with each other and, in fact, they may be in conflict. The planning agent must consider all these points of view when carrying out the process. The process must be transparent, and those charged with implementing the planning process must not make assumptions without thorough vetting by all parties concerned. All special interests in the project need to recognize the different modalities of the various parties in the process and must not assume that everyone in the venture shares their group's goals but may, in fact, have interests of their own which may lead in different directions. The constraints and activities of transactive planning are outlined in Figure 1.2.

Figure 1.2 sets out a classical conceptual model for tourism planning. Its implementation may be more complicated in actuality than it appears diagrammatically. The steps in the planning process are contained in the triangle in the middle of the diagram.

Vision creation addresses the question: What do we want this community (region country, etc.) to look and feel like over the long term that could be positively or negatively affected by this project? What is the overall aspiration of those who are to be directly affected by the plan? After all, their well-being must be at the center of the plan unless it is being intentionally forfeited for some larger national goal. In fact, participation by affected citizens, or their surrogates, should be fully engaged at this beginning stage and continue throughout the entire process. It is most likely that their engagement would be secured during the preplanning stage, as outlined earlier in this chapter. How this engagement is facilitated is of great importance to the overall strategy. Great skill in facilitation and group dynamics is required to manage this critical component of the exercise, and sound ongoing expertise should be sought to accomplish this part of the process effectively.

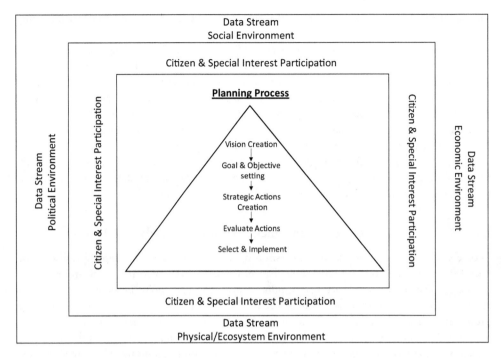

Figure 1.2   The comprehensive tourism plan

Goal and objective setting follows naturally from the vision statement as described above. Goals set out the large chunks of 'hoped-for achievements' that, if reached, will collectively realize the vision as outlined earlier in the planning process. Goals are not necessarily measurable but set out the direction in which the actions of the eventual plan will move. Objectives, on the other hand, are strategic measurable actions that describe what is to be done to accomplish the goals.

Flowing from the goals and objectives, the plan will *create strategic actions* including the preparation of the projects and programs that are determined to best achieve the objectives of the plan. It is at this stage that concrete proposals are prepared in detail outlining what exactly is to be constructed or instituted that will achieve the goals as outlined. The *evaluation of the proposed actions* is undertaken at this point in the process to determine the costs and benefits of what is being suggested. Costs and benefits are to be determined for all those who will be affected by the plan and not simply for the project proponents or for the national governments where the eventual project resides. Costs and benefits stretch far beyond economic indicators and include environmental and social indicators (value criteria) as well. A necessary step at this stage of the process is to collectively identify the value criteria on which the strategic actions will be judged. Most often a proposal is judged on economic criteria, who benefits and who loses. There are additional criteria, such as maintaining or enhancing sense of place, that may be just as important to local residents as economic measures. These criteria need to be determined and agreed to by all parties engaged in, or affected by, the plan. It is here where proposals are examined for their potential positive and negative impacts on the community and environment based on agreed-upon value criteria. Full social and environmental impact assessments must be undertaken on all proposals at this stage in the process.

A word of caution is needed at this point in the discussion. All too often, tourism planners start their community engagement at the strategic action stage of the planning process. This is particularly the case when the proponent—a resort company, for example—is driving the planning process. Neglecting to engage all interested parties at the beginning stage of the process (vision creation) because it may not appear to oblige the direct interests of the commercial enterprise will only serve to create mistrust in the community and generate hostility for the project. If presentations of proposals become the starting point for public input in the tourism plan, the project may run into stiff opposition because of the lack of sufficient information and the rationale on which the project is being offered. Although proponents of the project understand the plan from the beginning, locals will react negatively at this stage if for no other reason than out of fear if they have not been involved from the beginning and carried along to this stage of the process. In this scenario, the public may not even know the issues that need to be addressed, let alone have sufficient data on which to provide informed answers to those questions. In fact, the plan may not fit but be in opposition to the goals of the community. This is the reason why the planning process is contained within the boxes of *citizen and special interest participation* and the *four data streams: economic, social, political*, and *environmental*. Participation by locals and special interests must be embedded throughout the entire process and not simply seen as a hurdle to be overcome in the last stages of the planning process just to get a proponent's project approved. Surely, we are far beyond that regressive thinking in planning generally, and in tourism planning particularly. Public participation must not be turned into a marketing and sales activity but needs to be a true partnership between the community and any outside commercial enterprise that may have primary interest in the proposal.

The identification and creation of relevant and sufficient data that speak directly to the interest and well-being of the community are integral parts of the tourism planning process. The participation of the community in the research process is a highly desirable activity. Most important to this process is the prerogative of the participants in the plan to interpret all data that are thought to be germane to the plan. The interpretation of any data created or found that are considered relevant to the evaluation of proposals by any participant in the planning exercise is not the sole prerogative of the tourism planner. Interpretation of data is not a scientific but a political activity, and it is necessary for all parties in the process to provide their specific point of view on those data. This will provide for a rich debate and will speak to whether the proposed strategic actions address the vision, goals, and objectives set out earlier in the process. This provides an important feedback loop that, hopefully, will keep the process on track.

Tourism planning must be thought of as a component of a larger activity that is designed to increase the well-being of the area in question and not as an isolated, focused event. Tourism may provide one component of that wellness but not likely the only component.

Implementation is the final stage in the classical tourism planning tradition. This is the stage that is often given least attention and the place at which the process regularly breaks down. Tasks for implementing the project need to be identified, and responsibility for seeing that they get done must be assigned to individuals or committees. And, whereas this is easy to do for the construction of buildings and amenities, it is less straightforward for such areas as monitoring and evaluating the project for its success over the long term. Research to monitor the ongoing impacts of the development and arranging public presentations of those data are some of the tasks that often do not get assigned to an individual or small group and, consequently, fall by the wayside. The project is not over once the buildings are constructed and tourists start to flow into the area. Ongoing monitoring and evaluation of the tourist destination site are critical.

What does the future hold for tourism planning?

Planning ought to be viewed by everyone in the process as an aid to development and not as a hurdle or requirement that is put in the way of accomplishing a project. Planning that includes impact assessments is a fundamental instrument in coming to understand the nuances of any proposal before it becomes a reality, a reality that may be less than ideal for some involved if not well planned and monitored.

Future tourism development and planning for it will need to be grounded in a values framework. This approach may be quite different than the purely economic framework used exclusively in the past. First and foremost, all development, including tourism, must be rooted in an ethical protocol. Some of the most important elements of that ethical protocol will include, but not be exclusive to: the imperative of preserving local present and past culture and its artifacts; the conservation and preservation of the physical environment; the idea of equity and justice for all those affected by the plan and any eventual project; the imperative of not negatively impacting future generations; and the need to enhance social conditions for local populations, including economic circumstances.

In addition to the values framework and ethical imperatives outlined above, future tourism planning will need to pay special attention to: how decisions will be made in the planning process, and who should be involved and with what weight; how input to the process is made by all concerned and how that input is utilized in the decision-making process; and how the project is ranked in juxtaposition to other aspirations in the community and the process created to make those determinations.

The future of tourism planning will stretch far beyond the actual site-specific project and embrace a larger focus that considers how the proposed project fits into and affects the region in which it is embedded. Out of necessity, if not because of altruism, the tourism planning process will need to be wider ranging in substance and with regard to who is involved in the process than it is at present. The world is moving beyond a globalized economic system that is controlled by elites and experts and it will be more egalitarian and inclusive in the future. The ownership of the process must be communal and horizontal, not simply vertical and top–down, controlled by the tourism industry and political elite. Because of these changing conditions, transactional planning will take on a heightened role in determining the future of the world, including tourism development.

References

Appadurai, A. (2001). Grassroots globalization and the research imagination. In A. Appadurai, *Globalization* (pp. 8–32). Durham, NC: Duke University Press.

Bende, J. (2001). Towards an ethics of the future. In A. Appadurai, *Globalization* (pp. 104–133). Durham, NC: Duke University Press.

Graeber, D. (2004). *Fragments of an Anarchist Anthropology*. Chicago, IL: Prickly Paradigm.

Huyssen, A. (2001). Present pasts: Media, politics, amnesia. In A. Appadurai, *Globalization* (pp. 73–97). Durham, NC: Duke University Press.

Mbembe, A. (2001). At the edge of the world: Boundaries, territoriality, and sovereignty in africa. In A. Appadurai, *Globalization* (pp. 33–68). Durham, NC: Duke University Press.

Reid, D. G. (2003). *Tourism, Globalization and Development: Responsible Tourism Planning*. London: Pluto Press.

Reid, D. G. (2017). *Social Policy and Planning for the 21st Century: In Search of the Next Great Social Transformation*. London: Routledge.

2

TOURISM AND QUALITY OF LIFE

Perunjodi Naidoo and Prabha Ramseook-Munhurrun

Introduction

Tourism is viewed as an attractive vehicle of growth mostly in developing countries (Telfer & Sharpley, 2014); however, the challenge is not only to stimulate economic development but for tourism to be an engine of improved quality of life (QoL). This chapter explains the concept of QoL from a development approach and takes into account the perspectives of residents. In recent years, the concept of QoL has gained increasing attention in some regions of the world and at a global level. In fact, understanding the significance of QoL and its assessment can provide information on how well a country or a government is performing compared with other nations or previous governments. This chapter reflects on the emergence and growing importance of QoL in the field of tourism. It provides a theoretical review of the concept of QoL within the contexts of sustainable development. It also defines QoL and discusses key studies on QoL undertaken in the field of tourism.

Tourism, development and QoL

Tourism has been encouraged as a fundamental development policy for its potential to contribute to economic and social progress, in particular in developing countries (Telfer & Sharpley, 2014) by increasing government revenues, creating employment and acting as a facilitator for wider economic growth. However, its contributions to the QoL of destination communities is still disputed as, although tourism is an activity which undoubtedly brings economic benefits, the extent to which it has really enhanced the well-being of locals remains unclear (Naidoo & Sharpley, 2016). This is largely owing to the initial understanding of the concept of development, which was somewhat flawed and limited as it did not, for several decades, consider broader aspects of people's well-being. For generations, nations have assessed their success or failure based on measures of economic growth; however, an increase in traditional indicators of economic growth (e.g. GDP) does not necessarily translate into the quality of progress made by destinations (Uysal et al., 2016; Sirgy, 2002) such as reducing economic inequalities, empowering individuals, providing meaningful employment, or having access to better opportunities or better health for the community (New Economics Foundation, 2015).

Nevertheless, over time, the narrow understanding of the concept of development has evolved from a traditional economic conceptualisation to embrace a broader approach inclusive of human well-being (Naidoo & Sharpley, 2016). This is largely owing to arguments put forward by economists such as Sen (1990) who have criticised the restricted definition of development and disputed that the process of development should evolve to a human development approach expanding the capabilities of all people. This perspective is also adopted by the Human Development Report of the United Nations Development Programme:

> [T]he purpose of development is to offer people more options. One of the options is access to income – not as an end itself but as a means to acquiring human well-being. But there are other options as well, including long life, knowledge, political freedom, personal security, community participation and guaranteed human rights.
>
> *(UNDP, 1990)*

Development should focus on enlarging people's freedom, choices and opportunities and improving their well-being. The purpose is to ultimately expand the richness of human life rather than only increase the richness of the economy (UNDP, 2018). However, despite the shift in the development approach and the expanded notion of progress to focus on well-being, it has yet to be put into practice by many governments, particularly where tourism is concerned. For example, Novelli and Hellwig (2011) argued that there is little empirical evidence of the direct contributions of tourism to the Millennium Developmental Goals.

On a positive note, from a broader perspective, there have been a few recognised initiatives that have been taken at a global level and in some regions of the world with regard to QoL frameworks which have been adopted to measure societal progress. Happiness is increasingly considered as the proper measure of social progress and the goal of public policy. For example, the Happy Planet Index (HPI), a combination of human well-being and environmental measures, was introduced by the New Economics Foundation in July 2006. In 2011, The UN General Assembly passed a resolution, "Happiness: towards a holistic approach to development", acknowledging that happiness is fundamental to the well-being of people. The resolution also encouraged member nations to follow the example of Bhutan, which has adopted the Gross Happiness Index (GHI), taking a holistic approach towards progress and also considering non-economic components of well-being. The GHI consists of nine domains grouped under four pillars (good governance, sustainable socio-economic development, cultural preservation and environmental conservation). The nine domains comprise psychological well-being, health, education, cultural diversity and resilience, time use, good governance, community vitality, ecological diversity and resilience, and living standards.

The rising international importance of QoL is also reflected in the World Happiness Report, which was first released in 2012 and provided a foundation document for the UN high-level meeting on Well-being and Happiness: Defining a New Economic Paradigm. According to the World Happiness Report 2017, happiness should be at the core of a government's efforts to achieve both human and sustainable development. In the same report, the Head of UN Development also maintained that what really mattered to nations was the "quality of growth" and not the "tyranny of GDP" (Helliwell, Layard & Sachs, 2017). Moreover, there is increasing evidence that communities around the world believe that QoL is an important governmental goal (Naidoo, Pearce & Sharpley, 2017) and happiness should be part of government policy (Helliwell et al., 2012). For example, a survey carried out in the UK showed that 81% of the country's population thought that, instead of pursuing "greatest wealth", the government should instead target "greatest happiness" (BBC, 2006), demonstrating a strong commitment to improving the well-being of its population.

Quality of life

Many fields of study have embedded QoL within their research domain. Several definitions of QoL have emerged in the literature, and a number of models of QoL have been discussed. QoL has frequently been defined as the quality of people's experience of life (OECD, 2013) and has often been explained in terms of happiness, life satisfaction, good life and well-being (Veenhoven, 2012; Pearce, Filep & Ross, 2010; Diener, 2009; Moscardo, 2009). Veenhoven (2005: 61) suggests that "quality of life can be measured by how long and happy people live". Thus, QoL has been described as a multidimensional construct encompassing many aspects of people's lives and environments (Kim, Uysal & Sirgy, 2013; Schalock, 1996). From the literature, it can be gathered that there are broadly two types of QoL research: (1) objective measures (e.g. income, education) and (2) subjective measures (e.g. satisfaction with various aspects of life; Carneiro & Eusébio, 2015; Andereck & Nyaupane, 2011; Meng, Li & Uysal, 2010).

Objective measures of QoL

One of the widely used objective assessments of QoL is the Human Development Index which measures QoL through three dimensions: long and healthy life, education and income. In other scholarly research, QoL is also typically measured using other objective indicators such as economic well-being (e.g. literacy, housing and level of income), leisure well-being (e.g. access to parks and recreational facilities), environmental well-being (e.g. access to clean water, and low CO_2 emissions), health well-being (e.g. average life expectancy and healthcare; McCabe, Joldersma & Li, 2010; Schueller, 2009). These indices account for factors that are referred to as "facts of life" or "reality", while not taking into consideration the subjective components (Andereck & Jurowski, 2006).

Subjective measures of QoL

In contrast, from a subjective perspective, QoL research has its roots in positive psychology (Goodman et al., 2017; Schueller & Seligman, 2010; Ryff, 1989; Diener, 1984). Subjective well-being (SWB) is an overriding concept adopted in the discourse of QoL and places much stress on the 'subjective aspects' of human life, taking into account psychological responses, such as life satisfaction and personal happiness. The OECD (2013) defines SWB as "good mental states, including all of the various evaluations, positive and negative, that people make of their lives and the affective reactions of people to their experiences". SWB focuses on three main components which are positive affect (pleasant), negative affect (unpleasant) and life satisfaction (Brey, 2012). Life satisfaction, which is the cognitive dimension of SWB, comprises people's life conditions based on the positive and negative affect and, therefore, the evaluation of their life ranging from dissatisfaction to satisfaction (Brey, 2012; Diener, 2009). In that sense, SWB has to do with the general evaluation of one's life and the degree to which one experiences a sense of wellness (Deci & Ryan, 2008) with regard to the ongoing events in one's life.

The SWB measurement of QoL has gained much attention in recent years as it is argued that it provides a better alternative than objective well-being to assess QoL (Layard, 2005). Diener and Suh (1997) contend that subjective indicators are valid measures of what people judge to be important to their happiness and well-being. As Layard (2005) argues, "our feelings have sufficient objective reality to be taken very seriously". As a result the measurements of subjective indicators are essentially personal and based on the judgements of individuals regarding how they perceive their lives. Subsequently, the subjective experience is reliant on the perceptions and feelings of an individual (Andereck & Nyaupane, 2011). As QoL it is an outcome of the fulfilment of human needs and, as humans have multiple needs (Costanza et al., 2008), QoL can only be assessed from the perspectives of the individuals aspiring to those needs. It is also important to note that the definition of QoL is likely to be different across people and contexts (Cecil et al., 2010), and this poses challenges in its measurement. Nevertheless, in 2013, the OECD (2013: 10) designed guidelines for measuring SWB to assess the progress of countries based on three criteria, namely: (1) "Life evaluation – a reflective assessment on a person's life or some specific aspect of it"; (2) "Affect – a person's feelings or emotional states, typically measured with reference to a particular point in time"; and (3) "Eudaimonia – a sense of meaning and purpose in life, or good psychological functioning". As a result, the SWB model has been increasingly viewed as a useful measure to predict the sense of wellness and happiness at the individual level as well as at community and global levels.

QoL and sustainable development

In recent years, several authors have drawn the concept of QoL under the umbrella of sustainable development. Consistent with the criticisms of development outlined at the start of the chapter, authors argue that the goal of economic activity is to increase the well-being of societies (Naidoo & Sharpley, 2016; Costanza et al., 2009), hence, the importance of placing QoL at the centre of sustainable discourse and as the focus of a sustainable tourism development strategy for a destination. Useful measures of progress should reflect the degree to which society's economic, social, and ecological well-being is being considered (Costanza et al., 2007). This is because high levels of QoL are the results of the interplay among social, economic and environmental dimensions that together make people satisfied with their life, and these broad dimensions provide the resources to meet the aspirations of the community and enhance its QoL (Moscardo, 2009). Researchers and earlier studies have drawn attention to the negative outcomes of tourism development in developing countries (Naidoo & Pearce, 2016; Buzinde, Kalavar & Melubo, 2014; Telfer & Sharpley, 2014; Nunkoo, Gursoy & Juwaheer, 2010; Mbaiwa, 2005; Britton, 1982) such as unequal relations of dependency and inequitable socio-economic and spatial development. However, judiciously planned and well-developed tourist destinations with a focus on QoL can benefit the lives of residents, adding to the value of their experiences and making their lives more meaningful (Reisinger & Park, 2009). From a sustainable tourism development perspective, QoL provides a framework within which locals' prosperity can be attained (Boukas & Ziakas, 2016).

Studies drawing on the relationship between QoL and sustainable tourism have begun to emerge. For example, Moscardo and Murphy' study (2016) showed that tourism had potential value in supporting residents' QoL aspirations and sustainability. In contrast, Boukas and Ziakas's study (2016) showed that tourism in Cyprus only indirectly contributed to QoL as, although sustainable tourism is perceived as a valuable concept at governmental level, in practice, the focus was rather on tourist satisfaction instead of the well-being of residents. As a result, locals were largely treated as a component of the tourism product as opposed to a sustainable tourism approach being cultivated where locals' QoL was seriously considered as the outcome of tourism development. The findings of this case study also revealed that tourism planning was very much centralised, and locals' inputs were seldom included in decision-making. These studies and other scholarly work have focused on tourism development and its relationship with community well-being, which have increasingly gained attention in sustainable tourism literature over the past few years (e.g. Woo, Uysal & Sirgy, 2018; Naidoo & Sharpley, 2016; Vogt et al., 2016; Moscardo & Murphy, 2016; Buzinde et al., 2014).

Community well-being

Recent scholarly work in the field of tourism suggests that the outcome of sustainable tourism development is ultimately to enhance the well-being of destination communities (Moscardo et al., 2013). Community well-being is associated with the social, economic, cultural and political elements that maintain a community and satisfy the needs of its local people (Boukas & Ziakas, 2016). Hence, QoL can be seen as a multidimensional concept (Costanza et al., 2008) which aims to fulfil the multiple needs of the community, inclusive of the following: (1) the basic material requirements for a good life, including access to a secure and adequate livelihood, income and assets; (2) good health; (3) security, comprising access to a safe environment; (4) good social relations, comprising respect and cooperation that exist between individuals and groups; (5) freedom and choice, including the ability to acquire, experience and fulfil personal choices according to one's likes. In addition to meeting basic needs, QoL entails human beings needing a multitude of goods and services such as freedom, leisure, values, experiences and relationships, at the individual, community, national and global levels (Costanza et al., 2007, 2008). When these multiple needs are fulfilled at the personal and collective levels, both individuals and the community will benefit, because some aspects of well-being are mainly collective properties of a community (Petrosillo et al., 2013).

In this context, a good QoL requires a society that can rely on different types of capital (de Groot et al., 2010). In the same vein, Moscardo et al. (2013) contend that community well-being consists of multiple forms of capital: cultural, social, human, political, natural, financial and built capital (see Table 2.1). The authors further assert that sustainability also consists of enhancing all forms of capital, not just financial or built capital, but recognising that the natural environment capital is especially important for tourism because it cannot be replaced. Other factors such as social bonding, personal growth and support provided by the government also contribute to community well-being (Schueller, 2009). Additionally, variables such as human rights, democracy, equality, sustainability and welfare affect the levels of well-being across communities worldwide (Diener, Diener & Diener, 1995; Inglehart et al., 2008; Murphy, 2010). Empowerment is also seen as a factor which promotes community well-being through capacity-building (Schueller, 2009). Furthermore, governmental and non-governmental organisations should support communities in redistributing resources, alleviating poverty and promoting democracy. Community well-being

Table 2.1 Types of capital that contribute to community well-being

Capital	Description
Financial	Income, savings and access to funding for investment
Natural	Natural ecosystems and the assets, services and resources that they provide. This includes landscape, environmental systems, green spaces and conservation areas
Built	Physical facilities and infrastructure that communities have available for use, including buildings, transport systems, public spaces, technological systems and distribution systems for water, waste and energy
Social	Features of social networks such as trust, reciprocity and cooperation and social institutions and associations
Cultural	Values and symbols shared by human groups and manifested in things such as ritual and social activities, arts and crafts, spiritual practices, languages and celebrations
Human	The capabilities, skills, knowledge and health of the people who make up a community
Political	Ability to access political decision-making processes and influence governance

Sources: Emery & Flora, 2006; Fey, Bregendahl & Flora, 2006; Moscardo et al., 2013.

provides a more contemporary approach to understanding "the relationships between tourism and destinations and identifies in more detail how tourism detracts from or contributes to sustainability for destination regions" (Moscardo et al., 2013: 534). From this perspective, the goal of tourism development and sustainable policies should be much broader than economic growth, and income generated from the industry should be well utilised to enhance QoL.

Tourism impacts and QoL

Numerous studies have investigated residents' perceptions of tourism impacts, and a few have specifically investigated residents' perceptions of tourism impacts on QoL. Nawijn and Mitas (2012) contend that significant efforts have been made to understand tourists' behavior and its relationship with SWB, while simultaneously neglecting to explore residents perceptions on the subject. It is only in recent years that scholars have moved beyond tourism impact studies to the examination of the interconnectedness among the local population, tourism development and QoL. According to Andereck and Nyaupane (2011: 2), the difference essentially lies in terms of measurement, where tourism impact studies consider the way in which individuals perceive "tourism influences communities and the environment, whereas QoL studies (or well-being) are typically concerned with the way these impacts influence individual or family life satisfaction, including satisfaction with community, neighbourhood, and personal circumstances".

From the literature review, two types of studies may be identified: (1) studies about the impact of tourism on visitors' QoL (e.g. Dolnicar, Lazarevski & Yanamandram, 2013; Dolnicar, Yanamandram & Cliff, 2012; Carneiro & Eusébio, 2011) and (2) studies about the impact of tourism on residents' QoL (e.g. Woo et al., 2018; Suntikul et al., 2016; Kim et al., 2013; Andereck & Nyaupane, 2011; Meng et al., 2010; Andereck et al., 2007). This chapter focuses on the second perspective, as QoL has been identified as a critical goal of tourism development, and yet there is still a lack of attention paid to the subject. In the past few years, however, some efforts have been made to address this. For example, in 2016, the *Journal of Destination Management & Marketing* proposed a special issue on small island destinations and subjective well-being, with six case studies on small islands in different regions of the world which are referred to in this book chapter.

QoL measurement in tourism

There have been several attempts by researchers to assess QoL in the tourism industry, and various factors have been used. In the past ten years, there has been a rise in attention paid to this research area, and key articles from the year 2010 are summarised in Table 2.2. Andereck et al. (2007) constructed the tourism and quality of life (TQOL) measurement scale to explain the relationship between tourism development and QoL. Andereck and Nyaupane (2011) further developed the TQOL scale and identified eight domains: community well-being, urban issues, way of life, community pride and awareness, natural/cultural preservation, economic strength, recreation amenities, and crime and substance abuse. The study by Dolnicar et al. (2012) argued that total perceived QoL is a combination of satisfaction with several dimensions of life which can be grouped under two major domains, namely work and material well-being, and health well-being. Woo, Kim and Uysal (2015) divided these eight life domains into two groups: material and non-material domains. Consequently, Kim et al. (2013) proposed that residents' perceptions of tourism influence their sense of well-being in four domains: material, community, emotional life, and health and safety. Liang and Hui (2016) further pointed out that the TQOL indicators were incomplete as they excluded some widely accepted indicators of QOL, such as family life and personal well-being, which had also been adopted by others such as

Table 2.2 Indicators in tourism QoL studies

Authors	Type of QOL	TQoL indicators	Main results and relationships with QoL
Meng, Li & Uysal (2010)	Objective – China	Income, consumption compositions, residence quality, transportation, education, social security, health care, life expectancy, public security, employment	The greater the level of tourism development, the greater the level of QoL enjoyed by the population; tourism development level is positively related to most of the local residents' objective QoL
Andereck & Nyaupane (2011)	Subjective – Arizona, USA	Community well-being, urban issues, way of life, community pride and awareness, natural/cultural preservation, economic strength, recreation amenities, crime and substance abuse	Satisfaction with life domains has an influence on overall life satisfaction
Yamada et al. (2011)	Subjective – Indianapolis, USA	Health perception, wealth, safety, community contentment, cultural tourism development	The five assessed domains were positively related to life satisfaction
Yu, Chancellor & Cole (2011)	Subjective – Indiana, USA	Perceived social costs, environmental sustainability, perceived economic benefits	Economic and environmental impacts are positively related to community QoL; however, perceived social costs had no significant effect on QoL
Nawijn & Mitas (2012)	Subjective – Mallorca, Spain	Friends, family, interpersonal relationships, economic situation, job, neighbourhood, self, services and infrastructure, health and politics	The domains of health, interpersonal relationships, friends, and services and infrastructure impact on QoL. Perceived tourism impacts are associated with life satisfaction, the cognitive component of SWB, and not with the affective component of SWB
Abdul Ghani, Hafiza Azmi & Ali Puteh (2013)	Objective – 2 Malaysian islands	Employment, income	Employment and income significantly increase community well-being
Guo, Kim & Chen (2014)	Subjective – Shanghai, China	Public security, leisure time, family cohesion, community construction, societal atmosphere, health status, economic margin, and living cost	Tourism development has a positive influence on all the domains of quality of life
Kim, Uysal & Sirgy (2013)	Objective and subjective – Virginia, USA	Material life, community life, emotional life, health and safety	The four life domains positively influence overall QoL
Yu, Cole & Chancellor (2014)	Subjective – Indiana, USA	Community conditions (community opportunity, quality of environment in community, cost of living in community, community security); community services (public and private services)	Tourism development contributes to the difference in community QOL for residents

(continued)

Table 2.2 (continued)

Authors	Type of QOL	TQoL indicators	Main results and relationships with QoL
Woo, Kim & Uysal (2015)	Objective and subjective – (USA)	Material well-being, non-material well-being	The residents' perceived value of tourism development positively affects non-material and material life domain satisfaction and it also contributes to overall QoL. Overall quality of life is thus an effective predictor of support for further tourism development
Liang & Hui (2016)	Subjective – Shenzhen, China	Urban issues, community economic strength, family and personal well-being, community well-being, way of life, community awareness and facilities	Both residential status and the dimensions of QoL (except urban issues) positively impact on the future tourism development. Family and personal well-being was found to be an important domain of QoL
Naidoo & Sharpley (2016)	Subjective – Mauritius	Education and culture, socio–economic benefits, leisure, socio–environmental impacts, job and business opportunities, coastal environment, governance	Education and culture have a positive impact on well-being. Degradation of the environment and job and business opportunities negatively affect community well-being
Pratt, McCabe & Movono (2016)	Subjective and objective – 2 villages in Fiji (based on Bhutan's GHI)	Psychological well-being, health, time use, education, cultural diversity and resilience, good governance, community vitality, ecological diversity and resilience, living standard	Tourism development moderately influences the happiness of residents through combined effects of social, environmental, socio–economic, macroeconomic and cultural dimensions. Non-income factors have larger impact on happiness
Rivera, Lee & Croes (2016)	Subjective – Aruba	Macroeconomic, social, socio-economic, cultural, environmental	The residents in an income-dependent village were less happy than residents in a less tourism income-dependent village
Suntikul et al. (2016)	Subjective – Hue, Vietnam	Community well-being, community pride and awareness, natural/cultural preservation, crime and substance abuse, way of life, recreation amenities, economic strength, urban issues	Tourism provides residents with a sense of community well-being and community pride. However, although tourism brings jobs, there is dissatisfaction with the quality of employment available, and residents lack empowerment in policy-making and local government participation
Carneiro, Eusébio & Caldeira (2017)	Subjective – Portugal	Economic and social opportunities, calm and safety, public facilities and services, positive feelings	Tourism has a positive effect on all the four domains of QoL analysed. Positive feelings and public facilities and services had the highest effect on residents' overall QoL
Woo, Uysal & Sirgy (2018)	Subjective – USA	Perception of tourism impacts on material life, perception of tourism impacts on nonmaterial life, material life satisfaction, non-material life satisfaction	Both non-material life and material life influence overall life satisfaction

Nawijn and Mitas (2012). In addition, Liang and Hui's scale (2016) also assessed urban issues, community economic strength, community well-being, way of life, community awareness and facilities. Using Sirgy and Cornwell's community QoL model (2001) and modifying Andereck and Nyaupane's measurement approach (2011), Yu, Cole and Chancellor (2014) evaluated residents' perceptions of community quality of life in tourism development (TCQOL) in Indiana, USA, using four domains of community conditions, including community opportunity, quality of environment in community, cost of living in community and community security, and two domains of community services, namely public services and private services. Yamada et al. (2011) focused on subjective QoL and used five life domains – health perception, wealth, safety, community contentment and cultural tourism development – which were positively related to life satisfaction. Abdul Ghani, Hafiza Azmi and Ali Puteh (2013) investigated the objective well-being of residents on two Malaysian islands which have experienced tourism growth and reported that the significant increases in well-being of the residents are explained in terms of employment and income. In their measurements, other authors have also included economic and social opportunities/costs (e.g. Carneiro, Eusébio & Caldeira, 2017; Rivera, Lee & Croes, 2016; Naidoo & Sharpley, 2016; Yu, Chancellor & Cole, 2011). Measurements of QoL have also considered leisure, environment and culture (e.g. Naidoo & Sharpley, 2016; Guo, Kim & Chen, 2014; Andereck & Nyaupane, 2011).

Positive impacts of tourism on QoL

Studies have shown mixed results with regard to the contributions of tourism to QoL. Scholarly work such as Meng et al. (2010: 180) has demonstrated that the higher the level of tourism development, the more positive the impact on objective QoL. In their concluding remarks, the same authors cautioned that objective measures alone do not appropriately reflect QoL, and subjective assessments should also be considered to capture a more precise representation and thorough measurement. Other studies have also shown that economic factors have an impact on QoL (Abdul Ghani et al., 2013; Yu et al., 2011). As pointed out by Andereck et al. (2007), a higher personal standard of living, increased tax revenues, increased employment opportunities and economic diversity lead to an improved QoL. The results of some studies also reveal a higher impact of tourism on some dimensions of QoL related to access to services, facilities and attractions (e.g. retail shops, restaurants, festivals) created in the community as a result of tourism development (Andereck & Nyaupane, 2011; Andereck et al., 2005). The study by Rivera et al. (2016) showed that tourism development has modest positive impacts on the happiness of residents through the combined effects of social, environmental, socio-economic, macroeconomic and cultural dimensions.

The study by Carneiro and Eusébio (2015) suggested that interaction with visitors is important for residents to feel safer, and longer interactions between visitors and residents were important to enhance QoL. In addition, several studies revealed that tourism has an influence on host communities' QoL from a socio-cultural perspective as it helps them to have a secure job, set up their business, have solid ties with relatives, improve their education and add value to local traditions and culture (Ridderstaat, Croes & Nijkamp, 2016; Naidoo & Sharpley; 2016; Woo et al., 2015). Therefore, destinations also have to pay significant attention to non-material improvements in order to enhance the QoL of residents.

Negative impacts of tourism on QoL

Residents have also shown concerns with respect to tourism development and their QoL. Communities encourage tourism development as they expect economic benefits in the form of increased income, employment opportunities and increased tax revenues; unfortunately, this has led to negative economic effects. Studies have shown that, although tourism brings employment, it does not positively affect QoL (Suntikul et al., 2016; Naidoo & Sharpley, 2016). Other studies have noted that one of the most serious problems is the increase in cost of living for residents, which reduces their QOL and contributes to a lower approval level of tourism development (Liu & Var, 1986; Liang & Hui, 2016). Findings have also shown negative impacts of tourism on the physical environment which affect QoL more specifically with regard to resort development (Naidoo & Sharpley, 2016). The study of Suntikul et al. (2016) also showed that a lack of empowerment and involvement in tourism planning also affects QoL. Similar results have also been supported by Boukas and Ziakas (2016) in their study of QoL among Cypriots. It is also argued that, when economic benefits cause deterioration in social or physical environments, residents' QoL may decline (Jurowski & Gursoy, 2004; Roehl, 1999). Residents in a tourism destination may be forced to change their habits, daily routines, social beliefs and values, which can lead to psychological tension (Andereck & Jurowski, 2006) and, consequently, a lower quality of life (Yu et al., 2011). If residents do not see an improvement in their QoL, this can lead to visitors not being welcomed by residents, which jeopardises the stability of the tourism industry (Yu et al., 2011; Gursoy, Jurowski & Uysal, 2002).

Concluding remarks

There are three key observations from the literature review of relevance to the present discussion. First, QoL is a contemporary theme of research in tourism literature, and there is growing interest regarding the contributions of QoL for residents arising from tourism development. This is owing to several reasons, the main one being that QoL has been recognised as the ultimate goal of tourism development (Chancellor, Yu & Cole, 2011). Therefore, further research should be conducted to more clearly understand how to better enhance the positive contributions of tourism development to residents' QoL. It is important to further identify the factors which influence these impacts in order to properly plan for tourism so as to support the prosperity of the population and the sustainability of the industry and destination.

Second, despite the recent growth in awareness of QoL, there continue to be large gaps between governments' political agenda and policy implementation. To date, in several parts of the world, QoL awareness has yet to be extended beyond policies to incorporate changes into actual implementation. Although it is increasingly acknowledged that tourism development can bring improvement to destination communities, there are still significant barriers to developing, implementing and using better measurement of QoL. This may be because businesses whose financial success is established on continually increasing economic activity, as well as those institutions that are charged with collecting, managing and reporting on the current indicators, continue to rely on economic measures of QoL (Costanza et al., 2009). Another reason is that political commitment to QoL is also lacking, in part because, in several countries, focus still remains on GDP and also because efforts have yet to be made to ensure that government officials responsible for tourism development are made aware of the importance of QoL, so as to inform the planning and policy decisions that need to be made within their respective powers. A focus on QoL in tourism planning and marketing can bring real changes and progress to the well-being of locals through enhancing stakeholder involvement and designing interconnected actions to enhance QoL (Moscardo & Murphy, 2016). However, as with many other aspects of sustainability, discussions of QoL and tourism planning are both recent and uncommon in several destinations. Support for QoL should therefore be at the centre of the tourism planning process, where the government embraces a bottom–up approach referred to as 'inside–outside' planning (Boukas & Ziakas, 2016). The reason is that residents seem to have different opinions from government officers with regard to how tourism development can enhance their QoL. For example, policies grounded in the assumption that raising income will ensure greater well-being may be wrong, as income alone is not necessarily the most important driver of well-being (Croes, 2016), as shown from the review of studies presented in this chapter.

Third, on a positive note, several international institutions have acknowledged the importance of QoL and supported efforts for a more holistic assessment of well-being, as objective measures alone are not sufficient for appropriately assessing QoL. However, indicators of QoL still remain a challenge in terms of conceptualisation and assessment. It is not surprising that agreeing on what constitutes a happy life is somewhat problematic (Pratt et al., 2016). This leads to the question of how to measure QoL and its multiple dimensions. There is no unanimity on the measurement of QoL, and it is unlikely that there will be agreement on the subject, particularly owing to contextual factors that need to be considered. However, residents in each destination or community should identify indicators which are important to their own QoL, as measurement will bring destinations closer to sustainability goals. Moreover, assessment of QoL is also essential to provide a strong foundation on which to base policy changes, as it provides a tool to indicate where and whether improvements should be made (Delibasic et al., 2008). QoL assessments can be particularly significant for aiding economic and political agendas and can help governments design better policies to enhance the lives of the locals.

References

Abdul Ghani, N., Hafiza Azmi, N., & Ali Puteh, D. A. H. M. (2013). The impact of the tourism industry on the community's wellbeing on Langkawi and Redang Islands, Malaysia. *American-Eurasian Journal of Sustainable Agriculture*, 7, 389–396.

Andereck, K. L., Valentine, K. M., Knopf, R. C., & Vogt, C. A. (2005). Residents' perceptions of community tourism impacts. *Annals of Tourism Research*, 32, 1056–1076.

Andereck, K. L., & Jurowski, C. (2006). Tourism and quality of life. In G. Jennings & N. Nickerson (Eds.), *Quality Tourism Experiences* (pp. 136–154). Oxford: Elsevier.

Andereck, K. L., Valentine, K. M., Vogt, C. A., & Knopf, R. C. (2007). A cross-cultural analysis of tourism and quality of life perceptions. *Journal of Sustainable Tourism*, 15(5), 483–502.

Andereck, K. L., & Nyaupane, G. P. (2011). Exploring the nature of tourism and quality of life perceptions among residents. *Journal of Travel Research*, 50, 248–260.

BBC. (2006). Britain's happiness in decline. Available at: http://news.bbc.co.uk/2/hi/programmes/happiness_formula/4771908.stm (accessed 30 June 2015).

Boukas, N., & Ziakas, V. (2016). Tourism policy and residents' well-being in Cyprus: Opportunities and challenges for developing an inside-out destination management approach. *Journal of Destination Marketing & Management*, 5(1), 44–54.

Brey, P. A. E. (2012). Well-being in philosophy, psychology and economics, in P. A. E. Brey, A. R. Briggle & E. H. Spence (Eds), *The Good Life in a Technological Age* ((pp. 15–34). London: Routledge.

Britton, S. (1982). The political economy of tourism in the third world. *Annals of Tourism Research*, 9(3), 331–358.

Buzinde, C. N., Kalavar, J. M., & Melubo, K. (2014). Tourism and community well-being: The case of the Maasai in Tanzania. *Annals of Tourism Research*, 44, 20–35.

Carneiro, M. J., & Eusébio, C. (2011). Segmentation of tourism market using the impact of tourism on quality of life. *Tourism & Management Studies*, 7, 91–100.

Carneiro, M. J., & Eusébio, C. (2015). Host–tourist interaction and impact of tourism on residents' Quality of Life. *Tourism & Management Studies*, 11(1), 25–34.

Carneiro, M. J., Eusébio, C., & Caldeira, A. (2017). The influence of social contact in residents' perceptions of the tourism impact on their quality of life: a structural equation model. *Journal of Quality Assurance in Hospitality & Tourism*. DOI: 10.1080/1528008X.2017.1314798

Cecil, A. K., Fu, Y., Wang, S., & Avgoustis, S. (2010). Cultural tourism and quality of life: results of a longitudinal study. *European Journal of Tourism Research*, 3(1), 54–66.

Chancellor, C. C., Yu, C. P., & Cole, S. T. (2011). Exploring quality of life perceptions in rural mid-western (USA) communities: an application of the core-periphery concept in a tourism development context. *International Journal of Tourism Research*, 13(5), 496–507.

Costanza, R., Fisher, B., Ali, S., Beer, C., Bond, L., Boumans, R., Danigelis, N. L., Dickinson, J., Elliott, C., Farley, J., Gayer, D. E., MacDonald Glenn, L., Hudspeth, T., Mahoney, D., McCahill, L., McIntosh, B., Reed, B., Rizvi, S. A. T., Rizzo, D.M., Simpatico, T., & Snapp, R. (2007). Quality of life: an approach integrating opportunities, human needs, and subjective well-being. *Ecological Economics*, 61, 267–276.

Costanza, R., Fisher, B., Ali, S., Beer, C., & Bond, L. (2008). An integrative approach to quality of life measurement, research, and policy. *Sapiens*, 1(1), 17–21.

Costanza, R., Hart, M., Posner, S., & Talberth, J. (2009). Beyond GDP: The Need for New Measures of Progress. Pardee Paper No. 4. Boston: Pardee Center for the Study of the Longer-Range Future.

Croes, R. (2016). Connecting tourism development with small island destinations and with the well-being of the island residents. *Journal of Destination Marketing & Management*, 5(1), 1–4.

Deci, E. L., & Ryan, R. M. (2008). Facilitating optimal motivation and psychological well-being across life's domains. *Canadian Psychology*, 49, 14–23.

de Groot, R. S., Alkemade, R., Braat, L., Hein, L., & Willemen, L. (2010). Challenges in integrating the concepts of ecosystem services and values in landscape planning, management and decision-making. *Ecological Complexity*, 7, 260–272.

Delibasic, R., Karlsson, P., Lorusso, A., Rodriguez, A., & Yliruusi, H. (2008). Quality of life and tourism in Budečsko. Available at: www.cenia.cz/__C12572160037AA0F.nsf/$pid/CPRJ6WECYXIH/$FILE/SED%20Budec%20final%20report.pdf (accessed May 2014).

Diener, E. (1984). Subjective well-being. *Psychological Bulletin*, 95(3), 542–575.

Diener, E. (2009). *The Science of Well-Being: The Collected Works of Ed Diener*. Social Indicators Research Series, Volume 37. Dordrecht, Netherlands: Springer.

Diener. E., Diener, M., & Diener, C. (1995). Factors predicting the subjective well-being of nations. *Journal of Personality & Social Psychology*, 69, 851–864.

Diener, E., & Suh, E. (1997). Measuring quality of life: Economic, social, and subjective indicators. *Social Indicators Research*, 40, 189–216.

Dolnicar, S., Yanamandram, V., & Cliff, K. (2012). The contribution of vacations to quality of life. *Annals of Tourism Research*, 39(1), 59–83.

Dolnicar, S., Lazarevski, K., & Yanamandram, V. (2013). Quality of life and tourism: A conceptual framework and novel segmentation base. *Journal of Business Research*, 66, 724–729.

Emery, M., & Flora, C. B. (2006). Spiraling-up: Mapping community transformation with community capitals framework. *Community Development*, 37, 19–35.

Fey, S., Bregendahl, C., & Flora, C. (2006). The measurement of community capitals through research. *Online Journal of Rural Research and Policy*, 1(1), DOI: http://dx.doi.org/10.4148/ojrrp.v1i1.29

Goodman, F. R., Disabato, D. J., Kashdan, T. B., & Kauffman, S. B. (2017). Measuring well-being: a comparison of subjective well-being and PERMA. *The Journal of Positive Psychology*. doi.org/10.1080/17439760.2017.1388434

Guo, Y., Kim, S., & Chen, Y. (2014). Shanghai residents' perceptions of tourism impacts and quality of life. *Journal of China Tourism Research*, 10(2), 142–164.

Gursoy, D., Jurowski, C., & Uysal, M. (2002). Resident attitudes: a structural modeling approach. *Annals of Tourism Research*, 29, 79–105.

Helliwell, J., Layard, R., & Sachs, J. (Eds). (2012). World happiness report. Available at: www.earth.columbia.edu/sitefiles/file/Sachs%20Writing/2012/World%20Happiness%20Report.pdf (accessed 30 June 2015).

Helliwell, J., Layard, R., & Sachs, J. (2017). World happiness report 2017. Available at: https://s3.amazonaws.com/happiness-report/2017/HR17.pdf (accessed 5 May 2018).

Inglehart, R., Foa, R., Peterson, C., & Wetzel, C. (2008). Development, freedom, and rising happiness: a global perspective (1981–2007). *Perspectives on Psychological Science*, 3, 264–285.

Jurowski, C., & Gursoy, D. (2004). Distance effects on residents' attitudes toward tourism. *Annals of Tourism Research*, 31, 296–312.

Kim, K., Uysal, M., & Sirgy, M. J. (2013). How does tourism in a community impact the quality of life of community residents? *Tourism Management*, 36, 527–540.

Layard, R. (2005). *Happiness – Lessons from a New Science*. London: Penguin.

Liang, Z.-X., & Hui, T.-K. (2016). Residents' quality of life and attitudes toward tourism development in China. *Tourism Management*, 57, 56–67.

Liu, J. C., & Var, T. (1986). Resident attitudes toward tourism impacts in Hawaii. *Annals of Tourism Research*, 13, 193–214.

Mbaiwa, J. (2005). Enclave tourism and its socio-economic impacts in the Okavango Delta, Botswana. *Tourism Management*, 26(2), 157–172.

McCabe, S., Joldersma, T., & Li, C. (2010). Understanding the benefits of social tourism: linking participation to subjective well-being and quality of life. *International Journal of Tourism Research*, 12, 761–773.

Meng, F., Li, X., & Uysal, M. (2010). Tourism development and regional quality of life: the case of China. *Journal of China Tourism Research*. 6(2), 164–182.

Moscardo, G. (2009). Tourism and quality of life: towards a more critical approach. *Tourism & Hospitality Research*, 9(2), 159–170.

Moscardo, G., Konovalov, E., Murphy, L., & McGehee, N. (2013). Mobilities, community well-being and sustainable tourism. *Journal of Sustainable Tourism*, 21(4), 532–556.

Moscardo, G., & Murphy, L. (2014). There is no such thing as sustainable tourism: re-conceptualizing tourism as a tool for sustainability. *Sustainability*, 6, 2538–2561.

Moscardo, G., & Murphy, L. (2016). Using destination community wellbeing to assess tourist markets: a case study of Magnetic Island, Australia. *Journal of Destination Marketing & Management*, 5(1), 55–64.

Murphy, B. (2010). Community well-being: an overview of the concept. Nuclear Waste Management Organisation. Available at: www.nwmo.ca/uploads_managed/MediaFiles/1681_researchsupportprogram_communitywellbeingoverview.pdf (accessed August 2013).

Naidoo, P., & Pearce, P. L. (2016). Enclave tourism versus agritourism: the economic debate. *Current Issues in Tourism*. DOI: 10.1080/13683500.2016.1235554

Naidoo, P., Pearce, P., & Sharpley, R. (2017). The contributions of enclave tourism to community wellbeing in Mauritius: host community perspective. In A. Saufi, I. Andilolo, N. Othman & A. Lew (Eds), *Balancing Development and Sustainability in Tourism Destinations: Proceedings of the Tourism Outlook Conference 2015* (pp. 179–188). Singapore: Springer.

Naidoo, P., & Sharpley, R. (2016). Local perceptions of the relative contributions of enclave tourism and agritourism to community well-being: the case of Mauritius. *Journal of Destination Marketing & Management*, 5(1), 16–25.

Nawijn, J., & Mitas, O. (2012). Resident attitudes to tourism and their effect on subjective well-being: the case of Palma de Mallorca. *Journal of Travel Research*, 51(5), 531–541.

New Economics Foundation. (2015). The importance of measuring wellbeing, Available at: www.new economics.org/blog/entry/the-importance-of-measuring-wellbeing (accessed 30 June 2015).

Novelli, N., & Hellwig, A. (2011). The UN Millennium Development Goals, tourism and development: the tour operators' perspective. *Current Issues in Tourism*, 14(3), 205–220.

Nunkoo, R., Gursoy D., & Juwaheer, T. D. (2010). Island residents' identities and their support for tourism: an integration of two theories. *Journal of Sustainable Tourism*, 18(5), 675–693.

OECD. (2013). *OECD Guidelines on Measuring Subjective Well-being*. OECD Publishing. https://doi.org/10.1787/9789264191655-en

Pearce, P., Filep, S., & Ross, G. (2010). *Tourists, Tourism and the Good Life*. Abingdon, UK: Routledge.

Petrosillo, I. R., Costanza, R., Aretanoa, R., Zaccarelli, N., & Zurlini, G. (2013). The use of subjective indicators to assess how natural and social capital support residents' quality of life in a small volcanic island. *Ecological Indicators*, 24, 609–620.

Pratt, S., McCabe, S., & Movono, A. (2016). Gross happiness of a 'tourism' village in Fiji. *Journal of Destination Marketing & Management*, 5(1), 26–35.

Reisinger, Y., & Park, K. (2009). Community based sustainable tourism: quality of life as perceived by residents in tourism destinations. BEST EN Think Tank IX: The Importance of Values in Sustainable Tourism.

Ridderstaat, J., Croes, R., & Nijkamp, P. (2016). The tourism development-quality of life nexus in a small island destination. *Journal of Travel Research*, 55(1), 79–94.

Rivera, M., Lee, S. H., & Croes, R. (2016). Tourism development and happiness: a residents' perspective. *Journal of Destination Marketing & Management*, 5(1). DOI: 10.1016/j.jdmm.2015.04.002

Roehl, W. S. (1999). Quality of life issues in a casino destination. *Journal of Business Research*, 44(3), 223–229.

Ryff, C. D. (1989). Happiness is everything, or is it? Explorations on the meaning of psychological well-being. *Journal of Personality & Social Psychology*, 57, 1069–1081.

Schalock, R. L. (Ed.) (1996). *Quality of Life: Conceptualization and Measurement* (Vol. 1). Washington, DC: American Association on Mental Retardation.

Schueller, S. M. (2009). Promoting wellness: integrating community and positive psychology. *Journal of Community Psychology*, 37(7), 922–937.

Schueller, S. M., & Seligman, M. E. P. (2010). Pursuit of pleasure, engagement and meaning: relationships to subjective and objective measures of well-being. *The Journal of Positive Psychology*, 5, 253–263.

Sen, A. (1990). Development as capability expansion. In K. Griffen & J. Knight (Eds), *Human Development and the International Development Strategy for the 1990s*. London: Macmillan.

Sirgy, M. J. (2002). *The Psychology of Quality of Life*. Dordrecht, Netherlands: Kluwer.

Sirgy, M. J., & Cornwell, T. (2001). Further validation of the Sirgy et al.'s measure of community wuality of life. *Social Indicators Research*, 56(2), 125–143.

Suntikul, W., Pratt, S., Kuan, W. I, Wong, C. I., Chan, C. C., Choi, W. L., & Chong, O. F. (2016). Impacts of tourism on the quality of life of local residents in Hue, Vietnam. *Anatolia, an International Journal of Tourism and Hospitality Research*. DOI: 10.1080/13032917.2016.1138234

Telfer, D., & Sharpley, S. (2014). *Tourism and Development: Concepts and Issues*, 2nd ed. Clevedon, UK: Channel View.

United Nations Development Programme (UNDP). (1990). *Human Development Report 1990*. New York: Oxford University Press.

United Nations Development Programme (UNDP). (2018). Human development reports. Available at: http://hdr.undp.org/en/humandev (accessed March 2018).

Uysal, M., Sirgy, J., Woo, E. C., & Kim, H. (2016). Quality of life (QOL) and well-being research in tourism. *Tourism Management*, 53, 244–261.

Vogt, C., Jordan, E., Grewe, N., & Kruger, L. (2016). Collaborative tourism planning and subjective well-being in a small island destination. *Journal of Destination Marketing & Management*, 5(1), 36–43.

Veenhoven, R. (2005). Apparent quality-of-life in nations: how long and happy people live. *Social Indicators Research*, 71(1), 61–86.

Veenhoven, R. (2012) Happiness: Also Known as "Life Satisfaction" and "Subjective Well-Being". In K. C. Land, A. C. Michalos, & M. J. Sirgy (Eds), *Handbook of Social Indicators and Quality of Life Research* (pp. 63–77). Dordrecht, Netherlands: Springer.

Woo, E., Kim, H., & Uysal, M. (2015). Life satisfaction and support for tourism development. *Annals of Tourism Research*, 50, 84–97.

Woo, E., Uysal, M., & Sirgy, J. (2018). Tourism impact and stakeholders' quality of life. *Journal of Hospitality & Tourism Research*, 42(2), 260–286.

Yamada, N., Heo, J., King, C., & Fu, Y. (2011). Higher-level and lower-level life satisfaction of urban residents: the role of health perception, wealth, safety, community pride, and tourism development. *Journal of Quality Assurance in Hospitality & Tourism*, 12(3), 1–16.

Yu, C.-P., Chancellor, H. C., & Cole, S. T. (2011). Examining the effects of tourism impacts on resident quality of life: evidence from rural Midwestern communities in USA. *International Journal of Tourism Sciences*, 11, 161–186.

Yu, C.-P., Cole, S. T., & Chancellor, C. C. (2014). Assessing community quality of life in the context of tourism development. *Applied Research in Quality Life*, 11(1), 147–162.

3

OVERVIEW OF UNDERPINNINGS OF TOURISM IMPACTS

The case of Lisbon destination

Sandra Maria Correia Loureiro, Eduardo Moraes Sarmento, and João Ferreira do Rosário

Introduction

For decades, tourism industry growth has been regarded as an important contribution to economic activity in destinations owing to the new jobs created. Tourism is also associated with the exchange of ideas and culture, which can enrich the local population but can also bring bad habits and behaviors. The increased number of visitors can generate overcrowding, pollution, negative changes in landscape, and impacts on fauna and flora (e.g., Frent, 2016; Ribeiro, Pinto, Silva, & Woosnam, 2017).

Indeed, several destinations worldwide have opened up to, and invested in, tourism, turning it into a key driver of socio-economic progress through the creation of jobs and enterprises, export revenues, and infrastructure development (UNWTO, 2017), as happened in Portugal. Tourism has been boosted in the last two years and, at time of writing, is a major category of international trade in services (UNWTO, 2017). All Portuguese regions have seen increases in revenue, with the emphasis on Alentejo (+28.2% in total revenue and +24.0% in revenue from accommodation), Centro (+20.7% and +22.9%, respectively) and Lisbon (+17.9% and +20.7%, respectively; INE, 2018).

Lisbon has seen a sharp rise in the number of tourists in recent years, and between January and November 2017 more than 5.8 million tourists stayed in Lisbon hospitality infrastructures, a rise of nearly 10% over the same period in 2016 (INE 2018). The majority of tourists come for holidays, but many also visit for business reasons, including business conferences, as shown in the Lisbon's fifth place in international visitor growth (Global Destination Cities Index Mastercard, 2016). The reasons for this growth are global economic improvements, the unstable situation in North African countries as tourism destinations, and also several tourism prizes and excellent media coverage in recent years.

Recently, Lisbon has been given many awards, such as Europe's Leading Cruise Destination (World Travel Awards, 2016), Best City Break (World Travel Awards, 2017a), Europe's Leading Cruise Port (World Travel Awards, 2017b), and Best City of the Year (Wallpaper Design Awards, 2017), with nominations for many more and also several flattering articles in the news such as "Is Lisbon the coolest capital city in Europe?" (CNN, 2017) and similar articles in press all over the world, such as *New York Times*, *Financial Times*, *Monocle*, *The Guardian*, *Global*

Table 3.1 Tourism lodging capacity in Lisbon: guests in hotel establishments

2009	2010	2011	2012	2013	2014	2015	2016	2017
2,667	2,841	2,857	2,950	3,087	3,816	4,165	5,288	5,782
–	6.5%	0.6%	3.3%	4.6%	23.6%	9.1%	27.0%	9.4%

Source: INE, 2017.

Post, Hola, China Daily, and so on. Events such as Web Summit also place Lisbon as a city to at least visit, because of good work conditions for international start-ups.

All this promotion and evolution in tourism in Lisbon brought economic benefits but also some less positive aspects, because of the tourism pressure on infrastructure, mainly in terms of hospitality, with *alojamento local* (local accommodation) complaints from older Lisbon citizens in the more historical areas of the city, the growth of foreign residents in the same areas (including famous show-business stars such as Madonna), and also the surge in the numbers of hotels and "tourist shops" replacing Portuguese citizens and traditional Portuguese shops. This is seen by a number of Lisbon citizens as disqualifying Lisbon as a traditional Portuguese city.

In this context, two major questions emerge: (1) What are the major positive and negative tourism impacts? And (2) what is happening in a European city with one of the highest growth rates of tourism, as shown in Table 3.1?

Overview of underpinnings of tourism impacts

Past research dedicated to tourism impacts tends to point to three major impacts: economic, environmental, and social (e.g., Djurasevik & Nedelea, 2007; Correia, 2017; Ribeiro et al., 2017). In each category, we can find positive and negative impacts (Frent, 2016; Ribeiro et al., 2017; see Figure 3.1).

Many destinations have seen tourism as an economic activity that bring economic benefits – for instance, new business opportunities, new jobs, or tax revenue (e.g., Lindberg & Johnson, 1997; Oosterhaven & Fan, 2006; Dyer, Gursoy, Sharma, & Carter, 2007). Tourism may represent a complementary activity for agriculture, fishing, mining, or culture (Sinclair-Maragh & Gursoy, 2016). The positive economic impact of tourism generates income and new jobs, contributes to raising standards of living, improves public and transport infrastructures (e.g., Látková & Vogt, 2012; Kim, Uysal, & Sirgy, 2013; Woo, Kim, & Uysal, 2015). Local communities may have better material conditions with improved public infrastructure, such as parking, restrooms, water supply, sewers, sidewalks, and lighting. Transport infrastructure includes airports, public transportation, and upgraded roads (Ribeiro et al., 2017).

Notwithstanding the benefits, negative economic consequences also arise, such as price increases, increased use of resources, infrastructure costs, seasonality, and dependence on a single economic sector, creating enclaves or leakages (e.g., Saarinen, 2003; Goeldner & Ritchie, 2009; Zahra, 2013; Pratt, 2015; Sinclair-Maragh & Gursoy, 2016). Owners of tourism businesses often tend to offer low-paying jobs at minimum wage or lower (Kim & Uysal, 2003). The jobs connected to tourism tend to be seasonal (with unemployment in the off-season), with work often done by immigrants. Local entities can increase taxes to maintain facilities and transportation systems. Thus, prices tend to increase for inhabitants and tourists (e.g., food, housing), as well as infrastructure costs, whereas local or national government authorities can reduce investment in other fields (e.g., health or education; see, e.g., Stylidis &Terzidou, 2014).

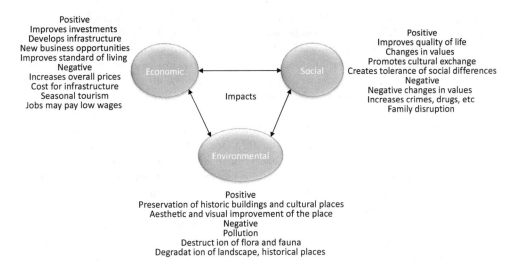

Figure 3.1   Overview of tourism impacts

Source: Authors' elaboration.

Tourism is usually associated with seasonality. During the periods where tourism flow decreases, inhabitants – tourism workers – suffer from low income or no income. This situation leads us to another risk – that is, the high risk of tourism investment. Private investors may see this activity involves high investment risks, and banks may be reluctant to fund lodgings, attractions, and other touristic projects. Therefore, destinations should not be economically dependent on tourism; rather, they must complement it with other economic activities (e.g., Frent, 2016; Sinclair-Maragh, 2017).

Some types of tourism can create enclaves (e.g., cruises or resorts). Tourists are confined to a location (e.g., the cruise ship or the accommodation) and tend to do not spend money at the destination (Frent, 2016). The economic benefits are restricted to the enclave and are not experienced in the surroundings.

The environmental category deals with the physical environment of a destination (Archer, Cooper, & Ruhanen, 2005). Destinations with high-value natural resources (e.g., beaches, lakes, mountains), museums, historic buildings, or heritage places are attractive to tourists. Tourism can generate income to preserve such natural places or restore monuments or historical areas, or even improve the visual and aesthetic appearance of a place (Tsai, Wu, Wall, & Linliu, 2016).

Tourism has also a dark side for the environment of a destination. The flow of people at the destination and the use of vehicles for transportation add to air, water, noise, waste, and visual (human crowding and traffic congestion) pollution (e.g., Taylor, 2001; Mason, 2003; Brida, Osti, & Barquet, 2010). In natural and city destinations, tourism can contribute to the destruction of flora and fauna and degradation of landscape, monuments, and historical areas. Likewise, inhabitants can learn to help tourists when disasters occur. The study by Tsai et al. (2016) explains that, in communities regularly exposed to the threats of typhoons and flooding (in Taiwan), residents have a high degree of awareness of tourism impacts. When disasters occur, community members can be prepared to form an effective joint defensive mechanism with local authorities. Members of the community can even help tourists in disaster situations.

Social impact is the third major category. Tourism encourages interactions between residents and tourists (Pelling, 2003). These interactions can benefit residents by providing new opportunities, new ideas, and knowledge that can be the seed for new behaviors. Tourists can push inhabitants to adopt a different moral code. The increased number of attractions, festivals, and cultural offers can improve the quality of life of inhabitants (e.g., Sharpley, 2014; Campo & Turbay, 2015). The change in attitude can have positive aspects by causing the inhabitants to accept the behaviors of other cultures, greater equality between genders, or other physiognomies (Gursoy, Chi, & Dyer, 2010; Nunkoo, Ramkissoon, & Gursoy, 2012; Stylidis & Terzidou, 2014). As Carneiro, Eusébio, and Caldeira (2017) claim, host–tourist social interaction may have a significant influence in all domains of quality of life, particularly relating to positive feelings (e.g., feeling proud to live in the place, feeling good), economic and social opportunities (e.g., job, recreational activities, financial resources, contact with people from different culture), and public facilities and services (e.g., public facilities, mobility, preservation of cultural heritage). Yet, tourists can also influence crime and accident rates (for instance, bringing in new drugs, gambling, alcoholism, or other diseases, or increased traffic heightening the risk of accidents; Deery, Jago, & Fredline, 2012; Stylidis & Terzidou, 2014; García, Vázquez, & Macías, 2015).

Deery et al. (2012) suggest several aspects as negative social impacts, such as overcrowding (the number of people in public areas), reduced numbers of parking places for residents, and traffic congestion. Tourists tend to enjoy the night and consume more alcohol, leading to increases in levels of noise, prostitution, and crime due to bad behavior and drug and alcohol abuse. The relationships and social exchange between groups of inhabitants and tourists can create friction owing to different moral and cultural standards (Lundberg, 2017).

Overview of tourism in Portugal

Portugal had 471,043 beds allocated to tourism in 2016, and, in 2018, the number reached 567,772 beds (PORDATA, 2018). In terms of balance of travel and tourism, in 2010 Portugal had a surplus of €4,648.45 million and, in 2016, it was €8,830.63 million (€12,580.55 million from exports and €3,848.92 million from imports; PORDATA, 2018).

Hotel establishments recorded 1.2 million guests and 3.1 million overnight stays in November 2017. Overnight stays in the internal and external markets accelerated to changing rates of +8.9% and +8.8%, respectively (+5.3% and +6.8% in October; INE, 2018). Total revenue grew by 15.5%, at a slower pace (18.2% in October), amounting to €178.0 million. Revenue from accommodation increased by 17.4% (22.7% in October), totaling €124.9 million (INE, 2018). Total revenue from hotel accommodation activity amounted to €178.0 million, and revenue from accommodation stood at €124.9 million (+15.5% and +17.4%, respectively), which represented a deceleration from the previous month (+18.2% and +22.7%, respectively, in October; INE, 2018).

The total contribution of travel and tourism to employment reached 967,500 jobs in 2017 (20.4% of total employment) and was expected to rise by 4.5% in 2018 to 1,011,500 jobs. By 2028, travel and tourism is forecast to support 1,151,000 jobs (24.9% of total employment), meaning an increase of 1.3% pa over the period (WTTC, 2018; see Figure 3.2).

In terms of visitor exports, which is a key component of the contribution of travel and tourism, Portugal generated €18.1 billion in visitor exports in 2017 and expects, by 2026, to achieve a total amount of €18.9 billion in expenditure, an increase of 2.5% pa (WTTC, 2018; see Figure 3.3).

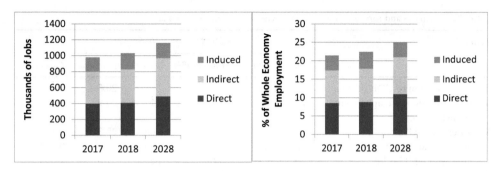

Figure 3.2 Total contribution of travel and tourism to employment in Portugal

Source: Redrawn data from WTTC (2018)

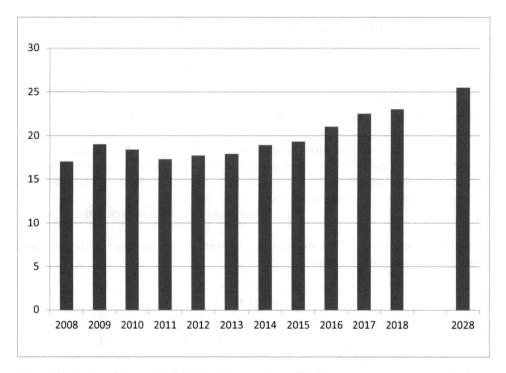

Figure 3.3 Foreign visitor exports in Portugal as percentage of total exports

Source: Redrawn data from WTTC (2018)

Taking into consideration the components of travel and tourism, we can admit that leisure travel spending (both inbound and domestic) was responsible for 85.6% of direct travel and tourism GDP in 2017 (€21 billion) against 14.4% for business travel spending (€3.5 billion; WTTC, 2018). Anyway, leisure travel spending was expected to grow by 4% in 2016 to €18.6 billion, 5.6% in 2018 to €22 billion, and 2.2% pa to €23.2 billion in 2026. On the other hand, business travel spending was expected to grow by 3.5% in 2018 to €3.7 billion and rise by 3.0% pa to €4.9 billion in 2028 (WTTC, 2018; see Table 3.2).

Table 3.2 Estimates and forecasts of tourism activity in Portugal – summary

Portugal	2017		2018	2028		
	Value	% of total	Growth (%)	Value	% of total	Growth (%)
Total contribution to GDP (US$bn)	38.0	17.3	5.1	50.8	20.5	2.4
Total contribution to employment (thousand jobs)	967.6	20.4	4.5	1.151	24.9	1.3
Visitor exports (US$ bn)	20.6	22.0	6.8	30.0	25.3	3.1
Domestic spending (US$ bn)	7.2	3.3	1.0	8.0	3.2	0.9
Leisure spending (US$ bn)	23.8	5.8	5.6	32.4	7.0	2.6
Business spending (US$ bn)	4.0	1.0	3.5	5.6	1.2	3.0
Capital investment (US$ bn)	3.6	10.2	7.4	5.4	12.5	3.3

Source: WTTC (2018)

Impacts of tourism: the case of Lisbon City

With the growth in numbers of tourists visiting Lisbon, it was expected that some infra-structures would feel the weight of that growth, mainly the transport and accommodation infrastructures. To address these problems, many investments are now being made and will be made in the near future.

Worx – Real Estate Consultants considered in its 2018 *Market Review* that:

> [it] is expected that touristic demand will remain high throughout 2018, sustained by the value for money offered in Portugal, and because of the safety factor, which has become increasingly important for tourists. In 2017, Portugal was voted the third most peaceful country in the world by the Global Peace Index.
>
> *(Worx – Real Estate Consultants, 2018, p. 18)*

Given this expected growth of tourism demand, what is expected to be done regarding the main infrastructures in the tourism market?

Airport

Humberto Delgado Airport (Lisbon) received nearly 27 million passengers in 2017, an 18.8% rise in traffic compared with 2016. Lisbon Airport is an airport in the middle of the city that has received continuous "upgrades," including, in August 2007, a second terminal, for domestic and low-cost flights, just to keep up with rising demand. Considering the location, any further structural expansion of the airport is impossible. Because of this, on the 75th anniversary of Lisbon Airport, November 13, 2017, Ana-Aeroportos de Portugal (the Portuguese airport management organization) presented the government with a proposal for more investment in the actual airport, to try to address passenger capacity in Humberto Delgado Airport with

> [the] duplication of shipping channels for all Schengen ports in Terminal 1 that do not yet have this facility. But also, the creation of two new non-Schengen boarding gates, or the ongoing installation of automatic lines in the security control, which will significantly increase passenger processing and the quality of the service provided. The planned investment also includes the renovation of the check-in area.
>
> *(ANA, 2017)*

On the same occasion, the ANA CEO also stated the need for a new airport in Montijo, using Montijo Air Base on the south bank of the Tagus River, an airport that, for now, is called Lisboa+1 Airport. The proposal has been presented to the government, and construction was expected to start by 2019.

Cruise tourism

Like the airport, the port of Lisbon is facing a huge problem with the rising number of passengers. Lisbon is also one of the biggest cruise terminals, with around half a million passengers and more than 300 cruise ships passing through Lisbon's cruise terminals, reflected in awards such as Europe's Leading Cruise Destination (World Travel Awards, 2016) and Europe's Leading Cruise Port (World Travel Awards, 2017a).With three cruise terminals already in Lisbon, Gares Marítima da Rocha Conde de Óbidos, Gare Marítima de Alcântara, and Terminal de Cruzeiros de Santa Apolónia, a new one was open on November 30, 2018, the Terminal de Cruzeiros de Lisboa.

A €77 million investment, the project provides a building with 13,800 square meters on three floors and capacity for 800,000 passengers per year, which represents an increase of 300,000 over the current total of the three terminals that already existed. The dock of the new terminal has 1,490 meters of pier for multi-length ships, with a draft up to 12 meters. The terminal allows the maximum boarding and disembarkation of 4,500 passengers, with parking for 360 vehicles and 80 tour buses or taxis, a panoramic terrace, and free Internet. A 2017 survey of Observatório de Turismo de Lisboa showed that each cruise passenger spends around €50 in Lisbon, with total revenues of nearly €30 million for the year.

In 2018, the national ports registered the passage of more than 1.3 million tourists on cruises and 947 stopovers, an increase compared with 2017 of 5% and 10%, respectively, and a new record. Of the six Portuguese port stops (Leixões, Lisbon, Setúbal, Portimão, Azores, and Madeira), all showed a positive increase in passengers embarking and disembarking. Lisbon was the one that added more stops, registering a movement of 330 cruise ships (APL, 2019). In 2018, the port of Lisbon achieved another record when the number of cruise passengers reached 577,603, 11% more than in 2017. The Port of Lisbon received 123 ships that made 339 stopovers, 3% more than in 2017.

The year 2018 was also a success for the turnaround segment that continued to grow significantly and became one of the best ever for the port of Lisbon. The year 2018 was notable for the 12th Seatrade Cruise Med conference in Lisbon, which had the biggest attendance ever and is one of the largest cruise fairs in the world.

And, last but not least, the port of Lisbon was awarded, for the third consecutive year and the fourth time, the prize of the best cruise port in Europe by the World Travel Awards.

Accommodation

All these tourists traveling to visit Lisbon naturally have an impact on accommodation infrastructure and business. The figures regarding the number of hotels and occupation have risen in recent years to adapt to the rising number of tourists visiting Portugal (more than 20 million in 2017), with Lisbon Metropolitan Area (18 municipalities including Lisbon, north and south of the Tagus River) reaching more than 6 million guest stays in 2017 (INE, 2018). These guests stay around two days, usually on city breaks, with the exact average length of stay declining marginally in the past few years, maybe because tourists who visit Portugal are more likely to also visit the rest of the country.

Nevertheless, even with this slowdown, total revenues in hotel establishments are rising (Figure 3.4) because the number of guests and the average revenue from available bedrooms are rising.

The total revenues include not only the room price, but also revenues from all other hotel services. There is a rise in the room revenues as a percentage of total hotel revenues, meaning that revenues from all other services beside the room itself are falling.

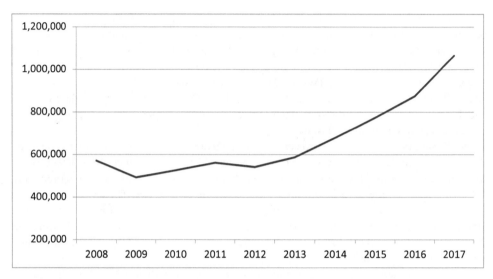

Figure 3.4 Total revenues in hotel establishments (Lisbon Metropolitan Area)

Source: INE (2018)

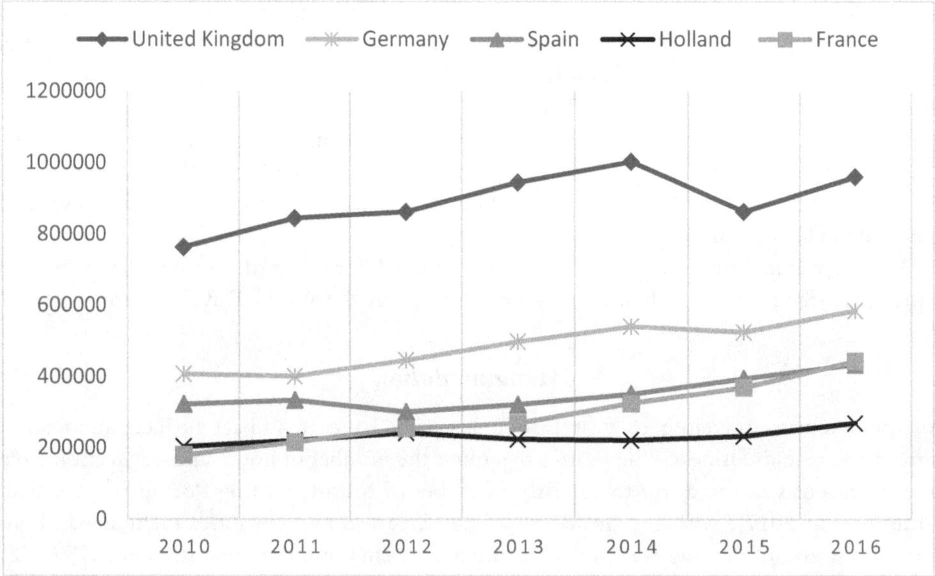

Figure 3.5 Evolution of tourists (sleeping nights) by country of origin

Source: INE (2018)

Considering visitors by country, nationwide, we can see that Portugal for many years has had more tourists from Britain and Spain, with a growing importance of "Other Countries" that include China and Russia (Figure 3.5).

In 2017, the United Kingdom, Spain, France, and Germany still represented 50% of all visitors, and there is expected to be a negative impact from Brexit, with the return of travel borders between Portugal and the United Kingdom.

Number of hotels

With all the growth dynamics in the sector, Lisbon has also seen growth in the number of hotels, mainly four-star hotels (Figure 3.6). By 2017, 44 new hotels had opened in Portugal, nearly a quarter of them in Lisbon, and mainly four-star hotels (Figure 3.6). The year 2017 also saw 80 new hotel projects in the country, an increase from the 50 new hotel projects submitted in 2016 (Worx – Real Estate Consultants, 2018). This was a 60% increase, following an increase of 47% between 2015 and 2016. Thus, between 2015 and 2017, in mainland Portugal, there were 164 new hotel projects. As expected,

> [T]he temporal dynamics show that hotel investment has increasingly moved out of Lisbon, dispersing geographically to less central markets. In fact, 60% of the growth in the number of new portfolio projects observed in 2017 took place in the non-metropolitan regions.
>
> *(Ricardo Guimarães, director of Confidencial Imobiliário, ECO, 2018a)*

In Lisbon, the new hotels were made from scratch but also from old buildings, with most of the original architecture – mainly the building façade – being kept. The building of new

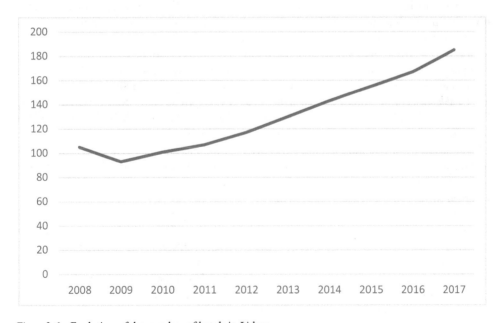

Figure 3.6   Evolution of the number of hotels in Lisbon
Source: INE (2018)

hotels from traditional Lisbon buildings has been subject to negative comments and opposition from Lisbon citizens and some political parties that want to preserve traditional Lisbon, without defacing it with an excess of tourists and hotels, losing the traditional Lisbon soul.

One of examples is the now abandoned DN building in Avenida da Liberdade, which was the office of one of the older Portuguese newspapers, *Diário de Notícias*, founded in 1864. It is expected to be transformed into a hotel or deluxe apartments that, even if the main structure is retained, will be at odds with the feelings of many Lisbon citizens.

Local accommodation

Regarding local accommodation, Lisbon has seen a big increase in all its neighborhoods, putting pressure on the local population that pays low rents, with landlords trying to dump residents from their apartments so that they can let them later at much higher prices as local accommodation; this also leads to local inhabitants complaining about "too many tourists in my neighborhood," even if a recent study (AHRESP, 2017, p. 40) showed that "the neighbor-hood's opinion on local accommodation is overall positive (32%), with parking and cleaning being pointed out as improving."

A recent study from the Institute of Planning and Development of Tourism (IPDT, 2018) showed rising tourist pressures on the city. Lisbon has more tourists per inhabitant (nine) than cities such as London (four) or Barcelona (five), with more than 4.5 million tourists visiting in 2017, a density of 300 tourists per square kilometer. This pressure, with local population complaints rising about the increased numbers of tourists visiting Lisbon, led the city council of Lisbon to initiate regulation measures for local accommodation.

As ECO (2018b) reports, local accommodation started with a city council study to analyze the maximum local accommodation capacity per city zone, a new local accommodation regula-tion office, and local accommodation quotas in each city zone, including the more vulnerable and traditional historic zones. There will also be a distinction made between "local housing" (the concept of home sharing) and "housing tourism" (houses are used 100% for tourism), with more restrictions in the latter case, because it is considered a hotel service, and the opening of a local accommodation offer will need authorization from the city council.

But what is the economic profile of the local accommodation in Lisbon? An Association of Hospitality, Restaurant and Related Services of Portugal study (AHRESP, 2017), *Valorization and Qualification of Local Accommodation in the Lisbon Region*, produced by ISCTE-IUL Marketing FutureCast Lab and Sítios – Serviços, Informação e Turismo, shed some light on this somewhat recent sector, using 2016 data. In 2016, this subsector employed more than 5,700 people, and 13,400 indirectly, accounting for 1% of the GDP of the metropolitan area of Lisbon (€285.9 million) and representing 18.6% of total tourist income in the area, with an indirect impact from tourist spending in Lisbon of €549.6 million, a daily average of €70 spent on food, leisure and entertainment, travel, and tourist attractions.

Considering the properties, the clear majority (86%) are apartments – nearly 7,000 in 2016, almost double the number in 2015, followed by housing (6.5%) and lodging establishments (5.6%). Lisbon local accommodation accounts for nearly 55,000 guests, a rise of 75% on 2015.

Although the news sometimes showed complaints of older citizens being pressed by landlords to leave their apartments that later will be let to tourists, 59% of the local accommodation prop-erties were vacant before, and 13% were used for own housing, but, in 19% of cases, properties went from rentals to housing to local accommodation.

The opportunities most cited by local accommodation owners are tourism demand from foreigners (85%), positive perceptions about Portugal (59%), and the demand for a personalized service (42%); considering their clients, the French (47%) and Spanish (28%) represent three-quarters of demand, with 45% being couples and 50% aged below 40 years.

With regard to the factors considered by guests when they choose local accommodation, the property location (72%) and other guests' comments (68%) are the main motivations. They also value the support of the host (69%), and half of them also consider the property's decor. Public transportation is the preferred means of transport for guests of local accommodation.

The occupancy rates are mainly 50–70% in low season and 70–90% in high season, with bookmarking made mainly with Booking.com (45%), followed by Airbnb, and with direct reservations at about 9%. Local accommodation promotion is made through Facebook by almost all respondents (98%), with a significant number (78%) advertising on standby platforms to attract customers.

Conclusions

This chapter contributes an overview of the economic, environmental, and social impacts of tourism as they have emerged in the literature. We also characterize and analyze a particular destination – Lisbon – experiencing growth in the number of tourists and the consequent impacts.

In this vein, considering the social and economic impacts of the growth of tourism in Lisbon, we can conclude that it has very positive aspects such as the growth of tourism-related jobs (including in the 45–66 age group), the growth of direct and indirect tourism revenues, and also the current or near-future improvements of infrastructure, such as the cruise port, airport upgrade, creation of a second airport for the city, and new accommodation units (mainly four-star hotels). Yet there are also some less positive impacts, which start to show their effects on the local population and even led to the first city countermeasures to try to minimize them.

The growth in the number of Lisbon hotels – some of them built on older buildings that were appreciated by the older, more traditional local population – the proliferation of local accommodation services, and the larger number of tourists throughout the year (and not only in summer, as was usual some years ago) in older and traditional city neighborhoods cause some pressure and discomfort for some population segments, which do not usually have great protest capacities, but which local or national government try to help if needed. Some of the older inhabitants are seeing their home rental contracts cancelled, because is more lucrative to let the same apartments to tourists. There is a wave of real-estate speculation in the city, with a rise in the cost of renting apartments.

When we look at the environmental impacts, Lisbon – as a destination – has faced increases in air pollution and the debris generated by the increase in people.

In the end, in Lisbon, we have:

- Infrastructure improvement;
- Rise of economic activity;
- Rise of tourism-related jobs;
- Boom in real estate and renting.

But these come with:

- Pressure on the quality of life in Lisbon, as citizens are living in locations crowded by tourists;
- Threats of home rental cancellation for the older citizens with cheap rents.

What can be done from here? While trying not to kill the goose that laid the golden eggs (economic activity and jobs related to Lisbon tourism), hospitality sector self-regulation measures and policy measures can be considered to try to mitigate pressures from tourism and real-estate and rent speculation, which have a negative impact on some Lisbon areas.

Moreover, deeper research must be carried out to analyze the positive and negative impacts of tourism on Lisbon (and other Portuguese cities), to ensure that appropriate measures are taken without pressure from local populations or the media.

References

AHRESP (Association of Hospitality, Restaurant and Related Services of Portugal). (2017). *Valorization and Qualification of Local Accommodation in the Lisbon Region.* Portugal: AHRESP.

ANA. (2017). *Lisbon Airport Celebrates 75 Years.* Retrieved from: www.ana.pt/en/corporate/press/2017/11/13/lisbon-airport-celebrates-75-years (accessed January 30, 2018).

APL. (2019). *Administration of the Port of Lisbon.* Retrieved from: www.portodelisboa.pt/portal/page/portal/PORTAL_PORTO_LISBOA/CRUZEIROS/NOTICIAS?notid=53296818 (accessed February 26, 2019).

Archer, B., Cooper C., & Ruhanen, L. (2005). The positive and negative impacts of tourism. In W.F. Theobald (Ed.), *Global Tourism* (3rd ed., pp. 79–102). Oxford: Elsevier Butterworth Heineman.

Brida, J. G., Osti, L., & Barquet, A. (2010). Segmenting resident perceptions towards tourism – a cluster analysis with a multinomial logit model of a mountain community. *International Journal of Tourism Research*, 12(5), 591–602.

Campo, A. R., & Turbay, S. (2015). The silence of the Kogi in front of tourists. *Annals of Tourism Research*, 52(0), 44–59.

Carneiro, M. J., Eusébio, C., & Caldeira, A. (2017). The influence of social contact in residents' perceptions of the tourism impact on their Quality of Life: a structural equation model. *Journal of Quality Assurance in Hospitality & Tourism*, Online September 12, 2017. DOI: 10.1080/1528008X.2017.1314798

CNN. (2017). *Is Lisbon the Coolest Capital City in Europe?* Retrieved from: https://edition.cnn.com/travel/article/lisbon-coolest-city/index.html (accessed February 2, 2018).

Correia, F. (2017). What meaning for sustainability? The role of tourism academics in securing impact. *Journal of Policy Research in Tourism, Leisure & Events*, 9(2), 224–227.

Deery, M., Jago, L., & Fredline, L. (2012). Rethinking social impacts of tourism research: a new research agenda. *Tourism Management*, 33, 64–73.

Djurasevik, S., & Nedelea, A. (2007). Comparing and contrasting the alternative methodologies available for evaluating the impact of tourism. *Journal of Tourism – Studies & Research in Tourism*, 4, 13–18.

Dyer, P., Gursoy, D., Sharma, B., & Carter, J. (2007). Structural modelling of resident perceptions of tourism and associated development on the Sunshine Coast, Australia. *Tourism Management*, 28(2), 409–422.

ECO. (2018a). *Foram registados 80 novos projetos para hotéis em 2017.* Retrieved from: https://eco.sapo.pt/2018/03/06/foram-registados-80-novos-projetos-para-hoteis-em-2017/ (accessed March 22, 2018).

ECO. (2018b). *Local Accommodation.* Retrieved from: https://eco.pt/2017/11/02/quotas-para-travar-alojamento-local-em-lisboa-avancam-em-2018/ (accessed March 22, 2018).

Frent, C. (2016). An overview on the negative impacts of tourism. *Journal of Tourism – Studies & Research in Tourism*, 22, 32–37.

García, F. A., Vázquez, A. B., & Macías, R. C. (2015). Residents' attitudes towards the impacts of tourism. *Tourism Management Perspectives*, 13, 33–40.

Global Destination Cities Index Mastercard. (2016). Retrieved from: https://newsroom.mastercard.com/wp-content/uploads/2016/09/FINAL-Global-Destination-Cities-Index-Report.pdf (accessed February 2, 2018).

Goeldner, Ch. R., & Ritchie, J. R. B. (2009). *Tourism Principles, Practices, Philosophies* (11th ed.). Holden, NJ: John Wiley.

Gursoy, D., Chi, C. G., & Dyer, P. (2010). Locals' attitudes toward mass and alternative tourism: The case of Sunshine Coast, Australia. *Journal of Travel Research*, 49(3), 381–394.

INE. (2017). *Lodging Capacity and Personnel Employed Survey (until 2004) Guests' Stay in Hotels and Other Accommodations Survey.* Retrieved from: www.ine.pt/xportal/xmain?xpid=INE&xpgid=ine_publicacoes&PUBLICACOEStipo=ea&PUBLICACOEScoleccao=107668&selTab=tab0&xlang=pt (accessed March 5, 2018).

INE. (2018). *Tourism Activity*. Portugal: INE.

IPDT (Institute of Planning and Development of Tourism). (2018). *Overtourism: Impacts, Challenges, Solutions*. Portugal: IPDT

Kim, K., & Uysal, M. (2003). Perceived socio-economic impacts of festivals and events among organizers. *Journal of Hospitality & Leisure Marketing*, 10(3/4), 159–171.

Kim, K., Uysal, M., & Sirgy, M. J. (2013). How does tourism in a community impact the quality of life of community residents? *Tourism Management*, 36, 527–540.

Látková, P., & Vogt, C. A. (2012). Residents' attitudes toward existing and future tourism development in rural communities. *Journal of Travel Research*, 51(1), 50–67.

Lindberg, K., & Johnson, R. L. (1997). Modeling resident attitudes toward tourism. *Annals of Tourism Research*, 24(2), 402–424.

Lundberg, E. (2017). The importance of tourism impacts for different local resident groups: a case study of a Swedish seaside destination. *Journal of Destination Marketing & Management*, 6(1), 46–55.

Mason, P. (2003). *Tourism Impacts, Planning and Management*. Amsterdam: Butterworth-Heinemann.

Nunkoo, R., Ramkissoon, H., & Gursoy, D. (2012). Public trust in tourism institutions. *Annals of Tourism Research*, 39(3), 1538–1564.

Oosterhaven, J., & Fan, T. (2006). Impact of international tourism on the Chinese economy. *International Journal of Tourism Research*, 8(5), 347–354.

Pelling, M. (2003). *The vulnerability of cities: Natural disasters and social resilience*. London: Earthscan.

PORDATA. (2018). *Data from Contemporary Portugal*. Retrieved from: www.pordata.pt (accessed January 22, 2018).

Pratt, S. (2015). The economic impact of tourism in SIDS. *Annals of Tourism Research*, 52(0), 148–160.

Ribeiro, M. A., Pinto, P., Silva, J. A., & Woosnam, K. M. (2017). Residents' attitudes and the adoption of pro-tourism behaviours: The case of developing island countries. *Tourism Management*, 61, 523–537.

Saarinen, J. (2003). The regional economics of tourism in Northern Finland: The socio-economic implications of recent tourism development and future possibilities for regional development. *Scandinavian Journal of Hospitality & Tourism*, 3(2), 91–113.

Sharpley, R. (2014). Host perceptions of tourism: a review of the research. *Tourism Management*, 42, 37–49.

Sinclair-Maragh, G. (2017). Demographic analysis of residents' support for tourism development in Jamaica. *Journal of Destination Marketing & Management*, 6(1), 5–12.

Sinclair-Maragh, G., & Gursoy, D. (2016). A conceptual model of residents' support for tourism development in developing countries. *Tourism Planning & Development*, 13(1), 1–22.

Stylidis, D., & Terzidou, M. (2014). Tourism and the economic crisis in Kavala, Greece. *Annals of Tourism Research*, 44, 210–226.

Taylor, P. J. (2001). Authenticity and sincerity in tourism. *Annals of Tourism Research*, 28(1), 7–26.

Tsai, C. H., Wu, T. C., Wall, G., & Linliu, S. C. (2016). Perceptions of tourism impacts and community resilience to natural disasters. *Tourism Geographies*, 18(2), 152–173.

UNWTO. (2017). *UNWTO Tourism Highlights – 2017 Edition*. Spain: UNWTO.

Wallpaper Design Awards. (2017). *Best City of the Year*. Retrieved from: www.kryptonfilmsinternational.com/2017/01/17/lisbon-is-2017s-best-city-according-to-wallpaper-magazine/ (accessed March 2, 2018).

World Travel Awards. (2016). *Europe's Leading Cruise Destination*. Retrieved from: www.worldtravelawards.com/award-europes-leading-cruise-destination-2016 (accessed March 2, 2018).

World Travel Awards. (2017a). *Europe's Leading Cruise Port*. Retrieved from: www.worldtravelawards.com/award-europes-leading-cruise-port-2017 (accessed March 2, 2018).

World Travel Awards. (2017b). *Best City Break*. Retrieved from: www.worldtravelawards.com/award-worlds-leading-city-break-destination-2017 (accessed March 2, 2018).

Woo, E., Kim, H., & Uysal, M. (2015). Life satisfaction and support for tourism development. *Annals of Tourism Research*, 50, 84–97.

Worx – Real Estate Consultants. (2018). *Worx Market Review*. Portugal: Worx.

WTTC (World Travel Tourism Council). (2018). *Travel & Tourism Economic Impact 2018 – Portugal*. Spain: WTTC.

Zahra, I. (2013). Tourism and its impact on Cox's Bazar, Bangladesh. *Journal of Tourism –Studies & Research in Tourism*, 15, 12–18.

4

TOURISM PLANNING: THE UNITED NATIONS WORLD TOURISM ORGANIZATION INSTO PROGRAMME

The example of Raglan, New Zealand

*Chris Ryan, Zhe Chen, Li Linrui and
Mary Anne Ramos Tumanan*

Why Raglan?

Raglan is a community of 1,143 households (2013 census) and a current estimated population of 5,320. It is estimated that about 477 properties are not fully occupied all year round, many of these being summer homes (or *baches* as they are known in New Zealand) that are either owner occupied or rented for summer. Located on the west coast of North Island of New Zealand, it is famed among surfers for possessing the longest left-hand break in the southern hemisphere. It has long been established as a surfing Mecca, as evidenced by Raglan being featured in the film *The Endless Summer*, made in 1966, and more recently it featured in the 2011 award-winning Indie adventure sports film *Last Paradise*. Adding to the traditional laid-back lifestyle that characterises Raglan as a surfing Mecca are the several painters, potters, craftspeople and alternative lifestylers. Among these one can list the wild-life photographer Janet Scott, the artist Elsa Lye and others whose work can be seen on www.raglanart.nz. Complementing this is a fund of stories, from those relating to the surfer Miki Dora who stayed at Raglan while escaping the FBI on a charge of credit card fraud to others of more importance to New Zealand, such as the success of the late Eva Rickard (1925–1997). She was a Maori activist who laid the groundwork for the Maori *hikoi* (mass participation marches) that helped establish the contemporary role of Maori in New Zealand today. Born in Raglan (for which the Maori name is Whāingaroa), her arrest in 1978 over protests about the Raglan golf course was a pivotal moment, along with the occupation of Bastion Point in Auckland, in leading to a reappraisal of the 1840 Treaty of Waitangi between the colonial government and the Maori chiefs.

Over the intervening years, Raglan has sought to retain its lifestyle and history even while the numbers of tourists have continued to grow. Based on various sources of information, including the recording of smartphone usage by Qrious (a market research company that is part of the New Zealand telco Spark), it has been estimated that, during the summer months, the numbers in Raglan exceed the town's population by some three to four times

(Waikato District Council, 2017). It has also been estimated that, during January 2018, the number of people congregated at just one of the Raglan beaches was the equivalent to the town's normal population (personal communication, R. Thorpe, 2018).

Raglan was also selected because of a link between the first author and participants in the local tourism industry. Early in the twenty-first century, he had been asked to undertake some research relating to the way in which Raglan residents were perceiving tourism, and what it was that they valued about the town and its lifestyle (Ryan & Cooper, 2004). What became evident was that Raglan possessed a strong sense of community, and this was evidenced in the way the community board and others came together to create their own vision of the town's future in the document *Raglan Naturally*. In that document, the community identified aspects of their built environment, the natural environment of harbour and sea, and features of their culture and community. Of note was that not only did the planning process include what they desired, but their vision additionally included a list of exclusions that included the development of high-rise, large hotels. As described below, this document has helped shape the planning policies of the local administration, the Waikato District Council (WDC).

The International Network of Sustainable Tourism Observatories (INSTO) Programme

Precursors and context

Concerns about environmental sustainability are not new. The contemporary legislative framework as established in much of the Western world can be traced back to the Industrial Revolution and the reaction to the pollution and poor working conditions caused by the new factories of the late eighteenth and early nineteenth centuries. In the United Kingdom, the 1833 Factory Act addressed the issue of young children working in the factories and banned the employment of those under the age of nine years. As the cities grew larger, problems of public health emerged owing to poor sanitation. The cholera outbreaks of the 1830s and again in the 1840s led to the deaths of literally hundreds of thousands (Gilbert, 2018). These pandemics in countries such as the United Kingdom and United States led to reforms in local administration and the commencement of investment in public utilities such as sewage disposal and water supplies. Public-spirited families such as the Chamberlains in Birmingham, UK, came to prominence based on large-scale public investment in urban infrastructure that effectively addressed the problems of cholera in the developed world (Petrie, 1938).

One can discern an emergent agenda concerning the natural environment and the creation of national parks among many nations in the 1930s, partly based on the advocacy of earlier environmentalists such as John Muir and the reform policies of politicians such as Franklin D. Roosevelt and their various counterparts around the world (Baird & Nelson, 1998). Similarly, reflecting the emerging concerns of increasing use of pesticides and the industrialisation of agricultural practices in the face of growing populations, the period immediately after the Second World War saw advances in town planning and rural legislative frameworks with an emphasis on trying to establish the consequences of development. The 1966 Santa Barbara oil spill gave rise to the National Environmental Policy Act of 1969 in the USA, which was followed by the creation of the Environmental Protection Agency in 1970. A green pressure group movement was becoming increasingly recognised as a political movement as well as an active pressure group and was active on a global scale, particularly in developed nations.

The emergence of a global concern was given voice in the Brundtland Commission and its report *Our Common Future* (World Commission on Environment and Development, 1987), and, together with the 1991 Rio Declaration (United Nations Conference on Environment and Development, 1992; both sponsored by the United Nations), the whole process of co-ordinated global action on sustainability was taken into an international dimension. Both forums recognised that sustainability required more than the simple rectification of degraded environments. Instead, the need was for programmes located within the respective socio-economic–political frameworks, with a focal point being the communities, their culture and lifestyles, and the economic opportunities that development might bring. Equally, there was an evident concern about the impacts of development on the environment, and the need to plan in ways that not only minimised negative impacts, but also enhanced natural and social environments. By the beginning of the twenty-first century, what had previously been factors often peripheral to goals of economic growth had now been reassessed. In the view of many, the adoption of environmentally friendly policies was itself the source of future growth. Equally, it seemed to many that such goals had to be adopted at local, national and international levels.

Consequently, with a new millennium, all the then 191 member nations of the United Nations established eight Millennium Development Goals (MDGs), which briefly were to:

- eradicate extreme poverty and hunger,
- achieve universal primary education,
- promote gender equality and empower females,
- reduce child mortality,
- improve maternal health,
- combat malaria, HIV/AIDS and other diseases,
- ensure environmental sustainability, and
- create a global partnership for development.

The target date for seeking to achieve these deliberately ambitious goals was 2015. Financing arrangements were established through the World Bank, the International Monetary Fund and the African Development Bank, and some US$50 billion of debt owed by the more impoverished nations was cancelled. Among others, Liu et al. (2016) noted that significant improvements had been made in child mortality, and other gains had been made, for example in primary education provision. By the same token, others had noted a need for more specific targets, especially in relation to food provision and its transport (Hawkes & Popkin, 2015). Generally, it was felt that progress had been made, and, in 2016, the United Nations replaced the eight original Millennium Goals with 17 separate but related Sustainable Development Goals. These are collectively also known as "Transforming Our World: The 2030 Agenda for Sustainable Development" – often shortened to the "2030 Agenda". Among these goals are the elimination of poverty and hunger; the provision of quality education; gender equality; clean water; affordable, clean energy; sustainable cities and communities; climate action; an enhancement of peace; and strong institutions and partnerships. The full list and further details are listed on web pages such as https://sustainable development.un.org/ and http://insto.unwto.org/about/ and their various submenus.

The INSTO Network

The INSTO Programme is one of the programmes developed by the UNWTO in conjunction with the United Nations Development Programme (UNDP) that seek to attain the objectives of the United Nation's SDGs. In a joint publication, *Tourism and the Sustainable Development Goals – Journey to 2030* (UNWTO, 2017), it is noted that public reporting on the progress of the goals is in itself, an important means of securing the desired objectives. It is also noted that 41 of the 64 Voluntary National Reviews made prior to December 2017 made reference to tourism, with frequent reference to Goals 8, 12 and 17. These goals are "Decent work and economic growth", "Responsible consumption and production" and "Partnerships for the goals". However, the UNWTO (2017) also points out that policymakers may be underestimating the contribution that tourism could make to other objectives, including those relating to the management of waste and of water supplies, and to the sustaining of communities and diversity.

When examining the INSTO Programme in operation as at December 2017, 21 observatories were operating in, among others, the USA, Spain, Brazil, and Greece. The greatest number of INSTO centres were in China and Indonesia. An examination of the web page www.insto.unwto.org indicates that many of the observatories are studying the impacts of tourism on local communities and the impacts on patterns of employment, culture and environment. A key parameter within these programmes is an insistence on a monitoring process that retains a thread of repetition in the research process. The concept is that tourism is a catalyst of change, even as tourism itself is reflective of wider socio-economic change, particularly in response to the emergence of Asian middle classes and the changes in transport and communication technologies. These latter changes permit more people to travel and a greater exchange of information. This ease of access to information feeds perceptions and expectations about tourist destinations, while at the same time arming the destination marketers with more information about the visitor.

Under these circumstances, the traditional "one-shot", cross-sectional survey of tourism impacts is of less value as an aid to policy-making and decision-making about destinations. Communities and local and state planning authorities require more instant information about changes in the tourism environment. Such information can come from a series of sources. Forecasts about the flow of tourist numbers in the immediate future are now available from a study of Google searches (Choi & Varian, 2012; Bangwayo-Skette & Skeete, 2015), and the ability to discern patterns of change can come from the repetitive research projects into resident and tourist perceptions of change, and the monitoring of economic and environmental data. Trends relating to speed of change, directions of change, volumes of changes and consequences of change require the establishment of starting points and the continuous collection of data in an organised fashion that can produce timely information to aid decision-making. The need for a sustained commitment requiring high levels of research expertise might in part explain the involvement of many universities from around the world. Again, details of the research institutions involved in the observatories can be found on the web page www.insto.unwto.org, and many of the observatories additionally possess their own web pages.

Consequently, the INSTO centres have tended to retain within their portfolios of research one or two constant modes of data collection. Some of the oldest continued monitoring programmes exist in China under the auspices of the College of Tourism Management at Sun Yat Sen University. Through the Monitoring Centre for UNWTO Sustainable Tourism Observatories (MCSTO), the research team headed by Professor Bao Jigang now manages (as at January 2018) 11 observatories scattered throughout China, from the far north-west, at Kanas, based on Tuva and Kazakh culture, to the south-west, in Xishuangbanna, an area of China where the Han are not the majority ethnic grouping, to the centre of China, with the UNESCO heritage sites in Anhui to the north-east with the city of Changshu. At the 2016 UNWTO Conference held at Passikudah, Sri Lanka, Yi Liu from Sun Yat-Sen University listed the activities of MCSTO and INSTO as monitoring change, collecting and compiling examples of good practice, stimulating local participation in development, engaging in capacity building, undertaking educational campaigns and providing opportunities for various stakeholders, including local authorities, which also included the provision of recommendations for future action.

Tourism impacts at Raglan

As noted above, during the summer period, the numbers of tourists staying in Raglan significantly swells the size of the population. At the time of writing (March 2018), the WDC is engaged in consultations over its 10-year plan that is designed to set general principles that will guide the shorter-term plans that the council makes, as is required by the Local Government Act of 2002. This will take the council through to 2018. The challenges the council is facing are significant, for it is the third fastest growing council region in New Zealand (Sanson, 2018). Visitor expenditure for the whole of the council in 2017 had increased by 10% in the prior 12-month period to a figure of NZ$124 million (US$91 million), and Raglan is the premier visitor destination within the council region. The total population residing in the council area is approximately 73,000, of whom 5,320 live in Raglan. Morgan (2018), the council's economic development planning officer, estimated the number of visitors in Raglan over the period of November 2016 to March 2017 as being about 145,000, drawing on data derived from Statistics New Zealand, Paymark (dealing with credit card transactions) and Qrious (researching cell phone calls).

Major challenges facing the WDC relate to roads, water and sewage (Waikato District Council, 2018), a problem common to many of New Zealand's councils. Much of this challenge arises from the expected growing population and a need to maintain current water supplies and sewage treatment. These issues are also common in Raglan. In 2016, there were, within four months, three significant waste water spills into Raglan Harbour after periods of heavy rain, when the existing methods of dealing with waste water were found to be deficient. Given the value of the harbour, not simply for tourism, but as a marine resource (for example, it is not uncommon to see orca in the harbour), a NZ$1.5 million per annum renewal programme was instituted (Waikato District Council, 2018) combined with other initiatives including educational programmes on the importance of keeping drains unblocked. The waste water charge on the rates was also increased by 13.9% for 12 months, with annual increases then to be decreased over time to 2%. Equally, by 2023–2024, a further expenditure of NZ$16.6 million on waste water treatment plant is planned, with a relocation of the water outfall as well.

Tourism imposes significant challenges for Raglan in terms of infrastructure needs and waste and water management. Although Raglan has only suffered a water shortage once, following an earthquake in November 2016, water tankers are not an uncommon feature of town life, as many of the rural properties outside the town are not on the town water supply, and this will include lifestyle blocks and farm stay operations providing accommodation for visitors. A combination of lower rainfall and growing numbers of tourists enjoying home and farm stays in the Raglan region has led to a greater need for water portage by large tankers. Equally, the council is engaged in road upgrading schemes and road straightening along the somewhat winding approach road to Raglan that comes from Hamilton. This benefits locals as well as tourists, as many Raglan residents are thought to work in Hamilton, and, equally, Raglan is a summer beach location for those who live in Hamilton.

The summer impact of tourism is clearly shown in data relating to waste management. For example, in July 2016 (a winter month in the southern hemisphere), the totals of glass and paper diverted from landfill as part of the waste management programme in Raglan were 29.7 and 10.00 tonnes, respectively. In February 2017 (the main month of summer), the respective figures were 77.74 tonnes and 16.62 tonnes. During the winter months, the community-owned Xtreme Zero Waste would be undertaking a household and business waste collection just once per week, but, in the summer months, that would increase to three collections per week (personal communication, Thorpe, 2018).

In the Ryan and Cooper (2004) report, and in research undertaken in 2016–2018 by the Waikato INSTO Programme, several aspects of community attitudes remained constant. Over the intervening period, the metrics of community attachment to Raglan remained high, and the INSTO reports reinforced this (Chen, Li, Tumanan & Ryan, 2017). Equally, the community retained strong visions of what Raglan was, and what it was they did not wish to occur. For example, both visitors and residents wanted local retail stores and cafes to remain in local ownership. Residents saw local ownership as being important in (a) retaining local proprietorship as a means of ensuring business interests would be aligned with the community desires so that (b) Raglan would retain a situation where it was not like other resort areas characterised by the presence of international brands such as McDonalds, Starbucks or large hotel chains. The community wished to retain its mix of simple one- or two-storey buildings, its ambience of laid-back local ownership and friendly culture. Visitors saw Raglan as retaining a "kiwi lifestyle" that many areas had lost. Part of that was that local stores were locally owned – and, hence, stores were not simply places where one purchased items, but also sources of information about local spots, how to reach them, and what one could do as a visitor.

The INSTO Programme collected both quantitative and qualitative data that confirm these impressions. For example, in 2017, the interim report provided to the Raglan Chamber of Commerce and the WDC noted:

> What is also evident is the congruence between many of the views expressed by tourists and residents. There are, though, some notable differences. Within the resident group there was some thought that Maori culture might be able to play a role in creating a tourism product, but not withstanding the significance of Raglan in the history of Maori activism, no tourist made mention of this. For the tourist Raglan is a relaxing beach side town set in a harbour seascape that is renowned for surfing, while offering access to a green landscape that fulfils the notion of a beautiful New Zealand of hills, pastures and waterfalls.
>
> *(Chen et al., 2017, para. 4.3, p. 17)*

That report also provided descriptive statistics as to how a sample of 400 residents regarded tourism using a 7-point scale, where '7' represented the highest level of agreement. Thus, on the item "It is important that any development over the next decade in Raglan is consistent with the character of Raglan", the mean score was 6.14. Figure 4.1 presents a Gaussian representation of the main themes generated from textual analysis of residents' comments.

Given the above commentary, it is not wholly surprising to note problems relating to sewage, the numbers of people, and so on, all associated with summer and tourists. The appearance of the word 'rent' is associated with anecdotal stories of tenants being asked to vacate premises in the summer because of the higher rents available from renting to tourists during the summer. An examination of web pages relating to Airbnb and Bookabach undertaken in March 2018 indicated the presence of more than 200 such private rentals being listed. The mean daily rate being charged was NZ$132 (US$97) for Airbnb and NZ$243 (US$178) for Bookabach, representing potentially significant higher returns for property owners when compared with the norm for weekly rents during the winter period.

The issue emerged in interviews. As noted by one respondent: "Rents for properties have climbed by over $100 to $150 per week in the last two years and it is getting to the point where local people cannot afford these, especially in the summer." Another local employer in the town gave evidence of an increasing difficulty in finding accommodation for new employees, both summer and full-time employees. This has led to the WRAP initiative, briefly described below.

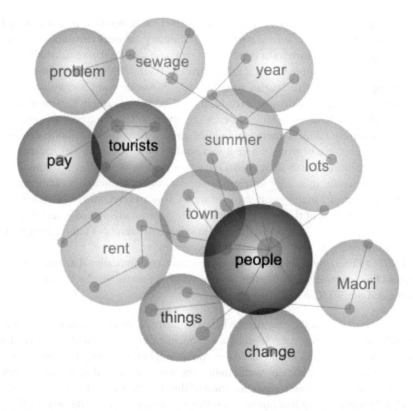

Figure 4.1 Gaussian representation of the main themes generated from textual analysis of residents' comments

Role of research for planning

As noted, the original community planning involved in the *Raglan Naturally* documentation has made an important contribution to the planning process. The document has, as noted, been continually referred to and eventually contributed to the WDC plan.

> Raglan will retain its seaside character as it grows, while protecting the Harbour. A sense of place will be fostered with the architecture and landscaping that complements both human scale and coastal setting. Industrial developments will be positioned to integrate with the topography so as to reduce the visibility of buildings and storage areas. The town centre will expand to accommodate an increased range of shops and services in Bankart Street, Bow Street and Wallis Street. A design guideline will promote a "Raglan look" for buildings in the town centre.
>
> *(Waikato, 2012, clause 1.6.1)*

The documentation is clearly consistent with the data reported above. Mention was made of the impact of growing summer rentals displacing those who rent properties during other times of the year. Four reactions emerged in the summer commencing 2017–2018. First, the local *iwi* (Maori tribe) made some arrangements to permit some displaced tenants to use the facilities of the Raglan Holiday Park (a camping and cabin area – see www.raglanholidaypark.co.nz/) for a fee of NZ$5 a night. Second, employers, including tourist industry employers, were finding it difficult to find accommodation for summer and full-time employees. Consequently, in 2017, an application was made to a local trust, the WEL Energy Trust, for funds to establish research into the problem. A working party was established under the acronym WRAP (Whaingaroa Raglan Affordable (Housing) Project) to look at the issues of housing affordability. Third, this project was then to be incorporated into the University of Waikato INSTO Programme of research. Finally, the WDC's proposed 10-year plan includes both industrial and residential development on the Rangitahi Peninsula – managed under the Rangitahi Peninsula Structure Plan. It is envisaged that, by 2022, the plan will involve four stages. In the first stage, 89 new residential buildings will be completed, with the basic infrastructure in place by June 2018. By 2022, 500 new homes will be completed, subject to planning controls designed to create a close community – for example, fences must have 50% permeability and, on streets, should not exceed 1.2 metres in height.

Although census data indicate that, of the working population, one-half to two-thirds may be commuting to Hamilton (at the time of writing, March 2018, data from the 2018 census had not been released), it is evident that tourism is a significant economic force within the township. The Hamilton–Waikato Regional Tourism Organisation (H–W RTO), in its Tourism Opportunities Plan, has noted Raglan as an emergent destination and, despite not having the iconic status of Hobbiton or the Waitomo Caves, it is recognised as a vibrant and growing tourism centre. Indeed, tourism is a thriving industry in Waikato. The H–W RTO plan initiated in 2014 targeted a tourist expenditure of NZ$1.35 billion by 2015. In March 2018, the actual recorded tourist expenditure for the previous 12 months was NZ$1.48 billion. In short, Raglan is part of a growing industry and contributes to that growth.

Discussion

The various councils and administrations in Raglan and the wider Waikato region have recognised the integrative nature of planning, and that the implications of tourism go beyond simply looking at tourist attractions and the need for satisfactory and memorable tourist experiences. Tourism interlinks with population trends of ageing, growth and movement and resultant needs in educational and health provision. A holistic perspective is required that takes into account social trends and the impacts created by tourism. People wish to live in attractive destinations characterised by social vibrancy and care for communities and environments. Tourism, as defined as people temporarily away from home for more than 24 hours and requiring accommodation, is a both a factor and a deficient way of assessing the impacts of tourism. Attractive tourist destinations such as Raglan become points of growth in regional economies, attracting second-home ownership and inbound investment in new businesses. In turn, in a community such as Raglan, communities seek to be involved in decision-making. Equally, means of accessing knowledge and community interaction are very much being strengthened by access to the internet. The local paper, the *Raglan Chronicle*, has a role in making people aware of events, both in print and on the internet. The community has its own active Facebook presence open to residents who voice their own opinions. The Community Board, the Raglan Chamber of Commerce and local Maori organisation engage in active debate about proposals affecting their community.

The exchange of opinion requires informed debate, and research is an important component of this debate. Research data come in many forms. Some require expenditure, and, as noted above, the WDC has commissioned data from bodies such a Qrious. Some of the data are derived from government, such as census data and the tourism and business statistics generated by the New Zealand Ministries of Statistics and Business Innovation and Employment. Equally, however, there remains a need for research that draws together these various sources and gives voice to the community in a structured and coherent manner.

The INSTO Programme based at Raglan is able to provide that input. Although in its early stages, the H–W RTO, the WDC and the Chamber of Commerce have made reference to the reports previously provided by the INSTO and are beginning to incorporate the data into planning considerations. Unlike the Chinese programmes referred to above, the Waikato research programme is embryonic, but it is already beginning to develop a stronger presence and informing debate. One of the advantages of the UNWTO initiative is that it requires a continuing commitment by the research stakeholder as it creates links with the other stakeholders – community, business and local administrations. One side benefit from an educational perspective is that it involves students in a 'real-life' programme of importance, thereby giving them experiences and skills involved in data collection, presentations and involvement with others outside the university. Equally, over time, as they perceive the unfolding plans and documentation of the various authorities, they can also see that their work has contributed to wider planning considerations.

References

Baird, C.J., & Nelson, M.P. (1998). *The great new wilderness debate*. Athens, GA: University of Georgia Press.

Bangwayo-Skette, P.F., & Skeete, R.W. (2015). Can Google data improve the forecasting performance of tourist arrivals? Mixed-data sampling approach. *Tourism Management, 46,* 454–464.

Chen, Z., Li, L., Tumanan, M.-A., & Ryan, C. (2017). *Perceptions of Raglan: the views of tourists and residents: a qualitative study – an interim report.* Hamilton, NZ: The University of Waikato Management School. Raglan INSTO Research Unit.

Choi, H., & Varian, H. (2012). Predicting the present with Google Trends. *Economic Record, 88*(s1), 2–9.

Gilbert, P.K. (2018). On cholera in nineteenth-century England. *BRANCH: Britain, representation and nineteenth-century history.* Ed. D.F. Felluga. Extension of *Romanticism and Victorianism on the Net* [website]. www.branchcollective.org/?ps_articles=pamela-k-gilbert-on-cholera-in-nineteenth-century-england (accessed 25 March 2018).

Hawkes, C., & Popkin, B.M. (2015). Can the sustainable development goals reduce the burden of nutrition-related non-communicable diseases without truly addressing major food system reforms? *BMC Medicine, 13*(1), 143.

Liu, L., Oza, S., Hogan, D., Chu, Y., Perin, J., Zhu, J., Lawn, J.E., Cousens, S., Mathers, C., & Black, R.E. (2016). Global, regional, and national causes of under-5 mortality in 2000–15: an updated systematic analysis with implications for the Sustainable Development Goals. *The Lancet, 388*(10063), 3027–3035.

Liu, Y. (2016). 2015–2016 MCSTO Work Report: on the way of exploring sustainability & harmony. Presentation at the UNWTO Conference "On Tourism: a catalyst for development, peace and reconciliation", Passikudah, Sri Lanka, 11–14 July. cf.cdn.unwto.org/sites/all/files/pdf/05._liu_yi.pdf (accessed 25 March 2018).

Morgan, C. (2018). *Whaingaroa Raglan: Planning for tourism.* Presentation to students involved in the Raglan INSTO Programme, 11 March. University of Waikato Management School.

Petrie, C. (1938). *The Chamberlain tradition.* New York: Frederick A. Stokes.

Ryan, C., & Cooper, C. (2004). Residents' perceptions of tourism development: the case of Raglan, New Zealand. *Tourism Review International, 8*(1), 1–17.

Sanson, A. (2018). *Consultation opens on the council's 10-year plan.* www.waikatodistrict.govt.nz/news/media-releases/article/2018/03/13/consultation-opens-on-the-council%27s-10-year-plan (accessed 28 March 2018).

United Nations Conference on Environment and Development. (1992). *Agenda 21, Rio Declaration, Forest Principles.* New York: United Nations.

United Nations World Tourism Organization (UNWTO). (2017). *Tourism and the Sustainable Development Goals – Journey to 2030*. Madrid: UNWTO.

Waikato District Council. (2012). *Waikato District Plan*. Huntly, NZ: Waikato District Council.

Waikato District Council. (2017). *Raglan Visitor Infrastructure Study – report by Strateg:Ease*. Huntly: NZ: Waikato District Council.

Waikato District Council. (2018). *Our vision: liveable, thriving and connected communities. The 10 year plan*. Huntly, NZ: Waikato District Council.

World Commission on Environment and Development. (1987). *Our Common Future*. Oxford: Oxford University Press.

5

THE IMPACTS OF TOURISM ON ANIMALS

Neil Carr

What is an animal?

"What is an animal?" is, at first glance, an easily answered question. It is simply anything that is a living being but not a plant or human. Yet this is an overly simplistic and humancentric view. However, there is an important point to be noted in this definition – namely, how humans have traditionally sought to distinguish themselves from animals. 'They' are animals and 'we' (humans) are not. This humancentric differentiation, which has sought to raise humans to a rarefied position, is the foundation upon which we have based our use, and justification of that use, of animals. We will return to this when discussing the issue of animal sentience, as well as the question of animal rights, welfare, and well-being, and our obligations, if any, to them. For now, it is sufficient to recognise that humans are actually just another animal, fundamentally no different from any other species. Such a recognition has led to the adoption of the term 'non-human animal' to differentiate between humans and animals while, at the same time, realising the fundamental similarity between them. Although we agree with this position, the term will not be employed in this chapter simply because it is so unwieldy. Rather, the terms 'animal' and 'human' will be used.

The initial simplistic definition of animals also highlights the point that any definition of them is a human social construct. Recognising this allows us to begin to provide more detail of how humans have defined and differentiated animals from us and from one another, and continue to do so. The first distinction we can draw is between wild and domesticated animals. The latter have been defined as being species that, over a number of generations, have been selectively bred by humans for specific purposes and/or traits (Clutton-Brock, 1989). Obvious examples include horses, pigs, cows, dogs, and sheep. Wild animals have been defined in opposition to this notion of domestication. For example, Usher (1986: 4) has defined wildlife as "a collective noun relating to non-domesticated species of plants, animals or microbes". Yet, as noted by Carr and Young (2018), these two definitions set up a binary state that is not an accurate representation of reality. Instead, as noted in Carr (2015), we need to think in terms of a continuum between wild and domesticated where behavioural traits associated with both types of animal exist within individuals to greater or lesser extents.

Even the notion of a wild–domesticated animal continuum based on behavioural traits is not sufficient to really begin to understand what an animal is. Instead, we must also study the relation between humans and animals, and the position in which we have placed animals. For domesticated animals, we need to distinguish between those that have become part of the human family, the pets and animal companions, and those that we utilise as tools or sources of food. The family pet dog and the milk cow on the dairy farm are both domesticated yet are generally perceived very differently by humans and, in the process, assigned different values. There is also a significant difference in how we view highly skilled domesticated animals and those that provide us with sustenance. Witness, for example, how we perceive the sheep that provide us with wool and meat versus the guide dog for the blind. Finally, the context in which we place and see animals matters in terms of how we identify and value them. For example, the black bear living in its natural habitat, such as the mountains of British Columbia, Canada, is viewed differently from the black bear wandering the streets of towns such as Whistler in the same region of Canada. The black bear confined to an enclosure at a zoo is also viewed differently from its 'wild' counterparts. The town bear is often seen as a pest; the zoo bear may be an attraction or poor substitute for the 'real thing', which is the bear living in the wild. It is this last bear that is most highly valued by human because we see it as the 'true' wild bear.

Perhaps a more meaningful – at least for understanding the impacts of tourism on animals – grouping of animals can be undertaken if we divide them up according to the notion that there are animals we love and those we hate. To this pairing could be added the category of those animals we simple ignore (Carr & Broom, 2018). These categorisations are, to an extent, personal to the individual and, therefore, just like the wild and domesticated categories, fuzzy rather than distinct constructs. However, it is clear that most of us certainly 'love' some types of animal that possess certain characteristics that are attractive to us. Clearly, the more characteristics we like that an animal possesses the more we will like it. This is what gives rise to the idea that there are specific flagship species that are highly effective in attracting tourists to destinations and tourist attractions such as zoos. The panda fits very clearly into this category. The opposite of love is hate, and this is the adjective we attach to those animals who possess traits most of us find repellent and/or that induce fear in us. Yet, in between the extremes of love and hate, there exist a range of animals – another continuum. Around the middle of this continuum are those animals we are simply ambivalent about, that we give little or no thought to, and that we just generally ignore (see Small, 2011, 2012, for a detailed discussion of the animal characteristics people love and which they hate and the associated animals). As noted earlier in this section, context, or the place where we encounter animals, still matters when we try to identify whether we love or hate an animal. For example, we may love to see a black bear, especially in the wild, but we would be very unlikely to be happy to see it in our house, a not-unheard-of experience in various parts of North America.

Animal rights and welfare

Whether we love or hate (or something in between) animals and whether we give conscious thought to them or ignore them have implications for the impact of tourism on animals, an issue which will be discussed later in the chapter. Before we arrive at that point, it is necessary to examine the concepts of animal welfare and animal rights. A more detailed discussion of these emotive issues can be found in Carr and Broom (2018) and Carr (2014). Briefly, rights and welfare are concepts that are fundamentally the same for humans and animals. Whether we should be concerned about animal rights and welfare is related to the notion of sentience and the question of whether animals are sentient beings. If they are seen to be, then animals can be said to have welfare needs, as opposed to objects owned by humans that have none. For example, the car we drive is an object. Despite attempts by Hollywood to anthropomorphise vehicles, in reality they do not have the capacity to think or feel. In contrast, the horses or dogs, for example, that many people own (from a legal perspective, in just the same manner as they own their car) are sentient beings, capable of experiencing feelings and emotions that, if not identical to those we as humans experience, are similar. If we recognise animals as sentient beings, then there are implications for the definition of their welfare needs and, consequently, for their rights to the actualisation of those needs and our obligations to ensure those needs are met.

Yet it is important to recognise that animal sentience is a highly contentious topic. Contemporary human society is grounded on the notion that animals are objects that lack human-like characteristics such as sentience. This has allowed us to differentiate ourselves from animals and to utilise them for our benefit without having to be concerned that we may be harming them. However, there is increasing recognition by humanity that animals are sentient beings, even if this sentience is potentially quantitatively and qualitatively different from ours. Consequently, we are seeing rising levels of concern surrounding animal welfare and a recognition of our obligations to ensure the welfare needs of animals are met. The historical conceptualisation of animals as lacking sentience is central to the impacts tourism has had, and continues to have, on animals. The contemporary recognition of animal sentience has implications for the future of the position of animals in the tourism experience, as will be discussed later in this chapter.

If we take the position that animals are sentient and that they have, as a result, welfare needs, we must then identify what those needs are and how we can assess them. Carr and Broom (2018) discuss the identification and assessment of animal welfare in detail. Such measurements can easily become reductionist, focusing on a science of animal welfare measurement that is sterilised and quantified. This can be very useful in that it can remove the tendency of humans to anthropomorphise and see animal welfare through human eyes and standards. However, such a reductionist approach also risks ignoring the reality that animal welfare is grounded in a human-constructed reality. Consequently, a middle ground for understanding animal welfare that navigates between positivistic scientific thinking and more interpretative social science approaches may actually yield valuable results.

Centrality of animals to the tourism experience

Animals are a central feature of the tourism experience, though they may not always be thought of as being so. Such is the all-pervasive nature of tourism that it is also a central feature of the lives of virtually all species of animal (Carr & Broom, 2018). The most obvious category contains those animals that are positioned in the tourism experience as attractions. Here we may think of everything from the animals that reside in the various zoos and associated entities that exist around the world to the horses that pull tourist carriages around many of the urban centres of Europe (see Figure 5.1, for example) and the vast array of animals that live in the 'wild'. A significant industry now revolves around the showing of these animals (including, for example, bears, mountain gorillas, whales, and sharks) to tourists.

In addition, we have witnessed the development of mass farm tourism experiences where tourists are able to get physically close to animals that play a central role in the content of many kitchen cupboards and fridges. Here, tourists may gaze upon, touch, and even feed a variety of domesticated animals.

Following on from the earlier discussion about animal attractiveness, the animal-oriented tourism industry tends to be focused around a relatively small number of animals that may be defined as charismatic, or box office material, as far as humans are concerned. These animals

Figure 5.1   Horse-drawn tourist carriage in central Salzburg, Austria

tend to be large furry mammals and are perceived as being intelligent (Carr, 2016). This focus by the tourism industry is based on the recognition that consumers will pay the most to see these desirable animals.

Tourists may wish to do a variety of things in relation to those animals that they actively enter the tourism environment in search of. Some may be focused on simply seeing an animal. Others may wish to take things a step further to gain a photograph of an animal, or to experience a close encounter with it, or even to touch it. Other people may seek to hunt and kill an animal, whereas others may seek a particularly culinary experience associated with a particular animal. All of these actions have potential welfare implications for the animals involved.

It is not just the box office animals that inhabit the tourist destination. Rather, a wide array of other animals do. These exist somewhere along the continua already mentioned. Yet to this must be added another layer which deals with the economic value of the animal to the tourist industry. As major attractions, the box office animals are highly valuable. At the opposite end of the scale, animals can actually detract from a tourism experience and, therefore, be a cost to the industry. Such animals are associated with those we hate, including reptiles and insects in particular (Cushing & Markwell, 2011). In between, as noted earlier in the chapter, there exist a range of animals to which varying levels of ambivalence are attached. Because of this ambivalence, there is relatively little economic value in them for the tourism industry.

In addition to existing in the tourism environment, as desirable sights or otherwise, animals are often employed as part of the tourist industry. Some of the earliest jobs animals had in the tourism experience involved performing for the tourists (i.e., elephant and camel rides, and dolphin and orangutan performances in aquaria and zoos). Today, the work of animals has expanded to incorporate a number of other roles, often, though not exclusively, filled by dogs. Included here are sniffer dogs at airports, meet and greet dogs at accommodation units, and stress relief dogs at airports (Carr, 2014). It is also necessary to recognise the increasing presence of animals, particularly – though not wholly – dogs, as guests within the tourism experience (Carr, 2017). This is linked to the increasingly central role pets in general, and pet dogs in particular, play in the lives of their humans (Carr, 2014).

The negative impacts of tourism on animals

The tourism industry and the desires of tourists have had, and continue to have, a wide range of negative impacts on a diverse array of animals. Zoos and aquaria are frequent targets of animal welfarists and rights activists. They point to distressed animals, housed in inadequate enclosures where their needs are not met and their mental and physical health is endangered. In addition, through the news we hear regular reports of animals being abused by tourists visiting zoos. Witness, for example, the reports of kangaroos being physically assaulted by visitors to Fuzhou Zoo, China, who were upset the kangaroos were not hopping across the landscape (Mosbergen, 2018). Although this may be extreme, the welfare of animals in zoos is regularly placed in danger by the behaviour of visitors that includes attempts to feed them and causing distress by tapping on the glass of enclosures. Zoos have also been accused of animal abuse through their control of individuals' breeding and the decisions made regarding animals deemed to be surplus to requirements. Here we have seen animals such as Marius the giraffe, killed and dissected in public, and his meat fed to the lions at Copenhagen Zoo in 2014 (Cohen & Fennell, 2016; Carr & Broom, 2018).

Zoos must also take at least some, though not all, of the blame for how we view animals and how their abuse for our amusement has been normalised. Perhaps the iconic example here is the chimpanzee tea party. This is not normal animal behaviour; rather, it is trained behaviour presented to visitors for their titillation, with little or no thought given to the negative implications for the welfare of the animals involved. More recently, this has led to complaints about animals being forced to 'perform' for the enjoyment of visitors, as discussed by John Sellar (2018).

Zoos are not the only part of the tourism industry that has a negative impact on animal welfare. Rather, concerns have been raised about virtually all types of wildlife tourism experience, both those constructed to cater to groups of tourists and ones undertaken by individual tourists independent of any tourism operator. The boats that take tourists to watch whales and orcas have been accused of disturbing the resting, feeding, and breeding patterns of these animals (Carr & Broom, 2018; Higham & Bejder, 2008). In addition, tourists seeking to get close to bears in North America have, for a long time, been accused of potentially damaging their welfare through attempts to feed them and putting their very lives at risk if they become habituated and, in turn, a danger to human well-being. When this occurs, bears are regularly shot as the ultimate solution (Carr & Broom, 2018). Yet, historically, the national parks in which these bears are to be found encouraged tourists to interact with the bears to the point where feeding wild bears at garbage dumps was provided as an attraction for tourists, and many park visitors hand-fed bears on the roadside from their cars (Biel, 2006).

Another example of the potential harm to animals associated with tourism is the contentious activity of trophy hunting. Cecil the lion is probably the most publicised recent case of a wealthy Western visitor to Africa killing an iconic animal to add to their virtual or physical trophy cabinet (Goodall, 2018). The case led to widespread discussion against the practice of trophy hunting, which may be most associated in the minds of the public with southern Africa, but is spread throughout much of the world. Riding the wave of public opinion against trophy hunting, many airlines banned the carrying of such trophies in an attempt to distance themselves from the practice, though there appears to have been a weakening of resolve as the story has faded from the front pages of the media.

Although the killing of iconic mammals by tourists or the tourism industry has often raised the ire of public opinion, the same has not been the case for fish, confirming the point noted earlier in the chapter that not all animals are valued equally by people. There is a multibillion-dollar global fishing tourism industry. It offers the opportunity for those interested in fishing as a sport to catch whatever type of fish they wish in increasingly diverse locations, from the rivers of Scotland to the remote islands of the South Pacific. Many operations conduct a strict catch and release policy that is designed to ensure that live fish are returned to the water after the fishermen (although not exclusively a male sport, it does appear to be dominated by men) have had their photograph taken with them (i.e., they have collected their trophy). Whether the fish survive this traumatic experience and the impact of it on their welfare are questions that have yet to be fully answered, but it is clear that it is an activity not without potential harm, though it can be argued that it is at least better than the fish being killed upon being landed by the fisherman.

Animals are also affected by tourism, not through being attractive to tourists, but for exactly the opposite reason, because they are deemed to be unattractive. Witness the myriad insects, such as cockroaches, mosquitos, ants, and wasps, eliminated in the name of human comfort in the tourism experience. Likewise, we can see the destruction of stray dogs in a variety of tourist destinations to save tourists from both potential attack and the distress of seeing such dogs (Galati, 2018; Osborn, 2011).

Animals are also killed by tourism operators once they are no longer of any economic benefit. For example, in the aftermath of the Vancouver Winter Olympics in 2010, a sled dog operator found himself with more dogs than he could cope with as visitor demand was not sufficient to pay the bills. As a result, the operator destroyed the surplus dogs (Carr, 2018; Fennell & Sheppard, 2011). This is similar to the horse and greyhound racing industries that slaughter animals that are deemed not to be fast enough or worth breeding from (Carr, 2015; Morris, 2014; Winter & Young, 2015).

Our lack of appreciation of animals when developing tourist resorts, attractions, and infrastructure has also historically seen the lives of many animals affected. For example, the development of hotels and resorts along the coastlines of the world has impacted the breeding grounds of turtles (Davenport & Davenport, 2006), and the development of air travel, including airports, has impacted the migratory routes of birds (Sodhi, 2002). In addition, the development of the cruise industry has contributed to the aquatic noise that is affecting the well-being of whales (Carr & Broom, 2018).

The position of pet animals within the tourism experience is also a potentially problematic one. Alongside an increasing trend of pets travelling with their owners on planes have been increasing reports of deaths of such animals and others suffering varying levels of distress from the experience (Carr, 2014). When in the holiday environment, pets may also experience welfare problems associated with the stress of being in an unfamiliar environment and being left alone in the holiday accommodation while their owners go out.

The positive impacts of tourism on animals

It has been argued that zoos are an institution that can act as an 'ark', a place where various species, threatened by extinction in the wild, may be preserved for a future time when the wild may be repopulated (World Association of Zoos and Aquariums, 2005). In addition, they are now promoted as educational centres, where people may come to learn about the value of protecting not just animals, but also their natural environment. The animals in this context play a vital role in helping to protect not just their wild brethren, but future generations as well (Carr & Broom, 2018). Examples of attempts to save viable breeding populations of animals in zoos abound and have spread across zoos and continents with the realisation of the importance of avoiding genetic inbreeding. There are also examples of animals that have been returned to the wild, such as the red-billed chough, by Jersey Zoo.

Animals in the wild may also benefit from the development of wildlife tourism. In a neo-liberal capitalist reality, wildlife tourism provides a viable economic alternative to the hunting and killing of animals. The premier example of this is the development of whale watching tourism. In the process, it is not only the animals that are protected, but also the environments they inhabit. Consequently, not only do the animals targeted by wildlife tourists benefit, but also all the wildlife that inhabits the same ecosystem. The potential of wildlife tourism to help protect animals in their natural habitat was enshrined in the *Buenos Aires Declaration on Travel & Tourism and Illegal Wildlife Trade* by the World Travel & Tourism Council in 2018.

The argument that animals' welfare can be improved through giving them an economic purpose is not restricted to those living in the wild. Instead, this applies to many domesticated animals. For example, there is the case of a pet boarding operation in Switzerland that began taking in unwanted huskies. These animals had been bought by people as status symbols or in

Figure 5.2   Heathrow airport birdlife (2018)

the mistaken belief that they would make lovely pets. Having 'rescued' several of these animals, the operators recognised that they needed to do something with them, both to help pay the bills associated with keeping multiple huskies and to keep them exercised and therefore content. Consequently, they set up a business providing sled dog tours to tourists.

The tourism industry infrastructure also has the potential to contribute to the well-being of animals. For example, the sparrow in Figure 5.2 that lives in Terminal 2 of Heathrow airport benefits from the warmth and food on offer while avoiding potential predators that cannot gain access to the terminal.

In addition, even otherwise unwanted and abandoned animals can see an increase in their welfare thanks to tourism. For example, in Whistler, Canada, the animal refuge (Whistler Animals Galore) allows tourists to spend time with the abandoned cats and even to take dogs awaiting a new home on walks. Occasionally, such animal–human meetings result in the tourist adopting an animal and taking it home with them. Whistler, as a very dog-friendly destination, also offers insights into the potential benefits of tourism for pet welfare. When human visitors are able to take their pets (particularly dogs) on holiday with them, there is the potential for the welfare of the latter to benefit through increased exercise during the holiday experience. For example, they may venture into the outdoors with their owners rather than being left behind in a boarding kennel.

Animal welfare: intention not attraction is where the truth lies

There are undoubtedly instances where the tourism industry has negative and positive impacts on the welfare of animals. However, we need to be careful not to ascribe positive or negative impacts to particular types of tourism or attraction, or particular species of animal. Instead, we need to look at the rationale behind the attraction, the operator's attention to animal welfare, and why they are concerned with animal welfare. For example, there are excellent examples of zoos that strive to ensure the welfare of their animals and those in the wild. Yet even these must exist within an economic reality that means that zoos must cater to the desires of the tourists (Carr & Cohen, 2011). In contrast, there are the worst examples of zoos who continue to focus solely on gaining a financial income from visitors. Any welfare concerns related to the animals in these zoos are only based on the earning potential of the animal, rather than its welfare for its own sake.

Focusing on animal welfare rather than human sensitivity forces us to re-examine the fate of Marius the giraffe. Seen from one perspective, his death was a waste, his dissection in public abhorrent, and the feeding of his meat to the lions beyond the bounds of reasonable action. From a different perspective, the dissection of Marius and the feeding of his meat to the lions offered an important educational experience to everyone, especially the children, who visited the zoo. It stripped the zoo of the veneer of social acceptability behind which the bloody reality of the wild is hidden in order to ensure the sensibilities of humans are not offended. Yet such sensibilities do nothing to educate visitors about the truth that wild animals are not the same as those we see in Disney movies. It is, therefore, the intention behind the action that must be judged, rather than the action itself, when assessing animal welfare. Furthermore, we truly need to focus on animal welfare rather than human sensitivities.

Conclusions: the future of animals in the tourism experience – hopes and fears

The impacts of tourism on animals highlighted in this chapter are, of course, only representative of a broader pattern. There is simply not the space to catalogue in this chapter all the specific ways tourism impacts animals. Set against and related to these impacts we are witnessing a growth in the desire of people to see and experience animals while on holiday. At the same time, we are seeing a growing awareness of the sentience of animals and concern for their welfare. This tourism growth may be seen both as a risk to the welfare of animals and a potential avenue to raise their welfare. As more tourists seek to experience animals in the wild, they come under increasing pressure, but, by experiencing them, more people may learn to truly appreciate them and care for them. This brings the issue of individual versus species welfare, raising the question of whether the two can be balanced, or if any suffering of an individual is 'worthwhile' if it benefits the species as a whole (see Carr & Broom, 2018, for more discussion on this point).

Increasing concern about the welfare of animals is having an impact on a range of tourism operators. Most recently, the public pressure brought to bear on aquaria that house dolphins and orcas in captivity has meant they have had to begin to reconsider their position. For example, in 2018, Vancouver Aquarium stated it would no longer be housing cetaceans (Lindsay, 2018). Pressure from tourists against myriad animal practices, some directly associated with tourism but others not, continues to grow. These practices include bull fighting in Spain, the consumption of dog meat in China, and the hunting of whales by Japan, among others.

Public opinion is also encouraging tourism operators to take better care of animals. It has seen zoos, faced with a significant downturn in visitor numbers in the 1980s as people turned away from dated animal-related practices, having to redesign their enclosures with a focus on increasing animal welfare and to cease practices such as elephant and camel rides that were undertaken solely for the enjoyment of visitors, without any consideration of animal welfare. Similarly, outside zoos, animal encounters are increasingly being encouraged to have a focus on animal welfare. Many tourism operators no longer work with attractions that do not conform to high standards of animal welfare. By effectively starving these attractions of visitors, the operators bring pressure on them to conform (Carr & Broom, 2018).

Yet we must question how effective animal welfare policies and practices are within the tourism experience. The vast majority of tourists seeking animal encounters are still focused on fulfilling their own desires, rather than the needs of the animal. This has led to questions about whether zoos can ever really educate and change the behaviour and attitudes of people to the benefit of captive and wild animals (Conway, 2003). Similar concerns can be levelled against wildlife tourism operators that offer an educational component to their visitors. In this context, it may be argued that, rather than aiding animals by catering to the desire of tourists to see them, not just in enclosed spaces like zoos but in their natural habitat, we are actually placing ever more stress on these animals and the environments that are their homes. Therefore, care must be taken to carefully consider how much tourism animals can actually cope with, and, if a neo-liberal model is to be pursued, then a balance must be struck between economic necessity and animal welfare that does not negate the latter either at the species or individual level. The explanation that tourism can be used as an economic justification for the survival of species cannot simply be used as an excuse to relegate animal welfare to a position that is subservient to human economic needs and desires. Likewise, when taking animal welfare into consideration, we need to consider it from the perspective of the animal rather than pandering to human views and sensitivities.

References

Biel, A. W. (2006). *Do (not) feed the bears: The fitful history of wildlife and tourists in Yellowstone*. Lawrence, KS: University Press of Kansas.

Carr, N. (2014). *Dogs in the leisure experience*. Wallingford, UK: CABI.

Carr, N. (2015). The greyhound: A story of fashion, finances, and animal rights. In N. Carr. (Ed). *Domestic animals and leisure*. Basingstoke, UK: Palgrave Macmillan. pp. 109–126.

Carr, N. (2016). Ideal animals and animal traits for zoos: General public perspectives. *Tourism Management*, 57: 37–44.

Carr, N. (2017). Recognising the position of the pet dog in tourism. *Annals of Tourism Research*, 62: 112–113.

Carr, N. (2018). Tourist desires, and animal rights and welfare within tourism: A question of obligations. In B. Grimwood, K. Caton, L. Cooke, & D. Fennell (Eds), *New moral natures in tourism*. Abingdon, UK: Routledge.

Carr, N., & Broom, D. (2018). *Tourism and animal welfare*. Wallingford, UK: CABI.

Carr, N., & Cohen, S. (2011). The public face of zoos: Balancing entertainment, education, and conservation. *Anthrozoos*, 24 (2): 175–189.

Carr, N., & Young, J. (2018). Wild animals and leisure: An introduction. In N. Carr & J. Young (Eds), *Wild Animals and Leisure: Rights and Welfare*. Abingdon: Routledge. pp. 1–11.

Clutton-Brock, J. (1989). *The walking larder: Patterns of domestication, pastoralism, and predation*. London: Unwin Hyman.

Cohen, E., & Fennell, D. (2016). The elimination of Marius, the giraffe: Humanitarian act or callous management decision? *Tourism Recreation Research*, 41 (2): 168–176.

Conway, W. (2003). The role of zoos in the 21st century. *International Zoo Yearbook*, 38: 7–13.

Cushing, N., & Markwell, K. (2011). I can't look: Disgust as a factor in the zoo experience. In W. Frost (Ed), *Zoos and tourism: Conservation, education, entertainment?* Bristol, UK: Channel View Publications. pp. 167–178.

Davenport, J., & Davenport, J. (2006). The impact of tourism and personal leisure transport on coastal environments: A review. *Estuarine, Coastal & Shelf Science*, 67: 280–292.

Fennell, D., & Sheppard, V. (2011). Another legacy for Canada's 2010 Olympic and Paralympic Winter Games: Applying an ethical lens to the post-games' sled dog cull. *Journal of Ecotourism*, 10 (3): 197–213.

Galati, D. (2018). Cats and dogs international. In N. Carr & D. Broom (Eds), *Tourism and animal welfare*. Wallingford, UK: CABI.

Goodall, J. (2018). Sport hunting tourism. In N. Carr & D. Broom (Eds), *Tourism and animal welfare*. Wallingford, UK: CABI.

Higham, J., & Bejder, L. (2008). Managing wildlife-based tourism: Edging slowly towards sustainability? *Current Issues in Tourism*, 11: 75–83.

Lindsay, B. (2018). Vancouver Aquarium will no longer keep whales, dolphins in captivity. *CBC News*. www.cbc.ca/news/canada/british-columbia/vancouver-aquarium-will-no-longer-keep-whales-dolphins-in-captivity-1.4492316?cmp=rss (accessed 19 January 2018).

Morris, S. P. (2014). The ethics of interspecies sports. In J. Gillett & M. Gilbert (Eds), *Sport, animals, and society*. New York: Routledge. pp. 127–139.

Mosbergen, D. (2018). Kangaroo dies after visitors at Chinese zoo hurl rocks to force her to jump. *Huffpost*. www.huffingtonpost.com/entry/kangaroo-china-dies-throw-rocks_us_5ada572ce4b00a1849cf477d?ncid=APPLENEWS00001 (accessed 21 April 2018).

Osborn, A. (2011). Ukraine accused of culling stray dogs ahead of Euro 2012. *The Telegraph*. www.telegraph.co.uk/sport/football/competitions/euro-2012/8931419/Ukraine-accused-of-culling-stray-dogs-ahead-of-Euro-2012.html (accessed 11 November 2013).

Sellar, J. (2018). Animal welfare and tourism: The threat to endangered species. In N. Carr & D. Broom (Eds), *Tourism and animal welfare*. Wallingford, UK: CABI.

Small, E. (2011). The new Noah's Ark: Beautiful and useful species only. Part 1. Biodiversity conservation issues and priorities. *Biodiversity*, 12 (4): 232–247.

Small, E. (2012). The new Noah's Ark: Beautiful and useful species only. Part 2. The chosen species. *Biodiversity*, 13 (1): 37–53.

Sodhi, N. (2002). Competition in the air: Birds versus aircraft. *The Auk: Ornithological Advances*, 119 (3): 587–595.

Usher, M. (1986). Wildlife conservation evaluation: Attributes, criteria and values. In M. Usher (Ed.), *Wildlife Conservation Evaluation*. London: Chapman & Hall. pp. 3–44.

Winter, C., & Young, W. (2015). Fatalities and fascinators: A new perspective on thoroughbred racing. In N. Carr (Ed), *Domestic animals and leisure*. Basingstoke, UK: Palgrave Macmillan. pp. 241–258.

World Association of Zoos and Aquariums. (2005). *Building a future for wildlife: The World Zoo and Aquarium Conservation Strategy*. Bern: WAZA Executive Office.

World Travel & Tourism Council. (2018). *Buenos Aires Declaration on Travel & Tourism and Illegal Wildlife Trade*. www.wttc.org/-/media/files/summits/buenos-aires-2018/wttc-buenos-aires-declaration-with-signatures.pdf (accessed 27 April 2018).

6

IMPACTS OF ELEPHANT TOURISM IN THAILAND

Eric Laws, Noel Scott, and John Koldowski

Introduction

Wildlife tourism

Wildlife tourism is tourism based on encounters with non-domesticated animals. These encounters can occur in either the animal's natural environment or in a captive setting. Wildlife tourism is often considered to be a way to obtain sustainable economic benefits while at the same time supporting wildlife conservation and local communities (Higginbottom, 2004). Although there is no reliable global estimate of the economic impact of wildlife tourism, it is clear that it involves large numbers of participants and is a significant travel motivator for many tourists. For example, an estimated 9 million people participated in whale watching in 1998, with total expenditure estimated to be above US$ 1 billion (Hoyt, 2001). Researchers estimated in 2015 that protected areas receive 8 billion visits a year globally, generating as much as US$600 billion in tourism expenditure annually (Balmford et al., 2015). Wildlife tourism can therefore contribute to sustaining local communities (The World Bank Group, 2018)

Academic study

Wildlife tourism is the subject of much academic debate and a developing stream of literature (Higham & Hopkins, 2015; Moorhouse, Dahlsjo, Baker, D'Cruze, & Macdonald, 2015; Reynolds & Braithwaite, 2001). It is seen as a way to improve support for environmental preservation (Tisdell & Wilson, 2001). Higginbottom and Scott (2004) identified a number of trends affecting wildlife tourism, including increasing commercial interest and tourist participation in a wide range of environments, target species, and types of activity. More recently, it is a growing area of concern regarding animal welfare, animal rights, and the morality of human exploitation of animals (Fennell, 2012, 2013; Kopnina, 2016). Numerous species and activities have been studied, including birds and bird-watching (Lawton, 2009; Partridge & Mackay, 1998; Steven, Morrison, & Castley, 2015), elephants (Keil, 2017), orangutans (Russell & Ankenman, 1996), monkeys (Knight, 2010), pandas (Cohen, 2010), sea turtles (Wilson & Tisdell, 2001), sharks (Catlin, Jones, Jones, Norman, & Wood, 2010), tigers (Thapa, Aryal, Roth, & Morley, 2017), and whale watching (Cunningham, Huijbens, & Wearing, 2012; Scarpaci & Parsons, 2017;

Valentine, Birtles, Curnock, Arnold, & Dunstan, 2004). Studies have examined cultural differences among wildlife tourists (Packer, Ballantyne, & Hughes, 2014) and operational matters such as feeding wildlife to alter animal behaviour so tourists can see them (Orams, 2002).

A range of types of wildlife interaction and venues for interactions have been described from fully natural settings, such as wildernesses, jungles, or deserts, which are not framed at all, and in which wild animals are not restrained in any way, to fully contrived settings, such as animal performances and shows in which captured animals, though they might appear wild, are in fact to different degrees tamed, trained, or humanised (Cohen, 2009). Typically, wildlife tourism has been studied either as zoo experiences (Carr, 2016; Clayton, Fraser, & Saunders, 2009; Kathleen & Lisa, 2005) or in natural settings such as safari parks (Akama & Kieti, 2003; Akama, Maingi, & Camargo, 2011; Bresler, 2011), but, to date, there has been little research in semi-captive settings (Kontogeorgopoulos, 2009b).

Elephant viewing

In situ elephant populations have been in decline for much of the last 200 years, driven by an inexorable combination of habitat loss and hunting for ivory, but with more recent and dramatic declines primarily driven by hunting in Africa (Cameron & Ryan, 2016). In Asia, poaching to capture baby elephants in the wild often results in the death of several protective female adults. Today, there are estimated to be 450,000–700,000 African elephants and between 35,000 and 40,000 wild Asian elephants. It should be noted that there is no consensus on elephant population numbers owing to the difficulty of counting those in the wild and the lack of registration of captive elephants (Talukdar & Choudhury, 2017)

Elephants are the largest land animals (megafauna), and their characteristics (memories, family structure, and family bonds) make them an iconic species (actually two species, African and smaller Asian elephants, or three if Sumatran elephants are included). Elephants are attractions often exhibited in zoos and were common in circus performances, although now rarely seen in the latter. Asian elephants have become iconic in many countries such as Thailand (Cohen, 2010), India, and Sri Lanka. There is thought to be an emotional (McIntosh & Wright, 2017) or aesthetic (de Pinho, Grilo, Boone, Galvin, & Snodgrass, 2014) reaction when viewing elephants, common to people from most countries.

Asian elephants

The Asian elephant (*Elephas maximus*) is smaller than its African cousin, but it may still weigh more than four tonnes and reach more than 3.5 metres in height (Santiapillai & Jackson, 1990). It is distinguished by its much smaller ears and rounded back, compared with the saddle back of the African species. Unlike African elephants, where both males and females have tusks, only Asian males carry them. Asian females have small tusks, which seldom show, but which may protrude beyond their lips. Therefore, ivory poaching does not threaten the survival of the Asian elephant as much as it does that of the African species. The Asian species is also smaller and relatively easier to train and control. Both Asian and African elephant populations are endangered.

The Asian elephant has been a part of the religious, cultural, and social activities of many societies. The folklore and cultures of Asian countries are rich in tales and anecdotes that confer on elephants a kind of superior intellect enabling them to live with people and yet not succumb to complete domestication. The elephant-headed Ganesh, son of Siva, is one of the most important gods of the Hindu pantheon. Hindu voyagers and settlers spread Ganesh worship through South East Asia, and Ganesh temples and images are found in Thailand, Indochina, and in Java and Bali in Indonesia (Santiapillai & Jackson, 1990). For Buddhists, too, the elephant has special significance. Gautama Buddha's mother, Maya, is said to have dreamt one night that a white elephant entered her side. Wise men told her that it was a sign she would give birth to a great man. White elephants feature in many Buddhist stories, have been revered for centuries, and were often donated to the Thai king (Santiapillai & Jackson, 1990).

There is a long tradition of using elephants for human purposes, as Locke (2013, p. 80) has explained:

> Variously representing weapons of war, emblems of prestige, symbols of divinity, objects of entertainment, icons of conservation, commodities for exchange, vehicles for labour, as well as intimate companions, elephants are animals caught up in human enterprises of power, wealth, worship, pleasure, and preservation. Feared or worshipped, killed or conserved, captured or maimed, appropriated for stories and symbols, they are animals with whom humanity is profoundly entangled.

Why Thailand?

Elephants in Thailand have been used for more than 4,000 years for the transport of goods, logging, war, or religious ceremonies (Sukumar, 1992). Thai elephants historically hold an important position in the local Thai culture (Worwag & Varga, 2017). They have played a special role in Thailand's history and have been employed as working animals for hundreds of years (Kontogeorgopoulos, 2009b). Elephants have been protected in Thailand since the late eighteenth century when the present Chakri Dynasty came to power, but long before that time they were already an integral part of Thai culture and the economy. As the national symbol and royal emblem of Thailand, Asian elephants (*Elephas maximus*) are infused into the fabric of Thai culture (Cohen, 2009). In 2004, an estimated 2,500–3,500 elephants remained in Thailand, accounting for roughly 5% of the total population worldwide (Blake & Hedges, 2004). Of these elephants in Thailand today, only 1,000 or so are wild – found almost exclusively in the Khao Yai National Park and the Thungyai-Huai Kha Khaeng Wildlife Sanctuaries – and the remainder are captive (Kontogeorgopoulos, 2009a).

Tourism is a more developed industry in Asia than in most parts of Africa. Thailand is one of Asia's leading tourist destinations (UNWTO & Global Tourism Economy Research Centre, 2016) and it has a strong and growing domestic tourism sector. Animals play a major and highly varied role in Thai tourism. The rich fauna of Thailand, including fish, butterflies, monkeys, gibbon, snakes, crocodiles, and elephants, is a significant tourism resource. The tourist authorities and entrepreneurs have promoted the manifold opportunities the kingdom offers to experience different species of animals, birds, insects, and fish (Cohen, 2009). Elephants are more deeply imbedded in the local culture than their African relatives, making them more suitable for use in tourism. Owing to the increase in demand for animal-related experiences, elephants started to be used in the tourism industry. Today, nearly every captive elephant works in the tourism industry, and the numbers are growing (Kontogeorgopoulos, 2009a).

Kontogeorgopoulos (2009a) suggests that the poor conditions in which captive elephants are kept prohibit them from interacting naturally with their herd, puts them into close proximity with elephants from different herds leading to tension between them, and separates babies from their maternal herd at a young age so that they do not properly learn how to behave or what to eat. When looking into differences among tourists' concerns about animal welfare, research has identified differences between different populations and trait groups (Phillips et al., 2012; Worwag & Varga, 2017). For example, in a study of students in European countries, those from former communist countries had the greatest concern for animal welfare, whereas students from Asian countries had the least (Phillips et al., 2012).

A case study: the Thai logging ban

Forestry work provided the main employment opportunities for elephants for centuries until the Thai government imposed a nationwide logging ban in January 1989. This was a political response to devastating landslides and floods in the northern mountains during that year's monsoon (Felardo, 2016; Sulaiman & Abdul-Rahim, 2015), the result of illegal overlogging on the steep slopes high above isolated villages. No more timber harvesting work was allowed after that, although some work continued for mahouts and elephants until 1992–1993, moving out logs that had already been felled and stacked in the forests. All logging licences issued to government agencies or private companies were cancelled. The Forest Industry Organisation held about 60% of the 306 logging licences and experienced the biggest impact in terms of earnings and employment for the foresters, mahouts, and elephants.

Responses to the logging ban

A mahout was essential in forestry for instructing his elephant which logs to move, and to where, and ensuring that the animals were properly fed and rested each day. The welfare of elephants is largely dependent on their economic value and utility to humans (Duffy & Moore, 2010), but it is the mahout who is directly responsible for an individual elephant. Some mahouts found work patrolling on their elephants as forest rangers. A second programme, "Bring Elephants Home", was introduced in 2006, where the government offered 8,000 baht a month for each mahout who agreed to relocate to a designated area in the Surin Province of Thailand. This project failed because Surin was already home to 1,000 captive elephants and could not support the newcomers, and the payment offered was too low to enable a mahout to support his family and an elephant.

The mahouts and their elephants quickly developed new opportunities in the tourism industry by presenting the traditional forestry skills such as dragging and stacking heavy logs and washing and feeding the elephants at camps. Rides were offered during which two tourists sat in a chair specially made to be strapped on the elephant's back while it was guided by a mahout. Bags of bananas or cut sugar cane could be purchased after the ride to feed the elephants. Games such as darts and football were easily adapted to elephants' abilities and added to the repertoire, and some camps introduced elephant painting shows with opportunities to purchase a painting.

The logging ban also resulted in "street wandering elephants" – unemployed mahouts took their elephants into cities and tourist areas to beg on the streets. In Bangkok, the practice was a danger to traffic and pedestrians (Pimmanrojnagool & Wanghongsa, 2001). In 2001, the Food and Agricultural Organisation and the Forest Industry Organisation expressed concerns regarding elephant welfare: they were working long hours (including at night) and they were being frightened by the noise and lights of city traffic, and walking on tarmac and concrete is painful to them and leads to potentially crippling disorders in the elephants' feet (Fowler, 2001). The national and local governments responded by banning elephants from urban areas, but the few other regulatory controls over elephant welfare, ownership, and use were not adequate. Tourism work in resorts and camps quickly attracted critical attention from wildlife care advocates, mainly NGOs, who raised public awareness of the (often) cruel methods used to capture and train elephants and criticised the poor living conditions to which most of the elephants were subjected.

Prior to the logging ban, the Thai forestry service had maintained a specialist Young Elephant Training School, which also provided Mahout training. It became obsolete and was closed. Since then, few, if any, sons have taken over their fathers' profession as mahouts. The skills and knowledge of handling elephants, accumulated over centuries in Thailand, are quickly disappearing.

Elephant camps

Another consequence of the logging ban was the establishment of elephant camps. Elephant camps rely on the mahouts to control the elephants, which are not easy to predict and could be very dangerous to visitors. The process of gaining control over the elephants starts early on in their captive life. It is often referred to as 'breaking-in', 'crush', or '*phajaan*'. All wild-caught and captive-bred elephants undergo what is harsh training in their early years to enable their use in riding and shows and also to enable their management in situations where visitors closely interact with the animals. This training process has been handed down from generation to generation and remains a cruel process (Kopnina, 2016).

Two types of camp can be distinguished: anthropocentric elephant camps, the purpose of which is to profit from tourist interest but which do little to benefit elephant welfare; and ecocentric camps, which are centered on concerns for elephant well-being. In anthropocentric elephant camps, the tourists' needs and wishes are prioritised. Elephants in anthropocentric camps work harder and are at greater risk of injury from activities which satisfy tourists' needs. On the other hand, elephants in ecocentric camps have more free time to interact with other elephants and more space to roam. Kontogeorgopoulos (2009b) and Cohen (2009) have discussed a number of camps in Thailand that vary significantly in terms of elephant conditions and visitor activities, as shown in Table 6.1.

Table 6.1 Characteristics of elephant camps in Thailand

Camp type	Factors
Poor venues	Rides last 15–30 minutes and usually follow identical paths; there may also be long queues for elephants, resulting in very short breaks between jobs. The stressful environment often also results in injuries to the elephants' heads from excessive use of bull hooks as they are forced to maintain a constant pace
Middle-ranking venues	Saddled rides are offered, with strict regulations about how many each elephant can give and for how long. Alternatively, they provide half-day or day-long activities where visitors learn to control, command and care for an individual elephant. This brings visitors into very close contact with the elephants, requiring a mahout who has full control of the elephant at all times
Better venues	These offer activities such as feeding and bathing elephants. This involves close, direct contact during the activities, but for the most part elephants are left to do what they like while visitors observe. The proximity to elephants poses a high risk of injury to visitors, with the added potential for disease transmission
Highest-ranking venues	No direct interaction between visitors and elephants is permitted. Visitors observe elephants behaving naturally, interacting with other elephants and browsing in the forest. Visitors regard these experiences as extremely rewarding. As there is no direct interaction between visitors and elephants, this type of venue is safest for visitors and least stressful for the elephants. Mahouts are trained to manage elephants humanely, using positive reinforcement training techniques rather than force. Visitor education about elephants is provided by knowledgeable staff

Elephant riding

Many tourists are attracted by the opportunity to ride an elephant, either in a captive setting or along forest tracks. A 2014 World Animal Protection survey of 1,700 tourists to Thailand concluded that 36% of the interviewed tourists had already been on, or planned to experience, an elephant ride (Schmidt-Burback, 2017). Many elephant camps for tourists provide elephant riding, in which two tourists mount the elephants from a high wooden platform, clambering into a specially made metal chair strapped to its back, assisted by a mahout who accompanies their tour. As they set off, a photo is usually taken and sold to the tourists on their return. Few of the mahouts speak much English, so there is little to be learned on a typical half-hour stroll along forest tracks around the camp. Rarely, a mahout will speak English quite well and offer a commentary on the plants the elephant browses on and respond to questions about elephant handling. At the end of the tour, after dismounting on to the platform, the tourists are usually taken to a stall where they can purchase bananas or sugar cane as treats for the elephant. This provides another photo opportunity. The elephant is soon led away, to take its place in the queue of its fellows awaiting their next job, out of sight of tourists. Often, they have to queue, unsheltered and unfed, in direct sunshine. Although of great interest to tourists, riding on an elephant's back can lead to physical damage to the elephant. Indeed, the majority of animals in such camps are kept in poor conditions (Schmidt-Burbach, Ronfot, & Srisangiam, 2015; Schmidt-Burback, 2017)

Moving to elephant-friendly tourism in Thailand

How can the conditions of elephants in Thailand be improved? Certainly, around the world, there is increasing concern for animal welfare and moves to improve the conditions of captive species. For example, *direct action* involving a picket of the attraction led to the cessation of dolphin performances at Brighton Aquarium. Following this case, there are no captive dolphin attractions in the UK, although there are dolphin shows in Australia (Sea World, 2018). Some captive dolphins from UK aquaria were transferred to the Caribbean Sea and released into the wild. This case demonstrates that customer demand had a direct effect on the conditions of animals in captivity and led to their release (Hughes, 2001). When applied to elephants in Thailand, we may envisage that there could be pickets outside elephant camps and the closure of such attractions. The problem, however, is what will happen to those elephants, as there is little protected land available to relocate them, and that land is already under pressure from illegal logging and other human activity.

An alternative is to continue the camps as tourist attractions using animals already in captivity, on the basis that there is no possibility of returning animals to the wild. In this case, the conditions in the camps would need improvement. As with dolphin attractions, it may be argued that, in this situation, the elephants may facilitate education and research about wildlife. Many authors have commented on the importance of education in animal welfare and wildlife conservation. Hammitt, Dulin, and Wells (1993) indicate that satisfaction with wildlife experiences serves the interests of conservation, and there is some experimental evidence for this proposition (Ballantyne & Packer, 2005). Information distributed at environmental parks may raise awareness of wildlife, the natural setting, and the human impact on it overall (Ballantyne, Packer, & Hughes, 2009). The effects, however, may be a short-term change in attitude rather than a longer-term behavioural change (Ballantyne, Packer, & Falk, 2011). The short-term liking experienced may affect questionnaire response on site but has little effect on attitudes in non-zoo contexts.

In the case of elephants in Thailand, the main factor leading to an improvement in their welfare occurred through the actions of trade channel members. There has been change in the ethical treatment of animals due to the impact of tourism operators. In 2010, TUI Nederland became the first tour operator to stop all sales and promotion of venues offering elephant rides and shows. It was followed soon after by several other operators, including Intrepid Travel, which, in 2013, was first to stop such sales and promotions globally. By early 2017, more than 160 travel companies had made similar commitments and now offer elephant-friendly tourism activities (Schmidt-Burback, 2017). More recently, TripAdvisor announced in 2016 that it would end the sale of tickets for wildlife experiences where tourists come into direct contact with captive wild animals, including elephant riding. This decision was in response to 550,000 people taking action to demand that the company stop profiting from the world's cruellest wildlife attractions (Schmidt-Burback, 2017). The result of these campaigns has been to improve the welfare of elephants in those camps that have been able to adapt and continue trading.

Discussion

Tourism has provided a step towards the preservation of elephants in a difficult environment (Kontogeorgopoulos, 2009a), but is only part of the story. Elephant camps have provided a means for elephants to be fed and housed, but clearly not in a manner that meets current welfare standards. Recent industry action has resulted in some improvement in conditions, but these changes are only partial improvements. The rehabilitation and reintroduction of elephants into protected areas would be a great outcome but is unlikely to occur, in part because of the lack of available land. Further, any solution is complicated by the linkages among tourism, community livelihoods, and conservation (The World Bank Group, 2018). Elephant camps provide income for mahouts and their families, as well as income for a regional community.

There is certainly a need for further research into the links between elephant welfare in captivity, visitor education, sustainability of elephants in the wild, and the income of local communities (Stone & Nyaupane, 2015). Much of the research on elephants is proprietary consultancy work, disseminated in peer-reviewed outlets in a fragmented manner. Several commentators have noted that government policy is consequently based on out-of-date or only partial knowledge (Spenceley, 2008).

Sin and Minca (2014, p. 96) note that:

> Elephant Camp[s] [are] a laboratory for reflecting on how questions of responsibility towards distant people and places, especially when actually enacted in place – which is what tourism does – often become a complicated affair, which is at the origin of new opportunities but also new tensions, of learning and but also misunderstandings, of neo-colonial practices but also of actual support to the local economy.

Many of the issues facing elephants are similar to those of other animals, and their protection requires attention (Markwell, 2018). Although each species has specific needs and problems (and also attracts the attention of different experts and enthusiasts), more research is required to establish general principles of wildlife conservation, captive animal welfare, and wildlife tourism. The issues of animal protection and the interaction of tourists with such animals are in need of further research. Some guidelines for tourist–wildlife interactions are available (ABTA, 2013), but further work is needed, drawing on a range of research approaches.

References

ABTA. (2013). *ABTA Animal Welfare Guidelines*. London: Association of British Travel Agents.

Akama, J. S., & Kieti, D. M. (2003). Measuring tourist satisfaction with Kenya's wildlife safari: a case study of Tsavo West National Park. *Tourism Management, 24*(1), 73–81.

Akama, J. S., Maingi, S., & Camargo, B. A. (2011). Wildlife conservation, safari tourism and the role of tourism certification in Kenya: a postcolonial critique. *Tourism Recreation Research, 36*(3), 281–291.

Ballantyne, R., & Packer, J. (2005). Promoting environmentally sustainable attitudes and behaviour through free-choice learning experiences: what is the state of the game? *Environmental Education Research, 11*(3), 281–295.

Ballantyne, R., Packer, J., & Falk, J. (2011). Visitors' learning for environmental sustainability: testing short- and long-term impacts of wildlife tourism experiences using structural equation modelling. *Tourism Management, 32*(6), 1243–1252.

Ballantyne, R., Packer, J., & Hughes, K. (2009). Tourists' support for conservation messages and sustainable management practices in wildlife tourism experiences. *Tourism Management, 30*(5), 658–664.

Balmford, A., Green, J. M., Anderson, M., Beresford, J., Huang, C., Naidoo, R., et al. (2015). Walk on the wild side: estimating the global magnitude of visits to protected areas. *PLoS Biology, 13*(2), e1002074. doi:10.1371/journal.pbio.1002074

Blake, S., & Hedges, S. (2004). Sinking the flagship: the case of forest elephants in Asia and Africa. *Conservation Biology, 18*(5), 1191–1202.

Bresler, N. C. (2011). On safari in Botswana: describing the product. *Tourism Analysis, 16*(1), 67–75.

Cameron, E. Z., & Ryan, S. J. (2016). Welfare at multiple scales: importance of zoo elephant population welfare in a world of declining wild populations. *PLoS One, 11*(7), e0158701. doi:10.1371/journal.pone.0158701

Carr, N. (2016). Ideal animals and animal traits for zoos: general public perspectives. *Tourism Management, 57*, 37–44.

Catlin, J., Jones, R., Jones, T., Norman, B., & Wood, D. (2010). Discovering wildlife tourism: a whale shark tourism case study. *Current Issues in Tourism, 13*(4), 351–361.

Clayton, S., Fraser, J., & Saunders, C. (2009). Zoo experiences: conversations, connections, and concern for animals. *Zoo Biology, 28*(5), 377–397.

Cohen, E. (2009). The wild and the humanized: animals in Thai tourism. *Anatolia, 20*(1), 100–118.

Cohen, E. (2010). Panda and elephant – contesting animal icons in Thai tourism. *Journal of Tourism & Cultural Change, 8*(3), 154–171.

Cunningham, P. A., Huijbens, E. H., & Wearing, S. L. (2012). From whaling to whale watching: examining sustainability and cultural rhetoric. *Journal of Sustainable Tourism, 20*(1), 143–161.

de Pinho, J. R., Grilo, C., Boone, R. B., Galvin, K. A., & Snodgrass, J. G. (2014). Influence of aesthetic appreciation of wildlife species on attitudes towards their conservation in Kenyan agropastoralist communities. *PLoS One, 9*(2), e88842. doi:10.1371/journal.pone.0088842

Duffy, R., & Moore, L. (2010). Neoliberalising nature? Elephant-back tourism in Thailand and Botswana. *Antipode, 42*(3), 742–766.

Felardo, J. (2016). A comparison of microeconomic and macroeconomic approaches to deforestation analysis. *EnvironmentAsia, 9*(1), 18–27.

Fennell, D. A. (2012). Tourism and animal rights. *Tourism Recreation Research, 37*(2), 157–166.

Fennell, D. A. (2013). Tourism and animal welfare. *Tourism Recreation Research, 38*(3), 325–340.

Fowler, M. E. (2001). An overview of foot conditions in Asian and African elephants. In B. Csuti (Ed.), *The elephant's foot: prevention and care of foot conditions in captive Asian and African elephants* (pp. 1–7). Iowa: Iowa State University Press.

Hammitt, W. E., Dulin, J. N., & Wells, G. R. (1993). Determinants of quality wildlife viewing in Great Smoky Mountains National Park. *Wildlife Society Bulletin, 21*(1), 21–30.

Higginbottom, K. (2004). Wildlife tourism: an introduction. In K. Higginbottom (Ed.), *Wildlife tourism: impacts, management and planning* (pp. 1–14). Altona, VIC: Common Ground.

Higginbottom, K., & Scott, N. (2004). Wildlife tourism: a strategic destination approach. In K. Higginbottom (Ed.), *Wildlife tourism: impacts, management and planning* (pp. 253–277). Altona, VIC: Common Ground.

Higham, J., & Hopkins, D. (2015). Wildlife tourism: "call it consumption". In D. Scott, C. M. Hall, & S. Gössling (Eds), *The Routledge handbook of tourism and sustainability* (pp. 280–293). London: Routledge.

Hoyt, E. (2001). *Whale watching 2001: worldwide tourism numbers, expenditures, and expanding socio-economic benefits*. Yarmouth Port, MA: International Fund for Animal Welfare.

Hughes, P. (2001). Animals, values and tourism: structural shifts in UK dolphin tourism provision. *Tourism Management, 22*, 321–329.

Kathleen, K., & Lisa, T. F. (2005). Lions and tigers and bears, oh my! An examination of membership communication programs among our nation's zoos. *Journal of Hospitality & Leisure Marketing, 12*(1/2), 57–78.

Keil, P. G. (2017). Uncertain encounters with wild elephants in Assam, Northeast India. *Journal of Religious & Political Practice, 3*(3), 196–211.

Knight, J. (2010). The ready-to-view wild monkey: the convenience principle in Japanese wildlife tourism. *Annals of Tourism Research, 37*(3), 744–762.

Kontogeorgopoulos, N. (2009a). The role of tourism in elephant welfare in Northern Thailand. *Journal of Tourism, 10*(21), 1–19.

Kontogeorgopoulos, N. (2009b). Wildlife tourism in semi-captive settings: a case study of elephant camps in northern Thailand. *Current Issues in Tourism, 12*(5–6), 429–449.

Kopnina, H. (2016). Wild animals and justice: the case of the dead elephant in the room. *Journal of International Wildlife Law & Policy, 19*(3), 219–235.

Lawton, L. J. (2009). Birding festivals, sustainability, and ecotourism: an ambiguous relationship. *Journal of Travel Research, 48*(2), 259–267.

Locke, P. (2013). Explorations in ethnoelephantology: social, historical, and ecological intersections between Asian elephants and humans. *Environment & Society, 4*, 79–97.

Markwell, K. (2018). An assessment of wildlife tourism prospects in Papua New Guinea. *Tourism Recreation Research*, 1–14. doi:10.1080/02508281.2017.1420008

McIntosh, D., & Wright, P. A. (2017). Emotional processing as an important part of the wildlife viewing experience. *Journal of Outdoor Recreation & Tourism, 18*, 1–9.

Moorhouse, T. P., Dahlsjo, C. A. L., Baker, S. E., D'Cruze, N., & Macdonald, D. W. (2015). The customer isn't always right: conservation and animal welfare implications of the increasing demand for wildlife tourism. *PLoS One*. doi:10.1371/journal.pone.0138939

Orams, M. (2002). Feeding wildlife as a tourism attraction: a review of issues and impacts. *Tourism Management, 23*(3), 281–293.

Packer, J., Ballantyne, R., & Hughes, K. (2014). Chinese and Australian tourists' attitudes to nature, animals and environmental issues: implications for the design of nature-based tourism experiences. *Tourism Management, 44*(0), 101–107.

Partridge, C., & Mackay, K. J. (1998). An investigation of the travel motives of bird watchers as a nature based tourist segment. *Journal of Applied Recreational Research, 23*(3), 263–287.

Phillips, C. J. C., Izmirli, S., Aldavood, S. J., Alonso, M., Choe, B. I., Hanlon, A., et al. (2012). Students' attitudes to animal welfare and rights in Europe and Asia. *Animal Welfare – The UFAW Journal, 21*(1), 87.

Pimmanrojnagool, V., & Wanghongsa, S. (2001). *A study of street wandering elephants in Bangkok and the socio-economic life of their mahouts.* Paper presented at the Giants on Our Hands: Proceedings of the International Workshop on the Domesticated Asian Elephant, 5–10 February, Bangkok, Thailand.

Reynolds, P. C., & Braithwaite, D. (2001). Towards a conceptual framework for wildlife tourism. *Tourism Management, 22*(1), 31–42.

Russell, C. L., & Ankenman, M. J. (1996). Orangutans as photographic collectibles: ecotourism and the commodification of nature. *Tourism Recreation Research, 21*(1), 71–78.

Santiapillai, C., & Jackson, P. (1990). *The Asian elephant.* Gland, Switzerland: IUCN.

Scarpaci, C., & Parsons, E. C. M. (2017). Recent advances in whale-watching research. *Tourism in Marine Environments, 12*(2), 125–137.

Schmidt-Burback, J. (2017). *Taken for a ride, the conditions for elephants used for tourism in Asia.* Retrieved from: www.worldanimalprotection.org.au/sites/default/files/au_files/taken_for_a_ride_report.pdf

Schmidt-Burbach, J., Ronfot, D., & Srisangiam, R. (2015). Asian elephant (*Elephas maximus*), pig-tailed macaque (*Macaca nemestrina*) and tiger (*Panthera tigris*) populations at tourism venues in Thailand and aspects of their welfare. *PLoS One, 10*(9), e0139092. doi:10.1371/journal.pone.0139092

Sea World. (2018). *Our position.* Retrieved from: https://seaworld.com.au/animals-rides-and-shows/animals/our-position.aspx

Sin, H. L., & Minca, C. (2014). Touring responsibility: the trouble with "going local" in community-based tourism in Thailand. *Geoforum, 51*, 96–106.

Spenceley, A. (2008). Implications of responsible tourism for conservation and development. In A. Spenceley (Ed.), *Responsible tourism: critical issues for conservation and development* (pp. 361–374). Milton Park, UK: Earthscan/James & James.

Steven, R., Morrison, C., & Castley, J. G. (2015). Birdwatching and avitourism: a global review of research into its participant markets, distribution and impacts, highlighting future research priorities to inform sustainable avitourism management. *Journal of Sustainable Tourism, 23*(8–9), 1257–1276.

Stone, M. T., & Nyaupane, G. P. (2015). Protected areas, tourism and community livelihoods linkages: a comprehensive analysis approach. *Journal of Sustainable Tourism, 24*(5), 673–693.

Sukumar, R. (1992). *The Asian elephant: ecology and management.* Cambridge: Cambridge University Press.

Sulaiman, C., & Abdul-Rahim, A. (2015). Logging ban policy and its impact on international trade in forest products: the case of Thailand. *International Journal of Green Economics, 9*(3–4), 242–257.

Talukdar, N. R., & Choudhury, P. (2017). Population structure of wild Asiatic elephant in Patharia Hills Reserve Forest, Karimganj, India: a plea for conservation. *Journal of Entomology & Zoology Studies, 5*(2), 1493–1498.

Thapa, B., Aryal, A., Roth, M., & Morley, C. (2017). The contribution of wildlife tourism to tiger conservation (*Panthera tigris tigris*). *Biodiversity, 18*(4), 168–174.

The World Bank Group. (2018). *Supporting sustainable livelihoods through wildlife tourism.* Retrieved from: http://documents.worldbank.org/curated/en/494211519848647950/Supporting-sustainable-livelihoods-through-wildlife-tourism

Tisdell, C., & Wilson, C. (2001). Wildlife-based tourism and increased support for nature conservation financially and otherwise: evidence from sea turtle ecotourism at Mon Repos. *Tourism Economics, 7*(3), 233–249.

Valentine, P. S., Birtles, A., Curnock, M., Arnold, P., & Dunstan, A. (2004). Getting closer to whales – passenger expectations and experiences, and the management of swim with dwarf minke whale interactions in the Great Barrier Reef. *Tourism Management, 25*(6), 647–655.

Wilson, C., & Tisdell, C. (2001). Sea turtles as a non-consumptive tourism resource especially in Australia. *Tourism Management, 22*, 279–288.

UN World Tourism Organization (UNWTO) & Global Tourism Economy Research Centre. (2016). *Asia tourism trends 2016.* Retrieved from: http://asiapacific.unwto.org/publication/unwtogterc-annual-report-asia-tourism-trends-2016-edition

Worwag, S. S., & Varga, P. (2017). Tourists' animal welfare considerations – elephant tourism in Thailand. In C. Lee, S. Filep, J. N. Albrecht, & W. J. L. Coetzee (Eds), *CAUTHE 2017: time for big ideas? Re-thinking the field for tomorrow* (pp. 419–428). Dunedin, NZ: Department of Tourism, University of Otago.

WWF. (2015). *Global welfare guidance for animals in tourism.* Retrieved from

PART II

Economic impacts of tourism

7

ECONOMIC IMPACTS OF TOURISM

Orhan Icoz and Onur Icoz

Introduction

Tourism is a significant economic activity in most countries around the world owing to its numerous benefits for societies and contributions to local and national economies. Despite a great acceptance of this phenomenon, the economic importance of tourism and travel for a region or a country is usually underestimated, and it extends well beyond the core sectors of this industry. The crucial role of the tourism industry in the world economy and the positive effects of tourism development on a nation's economy are commonly accepted by many authorities (Chen, 2008). Moreover, tourism can indirectly influence other sectors and sociocultural structures by improving local living standards as the reflections of economic impacts of tourism on communities (Dritsakis, 2004).

The economic impacts of visitors' presence in destinations result from the fact that tourists spend their money on a wide variety of goods and services. These impacts of tourism can also affect *private-sector entities, public revenues,* and *investments* in different ways. The revenues obtained from tourism can have the potential to affect local or national economies. But, as indicated above, the more favorable revenues are the earnings from international tourism, because visitor expenditures can be seen as an injection of foreign money into the local economy, thus creating new levels of consumer demand (Harcombe, 1999), and it is well known that foreign exchange revenues from international tourism can be utilized to import capital goods for the production of goods and services, which in turn aids the growth of the national economy (McKinnon, 1964). Depending on these benefits, many communities have turned to tourism as an alternative means of selling something to other countries (Hughes and Shields, 2007).

In the major tourism destinations, the increase in the number of tourists has been parallel to the increase in the *gross domestic product* (GDP), giving place to a greater growth in employment and wealth than in a lot of economies that do not specialize in tourism and leading to growth and employment rates higher than in those economies (Capó and Valle, 2008).

In order to understand and evaluate the relative importance of tourism for an economy, it is important to measure its effects precisely. However, there is great difficulty in measuring the economic effects of tourism, as it is a cross-sector consisting of multiple businesses in different branches of activity offering services to the tourists. In other words, tourism is generally regarded as an industry, although really it is a mixture. To get round the problem of its definition, analyses of tourism's impacts on the economy are generally demand-oriented, that is they are based on tourist spending in a particular region. Tourists consume an extraordinarily broad range of goods and services supplied by different types of business during their holiday. Therefore, tourist expenditures spread over the other sectors and industries where they spend. Thus, direct spending can easily be identified by collecting data, but other types of spending are only estimated based on the calculations and methodologies developed by the authors. These methodologies will be discussed in the further sections of this chapter.

Tourism as economic activity

Tourism as an economic activity is considered as the cluster of production units in different industries that provide consumption goods and services demanded by visitors. Such industries are called *tourism industries*, because visitor acquisition represents a significant share of their supply the production of which, in the absence of visitors, would cease to exist in a meaningful quantity (UNWTO and ILO, 2014, 17). Over the past six decades, tourism has experienced continued expansion and diversification to become one of the largest and fastest-growing economic sectors in the world. Tourism has created continuing growth over time, despite some economic downturns, demonstrating the sector's strength and resilience (UNWTO, 2017). International tourist arrivals have increased from 25 million globally in 1950 to 1,322 million in 2017. Likewise, international tourism receipts earned by destinations have surged from only US$2 billion in 1950 to US$1,220 billion in 2016 (UNWTO, 2017). This strong momentum was expected to continue in 2018 at a rate of 4–5%.

These figures indicate that tourism is a major category of international trade in services and the *third* largest export industry in terms of global earnings after *chemicals* and *fuels*, representing 7% of the world's exports in *goods and services*, and this industry is responsible for 1 out of 11 jobs and 10% of the world's economic output (World Trade Organization, 2016; WTTC, 2018). In many developing countries, tourism is the top export category. In addition to receipts earned in destinations, international tourism also generated US$216 billion in exports through international *passenger transport services* rendered to nonresidents in 2016, bringing the total value of tourism exports up to US$1,4 trillion (UNWTO, 2017).

Tourism continued to show its resilience in 2017, contributing direct GDP growth of 3.1% and supporting 6 million net additional jobs in the sector. In total, tourism generated US$8.2 trillion (10.4% of global GDP) and 313 million jobs in 2017. The sector accounted for 6.5% of total global exports and almost 30% of total global service exports (Table 7.1). The direct contribution of travel and tourism to GDP growth is expected to support more than 380 million jobs by 2027 (WTTC, 2018). All these figures show the size and significance of tourism as an economic activity, particularly for small economies (WTO, 2016).

Tourism and national economies

Tourism has played an increasingly significant role in the economic growth of many countries for more than 60 years. Depending on the volume of visitor expenditures, the development of tourism in a region creates different benefits and costs in many fields of the local economy. These benefits and costs may change in terms of their effects, depending on the economic structure of the countries. The most significant difference concerning the effects of tourism on economies may appear between developed and less-developed countries (Icoz, 2005, 183). In developing countries, GDP is typically low, income and wealth distribution is unfair, unemployment rates are substantial, and industrial progress is relatively slow owing to insufficient human and capital stocks. Therefore, these countries are more interested in tourism than

Table 7.1 Direct and total contribution of tourism and travel by selected countries (2017)

Countries	Direct contribution to GDP, US$ bn (% of GDP)	Total* contribution to GDP, US$ bn (% of GDP)	Direct contribution to employment, number of jobs (% of total)	Total* contribution to employment, number of jobs (% of total)	Visitor exports, US$ bn (% of total exports)
China	402.3 (3.3)	1,349.3 (11.0)	28,250,000 (3.6)	79,900,000 (10.3)	125.3 (5.2)
Croatia	6.0 (10.9)	13.7 (25.0)	138,000 (10.1)	320,500 (23.5)	11.02 (39.0)
France	93.9 (3.6)	232.0 (8.9)	1,192,000 (4.2)	2,830,500 (10.0)	50.3 (6,5)
Greece	16.2 (8.0)	39.7 (19.7)	459,000 (12.2)	934,000 (24.8)	19.5 (28,4)
Italy	106.8 (5.5)	253.5 (13.0)	1,490,500 (6.5)	3,394,500 (14.7)	44.9 (7,4)
Japan	107.4 (2.2)	331.2 (6.8)	1,098,500 (1.7)	4,171,500 (6.4)	35.3 (4,1)
Malta	1.7 (14.2)	3.2 (27.1)	31,000 (15.7)	55,500 (28.3)	1.9 (12.3)
Spain	70.9 (5.4)	196.2 (14.9)	930,500 (4.9)	2,838,500 (15.1)	75.4 (16,4)
Turkey	32.0 (3.8)	98.4 (11.6)	462,000 (1.6)	2.093,500 (7.4)	31.3 (14.8)
UK	93.5 (3.7)	266.1 (10,5)	1,716,500 (4.9)	4,055,000 (11.6)	35.6 (4,7)
USA	509.4 (2.6)	1,501.9 (7.7)	5,285,500 (3.4)	13,668,000 (8.9)	200.7 (8,6)
World total	2,570.0 (3.2)	8,272.3 (10.4)	118,454,000 (3.8)	313,221,000 (9.9)	1,494.2 (6.5)

Note: * The sum of *direct*, *indirect* and *induced contributions*

Source: WTTC, 2018 (data compiled by the authors).

others are, as it has low technology requirements and high potential to create more employment opportunities owing to its service nature (Dritsakis, 2004).

In developed countries, the tourism industry is only one productive part of economic diversity, and, hence, economic dependency on tourism is weak, the tourism industry's relative share of GDP is low, and, for most cases, this share is not more than 5% (Table 7.1). Therefore, developed countries primarily see tourism as an industry that offers adequate and favorable tourism services for their citizens. The objective of tourism managers is to create opportunities for their nationals to participate in tourism as much as possible. In developing countries, on the other hand, the basic objective is to increase the socioeconomic benefits of tourism, concentrating on the supply-side investments of the market. Tourism also provides a possible means for lower-income countries to escape from the low product quality, low expenditure, and low income pattern which generally constraint their development (Sinclair and Stabler, 1997, 149). For these reasons, the relative share and significance of the tourism industry in their economies is high enough that it may create overdependence on tourism to an undesirable level. Tourism's share of GDP may reach up to 15% in some of these countries (Table 7.1).

However, tourism is considered an efficient source of foreign money, employment, and investment, and it has a *comparative advantage* owing to natural endowments and almost *zero opportunity cost* for resource use if tourism production is relatively efficient (Lickorish and Jenkins, 1997, 53; Sinclair and Stabler, 1997, 128; Zhang and Jensen, 2005); the major threat awaiting less-developed countries is the fact that they may heavily be influenced by international demand fluctuations and negative external economies caused by industrial tourism.

Economic impacts of tourism

It is widely accepted that the tourism industry has a *positive* influence on the local economy by resulting in effects such as *economic diversity*, *revenues*, *jobs*, and *tax revenue* (Brida, Osti, and Faccioli, 2011). However, tourism also brings some *negative* economic impacts for

Table 7.2 Economic impacts of tourism

Positive impacts/benefits	Negative impacts/costs
• contributions to balance of payments • generation of income and government revenues • improvement of economic structure • more employment opportunities • investment and development • public utilities and infrastructure • new business opportunities • encouragement of entrepreneurial activity • gender structuring of tourism employment	• increases in the price of goods/services and the cost of living • additional infrastructure costs • competition for land with other economic uses • profits exported by owners • import leakages • overdependence on tourism • increased propensity to import • external costs

Source: Kreag, 2001, and Mathieson and Wall, 1982, 52.

destinations as it leads to *price increases* in real estate property, goods, and services, as well as many others. In a broad context, tourism development contributes to both profits and costs to the local economy, as higher demand from tourists will significantly influence an increase in prices (Marzuki, 2012). Table 7.2 summarizes overall *positive* and *negative* economic impacts of tourism development.

The economic impact of tourism can be summarized as follows: (a) it is a powerful economic force providing *employment, foreign exchange earnings*, and *tax revenue*; (b) visitors are generators of economic impact for a destination area, directly from their spending and indirectly from the tourism multiplier effect. All positive and negative economic impacts of tourism are discussed under the headings of the benefits and costs of tourism.

Economic benefits of tourism

Tourism expenditures and investments in a destination provide a significant amount of income and create jobs for the local community. Particularly, the economic benefits are the major reasons for governments to get involved with development of tourism. The most prominent economic benefits of tourism are as follows:

Income creation

The economic impact of tourism is a function of the size of domestic and international visitor expenditures (Goeldner, Ritchie, and McIntosh, 2000, 412). Tourists usually buy a wide range of goods and services while visiting a region. They spend money in the region and demand goods and services supplied by local firms (Baaijens, Nijkamp, and Montfort, 2010). These expenditures generate considerable economic benefits for local businesses (Caughlan, 1998, 5). The income and employment resulting from purchases from local businesses represent monetary injections into the economy. As tourism generates significant economic impact on an economy, the industry is gaining growing importance for all stakeholders (Mazumder, Al-Mamun, Al-Amin, and Mohiuddin, 2012, 270). For most economies, tourism income may be seen as better than other income earned from the export of tangibles because much of it is received for *services* whose import potential is zero (Lundberg, Stavenga, and Krishnamoorthy, 1995, 139).

In a labor-intensive industry such as tourism, the greater proportion of income is likely to be derived from *wages* and *salaries* paid to those working in jobs *either* directly serving the needs of tourists or benefiting indirectly from tourists' spending (Holloway, 1999, 46) and it is also generated from *interest, rent,* and *profits* on tourism businesses. Taxation on tourism activities, such as *value added tax, hotel bills,* and *fuel* used by tourists, and *other direct forms of taxation,* which countries may choose to levy on tourists to raise additional *public income,* is another source of tourism impact on income (UNWTO and ILO, 2014, 24). In addition, income generation results not only from expenditures by foreign tourists, but also from the associated increases in private investment and public expenditure (Sinclair and Stabler, 1997, 139).

Increases in production and sales volumes through tourism can lead to increases in local individual income and contribute to government revenues (Frechtling, 1994; Gasparino, Bellini, Del Corpo, and Malizia, 2008). This is the first type of economic impact on the economy, also known as *direct effects* of tourism expenditures. An increase in demand from tourism will raise prices for products, semi-products, and production factors (Dwyer, Forsyth, and Spurr, 2004). Also, real property values and returns on capital invested in tourist facilities can be affected (Frechtling, 1994); this is the *second type* of economic impact described as *indirect effects* that result from the re-spending of the initial tourist spending. A third category, *induced effects,* emerge if an increase in employment caused by direct and indirect effects results in an increase in income to be spent by households. This means that other sectors of the economy take advantage, because of an increased demand for goods and services as well (Otgaar and Klijs, 2010). The *induced effects* are the impact of tourism arising from people in the host community spending revenue from tourism profits and wages for their own different needs such as housing, education, health, and so on (Muñoz, Muñoz, and Pérez, 2016).

The greatest changes in economic structure probably arise when the transformation is from a traditional agricultural production economy to one dominated by tourism in rural destinations. Many of the changes can be the result of *demographic pressures, technological progress,* and *employment opportunities* outside the rural economy. Tourism has often contributed to the acceleration of such changes, but is not always a major cause (Mathieson and Wall, 1982, 85). The result is the changing profile of tourism revenue earners.

Contribution to balance of payments

An important indicator of the role of international tourism is its generation of foreign exchange earnings and contributions to the balance of payments. The balance of payments is "an account which shows a country's financial transactions with the rest of the world" and it records inflows and outflows of currency. It is a statement that takes into account the value of all goods, services, and capital loans (Vanhove, 2005, 178). This account is composed of two main parts: (1) *The current account,* which includes goods, services, incomes, and current transfers; and (2) *the capital and financial account,* which refers to capital transfers and acquisition disposal of non-produced, financial, and nonfinancial assets and liabilities (Vanhove, 2005, 178).

In this account, inbound tourist spending is considered as an *invisible export,* and outbound tourist spending is seen as an *invisible import* (Smith, 1991, 270; Holloway, 1999, 50). So, the total value of receipts minus the total payment made during the year represents a country's *balance of payments* on the tourism account. The money that a large number of inbound tourists spend in a country can make a considerable contribution to its balance of payments (Kumar and Hussain, 2014). The contribution of tourism to the balance of payments is measured as *net travel balance,* which shows the difference between tourism earnings from visitors and resident expenditures outside the country. A positive net balance is clearer in traditional tourism destination countries (Spain, France, and Italy) and most developing countries.

Many countries are bearing large foreign trade deficits and they are searching for measures to balance the payments. Despite some of the critiques of tourism industry, most countries view the possibility of expanding the tourist industry with favor. The relationship between the balance of payments and tourism is very attractive for policymakers and causes them to search for guidance on the continuity of enlarging this industry (Mathieson and Wall, 1982, 56).

The generation of employment

Employment, together with income generation, is the most obvious benefit of tourism development (Vanhove, 2005, 199). Tourism can generate jobs directly through *hotels*, *restaurants*, *transportation*, and so on, and indirectly through the supply of *goods and services* needed by partly tourism-related businesses that are not directly associated with the sector, such as *construction*, *banking*, and *local transport*. According to the latest statistics, this industry supports some 10% of employment worldwide (UNWTO, 2017). These data show the importance of tourism to the creation of job opportunities all around the world. Especially in underdeveloped countries, tourism is able to employ more people than other industries. Moreover, if an area suffers from declining industries and levels of unemployment are high, tourism can be a way of revitalizing that area and creating employment opportunities (Filiposki, Ackovska, Angelovska, and Metodieski, 2016).

The impact of tourism industries on employment is brought about in three ways:

- *Direct employment* in the tourism industries such as hotels, travel businesses, and government organizations (Leiper, 1979),
- *Indirect employment* in the sectors supplying inputs to the tourism industries,
- *Induced effect* on employment as a result of subsequent rounds of spending.

Total effect on employment is also reflected in the employment multiplier (ESCAP, 1990). Tourism also brings about changes in the pattern of employment. Studies of employment in tourism have indicated the ways in which it is structured by gender. In most countries, jobs in the transport sector are fulfilled by men, for instance, whereas those in accommodation and catering are undertaken by women. An inflow of foreign tourists is accompanied by the construction of large hotels in which many younger and more educated women have obtained employment in developing destinations (Sinclair and Stabler, 1997, 145).

However, some authors draw attention to the negative aspects of tourism employment due primarily to its *transient* nature, such as high turnover rates, seasonality (Albrecht, 2000; ILO, 2010), a flexible workforce based on part-time, temporary contracts, and agency work far more common than in any other industry. Further, employment in the tourism industries involves a disproportionately high degree of employers/owners/proprietors, as well as own-account workers. Some also argue that economic dependency on service-sector jobs contributes to income differences in urban versus rural locations (Jensen and Tienda, 1989; Lichter 1989). Noting that service sectors tend to employ more female workers, some researchers argue that economic dislocation and lower marriage rates are more prevalent in communities where service-sector jobs predominate (Albrecht, 1998).

When it comes to measurement of the contribution of tourism to employment, it should be admitted that it is more difficult to measure employment in tourism than is the case for many other industries owing to the above-mentioned reasons where exact measurement is almost impossible (Wood, 1992; Smeral, 2004). Data and measurements are frequently based on the labor statistics collected by public organizations, observations, and estimations.

Investment and development

Tourism development generates dynamic impacts and contributions to infrastructure improvements in destination countries, because tourism can induce the local government to make infrastructure improvements such as better water and sewage systems, electricity, communication, and public transportation. Growth in tourism typically leads to development of restaurants, retail establishments, and other tourism-related businesses. These investments contribute to improving the living standards of residents, as well as to encouraging long-term economic growth, and local people can also benefit from the improved facilities that are needed to attract and satisfy visitors (Mathieson and Wall, 1982; Blake, Arbache, Sinclair, and Teles, 2008; Spenceley and Meyer, 2012; Kumar and Hussain, 2014).

The benefits that business travel brings to international trade also foster investment by domestic firms and foreign investors. Foreign direct investments bring new capital, technology, more knowledgeable people, know-how, and extra demand for local supplies and improvements in trade balances (Oxford Economics, 2011, 43; UNWTO and ILO, 2014). It can also create new products and provide opportunities for local businesses further down the supply chain, and policymakers encourage more investment in tourism facilities in order to attract more tourists to peripheral regions (Zhang and Jensen, 2005). Once tourism is shown to be successful, private developers or government agencies are often willing to invest even further. Economists refer to this process as the "accelerator concept" (Holloway, 1999, 51)

Tourism, on the other hand, can be recognized as an economic activity that supports the growth of the "green economy," which is one of the long-term objectives of the tourism sector, and as an effective means of sustainable development (De Lacy and Lipman, 2010). As an extension of the green economy, green tourism brings new demand which motivates less use of transport and heavy infrastructure, as well as a better regional distribution of tourism flows.

Economic costs of tourism

As the positive economic impacts of tourism are widely accepted all over the world, the fact is that this industry may cause some negative economic effects which cannot be underestimated. The most commonly mentioned negative impacts are explained in the following sections.

Leakages

The term "leakage" has been mentioned for half a century in economics. It is defined as "financial processes through which less money gets back into the economy" (Rátz and Puczkó, 2002, 82) and is considered as the monetary loss from a region or other hidden costs through tourism (De Cuello, 2001; Cooper, Fletcher, Gilbert, and Wanhill, 2008, 136). This could be because the tourism businesses are owned by foreign companies, and some of their earnings (i.e., profits, wages/salaries, fees, and royalties) are transferred to the home countries, also known as "export leakage" (Supradist, 2004, 20; Kumar, Hussain, and Kannan, 2015). This type of leakage is not considered to be direct leakage, as the main source of money is tourist spending anyway. Therefore, the most significant leakage caused by tourism is "import leakage" (Supradist, 2004, 22), where tourists demand goods that the host country cannot produce and supply. According to some experts, import-related leakage for underdeveloped countries and small economies is on average between 40% and 50% of gross earnings, whereas the same figure for advanced and diversified economies is only between 10% and 20% (Ardahey, 2011).

Overdependence

Many destinations, even countries, may be highly dependent on tourism. Without tourism, most of the businesses (hotels, restaurants, etc.) would struggle, as they are not places that locals visit every day. When destinations become overdependent on tourism, they make themselves vulnerable to changes in tourist demand (Mathieson and Wall, 1982, 87). Tourism is a susceptible industry and is heavily influenced by socioeconomic and political changes, both domestic and international. For instance, areas with political unrest have lost out on tourists, who prefer to travel to other relatively stable destinations. In order to avoid economic disruption due to changes in demand, tourism destinations should support a diversified tourist industry and base economy (Ardahey, 2011). Therefore, overreliance on the tourist industry carries some risk to tourism-dependent economies. For example, economic recession or downturn, the impacts of natural disasters, such as tropical storms, and changing tourist preferences may all have a harmful effect on tourism-dependent destinations (Harcombe, 1999). Similarly, the strategy of dependence on a single market or a few markets is also crucial. Changes in the economic conditions or fashions in these limited-number tourist markets, as well as changes in political conditions and travel links, can have a significant effect in the destination economy (Bull, 1998, 186).

Inflationary effects

The relationship between tourism and inflation is more complex, temporal, and frequently local. A high inflow of tourists during a season may cause a rise in prices of many goods and services in the destination. Some authors suggest that it is undeniable that in tourist areas the prices for products and services are, in general, higher than in regions where there is very little or no tourism, and that in holiday destinations the prices for tourist services are higher in the peak season than in the rest of the year. This upswing of prices is frequently greater in underdeveloped regions than in richer ones (Vanhove, 2005, 175). The consequences of increases in prices may arise in many different ways. Wealthy tourists will be able to purchase products at higher prices, and, when suppliers recognize that this increases their profits, they continue to raise the prices further (Mathieson and Wall, 1982, 88). Consequently, local residents are forced to pay more and may even have to travel further in order to get what they need, as local enterprises concentrate on a more limited range of products.

On the other hand, mass or industrial tourism makes land and real estate prices higher as well. Development of tourism brings additional demand for land, and competition from potential buyers forces the price of land to rise. Locals are compelled to pay more for their homes (Vanhove, 2005, 176). Inherently, there are losers and winners as a result of these price increases for land. Indeed, the losers are those local people who have fixed incomes, such as wages and salaries, while the winners are landowners and traders. In the long run, this may be a problem for visitors, if prices are to rise in a stable manner. The primary danger is the displacement of tourists to cheaper destinations due to the unbearably higher prices in the region.

Unpaid costs

As an economic reality, many projects in tourism escalate many economic, social, and/or environmental costs for which the investor does not want to pay, and a third party has to pay the cost (Vanhove, 2003). This outlay is defined as "unpaid cost" in economics. Most obvious examples are environmental pollution and traffic congestion. The local residents have to pay these costs caused by tourism growth. The *opportunity cost* in such situations, on the other hand, is the cost of using scarce resources for tourism, either as consumption or development, as opposed to using the money for alternative, perhaps more society-related purposes. For example, it is assumed that resources allocated to the tourism industry are resources removed from other activities such as agriculture, which represents a forgone opportunity for the regional economy (Lundberg et al., 1995, 28). Likewise, if labor or land is used for tourism, its social cost to an economy is its opportunity cost or the cost of the opportunity of using it in the next best activity (Vanhove, 2005, 176). Therefore, tourism should be carefully planned and managed for efficient resource allocation and use in developing regions where resources are mostly scarce.

Enclave tourism

When tourists stay for their entire holiday at the same resort, which provides everything they demand and where they make all their expenditures, not much opportunity is left for locals to earn from tourism. For example, as widely observed in developing countries, all-inclusive accommodation generates the largest amount of revenue, but its impact on the local economy is smaller per dollar of revenue than other hotels. Similarly, in a region or destination, intense revenue leakages due to the above-mentioned reasons might create enclave resort conditions, where buyers are discouraged from spending their money outside the hotels, and where most of the goods are supplied from the local community (Freitag, 1994). The process of "enclavisation" in tourism has been a result of the need for exclusivity of the product and dependability of income. However, enclave models that signify a high concentration of tourism activities in a closed geographic area often result in little benefit to the local economy. Furthermore, there is a less social interaction and sometimes greater environmental impact owing to the intensity of development (Equations, 2008, 8).

Measurement of economic impacts

Notwithstanding the effects of tourist expenditures on economies are widely accepted all over the world, attempts to identify or measure the impacts of tourism are always difficult, because it is not easy to distinguish between the money spent by tourists and inhabitants in local businesses. The main obstacle to identifying the monetary effects of tourism is the fact that this industry is neither acknowledged as a single industry nor regarded as an isolated economic activity. So, its contribution to the development of economies cannot be definitely measured. In resorts, on the other hand, even such businesses might be highly dependent upon visitor spend where a large number of tourists are in self-catering facilities. However, several methods have been developed by a number of authors in order to estimate and analyze the economic impact of tourism. The most widely used methods aimed to measure the economic impacts of tourism are explained in the following.

Tourism multipliers

Tourism's contribution to income in an area is boosted by a phenomenon known as the tourism multiplier. This arises because money spent by tourists in the area will be re-spent by the earners, expanding the total. The multiplier, by definition, is the factor by which tourist spend is increased in this process (Archer, 1977; Horwath Tourism and Leisure Consulting, 1981, 3; Wanhill, 1983; Var and Quayson, 1985; Holloway, 1999, 47) and it shows the relationship between an additional unit of tourist spending and the changes that result in the level of income in the economy. In theory, any income accruing to nonnationals resident in the area is extracted from the sum (Vanhove, 2005, 185). The basic purpose of multiplier methodology is to measure the secondary effects of tourist spending, and it takes account of the short-term effects of tourism on income and employment, but the models are not appropriate for examining its longer-term reflections in the economy. Empirical evidence about the role of tourism within the structural transformation of economies over the long run is limited but indicates that the common conception of the development process as a transition from an agriculture-based economy to manufacturing and thence to services may be misguided (Sinclair and Stabler, 1997, 141). Fletcher and Archer (1991, 37) suggested four different multipliers: (a) the *transaction multiplier*, (b) the *output multiplier*, (c) the *income multiplier*, and (d) the *employment multiplier*. They all relate the measure of total impact to the initial tourism expenditure.

Residual receipts

This is a model developed by R.D. Kreutzwiser in 1973 to estimate total visitor expenditures in a specific and relatively small region using secondary data (Smith, 1991, 281). The model assumes that the expenditures due to local consumption in a tourism destination are usually less than total local receipts, and the difference is attributed to visitors from outside the local area. The method begins with multiplying total household income in a region by the percent of this income spent on retail goods and services. Then, this total is subtracted from the sales of retail and service establishments in the region, and this *residual* is the amount attributable to tourists in the region (Frechtling, 1994, 10). However, the basic inadequacy of this approach lies in the fact that the method cannot categorize the expenditures by type of product purchased, type of business used by tourists, or type of visitor for detailed analysis and, especially, segmentation purposes.

Input–output models

The input–output model developed by W. Leontief in 1973 is a means of analyzing inter-industry transactions in the production process (Harmston, 1969; Frechtling, 1994, 32). It permits analysis of the flow of goods and services from one producer to another and from the final producer to the final purchaser. It covers all production and also provides a detailed understanding of the linkages among industries (Ritz, 1979).

Input–output analysis starts with the development of a table representing how transactions flow through an economy during a given period of time (Fletcher, 1989). The rows of the table show the sales of the sector, listed on the left, to every other industry and the final demand sectors, listed at the top of the columns (Lundberg et al., 1995, 143). Input–output tables represent the characteristics of an area's economy at a particular point in time. However, the weakness in the application of input–output tables to smaller areas, such as regions, is that the tables are usually constructed at the national level. Therefore, unless a specific region is an actual sample or representative of the country, the forecasts made in this way will easily be biased. In the case of tourism, the application of these models is further complicated by the fact that tourism consumption includes elements that do not belong to final demand but to intermediate consumption of activities instead.

Tourism satellite accounts

The tourism satellite account (TSA) methodology developed by WTO is essential for obtaining accurate measurements of the impact of tourism. It is used to supplement the system of national accounts by measuring the economic contribution of tourism and is a means of measuring the size of the tourism sector in an economy. The TSA estimates the worth of the tourism sector by combining the contributions of different goods and services across the economy. TSA has the ability to show maximum linkages to input–output models as well as to demonstrate results originating from product-specific records (Mazumder et al., 2012, 285).

The TSA's essential contribution is that it represents entire official figures, within the national accounts, for a tourism *"industry"*. Because the TSA is developed in a manner which is consistent with the national accounting system as a whole, it makes it possible to compare the tourism industry with other sectors of the economy, examine its components, and measure tourism's *added value* in a national economy. For instance, tourism's relative share of GDP and employment, the relative importance of tourism components to overall tourism activity, and their contribution to other non-tourism industries can all be determined (Dwyer, Forsyth, Spurr, and Ho, 2004, 27). The TSA can be used to evaluate the proportion of tourism activity per se (*resulting from tourism travel*) in branches typical of the tourism sector (Vellas, 2011). Alongside the TSA-based analysis, it is possible to measure the expected impacts of tourism by calculating its multiplier effects. The TSA can also be used to predict tourism-related employment.

Conclusion

The economic impacts of tourism have been researched in the literature on a large scale, but there has been substantially more interest in the positive economic effects than the negative ones. The research on the positive economic impacts has contributed to the broad optimism among policymakers concerning tourism's potential for fostering economic growth. However, as is well known, each coin has two sides, and there is no economic activity without its costs. Among the negative effects of tourism, the most widely discussed ones are inflation, financial leakage, infrastructure costs, and economic dependence. However, in recent years, as societies' awareness of the environmental problems grows worldwide, the costs of tourism begin to draw more attention than ever. So, we can expect that there will be more research on the negative impacts of tourism on economies.

To conclude, tourism is undeniably one of the more powerful operators of employment and wealth. Despite some turbulent times with the world recession, these facts are not likely to change. Therefore, policies should focus on the wealth-creating power of tourism rather than the creation of negative effects. Considering the positive and negative economic impacts of tourism, it could be concluded that, with short-term and long-term strategic planning and using the specific abilities and tourism products of developing countries, most of the economic problems can be solved through a well-planned and -managed tourism industry.

References

Albrecht, D.E. (1998). The industrial transformation of farm communities: Implications for family structure and socio-economic conditions. *Rural Sociology*, 63(1), 51–64.

Albrecht, D.E. (2000). Recreational and Tourism Development vs. the Decline of Agriculture in Southern Utah. In P.V. Schaeffer and S. Loveridge (Eds.), *Small Town and Rural Economic Development: A Case Study Approach*. Westport, CT: Praeger. pp. 107–115.

Archer, B.H. (1977). *Tourism Multipliers: The Stale of the Art*. Bangor, UK: University of Wales Press.

Ardahey, F.T. (2011). Economic impacts of tourism industry. *International Journal of Business & Management*, 6(8). https://doi.org/10.5539/ijbm.v6n8p206

Oxford Economics. (2011). Aviation: The Real World Wide Web. Oxford. www.oxfordeconomics.com/my-oxford/projects/128832 (accessed March 17, 2018)

Baaijens, S.R., Nijkamp, P., and Montfort, K.v. (2010). Explanatory meta-analysis for the comparison and transfer of regional tourist income multipliers. *Regional Studies*, 32(9), 839–849.

Blake, A., Arbache, J.S., Sinclair, M.T., and Teles, V. (2008). Tourism and poverty relief. *Annals of Tourism Research*, 35(1), 107–126.

Brida, J.G., Osti, L., and Faccioli, M. (2011). Residents' perception and attitudes towards tourism impacts: A case study of the small rural community of Folgaria (Trentino-Italy). *Benchmarking: An International Journal*, 18(3), 359–385.

Bull, A. (1998). *The Economics of Travel and Tourism*, 2nd ed. Melbourne, VIC: Addison Wesley Longman Australia.

Capó, J., and Valle, E. (2008). The Macroeconomic Contribution of Tourism. In A.D. Ramos and P.S. Jimenez (Eds.), *Tourism Development: Economics, Management and Strategy*. New York: Nova Science. pp. 201–226.

Caughlan, L. (1998). *Estimating the Economic Impacts of Tourism on the Economy of Grand County*. Unpublished Masters thesis, Colorado State University, Department of Agricultural and Resource Economics.

Chen, M.H. (2008). Causal Relations among Tourism Development, Exchange Rate, Exports and Economic Activity. In A.D. Ramos and P.S. Jimenez (Eds.), *Tourism Development: Economics, Management and Strategy*, New York: Nova Science. pp. 101–120.

Cooper, C., Fletcher, J., Gilbert, D., and Wanhill S. (2008). *Tourism: Principles and Practice*. Harlow, UK: Prentice Hall, Pearson.

De Cuello, E.P.L (2001). Financial Leakages from Tourism, Evaluation and Policy Issues for LDCs. In *Tourism in the Least Developed Countries*. Madrid: WTO. pp. 123–144.

De Lacy, T., and Lipman, G. (2010). Moving to Carbon Clean Destinations. In C. Schott (Ed.), *Tourism and the Implications of Climate Change: Issues and Actions*. Bingley, UK: Emerald Group. pp. 299–312.

Dritsakis, N. (2004). Tourism as a long-run economic growth factor: An empirical investigation for Greece using causality analysis. *Tourism Economics*, 10(3), 305–316.

Dwyer, L., Forsyth, P., and Spurr, R. (2004). Evaluating tourism's economic effects: New and old approaches. *Tourism Management*, 25, 307–317.

Dwyer, L., Forsyth, P., Spurr, R., and Ho, T. (2004). *Economic Impacts and Benefits of Tourism in Australia: A General Equilibrium Approach*. Gold Coast, QLD: CRC Sustainable Tourism.

Economic and Social Commission for Asia and the Pacific (ESCAP). (1990). *Guidelines on Input–Output Analysis of Tourism*. ST/ESCAP/836. New York: UN.

Equations. (2008). *Rights of the Child in the Context of Tourism Equations: A Compilation*. EQUATIONS–Equitable Tourism Options. UNIFEM through its project Promoting Collaboration in Responsibility in Tourism. www.equitabletourism.org

Filiposki, O., Ackovska, M., Angelovska, N.P., and Metodieski D. (2016). Socio-economic impacts of tourism. *Economic Development*, 18(1–2), 125–140.

Fletcher, J.E., and Archer, B.H. (1991). The Development and Application of Multiplier Analysis. In C.P. Cooper (Ed.), *Progress in Tourism, Recreation and Hospitality Management*, Vol. 3. London: Belhaven Press. pp. 28–47.

Fletcher, J.E. (1989). Input–output analysis and tourism impact studies. *Annals of Tourism Research*, 16(4), 514–529.

Frechtling, D.C. (1994). Assessing the Impacts of Travel and Tourism – Measuring Economic Benefits. In J.R.B. Ritchie, and C.R. Goeldner (Eds.), *Travel, Tourism and Hospitality Research: A Handbook for Managers and Researchers*. New York: John Wiley. pp. 359–365.

Freitag, T.G. (1994). Enclave tourism development: For whom the benefit roll? *Annals of Tourism Research*, 21(3), 538–554.

Gasparino, U., Bellini, E., Del Corpo, B., and Malizia, W. (2008). Measuring the impact of tourism upon urban economies: A review of literature. 13th Coalition Network Workshop. Venice.

Goeldner, R.G., Ritchie, B., and McIntosh, R. (2000). *Tourism: Principles, Practices and Philosophies*, 8th ed. New York: John Wiley.

Harcombe, D. (1999). The economic impacts of tourism. *ABAC Journal*, 19(2), 10–22.

Harmston, K.F. (1969). The importance of 1967 tourism to Missouri. *Business & Government Review*, 10(3), 5–12.

Holloway, J.C. (1999). *The Business of Tourism*. New York: Pearson Education Asia, Addison Wesley Longman.

Horwath Tourism and Leisure Consulting. (1981). *Tourism Multipliers Explained*. Published in Conjunction with WTO, November. http://horwathhtl.co.za

Hughes D.W., and Shields, M. (2007). Revisiting tourism regional economic impact: Accounting for secondary household employment. *The Review of Regional Studies*, 37(2) 186–206.

Icoz, O. (2005). *Tourism Economics* (in Turkish), 3rd ed. Ankara: Turhan.

ILO. (2010). Developments and challenges in the hospitality and tourism sector. Issues paper for discussion at the Global Dialogue Forum for the Hotels, Catering, Tourism Sector, November 23–24, Geneva.

Jensen, L., and Tienda, M. (1989). Nonmetropolitan minority families in the United States: Trends in racial and ethnic economic stratification, 1959–1986. *Rural Sociology*, 54(4), 509–532.

Kreag, G. (2001). The impacts of tourism. Minnesota Sea Grant. Retrieved November 15, 2010, from www.seagrant.umn.edu/tourism/pdfs/ImpactsTourism.pdf

Kumar, J., and Hussain, K. (2014). A review of assessing the economic impact of business tourism: Issues and approaches. *International Journal of Hospitality & Tourism Systems*, 7(2), 49–55.

Kumar, J., Hussain, K., and Kannan, S. (2015). Positive vs. negative economic impacts of tourism development: A review of economic impact studies. 21st Asia Pacific Tourism Association Annual Conference, May 14–17, Kuala Lumpur.

Leiper, N. (1979). The framework of tourism. *Annals of Tourism Research*, 6(4), 390–407.

Lichter, D.T. (1989). Race, employment hardship, and inequality in the American nonmetropolitan South. *American Sociological Review*, 54(3), 436–446.

Lickorish, L.J., and Jenkins, C.L. (1997). *An Introduction to Tourism*. London: Butterworth–Heinemann.

Lundberg, D., Stavenga, M., and Krishnamoorthy, M. (1995). *Tourism Economics*. New York: John Wiley.

Marzuki, A. (2012). Local residents' perceptions towards economic impacts of tourism development in Phuket. *Turizam: An International Scientific & Professional Journal*, 60(2), 199–212.

Mathieson, A., and Wall, G. (1982). *Tourism: Economic, Physical and Social Impacts*. Harlow, UK: Longman.

Mazumder, M.N., Al-Mamun A., Al-Amin, A.Q., and Mohiuddin, M. (2012). Economic impact of tourism – A review of literatures on methodologies and their uses: 1969–2011. In M. Kasimoglu (Ed.), *Visions for Global Tourism Industry – Creating and Sustaining Competitive Strategies*. London: InTech. pp. 269–294.

McKinnon, R. (1964). Foreign exchange constraint in economic development and efficient aid allocation. *Economic Journal*, 74, 388–409.

Muñoz, D.R.M., Muñoz, R.D.M., and Pérez, F.J.G. (2016). A sustainable development approach to assessing the engagement of tourism enterprises in poverty alleviation. *Sustainable Development*, 24, 220–236.

Otgaar, A.H., and Klijs, S. (2010). The regional economic effects of industrial tourism development. 50th European Congress of the Regional Science Association International, August 19–23, Jönkoping, Sweden.

Rátz, T., and Puczkó, L. (2002). *The Impacts of Tourism. An Introduction*. Hämeenlinna, Finland: Häme Polytechnic.

Ritz, P.M. (1979). The input–output structure of the U.S. economy. In *Survey of Current Business* (February). Washington, DC: U.S. Department of Commerce. pp. 34–72.

Sinclair, M.T., and Stabler, M. (1997). *The Economics of Tourism*. London: Routledge.

Smeral, E. (2004). Quandaries of the labour market in tourism exemplified by the case of Austria. *Tourist Review*, 59(4), 14–20.

Smith, S.L.J. (1991). *Tourism Analysis: A Handbook*. New York: Longman, John Wiley.

Spenceley, A., and Meyer, D. (2012). Tourism and poverty reduction: Theory and practice in less economically developed countries. *Journal of Sustainable Tourism*, 10(3), 297–317.

Supradist, N. (2004). *Economic Leakage in Tourism*. Masters thesis, Master of Science in Environmental Management and Policy, Lund, Sweden.

UNWTO. (2017). *Tourism Highlights*. www.e-unwto.org/doi/pdf/10.18111/9789284419029

UNWTO and ILO. (2014). *Measuring Employment in the Tourism Industries – Guide with Best Practices*. Madrid: UNWTO.

Vanhove, N. (2003). Externalities of sport and tourism investments, activities, and events. In P. Keller and T. Bieger (Eds.), *Sport and Tourism, 53rd AIEST Congress*. Athens: St-Gall.

Vanhove, N. (2005). *The Economics of Tourism Destinations*. Oxford: Elsevier Butterworth-Heinemann.

Var, T., and Quayson, J. (1985). The multiplier impact of tourism in the Okanagan. *Annals of Tourism Research*, 12(4), 497–514.

Vellas, F. (2011). The indirect impact of tourism: An economic analysis. Third Meeting of T20 Tourism Ministers. Paris, October 25.

Wanhill, S.R.C. (1983). Measuring the economic impact of tourism. *The Service Industries Journal*, 3(1). https://doi.org/10.1080/02642068300000003

Wood, R. (1992). Hospitality industry labour trends: British and international experience. *Tourism Management*, 13(3), 297–304.

World Trade Organisation (WTO). (2016). Tourism sector highlighted as important contributor to trade and development. www.wto.org/english/news_e/news16_e/bus_13jul16_e.htm

WTTC. (2018). *Travel and Tourism Economic Impact*. London, UK. www.wttc.org

Zhang, J., and Jensen, C. (2005). Comparative advantage in tourism: A supply-side analysis. 45th Congress of the European Regional Science Association, August 23–27, Amsterdam.

8

TOURISM AND INCOME INEQUALITY IN MAURITIUS

An empirical investigation

Sheereen Fauzel

Introduction

Mauritius is a tropical island and is renowned as a popular destination for tourists from all over the world looking for a high-end holiday. It has a wide range of natural attractions, with a subtropical climate, beautiful, clear beaches, and tropical fauna and flora complemented by a multi-ethnic, multicultural population that is friendly and welcoming. Moreover, Mauritius has high-class beach resorts and hotels. The hotel industry has constantly upgraded the quality of its service to fulfil the growing international demand from tourists. This industry has experienced massive growth over recent years. The island had around 18,000 visitors in 1970, and, in 2017, the number of visitors was approximately 1,300,000. The tourism sector is considered a main pillar of the Mauritian economy and has contributed massively towards economic growth. The industry generates around 40,000 direct employment jobs.[1] It has considerable advantages for the economy in terms of creating direct and indirect employment. As such, it is expected to contribute towards a reduction in income inequality in the country. Referring to the Kuznets curve hypothesis, and linking tourism development to economic development, as tourism expands it is considered to increase inequality and then reduce inequality with time as there is more development.

Referring to the literature, there is, to date, no study which has assessed the impact of tourism development on income inequality in Mauritius. As such, there is a need to analyse the implications of the dynamics of tourism expansion for the economy. To that end, although it is by and large acknowledged that there are benefits to be gained from tourism, unfortunately, however, it is also true that firms do pose certain problems in certain cases.

Given the above, the focus of this chapter is an attempt to fill such a gap and it aims to add to the existing literature by investigating the direct and indirect relationship between tourism development and income inequality in Mauritius. In this regard, this study uses a rigorous dynamic time series analysis, namely a dynamic vector error correction model (VECM), to carry out the proposed investigation. Such a procedure ensures that the dynamic behaviour of the time series under consideration is properly captured, while simultaneously catering for endogeneity and causality issues. Any feedback and indirect effects which might be present will also be detected within the VECM. The model also simultaneously allows the identification of any bidirectional and/or unidirectional causality between the variables of interest.

The rest of this chapter is organized as follows: the second section discusses the theoretical and empirical literature; the third section provides a brief overview of the evolution of the tourism sector and inequality in Mauritius; the fourth section defines the methodological approach used; the fifth discusses the findings from the study; and, in the final section, some conclusions are presented.

Literature review

The tourism sector is regarded as an important sector having important effects on the economy of a country. Many scholars have investigated the impact of tourism development on the economic growth of a country. For instance, the tourism-led hypothesis has been overwhelmingly discussed in various studies. This theory states that international tourism leads to a significant increase in economic growth. Papers such as those of Sinclair and Stabler (2002) and Samimi, Sadeghi, and Sadeghi (2011) prove this relationship in their studies. Apart from the creation of growth, tourism development has various spill-over effects on an economy. A boost in the tourism sector can help an economy to have structural diversification as well. For instance, we have the structural bonus hypothesis. This hypothesis states that, during industrial development, factor inputs shift to more productive branches (Timmer and Szirmai, 2000). Hence, structural change prompted by tourism development has the potential to promote productivity and economic growth. For instance, Fauzel, Seetanah, and Sannassee (2017) show that tourism development has positively influenced economic growth in Mauritius. In fact, they found that a 1% increase in tourist development contributed to a 0.45% increase in the economic growth of Mauritius. Similar results were obtained by Dritsakis (2004), Kim, Chen, and Jang (2006), and Eugenio-Martín, Morales, and Scarpa (2004). Indeed the tourism industry in Mauritius has recorded a consistently robust performance since 1995. Mauritius has also registered an impressive inflow of tourism receipts.

Tourism development can further spill over to employment in the country. Tourism can promote direct employment, indirect employment, and induced employment. For instance, the tourism industry employs local citizens in hotels, restaurants, and entertainment and tourist services which cater directly for tourists or through the multiplier effect (Haley and Haley, 1997). Furthermore, in view of the prevalence of service quality in the tourism sector, there is a constant demand for training which can only serve to upgrade the skills of local employees working in the industry. And in this regard, skill transfers are common practice for international hotels.

Klytchnikova and Dorosh (2009) argue in their paper that tourism revenues extend beyond hotel operators and employees, tour operators, restaurateurs, and shop workers who sell goods and services to tourists. Expenditure by tourists at least in part extends to local goods and services, which further raises output and incomes. The multiplier effect can thus be huge. The net impact of tourism on income generation and distribution depends on more than just the direct spending by tourists on various commodities and services. Likewise, poverty reduction impacts go beyond the employment and income generated by direct contacts with tourists as a function of multiplier effects of other sectors on output. Hence, the ultimate distribution of incremental revenues from increased production to household groups (poor and non-poor) also varies with several additional factors (labour and capital). This paper found that tourism expansion has benefitted both the economy and the poor in Panama. Pant (2011) investigated tourism's impact on income inequality using cross-country and panel data regressions. In his investigation, he found that the tourism sector has decreased gross income inequality in the sample of countries used in his study.

However, there are conflicting views on whether tourism reduces income inequality or not. For instance, it has been found that tourism expansion in a country with surplus tourist attractions can reduce income inequality. On the other hand, several scholars have found that tourism expansion can increase inequality. For instance, Alam and Paramati (2016) investigated the impact of tourism on income inequality in developing economies. Their investigation utilizes a balanced panel data set from 1991 to 2012 on 49 developing economies around the world. The study found that there is a long-run equilibrium relationship among the variables. Results from long-run elasticities indicate that tourism increases income inequality significantly. Further, the long-run elasticities on squared tourism revenue confirm the existence of the Kuznets curve hypothesis between tourism revenue and income inequalities, meaning that, if the current level of tourism doubles, then it will significantly reduce the income inequality in developing economies.

Similar findings were found by Raza and Shah (2017), who examined the relationship between tourism and income inequality in the top 43 tourist arrival countries by using the data over the period of 1995–2015. The investigation applied advanced econometric techniques which include cross-sectional augmented IPS (CIPS) unit root test, bootstrap co-integration, Pedroni co-integration, fully modified ordinary least squares, and a heterogeneous panel causality technique. They found that that all the variables are co-integrated in the long run. That is, tourism has a positive effect on income inequality overall and in the regional sample. Furthermore, the Kuznets curve hypothesis was also tested and found to exist. This concludes that, if the examined countries increase their tourism revenue, this will help them to reduce income inequality.

Another strand of literature shows that inequality in various regions is increased owing to international tourism development. This was found in the studies by Göymen (2000) and Seckelmann (2002) for the case of Turkey as developed and coastal locations receive more tourism-related investments and superior policies. Hence, given such a situation, these regions have grown much faster, and therefore regional inequality is further enlarged. On the other hand, Krakover (2004) compared the centre and peripheries in Israel and noted that Israel's tourism success in reaching balanced regional economic development is due to special situations, namely, the size of the country, government policies, and security issues. Based on a conditional convergence model, Proença and Soukiazis (2008) observed that international tourism has a noticeable influence on decreasing regional gaps among different locations in Spain, Italy, Greece, and Portugal. Also, Soukiazis and Proença (2008) show that tourism increases the convergence rate within Portugal's NUTS-2 and NUTS-3 regions.

Moreover, when domestic tourism is greater than international tourism both in terms of economic contribution and size, then domestic tourism has the capacity to reduce disparities in less-developed countries (Massidda & Etzo, 2012). In relation to this argument, Seckelmann (2002) argued that south-eastern Turkey and other less-developed regions with more natural and historical resources attract more domestic tourists, which is considered to be an instrument to achieve balanced regional development. Also, Haddad, Porsse, and Rabahy (2013) applied an input–output model to empirically study the regional effect of domestic tourism and found that domestic tourism narrows regional disparity in Brazil.

Li, Chen, Li, and Goh (2016) examined the role of tourism development in reducing regional income inequality in China. The study proposed a spatiotemporal autoregressive model to capture spatial and temporal dependence as well as spatial heterogeneity. They included tourism development as a conditional convergence factor in order to examine whether the convergence speed was accelerated by regional tourism development. They also tested the effects of international and domestic tourism in narrowing regional inequality, both globally and locally. The empirical results indicated that tourism development contributes significantly to the reduction of regional inequality, with domestic tourism making a greater contribution than international tourism.

Income inequality can be affected by other variables as well. For instance, the paper by Bulíř (2001) contributed to the income inequality literature that is based on the traditional Kuznets model. He found that development, state employment, fiscal redistribution, and price stability improve income inequality in a given country. The positive impact of price stability on income distribution is found to be nonlinear. The reduction in inflation from hyperinflationary levels significantly lowers income inequality, and further reduction towards a very low level of inflation seems to bring about negligible additional gains in the Gini coefficient.

Also, inequality can be affected by GDP and vice versa. Hence, it can be said that there is a causal link between GDP and income inequality. Such a finding is found by Brueckner and Lederman (2017), whereby the initial distribution of wealth affects aggregate level of output and investment in the short run and long run.

Analysing the literature, it can be observed that there is mixed evidence on the relationship between tourism development and income inequality. Moreover, it is as clearly perceived that economic growth, inflation, and unemployment all have a significant impact on income inequality.

Overview

Mauritius is a small multicultural island state that has made a great effort to foster equal opportunity for all. The economy, which was a monocrop one based on the sugar sector, has now been transformed into a well-diversified economy. The first phase of economic transformation occurred with the boom of the EPZ sector in the 1980s. This transformation generated lots of employment and growth in the Mauritian economy. This was followed by development in the tourism sector.

The island's clear postcard beaches, calm sea conditions, tropical fauna and flora, complemented by a multi-ethnic, multicultural population that is friendly and welcoming, have contributed to massive tourism development in the country. These tourism assets are Mauritius's main strengths, especially as they are backed up by top-class beach resorts and hotels and reliable and operational services and infrastructures. The hotel industry in Mauritius is a very well-organized industry. The industry has constantly upgraded the quality of accommodation to cater to the demands of the international traveller. Many resorts and hotels have been equipped with the latest technology and services for the indulgence of tourists, with a large variety of services such as saunas, massages, private hot tubs, and well-designed gardens, providing a fairylike atmosphere (see the Mauritius Attractions website).[2]

This sector has contributed a lot towards the economic growth of the country. Tourist arrivals in 2017 reached around 1,341,860, and tourism receipts were about 60.3 billion Mauritian rupees. Tourist arrival in Mauritius has consistently grown in recent years, and, following the government efforts to develop the local tourism sector, it is most likely therefore that the tourism sector will continue growing in coming years. Also, the government has been putting much effort into developing the tourism sector by setting clear policies, eliminating bureaucratic procedures, offering incentives, and creating an environment conducive to investment. Figure 8.1 shows the evolution of tourist arrivals in Mauritius, and the growth can clearly be observed.

However, regarding income inequality and poverty in the country, it can be observed that some proportion of the population is still left out. The Mauritians of African origin are disproportionately present within that group. We can still see jobless growth, growing inequality, and inequalization in the country. The main pillars of the economy remain the tourism and financial sectors; however, the country is experiencing rising unemployment.

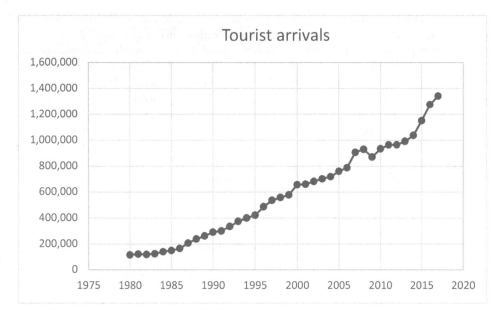

Figure 8.1 Evolution of tourist arrivals in Mauritius

Source: Author computation.

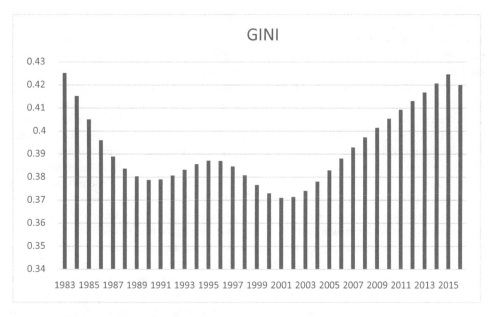

Figure 8.2 Evolution of GINI coefficient in Mauritius

Source: Author computation.

It is now struggling to maintain growth rates at reasonable levels, but the rising inequality and poverty, as well as other associated problems, constitute major challenges. Mauritius has growing unemployment, which currently hovers around 7% and is much more concentrated among women. This rapid increase in youth and female unemployment is very serious, mainly in a context of growing inequalization and rising poverty (Bunwaree, 2014). Inequality in Mauritius has been rising. Measured by the Gini coefficient, inequality in Mauritius is now high. Referring to the World Bank's report "Mauritius – Inclusiveness of growth and shared prosperity", it says "On inequality, Mauritius also fared well compared to its peer middle-income countries, with a Gini coefficient 0.39 in 2012. On the negative side, Mauritius' growth has not been equally shared" (Sulla et al., 2015, p. xi).

Figure 8.2 shows the evolution of the Gini coefficient in Mauritius.

Methodology

Model specifications

The main objective of this study is to investigate the relationship between tourism and income inequality in Mauritius for a period of 34 years (1983–2016). This section describes the model adopted and the empirical indicators of tourism, inequality, and other control variables used in the model. The basic specification of the model is based on the principles of some earlier studies carried out by Pant (2011) and Li et al. (2016). In this regard, the econometric model takes the following functional form:

$$INQ = f(TOU, RGDP, UNEM, DEF, EDU) \tag{1}$$

The model is used to analyse the impact of tourism development on income inequality, which is measured by the Gini coefficient in Mauritius. The variable of interest in this study is tourism development and it is measured by tourists' arrivals. The reason for emphasising tourism is inspired by economic theories. For instance, the Heckscher–Ohlin theorem states that the relative abundance of a country's factor of production will provide the country with a comparative advantage in the production of the goods that use the relatively abundant factor extensively. As per this theory, tourism is relatively more labour-intensive and, hence, it has a comparative advantage because of the excessive quantity of cheap labour. As per this theory, tourism becomes more predominant because of a great amount of the exclusive properties of a country such as sea, sun, climate, mountains, and so on. Likewise, it also converts untradable goods into tradable because both the production and consumption of tourism take place at the destination. Hence, there is an increase in tourism receipts as well as the creation of employment in the country. It thereby allows the reduction of income inequality. Hence, *tourism development* has the potential to reduce the income inequality in the country.

Furthermore, the relationship between aggregate output and the distribution of income is an important topic in macroeconomics. Accordingly, economic theory suggests that there is a link between inequality and aggregate output, and that the effects differ between rich and poor countries. Referring to the work by Galor and Zeira (1993), a model is suggested whereby the credit market imperfections and indivisibilities in human capital investment are used to show that inequality affects aggregate output in the short run as well as in the long run. This model forecasts that the effect of inequality differs across countries and time depending on initial wealth. Brueckner and Lederman (2017) suggest that a causal link exists between inequality and GDP, whereby the GDP of the country also affects income inequality. Hence, the variable *GDP per capita* is included in the model to investigate this link.

114

In addition, it has been observed that income inequality and human capital are linked. Various studies shows that, in poor countries, income inequality and human capital are significantly positively correlated. In rich countries, the relationship between income inequality and human capital is negative (Brueckner and Lederman, 2017). Hence, the secondary enrolment rate is included to capture the link between income inequality and human capital in Mauritius.

Inflation is seen to affect the cost of living of workers and reduces their purchasing power. In fact, fewer studies have been done on the link between inflation and income inequality. As observed by Hudson, Roth, Madden, and Hudson (2015), as inflation goes up, income inequality decreases, reaches a minimum level, and then starts rising again. The findings of their paper show the existence of the Kuznets hypothesis across the countries. Hence, the GDP deflator is included in the model to investigate the link between inflation and income inequality.

Work income is considered to be very important to households' economic status. Households that receive no income from work have far lower levels of overall income and expenditure than households that do receive some income from work. The study by Tregenna and Tsela (2012) shows that the rate of unemployment accounts for a significant part of earnings inequality.

The econometric specification for the present study can be written as follows, as derived from Equation 1:

$$\ln INQ_t = \alpha_0 + \beta_1 \ln TOU_t + \beta 2 \ln GDPt + \beta_3 \ln UNEM_t + \beta_4 \ln DEF_t + \beta_5 \ln EDU_t + \mu_t \qquad (2)$$

where t denotes the time dimension, and the natural logarithms of the variables are employed for ease of interpretation (that is, in percentage terms).

Estimation issues

A VAR approach is used to delineate the relationship between tourism development and income inequality. Such an approach does not impose a priori restriction on the dynamic relations among the different variables. It resembles simultaneous equation modeling, whereby several endogenous variables are considered together. Hence, the VECM linking short-term and long-term causality between tourism and inequality is set as follows:

$$\Delta \ln INQ_t = \alpha_0 + \sum_{j=1}^{n} \alpha_1 \Delta \ln TOU_{t-j} + \sum_{j=1}^{n} \alpha_2 \Delta \ln GDP_{t-j} + \sum_{j=1}^{n} \alpha_3 \Delta \ln UNEM_{t-j} +$$
$$\sum_{j=1}^{n} \alpha_4 \Delta \ln DEF_{t-j} + \sum_{j=1}^{n} \alpha_5 \Delta \ln EDU_{t-j} + \eta ECT_{t-1} + \varepsilon_t \qquad 3$$

The coefficient of the error correction term (ECT_{t-1}) indicates whether there exists a short run relationship among the time series variables.

Furthermore, applying regression to time series data may generate spurious results (Granger and Newbold, 1974; Phillips, 1986), given the possibility of non-stationarity data. As such, undertaking a check as to the stationarity of data is a prerequisite for applying the co-integration test. As a result, the augmented Dickey–Fuller (ADF) test (Dickey and Fuller, 1979, 1981) and the Elliot–Rothenburg–Stock point optimal were applied.

Analysis of findings

From the application of the ADF (Dickey and Fuller, 1979) and Elliot–Rothenburg–Stock point optimal unit-roots tests, it is observed that all the variables are integrated of order 1 and stationary in the first difference. The Johansen maximum likelihood approach is subsequently used to test the presence of co-integration in a vector error correction model in both specifications. Trace statistics and maximal eigenvalue confirm the presence of co-integration, and thus it is concluded that a long run relationship exists in both the above specifications.

Empirical results

The long-run dynamic estimate of Equation 2 is reported below:

$$lnINQ = -4.994 - 0.105lnTOU + 0.465lnGDP + 0.034lnUNEM + 0.0008lnDEF - 0.127 \ln EDU$$

$$*** \qquad *** \qquad *** \qquad *** \qquad *** \qquad **$$

** significant at 5%, ***significant at 1%

The long-run equation yields motivating results. As the main research objective of the study is to analyse the impact of tourism development on income inequality growth in Mauritius, an analysis of the results for the variable LTOU is done first. From the results, it is observed that tourism development has contributed towards reducing income inequality in the economy in the long run, as supported by the negative and significant coefficient of the variable. In fact, a 1% increase in tourism development reduces income inequality by 0.11%. This result is in line with Pant (2011), who investigated tourism's impact on income inequality using cross-country and panel data regressions. His results from the regression analyses show that the tourism sector has decreased gross income inequality in the sample of countries used in his study. Regarding the Mauritian economy, it has undergone a complete transformation since independence. From a monocrop agricultural economy, it has transformed into a well-diversified economy with agro-industry, manufacturing, financial services, tourism, retail trade, and information and communication technology as its main pillars (Three year strategic plan report, Mauritius, 2017).[3] Tourism has contributed towards boosting direct, indirect, and induced employment in both the long run and short run in Mauritius (Fauzel, 2016). This can partly explain the results obtained above. When workers are able to obtain an income, it can significantly reduce income inequality in the country.

Inflation is also included in the model to investigate the impact of increases in general price levels on income inequality. The result shows that an increase in inflation increases income inequality (this supports the results of Bulíř, 2001). This result was predictable, as inflation leads to redistribution of income, and there is a tendency for wealth and income to flow to the rich.

Zooming in on the unemployment results, it can be seen that higher unemployment increases income inequality. Unemployment results in inequality when it continues for succeeding cycles. Unemployment, be it cyclical, structural, or frictional, adds to the despair of the unemployed. Human capital is seen to reduce inequality. The results are as expected and are negative and significant. On the global level, if we consider the case of developing countries, a great deal of effort has been made by these economies to eradicate illiteracy. As a result, the inequality in the distribution of education has been reduced by more than half (Castelló-Climent and Doménech, 2014).

Short-run regression

In the presence of co-integration, we subsequently estimate a VECM including the error correction term, which should allow for an investigation of the dynamic nature of the model. The VECM specification forces the long-run behavior of the endogenous variables to converge towards their co-integrated relationships, which accommodates short-run dynamics. In this study, the VECM is estimated using an optimum lag length of 1. The empirical results of the short-run estimates for Model 1 of the VECM are displayed in Table 8.1.

Table 8.1 is a composite table, where each column can be viewed and analysed as an independent function; that is, each column in the table corresponds to an equation in the VECM. The variable named in the first cell of each column is viewed as the dependent variable. The estimated coefficient of the explanatory variables is reported in the cells. Our focus will be on the first column.

Analysing the short-run estimates of Equation 1 – that is, the regression equation with inequality as the dependent variable – it may be argued that, in the short run, tourism development does have a negative effect on income inequality, albeit the coefficient being smaller, which tends to support the argument that such development takes time to have its full effect on income inequality. For instance, in Mauritius, tourism development has increased considerably from 1970 to 2017. There has been a 7,123% increase in tourists' arrivals. Hence, it can be argued that the results support the Kuznets curve hypothesis. With more tourism development, income inequality has decreased. In this instance, a 1-percentage-point increase in the growth rate of tourism leads to a 0.009-percentage-point decrease in the income inequality after one year. Additionally, but similar to the findings uncovered for the long-run equation, unemployment and inflation are also significant. Regarding the variable GDP, it can be observed that an increase in economic growth leads to a reduction in income inequality. For instance, a 1% increase in GDP has led to a 0.04% decrease in income inequality. This result supports the results of Brueckner and Lederman (2017).

Furthermore, and as discussed previously, the VAR/VECM framework allows us to gauge more interesting insights into endogeneity issues and also allows us to detect any potential indirect effects. Whereas our results show that tourism development influences income inequality, the results reported in Table 8.1 demonstrate that income inequality does not have any effect on tourism development in the country. In this regard, and more specifically referring to the tourism equation depicted in the third column of Table 8.1, it is observed that a reverse causation

Table 8.1 Short-run dynamics (dependent variable: TOU)

Error Correction:	D(LINQ)	D(LTOU)	D(LGDP)	D(LUNEM)	D(LDEF)	D(LEDU)
CointEq	−0.17372 ***	0.85414	−0.311766	3.38043	9.72623	−0.68933
D(LINQ(−1))	0.97298 *	−5.99704	−0.26959	1.84678	−53.8367	0.069603
D(LTOU(−1))	−0.00852 ***	0.09161	0.05654 **	−0.31054	−0.96675	−0.05669 *
D(LGDP(−1))	−0.04019 *	2.12541	−0.30685	0.83216	25.0088	−0.24755
D(LUNEM(−1))	0.00318 ***	0.10193	0.01474 **	0.18558	1.68012	−0.00024 *
D(LDEF(−1))	−0.00013 ***	0.00278 ***	−0.00223 ***	0.00635 **	−0.29880	0.00025 ***
D(LEDU(−1))	0.08917 **	−0.39602	−0.08816	0.63464	6.48259	0.37338
Constant	0.00142 ***	0.04970 **	0.049046 **	−0.02615 *	−1.24611	0.03378 **

Notes: *significant at 10%, ** significant at 5%, ***significant at 1%.

does not exist between income inequality and tourism development. Thus, the results demonstrate a unidirectional relationship flowing from tourism development to income inequality.

In addition, referring to Column 4 of Table 8.1, the above result confirms the tourism-led growth hypothesis, and, hence, an increase in the growth rates leads to tourism development in the present study in the short run.

Given the above, the overall results tend to provide support to the existence of a negative and significant relationship between tourism development and income inequality, both in the short run and in the long run for the case of Mauritius.

Conclusion

Based on the VECM framework adopted in this study, the main objective is to investigate the relationship that might exist between tourism development and income inequality in Mauritius over the period 1983–2016. Referring to the results, it is found that tourism expansion in the country reduced income inequality in the country, both in the long run and in the short run. In fact, the government has played an important role in developing the tourism sector in Mauritius. Various incentives have been given to investors in the tourism sector to boost investment in this field. For instance, liberalization policies have been adopted by the Mauritian government, and thereby foreign investment was allowed to flow into key tourism elements, such as restaurants, yachts, and travel agencies, among others. These policies have not only attracted more investment in the sector, but have also brought the capital needed for further investment, and also the necessary technological know-how and skills, and they have led to the construction of world-class hotels and villas. Direct and indirect employment has also increased to a large extent. Moreover, inflation and unemployment are seen to increase income inequality in the long run, whereas human capital reduces income inequality. Regarding the short-run results, a unidirectional relationship is observed flowing from tourism development to income inequality. Moreover, the results confirm the tourism-led growth hypothesis in the country.

Referring to the results obtained above, the government should further encourage the tourism sector to expand, given its numerous advantages for the economy. It also contributes towards reducing income inequality. The government has been encouraging the building of new hotels, increasing the number of rooms available on the island. It also came up with a policy to launch numerous integrated resort scheme projects and organize a selection of international cultural events. However, other policies could be adopted to further reduce inequality in the country. For instance, the adoption of the minimum wage in Mauritius could contribute to reducing inequality to a large extent. Policies to further increase access to education can also be successful, as well as the adoption of a more progressive tax system.

Notes

1 https://mauritiusattractions.com/mauritius-tourism-i-82.html
2 https://mauritiusattractions.com/mauritius-tourism-i-82.html
3 http://budget.mof.govmu.org/budget2017-18/2017_183-YearPlan.pdf

References

Alam, M.S., and Paramati, S.R. 2016. The impact of tourism on income inequality in developing economies: does Kuznets curve hypothesis exist? *Annals of Tourism Research, 61*, pp. 111–126.
Brueckner, M., and Lederman, D. 2017. *Inequality and Economic Growth: The Role of Initial Income*. The World Bank

Bulíř, A. 2001. Income inequality: does inflation matter? *IMF Staff papers, 48*(1), pp. 139–159.

Bunwaree, S. 2014. The fading developmental state: growing inequality in Mauritius. *Development, 57*(3–4), pp. 578–590.

Castelló-Climent, A., and Doménech, R. 2014. Human capital and income inequality: some facts and some puzzles. Retrieved from BBVA Research: www.bbvaresearch.com/wp-content/uploads/migrados/WP_1228_tcm348-430101.pdf

Dickey, D.A., and Fuller, W.A. 1979. Distribution of the estimators for autoregressive time series with a unit root. *Journal of the American Statistical Association, 74*(366a), pp. 427–431.

Dickey, D.A., and Fuller, W.A. 1981. Likelihood ratio statistics for autoregressive time series with a unit root. *Econometrica: Journal of the Econometric Society, 49*(4), pp. 1057–1072.

Dritsakis, N. 2004. Tourism as a long-run economic growth factor: an empirical investigation for Greece using causality analysis. *Tourism Economics, 10*(3), pp. 305–316.

Eugenio-Martín, J., Martín Morales, N., and Scarpa, R. 2004. Tourism and economic growth in Latin American countries: A panel data approach. FEEM Working Paper.

Fauzel, S. 2016. Tourism and employment spillovers in a small island developing state: a dynamic investigation. *Theoretical Economics Letters, 6*(02), p. 138.

Fauzel, S., Seetanah, B., and Sannassee, R.V. 2017. Analysing the impact of tourism foreign direct investment on economic growth: evidence from a small island developing state. *Tourism Economics, 23*(5), pp. 1042–1055.

Galor, O., and Zeira, J. 1993. Income distribution and macroeconomics. *Review of Economic Studies, 60*, pp. 35–52.

Göymen, K. 2000. Tourism and governance in Turkey. *Annals of Tourism Research, 27*(4), pp. 1025–1048.

Granger, C.W., and Newbold, P. 1974. Spurious regressions in econometrics. *Journal of Econometrics, 2*(2), pp. 111–120.

Haddad, E.A., Porsse, A.A., and Rabahy, W. 2013. Domestic tourism and regional inequality in Brazil. *Tourism Economics, 19*(1), pp. 173–186.

Haley, U.C., and Haley, G.T. 1997. When the tourists flew in: strategic implications of foreign direct investment in Vietnam's tourism industry. *Management Decision, 35*(8), pp. 595–604.

Hudson, S., Roth, M.S., Madden, T.J., and Hudson, R. 2015. The effects of social media on emotions, brand relationship quality, and word of mouth: an empirical study of music festival attendees. *Tourism Management, 47*, pp. 68–76.

Kim, H.J., Chen, M.-H., and Jang, S.C. 2006. Tourism expansion and economic development: the case of Taiwan. *Tourism Management, 27*, pp. 925–933.

Klytchnikova, I.I., and Dorosh, P.A. 2009. How Tourism Can (and Does) Benefit the Poor and the Environment-A Case Study from Panama. https://openknowledge.worldbank.org/handle/10986/10237

Krakover, S. 2004. Tourism development—centres versus peripheries: the Israeli experience during the 1990s. *International Journal of Tourism Research, 6*(2), pp. 97–111.

Li, H., Chen, J.L., Li, G., and Goh, C., 2016. Tourism and regional income inequality: evidence from China. *Annals of Tourism Research, 58*, pp. 81–99.

Massidda, C., and Etzo, I. 2012. The determinants of Italian domestic tourism: a panel data analysis. *Tourism Management, 33*(3), pp. 603–610.

Pant, S. 2011. *The Impact of Tourism on Income Inequality: An Econometric Assessment.* Doctoral dissertation, Reed College.

Phillips, P.C. 1986. Understanding spurious regressions in econometrics. *Journal of Econometrics, 33*(3), pp. 311–340.

Proença, S., and Soukiazis, E. 2008. Tourism as an economic growth factor: a case study for Southern European countries. *Tourism Economics, 14*(4), pp.791–806.

Raza, S.A., and Shah, N. 2017. Tourism growth and income inequality: does Kuznets curve hypothesis exist in top tourist arrival countries? *Asia Pacific Journal of Tourism Research, 22*(8), pp. 874–884.

Samimi, A.J., Sadeghi, S., and Sadeghi, S. 2011. Tourism and economic growth in developing countries: P-VAR approach. *Middle-East Journal of Scientific Research, 10*(1), pp. 28–32.

Seckelmann, A. 2002. Domestic tourism – a chance for regional development in Turkey? *Tourism Management, 23*(1), pp. 85–92.

Sinclair, M.T., and Stabler, M. 2002. *The Economics of Tourism, Advances in Tourism.* London: Routledge

Soukiazis, E., and Proença, S. 2008. Tourism as an alternative source of regional growth in Portugal: a panel data analysis at NUTS II and III levels. *Portuguese Economic Journal*, 7(1), pp. 43–61.

Sulla, V., Munoz Moreno, R., Da Maia, C.C.P., Klapper, L., Van Oudheusden, P., Guven, M.U., et al. 2015. *Mauritius – Inclusiveness of growth and shared prosperity* (English). Washington, DC: World Bank Group. http://documents.worldbank.org/curated/en/331711468190164152/Mauritius-Inclusiveness-of-growth-and-shared-prosperity

Timmer, M.P., and Szirmai, A. 2000. Productivity growth in Asian manufacturing: the structural bonus hypothesis examined. *Structural Change and Economic Dynamics*, 11(4), pp. 371–392.

Tregenna, F., and Tsela, M. 2012. Inequality in South Africa: the distribution of income, expenditure and earnings. *Development Southern Africa*, 29(1), pp. 35–61.

9

LOCAL ECONOMIC DEVELOPMENT, RURAL TOURISM AND COMMUNITIES

Southern African perspectives

Deserè Kokt and Johan Hattingh

Introduction

Tourism in rural areas has the potential to convert local resources, such as archaeological sites, deserts, forests and mountains, into economic value propositions that can create economic growth and employment (National Department of Tourism, 2012). According to Spenceley and Meyer (2012), some of the poorest regions in the world have rich cultural and natural assets that can attract tourists. As tourists travel to less developed regions, they spend money on travel, accommodation, excursions, food, drinks and shopping. This creates opportunities for communities to generate income by offering goods and services (Page & Connel, 2014; National Department of Tourism, 2017).

Local economic development (LED) is visible in a variety of forms in the international world, including aggressive place promotion, urban entrepreneurialism and community-based economic strategies. LED can manifest itself either in direct, community-based, pro-poor interventions and/or as pro-market endeavours. The purpose of LED is to promote economic growth and job creation in rural areas which could contribute to poverty alleviation and community upliftment. LED thus enables the creation of economic growth and prosperity by coordinating interaction with public, private and non-governmental sector partners.

In this regard, the Report on Economic Development in Africa (UNCTAD, 2017) asserts that LED is about local people working together to achieve sustainable economic growth that brings economic benefits and quality of life to all in the community. Therefore, the core focus of LED is partnerships, economic sustainability, job creation and the improvement of community well-being. This chapter provides a detailed background on LED by focusing on the importance of rural tourism, community-based tourism and route tourism and LED's potential to impact the livelihood of especially poor communities. Although the chapter reflects mostly on southern Africa, it provides valuable insights that can apply to other LED and rural tourism initiatives.

Explaining local economic development

LED could be viewed as an attempt to address socio-economic problems, including low economic growth, high levels of unemployment and poverty. LED offers an opportunity for local governments, the private sector and communities to work together in enhancing competitiveness and thus create sustainable growth for local areas. The goal of LED is further to create a conducive environment for business development, enhancing local skills and engaging with relevant stakeholders (Rogerson & Nel, 2016). The concept of LED has gained widespread acceptance internationally as a locality-based response to the challenges posed by globalisation, devolution and local-level opportunities and crises. LED is also firmly included on the agendas of many national governments and international agencies, such as the World Bank, that acknowledge its prominent role in urban development and business promotion.

The World Bank (2017) defines LED as the process by which public, business and nongovernmental sector partners work collectively to create better conditions for economic growth and sustainability. The purpose of LED is to build up the economic capacity of local areas to improve their economic future and create quality of life for all. Nel and Humphrys (1999) describe LED as the process by which individuals or organisations use resources to modify and/or expand economic activity to the benefit of the majority of community members. LED is essentially a process by which local government and/or community-based groups manage their existing resources and enter into partnership arrangements with the private sector, or with each other, to create new jobs and stimulate economic activity in a particular area.

A major international development organisation that has actively engaged in LED is the German Technical Cooperation Agency (GTZ). The GTZ maintains that LED is an:

> ongoing process by which key stakeholders and institutions from all spheres of society, the public and private sector as well as civil society work together to create a unique advantage for the locality and its firms tackle market failures, remove bureaucratic obstacles for local businesses and strengthen the competitiveness of local firms.
>
> *(Ruecker & Trah, 2007)*

The above definition emphasises that LED is an ongoing process and recognises that any effort to stimulate the economic growth of a local economy is bound to involve large-scale systemic change. The focus of GTZ is on a market-driven approach, and it considers LED activities as intrinsically opportunistic (Ruecker & Trah, 2007). The overall purpose of LED is to create an economic structure that facilitates and enables improved growth. The pursuit of growth is, however, not enough, and there should also be an emphasis on enhancing the quality of life of community members.

Hristova and Tast (2015) describe LED as a process by which local authorities cooperate with the public sector, business community and NGOs in order to create a more appropriate environment for economic development and decreased unemployment. Its objectives are to stimulate investments that will promote sustained growth in local communities. These definitions show that the core focus of LED concerns partnerships, economic sustainability, job creation and the improvement of quality of life and infrastructure at a local level.

According to the South African Local Government Association (Cohen, 2010), LED is achieved when a community's standard of living is preserved and increased through a process of human and physical development. These developments should be based on the principles of equity and sustainability. The concept of LED extends beyond focusing on economic growth as it is about creating development within local communities. It recognises that a necessary component of this development is the provision of employment and the generation of income to enable local communities to invest in the necessary services, facilities and infrastructure. The concept of 'community economic development' is closely related to LED, with the specific purpose to improve the quality of life of local communities (Cohen, 2010).

Global perspectives on local economic development

Europe acted as the cradle for the development of LED, which had its origins in the late 1960s and early 1970s – a period of global economic restructuring and decentralisation in the cities of the Global North. During this time, many former industries were in decline – including the textile industry, shipbuilding, steel-making and other heavy industries, and many relocated to overseas locations. Similar trends occurred in the US, where American multinationals, which initially benefitted the US economy, ended up hurting local economies when factories closed, leaving a trail of unemployment and depressed regions (Blakely & Leigh, 2010).

This global restructuring created a need to develop and adopt novel technologies, and new strategies were put in place to attract investments. This included policies on promoting LED that focused on retaining and attracting investments through place marketing and investment attraction, as well as offering incentives such as grants, tax breaks or loans, and the development of hard and soft infrastructure. The areas in decline were identified and rezoned for new development through special legislation to attract new public- and private-sector investments (Nel & Rogerson, 2005).

A mix of LED strategies was utilised, ranging from encouraging inward investment, fostering new innovation, nurturing creative environments and promoting start-ups to coordinating infrastructure investments and assisting small businesses to grow. Systemic competitiveness was increased by encouraging and supporting networking and collaboration between businesses, including public and private partnerships, supporting cluster growth and quality-of-life improvements among local communities. This competitiveness in regional, national and global markets informs current LED practices worldwide.

Pressure to stimulate LED has come from at least two main directions: On the one hand, there are expressions of uneven and inequitable outcomes in the economic landscape and, on the other hand, there are reflections of variability in the aspirations and concerns of actors about the pace and extent of local investment (Le Heron, 2009). Although LED was initially applied to Western Europe and North America, it subsequently spread to other parts of the world. With increasing globalisation and growing decentralisation, the 1990s saw a diffusion of LED ideas and practices from the Global North to the South. The difference in LED application between the North and South was that the North focused on the promotion of self-reliance in local spaces, whereas, in the South, it was applied as a coping strategy for underdeveloped areas.

Local economic development in southern Africa

Over the past two decades, sub-Saharan Africa has been greatly affected by decentralisation and reduced central state control in an period of accelerating globalisation (World Bank, 2017). One important area has been the spread and growth of LED as a component of development planning. The importance of LED across sub-Saharan Africa is signalled by the activities of the United Cities and Local Governments of Africa (UCLG-A). The UCLG-A is an association of local governments, individuals and entities that acts as a united voice and representative of local governments. As part of its mission of building African unity within and driving development through the grass roots, it identified LED as one of six priority areas for the period 2006–2015 (Swinburn, Yatta, Kreutz & Beez, 2007).

Although LED research is less prolific in African countries outside South Africa, many efforts have been made to establish LED as an alternative development approach across Africa. The main challenges and constraints that were identified were a lack of government capacity in many African countries, poor governance and data shortcomings, which often hamper the correct identification of a locality's strengths and weaknesses and, consequently, the making of well-informed policy choices. Local and regional governments generally face constraints such as a lack of funding and government capacity with regard to skills and infrastructure, which may obstruct the development and implementation of successful strategies (Rodríguez-Pose & Tijmstra, 2007).

Some misgivings exist as to whether an 'enabling environment' for the design and implementation of LED exists outside South Africa (Rodríguez-Pose & Tijmstra, 2007). Most of the research on African LED activities centres around the South African context, mainly because LED is legislated as a reform mandate for local governments (Nel & Rogerson, 2005; Rivett-Carnac, 2009; Rogerson, 2016). South Africa has become a laboratory for LED practice and research, and many LED-related aspects have been exported to other African countries. In the South African context, the most important policy documents on tourism are the White Paper on Development and Promotion of Tourism in South Africa (DEAT, 1996) the White Paper on Local Government (CoGTA, 1998), the National Development Plan: Vision 2030 (National Planning Commission, 2011) and the National Tourism Sector Strategy (NTSS) (National Department of Tourism, 2017).

The vision set out in the South African Tourism White Paper is to develop the tourism sector as a national priority in a sustainable manner so that it would contribute significantly to the improvement of the quality of life of every citizen. The South African Tourism White Paper further identifies the need to promote community participation in tourism, and many local authorities have embarked upon what often amounts to pro-poor tourism development strategies, such as the promotion of crafts, township visits (the so-called 'black residential areas' created under apartheid) and cultural tourism.

The White Paper on Local Government (South African Government, 1998) advocates that, 'Local Government should be committed to working with citizens and groups within the community to find sustainable ways to meet their social, economic and material needs and improve the quality of their lives'. The White Paper directly states that LED should be a developmental outcome of municipalities, as they can play an essential role in advancing the creation of jobs and boosting the local economy. Therefore, municipalities must first invest in the basics, such as providing good-quality, cost-effective services and making the local area a pleasant place to live and work (Rivett-Carnac, 2009). In terms of the White Paper, municipalities are given the responsibility towards the people within their area of jurisdiction and are, therefore, accountable for all actions. It also highlights the following challenges facing the South African municipalities:

- Addressing skewed settlement patterns, which can be considered functionally inefficient and costly,
- Addressing redistribution between and within local areas, as there is an extreme concentration of taxable economic resources in formerly so-called 'white' areas,
- Concentrating on creating viable municipal institutions for dense rural settlements close to the borders of the former homelands (areas created during apartheid such as Transkei) with minimal access to services and little or no economic base,
- Addressing the spatial separations and disparities between towns and townships and urban sprawl, and
- Creating municipal institutions which recognise the linkages and dependencies between urban and rural settlements.

The White Paper also puts forward tools, techniques and approaches to create a framework in which municipalities can develop their own strategies for meeting local needs and promoting the social and economic development of communities (South African Government, 1998).

In the neighbouring country of Namibia, LED is still in its infancy; however, the country adopted its White Paper on LED in 2008, supported by the GTZ. The GTZ is also behind the Local Economic Development Agency, which was set up within the Ministry of Regional and Local Government, Housing and Rural Development to support municipalities in developing LED strategies and processes. The vision in the Namibian White Paper acknowledges that national efforts are geared to enhance the conditions for greater global competitiveness in the country.

The White Paper on LED in Namibia further asserts that it is at the local and regional level that opportunities are identified through the active involvement of local people and the responsiveness of public and private actors. It does not prescribe any specific action to local players, but aims to create a common understanding of LED as a concept and provide practical examples of initiatives which are drawn from local and international LED practices. The White Paper also provides a framework for local and regional development and adds value to national development initiatives, without being prescriptive.

Local economic development through rural tourism

The term 'rural' can be explained as referring to areas of either low population density or poor economic development situated in non-First World urban areas. The concept of 'rural tourism' is explained by Gopal, Varma and Gopinathan (2008) as visiting an area dominated by natural and farming environments where specific natural, economic and sociocultural features are harmoniously integrated to create unique tourist products. Rural tourism is an activity that takes place in a rural setting and is aimed at tourists who wants to experience a rural lifestyle. This experience usually includes local arts and crafts, culture, adventure and heritage. Rural tourism represents a large portion of the tourism landscape in southern Africa.

Rural tourism is dependent on aspects such as infrastructure, connectivity and sanitation because it relies heavily on the movement of tourists to a particular area. The provision of basic infrastructure is critical for tourism growth and poverty alleviation, and a lack of infrastructure and other services may frustrate the development of rural tourism. Rural tourism centres around tourists' experiences and being exposed to aspects such as culture (e.g. visiting arts and crafts markets) and heritage, as well as adventure and other activities (Meyer & Meyer, 2015; Rivett-Carnac, 2009; Viljoen & Tlabela, 2006).

Rural tourism has become a developmental tool for many rural areas as it offers a means to foster long-term economic and social development. In this regard Viljoen and Tlabela (2006) have identified five features of rural areas:

- Rural areas are spaces where there are human settlements which occupy only small patches of land. Most of these patches of land are dominated by fields and pastures, woods and forest, water, mountains and deserts,
- Rural areas are places where the majority of people spend most of their time working on farms,
- Rural areas are characterised by an abundance of relatively cheap lands,
- Rural areas have high transaction costs, associated with long distances and poor infrastructure, and
- Rural areas have geographical destinations which increase the costs of political transactions and magnify the possibility of elite capture of urban bias.

There was a dramatic growth in rural tourism after World War II, especially owing to the advancement of transportation systems enabling tourists to travel to remote areas. During the first half of the 20th century, rural tourism played a major role in nation-building and became an integral part of diverse rural economies. In this sense, nature became a tourist product, and rural tourism began to dominate land usage. Cole (2009) links factors such as higher incomes, smaller families, changing demographics, lower transportation costs, improved living standards, peace and tranquillity, interest in healthy lifestyles, growing interests in heritage, the development of infrastructure, more hospitable environments for tourists and an increase in leisure time as reasons that contributed to the development of rural tourism. Rural tourism was further aided by raised living standards and the increase in ownership of motor vehicles during the 1960s and 1970s, which improved accessibility to rural areas.

Any form of tourism that provides access to rural life, local art, culture and heritage and that benefits the local community economically and fosters interaction between the tourists and the community can be termed rural tourism. A well-planned tourism destination could provide multiple points of interaction, combining sites of agri-tourism (e.g., wineries, orchards), ecotourism, cultural tourism, and outdoor sports and recreation opportunities (Smith, Davis & Pike, 2010). Rural tourism is therefore a subset of tourism that may consist of farm/agri-tourism, cultural tourism, nature tourism, adventure tourism and ecotourism.

Rural tourism can also imply agri-tourism or farm tourism. Farm tourism is when accommodation for rural tourists is provided on farms, and the core activity takes place in the wider rural area. Agri-tourism occurs when the purpose of the visit has a specific agricultural focus such as being with animals. Rural tourism can incorporate aspects that include not only farm tourism and agri-tourism, but also activities such as camping, staying in lodges, going on safari drives, visiting craft markets and/or cultural displays/villages, engaging in adventure sports, participating in hiking trails, visiting heritage sites, attending musical events or any other activity that takes place in a rural setting (Smith et al., 2010). Rural tourism in the southern African context usually showcases rural life, arts, culture and heritage to benefit local communities and enable interaction between the tourists and community members for a more enriching experience (Ministry of Regional and Local Government, Housing and Rural Development, 2008; National Department of Tourism, 2012).

Types of rural tourism

There are two types of rural tourism:

- The first type is 'pure' rural tourism that conjures up images of the unspoilt, idyllic countryside with activities related to enjoying the setting. This type of rural tourism typically targets a number of niche markets offering a range of the traditional, peaceful rural experiences such as hiking, fishing, picnicking, observing wildlife and enjoying the countryside and its people.
- The second type of rural tourism is a large-scale, high-impact phenomenon in which the rural location is less important. This type of tourism imposes urban values on the rural space and attracts large numbers of people. These people collectively participate in activities such as leisure shopping and competitive events such as cycle races, marathons, and 4×4 rallies.

As tourists want memorable experiences more than just service delivery, experiences form an integral part of tourism, and visitors travel away from their usual places of residence to seek new and different experiences. As rural tourism lends itself to poverty alleviation in rural areas where few other possibilities for economic development exist, it can often provide opportunities to women and the informal sector. This emphasises the pro-poor component of rural tourism (Rogerson, 2015), as it can place more product owners in a better position to offer authentic rural experiences to tourists.

The impact of rural tourism on local communities

As local communities are not always the proactive recipients of the benefits of tourism, they often negotiate and modify their environment to create opportunities. There may be negative consequences for using the resources of rural communities for tourism development. As the quality of available resources might diminish, it can limit further developments in a particular locality. Also, the deterioration of the quality of resources can have a negative impact on the tourist product and reduce the profitability of a destination, which can lead to less tourism (Rogerson, 2015).

Rural tourism can result in aggression against the environment and the way of life of local communities, with no real compensation for individual members. Local communities may be exposed to people that ascribe to different cultural values, which can influence their economic situation, morality, social structures, politics and local identity (Rivett-Carnac, 2009). Rural tourism might not generate sufficient income to recover considerable developmental costs. Although tourism could facilitate an inflow of income into a rural area, much of the economic gains could leak out of the area if local residents do not get their fair share of the profits. There should thus be proper respect between tourists and hosts, and local communities should fully participate in the activities. There should also be a fair distribution of economic gains and effective protection of the environment and local resources. Among the economic objectives set out in the South African Tourism White Paper, it is clear that tourism should be used to aid with LED and to promote tourism development in a balanced manner (DEAT, 1996; CoGTA, 1998).

Community-based tourism as a form of rural tourism

Community-based tourism (CBT) as a form of rural tourism and LED is based on the active participation of local communities (Rogerson, 2013). This places emphasis on ownership, management and the control of tourism projects by the local community. Active community participation in the development of their tourism industry is central to CBT. CBT should be regarded as a development strategy based on community resources, needs and decisions (Donaldson, 2013).

According to Zahra and McGehee (2013), tourism literature has advocated for the inclusion of local communities in tourism since the 1980s. Developing tourism from the local community level is considered crucial for the success of tourism at the national level. This is because communities play a key role in the sustainability of the tourism product, and their positive interaction with tourists helps to build a good image for a destination. Similarly, the Rural Tourism Strategy of South Africa (National Department of Tourism, 2012) points out that the goal of CBT is to benefit indigenous people and villagers through tourism ventures. It aims to ensure that the members of local communities have a high degree of control and/or ownership over the tourism activities and the resources required.

The UNTWO (2008) has guided many local communities to develop tourism under the principle of sustainability through the development of CBT projects. Telfer and Sharpley (2008) stress two major goals for CBT. The first is social sustainability, which implies community participation and shared socio-economic benefits. The second is respect for local cultures, identities, traditions and heritage; hence, communities and the people involved should be depicted in ways that are ethically sustainable and acceptable. CBT must, therefore, emphasise community empowerment and ownership as a means to sustain community growth.

Community participation, involvement and a sense of ownership are essential elements to ensure the sustainability, viability and success of LED and CBT (Meyer & Meyer, 2015). This focus on the community can be seen as a bottom–up approach to development, where the local people on the bottom line of the development ladder can take control of their future and tailor tourism development around their needs (Hamzah & Hampton, 2012). However, not all communities are suited to engage in CBT, and it is imperative that an assessment of a community's tourism potential should be made beforehand.

In assessing the potential for CBT development, the initial planning stage should begin with an inventory of potential tourism products within a community. Potential tourism products are known as 'CBT assets' and can range from nature-based activities, to local handicrafts, to cultural events (Cooper, Fletcher, Gilbert & Wanhill, 2005). Tourists are initially lured to an area because of its unique features; therefore, the assessment process should begin with an evaluation of the characteristics that make a community unique. Cultural assets, a destination's traditions and ways of life, are aspects that can form part of what a community can offer (Brida & Pulina, 2010). For this reason, it is important to involve communities in tourism development as this may reduce the negative impact of mass tourism.

CBT can empower local communities, improve skills and bring about a sense of ownership that is beneficial for the development of rural areas. In addition, CBT should ensure local control of activities to increase the benefits to community members. If community members are not involved in CBT initiatives, they may resent tourism and the influx of visitors to their area (Rogerson & Nel, 2016). Communities can be empowered through CBT in four ways: economically, psychologically, socially and politically.

In an economic sense, tourism may bring long-term financial benefits to a community. If the available funds are spread throughout the community, there may be notable improvements in local services and infrastructure. Tourism can psychologically enhance the self-esteem of community members because of outside recognition of the uniqueness and value of the local culture, natural resources and traditional knowledge. Increased confidence in the community may lead to members seeking further education and training opportunities.

On a social level, increased tourism may maintain or enhance the equilibrium within communities. Community cohesion may be improved as individuals and families cooperate to build a successful industry. On a political level, a community's political structure may provide a representational forum through which people can raise questions and concerns pertaining to tourism initiatives. This will ensure that agencies that initiate the implementation of new tourism ventures source the opinions of community members, ensuring that all members are represented in the decision-making processes (Scheyvens, 2002).

Communities are often split into various groups based on class, gender and ethnic origin, and certain families are likely to lay claim to privileges based on their status in the community. It is thus unlikely that community members will have equitable access and involvement in tourism development and its ensuing benefits. Another challenge mentioned by Scheyvens (2002) is that communities often lack information, resources and power in relation to other stakeholders in the tourism environment, which makes them vulnerable to exploitation. Some barriers to the implementation of CBT can relate to sociopolitical traditions, gender, ethnicity, accessibility of information, a lack of awareness, economic issues, a lack of cooperation and so on.

The South African Tourism White Paper identified a number of key factors hindering the tourism industry's potential to achieve meaningful growth and community benefit, which can also apply to tourism in Namibia. These factors include:

- Limited integration of communities and previously neglected groups,
- A lack of market access and market knowledge,
- A lack of interest on the part of existing operators to build partnerships with communities and non-traditional suppliers, and
- A lack of appropriate institutional structures (DEAT, 1996).

In addition to this, the international donor and research communities have raised concerns about the viability of CBT enterprises, questioning whether the significant amount of grant money provided by donors and NGOs to CBT enterprises is justifiable based on the benefits to the community and the environment. Communities, particularly rural ones, are often on the front line in service provisions but last to receive the benefits of their efforts. In Namibia, out of eight community–private sector joint ventures, initiated between 1996 and 1998, only two reached operational stage, while the remaining six did not realise their potential (Ashley & Jones, 2001).

CBT has demonstrated the potential to generate significant returns on conservation, socio-economic and business objectives as ventures have spread and evolved. However, most CBT projects have not contributed to local poverty reduction or delivered the envisaged sufficient incentives for conservation, which is a major concern. Although some CBT tourism schemes have been widely adopted, many under the guise of eco-tourism, their successes are questionable.

Route tourism as a way to enhance rural tourism

Route tourism is another way in which rural tourism, CBT and LED could be enhanced. The concept of 'route tourism' refers to an initiative designed to link together a group of tourism activities and attractions under a unified theme to promote local tourism by encouraging visitors to travel from one location to the next on a demarcated route (Rogerson, 2007). Route tourism can include a pro-poor element, namely an explicit agenda to include and promote business operations for poor communities.

The types and numbers of tourists that are attracted by route tourism vary considerably from one route to another. Route tourism can increase the economic benefits through the development of small businesses supplying goods and services, which significantly enhances job creation opportunities. Local product owners can expand their business when they are incorporated as part of a tourism route (Meyer, 2004). This especially applies to rural areas where the establishment of a tourism route can benefit local communities as it is envisaged that a route may lead to increased tourism.

Meyer (2004) argues that tourism routes and networks have been identified as a possible means to encourage community development. The heightened interest in community and pro-poor activities of rural LED has meant that route tourism has become increasingly important. In some parts of the world, the concepts of rural trails, heritage routes or scenic roads are used, particularly in the context of promoting rural tourism. One example of a heritage route with sponsorship by UNESCO is the Jesus Christ Route, a flagship project in Palestine which aims to mobilise a selection of cultural, religious and natural heritage resources (tangible and intangible) in the area to create internationally marketed, high-quality tourism products.

Cultural routes can be used as a developmental tool for marginal or rural areas because they have the potential to stimulate economic activity and bring tourists into local areas. Therefore, it is important to include local communities in the decision-making process, especially in the planning and developmental phase of route development. The Liberation Heritage Route in the Mpumalanga Province of South Africa had a participatory management approach. Much effort was made to include local communities by identifying and prioritising heritage sites to allow them more ownership (The Liberation Heritage Route, n.d.). The commitment to local small-business development should be central to any tourism route planning that is linked to LED objectives.

When the objectives of increasing the overall appeal of a destination, increasing the length of stay and spending by tourists, attracting new tourists or repeat visitors, and increasing the sustainability of the tourism product are met, diffusion of visitors and dispersal of income from tourism are likely to follow. Furthermore, the overall appeal of a destination is likely to increase, as well as the length of stay and the amount of money tourists spend in the region. Tourism routes should be initiated with the objective of attracting new tourists or repeat visitors to ensure the sustainability of the tourism product.

The main purpose of route tourism is to create historical, economic and cultural linkages between individual cities, smaller towns, tourist-historical cities and regions. A well-organised association (or forum) in control of a tourism route is an important component of route tourism and LED, as it may lead to the growth of not only the tourism route itself, but also the local region (Proos, Kokt & Hattingh, 2017).

Summary

This chapter provided an overview of the importance of LED in a developing-country context – hence the focus on southern Africa. Although some global perspectives were alluded to, the main focus was on the important role played by South Africa in advancing LED. Some of the mechanisms by which LED could be realised include rural tourism, CBT and route tourism. These mechanisms can only have a real impact on poor communities if there is collaboration between the various stakeholders and if communities share in the profits that can be generated through tourism development.

References

Ashley, C., & Jones, B. (2001). Joint ventures between communities and tourism investors: experience in South Africa. *International Journal of Tourism Research, 3*(5), 407–423.

Blakely, E.J., & Leigh, N. (2010). *Planning local economic development: Theory and practice*. Los Angeles, CA: Sage.

Brida, J.G., & Pulina, M. (2010). *A literature review on the tourism-led growth hypothesis*. Working paper. Cagliari, Sardinia.

CoGTA. (1998). *The White Paper on Local Government*. Retrieved from www.cogta.gov.za/cgta_2016/wp-content/uploads/2016/06/whitepaper_on_Local-Gov_1998.pdf

Cohen, D. (2010). SALGA LED position paper. Key issues in local economic development in South Africa and a potential role for SALGA. Retrieved from www.salga.org.za/Documents/Knowledge Hub/SALGA Position Papers/SALGA-Position-Paper-on-Local-Economic-Development.pdf

Cole, S. (2009). A logistic tourism model, resort cycles, globalization and chaos. *Annals of Tourism Research, 36*(4), 689–714.

Cooper, C., Fletcher, J., Gilbert, D., & Wanhill, S. (2005). *Tourism principles and practice*. Harlow, UK: Pearson Education.

Department of Environmental Affairs and Tourism (DEAT). (1996). The White Paper on the development and promotion of tourism in South Africa. Retrieved from www.tourism.gov.za/AboutNDT/Publications/Tourism%20White%20Paper.pdf

Donaldson, R. (2013). *Small town tourism in South Africa*. Stellenbosch, SA: Springer.

Gopal, R., Varma, S., & Gopinathan, R. (2008). Rural tourism development: constraints and possibilities with special reference to agri-tourism. In *Conference Tourism Proceedings*, New Delhi (pp. 512–523).

Hamzah, A., & Hampton, M.P. (2012). Resilience and non-linear change in island tourism. *Tourism Geographies*, 15(1), 43–67.

Hristova, S., & Tast, J. (2015). The emergence and significance of local economic development. *Economic Development / Ekonomiski Razvoj*, 17(3), 379–397. Retrieved from https://liverpool.idm.oclc.org/login?url=http://search.ebscohost.com/login.aspx?direct=true&db=bth&AN=112638021&site=eds-live&scope=site

Le Heron, R. (2009). 'Globalisation' and 'local economic development' in a globalising world: critical reflections on the theory-practice relation. In J.E. Rowe (Ed.), *Theories of local economic development: linking theory to practice* (pp. 93–111). Farnham, UK: Ashgate.

Meyer, D. (2004). Tourism routes and gateways: key issues for the development of tourism routes and gateways and their potential for pro-poor tourism. Retrieved from www.odi.org/sites/odi.org.uk/files/odi-assets/publications-opinion-files/4040.pdf

Meyer, D.F., & Meyer, N. (2015). The role and impact of tourism on local economic development: a comparative study. *African Journal for Physical Health Education, Recreation & Dance*, 211(2111), 197–214.

Ministry of Regional and Local Government, Housing and Rural Development. (2008). LED White Paper for Namibia. Retrieved from www2.giz.de/wbf/4tDx9kw63gma/Namibia_RLED_White_Paper.pdf

National Department of Tourism. (2012). The National Rural Tourism Strategy. Retrieved from www.tourism.gov.za/AboutNDT/Branches1/domestic/Documents/National Rural Tourism Strategy.pdf

National Department of Tourism. (2017). National Tourism Sector Strategy (NTSS) 2016–2026. Retrieved from www.governmentpublications.lib.uct.ac.za/news/national-tourism-sector-strategy-ntss-2016-2026

National Planning Commission. (2011). National Development Plan 2030. Retrieved from https://www.gov.za/issues/national-development-plan-2030

Nel, E. (2007). Critical reflections on urban and local development in Africa. *Environment & Planning C: Government & Policy*, 25(4), 459–465.

Nel, E., & Humphrys, G. (1999). Local economic development: policy and practice in South Africa. *Development Southern Africa*, 6(2), 277–289.

Nel, E., & Rogerson, C.M. (2005). *Local economic development in the developing world: the experience of southern Africa*. New Brunswick, NJ, and London: Transaction Press.

Proos, E., Kokt, D., & Hattingh, J.L. (2017). Marketing and management effectiveness of Free State section of Maloti Drakensberg Route. *South African Journal for Research in Sport, Physical Education & Recreation*, 39(1), 135–147.

Rivett-Carnac, K. (2009). Local economic development, tourism and land use choices. Retrieved from www.dbsa.org/EN/About-Us/Publications/Documents/DPD No 4. Local economic development, tourism and land use choices.pdf

Rodríguez-Pose, A., & Tijmstra, S.A.R. (2007). Local economic development in sub-Saharan Africa. *Environment & Planning C: Government & Policy*, 25(4), 516–536.

Rogerson, C.M. (2007). Tourism routes as vehicles for local economic development in South Africa: the example of the Magaliesberg Meander. *Urban Forum*, 18(2), 49–68.

Rogerson, C.M. (2013). Urban tourism, economic regeneration and inclusion: evidence from South Africa. *Local Economy: The Journal of the Local Economy Policy Unit*, 28(2), 188–202.

Rogerson, C.M. (2015). Tourism and regional development: the case of South Africa's distressed areas. *Development Southern Africa*, 32(3), 277–291.

Rogerson, C.M. (2016). Climate change, tourism and local economic development in South Africa. *Local Economy*, 31(1–2), 322–331.

Rogerson, C.M., & Nel, E. (2016). Planning for local economic development in spaces of despair: key trends in South Africa's 'distressed areas'. *Local Economy*, 31(1–2), 124–141.

Ruecker, A., & Trah, G. (2007). Local and regional economic development: towards a common framework for GTZ's LRED interventions in South Africa. Retrieved from http://citeseerx.ist.psu.edu/viewdoc/download?doi=10.1.1.496.44&rep=rep1&type=pdf

Scheyvens, R. (2002). *Tourism for development: empowering communities*. Themes in Tourism Series. Harlow, UK: Pearson Education.

Smith, S., Davis, N., & Pike, J. (2010). Rural tourism development: a case study of the Shawnee Hills Wine Trail in Southern Illinois. *Journal of Extension*, 48(5), 1–11.

South African Government. (1998). White Paper on the Development and Promotion of Tourism in South Africa. Retrieved from www.tourism.gov.za/AboutNDT/Publications/Tourism White Paper. pdf

Spenceley, A., & Meyer, D. (2012). Tourism and poverty reduction: theory and practice in less economically developed countries. *Journal of Sustainable Tourism*, 20(3), 297–317.

Swinburn, G., Yatta, F., Kreutz, C., & Beez, P. (2007). Local economic development network of Africa. Concept paper, United Cities and Local Governments of Africa (UCLGA). Retrieved from www.uclgafrica.org/AboutUCLGA.htm

Telfer, D.J., & Sharpley, R. (2008). *Tourism and development in the developing world (Routledge perspectives on development)*. Abingdon, UK: Routledge.

The Liberation Heritage Route. (n.d.). Retrieved from www.mpumalanga.com/routes/liberation-heritage-route-rt6094

UNCTAD. (2017). *Economic development in Africa, Report 2017*. Retrieved from http://unctad.org/en/PublicationsLibrary/aldcafrica2017_en.pdf

UNTWO. (2008). Tourism Highlights. Retrieved from www.e-unwto.org/doi/pdf/10.18111/9789284413560

Viljoen, J., & Tlabela, K. (2006). *Rural tourism development in South Africa: trends and challenges*. Pretoria: HSRC.

World Bank. (2017). What is local economic development? Retrieved from http://web.worldbank.org/WBSITE/EXTERNAL/TOPICS/EXTURBANDEVELOPMENT/EXTLED/0,,contentMDK:20185186~menuPK:399161~pagePK:148956~piPK:216618~theSitePK:341139,00.html

Zahra, A., & McGehee, N.G. (2013). Volunteer tourism: a host community capital perspective. *Annals of Tourism Research, 42*, 22–45.

10

TRACING THE ECONOMIC IMPACTS OF ADVENTURE TRAVEL

Paige P. Viren and Christina Beckmann

Introduction

The potential economic benefits of tourism draw many developed and developing countries to seek tourism development as a means of economic growth. This has often taken place without an adequate appreciation of the associated costs (Mathieson & Wall, 1982). The impacts of tourism have been the most researched area of tourism, and economic impacts have been examined more than any other type of impact. All forms of tourism have three main types of impacts: (a) economic, (b) environmental, and (c) sociocultural. Economic impacts are related to the balance of payments, income, and employment; environmental impacts are associated with the effects of tourism on both natural and built environments; and social impacts are connected to the effects of tourism on traditional lifestyles and the erosion of cultural heritage. Although there has been a focus on economic impacts, it is difficult to separate economic impacts from environmental and social impacts (Mason, 2003).

The principal motivations for a business or region to serve tourists are generally economic. An individual business is interested primarily in its own revenues and costs, whereas a community or region is concerned with the overall contribution of tourism to the economy, as well as its fiscal, environmental, and social impacts. USAID observes, "Developing countries particularly benefit from the tourism industry's positive economic, environmental, and social impacts, through the creation of jobs, preservation and celebration of indigenous culture, reduction of poverty, and promotion of environmental conservation (environmentally-friendly alternative livelihoods)" (Phillips & Faulkner, 2009, p. 4). Thus, a comprehensive understanding of the economic impacts of tourism is important for the tourism industry, government officials, and the community as a whole (Stynes, 1997).

Adventure travel has become a cornerstone of the tourism experience for many of the world's billions of tourists seeking to roam further afield in search of unique experiences. In 2014, the United Nations World Tourism Organization (UNTWO) published the *Global Report on Adventure Tourism*, and then UNWTO Secretary General Taleb Rifai noted that increased globalization has caused consumers to seek authentic experiences, and that adventure tourism will continue to be in high demand as a result. Expansion of adventure tourism creates immense opportunities for development, particularly in remote communities where adventure travel fuels the local economy, as well as generating income and employment. However, the growth of this segment also brings about the critical challenge of sustainable development, calling for careful and responsible tourism management. This chapter offers a case study analysis of adventure and mass tourism economic impacts in the Caribbean and Jordan based on the results of comprehensive analysis conducted by World Bank- and USAID-funded researchers.

Adventure travel definition and market value

Globally, tourism is estimated to account for one in ten jobs or 9.9% of global employment, generating US$7.6 trillion or 10% of global GDP in 2017 (World Travel & Tourism Council [WTTC], 2018). Adventure tourism, long assumed a niche in the tourism economy, has expanded from its technical, adrenaline-focused roots to encompass a broader mix of experiences. From trips that emphasize technical or "hard" adventure activities such as rock and ice climbing to "soft" adventure experiences with a central focus on hiking and bird-watching along with cultural activities, the adventure travel sector now has broad reach and the potential to drive sizeable impacts.

Given the aspirational nature of the term "adventure" – what constitutes an adventure for one person may be merely a routine excursion for another – defining adventure travel has been a matter of some debate. Recently, the Adventure Travel Trade Association (ATTA), in partnership with researchers at East Carolina University and *Outside* magazine, conducted a survey to sharpen its understanding of how consumers define adventure travel, and it published the definition shown in Figure 10.1 in 2017. The figure illustrates the modern definition of adventure travel established through this work.

On the left side of Figure 10.1, the essential components of an adventure travel trip are highlighted: nature, culture and activity. At the center of these three essential components is the "experience." Experience at the heart of adventure travel refers to the importance of not only taking into consideration the nature, culture, and activity components of the trip as individual ingredients, but also acknowledging that the way they are brought together into a whole experience is what constitutes an adventure. Note that the components are couched in a shaded circle

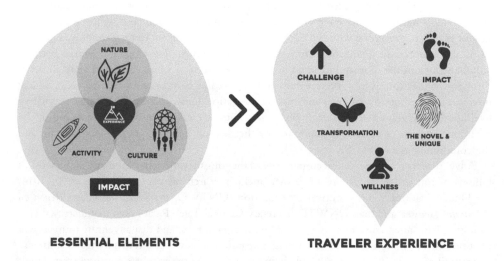

Figure 10.1 Definition of adventure travel
Source: Viren, Murray, Brown, and Beckmann, 2017.

with the word, "Impact." This is to emphasize to developers of adventure travel products that the impacts of their trips are important considerations – not only economic impact, but also environmental and social impacts.

On the right side of Figure 10.1, the traveler experience of adventure is illustrated. This part of the graphic highlights key motivations for adventure travelers and provides insight into how they are experiencing all the elements packaged for them by commercial tour operators. Adventure travelers are driven by a desire for mental and physical wellness, novel and unique experiences, challenge – whether physical or cultural – and often, ultimately, transformation. As with tour operators, travelers must also be keenly aware of their impact and strive to leave a positive impact on the environment and communities they visit.

A 2013 study conducted by the ATTA estimated the value of international adventure traveler consumers at US$683 billion, and the International Finance Corporation estimated it at US$745 billion, based on a 2017 report by Euromonitor International. The ATTA's projections are based on consumer research conducted in North America, South America, and Western Europe, and do not include Asian outbound markets or domestic adventure travel.

The key characteristics of adventure travel – its focus on nature conservation, celebration of local culture, and healthy outdoor activity – position it as an interesting development alternative for countries grappling with complex problems and clearly differentiate it from the mainstream tourism model which caught hold in the 1950s (Sezgin & Yolal, 2012). As such, the adventure travel sector finds itself the object of increasing interest from post-conflict and post-natural-disaster nations, international aid agencies, and conservation and climate activists. These people and agencies see adventure travel as a way to build stronger rural economies and provide possible business opportunities for large populations of young people. They also find the economic impacts of adventure travel can help bring a compelling financial argument for conservation to the table when natural resource extraction and transformation projects are being debated.

Figure 10.2 Value of international adventure travel consumers
Source: Projections based on ATTA, 2013.

Overview: adventure travel impacts

The tourism industry is one of the world's largest economic sectors. As noted in the UNWTO *Global Report on Adventure Tourism*, "the impacts of tourism are large and complex, not least because tourism can focus on the most vulnerable natural and cultural sites across the globe" (2014, p. 34). In many cases, opportunities for short-term financial gains are put before long-term environmental and cultural considerations. Impacts can be considered under the headings of positive and negative. Adventure tourism, like other forms of tourism, usually considers impacts in three main categories: (a) economic, (b) environmental, and (c) sociocultural.

It is vitally important for the tourism sector to focus its efforts to minimize the negative impacts of tourism, while protecting and enhancing local environments, biodiversity, and culture. The key to achieving balance between the positive and negative impacts is appropriate planning and management. When planned and managed properly, tourism can improve the local quality of life through economic development that enhances and protects the environment and culture.

When thoughtfully planned and managed, tourism can play a role in reducing poverty, fostering cultural understanding, and protecting biodiversity conservation. Like any tourism sector, adventure travel must be consciously planned and undertaken to maintain or enhance biological and cultural diversity and to be economically viable and socially equitable.

Tourism destinations can benefit in a number of ways from adventure travel, including job creation and the provision of strong incentives for conservation. In addition, it raises awareness of the many goods and services provided by biological diversity and of the need to honor cultural traditions and practices.

As stated by the UNWTO (2014, p. 34), adventure tourism

> has the potential to reconcile economic and environmental concerns and give practical meaning to sustainable development. Short- and long-term customer advocacy and financial support for marginal communities often springs from the transformative experiences that adventure travel can bring, with customers gaining an understanding of how their immediate, and sometimes ongoing, support can help preserve a destination's key cultural and natural capital.

Adventure tour operators can contribute to a sustainable vision for the sector by being mindful of their selection of service providers and vendors, as well as the activities they promote and facilities they utilize. As reflected in this chapter's case studies, choosing adventure travel has the compound benefit of contributing to both conservation and community development in a conservancy.

Economic

Overall, it appears that the economic impact of adventure travel is positive in most destinations, although there is always the potential for "leakages" (i.e., when revenue created in the local area does not stay locally, but instead is distributed outside the local economy) – particularly in developing countries where the industry is dominated by "foreign" enterprises. The economic impacts of adventure tourism include:

Positive:

- Direct and indirect job creation
- Contribution to foreign exchange earnings

- Generation of tax income for central and and local government
- Opportunities for development of small and medium-sized enterprises and family- and women-owned businesses
- Contribution to regional development.

Negative:

- Inflation
- Seasonality of demand can lead to underutilization of infrastructure
- Opportunity costs, with money invested in adventure tourism facilities not being available for other issues such as health and education
- Certain economies in developing countries can be overdependent on adventure tourism to the detriment of other economic sectors.

Environmental

Adventure tourism often involves direct contact with the physical environment; indeed, this environment is typically the main attraction for the adventure tourist. It can be argued that adventure tourism has had a positive impact on environmental conservation and cultural preservation because it has given the environment and the culture a monetary value and has afforded destinations a financial incentive for conservation. However, adventure tourism has had many negative impacts on the environment around the world as well. Environmental impacts include:

Positive:

- Tourism may stimulate measures to protect the environment, landscape, and/or wildlife
- Tourism can help to promote the establishment of national parks and/or wildlife reserves
- Tourism can promote the preservation of buildings/monuments (including, for example, UNESCO's World Heritage Sites)
- Tourism may provide the money via, for example, entrance charges to maintain historic buildings, heritage sites, and wildlife habitats.

Negative:

- Tourism can contribute to congestion in terms of overcrowding of people as well as traffic congestion
- Tourism can contribute to pollution and the depositing of nonbiodegradable waste
- Tourism may lead to damage and/or disturbance to wildlife habitats, especially in places where human presence has been limited, such as Antarctica or remote places
- Some activities involved cause damage to the environment: for example, climbing with artificial aids (e.g., sport climbing, where metal pegs are hammered into rock); high-volume safari tourism can disrupt both the feeding and breeding patterns of animals; diving can irretrievably damage coral reefs.

Given that the prime motivation in adventure tourism is often the desire to "get off the beaten path" and away from others tourists, this form of tourism has the potential to spread negative impacts throughout a wide geographical area if not appropriately managed. Adventure tourism developers are encouraged to think broadly about water use, waste management, and other environmental impacts resulting from exploration by well-meaning adventure travelers. Urban-based adventure tourism may have lower impacts, as the urban environment has been developed to support human presence in ways the remote wilderness areas have not.

Sociocultural impacts

Many adventure tourists from more developed countries (MDCs) visit less developed countries (LDCs) with very different cultures. This can have an array of impacts, some of which might be viewed as negative. Some positive impacts might include the work tourists can contribute to conservation and aid projects. In addition, the growth of tourism can spark a greater appreciation for local culture in both residents and visitors. As well, adventure tourism can provide job opportunities, particularly for women and young people. It also provides a relatively low-cost way to develop some locally owned businesses, such as guiding. Examples of sociocultural impacts include:

Positive:

- Revitalization of poor or nonindustrialized regions
- Rebirth of local arts and crafts and traditional cultural activities
- Creation of employment
- Revival of the social and cultural life of the local population
- Renewal of local architectural traditions
- Promotion of the need to conserve areas of outstanding beauty which have aesthetic and cultural value
- Encouragement of greater social mobility trough changes in employment from traditional agriculture to service industries, which may result in higher wages and better job prospects.

Negative:

- Tourists can behave in a manner that local people find offensive
- Cultural damage
- Specific issues such as drug abuse, prostitution, and crime in general
- Tourists can become role models for local young people because they are perceived to come from "advanced" countries. The copying of tourists' habits by young people can cause tension within families. This is known as the demonstration effect
- Sex tourism causes, or at least perpetuates, health problems and individual suffering at destinations
- Tourists giving local people gifts and money may encourage a culture of begging, which will harm the ability of the community to develop economically.

It is clear that the impacts of adventure tourism are both positive and negative, and they affect both urban areas and nonurban areas. We have discussed that adventure tourism has both positive and negative impacts on destinations. It seems that, in general, the economic impacts tend to be positive, and the environmental impacts and sociocultural impacts are a mixture. It has also been noted that the impacts are usually more marked in rural areas and wilderness zones than they are in urban areas, given the greater ability of urban areas to have a diverse economy (i.e., less dependent on one form of economic growth strategy). At the same time, it seems clear that the impacts are more pronounced when the destination is an LDC, rather than an MDC. Given the relative pros and cons involved with adventure tourism, we need a better understanding of the impacts of adventure tourism if we are to manage its development more effectively.

Adventure tourism economic impacts compared with mass tourism

The Caribbean: a case study

In the Caribbean, where warm island breezes and clear ocean waters have lured package tourists for decades, the World Bank commissioned a study in 2017 to analyze the economic impact of different types of tourism across several islands (WTTC, 2018). Although the dominant model of tourism in the Caribbean is vitally important to the regional economy, contributing almost 5% of GDP (US$17.9 billion) in 2016, it is also widely understood to provide little benefit to local people, with as much as 80% of every dollar "leaking" to companies based outside the region.

The WTTC report *Travel and Tourism Economic Impact 2017 Caribbean* forecast tourism in the region to rise, between 2017 and 2027, to US$26.7 billion, or almost 6% of total GDP in 2020; regional tourism planners are searching for new models (WTTC, 2017).

Enclave tourism is tourism localized within one area or organization, where all revenues generated revert back to one organization or business, and little goes back to the broader local economy (Healy & Jamal, 2017). As a result of enclave tourism, local businesses may see their chances of earning income from tourists severely reduced by the creation of "all-inclusive" vacation packages. When tourists remain at the same resort for their entire stay, which provides everything they need and where they will make all their expenditure, not much opportunity is left for local people to profit from tourism.

In the Caribbean, all-inclusive hotels generate the largest amount of revenue, but their impact on the economy is smaller per dollar of revenue than other accommodation types. All-inclusive resorts/hotels also import more nonlocal foods and employ fewer people per dollar of revenue than other hotels, thereby creating a smaller trickle-down effect on local economies.

The cruise ship industry provides another example of economic enclave tourism. Non-river cruises carried some 8.7 million international passengers in 1999. On many ships, especially in the Caribbean, guests are encouraged to spend most of their time and money on board, and opportunities to spend in some ports are closely managed and restricted.

A study conducted by researchers from American University reviewed the behaviors and spending patterns of two dominant types of visitor in this region: cruise tourists and all-inclusive tourists (Nikolova, Fernandes, & Shahidsaless, 2015). Results from this study indicated cruise tourists will stay at an island for a few hours and spend approximately US$50 per visit. All-inclusive visitors stay at their resort, typically as part of seven-day packages, and spend approximately US$1,000 per visit, most of which will stay at the resort. In contrast, adventure travelers were found to stay an average of eight days, spending approximately US$308 per day, for a total of US$2,710 per visit. Furthermore, adventure travel industry research indicates that the percentage of trip cost remaining in a local economy is about 65%, suggesting that, in the Caribbean, adventure tourists may deliver a greater, locally distributed revenue benefit than mass tourists.

When revenues generated by the three segments were compared, it was determined that US$10,000 in revenue could be generated by 200 cruise arrivals, ten all-inclusive visitors, or four adventure travelers. This information is especially interesting when put in the context of the region, where "overtourism" (i.e., tourism beyond normal levels of carrying capacity) from cruise passengers has resulted in damage to natural resources in the form of marine pollution and overuse by tourists of scarce fresh-water resources needed by locals. Understanding that the economic benefit of 200 cruise tourists can be achieved by four adventure travelers may help inform tourism investment and promotion strategies in the years to come.

Jordan: a case study

Shifting from the islands of the Caribbean to the deserts and wadis of the Near East, another example of adventure tourism's economic impact can be found in Jordan. Here, USAID was engaged in a five-year initiative, begun in 2013, to help underserved, impoverished communities improve their livelihoods and create new economic opportunities (USAID Jordan LENS, n.d.).

As in the Caribbean, the tourism context in Jordan has been dominated by the mass tourism model for many years. In Jordan, packaged tours are organized around a familiar circuit including the Dead Sea, Jerash, Um Qais, Madaba, Karak, Petra, and Wadi Rum, with visitors having a broad selection of international hotel brands to choose from for accommodation. Up until 2010, tourism in Jordan was on the increase and predicted to grow steadily. Following the "Arab Spring" in 2011, however, the industry suffered. Businesses built around high volume and rapid turnover of customers sustained significant losses, with many hotels and restaurants closing entirely. A need for new strategies arose, and adventure travel was identified as a form of tourism that might offer an alternative to the traditional model and diversify the standard portfolio.

In order to gauge the impact of adventure tourism on revenues and jobs within local communities in Jordan, the USAID LENS team developed an in-depth model for capturing the changes in local businesses. Their process involved examining national data sets such as input–output tables and conducting in-depth surveys with local businesses. The team modeled tourism using the mass tourism profile, as represented by Dead Sea resorts, and compared it with the adventure tourism profile, as represented by the Jordan Trail, a cross-country hiking trail.

The analysis revealed that mass tourism provides a direct economic impact to Jordan of US$66 million in tourism receipts, with US$6.2 million remaining in the local economy. Its indirect impact was captured at US$35 million, with US$8 million generated in the local economy. Altogether, this resulted in US$101 million generated in revenue, with 14% remaining in the local economy. In terms of jobs, mass tourism provides 1,523 local jobs, or 1.5 local jobs per US$100,000 in tourism receipts.

Adventure tourism, in contrast, provides a direct impact of US$4.4 million, with US$3.2 million remaining in the local economy. Its indirect impact is US$2.9 million, with US$1.6 million generated in the local economy. Altogether, adventure tourism was found to generate US$7.3 million in total revenue, with 65% remaining in the local economy. In terms of jobs, 2.62 local jobs were created per US$100,000 in tourism receipts.

The comparison of revenues remaining in the local economy, local jobs, and jobs created highlights the economic benefits of adventure tourism. It offers 51% more benefit in terms of money left in the local economy, 48% more local jobs, and 1.12 more local jobs created per US$100,000 than mass tourism. Although the actual dollar amount generated by the mass tourism efforts is larger, the adventure tourism efforts are expected to generate a broader dispersion of revenues throughout Jordan and create greater indirect expenditures in other complementary sectors, thereby creating less economic leakage.

Given the profile of adventure travelers – placing a premium on rugged and less developed locales, it was also speculated that adventure tourism might be more resistant to unpredictable shocks (e.g., terrorist attacks, political instability, health pandemics, and natural disasters) that in the past had such a negative effect on mainstream tourism enterprises.

Summary

As a significant form of human activity, tourism can have major impacts. These impacts are most visible in the destination region where tourists interact with the local economy, environment, culture, and society (Mason, 2003). Therefore, it is of value to consider tourism impacts under the headings of (a) economic, (b) environmental, and (c) sociocultural impacts.

As noted by Edmund Morris of the USAID Jordan LENS project (n.d.), "Adventure travel is not simply a 'new type of tourism' but should be considered as an approach to economic development that has far-reaching economic advantages over its counterparts." It is evident that adventure tourism has both positive and negative impacts on destinations. It seems that, in general, the economic impacts tend to be positive, and the environmental impacts tend to be negative, whereas the social impacts have provided mixed results. It has been shown that adventure tourism impacts are usually more marked in rural areas and wilderness zones than they are in urban areas. At the same time, it seems clear that the impacts are more significant when the destination is an LDC, rather than an MDC. We need a better understanding of the impacts of adventure tourism if we are to manage its development more effectively.

To better understand adventure tourism, we presented two case studies: the Caribbean and Jordan. The Caribbean case study presented a cautionary tale of enclave tourism and evidence to support adventure tourism as an alternative approach to tourism for economic growth. In the case of Jordan, it was noted that adventure tourism can demonstrate a positive contribution to the country's stability and the prospects for long-term investment, sparking increased foreign direct investment and generating indirectly "more jobs and more opportunities for businesses in a range of economic sectors" (USAID, 2017, p. 5).

People working at the intersection of conservation and business and looking for ways to drive awareness of the implications of climate change and slow or halt rising global temperatures (which are bringing about great loss of biodiversity and glacial ice melt) may embrace the economic arguments for adventure tourism as a way to achieve the sector's other benefits, which center on environmental and wildlife conservation.

Adventure travel experiences can increase consumer awareness of sustainable behavior such as recycling, elimination of single-use plastics, and many other concerns associated with the decline in environmental health. The economic benefits become the motivating force to help make an argument for adventure tourism and thereby hope to drive numerous conservation benefits. According to Guy Castley, Senior Research Fellow from the International Centre for Ecotourism Research at Griffith University, "Conservation benefits depend to a large degree on the choices we make: the destination we pick out, the travel options we choose, the activities we participate in, and how the money we spend is redistributed" (2011, n.p.). Adventure tourism, if planned properly, presents a platform from which to realize these benefits.

References

Adventure Travel Trade Association (ATTA). (2013). *Adventure tourism market study*. www.adventure travel.biz/research/adventure-tourism-market-study-2013/. Seattle, WA: ATTA.

Castley, G. (2011). Can tourism really have conservation benefits? https://theconversation.com/can-tourism-really-have-conservation-benefits-1337

Healy, N., & Jamal, T. (2017). Enclave tourism. In L.L. Lowry (Ed.), *International encyclopedia of travel and tourism* (pp. 418–419). Thousand Oaks, CA: Sage.

International Finance Corporation. (2017). *Niche markets global sizing, summary of market segments Papua New Guinea tourism program*. Papua New Guinea: Euromonitor International.

Mason, P. (2003). *Tourism impacts, planning and management*. Burlington, MA: Butterworth-Heinemann. www.mu.edu.et/iphc/images/liblary/Heritage/Heritage_Culture_and_Tourism/Tourism_Impacts_ Planing__devet.pdf

Mathieson, A., & Wall, G. (1982). *Tourism, economic, physical and social impacts*. London: Longman.

Nikolova, M., Fernandes, E., & Shahidsaless, R. (2015). *Strengthening tourism competitiveness in OECS countries: market analysis*. Washington, DC: The World Bank.

Phillips, J., & Faulkner, J. (2009). *Accessing sustainable funding and social impact capital. Sustainable tourism*. International Cooperation for Development, Online Toolkit and Resource Series. Washington, DC: USAID Tourism Investment and Finance.

Stynes, D. (1997). *Economic impacts of tourism: a handbook for tourism professionals*. Urbana-Champaign, IL: Tourism Research Laboratory at the University of Illinois at Urbana-Champaign.

Sezgin, E., & Yolal, M. (2012). Golden age of mass tourism: its history and development. In M. Kasimoglu (Ed.), *Visions for global tourism industry: creating and sustaining competitive strategies*. Rijeka, Croatia: Intech.

United States Agency for International Development (USAID). (2017). *USAID/Jordan local enterprise support project assessment of the mountaineering sector in Jordan*. Amman, Jordan: USAID Jordan Local Enterprise Support (LENS) Project.

United National World Tourism Organization (UNWTO). (2014). *Global report on adventure tourism*. Madrid: UNWTO. http://cf.cdn.unwto.org/sites/all/files/pdf/final_1global_report_on_adventure_ tourism.pdf

USAID Jordan Local Enterprise Support Project (LENS). (n.d.). *Jordan LENS*. Retrieved April 13, 2018, from https://jordanlens.org/node/45#field_ab_simage-section

Viren, P.P., Murray, A.K., Brown, T., & Beckmann, C. (2017). *North American travelers: Personal growth, new destinations, and immersive culture*. Prepared for the Adventure Travel Trade Association, May.

World Travel and Tourism Council (WTTC). (2017). *Travel and tourism economic impact 2017 Caribbean*. London, UK: WTTC.

World Travel and Tourism Council (WTTC). (2018). *World Travel and Tourism Council: travel & tourism economic impact 2018*. London: WTTC. www.wttc.org/-/media/files/reports/economic-impact-research/regions-2018/world2018.pdf

11

LONG-TERM ECONOMIC IMPACTS OF TOURISM

João Romão

Introduction

The continuous growth of tourism observed in recent decades can be measured by the number of journeys (more than 1 billion international arrivals in the world for the first time in 2012, 1.3 billion in 2017, and 1.8 billion expected for 2030), but also by the economic impacts of this activity: According to UNWTO (2018), tourism activities are responsible for 30% of global exports of services and 10% of GDP and employment at the global level. As will be discussed, these estimations raise several relevant methodological questions, but it is unquestionable that tourism plays an important role within contemporary economic dynamics.

This intense growth of tourism is clearly related to economic aspects, such as the generalized increase in discretionary income observed since the second part of the 20th century all over the world, despite important geographical differences and also relevant social inequalities within each country. As is characteristic of nonessential goods and services, tourism demand normally reveals high elasticity, both regarding fluctuations in prices (negative) and revenues (positive). This aspect is clearly illustrated by the importance achieved by China as an issuing market, reaching the position of third in the world in 2016, as a result of the implications of the economic performance of the country on the wages, well-being, and willingness to travel of its citizens. Other societal transformations (reduction of working hours or the importance of leisure and cultural enrichment within consumption patterns) also contribute to the rapid and intense growth of tourism in contemporary economies and societies.

Nevertheless, measuring the economic impacts of tourism raises important methodological questions. First of all, tourism is not an economic sector and it is not classified as such within national or regional economic accounts. In fact, tourism comprises a wide range of activities, including services related to accommodation, transportation, or the provision of food and beverages, but also related to entertainment, educational, cultural, or environmental activities, retail and shopping, or other leisure services. Obviously, these products and services, along with the facilities and infrastructures for their utilization and consumption, are normally used by tourists and by local residents in a tourism destination.

Besides the potential conflicts eventually emerging from the shared use of spaces, facilities, and services, this also imposes problems and difficulties with the assessment of tourism economic impacts, as it is generally not possible to make a precise distinction between the consumption made by local residents and that by tourists. Even accommodation, one of the most tourism-oriented services in a destination, is now largely shared by tourists and local residents as a consequence of the massification of house-sharing through Internet-based platforms. It is also noteworthy that most of the main territorial characteristics attracting tourists to a destination (material and immaterial cultural heritage, natural resources, lifestyles, landscapes, etc.) can be framed within the concept of common pool resources, which raises new theoretical and methodological problems when estimating the economic impacts of tourism. Taking these aspects and problems into consideration, this chapter starts with a presentation and discussion of different methods and techniques to evaluate the economic impacts of tourism, pointing out abundant references for a more detailed quantitative analysis in the next section.

Taking this problematic into account, the following section will discuss the long-term impacts of tourism development on regional economies, starting with a discussion of the different economic effects that can be observed throughout the life cycle of a tourism destination. These effects will depend on the specific conditions that characterize each destination, the type of tourism-related business developed, and their interrelation with the other local and regional economic sectors. Thus, the long-term economic impacts of tourism can be seen as an evolutionary process where variety, relatedness, or agglomeration effects will influence the local and regional economic structures, specialization patterns, and economic growth.

Next, the discussion will be centered on the role of tourism within the emergent "creative economies," in which products and services tend to integrate cultural and symbolic values, and culture is increasingly commoditized. The importance of personal experiences is especially important within these contemporary tendencies of production and consumption, along with a search for personalized products and services in different economic sectors, including tourism and recreation. Some specific characteristics of tourism activities (such as co-terminality, spatiality, and temporality, which imply that consumption and production occur at the same time, in the same place, and with direct interaction between producers and consumers) enhance the opportunities for the implementation of innovative processes of co-creation of tourism services. Moreover, taking into account the recognized importance of tourism and leisure within contemporary creative economies, the potential role of tourism within regional innovation networks will be discussed. Finally, the main ideas presented in this chapter will be summarized in the concluding section.

Tourism economic value

An important starting point to measure the economic importance of tourism in national or regional economies is the implementation of tourism satellite accounts (TSAs), as recommended by different international institutions with a relevant role in tourism policy and management (OECD, 2000; United Nations, 2010). Based on a combination of data from "conventional" economic accounts and survey data collected at each tourism destination, the main purpose of the TSA is to identify and distinguish the consumption made by local residents or tourists for each particular sector of activity (restaurants, transport, cultural, educational or entertainment facilities, transport services, shopping, etc.). This methodology allows the estimation of the effective contribution from tourism for the production of each economic sector.

As is easy to perceive, this task requires a large effort and a significant allocation of funds in order to deal with different types of problem, including a possible geographical concentration of tourism activities in some parts of the territories and a potential temporal concentration in some periods of the year. Thus, the accuracy of the results is largely dependent on the resources devoted by each country for its implementation. Moreover, different types of methodology or assumption underlying the analysis may be used in different countries, with the related problems when international comparisons are performed (in fact, many countries have not yet adopted TSA). Nevertheless, it is clear that these tools have gained higher accuracy with time, and efforts are been systematically pursued at the international level in order to support the definition of common technical standards (UNWTO, 2017).

The impacts of tourism on local, regional, or national economies comprise direct effects (related to the consumption of tourism products and services), indirect effects (related to the inputs of other products and services needed for the supply of tourism activities), and induced effects (related to the consumption made by employees involved within the provision of tourism products and services). Consequently, it is noteworthy that a multiplier effect on local economies arises from tourism consumption (once there are indirect and induced impacts, the total impact is larger than the impact of tourism consumption itself), the magnitude of which is determined by the interrelations established between tourism activities and the other economic sectors, as analyzed by Crompton, Jeong, and Dudensing (2016).

The impacts of tourism on other regional or national economic activities (and the economy as a whole) are often estimated using input–output tables. These tables measure the fluxes between the different sectors (in terms of both monetary flows and labor requirements) through the definition of "technical coefficients" (fixed parameters defining the quantity of a given product or service that is necessary for the production of another product or service). With this method, it is possible to estimate the impacts of variations in the production (or consumption) of one sector on the remaining economic structure. Thus, it is possible to estimate the potential impacts of an increase in tourism demand on regional or national economies.

Nevertheless, input–output tables are not always available at regional or local levels (as their estimation implies relatively high costs) or they not updated often enough in order to capture the structural transformations of the economies. A major limitation of these methods is the fixed character of the "technical coefficients," implying that changes in productivity arising from technological or organizational innovations are not taken into account. Restrictions on the mobility of products and production factors between sectors, demand constraints, or feedback effects are other problems identified in the literature, leading to different developments, as observed by Polo and Valle (2012). Moreover, input–output tables can be used within computable general equilibrium or social account models aiming at identifying optimal solutions when an external shock (e.g., a decrease in tourism demand or the creation of a new infrastructure or facility) affects an economic system. Dwyer, Forsyth, and Spurr (2004) offer a systematic review of these methods.

It is also noteworthy that different types of asset with relevance to tourism attractiveness cannot be measured in terms of their market value, as they are not the objects of market transactions. This is the case with landscapes, natural parks, monuments, or other types of cultural heritage (including immaterial aspects), which implies the consideration of use values (the expected value assigned to the resource by the users) and nonuse values (such as emotional connection or perceived ecological or cultural importance), as Andersson, Armbrecht, and Lundberg (2012) observe. In this context, Choi, Lee, Lee, and Dattilo (2015) suggest three types of perceived value: the functional (difference between costs and benefits), the emotional (affective relation with the asset), and the reputational (notoriety of the resource). Different perceptions related to the characteristics and motivations of diverse types of user (Saayman and Saayman, 2014) normally lead to very different evaluations, implying the need to implement extensive surveys to achieve reliable results.

In order to support decisions about investment projects involving the creation of new infrastructures, facilities, services, or events (or the introduction of entrance fees for resources with free access), two types of method ("hedonic prices" and "stated preferences") are normally used in order to assess their perceived value, their potential impact, or the "willingness-to-pay" of possible users (Loomis, 2014; Weaver and Lawton, 2007). Assuming the travel cost to a particular destination to be a form of revealed preference, the "hedonic travel cost method" (Brown and Mendelsohn, 1984) offers a very objective and quantitative estimation for the value of a resource. Nevertheless, tourists normally visit more than one place (or attraction) during one trip, which makes it difficult to identify with precision the importance of a specific asset. On the other hand, the "contingent valuation method" (Wright and Eppink, 2016) is based on the aggregation of individual preferences expressed in surveys for the assessment of the willingness to pay for the utilization of a service or a visit to a place. Also requiring a large sample in order to deal with very diverse answers, this method raises the problem of distinguishing the stated willingness to pay from the real payment that would be made.

Most of the assets previously described, with relevant nonmarket values, can also be framed within the concept of "common pool resources" (CPRs; Ostrom, 2010). In fact, many essential (and probably the most important) resources determining the attractiveness of a tourism destination (material aspects such as natural resources and landscapes or monuments, but also immaterial elements related to local cultural heritage and lifestyles) can be defined as such (Briassoulis, 2002). CPRs are characterized by "subtractability" and "nonexcludability," implying a competition process among potential users for their consumption in which the utilization by one user can exclude or reduce the possibility of utilization by others, while it is difficult to impose limits to access them or to identify legitimate users.

Additional problems for the management of these resources relate to the different value each potential user assigns to them (Holden, 2005). Thus, free access to these resources may lead to overuse (the "free ride" problem) and degradation, and their communal character may reduce the incentive for preservation by individual users. In the case of tourism, it is noteworthy that local residents and external visitors normally assess the value of these resources differently and have different concerns about their preservation. On the other hand, the private appropriation of benefits arising from the commercial exploitation of these resources can also be unequal within a local community, raising problems of social and economic justice.

This is very clear for the case of tourism, as a large part of the expenses of tourists is normally concentrated in the transportation and accommodation services (Mullis, 2017), although they are attracted by common resources available to a local community, which does not necessarily benefit from tourism (or can even suffer negative consequences of massive forms of tourism, related to inflationary processes, congestion, or degradation of livability). Taking these aspects into consideration, Ostrom (2011) proposes general principles for CPR management, aimed at their integration into local processes of sustainable development, by taking into account the three pillars of sustainability (economic benefits, social equity, and environmental protection), while proposing the creation of participatory processes of decision-making involving local communities.

Tourism and economic growth

It is widely documented in the literature that the economic (and other) impacts of tourism are time-dependent, and they can be seen as an evolutionary process, as analyzed by Butler (1980) when proposing his tourism area life cycle model for the analysis of the historical process of development of a destination. Despite its limitations (observed by, among others, Agarwal, 1997, or Lagiewsky, 2006), this model offers a linear, simplified standard for the evolution of tourism areas with which each specific destination can be compared. Tourism-oriented activities emerge in a destination in the "involvement" and "exploration" stages, when spontaneous visitors discover a place, leading to a slow increase in the number of tourists and to the development of small-scale, locally based tourism-oriented businesses.

This situation tends to change if the destination reaches the "development" stage as a result of its increasing attractiveness. In such a case, travel starts to be organized, transportation services and infrastructures are developed, the number of visitors tends to increase, and new tourism-oriented facilities are implemented. Normally, this is a long-term process, involving public and private investments, from both local and external entrepreneurs. The high growth rates of tourism demand, the expectation of high returns on investments, and short payback periods reinforce the attractiveness of the tourism sector, eventually leading to decay in other economic activities, in terms of both regional production and employment.

As an example, a recent study in a tourism-dependent region in south Europe shows how the development of tourism was related to a significant increase in the construction sector and the provision of non-tradable services, while agriculture, fisheries, and manufacture lost importance within the regional context (Romão, Guerreiro and Rodrigues, 2016). Very similar results were obtained by Capó, Font, and Nadal (2007a) when they analyzed the development of tourism within the regional economies of the Balearic and Canary Islands, in Spain. This aspect is related to the concept of "Dutch disease," defined by Corden (1984) as a process of deindustrialization resulting from overexploitation (extraction) of natural resources, boosting the importance of non-tradable products and services.

Although the original formulation of this concept was related to the discovery and exploitation of natural gas in a region of the Netherlands, similar approaches to the case of tourism have been proposed (e.g., Copeland, 1991; Chao, Hazari, Laffargue, Sgro, and Yu, 2006). In a large study involving 134 countries and a long series of data, Holzner (2011) defined this problem as the "beach disease." Nevertheless, the empirical studies performed by all these authors (at different territorial levels, in different parts of the world) did not lead to the identification of a direct relation between tourism development and the emergence of processes of deindustrialization, suggesting that it is not possible to generalize the results to all tourism destinations.

When reaching the stage of development, a tourism destination necessarily comprises a broad set of products and services, revealing the potential of the tourism sector to mobilize resources, products, and services from the rest of the economy. Some common examples are agriculture, food industries, transport, energy production and consumption, entertainment activities, retail and shopping, ecotourism services, cultural and educational activities, or different support services supplied through information and communication technologies (ICT). On the other hand, the attraction of tourists to a destination generates agglomeration economies that contribute to the development of local markets, not necessarily related to the tourism sector, with a potential to support the emergence of innovative practices, products, and services (Liu, Nijkamp, and Lin, 2017).

Taking into consideration the close links between tourism attractiveness and the specific characteristics of places, the historical processes of development of a tourism destination, and the importance of local and regional inter-sectorial relations shaping them, it is not surprising that the conceptual and methodological developments related to evolutionary economic geography (EEG; Boschma and Martin, 2010) have recently been applied to the analysis of the tourism sector and its relation with local and regional processes of economic growth, as generally described and systematized by Brouder and Eriksson (2013). Focusing on more particular aspects, Ma and Hassink (2013) and Sanz-Ibáñez and Clavé (2014) linked the EEG approach to the life cycle analysis developed by Butler (1980), and the importance of the characteristics of the territory influencing the relation between tourism and economic growth was analyzed by Cárdenas-García and Sánchez-Rivero (2015).

Path-dependence, emphasizing the importance of past strategic choices shaping and constraining the possibilities of future development, is a crucial concept within the EEG theoretical framework, with relevant implications for the analysis of long-term processes of tourism development. Some of the causes of path-dependence proposed by Martin (2014) have particular implications for tourism: natural resources (when tourism attractiveness is mostly dependent on natural features, this constrains the range of tourism products and services that can be implemented); sunk costs related to local productive, physical, and infrastructural facilities (large-scale tourism-related investments, which are not necessarily useful for other economic activities, thus reinforcing the importance of tourism); agglomeration economies, economies of specialization, or spin-off firm birth (high growth rates of tourism demand during the development stage of a destination reinforces the attractiveness of this sector for the creation of new businesses); interregional linkages (resulting from multi-destination trips, which prompt co-evolutionary processes of tourism development among neighbor regions); and technological lock-in (concentration of knowledge and innovation capabilities tourism when this is a prominent sector may imply an overall reduction in the regional innovation dynamics if tourism is not connected with more technologically advanced sectors).

In this context, other concepts proposed by the EEG approach (such as relatedness, variety, or regional branching, as defined by Boschma, Coenen, Frenken, and Truffer, 2016) offer relevant insights in analysis of the interconnections between tourism, other economic sectors, regional economic structures, and long-term processes of economic growth. In fact, the differences among regions within these evolving structural aspects and the related path-dependency processes seem to be crucial determinants of the relations established between tourism dynamics and economic growth, as observed in several studies analysing the tourism-led growth hypothesis (TLG), which discusses the role of the tourism sector in promoting processes of economic growth (a review of studies of this type is offered by Brida, Cortes-Jimenez, and Pulina, 2016).

In an initial stage, the TLG seemed to be confirmed by a large number of studies addressing different territorial levels: international comparisons (Chen and Chiou-Wei, 2009; Cortes-Jimenez, and Pulina, 2010), national analysis (Balaguer and Cantavella-Jordá, 2002; Dritsakis, 2004; Kim, Chen, and Jang, 2006), and regional studies (Risso, Barquet, and Brida, 2010). In contrast, recent studies analyzing longer periods and based on larger data sets obtained different results. At the local level, Capó, Font, and Nadal (2007b) observed that the transformations that occurred within the regional economic structure during the development stage of tourism in Canary Islands led to a negative long-term impact on economic growth. Similarly, Adamou and Clerides (2010) concluded that the positive impacts of tourism on economic growth tend to disappear in the long run, when they analyzed this relation in 162 countries. Thus, these recent results seem to suggest that the impacts of tourism dynamics on local and regional economic growth depend on the evolutionary aspects of the life cycle of tourism destinations.

Tourism and the contemporary creative economy

Contemporary "Post-Fordist" societies are characterized by a double process of integration of cultural and symbolic values into the economic system, while culture is increasingly produced under commoditized forms (Scott, 2007). New production systems emerge, based on small and decentralized units, with high incorporation of creative work and intense utilization of ICT, often oriented to the creation of personalized products, adapted to the specific needs of different types of consumer. On the demand side, rising discretionary income (at least for part of the population) and changing lifestyles, with consumption patterns more oriented to aspects related to self-esteem and personal valorization, wellness, education, cultural interaction, or entertainment, also contribute to the emergence of these transformations, where personal experiences and immaterial aspects clearly influence consumption patterns.

This emergent economic system can be defined as "cognitive capitalism" (Scott, 2007) or as a "creative economy" (OECD, 2014), it being noteworthy that significant transformations have also occurred within tourism, not only resulting in a significant increase in the number of trips worldwide, but also in the rising importance of the concept of "experience" (Tussyadiah, 2014). This implies that the focus of tourism policies has gradually shifted towards concepts such as "livability" or cultural interaction, rather than the management of resources and facilities. Moreover, the concept of "co-creation" (Binkhorst and Dekker, 2009) has also emerged in the tourism literature, referring to the development of new products and services based on the interaction between producers and consumers (or even between consumers, as recently observed by Rihova, Buhalis, Gouthro, and Moital, 2018).

In fact, "co-terminality" (direct interaction between producers and consumers) is a distinctive characteristic of tourism services, with relevant economic implications. This aspect has been clearly enhanced by the development of ICT in recent decades, intensifying these interactive processes and the related fluxes of information. In a context of global competition between destinations to guarantee the supply of a competitive differentiated experience to an extremely segmented international market, where consumers have different motivations, needs, and preferences, interaction and information are crucial elements for the match between destination differentiation and market segmentation.

The generalization of the utilization of ICT before, during, and after travel, including the new developments related to Web 2.0 (social networks) and Web 3.0 (mobile devices), has transformed the tourism business, as observed by authors such as Buhalis and Law (2008), Hall and Williams (2008), Aldebert, Dang, and Longhi (2011) or Lo, McKercher, Cheung, and Law (2011). As well as constituting new sources of competitive advantage for the development of personalized services for specific consumers, ICT also contributed to increasing the autonomy and power of consumers (Tussyadiah and Fesenmaier, 2009; Wang, Weaver, and Kwek, 2016). Contemporary tourists can also have an active role in shaping the image of destinations (Kim and Fesenmaier, 2017) by sharing their experiences through online platforms (personal web pages or tourism-oriented websites), and service providers can develop long-term relationships with consumers (customer relation management) by using digital tools.

Two other important and distinctive characteristics of tourism as an economic activity are spatiality and temporality, implying that production and consumption occur at the same place and at the same time, enhancing the strict connection between tourism dynamics and territorial characteristics, including the local economic structures. Thus, the permanent interactions between suppliers and consumers occurring at the local level make each destination a repository of information about the preferences, motivations, behaviors, and satisfaction of visitors, although tourism services are normally provided by a large number of suppliers, creating a decentralized value chain.

Nevertheless, although some large tourism-oriented or digital companies have the tools and skills to process and integrate this information in their productive process, supporting the creation of innovative products and services (as is the case of companies using "big data" in order to track individuals' behaviors based on massive amounts of information), it is also noteworthy that most of the companies operating in the tourism sector are of small dimensions and have limited abilities to process and formalize the information received. In this sense, digital technologies can be used as tools of mass collaboration for the development of "coopetition" processes among local stakeholders, both for product development and for territorial governance (Sigala, 2012; Sigala and Marinidis, 2012). This potential and the importance of implementing participatory processes of tourism planning, management, and monitoring are framed within the concept of "smart tourism destinations" proposed by Boes, Buhalis, and Inversini (2016).

These aspects emphasize the importance of local and regional networks for the mobilization of local knowledge that can fuel innovation dynamics in the tourism sector. As Malakauskaite and Navickas (2010) observe, innovation can be seen as an evolutionary and path-dependent process (Martin, 2014), depending on the ability of each region to transform local resources into competitive products and services – the "territorial capital" defined by Capello, Caragliu, and Nijkamp (2011). Nevertheless, despite the apparent potential of tourism activities to develop strong synergies with a varied set of related sectors (Neffke, Henning, and Boschma, 2009), including creative or high-tech activities, a recent study involving a large group of European regions (Romão and Nijkamp, 2017) revealed weaker innovative performance in the regions where tourism has greater importance within economic structures.

Taking into account the existing conditions in tourism-dependent regions (including the concentration of knowledge, labor force, investment, and firm creation within this sector) and the contemporary approach to regional development based on the concept of "smart specialization" (focus on a small number of sectors, supported by knowledge capabilities based on endogenous resources in order to generate inter-sectorial spillovers, as defined by Foray et al., 2012), tourism seems to have a high potential to assume a central role within regional development processes. The achievement of this central role depends on the ability to generate stronger connections and innovation spillovers with the related sectors, through processes of "integrative diversification" (Benur and Bramwell, 2015), with the aim of diversifying the current tourism supply through the integration of new products and services that reinforce the linkages of tourism with other territorial resources and activities.

In particular, the prominent role of tourism within the contemporary creative economy and the importance of culture, education, and self-valorization as motivating factors for travelling open up important opportunities for the integration of tourism products and services in a larger range of creative activities. Moreover, contemporary approaches to culture emphasize its immaterial dimension and the role of the setting of cultural heritage for its preservation and valorization (UNESCO, 2001), which is assumed to be a crucial aspect for the enrichment of the tourism experience and the creation of higher value added by the tourism sector in each destination (UNWTO, 2003). OECD (2014) suggests the concept of "smart tourism" as an integrated economic approach that considers tourism as a central element of the creative economies, potentially establishing links with other cultural sectors and promoting higher levels of economic growth while reinforcing the singularity and uniqueness of each destination.

Along with the emergence of these new economic and touristic dynamics, where knowledge and creativity are prominent aspects, the role of cities has also been reinforced in terms of concentration of population and economic activities, and also as tourism destinations. As Currid-Halkett and Scott (2013) observe, contemporary cities promote the spatial agglomeration of the cultural sectors while disposing of high quantities of cultural infrastructures, facilities, services, and events. Tourism also benefits from these dynamics, as cities can offer a varied supply of services for different types of tourist, thus reducing the transaction costs for the enjoyment of different types of service (UNWTO, 2012). Finally, current efforts observed in many urban centers to increase livability (transport, public spaces, green areas, safety, security, etc.) and to attract skilled labor and economic activities may also reinforce city attractiveness for tourism.

Nevertheless, it is also possible to observe that contemporary urban dynamics implies a functional process of transformation of cities (Scott, 2017), with large processes of renovation of obsolete industrial areas, now reoccupied by creative activities and entrepreneurs. Similarly, urban centers tend now to be occupied by professionals in the creative sectors, often implying displacement of other sectors of the population to peripheral areas. These processes of "gentrification" potentially lead to increasing social and spatial inequalities in urban areas (Sassen, 2010), and tourism is often seen as an active agent in these processes.

In fact, the tourism sector benefits from the creative externalities increasing the attractiveness of certain areas as a result of the concentration of elements with cultural significance, but the massive presence of tourists in these areas also generates negative externalities for the living conditions of the local population (Romão, Kourtit, Neuts, and Nijkamp, 2018) by creating congestion, localized inflationary processes, or problems in the housing market. In this context, the emergence of organized social movements questioning and confronting tourism development is noticeable (Colomb and Navy, 2017), and UNWTO (2012) claims that the opportunities opened up by contemporary urban tourism dynamics imply new challenges for urban policies.

Concluding remarks

This chapter has analyzed different methodologies to assess the economic importance of tourism and to evaluate its economic impacts in terms of regional economic structures, specialization patterns, and long-term processes of economic growth. This discussion took into consideration the evolving character of tourism destinations, the fragmented and decentralized character of the value chain of tourism supply, and the different territorial characteristics that constrain the possibilities for tourism and economic development in each region. Finally, the opportunities for improvement of the performance of tourism activities and their interrelations with other economic sectors in contemporary creative economies have been addressed. In particular, this chapter has focused on:

- The tourism satellite account as a tool to evaluate the economic value of tourism;
- Different methods to estimate the structural impacts of tourism in regional or national economies;
- Different techniques to evaluate the nonuse value of tourism services, facilities, or infrastructures;
- The importance of an adequate management of "common pool resources";
- The evolving character of the impacts of tourism on local and regional economies throughout the life cycle of destinations;
- The potential negative impact of tourism on other productive economic sectors;
- The appropriateness of the conceptual framework related to evolutionary economic geography to analyze the economic evolution of tourism;
- The long-term relations between tourism and economic growth;
- The importance of tourism within contemporary creative economies;
- The opportunities for innovation and differentiation based on co-creation processes arising from the interactivity, spatiality, and temporality of tourism activities, along with the generalized utilization of ICT;
- The potential central role of tourism within regional innovation systems and smart specialization strategies for regional development; and
- The importance of cities for the contemporary creative economy, related opportunities for urban tourism, and potential negative implications.

References

Adamou, A., and Clerides, S. (2010) Prospects and limits of tourism-led growth: The international evidence. *Review of Economic Analysis*, *3*: 287–303.

Agarwal, S. (1997) The resort cycle and seaside tourism: An assessment of its applicability and validity. *Tourism Management*, *18*(2): 65–73.

Aldebert, B., Dang, R., and Longhi, C. (2011) Innovation in the tourism industry: The case of Tourism@. *Tourism Management, 32*: 1204–1213.

Andersson, T., Armbrecht, J., and Lundberg, E. (2012) Estimating use and non-use values of a music festival. *Scandinavian Journal of Hospitality & Tourism, 12*(3): 215–231.

Balaguer, J., and Cantavella-Jordá, M. (2002) Tourism as a long-run economic growth factor: The Spanish case. *Applied Economics, 34*(7): 877–884.

Benur, A., and Bramwell, B. (2015) Tourism product development and product diversification in destinations. *Tourism Management, 50*: 213–224.

Binkhorst, E., and Dekker, T. (2009) Towards the co-creation tourism experience? *Journal of Hospitality Marketing & Management, 18*(2–3): 311–327.

Boes, K., Buhalis, D., and Inversini, A. (2016) Smart tourism destinations: Ecosystems for tourism destination competitiveness. *International Journal of Tourism Cities, 2*(2): 108–124.

Boschma, R., Coenen, L., Frenken, K., and Truffer, B. (2016) Towards a theory of regional diversification. *Papers in Evolutionary Economic Geography*, 16.17.

Boschma, R., and Martin, R. (2010) The aims and scope of evolutionary economic geography. In: R. Boschma and R. Martin (Eds.), *The Handbook of Evolutionary Economic Geography*. Cheltenham, UK: Edward Elgar, pp. 3–39.

Briassoulis, H. (2002) Sustainable tourism and the question of commons. *Annals of Tourism Research, 29*(4): 1065–1085.

Brida, J.G., Cortes-Jimenez, I., and Pulina, M. (2016) Has the tourism-led growth hypothesis been validated? A literature review. *Current Issues in Tourism, 19*(5): 394–430.

Brouderm P., and Eriksson, R. (2013) Tourism evolution: On the synergies of tourism studies and evolutionary economic geography. *Annals of Tourism Research, 43*: 370–389.

Brown, G., and Mendelsohn, R. (1984) The hedonic travel cost method. *The Review of Economics & Statistics, 66*(3): 427–433.

Buhalis, D., and Law, R. (2008) Progress in information technology and tourism management. *Tourism Management, 29*: 609–623.

Butler, R. (1980) The concept of a tourism area life cycle of evolution: Implications for management of resources. *Canadian Geographer, 24*(1): 5–12.

Capello, R., Caragliu, A., and Nijkamp, P. (2011) Territorial capital and regional growth: Increasing returns in knowledge use. *Tijdschrift voor Economische en Sociale Geografie, 102*(4): 385–405.

Capó, J., Font, A., and Nadal, J. (2007a) Dutch disease in tourism economies: Evidence from the Balearics and the Canary Islands. *Journal of Sustainable Tourism, 15*(6): 615–627.

Capó, J., Font, A., and Nadal, J. (2007b) Tourism and long-term growth: A Spanish perspective. *Annals of Tourism Research, 34*(3): 709–726.

Cárdenas-García, P., and Sánchez-Rivero, M. (2015) Tourism and economic development: Analysis of geographic features and infrastructure provision. *Current Issues in Tourism, 18*(7): 609–632.

Chao, C., Hazari, B., Laffargue, J., Sgro, M., and Yu, E. (2006) Tourism, Dutch disease and welfare in a open dynamic economy. *Japanese Economic Review, 57*(4): 501–515.

Chen, C., and Chiou-Wei, S. (2009) Tourism expansion, tourism uncertainty and economic growth: New evidence from Taiwan and Korea. *Tourism Management, 30*(6): 812–818.

Choi, Y., Lee, W., Lee, C., and Dattilo, J. (2015) Valuation of mudflats in nature-based tourism: Inclusion of perceived value of festival experience. *Tourism Economics, 21*(4): 833–851.

Colomb, C., and Navy, J. (2017). *Protest and Resistance in the Tourist City*. London: Routledge.

Crompton, J.L., Jeong, J.Y., and Dudensing, R.M. (2016) Sources of variation in economic impact multipliers. *Journal of Travel Research, 55*(8): 1051–1064.

Copeland, B. (1991) Tourism, welfare and de-industrialization in a small open economy. *Economica, 58*(232): 515–529.

Corden, W. (1984) Booming sector and Dutch disease economics: Survey and consolidation. *Oxford Economic Papers, 36*: 359–380.

Cortes-Jimenez, I., and Pulina, M. (2010) Inbound tourism and long-run economic growth. *Current Issues in Tourism, 13*(1): 61–74.

Crompton, J.L., Jeong, J.Y., and Dudensing, R.M. (2016) Sources of variation in economic impact multipliers. *Journal of Travel Research, 55*(8): 1051–1064.

Currid-Halkett, E., and Scott, A.J. (2013) The geography of celebrity and glamour: Reflections on economy, culture, and desire in the city. *City, Culture & Society, 4*: 2–11.

Dritsakis, N. (2004) Tourism as a long-run economic growth factor: An empirical investigation for Greece using causality analysis. *Tourism Economics, 10*(3): 305–316.

Dwyer, L., Forsyth, P., and Spurr, R. (2004) Evaluating tourism's economic effects: New and old approaches. *Tourism Management, 25*: 307–317.

Foray, D., Goddard, J., Beldarrain, X., Landabaso, M., McCann, P., Morgan, K., and Ortega-Argilés, R. (2012) Guide to research and innovation strategies for smart specialisation. S3P, European Union, Regional Policy, Brussels.

Hall, C.M., and Williams, A.M. (2008) *Tourism and Innovation*. London: Routledge.

Holden, A. (2005) Achieving a sustainable relationship between common pool resources and tourism: The role of environmental ethics. *Journal of Sustainable Tourism, 13*(4): 339–352.

Holzner, M. (2011) Tourism and economic development: The beach disease? *Tourism Management, 32*(4): 922–933.

Kim, H., Chen, M., and Jang, S. (2006) Tourism expansion and economic development: The case of Taiwan. *Tourism Management, 27*(5): 925–933.

Kim, J., and Fesenmaier, D.R. (2017) Sharing tourism experiences: The posttrip experience. *Journal of Travel Research, 56*(1): 28–40.

Lagiewsky, R. (2006) The application of the TALC model: A literature survey. In: R. Butler (Ed.), *The Tourism Area Life Cycle, Vol 1: Applications and Modifications*. Clevedon, UK: Channel View, pp. 27–50.

Liu, J., Nijkamp, P., and Lin, D. (2017) Urban–rural imbalance and tourism-led growth in China. *Annals of Tourism Research, 64*: 24–36.

Lo, I., McKercher, B., Cheung, C., and Law, R. (2011) Tourism and online photography. *Tourism Management, 32*: 725–731.

Loomis, J.B. (2014) Economic valuation: Concepts and empirical methods. In: M, Fischer and P. Nijkamp (Eds.), *Handbook of Regional Science*. Berlin: Springer, pp. 973–992.

Ma, M., and Hassink, R. (2013) An evolutionary perspective on tourism area development. *Annals of Tourism Research, 41*: 89–109.

Malakauskaite, A., and Navickas, V. (2010) Relation between the level of clusterization and tourism sector competitiveness. *Engineering Economics, 21*(1). http://inzeko.ktu.lt/index.php/EE/article/view/11650

Martin, R. (2014) Path dependence and the spatial economy. In: M. Fischer and P. Nijkamp (Eds.), *Handbook of Regional Science*. New York: Springer, pp. 609–629.

Mullis, B. (2017) The growth paradox: Can tourism ever be sustainable? World Economic Forum. Available online at www.weforum.org/agenda/2017/08/the-growth-paradox-can-tourism-ever-be-sustainable/

Neffke, F., Henning, M., and Boschma, R. (2009) How do regions diversify over time? Industry related-ness and the development of new growth paths in regions. *Economic Geography, 87*(3): 237–265.

OECD. (2000) *Measuring the Role of Tourism in OECD Economies: The OECD Manual on Tourism Satellite Accounts and Employment*. Paris: OECD Publishing.

OECD. (2014) *Tourism and the Creative Economy*. Paris: OECD Publishing.

Ostrom, E. (2010) The challenge of common-pool resources. *Environment, 50*(4): 8–20.

Ostrom, E. (2011) Background on the institutional analysis and development framework. *The Policy Studies Journal, 39*(1): 7–27.

Polo, C., and Valle, E. (2012) Input–output and SAM models. In: L. Dwyer, A. Gill, and N. Seetaram (Eds.), *Handbook of Research Methods in Tourism: Quantitative and Qualitative Approaches*. Cheltenham, UK: Edward Elgar, pp. 227–260.

Rihova, I., Buhalis, B., Gouthro, M.B., and Moital, M. (2018) Customer-to-customer co-creation practices in tourism: Lessons from customer-dominant logic. *Tourism Management, 67*: 362–375.

Risso, W., Barquet, A., and Brida, J. (2010) Causality between economic growth and tourism expansion: Empirical evidence from Trentino-Alto Adige. *TOURISMOS: An International Multidisciplinary Journal of Tourism, 5*(2): 87–98.

Romão, J., Guerreiro, J., and Rodrigues, P.M.M. (2016) Tourism growth and regional resilience: The 'beach disease' and the consequences of the global crisis of 2007. *Tourism Economics, 22*(4): 699–714.

Romão, J., and Nijkamp, P. (2017) A spatial econometric analysis of impacts of innovation, produc-tivity and agglomeration on tourism competitiveness. *Current Issues in Tourism*. DOI: 10.1080/13683500.2017.1366434

Romão, J., Kourtit, K., Neuts, B., and Nijkamp, P. (2018) The smart city as a common place for tourists and residents: A structural analysis on the determinants of urban attractiveness. *Cities, 78*: 67–75.

Sassen, S. (2010) The city: Its return as a lens for social theory. *City, Culture & Society, 1*: 3–11.

Saayman, M., and Saayman, A. (2014) Who is willing to pay to see the Big 7? *Tourism Economics, 20*(6): 1181–1198.

Sanz-Ibáñez, C., and Clavé, S. (2014) The evolution of destinations: Towards an evolutionary and relational economic geography approach. *Tourism Geographies, 16*(4): 563–579.

Scott, A.J. (2007) Capitalism and urbanization in a new key? The cognitive-cultural dimension. *Social Forces, 85*(4): 1465–1482.

Scott, A.J. (2017) *The Constitution of The City.* Cham, Switzerland: Palgrave Macmillan.

Sigala, M. (2012) Exploiting web 2.0 for new service development: Findings and implications from the Greek tourism industry. *International Journal of Tourism Research, 14*: 551–566.

Sigala, M., and Marinidis, D. (2012) E-Democracy and Web 2.0: A framework enabling DMOS to engage stakeholders in collaborative destination management. *Tourism Analysis, 17*(2): 105–120.

Tussyadiah, I.P. (2014) Toward a theoretical foundation for experience design in tourism. *Journal of Travel Research, 53*(5): 543–564.

Tussyadiah, I.P., and Fesenmaier, D. (2009) Mediating tourist experiences. *Annals of Tourism Research, 36*(1): 24–40.

UNESCO. (2001) *Universal Declaration on Cultural Diversity.* Paris: UNESCO.

United Nations. (2010) *Tourism Satellite Account: Recommended Methodological Framework.* New York: UN Department of Economic and Social Affairs.

UNWTO. (2003) *Study on Tourism and Intangible Cultural Heritage.* Madrid: UNWTO.

UNWTO. (2012) *Global Report on City Tourism.* Madrid: UNWTO.

UNWTO. (2017) *Measuring Sustainable Tourism.* Madrid: UNWTO.

UNWTO. (2018) *World Tourism Barometer.* Madrid: UNWTO.

Wang, Y., Weaver, D.B., and Kwek, A. (2016) Beyond the mass tourism stereotype: Power and empowerment in Chinese tour packages. *Journal of Travel Research, 55*(6): 724–737.

Weaver, D., and Lawton, L.J. (2007) Twenty years on: The state of contemporary ecotourism research. *Tourism Management, 28*: 1168–1179.

Wright, W.C.C., and Eppink, F.V. (2016). Drivers of heritage value: A meta-analysis of monetary valuation studies of cultural heritage. *Ecological Economics, 130*: 277–284.

12

THE EFFECTS OF SMALL AND MEDIUM-SIZED TOURISM ENTERPRISES ON DESTINATIONS

Sevinç Aslan and Mithat Zeki Dinçer

Introduction

Small and medium-sized enterprises (SMEs) aim to provide more benefits to local destinations where they are located. As SMEs benefit from local sources, dependence on foreign resources is minimized. SMEs are able to adapt more quickly to market changes and, while providing a stable society, they cause less damage to the environment as well (Echtner, 1995: 123).

Tourism, as a sector dominated by SMEs, can create many opportunities for entrepreneurs in both formal and non-formal sectors. The socio-economic and environmental outcomes of entrepreneurship are important for the tourism activities of under-developed or developing communities (Kokkranikal & Morrison, 2011: 138). Along with this, small and medium-sized tourism enterprises (SMTEs) are essential for providing visitor satisfaction in a destination. These are businesses that mostly create individual experiences and a unique sense of place for visitors (Clarke, 2004: 194). Tourists want to be happy and peaceful in the visited destination during their tourism activities. Similarly, there may be a positive relationship between the perceptions of residents' tourism-related environmental impact and health/well-being. In this case, environmental policies and programmes should be formulated to increase the health and well-being of both residents and tourists in order to promote tourism development. Similar conclusions can be drawn about economic, cultural and social policies and programmers (Kim, Uysal & Sirgy, 2013: 528).

Small and medium-sized tourism enterprises and destination

Tourism has become an important sector for both developed and developing countries with the economic, social and environmental contributions it makes. However, there are also a number of adverse effects alongside the contributions tourism makes to the destination. Table 12.1 summarizes the positive and negative effects of tourism on three dimensions: economic, socio-cultural and environmental.

The tourism industry is dominated by SMEs; especially in the eastern Mediterranean basin, market characteristics (tourist attractions), socio-cultural characteristics (the traditional structure of the tourism sector, the role of families in terms of tourism entrepreneurship,

Table 12.1 General impacts of tourism on destination

Impacts	Positive	Negative
Economic	• Improving the standard of living • Increasing investment • Increasing business activity • Opportunities for local business • Employment opportunities • Revenue for local government • Funding for public services (e.g. health, police, fire services)	• Increasing property taxes • Increasing the price of goods and services • Increasing the price of land • Excessive demand • Problems with the protection of public spaces such as parks, beaches
Socio-cultural	• Upgrading facilities such as outdoor recreation facilities, parks and roads • Reducing crowdedness in theatres, movies, concerts and athletic events • Revitalizing cultures when dying customs are rejuvenated for tourists • Opportunities to socialize • Intercultural interaction	• Traffic congestion problems • Crowdedness in public areas • Contributing to social ills such as begging, gambling, drug trafficking, prostitution etc. • Uprooting traditional society • Deterioration of the traditional culture • Disruption of traditional cultural structures and behavioural patterns • Increasing noise level
Environmental	• Helps create a greater awareness of the need to preserve the environment by capturing its natural beauty for tourist purposes • Increasing investments in the environmental infrastructure of the host country • Tourism also thought to be a relatively clean industry, with fewer pollution problems compared with other types of industry	• The destruction of natural resources • Degradation of vegetation • Depletion of wildlife • Litter

Source: Adapted from Kim et al., 2013: 528, and Deery, Jago, & Fredline, 2012: 68.

general entrepreneur population) and geographical features strengthened the tendency towards small and family tourism enterprises (Bastakis, Buhalis & Butler, 2004: 151).

Considering the SMEs and tourism literature, it is important to agree a common definition of SMTEs (Akbaba, 2012: 33). Even defining SMEs can be challenging, as generalized classifications cannot be correctly adopted (Gunasekaran, Rai & Griffin, 2011: 5491). Academic studies generally try to formalize SME definitions based on the number of employees. However, it is not possible to say that there is a universal consensus on size. Definitions vary from country to country (Thomas, Shaw & Page, 2011: 965). When these definitions are examined, some institutions define small enterprises as "One which employs between 10 and 49 employees" and some others define it as "employing fewer than 50 people" (Akbaba, 2012: 33).

In the context of tourism, Morrison (1996: 400) defines a small tourism enterprise as a business that is "financed by one individual or small group and is directly managed by its owner(s), in a personalized manner and not through the medium of formalized management structure". SMTEs differ in terms of physical facilities, production/service capacity, market share and number of employees compared with large tourism facilities. Breen, Bergin-Seers, Jago and Carlsen (2005) have produced a more descriptive definition. Their conceptualization is as follows:

> Small and medium tourism enterprises comprise all businesses, which by their own definition, operate in the tourism industry and employ up to 100 employees. Specifically, micro businesses are those that employ between one and four workers, small businesses employ between five and 19 employees and medium businesses employ between 20 and 100 employees.
>
> *(Breen et. al, 2005: vi)*

SMTEs constitute the backbone of the tourism industry, as they undertake a significant part of the tourism output (Jones & Haven-Tang, 2005: 2). These enterprises are essential as local producers of cheap-import-substitute products for low-income groups, and they provide support to the sector by producing components, tools and spare parts for larger enterprises (Tambunan, 2005: 138). Small tourism enterprises prefer to offer their services directly to their customers, rather than seeing tourism as a trade. As well as low entry costs, local ownership and better local supply links are some of the characteristics of SMTEs (Wanhill, 2000: 133). It is important to consider the business environment and the sector in which they operate when analysing the business performance, characteristics or managerial aspects of these businesses (Akbaba, 2012: 32).

The tourism industry focuses on the marketing and creation of tourist experiences through "place commodification". Thus, destinations can be expressed as places marketed to meet the needs and desires of tourists (Smeral, 1998: 372). Destinations are areas where different businesses operate side by side under different market conditions. In other words, in the same destination, there are enterprises with largely different economic dynamics, depending on the interrelationship between market competition, product character and production style (Ioannides & Petersen, 2003: 416). According to Buhalis and Cooper (1998: 329), the tourism destination can be regarded as "the 'raison d'être' (reason) for tourism, providing an amalgam of tourism products such as facilities, attractions and activities which respond to the needs and wants of the tourists". Most tourism destinations include small SMTEs offering a wide range of tourist products and services, which are consumed under the brand name of the destination (Buhalis, 2000: 98).

There are a few characteristics associated only with SMTEs. Some of these can create obstacles to competitiveness at a destination where SMTEs are dominant. These are as follows (Jones & Haven-Tang, 2005: 10–14):

SMEs generate more interesting employment opportunities: The decision-making process is faster in SMTEs, communication is better, and employees are more involved in business decisions. Not being restricted by rules attracts potential employees to work in such enterprises.

Business failure rates: Tourism entrepreneurs generally focus on informal capital resources. More than half are dependent on personal and family savings (Shaw, 2004: 125). Along with that, small-scale businesses can be vulnerable in comparison with large-scale businesses (Scheyvens & Russell, 2012: 423). Therefore, they face more financial difficulties, which cause some businesses to close during the establishment phase. As a consequence, they tend to have a higher failure rate than that of large organizations (Terziovski, 2010: 892).

Flexibility and innovation: Flexibility can be reduced as larger firms increase their quality levels. Small businesses can benefit more from flexibility, especially because they have close relationships with customers.

Entrepreneurial motivations: Entrepreneurial activities can vary according to the person and entrepreneurship intention. Entrepreneurship is generally associated with the motivation to gain income, but in tourism this might as well include other motives, because tourism is driven by so-called lifestyle entrepreneurship (Ateljevic & Doorne, 2000: 280). The significance of such lifestyle motives related to tourism entrepreneurship is an important characteristic of small firms in this economic sector (Shaw, 2004: 125). Individuals can become tourism entrepreneurs to achieve their desired lifestyle. Besides this, there are some other types, such as women entrepreneurship, ethnic entrepreneurship and so on.

Business strategies: Strategies in small businesses can vary. Some businesses can use their resources appropriately for growth, whereas others are insufficient in terms of management.

Ease of entry leads to weak endemic business models: The fact that it is easy to enter the tourism industry can lead to the emergence of entrepreneurs who act with the mentality that "everyone can do it". But endemic business models can occur owing to managers who do not have sufficient skills in business and personnel management.

Fortress mentality and resistance to participation in the development of destination propositions: Businesses with a "fortress mentality" are closed against external elements. Small businesses may be affected through less formal channels (such as family, friends and social media comments) because it is hard to reach formal sources at the beginning, which causes businesses to have a more closed structure.

Lack of management skills and attitudes towards training: Small businesses experience financial difficulties, particularly in the establishment phase; this exacerbates the lack of management skills and has negative impacts on education, future investments and knowledge management and also creates serious effects for the future of individual tourism SMEs and, ultimately. the destination as well.

Poor market intelligence: Weak market knowledge prevents businesses from using their full potential. It is important that businesses know their target market well, in order to reach their goals. Businesses that consider the performance of their competitors and external changes are more likely to succeed (Wood, 2001: 286).

Lack of integrated approach to business planning and functionality: The lack of management skills and the negative view of education, future investments and knowledge management affect the future of individual SMTEs and also the destination.

Smaller-scale operations also face an additional challenge not faced by larger, foreign-owned enterprises: They have an extra responsibility to fulfil the social and cultural expectations of the wider community (Scheyvens & Russell, 2012: 426).

The dominance of SMTEs is particularly important in terms of achieving sustainability targets, especially those of destinations that are ecologically and economically sensitive. These initiatives are assumed to spread economic benefits and improve living conditions for local

Table 12.2 SMTEs' impacts on the destination

• Poor public transport infrastructure	• Increased health and safety regulations	• Lack of affordable housing and business properties
• Waste disposal – increased waste disposal costs	• Supply-chain pressures – increased demand from business customers to include social issues in tendering processes	• Increased regulatory environment
• Increased environmental regulations	• Staff recruitment and retention	• Delays in payment of contracts
• Litter	• Increases in cost of living	• Imposition of tax
• Lack of recycling facilities and lack of information on the benefits on recycling	• Social exclusion in local communities	• Lack of enforcement of regulations
• Congestion	• Retail crime	• Supply-chain understanding of regulations
• Lack of awareness of environmental risks and opportunities	• Low-level crime, anti-social behaviour (e.g., vandalism)	• Lack of competitive tendering opportunities
• Pollution incidents	• Lack of awareness of social risks and opportunities	• Lack of awareness of economic risks and opportunities
• Energy use – increased cost associated with energy use	• Poor reputation within the local community	• Impact of globalization on small businesses – international competition has increased, creating an imbalance of power
• Supply-chain pressures – increased demand from business customers to include environmental issues in tendering processes	• Image and profile of the subregions	• Planning regime
	• Media imbalance that does not present the destination in a positive light	
• Lack of facilities (e.g. parking spaces) in built-up areas	• Increased insurance costs and postcode discrimination	• Poor IT infrastructure

Source: Roberts, Lawson & Nicholls, 2006: 280.

people. In the sustainable tourism agenda of a destination, the "new tourist" plays a part that is highly likely to be well educated, environmentally friendly, sophisticated in terms of taste and consumption, and seeking authentic and customized experiences. SMTEs may be suitable to meet the needs and desires of these tourists. It is important to be able to measure the behaviour of SMTEs at this point (Roberts & Tribe, 2008: 590). In this respect, it is significant to know the adverse effects of SMTEs on the destination. Table 12.2 shows the risks to the destination of SMEs in general.

Economic effects

One of the most important developments in international tourism policy in the last 20 years is the growing interest in small businesses. SMEs have been recognized by policymakers as the industry's economic vitality and, at the same time, ironically, a barrier to innovation and growth. These and other uncertainties have encouraged academics to find out how these small businesses work and affect destinations (Thomas et al., 2011: 963).

Entrepreneurship associated with SMEs plays a key role in the creation of new enterprises and in the provision of employment. It stimulates the market by encouraging the competition (Ball, 2005: 2). Developing countries value SMEs for several reasons. The most important of these is the fact that, on average, while creating relatively high employment, SMEs achieve good productivity, in particular capital and all the factors taken together (i.e. total factor productivity). For this reason, in terms of productivity, SMEs are better than large enterprises at creating employment (Berry, Rodriguez & Sandee, 2002: 141). Also, SME supporters argue that SMEs increase competition and entrepreneurship and thus provide external benefits of efficiency, innovation and collective productivity growth throughout the economy (Beck, Demirguc-Kunt & Levine, 2005: 200).

SMEs constitute the driving force of industrial growth and development. This is fundamentally owing to the great potential of achieving the basic objectives of development as well as providing diversification and expansion of production and service. These enterprises use local raw materials and technology to help achieve their goals (Akingunola, 2011: 79). In addition, SMEs play an important role in successfully managing large-scale local and global supply chains (see also Husband & Mandal, 1999: 699). If large-scale companies want to be competitive, they have to select the appropriate partner companies (suppliers), most of which are SMEs. In order to develop a productive and sustainable supply chain, SMEs need to carefully consider their strategies, techniques and technologies (Gunasekaran et al., 2011: 5490).

SMEs play an important role in reducing poverty and, at the same time, make a significant contribution to the growth of emerging economies (Agbeibor, 2006: 40). The SME sector contributes to the economy through high levels of employment, job creation and rapid response to new markets (Kyriakidou & Gore, 2005: 193). SMEs also can enhance productivity through market participation and distribution of resources that conclusively provide poverty alleviation (Maksimov, Wang & Luo, 2017: 255).

Although market and institutional failures do affect the growth of SMEs, they are seen as the engine of economic development. In addition to the growing interest in subsidizing SMEs, there are also opinions that question the effectiveness of pro-SME policies. Critics are concentrating on the business environment that small or large businesses face. Low entry and exit barriers, effective contracting applications and access to financing characterize the business environment that is causing the competition (Beck & Demirguc-Kunt, 2006: 2932).

Recognizing that SMEs are dominant in tourism, tourism leaders are encouraging the growth of this sector to provide economic benefits from a healthy tourism sector. These positive economic impacts include job creation, GDP growth, foreign exchange earnings and foreign direct investment. Ensuring that these benefits are sustainable requires that tourism handle many difficulties, including misunderstanding about the nature of tourism, which is an important part of economic activities (Smith, 2006: 58). It is important to implement empirical studies besides theoretical ones in order to understand the role of the entrepreneur in generating tourist products and services and the importance of tourism enterprises in terms of regional economies. This kind of approach would make the point that tourism is an integral part of the economy (Ioannides & Petersen, 2003: 412).

SMTEs, which facilitate the rapid transfer of tourism expenditures into the local economy, have significant economic impacts on host communities. One of the most important effects is to increase the multiplier effect of tourism activities in the destination (Buhalis & Cooper, 1998: 330). These enterprises provide a stable employment environment, enabling the local economy to integrate with outside economies even during periods of recession (Buhalis & Main, 1998: 198), and also, owing to the great importance of fixed costs in large hotels, a predictable and seasonally constant demand such as business tourism is required. For this reason, the dominance of SMEs is an indispensable element in terms of ensuring the supply of accommodation around the country (Leidner, 2004: 41).

The most important adverse effect of SMTEs is on wages. Those working in the tourism sector in developed and developing countries receive lower salaries than those working in other sectors. This difference is wider in less developed countries with high unemployment rates, especially among unskilled workers. Informal employment relations in SMEs employing almost half of the workforce in hotels and catering businesses around the world contribute to unremunerated employment, child labour and other unacceptable forms of social exploitation (Neto, 2003: 215).

The informal sector is where the opportunities for small businesses are more common. For example, only a few families run hotels in Vietnam's Bai Chay. But, in tourism, local partici-pation constitutes 70–80% of the population. Apart from employees in hotels and restaurants, some women sell noodles on stalls, and some women and children are ambulant vendors. Anyone with a boat or motorcycle provides transportation services to tourists. But the informal sector is often ignored by politicians, which leads to damage to the economy (Ashley, Boyd & Goodwin, 2000: 3).

Environmental effects

As tourism is an energy-intensive sector, its environmental impacts are particularly significant at the local level. The relatively high energy consumption by hotels (such as the energy used for air conditioning, heating and cooking), as well as the fuel used for tourism-related transportation, can increase air pollution specifically. Local air and noise pollution, as well as the urban conges-tion associated with intensive tourism activities, can sometimes create discontent between locals and tourists visiting that destination (Neto, 2003: 217). Given the majority of SMEs and the diversity of pollution they create, it is important to know the environmental impacts of SMEs and how they perform in this regard (Seiffert, 2008: 1459). It is very difficult to assess the relationship between tourism and the environment. Large tourism operators are trying to take precautions in this regard by employing individuals who are responsible for the entire service chain and envi-ronmental affairs. As SMEs cannot control the value chain, they often take precautions through various collaborations and associations (Leidner, 2004: V).

Although the negative effects of SMEs on the environment are not very visible, there is an argument that their total impact is high (Gadenne, Kennedy & McKeiver, 2009: 45). Accommodation facilities are responsible for about 1% of all global emissions (Coles, Dinan & Warren, 2016: 399). Clearly, large-scale businesses are responsible for most of the observed pollution. In the case of pollution load and risk, despite small-scale enterprises not producing as much waste as larger industries, they still contribute to environmental pollu-tion (Frijns & Van Vliet, 1999: 970). Although it is very difficult to estimate the environ-mental impacts of small-scale enterprises at local and regional levels, it can be observed that their contribution is approximately 70% of the sectoral pollution in general (Hillary, 2004: 561). In the context of the tourism and hospitality industries, there are different opinions on the environmental impacts of these sectors. The consumption of natural resources is a con-stant challenge for all industries, although tourism industries do not use resources at high levels. But, even in countries that are very serious about resource usage, there is limited research on the impact of tourism SMEs on natural resources (Alonso & Ogle, 2010: 824). In particular, SMTEs may cause more pollution in natural areas by creating more density in certain regions.

There are an increasing number of commercial pressures on SMTEs to reduce environmental adverse effects to a minimum: substantial cost savings associated with effective management of waste and resources; increased protection against future cost increases (taxes, waste disposal and transport); market opportunities for environmental goods and services; demands made by insurance companies, financial institutions and stakeholders; and contract requirements (Friedman, Miles & Adams, 2000: 326). Also, small businesses have recognized that sustainability of the environment is necessary to protect the future of tourism (Berry & Ladkin, 1997: 434). Responsibility practices have recently been implemented by SMTEs to reduce the adverse effects on the destination in this regard. These practices, which have environmental, social and economic dimensions, are implemented through operational and organizational mechanisms. Although many of these businesses state that they are already taking action, there is still a long way to go (Garay & Font, 2012: 336). Small-scale enterprises generally do not have access to environmentally sensitive technologies that are compatible with their scale. Along with that, small-scale enterprises usually have limited space for the installation of treatment systems, and economic problems can prevent the installation and operation of pollution control facilities. Often, small-scale businesses operate in very competitive markets and only make marginal profits. So, adding environmental liability-related regulations to their costs can threaten their profitability (Frijns & Van Vliet, 1999: 971).

Sustainability is in perfect harmony with the lifestyles, habits and routines of most SMEs, and this positively correlates with improved performance. However, small businesses are hesitant to transfer their sustainability messages and to use sustainability actions to attract customers. It is therefore important to examine in more detail the initiatives undertaken by small businesses in ensuring sustainability in a destination (Font, Garay & Jones, 2016: 1447). Despite the fact that SMEs are widespread in the tourism industry, there are not enough data about the motives of these initiatives, the obstacles they have encountered, the measures applied and the effect of these measures, in terms of sustainability (Font et al., 2016: 1440). It is important to know the role of these initiatives in achieving the sustainable goals of the destinations. However, there is no mechanism to measure the exact size of this contribution (Roberts & Tribe, 2008: 575–576). Small firms in tourism are not willing to embrace the growing environmental agenda of the public sector to minimize the carbon footprint of tourism activities in order to reduce its contribution to CO_2 emissions and climate change (Thomas et al., 2011: 969). There are a number of motivating factors for and obstacles to SMTEs' fulfilment of social responsibility activities. Tamajón and Font (2013: 42) stated that the most important reasons (non-economic) for SMTEs exhibiting corporate social responsibility are environmental protection, community development and personal desire (lifestyle choice). Economic reasons are also important, but these are secondary. The most important economic reasons in this sense are cost reduction, marketing and image acquisitions, and legal requirements. Besides these, the most important obstacles that corporate social responsibility practices face are time, money and/or human resource limitations (Seiffert, 2008: 1447).

Many SMTEs lack strict environmental standards. Although professionally managed SMEs contribute to the development of the destination, those with unsatisfactory products and services undermine consumer confidence. Long-term customer satisfaction in tourism is dependent on the preservation of the natural and cultural resources of the destination (Clarke, 2004: 194). However, the implementation of environmental policies in SMTEs is usually constrained and does not receive sufficient support from owners or senior management (Chan, 2011: 4). The biggest problem for SMEs seems to be finding the money needed to invest in improvements to environmental performance. For this reason, an important barrier to the adoption and implementation of environmental monitoring systems may be related to costs (Chan, 2011: 7).

The dominance of small businesses and the heterogeneity of these enterprises in the tourism industry pose a particular challenge for the implementation of sustainable practices (Berry & Ladkin, 1997: 434).

Social effects

In recent times, businesses have become aware of the importance of establishing and managing positive relationships with the community. It is not only about social concerns, but also about providing support to the civil society (Russo & Perrini, 2010: 215). For small business owners, the most important social issue, in theory and in practice, is the health and well-being of the employees. The others are to be a good role model, to support local businesses and people, to help charities and to be sensitive to the environment (Spence & Lozano, 2000: 48), as well as supporting their industry and generating employment for others (Spence & Perrini, 2009: 22).

Small-scale locally controlled ventures such as traditional resorts, traditional food, music, leather goods, curio shops, camping sites, community tour operations, tourism activities such as hiking and canoe safaris, and SMTEs can have an important influence on the social environment (Mbaiwa, 2005: 169). Bike rental operations, small restaurants, retail operations and provision of accommodations are some of the examples that SMEs can create. Also, small and medium-sized hotel enterprises serve as a catalyst to provide significant power to communities, helping transform local resources into tourist products and services (Lordkipanidze, Brezet & Backman, 2005: 791). With these activities, SMTEs create employment opportunities especially for local people and drive the economic development of the region in which they are located. Thus, they provide various opportunities for social development (Jamieson, Goodwin & Edmunds, 2004: 12).

SMTEs can make a significant contribution to empowering women and alleviating poverty because of the significant number of jobs provided for women and unskilled workers in the industry (Neto, 2003: 215). Especially in recent years, the role of women in the economy and the importance of female entrepreneurship have increased. Women entrepreneurs have become important economic forces (Ball, 2005: 2). SMTEs owned by women bring in a unique value to the destinations where they are located (see also, Maksimov et al., 2017: 255). On one hand, woman can find an opportunity to work in tourism; on the other hand, they are able to generate income through the advantages of tourism. Also, being an SME owner is the aim of many marginalized people in society. Especially in destinations where ethnic minorities are concentrated, for such excluded groups, SMEs are an institutional reaction and provide employment as well as income (Blackburn & Ram, 2006: 76).

It is important not to evaluate the social impacts of SMTEs separately from their economic and environmental impacts. Whereas the local community pays the costs of tourism development such as the degradation of environmental resources, commercialization of landscapes and congestion, most of the economic benefits flow abroad and make tourism in the destination unsustainable (Batta, 2016: 19). In the name of every effort to improve local welfare, small-sized businesses can create a marginal situation. Support for these businesses could lead to some challenges to existing businesses, because it would cause the demand to be distributed among more enterprises (Fleischer & Felsenstein, 2000: 1009).

Many SMEs are too small to provide childcare facilities and operate in a market structure where they have limited and variable influence. They are also known for inconsistent employment practices. Another issue is that self-employed owners' economic status varies from high-paid hotel owner to low-paid owner of a small café. This leads to differentiation of access to resources and an unequal influence, as well as offering different life opportunities for business owners and employees (Blackburn & Ram, 2006: 77).

Conclusion

SMTEs have many effects on destinations. There are some positive impacts, such as employment and income generation, added value creation, less pressure on the environment, and social effects such as women's employment and poverty alleviation. They have some negative effects as well, such as informal employment, environmental pollution, noise, traffic and other issues. SMEs avoid social responsibility activities for different reasons. For example, SME owners think they have low environmental impact owing to the size of the business. They also believe that they have limited significance for sustainability and the environment. They prefer to be reactive rather than proactive in terms of the effects on the destination. Along with this, they do not have enough resources (monetary and institutional) to be sensitive compared with large businesses (Vernon, Essex, Pinder & Curry, 2003: 52). Small firm owners often do not see themselves as individuals who make great contributions and are responsible for ethical or moral issues. However, it can be indicated that they have a social role. They feel a sense of responsibility towards their employees and strive to protect their social rights and well-being beyond the law (Spence & Lozano, 2000: 49). According to research by Berry and Ladkin (1997) into small businesses in tourism:

- Awareness of tourism is a community activity consisting of small businesses with different backgrounds.
- The public sector needs to play a more active role in addressing sustainability issues.
- There is a need to identify what is encompassed by sustainable tourism.
- There is strong interest in "green" activities, but a desire to go for simple, open and commercially rational ideas.
- There is willingness to take part in activities that they will not spend too much time on. Many SME owners do not want to leave their businesses; they consider it is not affordable.
- Many have a strong interest in local issues, but have limited awareness of their impact on the environment.

References

Agbeibor Jr, W. (2006). Pro-poor economic growth: role of small and medium sized enterprises. *Journal of Asian Economics*, 17(1), 35–40.

Akbaba, A. (2012). Understanding small tourism businesses: a perspective from Turkey. *Journal of Hospitality & Tourism Management*, 19(1), 31–47.

Akingunola, R. O. (2011). Small and medium scale enterprises and economic growth in Nigeria: an assessment of financing options. *Pakistan Journal of Business & Economic Review*, 2(1), 78–97.

Alonso, A. D., & Ogle, A. (2010). Tourism and hospitality small and medium enterprises and environmental sustainability. *Management Research Review*, 33(8), 818–826.

Ashley, C., Boyd, C., & Goodwin, H. (2000). Pro-poor tourism: putting poverty at the heart of the tourism agenda. *Natural Resource Perspectives*, (51). www.odi.org/sites/odi.org.uk/files/odi-assets/publications-opinion-files/2861.pdf

Ateljevic, I., & Doorne, S. (2000). "Staying within the fence": lifestyle entrepreneurship in tourism. *Journal of Sustainable Tourism*, 8(5), 378–392.

Ball, S. (2005). The importance of entrepreneurship to hospitality, leisure, sport and tourism. *Hospitality, Leisure, Sport & Tourism Network*, 1(1), 1–14.

Bastakis, C., Buhalis, D., & Butler, R. (2004). The perception of small and medium sized tourism accommodation providers on the impacts of the tour operators' power in Eastern Mediterranean. *Tourism Management*, 25(2), 151–170.

Batta, R. N. (2016). SMEs and sustainable tourism – the case of an Indian Himalayan destination. *International Journal of Environment & Sustainability*, 5(1), 18–34.

Beck, T., & Demirguc-Kunt, A. (2006). Small and medium-size enterprises: Access to finance as a growth constraint. *Journal of Banking & Finance*, 30(11), 2931–2943.

Beck, T., Demirguc-Kunt, A., and Levine, R. (2005). SMEs, growth, and poverty: cross-country evidence. *Journal of Economic Growth*, 10, 199–229.

Berry, A., Rodriguez, E., & Sandee, H. (2002). Firm and group dynamics in the small and medium enterprise sector in Indonesia. *Small Business Economics*, 18(1–3), 141–161.

Berry, S., & Ladkin, A. (1997). Sustainable tourism: a regional perspective. *Tourism Management*, 18(7), 433–440.

Blackburn, R., & Ram, M. (2006). Fix or fixation? The contributions and limitations of entrepreneurship and small firms to combating social exclusion. *Entrepreneurship & Regional Development*, 18(1), 73–89.

Breen., J., Bergin-Seers, S., Jago, L., & Carlsen, J. (2005). *Small and Medium Tourism Enterprises: the Identification of Good Practice*. Queensland: CRC for Sustainable Tourism.

Buhalis, D. (2000). Marketing the competitive destination of the future. *Tourism Management*, 21(1), 97–116.

Buhalis, D., & Cooper, C. (1998). Competition or co-operation? Small and medium-sized tourism enterprises at the destination. In B. Faulkner, E. Laws & G. Moscardo (Eds), *Embracing and Managing Change in Tourism: International Case Studies*. London: Routledge, 329–351.

Buhalis, D., & Main, H. (1998). Information technology in peripheral small and medium hospitality enterprises: strategic analysis and critical factors. *International Journal of Contemporary Hospitality Management*, 10(5), 198–202.

Chan, E. S. (2011). Implementing environmental management systems in small-and medium-sized hotels: obstacles. *Journal of Hospitality & Tourism Research*, 35(1), 3–23.

Clarke, J. (2004). Trade associations: an appropriate channel for developing sustainable practice in SMEs? *Journal of Sustainable Tourism*, 12(3), 194–208.

Coles, T., Dinan, C., & Warren, N. (2016). Energy practices among small-and medium-sized tourism enterprises: a case of misdirected effort? *Journal of Cleaner Production*, 111, 399–408.

Deery, M., Jago, L., & Fredline, L. (2012). Rethinking social impacts of tourism research: a new research agenda. *Tourism Management*, 33(1), 64–73.

Echtner, C. M. (1995). Entrepreneurial training in developing countries. *Annals of Tourism Research*, 22(1), 119–134.

Fleischer, A., & Felsenstein, D. (2000). Support for rural tourism: does it make a difference? *Annals of Tourism Research*, 27(4), 1007–1024.

Font, X., Garay, L., & Jones, S. (2016). Sustainability motivations and practices in small tourism enterprises in European protected areas. *Journal of Cleaner Production*, 137, 1439–1448.

Friedman, A. L., Miles, S., & Adams, C. (2000). Small and medium-sized enterprises and the environment: evaluation of a specific initiative aimed at all small and medium-sized enterprises. *Journal of Small Business & Enterprise Development*, 7(4), 325–342.

Frijns, J., & Van Vliet, B. (1999). Small-scale industry and cleaner production strategies. *World Development*, 27(6), 967–983.

Gadenne, D. L., Kennedy, J., & McKeiver, C. (2009). An empirical study of environmental awareness and practices in SMEs. *Journal of Business Ethics*, 84(1), 45–63.

Garay, L., & Font, X. (2012). Doing good to do well? Corporate social responsibility reasons, practices and impacts in small and medium accommodation enterprises. *International Journal of Hospitality Management*, 31(2), 329–337.

Gunasekaran, A., Rai, B. K., & Griffin, M. (2011). Resilience and competitiveness of small and medium size enterprises: an empirical research. *International Journal of Production Research*, 49(18), 5489–5509.

Hillary, R. (2004). Environmental management systems and the smaller enterprise. *Journal of Cleaner Production*, 12(6), 561–569.

Husband, S., & Mandal, P. (1999). A conceptual model for quality integrated management in small and medium size enterprises. *International Journal of Quality & Reliability Management*, 16(7), 699–713.

Ioannides, D., & Petersen, T. (2003). Tourism "non-entrepreneurship" in peripheral destinations: a case study of small and medium tourism enterprises on Bornholm, Denmark. *Tourism Geographies*, 5(4), 408–435.

Jamieson, W., Goodwin, H., & Edmunds, C. (2004). *Contribution of tourism to poverty alleviation: pro-poor tourism and the challenge of measuring impacts* [Online]. Bangkok: United Nations Economic and Social Commission for Asia and the Pacific. http://haroldgoodwin.info/resources/povertyalleviation.pdf (accessed 1 February 2015).

Jones, E., & Haven-Tang, C. (2005). Tourism SMEs, service quality and destination competitiveness. In E. Jones & C. Haven (Eds), *Tourism SMEs, Service Quality and Destination Competitiveness*. London: CABI, 1–24.

Kim, K., Uysal, M., & Sirgy, M. J. (2013). How does tourism in a community impact the quality of life of community residents? *Tourism Management*, 36, 527–540.

Kokkranikal, J., & Morrison, A. (2011). Community networks and sustainable livelihoods in tourism: the role of entrepreneurial innovation. *Tourism Planning & Development*, 8(2), 137–156.

Kyriakidou, O., & Gore, J. (2005). Learning by example: benchmarking organizational culture in hospitality, tourism and leisure SMEs. *Benchmarking: An International Journal*, 12(3), 192–206.

Leidner, R. (2004). *The European Tourism Industry: a Multi-sector with Dynamic Markets: Structures, Developments and Importance for Europe's Economy*. Luxembourg: Office for Official Publications of the European Communities.

Lordkipanidze, M., Brezet, H., & Backman, M. (2005). The entrepreneurship factor in sustainable tourism development. *Journal of Cleaner Production*, 13, 787–798.

Maksimov, V., Wang, S. L., & Luo, Y. (2017). Reducing poverty in the least developed countries: the role of small and medium enterprises. *Journal of World Business*, 52(2), 244–257.

Mbaiwa, J. E. (2005). Enclave tourism and its socio-economic impacts in the Okavango Delta, Botswana. *Tourism Management*, 26(2), 157–172.

Morrison, A. (1996). Marketing the small tourism business. In A. V. Seaton & M. M. Bennett (Eds.), *Marketing Tourism Products: Concepts, Issues, Cases*. London: International Thomson Business Press, pp. 399–418.

Neto, F. (2003, August). A new approach to sustainable tourism development: moving beyond environmental protection. *Natural Resources Forum*, 27(3), 212–222.

Roberts, S., Lawson, R., & Nicholls, J. (2006). Generating regional-scale improvements in SME corporate responsibility performance: lessons from Responsibility Northwest. *Journal of Business Ethics*, 67(3), 275–286.

Roberts, S., & Tribe, J. (2008). Sustainability indicators for small tourism enterprises – an exploratory perspective. *Journal of Sustainable Tourism*, 16(5), 575–594.

Russo, A., & Perrini, F. (2010). Investigating stakeholder theory and social capital: CSR in large firms and SMEs. *Journal of Business Ethics*, 91(2), 207–221.

Scheyvens, R., & Russell, M. (2012). Tourism and poverty alleviation in Fiji: comparing the impacts of small-and large-scale tourism enterprises. *Journal of Sustainable Tourism*, 20(3), 417–436.

Seiffert, M. E. B. (2008). Environmental impact evaluation using a cooperative model for implementing EMS (ISO 14001) in small and medium-sized enterprises. *Journal of Cleaner Production*, 16(14), 1447–1461.

Shaw, G. (2004). Entrepreneurial cultures and small business enterprises in tourism. In A. A. Lew, C. M. Hall & A. M. Williams (Eds), *A Companion to Tourism*. Oxford: Blackwell, 122–134.

Smeral, E. (1998). The impact of globalization on small and medium enterprises: new challenges for tourism policies in European countries. *Tourism Management*, 19(4), 371–380.

Smith, S. L. (2006). How big, how many? Enterprise size distributions in tourism and other industries. *Journal of Travel Research*, 45(1), 53–58.

Spence, L. J., & Lozano, J. F. (2000). Communicating about ethics with small firms: experiences from the UK and Spain. *Journal of Business Ethics*, 27(1–2), 43–53.

Spence, L., & Perrini, F. (2009). Practice and politics: ethics and social responsibility in SMEs in the European Union. *African Journal of Business Ethics*, 4(2), 20–31.

Tamajón, L. G., & Font, X. (2013). Corporate social responsibility in tourism small and medium enterprises evidence from Europe and Latin America. *Tourism Management Perspectives*, 7, 38–46.

Tambunan, T. (2005). Promoting small and medium enterprises with a clustering approach: a policy experience from Indonesia. *Journal of Small Business Management*, 43(2), 138–154.

Terziovski, M. (2010). Innovation practice and its performance implications in small and medium enterprises (SMEs) in the manufacturing sector: a resource-based view. *Strategic Management Journal*, 31(8), 892–902.

Thomas, R., Shaw, G., & Page, S. J. (2011). Understanding small firms in tourism: a perspective on research trends and challenges. *Tourism Management*, 32(5), 963–976.

Vernon, J., Essex, S., Pinder, D., & Curry, K. (2003). The "greening" of tourism micro-businesses: outcomes of focus group investigations in South East Cornwall. *Business Strategy and the Environment*, 12(1), 49–69.

Wanhill, S. (2000). Small and medium tourism enterprises. *Annals of Tourism Research*, 27(1), 132–147.

Wood, E. (2001). Marketing information systems in tourism and hospitality small and medium-sized enterprises: a study of Internet use for market intelligence. *International Journal of Tourism Research*, 3(4), 283–299.

Further Reading

Alonso-Almeida, M. D. M., Bagur-Femenias, L., Llach, J., & Perramon, J. (2018). Sustainability in small tourist businesses: the link between initiatives and performance. *Current Issues in Tourism*, 21(1), 1–20.

Armenski, T., Dwyer, L., & Pavluković, V. (2018). Destination competitiveness: public and private sector tourism management in Serbia. *Journal of Travel Research*, 57(3), 384–398.

Buffa, F., Franch, M., & Rizio, D. (2018). Environmental management practices for sustainable business models in small and medium sized hotel enterprises. *Journal of Cleaner Production*, 194, 656–664.

Giama, E., & Papadopoulos, A. M. (2018). Carbon footprint analysis as a tool for energy and environmental management in small and medium-sized enterprises. *International Journal of Sustainable Energy*, 37(1), 21–29.

Hussain, M. D., Bhuiyan, A. B., Said, J., & Halim, M. S. B. A. (2017). Eradicating poverty through micro, small, and medium enterprises: an empirical exploration. *MAYFEB Journal of Business & Management*, 1, 42–49.

Shariff, N. M., Abidin, A. Z., & Bahar, M. R. (2018). Corporate governance model in the Malaysian tourism small and medium-sized enterprises. *Advances in Social Sciences Research Journal*, 5(2), 115–123.

13

ECONOMIC IMPACT OF VISITOR (TRADER) HARASSMENT ON TOURIST DESTINATIONS AND WHAT TOURISM LEADERS CAN DO ABOUT IT

Annmarie Nicely and Karla "Gabbie" Morrison

Introduction

Visitor harassment is a major problem in many tourist destinations across the world (Visitor Harassment Research Unit at Purdue, 2018), and tourism leaders globally have been seeking answers on how best to solve it. Though few, over the last two decades there have been important studies conducted on the phenomenon. Therefore, the goal of this chapter is to share the findings of both published and unpublished research on the topic. Specifically, the chapter looks at: (1) critical requirements for visitor harassment, (2) the economic impact of visitor harassment on tourist destinations, and (3) ways tourism leaders might reduce the negative financial impact of these behaviors on their local tourist destinations. Also included in the chapter is a series of activities to assist readers to apply some of the research findings discussed to an actual visitor harassment problem at a local tourist destination.

There are three broad categories of visitor harassment: institutional, sexual, and trader harassment. *Institutional harassment* is the aggravation of visitors by representatives of the state, such as local police officers, customs officials, and immigration officers (J. L. McElroy, Tarlow, & Carlisle, 2007). *Sexual harassment* is unwanted advances of a sexual nature directed toward visitors by individuals at the destination (de Albuquerque & McElroy, 2001; Kozak, 2007; J. L. McElroy et al., 2007; Rathnayake & Wijesundara, 2015; Skipper, 2009). *Trader harassment* is the bothering of visitors by micro-traders at the destination (de Albuquerque & McElroy, 2001; Kozak, 2007; J. L. McElroy et al., 2007; Nicely & Mohd Ghazali, 2014; Skipper, 2009). Of the three broad types, the harassment of visitors by micro-traders is the most common (Griffin, 2003; J. L. McElroy et al., 2007). The focus of this chapter is on the last. Therefore, visitor harassment within the present context is trader harassment.

Requirements for visitor (trader) harassment

There are three critical features of trader harassment. First, the selling behavior is unwanted or undesired by the visitor (de Albuquerque & McElroy, 2001; Griffin, 2003). Second, the trading behavior causes the visitor to feel angry, afraid, and/or sad (Griffin, 2003; Nicely & Mohd Ghazali, 2014). Third, the selling behavior is usually frequent and/or aggressive. Illegal, immoral, and dishonest small-trade behaviors have also been characterized as harassment by visitors. The first two features mentioned are established in the scholarly literature. However, in 2019 the latter two are not. An analysis of blog postings by one of the authors of this chapter on visitor harassment episodes around the world revealed recurrent use of the words "annoying", "badgering", "bothering", "continuous", "constant", "hounding", "incessant", "nagging", "persistent", and "unrelenting" when describing such behaviors, which suggests an important feature of the phenomenon is the frequency of the behavior. The same analysis also revealed significant use of the words "abusive", "intimidating", "threatening", "coercing", "pushy", and "insistent", which suggests another important feature of the behavior is aggressiveness. The final observation from the blog postings on trader harassment concerned visitors being asked to purchase items and services they believe to be illegal or immoral, such as counterfeit goods, drugs, and/or sex. There was also frequent reference made in the same blog postings of being cheated and overcharged by micro-traders. Most of the blog postings analyzed were from the travel website TripAdvisor and described visitor (trader) harassment episodes that occurred during the period 2010–2018.

One study, conducted on the Caribbean island of Jamaica, revealed a series of selling behaviors visitors characterized as harassment (Nicely & Mohd Ghazali, 2014), all of which satisfied one or more of the criteria mentioned above, such as, when a micro-trader trailed the visitor during the *solicitation phase* of the trading process, or when a micro-trader directed abusive language toward the visitor during the *sale refusal phase* of the trading process, or when a micro-trader overcharged a visitor during the *sale phase* of the trading process, or when a micro-trader demanded a tip during the *after sale phase* of the trading process (Nicely & Mohd Ghazali, 2014).

Simply defined, a *micro-trader* is someone who is self-employed or works for a business that employs fewer than ten persons and who sells legal or illegal goods and services directly to visitors. Some micro-traders are part of the informal economy of a tourist destination. However, there are some whose business is regulated and, hence, part of a destination's formal economy. There are a minimum of 16 different types of micro-trader that operate at tourist destinations around the world. Some examples include *informal tour guides and transportation operators* such as taxicab drivers and *food vendors and shop operators* such as fruit vendors. Figure 13.1 shows the types of micro-trader that operate at tourist destinations across the world.

Activity 1a: Visitor (trader) harassment behaviors at local tourist destination

In your work group, identify a tourist destination in your area where intense visitor (trader) harassment has been reported. Use various archival sources (such as blog postings and newspaper articles) to determine ways micro-traders in this community harass visitors. Compare the list of trader harassment behaviors discovered to those listed in the Nicely and Mohd Ghazali (2014) study.

Activity 1b: Types of micro-trader at local tourist destination

Use Figure 13.1 to identify the types of micro-trader that operate in the community identified earlier. State the types discovered. Provide examples of each.

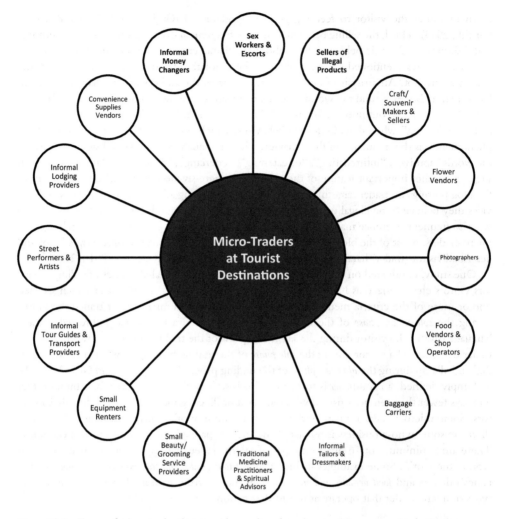

Figure 13.1 Types of micro-trader that provide goods and services to visitors at tourist destinations

Economic impact of visitor (trader) harassment at tourist destinations

According to two studies, one concerning Turkey and the other Sri Lanka, visitor harassment can have a deleterious effect on visitors' satisfaction with their vacation experience (Kozak, 2007; Pathirana & Athula Gnanapala, 2015). In the Turkey study, it was found that the phenomenon can have a significant negative effect on visitors' overall satisfaction with the destination (Kozak, 2007), and, in the Sri Lanka study, it was discovered that the phenomenon can result in visitor dissatisfaction with the destination and diminish their overall impression of the location (Pathirana & Athula Gnanapala, 2015).

One conflicting finding from the scholarly literature is the effect of visitor (trader) harassment on visitors' loyalty intention toward a destination, in particular on their intention to revisit the destination and recommend the destination to others. Two of three studies that examined this found no significant negative effect of visitor (trader) harassment on such intentions. For example, Skipper (2009) found no significant difference between those harassed and those not harassed on their: (1) impression of the destination, (2) intention to return to the destination, and intention to recommend the destination to others. Chepkwony (2013) also found no significant negative effect of visitor (trader) harassment on visitors' intention to revisit the destination. In fact, the researcher found the majority of visitors harassed stated they would return to the destination despite their harassment episode (Chepkwony, 2013). However, Kozak (2007) found that visitor (trader) harassment had a deleterious effect on visitors' intention to revisit the destination. It is important to note Skipper (2009), Chepkwony (2013), and Kozak (2007) looked at visitor harassment in Jamaica, Kenya, and Turkey, respectively.

There may be factors that would cause a visitor to be loyal to a destination after experiencing harassment by local micro-traders. What factors could explain these unusual findings at tourist destinations in Jamaica and Kenya? This question was explored in a pilot study detailed in the final section of this chapter.

However, one important loyalty intention not examined in previous studies published on the undesired selling practice was the effect of visitor (trader) harassment on visitors' intention to support the micro-traders in the future. Visitors' support of local micro-traders is important for the high retention of tourist dollars in these communities. The pilot study found much fewer visitors willing to support local micro-traders than to both recommend and return to the destination after an intense visitor (trader) harassment episode. However, this finding must be viewed with caution as it was a preliminary study.

Therefore, it is clear from previous research that visitor (trader) harassment can negatively impact a visitor's overall satisfaction with a destination. It is likely to impact the willingness of visitors to support micro-traders at the destination as well. Most important is that the phenomenon is likely to limit a destination's economic return from its tourism activities.

Activity 2: Economic impact of visitor (trader) harassment on a local tourist destination

In your work group, determine the impact of visitor (trader) harassment on the tourist destination identified in Activity 1a. Interview a few visitors in this community who personally experienced trader harassment while on vacation at the destination and ascertain whether they would return to the destination, recommend the destination to others, and support the micro-traders in the near and distant future. Finally, from those who indicated they will return to the destination, recommend the destination to others, and support the micro-traders in the future, determine why they would do so. Compare the findings of your mini-study with those mentioned in this chapter.

Reducing negative impact of visitor (trader) harassment

Two general ways tourism leaders can reduce the negative financial impact of visitor (trader) harassment on their local tourist destinations is by implementing measures that would: (1) reduce the unwanted selling behaviors over the long term and (2) ensure certain aspects of their tourist destinations are strong.

Reducing harassment behaviors

According to one study, for tourism leaders to reduce micro-traders' harassing selling behaviors over the long term, they must do the following. First, they must adjust the perpetrators' thoughts about both the undesired and desired selling behaviors. Second, they must introduce them to the desired selling behaviors. Third, they must reinforce among them the desired selling behaviors (Figure 13.2). Concerning the adjustment of their thoughts about the desired and undesired selling behaviors, perpetrators of visitor harassment must be convinced that non-harassing selling behaviors are good, supported, and easy, and that the alternative behaviors are bad, not supported, and difficult. Meanwhile, when introducing the desired selling behaviors, the rudiments of such behaviors must be taught and continuously modeled, and opportunities must be created for them to both observe and practice the wanted selling behaviors (Figure 13.2). Finally, when it comes to fortifying the desired selling behaviors among the target population, positive and negative reinforcement strategies must be used. For example, rewards must be given to those who consistently demonstrate the desired selling behaviors, and benefits must be removed from those who do not. Also, to stop the undesired selling behaviors over the short term, punitive actions must be taken.

Having been revised, the model is now called the *model for sustainably reducing local micro-traders' harassment-related selling behaviors* (SR-MT-HSB). The three most notable differences between the previous and updated model include the following. First is the inclusion of the term "local micro-traders" in the title: What is now known is that there are different types of micro-trader who harass visitors at tourist destinations—locals and migrants (Kitching, 2014). The focus of the first model was on local micro-traders; however, the word "local" was omitted from in the initial title. Second, the term "aggressive selling behaviors" was changed to the more inclusive term "harassment-related behaviors". Finally, the control perception construct in the previous model was changed from "convince micro-traders non harassment-related selling behaviors rewarding" to "convince micro-traders non harassment-related selling behaviors easy". It is now known, from both learning and visitor harassment literature, that believing a task is easy is an important driver of human behavior (Figure 13.2). Figure 13.2 shows the SR-MT-HSB Model.

Therefore, one way tourism leaders can reduce the negative economic impact of visitor (trader) harassment on destinations is by crafting a comprehensive program with goals addressing each area of the SR-MT-HSB model (Figure 13.2). The reason is the less frequently trader harassment occurs, the more satisfied visitors will be with their vacation experience at the destination. Initial research also seems to suggest less intense visitor (trader) harassment will result in greater visitor support of local micro-traders, and the more visitors support local micro-traders, the more tourist dollars will remain in host communities.

Over the years, researchers have proposed a plethora of ways tourism leaders can reduce negative visitor (trader) harassment at their tourist destinations. The ten types of initiative researchers proposed over the years include:

1 Data and information gathering;
2 Information sharing/media;
3 Physical infrastructure improvement;
4 Legislative;
5 Process;
6 Work group structure;
7 Policing;
8 Education and training;
9 Social and funding; and
10 Recognition initiatives.

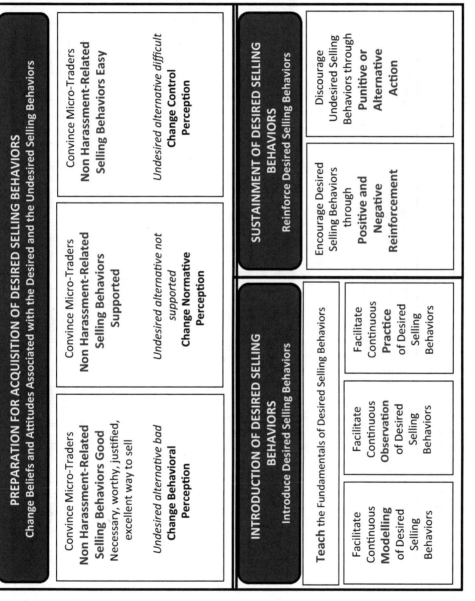

Figure 13.2 Model for sustainably reducing local micro-traders' harassment-related selling behaviors (SR–MT–HSB) at a tourist destination

Table 13.1 Suggestions from the academic community on how tourism leaders may reduce trader harassment at tourist destinations

Major types of program / initiative suggested	Specific programs / initiatives suggested	Source
Data / information gathering	Have systems in place to systematically measure the effectiveness of existing trader harassment mitigation programs. Use data gathered to make policy improvements.	J. McElroy, Tarlow, & Carlisle, 2007; Nicely & Armadita, 2017
	Have systems to gather visitor reports of trader harassment.	Chepkwony & Kangogo, 2013; Khajuria & Khanna, 2014; Rathnayake & Wijesundara, 2015; Wen & Yina, 2015
	Have systems to gather information from residents on how to improve their community's tourism sector	Griffin, 2003
	Commission studies looking at the economic benefits to micro-traders when they harass and do not harass visitors. Use the findings to convince them harassment is bad or to implement policies that will make harassing visitors an unprofitable option for micro-traders	Nicely, Day, Sydnor, & Mohd Ghazali, 2015
Information sharing / media	Inform visitors to locations known for trader harassment of the following: 1 Gratuity expectations for the area; 2 Prices for certain micro-trader products and services such as transportation; 3 Local currency comparisons; 4 Types of trader harassment behavior they are likely to experience in the area; 5 Services available to protect them from trader harassment; 6 Hassle-free routes and locations at the tourist destination; 7 Appropriate responses to trader harassment behaviors when experienced; 8 Safety precautions they should take to protect themselves from negative trader harassment; and 9 Their rights and recourses if harassed by micro-traders.	Badu-Baiden, Adu-Boahen, & Otoo, 2016; Boakye, 2012; Dunn & Dunn, 2002a; Griffin, 2003; Harris, 2012; Khajuria & Khanna, 2014; J. McElroy et al., 2007; Nicely, 2015; Nicely & Armadita, 2017; Rathnayake & Wijesundara, 2015
	Reduce the number of all-inclusive hotels at the destination. Other forms of tourism should also be promoted, such as heritage and community tourism. [The proliferation of all-inclusive hotels has been blamed for high levels of trader harassment]	Rhiney, 2012

Develop and conduct public awareness campaigns to improve local attitude toward tourism and visitors. The campaigns should address the following:	Dunn & Dunn, 2002a, 2002b; Griffin, 2003; Kozak, 2007; J. McElroy et al., 2007)
1 Positives and negatives of the local tourism sector (the negative being visitor harassment);	
2 Importance of tourism to the local economy (such as to gross domestic product, jobs, etc.);	
3 Importance of protecting visitors;	
4 The issue that not all visitors are wealthy;	
5 Importance of making visitors feel welcomed;	
6 Dos and don'ts locals should consider when interacting with visitors; and	
7 Outcomes if trader harassment levels are not tamed.	
Encourage domestic tourism by offering special rates to locals at local hotels and attractions.	Griffin, 2003
Create programs that would inform micro-traders, in particular, of the importance of tourism and tourists as well as of the consequences of trader harassment.	J. McElroy et al., 2007; Pathirana & Athula Gnanapala, 2015; Wen & Yina, 2015
Use respected micro-traders to spread the destination's anti-harassment message.	Nicely et al., 2015
Have marketing campaigns for micro-trading communities such as markets at the destination.	Nicely et al., 2015
Implement a fixed-price policy for micro-trading at tourist destinations. Make displaying of prices an important component of the policy.	Boakye, 2012; Harris, 2012; Khajuria & Khanna, 2014; Nicely, 2015
Encourage product diversification among members of the micro-trading community.	Dunn & Dunn, 2002a
Ensure adequate lighting at locations visitors frequent.	J. McElroy et al., 2007
Implement a surveillance system to monitor micro-trading activities.	Harris, 2012
Ensure vending spaces are comfortable.	de Albuquerque & McElroy, 2001; Griffin, 2003
Physical infrastructure Use open layout and designs for micro-trading communities such as markets.	Nicely, 2015; Nicely et al., 2015

Table 13.1 (continued)

Major types of program / initiative suggested	Specific programs/initiatives suggested	Source
Legislative	Create laws making visitor harassment illegal. Make penalties for visitor harassment behaviors clear.	Badu–Baiden et al., 2016; Chepkwony, 2013; Chepkwony & Kangogo, 2013; de Albuquerque & McElroy, 2001; Griffin, 2003; Prakash, 2013
Process	Create system to effectively vet and license micro–traders in tourism communities.	Chepkwony, 2013; Griffin, 2003
Work group structure	Establish a committee of tourism stakeholders to address the problem of trader harassment	de Albuquerque & McElroy, 2001; J. McElroy et al., 2007; Pathirana & Athula Gnanapala, 2015; Wen & Yina, 2015
	Implement incentive programs that would reward all-inclusive hotels that take steps to help local micro-traders improve their small-trade practices.	Nicely et al., 2015
	Create a special police unit to tackle visitor (trader) harassment. Ensure the members of this team are: multilingual, extroverted, and enjoy working with visitors. Have members of this team patrol tourist hotspots on foot	de Albuquerque & McElroy, 2001; J. McElroy et al., 2007
Policing	Have in place systems that ensure swift response to reports of visitor (trader) harassment.	Khajuria & Khanna, 2014
	Ensure adequate police presence in tourism areas during peak season.	Dunn & Dunn, 2002a
	Ensure prices charged to visitors by micro–traders are frequently monitored.	Khajuria & Khanna, 2014
	Target unlicensed micro-traders.	de Albuquerque & McElroy, 2001
	Tackle large drug and currency dealers with joint police/military operations.	Dunn & Dunn, 2002a
	Ensure members of the special police unit know how to handle visitor harassment complaints.	de Albuquerque & McElroy, 2001
Education & training	Make vocational skills training available to redirect residents who engage in the sale of illegal products and services to visitors (such as drugs and sex) to other viable professions.	Dunn & Dunn, 2002b; Rhiney, 2012

	Develop local appreciation for tourism by incorporating tourism into the school curriculum at the primary, secondary and tertiary levels.	Chepkwony & Kangogo, 2013; Dunn & Dunn, 2002a; Harris, 2012; Kozak, 2007; Nicely, 2015; Nicely et al., 2015; Rathnayake & Wijesundara, 2015; The Travel Foundation, 2013
	Teach micro-traders the fundamentals of good micro-trading, in particular: 1 Behaviors desired, undesired, and why; 2 How to engage in the desired selling behaviors; 3 How to prevent their engagement in the undesired selling behaviors; 4 The language of non-aggressive small trade; 5 How to manage their performance (such as how to learn, interact with important others, and manage stress); 6 How to improve the quality of the products they have for sale; and 7 Bookkeeping.	
	Develop and maintain a knowledge repository for micro-trading in the tourism sector to support micro-traders unlearning the undesired behaviors and acquiring the desired ones.	Nicely, 2015
	Ensure the following techniques are used when teaching micro-traders the fundamentals of effective micro-trade: cooperative learning, dialogue, questioning and critiquing, reflection, and analysis.	Nicely, 2015
	Ensure trainers model the behaviors they would like to see micro-traders demonstrate.	Nicely, 2015
Funding & social	Establish support initiatives for micro-trading communities with a reputation for not harassing visitors.	Nicely et al., 2015
Recognition	Have programs that would reward locals who report micro-traders who engage in harassment behaviors (such as cheating).	Harris, 2012
	Have in place programs rewarding micro-traders who do not harass visitors.	Nicely et al., 2015
Other	Implement programs integrating micro-traders into the mainstream tourism industry.	Dunn & Dunn, 2002b; Griffin, 2003; J. McElroy et al., 2007

In addition, researchers have proposed that various groups must be targeted using these initiatives if a destination's visitor (trader) harassment problem is to be effectively cauterized. The four populations researchers suggest tourism leaders target include: visitors to the area, the wider local community, other tourism stakeholders, and the micro-traders themselves. Table 13.1 lists specific programs and initiatives researchers suggest would reduce visitor (trader) harassment levels at tourist destinations.

Activity 3a: Beliefs of harassers at local tourist destination

In your work group, ascertain the beliefs shared by micro-traders in the community identified in Activity 1a. From the list of beliefs, identify those that suggest micro-traders in the community believe harassing visitors is good, supported, and easy, and those that suggest the alternative is bad, not supported, and difficult.

Activity 3b: Mitigation program for local tourist destination

Use your work group's response to Activities 1–3a, as well the contents of this chapter, to create a comprehensive anti-harassment program. The goal of the program should be to reduce visitor (trader) harassment levels in the target community. Include the following in your group's response:

1   Description of the micro-trade community;
2   Description of the trader harassment problem in the community;
3   Goals of the program;
4   Objectives of the program; and
5   Specific initiatives to be implemented and the entities that should be in charge.

Share the details of your trader harassment mitigation program with a team of tourism and learning experts for feedback. Revise the program accordingly.

Overcoming harassment by strengthening specific aspects of the destination

Another way tourism leaders may reduce the negative economic impact of visitor (trader) harassment on destinations is by ensuring other aspects of their tourist destinations are strong. This was the finding of a pilot study conducted by the present authors looking at reasons visitors reported positive loyalty intentions after personally experiencing an intense trader harassment episode at the tourist destination. Three loyalty intentions were examined: visitors' intention to return to the destination, recommend the destination to others, and support the micro-traders in the future. Three groups of visitors were examined: international, domestic, and diaspora visitors. The number of diaspora visitors in the sample was extremely small, and, as a result, their comments were excluded from the findings reported.

Data for the qualitative survey research were collected between February 2015 and August 2016. One hundred and thirty respondents (130) answered the study's critical questions.

The 130 respondents were individuals who visited a tourist destination within five years before completing the survey, had experienced intense trader harassment, and indicated they would return to the destination, recommend the destination to others, and/or support their micro-traders in the future. Closed-end survey items were used to confirm they both experienced intense trader harassment and had positive loyalty intentions toward the destination afterwards. Most of the study's data, in particular the reasons the respondents would be loyal to the destination after an intense visitor (trader) harassment episode, were analyzed using thematic content analysis.

Of the 130 respondents, 55.4% were female and 44.6% male. Also, 70.8%, 26.2%, and 2.3% were international, domestic, and diaspora visitors, respectively. The study's participants were also originally from eight of the nine cultural regions across the world. No member of the sample was originally from the Pacific Islands. However, most of the respondents were originally from North America (66.9%), followed by East Asia (15.4%), and Southeast Asia (5.4%). The 130 respondents reflected on visitor (trader) harassment episodes personally experienced in 54 cities across 24 countries, but most of the episodes they described occurred in cities and countries in Latin America and the Caribbean (30.8%), Northern America (21.5%), and Europe (19.2%). The results of the pilot study are reflected in Figures 13.3 and 13.4. It is important to note that only reasons provided by three or more respondents were reported in Figures 13.3 and 13.4.

From the pilot study, it appears tourism leaders may be able to overcome the negative economic effects of intense visitor (trader) harassment on their tourist destinations if the following are maintained at strong levels:

1 Enjoyment and fun factor;
2 Natural beauty and attractiveness;
3 Uniqueness;
4 History and culture;
5 Connections between visitors and the destination (such as with local family members and friends);
6 Likeability of local residents (in particular, their honesty, kindness, and goodness toward visitors);
7 Visitors' exposure to positives (even exceptional) about the destination;
8 Visitors' knowledge of how to effectively avoid micro-trader harassment;
9 Visitors' knowledge of how to effectively cope with micro-trader harassment;
10 Visitors' knowledge of how to form relationships with micro-traders that do not harass visitors;
11 Visitors' understanding that such behaviors are normal; and
12 Visitors' low encounter with trader harassment at the destination.

There were a few other noteworthy observations from the study. First, the percentage of respondents (international and domestic) who indicated they would support the micro-traders in the future although they were harassed by them was small—24%—versus 70% of the sample who indicated they would return to the destination. Second, only 12% of domestic visitors in the sample indicated they would support the micro-traders in the future after their intense trader harassment episode.

Another way tourism leaders may overcome negative trader harassment at their tourist destinations is by appealing for visitor understanding as they take steps to reduce the undesired selling behaviors. This is a highly feasible solution, as one study found visitor sympathy to be

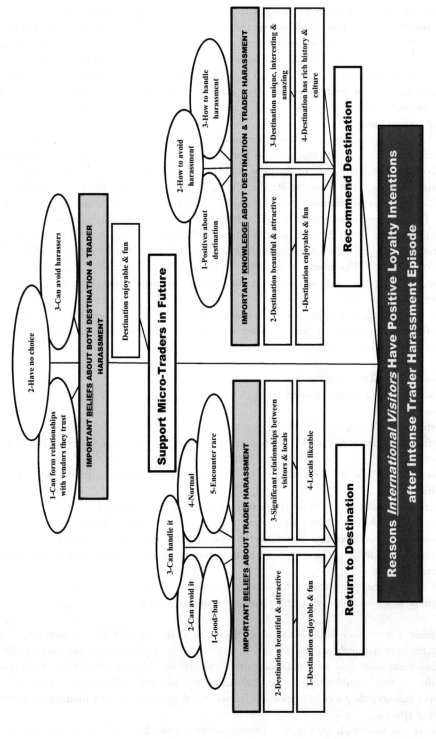

Figure 13.3 Factors that cause international visitors to have positive loyalty intention toward a destination after an intense trader harassment episode

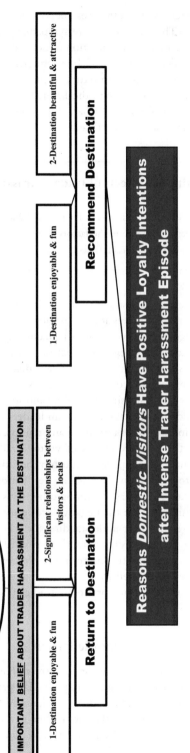

Figure 13.4 Factors that cause domestic visitors to have positive loyalty intention toward a destination after an intense trader harassment episode

a significant predictor of intention to both recommend a destination to others and support its micro-traders in the future. Therefore, the more sympathetic a visitor becomes after a trader harassment episode, the greater his or her intention to both recommend the destination to others and support its micro-traders in the future. Interestingly, sympathy was not found to be a significant predictor of visitors' intention to return to the destination after a trader harassment episode (Nicely & Armadita, 2018). Despite the latter, the willingness of visitors to support micro-traders at the destination after a visitor harassment episode is an important and valuable finding for tourism leaders from affected destinations.

Activity 4: Overcoming the effects of trader harassment

Use the findings of the pilot study as reflected in Figures 13.3 and 13.4 to develop a list of actions your work group would perform to ensure the factors listed in the figures are preserved or maintained at high levels. List three ideas for each factor.

In summary, visitor (trader) harassment is an undesired or unwanted selling behavior directed toward visitors by micro-traders at a tourist destination. These behaviors often cause visitors to experience a range of negative emotions. According to previous research, although the problem might have little or no negative effect on visitors' intention to return and recommend a destination, it is likely to have a significant deleterious effect on the amount of foreign exchange retained by tourism communities. Two broad approaches were discussed to address the problem: Reduce the undesired behaviors and strengthen critical areas of the destination. To reduce the undesired behaviors, tourism leaders should identify and address the beliefs fueling these behaviors as well as introduce and reinforce the desired selling behaviors. Meanwhile, to overcome the negative effects of visitor (trader) harassment, tourism leaders should ensure the destination is enjoyable and fun, beautiful and attractive, with strong relationships between visitors and individuals at the destination (such as family and friends), and the area's history and culture preserved, among other considerations. It was discovered as well that tourism leaders can minimize the negative economic effect of trader harassment on the destination by appealing for visitor understanding (Nicely & Armadita, 2018). Also, one reason visitors have strong positive loyalty intentions toward a destination after experiencing extreme harassment by its micro-traders relates to "other" elements at the destination. Some of these elements are highlighted in Figures 13.3 and 13.4; however, these elements were not explored in either the Jamaica or Kenya studies (Chepkwony & Kangogo, 2013; Skipper, 2009).

Acknowledgment

Special thanks are due to members of the Visitor Harassment Research Unit at Purdue team for their work on projects mentioned in this study, in particular: graduate students Filza Armadita, Shweta Singh, and Dan Zhu, and undergraduate students Aidan Selvia, Soyoung Yoo, and Lara Eichhron. The Visitor Harassment Research Unit is a research group. Its is based in the School of Hospitality & Tourism Management at Purdue University in West Lafayette, Indiana, USA.

References

Badu-Baiden, F., Adu-Boahen, E. A., & Otoo, F. E. (2016). Tourists' response to harassment: A study of international tourists to Ghana. *Anatolia, 27*(4), 468–479.

Boakye, K. A. (2012). Tourists' views on safety and vulnerability. A study of some selected towns in Ghana. *Tourism Management, 33*(2), 327–333.

Chepkwony, R. (2013). The magnitude and effects of tourist harassment on repeat visits: A case study of Kenya's coastal city of Mombasa. *International Journal of Current Research, 5*(10), 2978–2981.

Chepkwony, R., & Kangogo, M. (2013). Nature and factors influencing tourist harassment at coastal beach of Mombosa. *International Research Journal of Social Sciences, 2*(11), 17–22.

de Albuquerque, K., & McElroy, J. L. (2001). Tourist harassment: Barbados survey results. *Annals of Tourism Research, 28*(2), 477–492.

Dunn, H., & Dunn, L. (2002a). *People and Tourism*. Kingston, Jamaica: Arawak.

Dunn, H., & Dunn, L. (2002b). Tourism and popular perceptions: Mapping Jamaican attitudes. *Social & Economic Studies, 51*(1), 25–45.

Griffin, C. (2003). *The Caribbean Tourism Integrated Standards Project: Analysis and policy recommendations re harassment of and crime committed by and against tourists in the Caribbean*. San Juan, Puerto Rico.

Harris, L. C. (2012). "Ripping off" tourists: An empirical evaluation of tourists' perceptions and service worker (mis)behavior. *Annals of Tourism Research, 39*(2), 1070–1093.

Khajuria, S., & Khanna, S. (2014). Tourism risks and crimes at pilgrimage destinations—A case of Shri mata Vaishno Devi. *International Journal of Event Management Research, 8*(1), 77–93.

Kitching, C. (2014, September 8). Pushy Thai beach vendor arrested after kicking sand and pushing tourist who refuses to rent a sunlounger from him news article. *Daily Mail*. Retrieved from www.dailymail. co.uk/travel/travel_news/article-2747731/Pushy-Thai-beach-vendor-arrested-kicking-sand-pushing-tourist-refuses-rent-sunlounger-him.html

Kozak, M. (2007). Tourist harassment: A marketing perspective. *Annals of Tourism Research, 34*(2), 384–399.

McElroy, J., Tarlow, P., & Carlisle, K. (2007). Tourist harassment: Review of the literature and destination responses. *International Journal of Culture, Tourism & Hospitality Research, 1*(4), 305–314.

McElroy, J. L., Tarlow, P., & Carlisle, K. (2007). *Tourist Harassment and Responses*. Wallingford, UK: CAB International.

Nicely, A. (2015). Reversing visitor harassment through deliberate intelligence building strategies. *Tourism Culture & Communication, 115*(2), 19.

Nicely, A., & Armadita, F. (2017). How resilient are repeat visitors to trader harassment? *Tourism Management Perspectives, 23*, 154–156.

Nicely, A., & Armadita, F. (2018). Sympathy and loyalty intention after visitor harassment. *International Journal of Culture, Tourism & Hospitality Research, 12*(1), 47–58.

Nicely, A., Day, J., Sydnor, S., & Mohd Ghazali, R. (2015). Sustainably changing small traders' harassment behaviors—A theoretical framework. *Tourism Management, 47*, 273–285.

Nicely, A., & Mohd Ghazali, R. (2014). Demystifying visitor harassment. *Annals of Tourism Research, 48*, 266–269.

Pathirana, D. P. U., & Athula Gnapala, W. K. (2015). Tourist harassment at cultural sites in Sri Lanka. *Tourism, Leisure & Global Change, 2*, 42–56.

Prakash, D. H. (2013). The role of physical clues in detection of crimes. *International Research Journal of Social Sciences, 2*, 16–23.

Rathnayake, R., & Wijesundara, W. (2015). Tourist perception on harassment in Sri Lanka (with special reference to Mount Lavinia). *International Journal of Scientific & Research Publications, 5*(4).

Rhiney, K. (2012). The Negril tourism industry: Growth, challenges and future prospects. *Caribbean Journal of Earth Science, 43*, 25–34.

Skipper, T. (2009). *Understanding tourist–host interactions and their influence on quality tourism experiences*. Master of Arts thesis, Wilfred Laurier University, Ontario, Canada.

The Travel Foundation. (2013). *An all inclusive approach to improving livelihoods and reducing tourist hassle*. Retrieved from: www.thetravelfoundation.org.uk/green_business_tools/reducing_tourist_hassle

Visitor Harassment Research Unit at Purdue. (2018). Non-academic articles. Retrieved from www.purdue. edu/hhs/htm/research/visitor-harassment-research-unit/non-academic-articles.html

Wen, J., & Yina, L. (2015). The tourist harassment based on the marketing. *American Journal of Industrial and Business Management, 5*, 110–113.

14

THE EXTRAORDINARY LEAGUE OF RURAL WOMEN ENTREPRENEURS OF MALAWI

The socio-economic impacts of tourism in Malawi

Gerald Milanzi

Introduction

The relevance of entrepreneurship in the modern world stems from its integral role as catalyst for economic growth and development, as well as a source of innovation (Ribeiro-Soriano, 2017). Furthermore, a vast literature has propagated entrepreneurship's influence in job creation (Acs, Autio & Szerb, 2001; Litwin & Phan, 2013; Gittell, Sohl & Tebaldi, 2014). Nielsen's (2016) survey in Denmark situates entrepreneurship beyond job creation in an economy stabilisation block, cushioning governments against external changes arising through political turmoil. Nevertheless, beyond the pursuit of micro national benefits, the emergence of entrepreneurship on a regional and global scale, as both a socio-economic and political frontier, establishes itself within the core policies of international organisations such as the European Union, World Bank and the Organisation for Economic Co-operation and Development (Perkmann, 2002; Naude, 2016; World Bank, 2013). For the Southern Africa Development Community (SADC), however, entrepreneurship has been integrated into the economic development policies across the region as a tool for poverty eradication and, more importantly, as a strategy for implementing gender equality (EU, 2010; SADC Secretariat, 2008; van Welsum, 2016).

The customary rooted marginalisation of women in sub-Saharan Africa exposes women to obstacles and challenges which include, among others, inadequate access to technology, education and, more importantly, finance (Shackleton, Ziervogel, Sallu, Gill & Tschakert, 2015; BSR Women Economic Empowerment, 2016). The discussion of female entrepreneurship emanates from such a perspective: the significance of entrepreneurship as a means of achieving financial independence for women. Considering that close to 70% of the poor population in SADC are women, the majority of whom reside in rural areas (Semafumu, 2004), the intermediary role of entrepreneurship in empowering rural women to achieve equal economic and societal status acquires a superlative level in many African countries. A recently implemented gender policy in Malawi has such a purpose: to bridge the socio-economic gaps encountered by females in Malawian society (GoM, 2015). And, from the Malawi Growth and Development Strategy (MGDS), entrepreneurship and tourism serve as tools for removing economic hurdles encountered by the poor, the majority of whom are women (GoM, 2017). Such a background affords women entrepreneurship studies to focus on strategies for advancing female entrepreneurship, financing options and development of sustainable business projects. McGowan, Redeker, Cooper and Greenan (2012) and Winn (2004) support this by emphasising that studies on female entrepreneurship should be executed for the purpose of understanding and acknowledging female entrepreneurs to succeed within the purview of women. Such remarks emanate from Marlow and Patton (2005) and Padavic and Reskin (2002), who observe that the majority of studies on female entrepreneurship focus on differences between male and female entrepreneurs. Nevertheless, although gender-based comparative entrepreneurial studies can assist in illuminating possible conflicts and obstacles encountered by women entrepreneurs, to a larger extent they are perceived as a justification for male dominance (Baker, Aldrich & Liou, 1997) in the realm of entrepreneurship and, as such, regress efforts invested in equalising gender and acknowledging female entrepreneurs' contribution all over the world.

The contribution of this research to the body of knowledge is twofold, highlighting (1) the role of female entrepreneurs in rural communities and (2) the role of tourism in propelling female-led businesses and its impact on society. The findings of this study are relevant to the discourse of gender equality and the role of tourism in rural areas of Malawi. The chapter is structured as follows: First, there is an overview of female entrepreneurship literature across the globe, and Africa is discussed. This is followed by a discussion on the effect of assumed power variances between males and females in society. The role of tourism in propagating entrepreneurship is further reviewed, followed by the background to the study. Thereafter, the research results are presented and discussed.

The female force sweeping across the globe – women in entrepreneurship

Baum's (2013) observation that the influence and accomplishments of rural female entrepreneurs are rarely celebrated by the highest prestigious awards testifies to society's embedded seclusion of female entrepreneurs and their contribution on the socio-economic front globally. Although some studies have predicted and reinforced the notion that men are more likely to start and be successful at businesses than women (Reynolds, 2004; Bengtsson, Sanandaji & Johannesson, 2012), the Global Entrepreneurship Monitor report by Kelly, Brush, Greene and Litovsk (2011) depicts a positive trajectory of female entrepreneurship sweeping across the globe. In their 2010 global report (GEM, 2010), more than 100 million women, in close to 60 countries, started their own entrepreneurial businesses – a representation of 52% of the aggregated population. Similarly, Stange, Oyster and Sloan (2016) observed that, in the period between 1966 and 2006, female-owned enterprises grew at close to twice the rate of all US firms and accounted for 40.2% of all businesses in America, a contrast to only 700,000 women who owned businesses in 1976, accounting for a meagre 4.6% of all US businesses (Greene, Hart, Gatewood, Brush & Carter, 2003). Bennett and Dann's (2000) assertion that women outnumbered men on self-employment ratings in the USA, UK and Australia further emphasise women's progress in diverse aspects, hence a need to recognise the wide contribution of women on social and economic frontiers across the globe.

Regarding the growing dominance of female entrepreneurs, GEM (2010) findings acknowledge the effect of female entrepreneurship on the global economy, particularly through job creation and the distribution of wealth among the underrepresented section of society. However, to sustain such impacts, according to Abubakar, Abu Mansor and Djafar (2013), requires changing the gender equality landscape. Klapper and Parker's (2010) examination of the role of gender

equality in entrepreneurship revealed the significant contribution of gender-based discriminatory laws and regulations to the thwarting of female-engineered entrepreneurial progress. A
further analysis of the effect of gender on women entrepreneurs by Bajpai (2014) pinpointed
the role of traditions or customary values as a significant deterrent to balancing roles and responsibilities in many societies. Such culturally induced barriers have the potential to increase the
gender disparities that expose women to challenges in obtaining finances and education and in
executing their entrepreneurial endeavours (Ginige, Amaratunga & Haigh, 2007), Despite these
challenges, however, female entrepreneurship's contribution to the realms of global social transformation and economic growth remains positive (Bennett & Dann, 2000)

Incredible female entrepreneurs across Africa

Seen in evidence provided by the World Economic Forum (WEF), the ascendancy of African
women on an entrepreneurial platform has been remarkable. The WEF (2011) reports that
Africa's record of a growing proportion of female entrepreneurs in the world not only signifies
women's contribution to societies on a regional basis, but also exemplifies the magnitude of
female-owned businesses' exponential development to play a critical role in diverse development matters in Africa. Studies carried out by the Gates & Clinton Foundation (2015) exqui-
sitely capture the phenomenon of African female entrepreneurship by reporting that 41% of
women in Nigeria participate in entrepreneurship, compared with roughly 10% in the USA
and only 5.7% in the UK. Of special interest, however, is the dominance of female-owned
business in sub-Saharan Africa. With natural disasters such as famine and hunger coupled with
the devastating effects of HIV/AIDS, the sub-Saharan region falls among the poorest regions
in the world (Sahn, 2004). Arguably, the retrogressive effects of such disasters on growth and
development can eventually deter female-led entrepreneurial initiatives within the region. In
that regard, the 26% surge of nascent female entrepreneurs in sub-Saharan Africa (GEM, 2017),
the highest in the world, registers a fascinating phenomenon. Affirming the trend, Kitching and
Woldie's (2004) statistics indicate an impressive 80% participation of women in the informal
sector in sub-Saharan Africa. Such facts depict the integral economic strides women in sub-
Saharan Africa have achieved in what is perceived as a male-dominated territory, but the impact
of such progress transcends economic benefits. Dzisi's (2008) study on female entrepreneurs
in Ghana illustrates top economic-based contributions to the improvement of family life by
rural women. Similarly, studies by Otoo, Joan, Germaine and James (2011) in Ghana, Bradley,
McMullen, Artz and Simiyu (2012) in Kenya, and Manda (2015) in Malawi amplify the role
of women's entrepreneurship in rural poverty reduction. Although the gap between male- and
female-owned SMEs is slightly lower in Malawi, with women reported to own 46% of micro,
small and medium enterprise (Finmark Trust, 2012), women contribute close to 70% of agricultural labour in Malawi. Such female representation suggests the unequivocal contribution of
women in the major economic sphere in Malawi. Ignoring female entrepreneurs' impact in this
regard not only defies the essence of economic growth and development principles, but also
downplays the positive change that women bring to the society in every aspect.

This necessity-based female entrepreneurship (Ernst & Young, 2011; Clappaert, 2012;
Welsh, Kaciak & Ahmed, 2013; Amin, 2010) tackles hunger and starvation, illiteracy eman-
cipation and access to affordable health care for families. It is probably through such goals that
female entrepreneurs' contribution creates ripple benefits to societies. On a different note, the
uniqueness of female entrepreneurs' goals accentuates the irrelevance of comparing the impacts
of female-driven entrepreneurship with those of male-driven entrepreneurship. From Perry's
(2002) perspective, deploying male-dominated, traditional financially dependent standards in

evaluating the success of female entrepreneurs is futile. In the article, female entrepreneurs' success is judged by whose standards? Marlow and Strange (1994) eloquently elaborate on this position by affirming that women perform more significant and challenging roles than men, and some of their tasks cannot be financially weighed and yet are vital for entrepreneurship and society. Such comments highlight the importance of studying female entrepreneurship from a female perspective, rather than in the shadow of men. Weighing into the discussion, Ahl (2006) and Calas, Smircich and Bourne (2009) argue that a debate on female entrepreneurs' intentions in itself alludes to the discriminatory notion that entrepreneurship is a male task. Arguably though, instigating such debates can expose the profound effect female entrepreneurs have in diverse societies and the variability of entrepreneurial objectives apart from pure economic gain. For instance, Halkias, Nwajiuba, Harekiolakis and Caracatsanis's (2011) studies in Nigeria vindicate women's participation in entrepreneurship as central to the pursuit of their own family's and their extended family's improved quality of life. Brush, Carter, Gatewood, Greene and Hart (2006) and Dzisi (2008), in Ghana, report that the majority of female respondents preferred fulfilment to economic gain, whereas Meyer and Landsberg (2015) centre on the need for independence as a critical driver for female-led businesses. Although this discussion explores the incredible work by African women entrepreneurs, the need for independence disavows geographical boundaries.

For example, McGowan et al.'s (2012) research on female entrepreneurs in Ireland centres on the quest for fulfilment and independence; likewise, Bennett and Dann (2000), in Australia, identify the need for independence as a principle driving force towards female entrepreneurship. Indisputably, the quest for independence originates in the state of being dependent. In patriarchal cultures, women are required to be passive, humble and dependent on their husbands; rarely are women permitted to mingle with networks comprising menfolk other than their spouses (Zakaria, 2001; Woldie & Adersua, 2004; Bawa, 2012; Shahnawaz, 2015). Such male-controlled culture embodiment breeds the quest for independence, and entrepreneurship provides that route to financial freedom. In this respect, tackling the cultural components that propel gender inequality and underrepresentation of women in the spheres of entrepreneurship postulates a critical path towards fostering inclusive economic growth and minimising societal power variances.

Power variances – the male versus female society power equation

The male versus female presumed locus of power variances exert a potentially influential force towards the marginalisation of women in society; within the gender stereotypes lies the assumption that women are not meant for entrepreneurship. Such remarks originate from the substantial literature that has explored the marginalisation of women in entrepreneurial and other society endeavours (Bruni, Gherardi & Poggio, 2004; Hallward & Stewart, 2018; Azmi, 2017; Tur-Porcar, Mas-Tur & Belso, 2017). For example, the World Bank (2014) acknowledges the challenges that women encounter in accessing capital compared with men in sub-Saharan Africa. Iheduru's (2002) studies in Nigeria advance the deterrent influence of cultural beliefs in orchestrating the dominance of men in decision-making while downplaying the pivotal role of women in society. This is despite Bardasi, Blackden and Guzman's (2007) pivotal findings that women in Nigeria contribute more towards the economy than men. Such culturally perpetuated unequal distribution of power situates women in housekeeping roles, advancing a premise that deems entrepreneurship a task for men. As noted by Chitsike (2000), owing to cultural impediments in some of the rural and urban parts of Zimbabwe, it remains taboo for females to travel away from home for business, whereas it is unquestionably permissible for men. In Malawi, according to Action Aid (2017), cultural beliefs demand that women offer obedience to their husbands and devotion to managing their household, which eventually curtails women's participation in entrepreneurial activities.

The cultural effect on gender power variances within societies obscures the capacity of rural women for education, amassing capital assets for development and entrepreneurial financing options (Chitsike, 2000; Zakaria, 2001; Marthur-Helm, 2005). The resultant effect is the under-utilisation of female potential in societies. The ILO (2016) assessment of potential utilisation between genders asserts that 22% of males' potential is under-utilised as opposed to a staggering 50% of unexploited female potential. It is therefore remarkable to note that, despite under-utilisation of female potential, women were still responsible for contributing more than men towards the national economy in Nigeria, owning 80% of informal sector businesses and more than 70% of labour in Malawi. Additionally, women owned more than half of the micro entre-preneurs in Southern Africa, more than 40% of budding businesses in America, and close to 40% of small and medium enterprises in Asia (World Bank, 2011; Bardasi et al., 2007; Finmark Trust, 2012). From this perspective, it is possible to hypothesise the positive derivatives of minimising gender-based power variances. Curtailing traditionally orchestrated power gaps between male and females does lead to an improved global economy.

Impacting entrepreneurship – the tourism way

The conjectured direct and indirect effects of tourism on a country's macro and micro lev-els are accentuated in several ways. Lemma (2014) has argued for existing unsurmountable progressive effects of tourism through gross domestic product and employment measures for both developing and developed countries. Coincidentally, regardless of the sector, authors such as Carree and Thurik (2006), Braunerhjelm (2010) and Hartog, van Praag and van der Sluis (2010) have argued for the exact contribution of entrepreneurship towards economies. The symbiotic accord of tourism and entrepreneurship in propelling national and local economies avails itself in diverse dimensions. The growth of private tourism investments (Ashley, Boyd & Goodwin, 2000), for instance, marks the entrepreneurship principle of opportunity recogni-tion from which the tourism sector profits, consequently leading to tourism impacts on job and business creation. Likewise, tourist spending (Disegna & Osti, 2016) exerts a profound effect on employment and the establishment of new businesses, which equally signifies the role of tourism in spurring entrepreneurship.

Studies conducted in Okavango Delta in Botswana attest to another critical role of tourism: alleviating poverty within local communities through tourism-dependent businesses (Mbawa, 2003). Weighing into the poverty alleviation discussion, Hall (1995) and Lemma (2014) argue that the capability of tourism to reduce poverty depends on the nature of linkages between tourism and local economies; the greater the linkage between tourism and the local economy, the greater the propensity for tourism to boost the local economy. If materials are sourced from local communities, the potential for tourisms to positively impact on local entrepreneurial businesses is apparent.

In Malawi, for instance, as observed by Chirwa (2008), the majority of small and medium businesses that can provide such linkages are owned by women, who coincidentally reside in the rural areas. Deen, Harilal and Achu (2016) similarly observed a significant presence of female-owned small and medium tourism-dependent businesses in South Africa playing a vital role in alleviating poverty. Adjudicating the role of tourism in poverty alleviation, Roethlisberger (2017) explains that well-planned tourism efforts can foster inclusive growth by accommodat-ing the marginalised sections of society. Essentially, a three-way connection exists between tourism, female participation and national development. On enhancing female participation, the UNWTO and UN Women (2011) report that women constitute half the tourism workforce and that, in comparison with other sectors, tourism has twice as many female employers. Although such contributions have been observed, the gender stereotype within the sector continues to hamper significant progress. Mkono (2012), in Zimbabwe, cites the concentration of female workers in the lower-paid levels of the organisation, compared with male-dominated managerial positions. Likewise, Stephen, Isaac, George and Dominic (2014) in Kenya, Stone, Stone and Mbaiwa (2017) in Botswana, and Mrema (2015) in Tanzania extrapolate similar findings in their studies. In Malawi, research pertaining to differing levels of gender employment in tourism is scanty. Nevertheless, literature on the influence of tourism on economic perspectives is accessible. A study of household-level impacts of tourism by Snyman (2012) concedes that tourism significantly improves rural household incomes and overall social welfare. On the other hand, although Gartner and Cukier (2012) acknowledge the role of tourism in the creation of employment opportunities for local residents in Malawi, their research fails to guarantee the positive effects of tourism on local people in the long run.

The inconclusive effects of tourism on local people and economies perhaps emanate from the perceived detrimental effects of tourism. As noted by Glasson, Godfrey and Goodey (1995), most major tourism infrastructures and services are provided by foreign investors who, in their quest for development, control local resources and externalise a chunk of funds to their overseas headquarters. In the long run, according Prosser (1994), foreign firms display a tendency towards increasing short-term profits, a practice that leads to environmental degradation, massive job cuts and the devaluing of local communities' cultures. The causality effect of tourism to culture is inconclusive. Shishmanova (2015), for instance, argues for tourism's ability to preserve local cultures, whereas Ursache (2015) contends that tourism's capacity to weaken local traditions stems from local people's inclination to imitate tourist cultures. The imitation process aftermath leads not only to the dissolution of local cultures, but also to commercialisation of relationships in communities as well. It is interesting to note how the concept of imitation in tourism can have an antagonistic effect on local people. Stronza and Gordillo (2008) and Jamieson, Goodwin and Edmunds (2004) explore imitation as a source of imparting knowledge, skills and broader experiences; likewise Johannessen, Olsen and Lumpkin (2001), who attributed imitation to a source of innovation.

Evidently, measuring tourism impacts in developing countries and balancing the economic contributions against the social effects of tourism remain a conundrum.

Malawi the context – study background

Malawi's population of 18 million is a miscellany of ethnic diversity. Located in the southern part of Africa and covering 45,747 square miles, Malawi is also known as the "Warm Heart of Africa" because of the kindliness and the beaming smiles of its people. Covering a third of landlocked Malawi, Lake Malawi stretches from the southern to the northern region of the country. Ranked as the third largest fresh-water lake in Africa, Lake Malawi attained UNESCO World Heritage Site status on the basis of its harbouring the largest number of fish species in the world, and this indicates the competitiveness of Malawi as a tourist destination (UNESCO, 2013). Furthermore, its combined cultural richness and vast natural resources, including parks and wildlife reserves (World Bank, 2010), show Malawi's touristic flare. The Lonely Planet named Malawi as one of the top ten countries to visit in 2014 and, recently, the Rough Guides, an international travel guidebook, listed Malawi third in the top 18 countries to visit in the world (www.lonelyplanet.com; Rough Guides, 2018). Though the entire sub-Saharan region has exhibited an increase in tourism trends, with South Africa and Madagascar (up 13% and 20%, respectively) as the top growing tourist attraction earners, travel and tourism contributed 7.2% to Malawi's GDP in 2016 and 7.7% in 2017, surpassing the 4.7% rise expected (UNWTO, 2017; WTTC, 2016, 2018).

The World Bank (2010) identified tourism in Malawi as a promising substitute for tobacco as a major foreign exchange earner. However, deficiencies in accommodation investment, existing poor-quality accommodation facilities (Nsiku & Kiratu, 2009) and inaccessible roads to major tourist attraction sites (Zidana, 2015) restrict tourism's potential contribution to Malawi's economy.

Despite such inefficiencies, Malawi registered a remarkable 12–37% tourism growth rate between 1995 and 2015 (NSO, 2009; World Bank, 2010). And yet, despite such growth, rural poverty remains an economic hurdle in Malawi (World Bank, 2011). It is from this perspective that, in the MGDS (GoM, 2017), tourism is highly regarded as a strategy to reduce rural poverty. Considering that the majority of tourism attraction sites and establishments are located in rural areas, and that the majority of the poor in Malawi are women (Chimangeni, 2015; Chirwa, 2008), the role of tourism in propelling pro-poor growth becomes vital. This research therefore has been instituted to explore the effects of female entrepreneurs in rural communities and the perceived role of tourism in spurring female entrepreneurship in Malawi.

Research methodology

The study was conducted in two regions: Salima in the central region and Nkhata Bay in the northern region on the shores of Lake Malawi. Using purposive sampling and adopting a qualitative approach, unstructured interviews were conducted with a total of 30 women, 15 from each region. The use of unstructured interviews was chosen with the purpose of discovering the diverse issues that women entrepreneurs encounter in the tourism sector. Salima and Nkhata Bay are among the top tourist destinations in Malawi. The presence of women-led businesses in both tourist attraction sites is notable: women sell their products at the roadside and at entrances to tourist sites, attracting tourists towards their product and services; hence their suitability for the purposes of the study.

Participants were informed about the purpose of the research and that participation was voluntary. The interviews revolved around the following themes:

- The nature of female-led entrepreneurial initiatives.
- The impact of tourism on women-led businesses.
- Factors affecting female-led businesses.
- The purpose of pursuing entrepreneurship.

The criteria for inclusion in the study were based on the interpretation that any female who owned or managed a business (OECD, 2004) operating in the spheres of tourist attraction sites or offering products and services for the attention of tourists qualified as a female entrepreneur. After data collection through recorded interviews, content analysis was employed for data analysis, and themes were extracted from the interview data.

Limitations of the study

The main limitation of the study was the lack of data from women pursuing entrepreneurial businesses within the tourism sector in the southern region of Malawi, which potentially affected the generalisation of the findings.

Significance of the study

Stemming from Baum's (2013) observations that rural women's achievements are rarely acknowledged, in many aspects this study highlights the significance of female entrepreneurs in the society. Not only does the study highlight the extraordinarily abilities of women to inter-weave entrepreneurship with domestic roles, it also contributes to the currently minute amount known about female entrepreneurs in Malawi.

Findings

The research findings were reported based on the main themes of the prescribed unstructured interviews.

Analysis and discussion

Demographic of the respondents

The demographic age breakdown of the 30 female entrepreneurs interviewed ranged from 18 to 45 years old. All the participants were married and, at the time of the study, were living with their husbands. However, none of the respondents' husbands were reported to be interested in managing or running business affairs. All participants had more than two but fewer than six children and were supporting two or more extended family members. Out of the 30 female interviewees, 5 had never attended school, and 25 had never progressed with education above primary school. These findings correlate the notion of growing illiteracy levels among rural women in sub-Saharan Africa (Chitsike, 2000). Furthermore, the findings concur with Mandipaka (2014) that female entrepreneurs tend to lack the support of their husbands. The lack of support from family members inevitably has a detrimental effect on the growth of female-led entrepreneurial ventures.

The nature of female-led entrepreneurial initiatives

The findings revealed that women in in both regions engaged in similar types of business. The findings are illustrated in Tables 14.1 and 14.2.

Table 14.1 Nature of female-led businesses in Nkhata Bay, Malawi

Nature of business	Number of respondents	Age of business	Number of businesses/branches
Restaurant (food processing)	8	2–6 yrs	1
Retail (hawkers)	1	1–5 yrs	1
Supplying fruit and vegetables	2	Less than 1 yr	1
Arts and crafts	4	5–10 yrs	1

Table 14.2 Nature of female-led businesses in Salima, Malawi

Nature of business	Number of respondents	Age of business	Number of businesses/branches
Restaurant (food processing)	7	1–5 yrs	1
Retail (hawkers)	3	1–5 yrs	1
Selling clothes	1	1–2 yrs	1
Arts and crafts	4	5–10 yrs	1

These findings affirm those of McDade and Spring (2005) and the OECD (2004) that women entrepreneurs tend to cluster around micro, small and medium businesses. The majority of the respondents were either involved in food production and related services or arts and crafts businesses, on a small scale. From the respondents' perspectives, the choice of such types of business originates in the possession of skills learned in childhood and access to raw materials.

> I don't need someone to teach me how to cook my local dish. I have been cooking ever since I was five.
>
> *(Respondent 1, owner of a restaurant in Salima)*

Such a comment illustrates rural women entrepreneurs' ability to identify business opportunities based on informally acquired human capital (Dzisi, 2008) and culturally nurtured skill sets. Furthermore, the utilisation of informally acquired human capital allows women entrepreneurs to engage in business with little investment in acquiring new skill sets. However, the lack of formal skills, according to Degroot (2001), prevents substantial growth of female-led businesses. This would probably explain why none of the interviewed entrepreneurs had other business branches, despite the majority having operating for more than 5 years.

The role of female entrepreneurship in Salima

Data analysis was carried out with the intention of understanding the role female-led businesses play in their communities. It indicated an intrinsic desire to satisfy family financial obligations. The majority of the respondents emphasised that engaging in business was the only option to make ends meet and offer their families a comfortable life.

> Business affords us a chance to have money for food, clothes and most importantly pay rent. When I sell food, everyday I know I will have a little or sometimes more money for my family depending on the tourist season. I am always happy when tourists arrive because I know I will make money. When they come here they need food right? The food selling business allows me to look after my family, pay school fees for my children and pay medical bills. This is why I do business.
>
> *(Respondent 2, owner of a restaurant in Nkhata Bay)*

This quote agrees with Bradley et al.'s (2012) conclusion that tourism offers an opportunity to improve family life and eventually contributes towards alleviating poverty in rural communities. Furthermore, it accentuates Ernst & Young's (2011) and Halkias et al.'s (2012) assertions that women entrepreneurs' key objective centres on satisfying family obligations. A further analysis also revealed that pursuing entrepreneurship was the only alternative to employment, considering that majority of the respondents had not pursued education to an employable level. These findings concur with the findings of the World Bank (2010) and Zakaria (2001) that the growing levels of illiteracy among females in rural areas of Africa bind women to small businesses as an only alternative means of earning a living. However, it was interesting to note that employment was still not an option, even if the interviewed women had employable qualifications.

> It is my duty to look after the children and manage household. This is how I was brought up. There's no way I can go to work and leave my husband at home to cook for himself and the children. What kind of a woman does that? In this village every

married woman knows that it is their duty to look after their husbands, I have to make sure that food is available for everyone.

(Respondent 3, hawker–owner in Salima)

Such a remark manifests the effect of deeply entrenched cultural values and norms on females in society (Mungai & Ogot, 2012), imposing on them the role of obedient domestic care-taker, as propagated by male-dominated cultures (Action Aid, 2017). Considering that the husbands of almost all of the respondents were not employed nor participated in the business affairs, pursuing entrepreneurship for some females can arguably be seen as the only means of fulfilling their assumed cultural obligations. Furthermore, the studies confirm the growing impact of gender inequality rooted within families and propagated by society (Abubakar et al., 2013) and how such unequal distribution of responsibilities eventually deters female entrepreneurship endeavours in Malawi.

Factors affecting female-led businesses

Numerous researchers have commented on the challenges that women entrepreneurs encounter in raising finance for their businesses (Chinomona & Maziriri, 2015; Barr, 2015; Markovi, 2007). The research findings back up the aforementioned researchers on this subject: the respondents acknowledged that raising finance was a hurdle impacting the start and growth of their businesses. According to the respondents, high collateral demands from banks disbar women from obtaining loans. As an alternative, village savings banks evolve as lending houses. However, the growing number of women participants in village banks increases the challenges further by delaying loan disbursement time. Further challenges as per the findings relate to lack of support from the society and their partners or husbands:

> Whilst acknowledging that it is my role to manage my house, if I was able to get assistance with the business especially from my husband, our finances could have had improved. My husband has not worked for more than five years now, and most of the times he always asks for sales revenues and uses that to buy alcohol.
>
> *(Respondent 4, vegetable and fruit seller in Salima)*

> It is very difficult to complain to anyone not even my relatives because the blame will come back to me. If I complain about the lack of help, it will seem as if I am the one failing to take care of the family. The society doesn't help much in these issues you know. I even get verbal abuses from other customers and the rude boys who sometimes buy my products and refuse to pay. They know am a woman so I cannot compete with them. What can I do? I just let them leave.
>
> *(Respondent 6, hawker in Nkhata Bay)*

Rooted in the culture, the above comments illustrate how social culture values deter the progress of female entrepreneurs (Mordi, Simpson, Singh & Okafor, 2010) and, significantly, how they perpetuate the abuse and harassment of women in the society. Almost all of the respondents alluded to the effect of increased responsibilities as factors antagonistic to entrepreneurship. From such findings, we can extrapolate that rural women entrepreneurs assume extra family tasks compared with their male counterparts. Furthermore, the study concurs with Bajpai's (2014) assertion that gender inequality remains a challenge for female entrepreneurs.

The impact of tourism from the women entrepreneurs' perspective

Tourism propagates developmental opportunities for small businesses (Othman & Rosli, 2011). The findings revealed the causal dependency of women-led enterprises on tourism. The respondents acknowledged that tourism was the sole factor contributing to the establishment of businesses within their communities.

> My business depends on tourist, when there are no tourists, my business and family struggles. We cannot afford to buy some of the basic necessities and more importantly raise university fees for my son.
>
> *(Respondent 7, arts and crafts vendor in Nkhata Bay)*

> Tourism brings opportunities for us to make some money. When the tourist arrives, we ask what their interests are and what they intend to buy, our businesses depends on their needs.
>
> *(Respondent 8, arts and crafts vendor in Salima)*

Mbaiwa (2003), Disegna and Osti (2016) and Ashley et al. (2000) have argued for the influence of tourism in the proliferation of small and medium enterprises in rural areas, which eventually strengthens the bonds between the community and the tourism sector. The findings agree with the aforementioned argument by illustrating the propensity of tourism to offer entrepreneurial opportunities for rural women in Malawi.

> I have managed to build my current house by supplying vegetables to lodges and hotels, I don't know if I could have done this if it wasn't for tourism.
>
> *(Respondent 9, owner of restaurant in Salima)*

The above quote illustrates the positive effect of tourism in rural areas. As argued by Disegna and Osti (2016) and Mbaiwa (2003), tourism has the potential to alleviate poverty and improve the quality of life of the rural masses.

Despite the essential contribution tourism makes in the proliferation of small and medium businesses, the female entrepreneurs noticed the sprouting of illegal businesses within their communities. According to the respondents, in a quest for fun, some tourists look for or bring illegal drugs such as cocaine and Indian hemp into their communities. Concurring with Ursache (2015) and Türker and Öztürk (2013), these findings affirm the role of tourism in negating community cultural values.

Stronza and Gordillo (2008) and Jamieson et al. (2004) posited the role of tourism in imparting knowledge, innovation and skills. The findings of this study correlate well with such assertions. According to the women entrepreneurs, in their quest to offer the right services and products to the tourists, some of the tourists are kind enough to guide them through the process of developing or offering the service.

> Through tourist, we have learnt how to make a very soft home made Peanut Butter and Jam. Now we are able to make these products and sell them to the whole community not just the tourist.
>
> *(Respondent 10, hawker–owner in Salima)*

Through such interaction, women entrepreneurs and other members of the society acquire skills and knowledge and manage to innovate with products and services to suit their clientele.

Regardless of such contributions, however, the negative consequences of interacting with tourists, according to the respondents, can be observed through the overt, unacceptable changes in youth behavior in their community (Ursache, 2015). According to the respondents, some of the youth refrain from attending school, with a view to guiding tourists for easy money and access to new technology. Eventually, the youth assimilate what is construed to be culturally unacceptable behavior within their communities. These findings augment the assertions that tourism has the potential to distort community values (Shishmanova, 2015), but also, more importantly, contributes towards the growing levels of illiteracy which eventually negate efforts expended towards the eradication of poverty in rural communities.

A further discourse on the involvement of tourists in community activities revealed that tourism also offers a chance to improve structural development in their communities (Hundt, 1996).

> Tourism assisted us in building a new primary and nursery school for the community. Our children are able to pursue education in well built infrastructure, not only do we use them for school but we are able to hold community meetings in the same buildings. Tourism has aided infrastructure development in our communities.
>
> *(Respondent 11, arts and crafts vendor in Nkhata Bay)*

Such a comment confirms the positive ripple effects of tourism on rural communities. Simkute (2017), however, has argued that, although such developments are of critical importance to rural communities, the act and the manner in which they are executed promote the "white saviour complex", which reinforces racism and the gap between indigenous inhabitants and tourists. Supporting Simkute's comments, the findings revealed the role of tourism in propagating segregation and racism.

> Some tourists are kind, they are eager to learn and respect us the way we are. Some of the tourist are very violent and use foul language. It really feels bad to be chased within your own village by a stranger. You see when we are canvassing and selling our products some of the tourist actually chase as away instead of politely acknowledging that they are not interested in our products and services.
>
> *(Respondent 12, vendor of fruit and vegetables)*

Such abusive, gender-engineered aggravation has the potential to create hostility between local communities and tourists. The marauding effect of such hostility can reverse the economic contribution tourism makes to rural communities (Mbaiwa, 2008; Akama, 1996).

Conclusion

To conclude, entrepreneurship displays the capabilities to positively impact rural communities both on the social and economic frontiers, especially through the participation of women. However, women involved in entrepreneurship are met with a plethora of challenges, including lack of support from their partners, inadequate finances and harassment, which in most cases are rooted in gender and culture. The findings of this study support the fact that rural women extraordinarily merge and execute both domestic and income-generating roles within their families. Their income-generating activities centre on fulfilling family financial obligations and promoting a good quality of life within their extended families. Regardless of such contributions, however, rural women's impact on society is hardly acknowledged. It is this lack of recognition that drives gender inequality and regresses possible effort to equalise gender roles.

On the other hand, the effect of tourism in Malawi remains a conundrum; with the lack of statistical or qualitative formulae to weigh positive versus negative impacts of tourism, it remains a challenge to pinpoint the overall contribution of tourism in Malawi. The role of tourism in the establishment of women-led businesses is profound. Through the creation and development of small and medium enterprises run by women, families' financial requirements were met or enhanced. Furthermore, tourism played a vital role in improving infrastructure, as well as imparting skills and knowledge. Despite such contributions, tourism's role in perpetuating cultural distortion, juvenile delinquency and abuse against women remains pronounced.

The implications of these findings are essential. The role of tourism in the MGDS is critical to eradication of poverty. These findings highlight the prime role of addressing cultural components in balancing gender roles as a critical component in operationalising policies aimed at eradicating poverty in Malawi. Furthermore, development of mechanisms that could enhance the recognition of female entrepreneurs in the society could play a critical role in promoting female entrepreneurship.

Additionally, there is a need for future studies to investigate further the contribution of rural women to the society and identify measures with which their contributions can be acknowledged.

References

Abubakar, S., Abu Mansor, S., & Djafar, F. (2013) Assessing the factors that influence entrepreneurship in Nigeria. *Journal of Entrepreneurship and Management, 2*(3), 1–11.

Acs, J.Z., Autio, E., & Szerb, L. (2001) National systems of entrepreneurship: measurement issues and policy implications. *Research Policy, 43*, 476–494.

Action Aid. (2017) Women's economic empowerment in sub-Saharan Africa. Recommendations for Business Action 2017. Report, 1–69. Available from: www.Bsr.Org/Reports/Bsr_Womens_Empowerment_Africa_Main_Report.Pdf (accessed 18 April 2018).

Ahl, H. (2006) Why research on women entrepreneurs needs new directions. *Entrepreneurship Theory & Practice, 30*(5), 595–621.

Akama, S.J. (1996) Western environmental values and nature based tourism in Kenya. *Tourism Management, 17*(8), 567–574.

Amin, M. (2010) Gender and firm size: evidence from Africa. *Economic Bulletin, 30*(1), 663–668.

Ashley, C., Boyd, C., & Goodwin, H. (2000) Pro-poor tourism: putting poverty at the heart of the tourism agenda. *Natural Resource Perspectives, 51*, 1–6.

Azmi, G.A.I. (2017) Muslim women entrepreneurs' motivation in SMEs: a quantitative study in Asia Pacific countries. *Asian Economic & Financial Review, 7*(1), 27–42.

Bajpai, C.G. (2014) African women entrepreneur: problems, challenges and future opportunities. *International Journal of Managerial Studies & Research, 2*, 16–18.

Baker, T., Aldrich, H., & Liou, N. (1997) Invisible entrepreneurs: the neglect of women business owners by mass-media and scholarly journals in the USA. *Entrepreneurship & Regional Development, 9*(3), 221–238.

Bardasi, E., Blackden, C.M., & Guzman, J.C. (2007) Gender, entrepreneurship and competitiveness in Africa. In *Africa Competitiveness Report*, chaps 1–4, 1–18. Washington DC: World Bank.

Barr, S.M. (2015) Minority and women entrepreneurs: building capital, networks, and skills. The Hamilton Project Discussion Paper 2015-03, 1–32. Brookings Institution.

Baum, T. (2013) International perspectives on women and work in hotels, catering and tourism. Bureau for Gender Equality. Working Paper No. 289. International Labour Office. Geneva, pp. 1–75.

Bawa, S. (2012) Women's rights and culture in Africa: a dialogue with global patriarchal traditions. *Canadian Journal of Development Studies/Revue canadienne d'études du development, 33*(1), 90–105.

Bengtsson, O., Sanandaji, T., & Johannesson, M. (2012) The psychology of the entrepreneur and the gender gap in entrepreneurship. IFN Working Paper No. 944. Available at SSRN: https://ssrn.com/abstract=2542144

Bennett, R., & Dann, S. (2000) The exchange experience of Australian female entrepreneurs. *Gender, Work & Organisation, 7*(2), 75–83.

Bradley, S.W., McMullen, J.S., Artz, K., & Simiyu, E.M. (2012) Capital is not enough: innovation in developing economies. *Journal of Management Studies*, *49*(4), 5–30.

Braunerhjelm, P. (2010) Entrepreneurship, innovation and economic growth. Working Paper. Past experiences, current knowledge and policy implication. Swedish Entrepreneurship Forum, pp. 1–79.

Bruni, A., Gherardi, S., & Poggio, B. (2004) Entrepreneur mentality, gender and the study of women entrepreneurs. *Journal of Organisation Change Management*, *17*(3), 256–268.

Brush, C.G., Carter, N., Gatewood, E., Greene, P., & Hart, M. (2006) *Growth-Oriented Women Entrepreneurs and Their Business: A Global Research Perspective*. New Horizons in Entrepreneurship Series. Cheltenham, UK: Edward Elgar, pp. *205*, 393.

BSR Women Economic Empowerment. (2016) Business action for women's economic empowerment in Sub-Saharan Africa. Preview of an upcoming report with opportunities for apparel, telecommunications and mining sectors. William and Flora Hewlett Foundation. Available at: www.bsr.org/files/Business_Action_Womens_Empowerment_Africa_2016.pdf (accessed 4 March 2018).

Calas, M., Smircich, L., & Bourne, K. (2009) Extending the boundaries: reframing 'entrepreneurship as social change' through feminist perspectives. *Academy of Management Review*, *3*(34), 552–659.

Carree, M.A., & Thurik, A.R. (2006) *The Handbook of Entrepreneurship and Economic Growth*. Northampton, UK: International Library of Entrepreneurship, pp. 1–11.

Chimangeni, C.P. (2015) The benefits of tourism from community perspective of Chembe Village, Malawi. A research report submitted to the Faculty of Commerce, Law and Management at The University of the Witwatersrand.

Chinomona, E., & Maziriri (2015) Challenges facing women entrepreneurs in the Gauteng Province of South Africa: the Clute Institute Women in Action. *International Business & Economics Research Journal*, *14*(6), 1–16.

Chirwa, E.W. (2008) Effects of gender on the performance of micro and small enterprises in Malawi. *Development Southern Africa*, *25*(3), 347–362.

Chitsike, C. (2000) Culture as a barrier to rural women entrepreneurship: experience from Zimbabwe. *Gender & Development*, *8*(1), 71–77.

Clappaert, S. (2012) Entrepreneurs and women: keys to growth in Africa. Inter Press Service News Agency. Available at: www.ipsnews.net/2012/10/entrepreneurs-and-women-keys-to-growth-in-africa/ (accessed 4 March 2018).

Deen, A., Harilal, V., & Achu, N.F. (2016) Women in tourism: experiences and challenges faced by owners of small accommodation establishments. *African Journal of Hospitality, Tourism and Leisure* (special edition), *5*(3) Issn: 2223-814x

Degroot, U.T. (2001) Women entrepreneurship development in selected African countries. United Nations Industrial Development Organization, Investment Promotion and Institutional Capacity Building Division, Private Sector Development Branch. Working paper 7, 5–28.

Disegna, M., & Osti, L (2016) Tourists' expenditure behaviour: the influence of satisfaction and the dependence of spending categories. *Tourism Economics*, *22*(1), 5–30.

Dzisi, S. (2008) Entrepreneurial activities of indigenous women: a case of Ghana. *Journal of Enterprising Communities, People & Places in the Global Economy* 2(3), 254–264.

Ernst & Young. (2011) *Women of Africa: A Powerful Untapped Economic Force for the Continent*. EYGM Limited, 7–25.

European Union Commission (EU). (2010) Communication from the Commission to the European Parliament, the Council, the European Economic and Social Committee and the Committee of the Regions. Strategy for equality between women and men. Available at: www.eur-lex.europa.eu/legal-content/EN/TXT/PDF/?uri=CELEX:52010DC0491&from=EN (accessed 20 February 2018).

Finmark Trust. (2012) FINSCOPE Malawi MSME Survey. Available at: https://finmark.org.za/finscope-malawi-2012-msme-survey/ (accessed 5 March 2019).

Gartner, C., & Cukier, J. (2012) Is tourism employment a sufficient mechanism for poverty reduction? A case study from Nkhata Bay, Malawi. *Current Issues in Tourism*, *15*(6), 545–562.

Gates & Clinton Foundation. (2015) The full participation project. No ceilings. Available at: www.noceilings.org/entrepreneurs/ (accessed 4 February 2018).

Ginige, K., Amaratunga, D., & Haigh, R. (2007) Gender stereotype: a barrier for career development of women in construction. Built Environmental Education Conference, 1–10.

Gittell, S., Sohl, J., & Tebaldi, E. (2014) Do entrepreneurship and high-tech concentration create jobs? Exploring the growth in employment in U.S. metropolitan areas from 1991 to 2007. *Economic Development Quarterly*, *3*(28), 244–253.

Glasson, J., Godfrey, K., & Goodey, B. (1995) *Towards Visitor Impact Management: Visitor Impacts, Carrying Capacity and Management Responses in Europe's Historic Towns and Cities*. Aldershot, UK: Averbury, 170–189.

Global Entrepreneurship Monitor (GEM). (2010) Women's Report. Available at: www.gemconsortium. org/docs/768/gem-2010-womens-report (accessed 20 February 2018).

Global Entrepreneurship Monitor (GEM). (2017) Women's Entrepreneurship 2016/2017 Report. Smith's College. *Financial Education and Entrepreneurship Research*, 6–58.

Government of Malawi (GoM). (2017) The Malawi Growth and Development Strategy (MGDS). Iii Building a Productive, Competitive and Resilient Nation. Available at: https://Cepa.Rmportal. Net/Library/Government-Publications/The-Malawi-Growth-And-Development-Strategy-Mgds-Iii-1-233 (accessed 5 February 2018).

Government of Malawi (GoM). (2015) National Gender Policy, 1–57. Available at: https://Cepa. Rmportal.Net/Library/GovernmentPublications/National%20gender%20policy%202015.Pdf (accessed 23 February 2018).

Greene, G.P., Hart, M.M., Gatewood, J.E., Brush, G.C., & Carter, M.N. (2003) Women entrepreneurs: moving front and center: an overview of research and theory, 1–47.

Halkias, D.C., Nwajiuba, N., Harekiolakis, N., & Caracatsanis, S.M. (2011) Challenges facing women entrepreneurs in Nigeria. *Management Research Review*, 34(2), 221–235.

Hall, C.M. (1995) *Tourism, Ecotourism and Protected Areas*. Gland, Switzerland: IUCN, 149–150.

Hallward, M., & Stewart, C. (2018) Challenges and opportunities facing successful women in Morocco. *Journal of North African Studies*, 23, 871–895.

Hartog, J., van Praag, M., & van der Sluis, J. (2010) If you are so smart, why aren't you an entrepreneur? Returns to cognitive and social ability. Entrepreneurs versus employees. *Journal of Economics & Management Strategy*, 19(4), 947–989.

Hundt, A. (1996) Impact of tourism development on the economy and health of third world nations. *Journal of Travel Medicine*, 3(2), 107–112.

Iheduru, N.G. (2002) Women entrepreneurship and development: the gendering of microfinance in Nigeria. Paper presented at the 8th International Interdisciplinary Congress at Makerere University, Kampala, Uganda Women, 21–26.

ILO. (2016) *Women's Entrepreneurship Development, Sustainable Enterprise Programme. Encouraging Women Entrepreneurs for Jobs and Development*. Geneva: ILO, 1–3.

Jamieson, W., Goodwin, H., & Edmunds, C. (2004) Contribution of tourism to poverty alleviation: pro-poor tourism and the challenge of measuring impacts. For Transport Policy and Tourism Section, Transport and Tourism Division UN ESCAP. 1–38.

Johannessen, J.A., Olsen, B., & Lumpkin, G.T. (2001) Innovation as newness: what is new, how new, and new to whom? *European Journal of Innovation Management*, 4(1), 20–31.

Kelly, D.J., Brush, C.G., Greene, P.G., & Litovsk, Y. (2011) Global Entrepreneurship Monitor, Women's Report, 2–56. Available at: www.babson.edu/Academics/centers/blank-center/global-research/gem/ Documents/GEM%202010%20Womens%20Report%20V2.pdf (accessed 2 March 2018).

Kitching, B., & Woldie, A. (2004) Female entrepreneurs in transitional economies: a comparative study of businesswomen in Nigeria and China. In *Proceedings Hawaii International Conference on Business*, Honolulu, HI.

Klapper, L.F., & Parker, S.C. (2010) Gender and the business environment for new firm creation. *The World Bank Research Observer*, 26(2), 237–257.

Lemma, A.F. (2014) Tourism impacts: evidence of impacts on employment, gender, income. Overseas Development Institute, 1–22.

Litwin, A.S., & Phan, P.H. (2013). Quality over quantity: re-examining the link between entrepreneurship and job creation. *Industrial & Labor Relations Review*, 66(4), 833–873.

Manda, M. (2015) Malawi Situation of Urbanisation Report 2015. Lilongwe: Ministry of Lands and Housing.

Mandipaka, F. (2014) An investigation of the challenges faced by women entrepreneurs in developing countries: a case of King Williams Town, South Africa. *Mediterranean Journal of Science*, 5(27), 1–7.

Markovic, R.M. (2007) *The Perspective of Women's Entrepreneurship in the Age of Globalization*. Charlotte, NC: Information Age, 3–185.

Marlow, S., & Patton, D. (2005) All credit to men? Entrepreneurship, finance and gender. *Entrepreneurship Theory & Practice*, 29, 717–735.

Marlow, S., & Strange, A. (1994) Female entrepreneurs – success by whose standards? In M. Tanton (Ed.), *Women Management: A Developing Presence*, 172–184. London: Routledge.

Marthur-Helm, B. (2005) Equal opportunity and affirmative action for South African women: a benefit or barrier? *Women in Management Review, 20*(1), 56–71.

Mbaiwa, J.E. (2003) The socio-economic and environmental impacts of tourism development in the Okavango Delta, Botswana. *Journal of Arid Environments, 54*(2), 447–467.

Mbaiwa, J.E. (2008) The socio-cultural impacts of tourism development in the Okavango Delta, Botswana. *Journal of Tourism & Cultural Change, 2*(3), 163–185.

McDade, B., & Spring, A (2005) The "new generation of African entrepreneurs": networking to change the business climate for business and private sector-led development. *Entrepreneurship & Regional Development, 17*(1), 17–42.

McGowan, P., Redeker, L.C., Cooper, Y.S., & Greenan, K. (2012) Female entrepreneurship and the management of business and domestic roles; motivations, expectations and realities. *Entrepreneurship & Regional Development, 24*(1–2), 53–72.

Meyer., N., & Landsberg, J. (2015) Motivational factors influencing women's entrepreneurship: a case study of female entrepreneurship in South Africa. World Academy of Science, Engineering and Technology, *International Journal of Economics & Management Engineering, 9*(11), 1–6.

Mitchell, B.C. (2004) Motives of entrepreneurs: a case study of South Africa. *The Journal of Entrepreneurship, 13*(2), 167–183.

Mitchell, J., & Ashley, C. (2010) *Tourism and Poverty Reduction: Pathways to Prosperity.* London: Earthscan, 1–20.

Mkono, M. (2012) Women in hotel management in Zimbabwe: career ambitions, progression tactics, and career challenges. *Tourismos: An International Multidisciplinary Journal of Tourism, 7*(2), 165–181.

Mordi, C., Simpson, R., Singh, S., & Okafor, C. (2010) The role of cultural values in understanding the challenges faced by female entrepreneurs in Nigeria. *Gender in Management. An International Journal, 25*(1), 5–21.

Mrema, A.A. (2015) Tourism and women empowerment in Monduli District. *African Journal of Hospitality, Tourism & Leisure, 4*(2) Issn: 2223-814x.

Mungai, N.E., & Ogot, M. (2012) Gender, culture and entrepreneurship in Kenya. *International Business Research, 5*(5), 1–9.

National Statistical Office (NSO). (2009) Tourism Report 1. Available at: www.Nsomalawi.Mw/Images/Stories/Data_On_Line/Economics/Tourism_Report_2009/2009%20tourism%20report.Pdf (accessed 5 March 2018).

Naude, W. (2016) Is European entrepreneurship in crisis? Iza Discussion Paper No. 9817.1-14, Available at: https://Ssrn.Com/Abstract=2750300 (accessed 12 January 2018).

Nielsen, P.S. (2016) Entrepreneurship orientation in policy making. A determinant of collaboration and organisational adaptability in entrepreneurship policy delivery. *International Journal of Entrepreneurship & Innovation, 17*, 43–54.

Nsiku, N., & Kiratu, S. (2009) Sustainable development impacts of investment incentives: a case study of Malawi's tourism sector. Winnipeg, Canada: International Institute of Sustainable development.

OECD. (2004) Promoting entrepreneurship and innovative SMEs in a global economy: towards a more responsive and inclusive globalization. In *Proceedings of OECD Conference in Women Entrepreneurship; Issues and Policies.* OECD, Instabul, 13–14.

Othman, P., & Rosli, M. (2011) The impact of tourism on small business performance: empirical evidence from Malaysian Islands. *International Journal of Business & Social Science, 2*(1), 1–11.

Otoo, M., Joan, F., Germaine, I., & James, E.D. (2011) Women entrepreneurship in West Africa: the Cowpea street food sector in Niger and Ghana. *Journal of Developmental Entrepreneurship, 16*(1), 36–37.

Padavic, I., & Reskin, F.B. (2002) *Women and Men at Work. Sociology for New Century.* 2nd ed. Thousand Oaks, CA: Pine Forge Press, 1–159.

Perkmann, M. (2002) Euro regions: institutional entrepreneurship in the European Union. In: M. Perkmann & N. Sum (Eds), *Globalization, Regionalization, and Cross-Border Regions.* Basingstoke, UK: Palgrave Macmillan, 103–124.

Perry, S. (2002) A comparison of failed and non-failed small businesses in the United States. *Journal of Developmental Entrepreneurship, 7*, 415–428.

Prosser, R. (1994) Societal change and the growth in alternative tourism. In: E. Carter & G. Lowman (Eds), *Ecotourism. A Sustainable Option.* New York: John Wiley, 19–37.

Reynolds, P.D. (2004) Nature of business start-ups. In W.B. Gartner & K.G. Shaver (Eds), *The Handbook of Entrepreneurial Dynamics. The Process of Business Creation.* Thousand Oaks, CA: Sage, pp. 244–258.

Ribeiro-Soriano, D. (2017) Small business and entrepreneurship: their role in economic and social development. *Entrepreneurship & Regional Development, 29*(1–2), 1–3.

Roethlisberger, C. (2017) Tourism in Africa: an opportunity for fostering inclusive growth. Geneva, WTO Public Forum, 27 September 2017. Available at: www.wto.org/English/Forums_E/Public_Forum17_E/S36_Claudia_Roethlisberger.Pdf (accessed 3 January 2018).

Rough Guides. (2018) *The Rough Guide to Malawi*. Available at: www.roughguides.com/best-places-to-travel/the-rough-guide-to-2018/malawi/ (accessed 6 January 2018).

SADC Secretariat. (2008) Regional Economic Integration: A Strategy for Poverty Eradication towards Sustainable Development. The Regional Poverty Reduction Framework. 18–20 April 2008, Pailles, Mauritius. SADC International Conference on Poverty & Development. 1–77. Available at: www.sadc.int/files/6713/5293/3545/The_Regional_Poverty_Reduction_Framework.pdf (accessed 3 February 2018).

Sahn, D. (2004) Growth and poverty reduction in sub-Saharan Africa: macroeconomic adjustment and beyond. *Journal of African Economies, 13*, 66–95.

Semafumu, R. (2004) Protocol to the African Charter On Human and Peoples' Rights on the Rights of Women in Africa: Research Report. Harnessing A Potential Force for Positive Changes. Commisioned by Oxfam Gb Southern African Regiona Study, 1–6.

Shackleton, S., Ziervogel, G., Sallu, S., Gill, T., & Tschakert, P. (2015) Why is socially just climate change adaptation in sub-Saharan Africa so challenging? A review of barriers identified from empirical cases. *WIREs Climate Change, 6*, 321–344.

Shahnawaz, M.R. (2015) Preliminary investigation of Emirati women entrepreneurship in the UAE: motivating factors, challenges and government initiatives. *International Journal of Scientific & Technology Research, 4*(8), 50–61.

Shishmanova, M. (2015) Cultural tourism in cultural corridors, itineraries, areas and cores networked. *Procedia – Social and Behavioral Sciences, 188*, 246–254.

Simkute, T. (2017) Decommodifying volunteer tourism? Insights from nordic non-governmental organisations. University of Lapland, Tourism Research.

Snyman, L.S. (2012) The role of ecotourism employment in poverty reduction and community perceptions of conservation and tourism in Southern Africa. *Journal of Sustainable Tourism, 20*(3), 395–416.

Stange, M.Z., Oyster, K.C., & Sloan, E.J. (2016) *Encyclopedia of Women in Today's World*. Thousand Oaks, CA: Sage, 207–209.

Stephen, O.M., Isaac, K.M., George, M., & Dominic, K.R. (2014) Women employment in tourism businesses: a case study of Eldoret Town, Kenya. *African Journal of Tourism & Hospitality, 1*(1), 27–38.

Stone, S.L., Stone, M.T., & Mbaiwa, E.J. (2017) Tourism in Botswana in the last 50 years: a review. Special Issue on Environment, Tourism and Contemporary Socio-economic Issues in the Okavango Delta and other Ecosystems. *Botswana Notes & Records, 49*, 1–76.

Stronza, A., & Gordillo, J. (2008) Community views of ecotourism. *Annals of Tourism Research, 35*(2), 448–468.

Türker, N., & Öztürk, S. (2013) Perceptions of residents towards the impacts of tourism in the Küre Mountains National Park, Turkey. *International Journal of Business & Social Science, 4*(2), 1–12.

Tur-Porcar, A., Mas-Tur, A., & Belso, J.A. (2017) Barriers to women entrepreneurship. Different methods, different results? *Quality & Quantity, 51*(5), 2019–2034.

UNESCO. (2013) UNESCO Convention concerning the Protection of the World Cultural and Natural Heritage. World Heritage Committee, 37th session, Phnom Penh. Cambodia, 16–27 June.

UNWTO. (2011) UN Woman. The global report on women in Tourism 2010. Preliminary findings. Available at: www2.unwto.org/sites/all/files/pdf/folleto_globarl_report.pdf (accessed 23 January 2018).

UNWTO. (2017) Tourism highlights, 1–16. Available at: www.e-unwto.org/doi/pdf/10.18111/9789284419029 (accessed 19 March 2018).

UNWTO & UN Women. (2011) Global Report on Women in Tourism, Preliminary Findings, 1–12. Available at: www2.unwto.org/sites/all/files/pdf/folleto_globarl_report.pdf (accessed 4 March 2018).

Ursache, M. (2015) Tourism – significant driver shaping a destinations heritage. *Science Direct, 188*, 130–137.

Welsh, D.H.B., Kaciak, E., & Ahmed, S. (2013) Sudanese women entrepreneurs. *Journal of Developmental Entrepreneurship, 18*(2), 1–18.

van Welsum, D. (2016) Background paper Digital Dividends World Development Report Enabling Digital Entrepreneurs. World Bank Group, 1–10. Available at: http://Pubdocs.Worldbank.Org/En/354261452529895321/Wdr16-Bp-Enabling-Digial-Entrepreneurs-Dwelsum.Pdf (accessed 1 April 2018).

Winn, J. (2004) Entrepreneurship: not an easy path to top management for women. *Women in Management Review*, *19*(3), 143–153.

Woldie, A., & Adersua, A. (2004) Female entrepreneurs in a transition economy, business women in Nigeria. *International Journal of Social Economics*, *31*(1), 78–93.

World Bank. (2010) Malawi Travel & Tourism: Realizing the Potential. Finance and Private Sector Development, Africa Region Report No. 62353-MW.

World Bank. (2011) Women Gender Report, Women in Entrepreneurship, 1–18. Available at: http://Siteresources.Worldbank.Org/Ecaext/Resources/258598-1322580725430/Chapter3.Pdf (accessed 2 January 2018).

World Bank. (2013) World Bank Group Support for Innovation and Entrepreneurship: An Independent Evaluation. Available at: http://Ieg.Worldbankgroup.Org/Sites/Default/Files/Data/Reports/Innovation_Eval.Pdf (accessed 3 February 2018).

World Bank. (2014) *Gender at Work. A Companion to the World Development Report on Jobs*. Washington, DC: World Bank.

World Economic Forum (WEF). (2011) The African Competitiveness Report, the World Bank and the African Development Bank. 3–215. Available at: http://siteresources.worldbank.org/INTAFRICA/Resources/The_Africa_Competitiveness_Report_2011.pdf (accessed 2 March 2018).

World Travel & Tourism Council. (2016) Economic Impact, 1–20. Available at; www.wttc.org//media/files/reports/economic%20impact%20research/regions%202016/world2016.pdf (accessed 19 March 2018).

World Travel & Tourism Council. (2018) Travel and Tourism Economic Impact Malawi. Available at: www.wttc.org/-/media/files/reports/economic-impact-research/countries-2018/malawi2018.pdf (accessed 3 March).

Zakaria, Y. (2001) Entrepreneurs at home: secluded Muslim women and hidden economic activities in northern Nigerian. *Nordic Journal of African Studies*, *10*(1), 107–123.

Zidana, R. (2015) Macroeconomic determinants of tourism sector performance in Malawi. *International Journal of Social Science & Humanities Research*, *3*(4), 481–491.

15

THE ROLE OF TOURISM IN POVERTY ALLEVIATION IN MAURITIUS

Boopen Seetanah

Introduction

It is a fact that tourism development is now widely used as a strategy to enhance economic well-being and to reduce the level of poverty in developing countries. Many countries, especially developing countries, have also tried to add tourism to the list of important economic sectors in which to pursue economic growth (Croes & Vanegas, 2008). Hawkins and Mann (2007) stated that approximately 80% of the 56 countries with a poverty reduction policy recognized tourism as an ingredient for poverty reduction. Saayman, Rossouw and Krugell (2012) also suggested that tourism earnings could be a tool to reduce poverty, provided that appropriate policies on the labour market and human resource development are present. At the multilateral level, the United Nations Conference on Trade and Development (UNCTAD),[1] the World Tourism and Travel Council (WTTC) and the United Nations World Tourism Organization (UNWTO)[2] strongly support a change in prevailing economic development strategies, arguing that tourism development can play a significant role in poverty reduction and in economic growth for the developing world (Croes & Vanegas, 2006, 2008; Cortés-Jiménez, Pulina, Prunera & Artis, 2009; Croes, 2012; Vanegas, 2014).

Although tourism and poverty reduction have been linked since the 1960s, the search to establish a direct empirical link between the two has been very recent. There exists a large strand of the empirical literature which assesses the impact of tourism development on the economic growth of countries, and an overwhelming majority of studies have confirmed the tourism-led growth (TLG) hypothesis (see Balaguer and Cantavella-Jorda, 2002; Dritsakis, 2004; Durbarry, 2004; Katırcıoğlu, 2009; and Seetanah, 2011, among others). Although one would argue that a positive effect of tourism in accelerating growth would also imply that this would in turn trickle down to alleviate poverty (as, on the other hand, economic growth has been empirically confirmed to impact on poverty alleviation), empirical work on the direct relationship between tourism development and poverty has been scant, and tourism researchers tend to neglect the link between tourism and poverty alleviation (Zhao & Ritchie, 2007; except for rare work by Croes and Vanegas, 2008; Blake, Arbache, Sinclair & Teles, 2008; Croes, 2014; Vanegas, Gartner & Senauer, 2015). The UNWTO (2002) argued that tourism, with the requisite of travel to a destination, is a sector that is likely to lead to poverty reduction as the tourist consumes a bundle of services and non-traded goods locally from more than one supplier. This implies that many different service suppliers participate in creating a tourism experience. This could create the opportunity for poor, marginal and remote areas to benefit from the advantages (increased employment opportunities, higher income levels and a trickle-down effect) that tourism spending may bring to a destination.

In order to improve our understanding of the tourism–poverty link, the current study aims to assess how tourism affects poverty beyond its effects on growth for the case for a tourism-dependent island economy, namely Mauritius. It investigates whether an empirical relationship between tourism and poverty reduction exists and measures the specific effects on poverty decline. Specifically, the study attempts to answer three interrelated questions. First, is there a relationship between tourism development and poverty decline? Second, in the eventuality of a relationship, what is the nature of that relationship? Third, what is the direction of the relationship? The study will focus on the tourist-dependent island of Mauritius and will employ a dynamic time series analysis over the period 1987–2017. Mauritius represents a good case study as it is one of the best performers of the continent and, moreover, is a tourist-dependent economy. It has been relatively successful in achieving a decent poverty level since its independence. In order to gauge the effect of tourism, an aggregate poverty model specification will be augmented to include a tourism development proxy while including the classic determinants of poverty as well. The study is expected to supplement the dwarf literature on the direct empirical relationship between tourism and poverty reduction and will be useful for policy implications.

This rest of this chapter is organized as follows: the following section looks into the theoretical and empirical review, the third section discusses the model specification and the methodology and analyses the findings, and the fourth section has the conclusions.

Related literature

Theoretical underpinning

Theoretically, tourism as a sector is linked to poverty alleviation through its benefits in the development of local economies (Ashley, Boyd & Goodwin, 2000; Ashley, Goodwin & Roe, 2001). Tourist visits provide opportunities for selling additional goods and services (e.g. agricultural products and handicrafts, among others) produced by locals, including the poor. The resulting income and employment generation is likely to cut down poverty levels, particularly the income poverty of the local residents, including the poor.

Moreover, the poor can reduce their poverty if tourism is used to support essential items such as health and education services, and this eventually helps to enhance their well-being and capabilities and thus alleviates poverty. As such, tourism offers a crucial opportunity to diversify local economies. Remote areas particularly attract tourists because of their origin, cultural, wildlife and landscape value, creating new income-generating activities and employment opportunities. Benefits may also be obtained as infrastructure and social service facilities are often established or improved using earnings from tourism. It has been argued that tourism offers labour-intensive and small-scale opportunities compared with other non-agricultural activities, and the sector is particularly engaged in employing a high proportion of women. It also give much importance to natural resources and culture, which may feature among the few assets belonging to the poor.

There are also indirect incomes and employment generated from tourist purchases outside the hotel business, which sometimes may be more important than the direct effects, but once again are hard to estimate. De Kadt (1979) indicates that tourists usually spend less than two-thirds of their expenditure on typical tourist hotels and restaurants. Therefore, the rest is spent elsewhere, on souvenirs and transport services, and on indirect services provided to tourists, such as food and other items supplied to hotels and restaurants, construction facilities, capital goods and the tax collected on this expenditure

Increased tourism spending also means heightened employment opportunities for the poor. A report by ECLAC (2007) suggested that tourism offers the greatest potential for job creation in Nicaragua in its search to defeat poverty. Besides the number of jobs created, tourism seems to provide better-quality jobs in terms of providing healthier, safer and more pleasant working conditions than other economic sectors in Nicaragua. Lengefeld and Beyer (2006) found that, although the hotel sector may offer lower wages than, for example, the sugar industry, hotel employees have permanent contracts and better fringe benefits, such as a bonus and paid leave. A word of caution: Pay in tourism jobs is comparatively lower than the average pay in the country (ECLAC, 2007), and jobs seem affected by seasonality (Ferguson, 2010).

Government tax revenues, both direct and indirect, are also an important benefit of tourism. Early evidence for sampled countries provides estimates for tax revenue in the order of 20% of (gross) tourist receipts. On average, 10% of gross tourism receipts go to government revenue in the Caribbean countries, compared with 20% reported in Tunisia and Kenya (Bryden, 1973). World Bank estimates from tourist projects show that budgetary receipts generated by tourist expenditures are in the range of one-fifth to one-third of tourist receipts. In the Maldives, in 1984, tourism accounted for 40% of government revenues. A study by the UNWTO (1988) indicated that it was common for 'tourist countries' to get between 10 and 25% of their fiscal revenues from tourism. The proportion may go up to 50% for smaller, specialized tourist countries such as the Bahamas. Rising incomes for individuals and households mean the government would receive higher taxes which would increase the government's capacity to invest in infrastructure, health, education and other services relevant for the poor (Hara, 2008).

Interestingly, there is also a causal relationship between tourism and foreign direct investment (FDI; which in itself has been argued to be pro-poor in nature). Tourists demand goods and services such as accommodation, food, transportation services and entertainment, among others, in the destination country, and it is a fact that, in most developing countries, this puts pressure on the current level of production which needs to be increased to meet this increasing demand. Tang, Selvanathan and Selvanathan (2007) argued that investment, particularly FDI, would eventually expand. Moreover, they argued that FDI would increase as the international hotel chains are usually attracted by the prospects of growing tourism demand and would thus attempt to capitalize on their brands. Sandford and Dong (2000) further argued that international tourism gives potential investors the opportunity to obtain 'first-hand knowledge' and 'ground information' on the economic and business environment of the host country, and, as a result, investment possibilities could be identified and made in more confidence. FDI has been widely documented to be pro-poor in itself. FDI can have direct and indirect impacts on poverty reduction in the host country. The indirect impact of FDI on the reduction of poverty is through economic growth which results in the improvement of living standards due to the increase in GDP and improvements in technology and productivity, as well as the economic environment (Bende-Nabende & Ford, 1998; Borenzstein, de Gregorio & Lee, 1998; Kakwani, 2000; Seetanah & Khadaroo, 2007). The direct impact of FDI on poverty can be seen through the increase in employment and the reduction of people living below the poverty line, resulting from the increase in the demand for employment and the improvement of workforce and safety nets. Studies that have found a positive impact of FDI on poverty reduction include Hung (1999), Reiter and Steensma (2010), Ucal (2014), Israel (2014) and Soumare (2015).

However, there are some potentially adverse effects which may arise from tourism development. These may include the transfer of tourism revenue out of the host country and also potential exclusion of local businesses, inhabitants and local products. In general, it is therefore possible that the poor may gain few direct economic benefits from tourism while bearing many of the costs and, hence, fail to reduce their poverty. Shah and Gupta (2000) also posited that not much attention has been paid to the impact that diversion of natural resources for tourist facilities would have on local communities. They further noted that tourism is a complex sector mainly driven by the private sector – often large international companies – with the latter having negligible interest in the quest to alleviate poverty in the local community.

Furthermore, leakages also occur, owing to the use of imported skilled labour and luxury products, repatriation of profits by international companies, and the considerable role of marketing, transport and other services based in the originating country. As a matter of fact, up to 85% of the estimated benefits of tourism are 'leaked out' of developing countries (cited in Bolwell and Weinz, 2008), owing mainly to the power of international tour operators (Brohman, 1996), foreign ownership and the high import propensity of tourism (Jules, 2005). Clancy (2001, p. 101) also added that tourism employment could be 'seasonal, low-paying and exploitative' in a few cases, and Dwyer, Forsyth, Madden and Spurr (2000) posited that tourism employment is more often secured by those with skills and not necessarily accessible to the poor.

Related empirical literature

Although tourism and poverty reduction have been linked since the 1960s, the search to establish an empirical link between the two has been very recent. The search can be classified in two strands: The first refers to the establishment of a link between tourism and economic growth and is grounded in the debate on the TLG hypothesis. It asserts that tourism is growth-oriented and implicitly assumes that growth will trickle down to the poor. The second refers to the attempt to establish a direct empirical link between tourism and poverty reduction.

The first strand – that is, the TLG hypothesis – contains country-specific and cross-sectional studies. Evidence from country-specific studies includes earlier work from Ghali (1976), who assessed the contribution of tourism to the economics of income in the case of Hawaii. The author found that tourism has had a positive and significant growth effect. A similar result is confirmed by Balaguer and Cantavella-Jorda (2002) for the case of Spain, and Dritsakis (2004) for the case of Greece. Evidence supporting the TLG hypothesis is also confirmed for emerging economies such as Mauritius (Durbarry, 2004), Indonesia (Sugiyarto, Blake & Sinclair, 2003) and South Africa (Akinboade and Braimoh, 2010). Other studies have tested the hypothesized link in cross-sectional and panel data settings, including Eugenio-Martin, Martín-Morales and Sinclair (2008) for the case of developing economies, and Seetanah (2011) for the case of a sample of island economies. Lanza and Pigliaru (2000) and Brau, Lanza and Pigliaru (2007) further reported that small states are likely to grow quickly when they are highly specialized in tourism, and Sequeira and Nunes (2008) confirmed a positive association between tourism receipts and the growth rate of tourist-specialist countries. However, it is noteworthy that there are some studies that could not confirm a positive tourism–growth link; for instance, Eugenio-Martin, Martín-Morales and Scarpa (2004) observed that tourism was not always related to the economy in the case of Latin America, being growth-conducive only in medium- and low-income countries. Oh (2005) could not establish a catalytic effect of tourism on growth, but rather found a significant positive relationship between growth and tourism for the case of Korea. Taking the Balearics and Canary Islands as case studies, Nowak and Sahli (2007) reported that tourism spending could even have led to welfare losses and early symptoms of the Dutch disease. For the case of Turkey, Katırcıoğlu (2009) could not confirm any significant causal relationship between tourism and economic growth, and, more recently, Kim and Lee (2012) reported similar evidence from the case of a newly industrialized country, namely South Korea.

The second strand of the literature has dwelled on a more direct link between tourism and poverty. Indeed, a sizeable part of this literature exists at the micro level, either including a single enterprise (lodge, resort or community business), a cluster of enterprises or related enterprises (see, for example, Elliot & Mwangi, 1998; Gujadhur, 2012; Halstead, 2003; Murphy & Halstead, 2003; Mulonga & Murphy, 2003; Clauzel, 2005; McNab, 2005; Hainsworth, 2008; and Lengefeld & Beyer, 2006, among others). Empirical methods used in such micro-level studies have been based mainly on sustainable-livelihoods analysis (non-financial impacts on the local community) and micro-economic analysis of enterprise operations (that is, based on revenues, profits and wages, among others).

A number of recent studies have provided some broader perspectives to the debate and have recently moved towards macroeconomic approaches, and this relates to analysis based mainly on either simulation models such as computable general equilibrium models (CGEs) or econometric methods based on time series and cross-sectional data sets (Winters, Corral & Mora, 2013). It remains a fact that relatively few studies have examined an empirical link between tourism and poverty reduction at the macroeconomic level. Among those studies is the pioneering work of Ashley et al. (2000, 2001), who reported that tourism could contribute to poverty alleviation by providing job opportunities to economically vulnerable groups of society in the production of goods and services related to tourism. The authors assessed pro-poor tourism experiences in six country case studies and discussed the fact that, whereas tourism activities are seen to have sizeable poverty reduction impacts at the regional level, such may not be the case at the national level. They argued that such impacts are dependent on the scale of tourism within the economy and on the capacity for it to change towards more pro-poor activities.

Croes and Vanegas (2008) used a vector autoregressive (VAR) approach for the case of Nicaragua and reported a uni-causal link between tourism development and economic expansion, and between tourism and poverty reduction. The authors posited that the relationship between tourism, economic growth and poverty reduction was related to the 'democratization of the dollar' by stressing the employment, income and opportunities for participation that are derived from a transfer of wealth and income from residents (tourists) of wealthier countries to developing countries (recipients). Blake et al. (2008), on the other hand, employed a CGE to assess the contribution of tourism to poverty reduction in Brazil and found that tourism benefits the lowest-income households, albeit to a lesser extent than higher-income groups.

Croes (2014) investigated the role of tourism in fighting absolute poverty, beyond its effects on economic growth, in two developing countries, namely Nicaragua and Costa Rica. Using an error correction model, the results revealed that, whereas tourism reduced the level of poverty for the case of Nicaragua, in Costa Rica, which enjoys a higher level of economic development than Nicaragua, tourism does not seem to affect the poor. The findings from the two developing countries exhibit differing impacts of tourism development with, hence, differing policy implications. Indeed, Vanegas et al. (2015) extended the study to examine the existence of a long-run relationship between extreme poverty reduction and agricultural, manufacturing and tourism development using an autoregressive distributed lag approach. The authors reported that the poverty reduction effect was statistically significantly greater than that of agriculture and manufacturing for both countries.

More recently, Kim, Song and Pyun (2016) researched the relationship between tourism, poverty and economic development for a panel of 69 developing countries for the period 1995–2012. The authors confirmed that tourism had heterogeneous effects on the poverty ratio with some threshold effects – that is, depending on a country's income per capita. Indeed, the poverty-reducing effects of tourism development was only found for the least developed countries. Rodríguez, Casas-Jurado and García-Fernández (2017) analysed the impact of tourism on poverty using a fixed effects model based on a panel data set of Peruvian departments for the period 2001–2013. Their findings suggested that tourism was important for the poor, but the benefits did not reach the extreme poor. Low community participation coupled with a weak macro environment were identified as elements impeding poverty alleviation through tourism.

However, it is noteworthy that there are also a few studies that could not establish any poverty-alleviation effect of tourism. For instance, Mbaiwa (2005) observed that tourism development in Botswana was accompanied by a higher level of poverty, thereby implying that tourism was not sustainable in reducing poverty. However, the authors noted that the overwhelming concentration of multinational safari operators in the country relative to local operators was not taken into account. Wattanakuljarus and Coxhead (2008) confirmed the same for the case of Thailand and posited that, although Thailand is a highly tourism-intensive economy and tourism development has raised aggregate household incomes, it has, however, worsened income distribution. Saayman et al. (2012) showed that increased tourism in South Africa led to an increase in the country's real growth rate, but that a decrease in the household expenditure of the poor and increased unemployment rates were also noted.

Methodology and analysis

The study follows the recent research on tourism and poverty by Kim et al. (2016) and Rodríguez et al. (2017) and also on classical studies by Ravallion and Datt (1996) and Ghura, Leite and Tsangarides (2002) whereby poverty is modelled at the macroeconomic level using the aggregate poverty function as per Equation 1 below. The study covers the 31-year period ranging from 1987 to 2017 inclusive, because of data availability. The explanatory variables of the poverty model pertain to the following determinants, namely: economic growth, income inequality, employment, human capital and financial development. For the sake of the study, tourism arrival is included to account for tourism development.

The proposed economic model is specified as follows:

$$POV = f(GDP, INEQ, EMP, EDU, TOURIST) \tag{1}$$

where *POV* is the dependent variable and measures the level of poverty in the country and is measured by the poverty head count ratio.

Explanatory variables: macroeconomic determinants of poverty

In the long run, economic growth is the key to the alleviation of absolute poverty as it creates the resources to raise incomes. Real GDP per capita (*GDP*) is the measure used to account for the above. Such a measure also simultaneously captures macroeconomic performance, which is commonly considered to be a key determinant of poverty (DeFina & Thanawala, 2004; Freeman, 2001; Gundersen & Ziliak, 2004; Mishel, Bernstein & Allegretto, 2005; Sawhill, 1988).

Progress in reducing rates of poverty through economic growth depends crucially on its distributional characteristics. This is particularly true for statistical measures of poverty, as relatively high numbers of people are clustered around typical poverty lines. In theory, a country could enjoy a high average growth rate without any benefit to its poorest households, if income disparities grew significantly – that is, if the rich got richer while the incomes of the poor stagnated or declined. This is unlikely, however; income distribution tends to be stable over time and rarely changes so much that the poor would experience an absolute decline in income while average incomes grew in a sustained fashion. Danziger and Gottschalk (1995) and Iceland (2003) found that declining economic inequality served to reduce poverty. Freeman (2001) and Gundersen and Ziliak (2004) also found that income inequality was associated with higher poverty. The variable used to proxy for inequality (*INEQ*) is the Gini coefficient.

The potential link between employment and unemployment rates, work hours and poverty has been well documented in the literature (see Atkinson, Rainwater & Smeeding, 1995; Kenworthy, 2004; Bernstein & Baker, 2003; and Iceland, Kenworthy & Scopilliti, 2005). To capture the employment effect (*EMP*) above effect, we use the employment level of the country.

The role of human capital, in the form of education, experience, skills, training and health, has often been emphasized as a particularly important determinant of income or production (Mincer, 1958; Schultz, 1988). Given a conducive environment, the productivity of the labour supplied by the poor is an important determinant of their ability to benefit from enhanced opportunities, and an important determinant of labour productivity is human capital in the form of, for example, education and health. Studies from Ackland and Falkingham (1997) showed that secondary education reduces the probability of being poor in comparison with both primary and higher education. It should be noted that education may affect economic welfare in many different ways. For example, it may influence both returns within economic activities and access to such activities. In addition, education may limit fertility and thus reduce the number of dependent children. So, education may raise income, increase access to non-farm employment, improve the ability to set up a household business and improve productivity in farming. Furthermore, owing to lack of education and skills, the poor tend to be less mobile (across sectors and regions) than better educated workers and are, therefore, often unable to switch jobs and capitalize on available employment opportunities. To measure human capital (*EDU*), we use the secondary enrolment ratio over the period of study.

Having established the theoretical and empirical link between the role of tourism and poverty alleviation, a measure of tourism development, namely the number of tourism arrivals (*TOURISM*) in the country, is used to measure tourism development. The data source is Statistics Mauritius (2019).

The econometric function is thus written as follows:

$$pov = \alpha + \beta_1 growth + \beta_2 ineq + \beta_3 emp + \beta_4 edu + \beta_5 tourism + \varepsilon \tag{2}$$

The lower-case letters denote the log of the respective variables, and such a transformation is undertaken for ease of interpretation and comparability of estimated coefficients.

Endogeneity and dynamic issues: the VAR specification

Given that the variables are stationary of the same order – that is, at first difference (tested using the augmented Dickey–Fuller and Phillips–Perron tests) – the second step is to check for a co-integration test or long-run co-integration relationship among the variables. The Johansen co-integrating test (Johansen, 1988; Johansen & Juselius, 1990) has been used, and the result has confirmed the presence of co-integration. An often ignored element in the modelling of the determinant of poverty at the macroeconomic level has been the control for simultaneous interactions between the variables in the specified equations. In fact, the static single-equation framework often adopted by an overwhelming number of studies fails to take into account the presence of dynamic feedback among relevant variables. Accordingly, a VAR approach is thus used to delineate the relationship between trade and poverty. Such an approach does not impose a priori restriction on the dynamic and endogenous relations among the different variables. It resembles simultaneous equation modelling, whereby several endogenous variables are considered together. Moreover, in the presence of co-integration, this framework allows us to generate both short-term and long-term associations between climate change and tourism. The long run results are summarized in Table 15.1.

The long-run estimates yield quite interesting results, and it can be noted that tourism development has had a negative and significant effect on the level of poverty for the island, albeit with a relatively low impact compared with the other factors included in the model. The estimated coefficient of -0.221 indicates that a 1% increase in tourism arrival in the island has been associated with a reduction of 0.2% in the level of poverty. Such a finding confirms the empirical results of Croes and Vanegas (2008), Croes (2014) and Vanegas et al. (2015), who used an econometric approach to model the tourism link. The relatively small coefficient obtained is more in line with the results of Li, Chen, Li and Goh (2016), who posited that the poverty-reducing effects of tourism development were found to be greater for the least-developed countries.

The findings further confirm that, in the long run, economic growth is the key to the reduction of absolute poverty as it creates the resources to raise incomes. For instance, a 1% increase in real GDP has led to a 0.47% decrease in poverty level. This result is in line with Squire (1993), who regressed the rate of poverty reduction against its rate of economic growth and found that a 1% increase in the growth rate reduced the poverty headcount (US$1 per person per day) by 0.24%. Empirical work from Bruno, Ravallion and Squire (1998) for 20 developing countries and Akmal, Ahmad, Ahmad and Butt (2007) for the case of Pakistan also confirmed a negative relationship between trade and poverty reduction.

However, the poverty-reducing effect of growth tends to be mitigated by a rise in inequality, as witnessed by the negative and significant coefficient of *ineq*, and this is in line with studies by Freeman (2001) and Gundersen and Ziliak (2004) who also found that income inequality was associated with higher poverty The relatively high, significant coefficient of human capital confirms that the latter is a key determinant of labour productivity, which in turn significantly affects the ability of the urban poor to benefit from enhanced opportunities. A higher level of education also helps the urban poor to be more mobile so that they can switch jobs and capitalize on available opportunities. Employment has had a positive effect on the poverty fight, confirming the literature (see Ackland & Falkingham, 1997, for confirmatory findings).

Table 15.1 The long-run VAR estimates

	Poverty equation Dependent variable: Pov	GDP equation Dependent variable: gdp	Tourism equation Dependent variable: tourism
pov		−0.234**	−0.134*
Gdp	−0.474***		0.325**
Ineq	0.284**	0.123	−0.143
Emp	−0.282**	0.274***	0.129
Hc	−0.409***	0.543***	0.212***
Tourism	−0.221**	0.428***	

Notes: * Significance at 10%; ** significance at 5%; ***significance at 1%

The VAR framework enables us to focus on additional insights. For instance, from the *gdp* equation, tourism is confirmed to be growth-conducive, thus validating the TLG hypothesis for the country, at the same time implicitly implying that growth will trickle down to the poor. Interestingly, such a finding is a rejoinder to numerous studies on emerging and developing countries (Durbarry, 2004; Seetanah, 2011; Sugiyarto et al., 2003; Eugenio-Martin et al., 2008; Akinboade & Braimoh, 2010). As such, by focusing on the tourism equation (fourth column in Table 15.1), it can be observed that the coefficient of poverty is negative and significant, although relatively low, suggesting that tourists are sensible to some extent to the poverty level of the country. This confirms the existence of a bi-causal relationship between tourism and poverty. The level of development (as measured by *gdp*) and human capital (*edu*) are also found to be ingredients of tourism development.

In the presence of co-integration, a vector error correction model (VECM) was subsequently estimated and it includes an error correction term which should allow for an investigation of the dynamic nature of the model and also for estimation of the short-run estimates.[3] In fact, the VECM specification forces the long-run behaviour of the endogenous variables to converge towards their co-integrated relationships, which accommodates short-run dynamics. In this study, the VECM is estimated using an optimum lag length of 1. The negative and significant ECM term confirms the existence of a long-run stable relationship with respect to the poverty equation. Analysing the main variable of interest to us, tourism, it can be noted that, in the short run, it has a positive and significant impact on poverty reduction. However, the result is very small, and it can, hence, be argued that tourism takes time to have its full effect on poverty alleviation.

The positive and significant coefficient of the lagged dependent (0.29) variable suggests that poverty is a vicious cycle, as the responsiveness of current period poverty measures with respect to their respective last-year values is high and significant, thereby confirming the existence of dynamism and endogeneity in the modelling framework. This result is in line with Seetanah and Khadaroo (2009).

Conclusions

Although there exists a large strand of the empirical literature that focused on the impact of tourism development on the economic growth of countries, assuming that growth will trickle down to assist in poverty alleviation, empirical work on the direct relationship between tourism development and poverty has been relatively rare. This research assessed the direct empirical link between tourism and poverty levels for the case of the tourist-dependent island of Mauritius by employing a dynamic time series analysis, namely a VAR framework, over the period 1987–2017 in an augmented aggregate poverty function.

The findings suggest that tourism development has had a negative and significant effect on the level of poverty for the island, although with a relatively low impact compared with other classical factors in the aggregate poverty model. Such a result tends to be aligned with those of Li et al. (2016), who reported that the poverty-reducing effects of tourism development were found to be relatively small for upper-middle-income economies. Moreover, in the long run, economic growth is confirmed to be a key ingredient in alleviating absolute poverty, and the poverty-reducing effect of growth tends to be mitigated by a rise in inequality. Employment and education level are also proved to be important in the quest for poverty alleviation. Interestingly, tourism development is observed to be growth-conducive, confirming the TLG hypothesis and thus providing an indirect path to poverty reduction as well. Finally a bi-causal relationship between tourism and poverty is observed, suggesting that tourists are sensible to some extent (although quite a small extent, as judged by the coefficient) to the poverty level of the country.

The implication of the study is twofold. Existing studies on the direct link between tourism and poverty are at best scant, and, moreover, most of the studies have focused on case studies in specific regions, which makes it difficult to obtain a broader (global) picture of the tourism–poverty link. Studies dealing with relatively large panel sets (and disaggregated by income group as well) over a reasonable time frame are important for further understanding of the hypothesized links and for more insights.

At the policy implications level, it seems clear that promoting the tourism sector appears to be the proper pathway. Policy interventions could include a government's alignment of economic and budgetary incentives with social costs and benefits to stimulate investment in this sector (for example, hotels and restaurants, among others). As the tourism sector is also linked with the informal economy (whereby the poor are most likely to engage with tourism), the government should aim at a more enabling environment for enterprise. Moreover, the authorities should market destinations more aggressively in an attempt to enhance international tourism demand and spending (including in products that directly benefit the local economy).

Appendix

Table 15A.1 Some key figures about the Mauritian tourism sector and poverty

	1990	2000	2010	2013	2016
Population of MUS	1,080,000	1,186,140	1,195,433	1,259,838	1,275,227
No. of hotels	75	95	97	107	111
Tourist arrivals	291,550	656,543	702,018	993,106	1,275, 227
Tourism receipts (% of GDP)	10%	14%	17%	18%	20%
Proportion of poor people (national poverty line)	14.2	11.8	12.3	9.8	6.3
Proportion of poor people (US$ 1 per day)	<1	<1	<1	<1	<1
Proportion of poor people (US$ 2 per day)	2.9	2.5	2.2	<2	<2
Gini coefficient	0.396	0.381	0.36	0.414	0.400
HDI	0.62	0.673	0.748	0.769	0.781

Notes

1 UNCTAD (1998, n.p.) posits that, 'tourism is the only major sector in international trade in services in which developing countries have consistently had surpluses'.

2 The UNWTO responded to this challenge by setting up the Sustainable Tourism-Eliminating Poverty (ST-EP) Initiative, which was meant to promote poverty alleviation through sustainable tourism development projects. Since 2002, it has specifically recommended the adoption of pro-poor approaches (WTO, 2002, 2004). Moreover, the UNWTO New Year message for 2007 read, 'this year . . . should be a year to consolidate tourism as a key agent in the fight against poverty and a primary tool for sustainable development' (UNWTO, 2007).

3 The results for the short-run estimates are not presented in this research but are available upon request.

References

Ackland, R., & Falkingham, J. (1997). 'A profile of poverty in Kyrgyzstan', in J. Falkingham, J. Klugman, S. Marnie & J. Micklewright (Eds), *Household Welfare in Central Asia*, pp. 81–99. Basingstoke, UK: Macmillan Press.

Akmal, S. M., Ahmad, Q. M., Ahmad, M. H., & Butt, M. S. (2007). 'An empirical investigation of the relationship between trade liberalization and poverty reduction: a case for Pakistan', *The Lahore Journal of Economics*, *12*(1): 99–118.

Ashley, C., Boyd, C., & Goodwin, H. (2000). 'Pro-poor tourism: who benefits? Perspectives on tourism and poverty reduction. *Annals of Tourism Research*, *35*(2), 616–618.

Ashley, C., Roe, D., & Goodwin, H. (2001). 'Pro-poor tourism strategies: making tourism work for the poor; a review of experience', Pro-Poor Tourism Report No. 1, April.

Akinboade, O., & Braimoh, L. (2010). 'International tourism and economic development in South Africa: a Granger causality test', *International Journal of Tourism Research*, *12*: 149–163.

Atkinson, A. B., Rainwater, L., & Smeeding, T. (1995). *Income Distribution in OECD Countries: The Evidence from the Luxembourg Income Study (LIS)*. Paris: OECD.

Balaguer, J., & Cantavella-Jorda, M. (2002). 'Tourism as a long-run economic growth factor: the Spanish case', *Applied Economics*, *34*(7): 877–884.

Bende-Nabende, A., & Ford, J. L. (1998). 'FDI, adjustment and endogenous growth: multiplier effects from a small dynamic model for Taiwan, 1959–95', *World Development*, *26*(7): 1315–1330

Bernstein, J., & Baker, D. (2003). *The Benefits of Full Employment*. Washington, DC: Economic Policy Institute.

Blake, A., Arbache, J. S., Sinclair, M. T., & Teles, V. (2008). 'Tourism and poverty relief', *Annals of Tourism Research*, *35*(1): 107–126.

Bolwell, D., & Weinz, W. (2008). 'Reducing poverty through tourism.' Working Paper, International Labour Office, ILO Sectoral Activities Programme. Geneva: ILO.

Borenzstein, E., de Gregorio, J., & Lee, J. W. (1998). 'How does foreign investment affect economic growth?', *Journal of International Economics*, *45*: 115–135.

Brau, R., Lanza, A., & Pigliaru, F. (2007). 'How fast are small tourism countries growing? Evidence from the data for 1980–2003', *Tourism Economics*, *13*(4): 603–614.

Brohman, J. (1996). 'New directions for tourism in third world development', *Annals of Tourism Research*, *23*(1): 48–70.

Bruno, M., Ravallion, M., & Squire, L. (1998). 'Equity and growth in developing countries: old and new perspectives on the policy issues', in V. Tanzi & K. Chu (Eds), *Income Distribution and High-Quality Growth*, pp. 117–146. Cambridge, MA: MIT Press.

Bryden, J. M. (1973). *Tourism and Development: a Case Study of the Commonwealth Caribbean*. Cambridge, UK: Cambridge University Press.

Clancy, M. (2001). 'Mexican tourism: export growth and structural change since 1970', *Latin American Research Review*, *36*: 128–150.

Clauzel, S. (2005). 'Community development through tourism: feasibility and demonstrativeness – lessons learned from the Saint Lucia Heritage Tourism Programme.' Castries, St Lucia.

Cortés-Jiménez, I., Pulina, M., Prunera, C.R. & Artis, M. (2009). 'Tourism and exports as a means of growth.' Research Institute of Applied Economics Working Papers 2009/10. Retrieved from: www.ub.edu/irea/working_papers/2009/200910.pdf

Croes, R. (2012). 'Assessing tourism development from Sen's capability approach', *Journal of Travel Research*, *51*(5): 542–554.

Croes, R. (2014). 'The role of tourism in poverty reduction: an empirical assessment', *20*(2): 207–226.

Croes, R., & Vanegas, M. (2006). 'Tourism and poverty alleviation: real promise or false premise?' Paper presented at the Second International Conference on Tourism Economics, Palma de Mallorca, Spain, 18–20 May.

Croes, R., & Vanegas, M. (2008). 'Cointegration and causality between tourism and poverty reduction', *Journal of Travel Research*, *47*: 94–103.

Danziger, S., & Gottschalk, P. (1995) *America Unequal*. Cambridge, MA: Harvard University Press. New York: Russell Sage Foundation.

DeFina, R. H., & Thanawala, K. (2004). 'International evidence on the impact of transfers and taxes on alternative poverty indexes', *Social Science Research*, *33*: 322–338.

de Kadt, E. (1979). *Tourism: Passport to Development? Perspectives on the Social and Cultural Effects of Tourism in Developing Countries*. New York: Oxford University Press, published for the World Bank and UNESCO.

Dritsakis, N. (2004). 'Tourism as a long-run economic growth factor: an empirical investigation for Greece using causality analysis', *Tourism Economics, 10*(3): 305–316.

Durbarry, R. (2004). 'Tourism and economic growth: the case of Mauritius', *Tourism Economics, 10*(4): 389–401.

Dwyer, L., Forsyth, P., Madden, J., & Spurr, R. (2000). 'Economic impacts of inbound tourism under different assumptions regarding the macroeconomy', *Current Issues in Tourism, 3*(4): 325–363.

ECLAC. (2007). *Panorama Social 2006*. Santiago de Chile: ECLAC.

Elliott, J., & Mwangi, M. (1998). 'Developing tourism in Laikipia – who benefits?' African Wildlife Foundation Discussion Paper CEC-DP-3.

Eugenio-Martin, J., Martín-Morales, N., & Scarpa, R. (2004). 'Tourism and economic growth in Latin American countries: a panel data approach.' FEEM Working Paper 26. Available at: www.feem.it/userfiles/attach/Publication/NDL2004/NDL2004-026.pdf (accessed 10 February 2015).

Eugenio-Martin, J. L., Martín-Morales, N., & Sinclair, M. T. (2008). 'The role of economic development in tourism demand', *Tourism Economics, 14*(4): 673–690.

Ferguson, C. (2010). 'Principles of transitional care for young people with longstanding continence problems', *Nursing Times, 106*: 47.

Freeman, R. B. (2001). 'The rising tide lifts', in S. Danziger & R. Haveman (Eds), *Understanding Poverty*, pp. 97–126. Cambridge, MA: Harvard University Press. New York: Russell Sage Foundation.

Ghali, A. (1976). 'Tourism and economic growth: an empirical study', *Economic Development & Cultural Change, 24*, 527–538.

Ghura, D., Leite, C. A., & Tsangarides, C. (2002). 'Is growth enough? Macroeconomic policy and poverty reduction.' International Monetary Fund Working Paper WP/02/118.

Gujadhur, T. (2012). 'Tourism and poverty reduction: lessons learned and good practices in the Greater Mekong Region.' Manila: ADB/SNV Asia.

Gundersen, C., & Ziliak, J. P. (2004). 'Poverty and macroeconomic performance across space, race, and family structure', *Demography, 41*: 61–86.

Hara, T. (2008). *Quantitative Tourism Industry Analysis: Introduction to Input–Output, Social Accounting Matrix Modeling and Tourism Satellite Accounts*. Burlington, MA: Elsevier.

Hainsworth, D. (2008). 'Community tourism and broad-based local development: the case of Doi village, Thua Then Hue province, Vietnam', in W. Jamieson (Ed.), *Tourism and Community Development – Asian Practices*, pp. 121–134. Madrid: UNWTO

Halstead, L. (2003). 'Making community-based tourism work: an assessment of factors contributing to successful community-owned tourism development in Caprivi, Namibia.' DEA Research Discussion Paper 60. Windhoek: MET.

Hawkins, D., & Mann, S. (2007). 'The World Bank's role in tourism development', *Annals of Tourism Research, 34*(2): 348–363.

Hung, T. T. (1999). 'Impact of foreign direct investment on poverty reduction in vietnam.' IDS Program, GRIPS.

Iceland, J. (2003). 'Why poverty remains high: the role of income growth, economic inequality, and changes in family structure, 1949–1999', *Demography, 40*: 499–519.

Iceland, J., Kenworthy, L., & Scopilliti, M. (2005). 'Macroeconomic performance and poverty in the 1980s and 1990s: a state-level analysis.' Discussion Paper 1299-05. Institute for Research on Poverty, University of Wisconsin. Available at: www.irp.wisc.edu

Israel, A. O. (2014). 'Impact of foreign direct investment on poverty reduction in Nigeria', *Journal of Economics & Sustainable Development, 5*(20).

Johansen, S. (1988). 'Statistical analysis of cointegration vectors', *Journal of Economic Dynamics & Control, 12*: 231–254.

Johansen, S., & Juselius, K. (1990). 'Maximum likelihood estimation and inference on cointegration: with the application to the demand of money', *Oxford Bulletin of Economics & Statistics, 52*: 169–210.

Jules, S. (2005). *Sustainable Tourism in St Lucia: A Sustainability Assessment of Trade and Liberalisation of Tourism Services*. Winnipeg, Canada: International institute for Sustainable Development.

Kakwani, N. (2000). 'Growth and poverty reduction: an empirical analysis', *Asian Development Review, 18*(2): 74–84.

Katırcıoğlu, S. (2009). 'Revisiting the tourism-led growth hypothesis for Turkey using the Bounds test and Johansen approach for cointegration', *Tourism Management, 30*(1): 17–20.

Kenworthy, L. (2004). *Egalitarian Capitalism*. New York: Russell Sage Foundation.

Kim, N., & Lee, C. K. (2012). 'Granger causality among tourism development, foreign direct investment and economic growth: the case of Korea', *Korean Journal of Tourism Research*, 27(3): 43–57.

Kim, N., Song, H., & Pyun, J. H. (2016). 'The relationship among tourism, poverty, and economic development in developing countries: a panel data regression analysis', *Tourism Economics*, 22(6): 1174–1190.

Lanza, A., & Pigliaru, F. (2000). 'Why are tourism countries small and fast growing?', in A. Fossati & G. Panella (Eds), *Tourism and Sustainable Economic Development*, pp. 57–69. Dordrecht, Netherlands: Kluwer.

Lengefeld, K., & Beyer, M. (2006). 'CSR beyond charity: how the core business of all-inclusive resorts contributes to poverty alleviation and local development in the Caribbean and Central America.' Paper presented at the VIth Corporate Social Responsibility for Sustainable Tourism, University of Girona, Spain, 13–16 June.

Li, H., Chen, J. L., Li, G., & Goh, C. (2016). 'Tourism and regional income inequality: evidence from China', *Annals of Tourism Research*, 58: 81–99.

Mbaiwa, J. (2005). 'The problems and prospects of sustainable tourism development in the Okavango Delta, Botswana', *Journal of Sustainable Tourism*, 13(3): 203–227.

McNab, D. (2005). *Impacts of Pro-poor Tourism Facilitation with South African Corporates: Monitoring and Evaluation Report of the Pro-Poor Tourism Pilots Project*. London: Overseas Development Institute.

Mincer, J. (1958). 'Investment in human capital and personal income distribution', *Journal of Political Economy*, 66(4): 281–302.

Mishel, L., Bernstein, J., & Allegretto, S. (2005). *Poverty in the State of Working America, 2004–05*. An Economic Policy Institute book. Ithaca, NY: ILR Press.

Mulonga, S., & Murphy, C. (2003). 'Spending the money: The experience of conservancy benefit distribution in Namibia up to mid-2003.' DEA Research Discussion Paper No. 63. Windhoek: DEA.

Murphy, C., & Halstead, L. (2003). '"The person with the idea for the campsite is a hero." Institutional arrangements and livelihood change regarding community-owned tourism enterprises in Namibia.' DEA Research Discussion Paper 61. Windhoek: MET.

Nowak J. J.,. & Sahli, M. (2007). 'Coastal tourism and "Dutch diseases" in a small island economy', *Tourism Economics*, 13(1): 49–65.

Oh, C.-O. (2005). 'The contribution of tourism development to economic growth in the Korean economy', *Tourism Management*, 26: 39–44.

Ravallion, M., & Datt, G. (1996). 'How important to India's poor is the sectoral composition of economic growth?', *World Bank Economic Review*, 10(1): 1–25.

Reiter, S. L., & Steensma, H. K. (2010). 'Human development and foreign direct investment in developing countries: the influence of FDI policy and corruption', *World Development*, 38(12): 1678–1691.

Rodríguez, C. M., Casas-Jurado, A. C., & García-Fernández, R. M. (2017). 'Tourism and poverty alleviation: an empirical analysis using panel data on Peru's departments', *International Journal of Tourism Research*, 19(6): 746–756.

Saayman, M., Rossouw, R., & Krugell, W. (2012). 'The impact of tourism on poverty in South Africa', *Development Southern Africa*, 29(3): 462–487.

Sandford, D. M., & Dong, H. (2000). 'Investment in familiar territory: tourism and new foreign direct investment', *Tourism Economics*, 6(3): 205–219.

Schultz, T. P. (1988). 'Education investments and returns', in H. Chenery & T. N. Srinivasan (Eds), *Handbook of Development Economics*, vol. 1. Amsterdam: North-Holland Press.

Seetanah, B. (2011). 'Assessing the dynamic economic impact of tourism for island economies', *Annals of Tourism Research*, 38(1): 291–308.

Seetanah, B., & Khadaroo, A. J. (2007). 'Foreign direct investment and growth: new evidences from SSA countries.' Available at: http://citeseerx.ist.psu.edu/viewdoc/download?doi=10.1.1.489.4815&rep=r ep1&type=pdf

Seetanah, B., & Khadaroo, J. (2009). 'An analysis of the relationship between transport capital and tourism development in a dynamic framework', *Tourism Economics*, 15(4): 785–802.

Sequeira, T., & Nunes, P. (2008). 'Does tourism influence economic growth? A dynamic panel data approach', *Applied Economics*, 40: 2431–2441.

Sawhill, I. V. (1988). 'Poverty in The U. S.: why is it so persistent?', *Journal of Economic Literature*, 26(September): 1073–1119.

Shah, K., & Gupta, V. (2000). *Tourism, the Poor and Other Stakeholders: Experience in Asia*. London: ODI.

Soumare, I. (2015). 'Does foreign direct investment improve welfare in North Africa?', *Applied Economics*, 47(51): 1–24.

Squire, L. (1993). 'Fighting poverty', *American Economic Review Papers & Proceedings*, *83*(2): 377–382.

Statistics Mauritius. (2019). National Accounts. Ministry of Finance and Economic Development. Port Louis. http://statsmauritius.govmu.org/English/

Sugiyarto, G., Blake, A., & Sinclair, M. T. (2003). 'Tourism and globalization: economic impact in Indonesia', *Annals of Tourism Research*, *30*(3): 683–701.

Tang, S., Selvanathan, E. A., & Selvanathan, S. (2007). 'The relationship between foreign direct investment and tourism: empirical evidence from China', *Tourism Economics*, *13*(1): 25–39.

Ucal, M. S. (2014). 'Panel data analysis of foreign direct investment and poverty from the perspective of developing countries', *Social & Behavioral Science*, *109*: 1101–1105.

United Nations Conference on Trade and Development (UNCTAD). (1998). 'Developing countries could target tourism to boost economic growth.' Available at: http://unctad.org/en/pages/PressReleaseArchive.aspx?' ReferenceDocId¼3243 (accessed 24 January 2015).

United Nations World Tourism Organization (UNWTO). (1988). *Tourism Highlights*. Madrid: UNWTO.

United Nations World Tourism Organization (UNWTO). (2002). *Tourism and Poverty Alleviation*. Madrid: UNWTO.

United Nations World Tourism Organization (UNWTO). (2004). *Tourism and Poverty Alleviation: Recommendations for Action*. Madrid: UNWTO.

United Nations World Tourism Organization (UNWTO). (2007). *Increase in Tourism to Fight Poverty – New Message from UNWTO*. Madrid: UNWTO.

Vanegas, M. (2014). 'The triangle of poverty, economic growth, and inequality in Central America: does tourism matter?', *Worldwide Hospitality & Tourism Themes*, *6*(3): 277–292.

Vanegas, M., Gartner, W., & Senauer, B. (2015). 'Tourism and poverty reduction: an economic sector analysis for Costa Rica and Nicaragua', *Tourism Economics*, *21*(1): 159–182.

Wattanakuljarus, A., & Coxhead, I. (2008). 'Is tourism-based development good for the poor? A general equilibrium analysis for Thailand', *Journal of Policy Modeling*, *30*: 929–955.

Winters, P., Corral, L., & Mora, A. M. (2013). 'Assessing the role of tourism in poverty alleviation: a research agenda', *Development Policy Review*, *31*(2): 177–202.

Zhao, W., & Ritchie, J. R. B. (2007). 'Tourism and poverty alleviation: an integrative research framework', *Current Issues in Tourism*, *10*(2–3): 119–143.

PART III

Sociocultural impacts of tourism

16

SOCIOCULTURAL IMPACTS OF TOURISM

Ozlem Tekin and Roya Rahimi

Sociocultural impacts of tourism

Tourism is not only an economic phenomenon, but also an international event that has an important impact on the social structures of societies and people. In order to understand the basic effects that tourism has on social structures, the effects of individual, social structure, and culture must be known. In this case, it is necessary to make an assessment from the socio-logical perspective of tourism. For people living in tourism development areas, living standards increase, together with tourism activities, employment, and various entrepreneurial activities, and there are also contributions to side sectors. Opportunities also arise for women to participate economically in the workforce. Local people can also benefit from the infrastructure investments that are developed by tourism (Avcıkurt, 2015: 64). Besides the positive effects, there are also negative social effects on touristic destinations. For example, changes in religious attitudes, clothing, behavioural rules, and tradition are the main elements of these changes. Tourism is interpreted as an "element of change" in many regions for this reason. This change can be indistinguishable when spread over a long period of time. Local people may not agree with the sociological change. Especially in underdeveloped countries, it can be said that, as tourism develops, the size of social structure, value judgements, and spiritual criteria and customs exhibit changes, and social behaviours start to show their tendency to change. Tourism creates changes in value trends, family structure, lifestyle, cultural activities, and perpetration. For this reason, local people may have a negative attitude towards tourism activities, and tourists particularly. At this point, it is important that tourism development be managed well. But today, development and change in the world, which is defined as a global village, take place through development and the media (Jenkins, 1997: 13).

The complex effects of tourism are almost impossible to measure thoroughly because quite a few of them are barely distinguishable and generally are revealed in unexpected ways. In other words, it is possible to mention several effects that are difficult to monitor or keep track of besides the primary, secondary, and tertiary effects. The interaction of these effects leads to further changes. For instance, the safaris organized in the national parks in Africa limit the feeding and living spaces of the wildlife. The protection of wildlife might serve for touristic development and thus contribute to the economy of the country having such resources. However, the creation of national parks causes the growing African population to engage in agriculture in less productive lands which will barely meet the needs of the population. Special effects are observed on ethnic or cultural minorities and on unique types of wildlife and vegetation. The specialty of such areas attracts tourists, although touristic activities might be very dangerous for them (Mathieson and Wall, 1992: 5–6).

Doxey's irridex model

For investigating the relationships between tourists and local people, Doxey's (1976) irridex model can be useful. According to this model, the attitude of the host community can be considered as four different stages: *euphoria, apathy, irritation,* and *antagonism.* In the first stage, euphoria, people are enthusiastic and thrilled about welcoming tourists to the region for the first time and making an economic profit. In the second stage, the industry expands in the region, and an increase is seen in the number of tourists. Gradually, the euphoria felt in the first stage is replaced by indifference. In the third stage, existing enterprises and quality begin not to meet the increasing demands of tourists, and, thus, attempts are made to increase supply. As a result of fast development without a concrete plan, tourism reaches a level that is disturbing owing to the harm it causes to nature. At this stage, changes or irreversible destruction in nature begin to stand out, and people start blaming tourism, tourists, and the local administration. In the last stage, tolerance of tourists is gradually replaced by anger and intolerance, and people begin to show their anger by associating increasing prices with tourism. The duration of these stages and whether the society in such regions will go through all stages should be discussed further (Gürbüz, 2002).

Tourism and the host community

The factors that impede communication between tourists and the host community can be summarized as follows (cited by Gürbüz, 2002):

- Tourism establishments' meeting all needs of tourist groups.
- Conflicts resulting from different languages.
- The host community's fear of tourists and their hesitant and prejudiced behaviour.
- Negative attitudes shown by both sides towards the other.
- Tourists' being there only for a short time for recreation and leaving the region soon.

The reasons that might account for communication problems between tourists and local people can be explained by social distance, as well. Social distance is a factor that is used to understand differences between individuals. Thus, it plays a role in ensuring that local people view tourism positively and in increasing the relationship between tourists and local people, as well as increasing the time that tourists spend in that region (Sinkovics and Penz, 2009). It is also worth mentioning that tourist guides play a crucial role in the communication and interaction between tourists and local people (Avcıkurt and Karaman, 2007: 424). Tourism is an intercultural activity, and so it is likely that a cultural gap emerges at any place where tourists and local people come together. Tourist guides are the agents that fill this gap (Köroğlu, 2009: 1336) as they play an important role in intercultural relationships. They encourage tourists to meet local people and provide opportunities for both sides to interact.

The social effects of tourism are becoming more apparent both to tourists and local people. The social impacts of tourism development in a tourism destination are explained by different authors in different dimensions. These effects can be summarized as follows (Gürbüz, 2002):

- The exchange of information between people who come from different backgrounds and their contribution to world peace as a result of the friendships and ties built up through tourism.
- The increase in the level of education and culture of the host community as a result of its members feeling a need to read and research more to be able to communicate with tourists.
- Increasing enthusiasm of local people to learn a foreign language to be able to meet different cultures, make friends, and help tourists vising the region.
- Protection of cultural values to prevent them from being undermined by tourism.
- Increasing urbanization in touristic rural regions.
- New employment opportunities created in rural regions with the development of the tourism industry have contributed to the integration of urban civilizations through the adoption of cultural values in modern industrial civilizations. With the increase in tourism establishments in rural regions, the uniformity in such regions is disrupted, whereas the number of groups with different characteristics and structures increases.
- Tourism increases the national consciousness in a country and encourages local people to be proud of their cultural values.

Tourists inevitably interact with local people or tourism workers in the destinations they visit. In these encounters, tourists are foreign to local people, and local people are foreign to tourists. This perception is not about individuals themselves, but about the personality, feelings, lifestyles, cultures, and ways of behaviour. The exchange that comes out of this encounter sets the frame of the sociocultural effects of tourism. With tourism, it becomes possible for people from different backgrounds and cultures to get to know one another, get rid of their prejudices, and build healthy relationships based on friendship (Akova, 2006). This, without doubt, contributes to world peace. The structure of tourism that emerges from the relationships between tourists and local people, tourists and tourism workers, and local people and tourism workers, and contributes to social interactions, plays an important role in providing a peaceful environment. These contributions made by tourism can be associated with realism and liberalism theories, as well as "social contract theory" in social psychology. The social contract theory through which Allport introduced his principal assumptions in *The Nature of Prejudice* (Allport, Clark, and Pettigrew, 1954) is regarded as one of the most effective strategies used to reduce prejudices between groups and has been employed for many years (Pettigrew and Tropp, 2006).

Tourism is an activity by which people can see different geographies and build social relationships with other people with whom they would not come together otherwise. Tourists might be worried about a conflict of culture in the countries they visit as a result of the different ethnic structures, religious groups, values, lifestyles, and languages. However, raising the awareness of people about tourism and welcoming tourists well contribute to tourists' satisfaction and their having a positive approach to a society about which they previously held prejudices. When they travel, people are interested in souvenirs, artwork, handicrafts, and materials that bear cultural traces. This attention paid by tourists contributes to the promotion of artists and the protection of cultural values. The emergence of new professional groups can also be counted among the positive effects of tourism.

People living in touristic areas have a tendency to learn foreign languages, read, and research in order to be able to communicate well with tourists, get to know them, and engage in commercial relations, all of which increases the level of education and culture of the local people. Thus, different cultures get to know one another and contribute to world peace. Within the scope of the sociocultural effects of tourism, it is worth mentioning that tourism affects the demographic characteristics of the local people. The extent of the labour demand in tourism attracts young people to touristic regions and leads to a lowering of the average age in the region.

The effects of tourism on attractions that increase touristic demand are also fairly important. As local people become more aware of the fact that tourists spend time and money on tasting the traditional dishes of that region while they stay there, and income increases thanks to the cultural heritage that offers attractions, they begin to protect the tangible and intangible heritage. With tourism, traditional handicrafts, performances, and traditions and customs can be presented in a more conscious way; otherwise, they might be forgotten or it might be difficult to pass them on to the next generations. The tourism industry helps local people realize how important it is to ensure the sustainability of their cultural heritage.

When local people become aware of the positive effects of tourism, they directly support the development of the industry and take part in this process.

As for the indicators of the negative effects of tourism, they can be summarized as follows (Kozak, Akoğlan, and Kozak, 1997):

- Changes in values, beliefs, and clothes in the region hosting tourists.
- The "foreignization" of the language of the country as a result of foreign words entering into the language by means of tourism.
- The replacement of valuable artworks with artificial works; replacement of the aesthetic appearance of architectural structures with ruins of disharmonious buildings; gradual change in the music tastes of local people.
- The replacement of sentimental values such as friendship and hospitality in relationships by economic interests.
- Changes in the lifestyle of the people living in touristic regions (for example, local people begin to go to pubs, cinemas, night clubs, casinos, etc., for entertainment after work).
- Local people envy the lifestyle of tourists and begin to imitate them. However, tourists actually behave differently on holiday and do things that are out of the ordinary for them, which becomes particularly obvious in their expenditures. They work for a certain period of the year to save money for their holiday and visit touristic regions to spend this money.
- The emergence of cultural conflicts as a result of tourists' improper behaviour which is contrary to the traditions, customs and lifestyles, and values of the host community.
- Differences in the standards of living between the visiting and host countries; the emergence of feelings of jealousy in the host community as its members come to think that they are responsible for serving tourists.
- The emergence of racial tensions in areas where there are obvious racial differences between tourists and local people.

Regarding the undesired social effects of tourism, it is possible to say that tourism affects cultural identity, traditions, and regional character negatively. Tourists' lifestyle, way of speaking, clothing, and attitude, which are unfamiliar to local people, can cause negative consequences in the host community. Also, differences in religious and cultural values might lead to a negative dialogue. Besides, tourists' insulting attitudes regarding the lifestyle of local people or their disrespectful behaviour about the daily routine of locals might result in many serious problems. However, the differences in tourists' cultural structures and values might also spark envy in young people in the host community, which ends up with cultural degeneration. This situation falls within the scope of the effects of tourism on moral values. The effect of tourism on the use of substances such as alcohol and drugs is among the consequences resulting from moral change. In addition, local people might feel uncomfortable and consider migrating when the carrying capacity of the tourism destination is exceeded. The opposite situation can take place too: People experiencing economic difficulties in rural areas might consider migrating to tourism destinations in the hope of becoming rich, which would negatively affect countries' population distribution.

As suggested by Lea (2001), tourism is a cultural interaction which can lead to positive and negative consequences. The quality of intercultural contact is determined by the profile and expectations of tourists, the attraction of the environment where the contact takes place, and the role of the staff (e.g. tourist guides) who introduce the culture. In summary, the cultural effects of tourism come to light in the form of change in religious beliefs, attitude, values, lifestyles, and language and art.

Another important problem emerging with the development of the tourism industry is the materialization of human relations and the degeneration of social values because of commercial concerns. It is possible that misunderstandings and conflicts arise owing to differences in language, traditions, beliefs, and behaviour. Fast development in the tourism industry leads to changes that come from the outside and are not understood or controlled well by the local society, which destroys the diversity of local and regional social structures.

Today, tourism is still associated with the gender identity of women by some people, although the status of women in the tourism industry has considerably improved in comparison with 30 years ago. Some researchers suggested that the female body was used a means of marketing and media in the tourism industry; accordingly, the journalists working for tourism promotion considered this industry as a male-dominant industry, the negative effects of which could be seen in the media (Dincer, Akova, Ertugral, and Ciftci, 2016). In the tourism industry, the problems associated with female employment do not solely exist because of people working in this area. The perspective of women, families, and the society regarding the concept of tourism also contributes to such problems. According to studies, more than half of the female population do not have the support of their family and, thus, find themselves in conflict in terms of familial and professional roles. In other words, the psychology and roles of women can be counted among the external factors that prevent their employment in the tourism industry (Li and Leung, 2001). When the sectoral distribution of female employment across the world is considered, it can be said that positive developments have taken place in the service industry over the years. Whereas 695,804,000 women were employed in 2015 (with a share of 55.1%) in the service industry, their numbers reached 708,176,000 in 2016, creating a higher share of female employment, 55.5%. For example, the employment rate of women in the tourism industry in Turkey has increased from 20% to 29.9% since 2006 according to a report from Eurostat, the European Statistical Office. This increase points to the leadership of women in the tourism sector in Turkey.

In order to eliminate the negative effects of tourism activities, the number of visitors can be limited before local people realize that "the benefits of tourism do not compensate for the burden of welcoming tourists and the negative situations that come along". Here, the question of "How many visitors are enough?" should be discussed, although the answer would completely depend on the carrying capacity of touristic areas (Uysal and Baloğlu, 1994: 36). Carrying capacity can be described as the saturation point before resources are negatively affected, tourist satisfaction decreases, or a detrimental effect is caused to the economy and culture of the host region.

Types of carrying capacity for tourism destinations

Many authors specify four types of carrying capacity, these being economic, psychological, ecological, and social (Holden, 2002: 141; Hall, 2001: 137).

Ecological carrying capacity

Ecological carrying capacity is about the effect of tourism on the physical environment. It refers to the limit of human activities that might cause undesirable changes to the environment.

Social carrying capacity

Touristic development leads to changes in the social characteristics of a host region. Social carrying capacity enables the development of tourism to the extent where local people are not faced with negative consequences (Saveriades, 2000). Described also as local people's limit of tolerance of the presence of tourists (Fennell, 2002: 48), social carrying capacity also refers to the level where the society is not affected by the presence of tourists (Newsame, 2002). It shows the level of tolerance of the host region. Thus, it can be considered as the level of maximum use that does not cause undesired consequences in the host community.

Psychological carrying capacity

This refers to the lowest satisfaction level obtained as a result of the tourism experience. Holden (2002) indicates that psychological carrying capacity shows the satisfaction level of tourists about the destination they visit. To Saveriades (2000), the psychological carrying capacity is the saturation point that tourists can tolerate before a tourism destination loses its attraction. It can also be described as the quality of activities that tourists mostly accept to before they begin to be dissatisfied. Psychological carrying capacity is the lowest satisfaction level that tourists are ready to tolerate. They compare their expectations before that visit to the destination with the possibilities offered at the destination. When tourists realize that they are more dissatisfied than the lowest level they could expect, they begin to look for other destinations.

Economic carrying capacity

Economic carrying capacity refers to the tolerance of the local economy to tourism activities. It is the balance between the benefits and costs of tourism in the region. Excessive dependence on tourism results from neglect of other sectors. Each carrying capacity is dependent on the others; however, it might not have a direct effect on other capacities when a certain threshold is exceeded in one of them.

Components of social impacts in the tourism industry

To examine the components that constitute the social effects of tourism, it is necessary to understand the concept of social structure. Radcliffe Brown argues that "all social relations that are interpersonal, is a part of it. When the social structure is examined, concrete reality are the existing relationships that bring together certain people" (Doğan, 1998: 131). Thus, social structure is the structural form of interpersonal relations (Table 16.1).

Tourism is a key activity that shows a versatile effect in starting the social evaluation process and ensuring the foreign expansion of an area. In this regard, tourism provides a convenient environment and conditions to further shape the functional differentiation in workplaces in small towns where people engage in tourism or agriculture; to increase the dependence on a market economy; to change the living standards and consumption norms in line with

Table 16.1 The effects of tourism on social structures and their components

Effects	Examples
Demographic effects	Population size, age, gender, rise and decline of the population in touristic regions, etc.
Occupational effects	Changes in occupations, professionalism, distribution of age and gender in some professions
Cultural effects	Changes in traditions, religion, and language
Changes in values	Values, role of gender, and ethics (crime, prostitution, etc.)
Changes in consumption	Education, infrastructure, products, and spending
Environmental effects	Pollution, ecology, and overcrowding

growth; to increase the relationships with the external environment; to eliminate prejudices and attitudes that reflect a self-enclosed approach; and to create social change in a socio-economic framework (Eralp, 1974: 6–7).

Tourism and crime

Fast development in tourism might create an opportunity for crime to spread in tourism destinations which have not gone through an urban renewal in parallel to this development. The increasing flow of tourists to a region during certain seasons results in a crowd that reaches the limits of capacity in a region and even exceeds it. Also, it creates suitable conditions for crimes to be committed while the region experiences temporary immigration waves owing to the arrival of seasonal workers. Additionally, it becomes easier for criminals to escape and hide if the size of a police force is not increased in parallel to this temporary increase in population, making it difficult to control criminal activities in the region (Çakmakçı, 2015).

Based on the map on which they showed the geographical distribution of crimes, Hooghe, Vanhoutte, Hardyns, and Bircan (2011) indicate that crime rates can be extraordinarily high in touristic regions. On the one hand, it is likely that a calculation error is made in crime rates owing to the increase in the population in such regions during summer months. However, it is pointed out that tourism has an effect on crime rates. Hooghe et al. (2011) also argue that it is not known who commits crimes or whether they are linked to some forms (e.g. gambling, drugs) of tourists' criminal behaviour. They also suggest that mass tourism can be associated with the destruction of local society order and a decline in the level of collective empowerment of the society.

Conclusion and suggestions

One of the biggest and fastest-growing industries in the world, tourism has become a significant economic and social phenomenon (Rahimi and Gunlu, 2016; Rahimi, 2017; Bihamta, Jayashree, Rezaei, Okumus, and Rahimi, 2017; Rahimi and Akgunduz, 2017; Rahimi and Kozak, 2017). The development of tourism has led to a lot of economic, environmental, and social effects in tourism destinations. The current studies on tourism investigate the economic, social, and physical effects of tourism on establishments dedicated to meeting the demands of tourists, as well as the effects on host communities. These studies consider the motivations and experiences of tourists, the expectations and views of local people, as well as the roles of establishments and enterprises that regulate the relationship between tourists and host communities. There are general views with regard to the effects of tourism in both economic and social terms.

In fact, this industry has revived employment and investment in several countries, determined land use and the economic structure, besides having positive effects on the balance of payments.

The main aim of developing tourism in an area should be to maximize the benefits and minimize the costs and negative effects. Thus, it is essential that a tourism development plan involves local people both in terms of meeting all their demands and facilitating the implementation of the plan. The effects of tourism on the social environment refer to the effects on relationships between people and on the community. These relationships and effects have both positive and negative effects on people, the environment, culture, and customs. For this reason, it is important to ensure a progressive development, raise the host community's awareness of tourists, and make sure they prepare themselves for tourism. As the type and level of social effects resulting from tourism can be affected by the intermediary establishments that bring tourists to a region, the training of such establishments is also very important. Accordingly, a type of tourism which is suited to the sociocultural values of the host community should be adopted. Another important point is to make sure that desired or undesired types of tourist visit or do not visit a destination, using selective marketing techniques. Implementation of a tourism plan based on protecting cultural heritage is a significant approach for preventing cultural erosion. Similarly, providing information to local people about the benefits of tourism, as well as the costs of it, and the provision of the same information to tourists visiting a destination or the staff working in that destination will prevent intercultural conflict. It is essential that the host community is informed about the potential positive and negative consequences of tourism and attempts are made to prevent negative consequences. Host communities should not perceive tourists just in terms of economic gain. It is also worth noting that the culture in tourism regions is not always affected negatively. In conclusion, it is vital that the host community is informed in the first place in order to eliminate the consequences of negative situations that might occur between tourists and the host community.

The factors that turn people on to tourism can be handled in two main groups, being natural and human factors. Climate conditions, geographical formations, and natural beauty are natural factors that attract people to certain places. Summer, sea, health, and winter tourism can be given as examples of this group. On the other hand, cities and artworks that are important for familial, religious, historical, or cultural reasons, education, congress, and business meetings, and sports and cultural activities are human factors that turn people on to tourism. Tourism activities are of considerable importance for people's relaxation, recreation, entertainment, or learning, as well as having a significant economic value for countries.

With its various components in the service industry, tourism is a sector that provides valuable benefits such as foreign currency inflow, balance of payments, added value, branding, presentation of countries, promotion of other sectors, and employment. Owing to the labour-intensive structure of the tourism sector, people play an important role that brings into play other complex factors and feelings. Thus, people's interaction with psychological, social, and environmental conditions should be investigated as well.

Social changes are observed on a limited scale when the economic, education, and cultural levels of tourists and local people are similar. Otherwise, the extent of the social change becomes wider (Demircioğlu, 1997: 137).

As indicated in the literature concerned, the socio-economic effects of tourism are abstract and cannot be seen most of the time. However, its social effects are permanent, and it is not possible to undo them. Considering the social effects of tourism, the focus is mostly on "the host society" in this industry. The social sustainability of tourism can be described as the ability of the society to sustain harmonious interactions and relationships with the visitors (at a national or local scale), in the short or long term. This approach requires the presence of harmony in bilateral relations in order to eliminate any unfavourable situation that might occur between the local society and tourists. The cultural differences between the local society and visitors can be associated with several factors such as fundamental values, ways of thinking, religious beliefs, traditions, customs, lifestyles, ways of behaviour, dressing styles, and the attitude towards foreign people.

From a wider perspective, it can be said that tourism has environmental, economic, and social effects. Sustainable tourism aims to increase the positive effects to the maximum level and to reduce the negative ones to the minimum. With some measures, a good outcome can be obtained from tourism activities, both in economic and sociocultural aspects. The most important of these measures is the evaluation of the attitude of local society towards tourism. The attitude of local society also plays a determining role in achieving sustainable tourism. Thus, it is recommended to widen the scope of studies on "social tourism" in order to increase the health and social well-being of families and individuals.

References

Akova, O. (2006). Yerel Halkın Turizmin Etkilerini Algılamalarına ve Tutumlarına Yönelik Bir Araştırma. *Akademik İncelemeler Dergisi (AID)*, 1(2): 77–109.

Allport, G.W., Clark, K., and Pettigrew, T. (1954). *The Nature of Prejudice*. Cambridge, MA: Addison-Wesley.

Avcıkurt, C. (2015). *Turizm Sosyolojisi Genel ve Yapısal Yaklasim*. 4. Baskı. Ankara: Detay Yayıncılık.

Avcıkurt, C., and Karaman, S. (2007). *Ulusal Türkiye Turizm Kongresi, Sakarya Üniversitesi Karasu Meslek Yüksek Okulu Kongre Bildiri Kitabı*, 419–431, Ankara: Detay Yayıncılık.

Bihamta, H., Jayashree, S., Rezaei, S., Okumus, F., and Rahimi, R. (2017). Dual pillars of hotel restaurant food quality satisfaction and brand loyalty. *British Food Journal*. DOI: 10.1108/BFJ-07-2016-0344

Çakmakçı, E. (2015). Turizm ve Suç Arasındaki İlişki ve Suçun Önlenmesine Yönelik Teoriler. *Turizm Akademik Dergisi*, 2(1): 49–59.

Demircioğlu, A.G. (1997). Turizm Çevre Etkileşimi Bakımından Sürdürülebilir Turizm Planlaması. *Dokuz Eylül Üniversitesi İİBF Dergisi*, 12(2): 135–147.

Dincer, F. İ., Akova, O., Ertugral, S. M., and Ciftci., M. A. (2016). Türkiye'de Turizm Sektöründe Kadın İstihdamı: İmkanlar ve Engeller. *Eurasian Academy of Sciences Social Sciences Journal*, 1: 379–395.

Doğan, I. (1998). *Sosyoloji*. İstanbul: Sistem Yayıncılık.

Doxey, G. (1976). *When Enough's Enough: The Natives Are Restless in Old Niagara*. Heritage Canada.

Eralp, Z. (1974). *Socio-Economic Effects of Tourism towards Communal Changes*. Ankara: Ankara University Press.

Fennell, D. A. (2002). *Planning Natural Resource-Based Tourism Programs*. Cambridge, MA: CABI.

Gürbüz, A. (2002). Turizmin Sosyal Çevreye Etkisi Üzerine Bir Araştırma. *Teknoloji*, 5(1–2): 49–59.

Hall, C. M. (2001). *Geography of Tourism and Recreation: Environment, Place and Space*. Florence, SC: Routledge.

Holden, A. (2002). *Environment and Tourism*. Florence, SC: Routledge.

Hooghe, M., Vanhoutte, B., Hardyns. W., and Bircan, T. (2011). Unemployment, inequality, poverty and crime: spatial distribution patterns of criminal acts in Belgium, 2001–06. *British Journal of Criminology*, 51: 1–20.

Jenkins, C. L. (1997). World Tourism Leaders' Meeting on Social Impacts of Tourism, Final Report. WTO, Manila, 22 May.

Köroğlu, O. (2009). İstanbul 2010 Avrupa Kültür Başkenti Uygulamaları Kapsamında Turist Rehberliği Eğitim Programları, 10. Ulusal Turizm Kongresi, Mersin, 1335–1345.

Kozak, N., Akoğlan, M., and Kozak, M. (1997). *Genel Turizm*. Ankara: Anatolia Yayınları.

Lea, J. (2001). *Tourism and Development in the Third World*. London and New York: Routledge.

Li, L., and Leung, R. W. (2001). Female managers in Asian hotels: profile and career challenges. *International Journal of Contemporary Hospitality Management*, 13(4): 189–196.

Mathieson, A., and Wall, G. (1992) *Tourism: Economic, Physical and Social Impacts*. London: Longman Specific and Technical, Longman Singapore.

Newsame, D. (2002). *Natural Area Tourism: Ecology, Impacts and Management*. Clevedon, UK: Channel View Publications.

Pettigrew, T., and Tropp, L. R. (2006). A meta-analytic test of intergroup contact theory. *Journal of Personality & Social Psychology*, 90(5): 751–783.

Rahimi, R. (2017). Customer relationship management (people, process and technology) and organisational culture in hotels: which traits matter? *International Journal of Contemporary Hospitality Management*, 29 (5). DOI: 10.1108/IJCHM-10-2015-0617

Rahimi, R., and Akgunduz, Y. (2017). Driving force analysis of East European students to study tourism and hospitality in the UK. *Anatolia*, 28(2): 224–238.

Rahimi, R., and Gunlu, E. (2016). Implementing customer relationship management (CRM) in hotel industry from organisational culture perspective. *International Journal of Contemporary Hospitality Management*, 28(1): 89–112.

Rahimi, R., and Kozak, M. (2017). Impact of customer relationship management on customer satisfaction: the case of a budget hotel chain. *Journal of Travel & Tourism Marketing*, 34(1): 40–51.

Saveriades, A. (2000). Establishing the social tourism carrying capacity for the tourist resorts of the east coast of the Republic of Cyprus. *Tourism Management*, 21(2): 147–156.

Sinkovics, R. R., and Penz, E. (2009). Social distance between residents and international tourists – implications for international business. *International Business Review*, 18: 457–469.

Uysal, M., and Baloğlu, S. (1994). *Destinasyonun Yasam Süresi ile Tasıma Kapasitesi Arasındaki Iliski*. Ankara: Anatolia Ocak-Haziran Mina Ofset.

17

SOCIAL IMPACTS OF TOURISM

A critical literature review on the interrelation between well-being and tourism in the case of seniors

Edina Kovács, Kornélia Kiss, Ivett Pinke-Sziva, and Gábor Michalkó

The issues of aging

In the literature, there is no consensus regarding who is considered to be old. The economics-related international literature refers to this – still undefined – group either as *seniors, older adults*, or, elsewhere, *elderly* or *aged*. For instance, Tiago, Couto, and Faria (2016) focus on people above 65 years, but, in their research, not only does age matter, but also employment status. Therefore, their tourism activity-related studies include only participants who are above 65 and are pensioners at the same time. However, Barska and Śnihur (2017), whose research concentrates on the innovation-adaptation attitudes of seniors, define the age of 55 as the beginning of being old, just as Pilar Díaz-López et al. (2017) did in their studies, and Nosraty, Jylhä, Raittila, and Lumme-Sandt (2015) concentrated specifically on the Methuselah-aged, the cohort older than 90 years. A while ago, Logan, Ward, and Spitze (1992) thoroughly studied the subjective age perception of older adults and pointed out that people rather link certain life events, not their absolute age, to being *young* or *old*. This subjective age perception, however, undoubtedly results in enormous differences among groups of people of the very same age, which cannot be ignored in the long term.

The fact that there is no consensus among researchers about who exactly belongs to the category of elderly, clearly shows that how heterogeneous this group is (Coughlin 2017, Tempest, Barnatt, and Coupland 2002). Despite the fact that – unlike in the case of other age groups – we tend to see older people as one large, homogeneous group, it is essential to be aware of the fact that, in their case too, there are quite different segments based on their:

- financial situation,
- health condition,
- abilities,
- qualifications, experiences, path of life, and
- personality.

Consequently, their needs, possibilities, and preferences are radically different as well (Coughlin 2017). Knowing these differences, it is rather controversial that most of the businesses operating in the private sector – and, therefore, hinging on their own ability to quickly adapt to market changes and consumer needs for survival – still do not consider older people as a potential and lucrative target group (Coughlin 2017). More than one and a half decades ago, Tempest et al. (2002) already drew attention to the urgent need to realize and change the traditional image we have in mind about old age, in order to reflect the actual situation.

Before the spread of state-supported pension systems, being *retired*, or more exactly the phase of their life when they had to pull back from the labor market was equal to a complete disaster for people and not only meant an absolute cut in their regular payments, but was also followed by diminishing social status. Therefore, most people desperately tried to avoid this stage of their life as long as possible. Despite the unpleasant narrative of old age, the laws of biology, as we all know, make it certain that the physical performance and energy levels of the human body significantly decrease by time, and, after a certain age, we have to admit that mental deterioration is also unavoidable, or at least mental abilities cannot compete with those of the younger generations. However, we must not forget that these inevitable changes happen at quite different ages – even during a certain age range – and different pace and intensity in the case of each person (Coughlin 2017).

Many researchers have addressed the problem of coping with loneliness, isolation, and the feeling of uselessness in old people who have already fallen out of the labor market and whose children have already grown up (Hawkley and Cacioppo 2013, Yang and Victor 2011). However, what seems to be a disadvantage on one side could be easily turned to an advantage on the other, if knowledge, willingness, a supportive environment, and the proper set of tools are available. The loneliness of seniors – lacking all types of family- or work-related commitments, but matched with good health – could be used for many multifunctional purposes, if there is enough motivation on both sides. Incentives such as programs for motivating life-long learning (Sulyok 2011) or activities aimed at ambitions for self-realization missed in earlier stages of life (Pachana 2017) could be launched with great success and could run effectively in the long term. The question is only where and how to open up more opportunities and space for these incentives to grow and bloom.

The phenomena of aging societies

Given the data produced by official national statistical bureaus and the results of regular censuses, it is undoubted that the population – especially in developed regions, but also in most developing countries – is rapidly aging (Eurostat 2015, UN 2015, KSH 2012). The reasons behind global aging are quite diverse; however, the following two dominant trends can explain most of the phenomena very accurately:

- life expectancy at birth is increasing globally, and
- fertility rates are decreasing, which means the number of newborns per woman of child-bearing age is radically decreasing.

As the two above-mentioned trends are happening simultaneously, the reason behind the rapidly growing proportion of elderly in society is, therefore, not only the decreasing number of newborn babies, but also the extension in the average life span, which is now longer than ever before. This phenomenon is called the "*aging of society*" in the literature.

Taking a closer look at the demographic statistics, it is evident that the problem of aging is primarily affecting developed countries; however, it is unquestionable that it is a global phenomenon and, in the near future, it will bring up quite serious challenges for political 'and private-sector' decision- and policymakers (UN 2015). Whether concerning the pension scheme, or any other component of the social security system, or the labor market, or the market supply of goods and services designed especially according to the needs of older customers, the challenges we face are quite significant (Coughlin 2017, Bloom, Canning, and Fink 2008, Katsumata 2000). After grasping the importance of the issue, not only has the academic sphere recently started extensive research into the – inevitable, but quite predictable – demographic processes described above, but, with more or less intensity, political and private business leaders and organizations also seem to have taken the first steps to effectively prepare and adapt to the changing circumstances. The growing attention paid to the topic is also reflected by the quickly multiplying number of national and international action plans and strategies in the last few years (OECD 2017, UN 2015, KSH 2012).

As can be predicted from the definition of the phenomenon, the aging of societies means an increasing proportion of older people within the total population. Globally in 2015, the number of people aged 60 years and older rose to 901 million, which is 12.2 percent of the total population of Earth and – in absolute terms – a 48 percent increase compared with 607 million in 2000, which meant only 9.8 percent of the total population at that time. Based on the statistics, it is very likely that the pace of increase in the proportion of older people will be similarly intensive in the future. According to the forecasts, by 2030, the number of people aged 60 years or older will grow by 56 percent, reaching 1.4 billion worldwide and making up 16.4 percent of the total population. If all goes as estimated, by 2050, the number of people aged 60 or older will have more than doubled compared with the data for 2015, which means around 2.1 billion people, or 22 percent of the total population. Consequently, by the middle of the 21st century, every fifth person on Earth will be 60 years old or older (UN 2015). According to estimates from the United Nations, the tendency of aging will further proceed in the distant future and, by 2100, the number of people aged 60 or older will reach 3.1 billion (UN 2017).

The slimming shape of the population pyramid (i.e., the growing ratio of older people in society) brings completely new challenges to cope with not only for political and business decision-makers and strategists, but also for the whole of society itself (Goldman, Chen, Zissimopoulos, and Rowe 2018, Coughlin 2017, Moreno-Galbis and Sopraseuth 2014, Tempest et al. 2002, Farkas 2011). These challenges to be solved in the future are, for instance, the operation and sustainability of pension schemes as part of social security, the functioning of the healthcare system, and taking care of those old people who require permanent assistance.

Another tendency that is one of the results of the above-described demographic and social processes is the drastically shrinking size of families, especially in developed countries, but globally as well. Shrinking family size, on the one hand, is due to the fact that the younger generations are marrying and raising a family much later in life and also have fewer children than their ancestors, and, on the other hand, is because young adults (singles or couples) are aiming to move away from their parents and start an individual life in a separate household. Not to mention the growing number of marriages resulting in divorce.[1] The once-traditional multigenerational family models are being replaced by a pattern of smaller, two to four-member families (Euromonitor 2017). The fact that, in 1880 in the United States of America, only 23.5 percent of retired men above the age of 65 lived separately from their children (i.e., alone or with their spouse), and, by 1990, this number rose to 28 percent, from where it climbed to 80 percent by the end of the 20th century is quite telling (Coughlin 2017). A substantial amount of research has already been carried out about aloneness, or more precisely its potential result, the feeling of loneliness and its long-term effects, not only in the case of older people but in other stages of life as well (Hawkley and Cacioppo 2013, Yang and Victor 2011). However, the issue of loneliness and its effects on mental and physical health has outstanding importance for the elderly, and this can be interpreted as a challenge to be solved by different government- or privately financed initiatives or by society itself in the form of various practices rooted in social innovation.

Several studies have investigated the question of senior vulnerability in terms of dealing with inequalities and how to eliminate them, as inequalities have severe multiplier effects at this age (OECD 2017). The commitment of certain international organizations, such as the UN or the WHO, to this issue is reflected in their professional publications and research reports, in which they continuously address the challenges of aging societies and propose solutions and preparations (UN 2015, 2017, WHO 2015, HelpAge 2013). The international importance of the topic has been emphasized by the Second World Assembly on Ageing, organized in 2002 in Madrid, where the participants signed the Madrid International Plan of Action on Ageing (MIPAA), which highlights the idea of taking the needs, preferences, and unique characteristics of older generations into consideration when making development plans and strategies for future decades. The MIPAA draws governments' attention to the importance of establishing an environment where – usually deprived – older people benefit from the results of developments to the same extent as any other age groups do, and therefore their health and the level of their social- and economic well-being would increase. According to what was said at the above-mentioned Madrid convention, it is going to be more important than ever before for governments to intervene, either by establishing different public institutions or applying innovative solutions to fields such as housing, healthcare, employment, or elements of basic infrastructure in the future.

Quality of life, welfare, and well-being

Quality of life, welfare, and well-being is a popular area of interest for theoretical and applied research. In the past few decades, research in various areas of science – primarily psychology, sociology, economics (Bruni and Porta 2007), medical science, political science, environmental economics, but also, increasingly, regional sciences and social geography – has explored the role, characteristics, domains, and measuring methods of quality of life, welfare, and well-being on which many indicators of human development have been based (Easterlin 2001, Donovan, Halpern, and Sargeant 2002, Helliwell and Putnam 2004, Kahneman and Krueger 2006).

A significant part of the quality of life research conducted over recent decades has linked quality of life to objective factors influencing a human being and/or their subjective reflection. The objective factors include reliably measurable living conditions and living standards that can be assessed by an external viewer, and the subjective pillar is the person's own assessment or satisfaction with his/her life. The literature refers to the objective factors of quality of life typically as welfare or objective well-being (Michalkó, Kiss, and Kovács 2008). The subjective quality of life in Diener's' early works was "subjective well-being." Sen (1993) referred to it as living standard, Emmons (1986, cited in Sőrés 2013) as life satisfaction, Veenhoven (1993) as subjective joy, and Ryan and Deci (2001) as happiness.

Most of the concepts of well-being are built on the domains of subjective life. Halleröd and Seldén (2013) found that well-being is connected to one's health, life functions, social relationships, psychosocial problems (such as depression, anxiety), and materialism. Among the "domains" of well-being, employment, education, and housing are also frequently mentioned. The role of the environment as a factor in well-being has been emphasized by several recent pieces of research (Knight, Rosa, and Schor 2013, NEF 2014). Some well-being research (EIU 2005) examines areas such as political stability, political freedom, gender equality, and environmental protection. Villamagna and Giesecke (2014) define well-being as a multidimensional value based on material (food, water, housing) and non-material (health, social cohesion, security) needs.

Diener (1984) includes both cognitive and affective elements, with three components of pleasant and unpleasant feelings and satisfaction with life. Veenhoven (1984), who built his concept of well-being on Diener's work, found in his early work that both the affective and the cognitive dimensions of well-being played an important role. Happiness in the later works of Veenhoven is a synonym for well-being; in other words, Veenhoven sees the essence of actual quality of life in how people enjoy their own lives.

Waterman (1993) and Ryan and Deci (2001) distinguish between two types of well-being in their use of words: eudemonic happiness, which attracts activities, and hedonistic happiness, with positive emotions satisfying our needs. Helliwell (2003) considers eudemonic and hedonic happiness equally important, but others (Waterman 2008) believe eudemonic happiness is more important. Kjell (2011) analyzed both forms of happiness – eudemonic and hedonistic.

Well-being, leisure, and tourism

Well-being is derived from different factors, or better to say it can be associated with various factors, one of which is leisure time. The relationship between well-being and leisure has been studied and proven in the past few decades. Diener and Suh (1997) considered leisure an important factor in well-being. London, Crandall, and Seals (1977) examined the relationship between satisfaction with leisure and satisfaction with life; Coyle, Lesnik-Emas, and Kinney (1994) and Mactavish, Mackay, Iwasaki, and Betteridge (2007) examined the same question in special segments. According to Diener, high welfare is closely related to satisfaction, positive effects, and factors of life such as work and leisure. Today, quality of life and well-being in the context of tourism mean more than verifying the relationship between the two domains: Budruk and Phillips (2011) present, for example, concepts and models for quantifying the effects of leisure and tourism activities on the quality of life.

Leisure activities have a number of positive effects. Participation in active or passive activities reduces stress, generates positive feelings, enhances self-esteem, and strengthens social relationships, thereby balancing and contributing to life satisfaction (Jeffres and Dobos 1993, Iso-Ahola and Mannell 2004, Iwasaki, Mannell, Smale, and Butcher 2005, Ateca-Amestoy, Serrano-del-Rosal, and Vera-Toscano 2008, Spiers and Walker 2009).

Csíkszentmihályi and Hunter (2003) and Wong and Csíkszentmihályi (1991) examined the relationship between generally active life and "happiness." A number of pieces of research deal with the correlation between well-being and leisure activities (Haworth and Evans 1995, Csíkszentmihályi and Lefevre 1989, Fox 1999, Pine and Gilmore 1999, Diener and Seligman 2002, Green, Oades, and Grant 2006, York and Wiseman 2012, Silverstein and Parker 2002). Haworth (2010) emphasizes that activity for the elderly is useful not only for material living, but also for mental well-being.

Dolnicar, Yanamandram, and Cliff (2012) examined 14 studies carried out between 1976 and 2009. They stated that tourism, as part of leisure, appears in half of the research as a well-being factor, but has been studied in a single study as a separate element.

Incorporating tourism into well-being-focused research is clearly related to Uysal, Perdue, and Sirgy. Their research (Neal, Sirgy, and Uysal 1999, Sirgy 2001, Sirgy and Cornwell 2001, Neal and Sirgy 2004, Neal, Uysal, and Sirgy 2007, Sirgy, Krueger, and Lee 2010, Uysal, Perdue, and Sirgy 2012) has provided a great deal of impetus for research on its contexts, and so, today, many research, theory, and synthesis studies deal with the relationship between well-being and tourism (Gilbert and Abdullah 2004, Corvo 2011, Nawijn, Marchand, Veenhoven, and Vingerhoets 2010, Nawijn 2010, Puczkó and Smith 2011, Filep 2012). Another major part of the research on the relationship between quality of life, well-being, and tourism is related to the economic, socio-cultural, and environmental impacts of tourism (Puczkó and Rátz 1998).

Uysal, Neal, and Sirgy examined the effects of tourism on the quality of life for both tourists and locals. Although McCabe, Joldersma, and Li (2010) believe that, despite the increasing popularity of tourism, the impact of travel on the level of happiness of tourists has not been proven, most well-being and tourism-focused research justifies the impacts of tourism on tourists' and locals' quality of life of life/well-being (Dolnicar et al. 2012).

The impact of tourism on the well-being of tourists

Tourism can improve the well-being of tourists in two ways. First, through the direct effects of the departure, where we distinguish three phases: before the trip (the effect of expectation), during the journey (the effect of the experience), and after the journey (the following effect). Second, the experience can indirectly contribute to everyday happiness, for example by recall of memories of experiences. The recall is supported by memories, photos, feelings, and impressions of travel experiences (Nawijn 2010).

According to the study analyzing the 13 well-being factors of Sirgy et al. (2010), it is proven that the positive and negative emotions associated with travel affect our satisfaction with our leisure time and other areas of our lives (love, family, social relationships). Richards (1999) refers to the relationship between quality of life and social well-being by emphasizing that leisure-time travel contributes to the quality of our life in the social context, as well as regarding the personal development of the individual.

Concerning the results of research on well-being and tourism from the point of view of consumers, the followings can be outlined:

- The impact of tourism on the quality of life of tourists is small but measurable (Kemp, Burt, and Furneaux 2008, Neal 2000, Dolnicar et al. 2012, Gilbert and Abdullah 2004, Nawijn et al. 2010, Sirgy et al. 2010). Some research (Milman 1998) has demonstrated the effects of tourism on the quality of life of consumers in a narrower segment.
- Some of the research analyzing the well-being aspect of tourism before, during, and after travel (Strauss-Blasche, Ekmekcioglu, and Marktl 2000, Westman and Eden 1997, Westman and Etzion 2001) reports the stress-reducing and/or health-improving effect of travel. De Bloom et al. (2009), however, emphasize that these effects are only for a short period of time.
- Nawijn (2010), Gilbert and Abdullah (2004), Kemp et al. (2008), and Lounsbury and Hoopes (1986) did not reveal any link between the length of the trip and the improved "happiness level," whereas Neal and Sirgy (2004) and Neal et al. (2007) confirmed the relationship between travel length and satisfaction and happiness in travel.
- Nawijn's (2010) research on the long-term impact of tourism among regular travelers has shown that the level of pre-journey happiness is slightly higher than in the case of occasional tourists. There is no difference in the level of post-trip happiness.

The first move towards modeling the effects of satisfaction with tourism services on life satisfaction is related to Neal et al. (1999).

The impact of tourism on the well-being of locals

In recent decades, the attitudes of tourists in tourism destinations and the impact of tourism on the local population have been popular research topics. As mentioned earlier, a significant part of the tourism-specific quality of life and subjective life-quality research has been the result of this research area. For example, the three groups of tourism impacts identified by Puczkó and Rátz (1998) have many aspects of quality of life.

- The link between economic impacts and the quality of life of the local population partly focuses on the fact that tourism creates jobs and generates income and economic benefits, which contribute to the objective well-being of locals.
- A good example of the relation between socio-cultural impacts and the quality of life of the local population is the connection between the role of tourism in destroying cultural and traditional social structures and social well-being.
- The effects of tourism on the physical environment and the quality of life of the local population are closely linked to the fact that a significant part of the physical impact of tourism is directly in the habitual residence of locals.

The above-described examples, which are largely incomplete, clearly illustrate that the effects of tourism affect both the pillar and the factors of quality of life. Although the identification of the effects of tourism on the quality of life of local populations can be considered as a new research field, examples from this area can be found, by both international and Hungarian researchers (Andereck and Nyaupane 2010, Michalkó, Rátz, and Irimiás 2010.)

Smith and Diekmann (2017) point out that nowadays the importance of developing ethical and responsible forms of tourism (sustainable tourism, ecotourism, slow tourism, and corporate social responsibility) which enhance the well-being of destinations and their residents is growing, and there is also an extensive literature on it. It is also acknowledged that there is an emerging body of literature on (cultural) ecosystem services, which is partly focused on human well-being, but – except for a couple of cases – "the connections to tourism have so far been under-explored" (p. 2).

Based on the quality of life factors of Rahman et al., Puczkó and Smith (2011) created the Budapest model which contains the connection between the quality of life and affecting factors such as travel, family, friends (social), work, material wealth, belonging, personal security, the environment, and emotional well-being. These factors are relatively objectively measurable; however, owing to the characteristics of tourism as a special service, it is necessary to add further subjective dimensions to the model. The factors that influence the subjective aspects of the quality of life of the Budapest model are the evaluation of travel as activity, visitor motivations, characteristics of travel, characteristics of the tourism destination, and the effects of tourism. The model, which presents the perceivable mapping of general quality of life factors in tourism, synthesizes 11 objective, statistically measurable parameters.

Well-being-focused tourism research among the elderly

Lately there has been a substantial amount of research investigating whether the results of the above-mentioned studies are equally relevant in the case of only older people and in terms of the whole society (Betts Adams, Leibbrandt, and Moon 2011, Easterlin 2006). The components of well-being of old people and the factors influencing it are not significantly different from those of other age groups; however, based on the idea of Erikson's (1950) *development theory*, we can conclude that, in their case, their expectations and goals (which impact their well-being through the level of satisfaction they feel) are strongly shaped by the awareness of mortality and the feeling of time passing. Following the results of Dolan, Peasgood, and White (2008), in an "optimal" case, the curve reflecting the level of well-being throughout one's lifespan is supposed to be U-shaped, as traditionally age and well-being (measured on a scale) are not inversely proportional (Kiss 2015, Dolan et al. 2008). Therefore, with the great – and still rapidly increasing – number of possibilities available for older people nowadays, it should not be obvious that age-related mental and physical changes cause a drop in the level of well-being.

Supply-side research

As has already been mentioned, in the case of retired older adults, the way they spend their tremendously increased amount of free time is crucial. Many among them find their way back to the labor market, and some commit themselves to voluntary work. However, there is a complete lack of research results about the exact impact of involving the retired elderly in the supply side of the tourism sector (i.e., as employees) on their level of well-being.

Demand-side research

Among others, the findings of Betts Adams et al. (2011) and the results of some later studies (Ponomarenko 2016, Bender 2012) also support that actively taking part in social interactions and/or engaging in different leisure-time activities contribute to the rising level of well-being of older people.

According to several pieces of research, the senior or gray tourist segment is gaining more and more relevance nowadays (Tiago et al. 2016, Chen and Shoemaker 2014) and plays an important role in tourism from several aspects:

- This segment possesses enough leisure time and economic power to be a relevant segment in tourism, particularly in domestic tourism, in which area they stay longer and spend more (Demunter 2012).
- Albu, Chaşovschi, Müristaja, Tooman, and Patiar (2015) highlight the fact that the gray segment travels in the off-season period, supporting the highly seasonal areas, and, in the main seasons, they take a part in family travel, increasing spending.
- Souca (2010) focuses on the safety-seeking behavior of seniors and points out that the gray generation seeks safe places and returns to these places regularly.

However, this segment seemed to be quite homogeneous according to earlier studies, but the newest ones proved the relevance of further segmentation in this area as well. Considering the research by Huang and Petrick (2010), older travelers nowadays travel more and longer distances than previously, though, after reaching the age of 60 years, health aspects can mean constraints. Chen and Shoemaker (2014) distinguish the so-called "younger seniors," aged in their 60s, who feel younger and search for new experiences and activities. Tiago et al. (2016) created four different clusters among senior European tourists as follows: explorers (who travel longer distances), livewires (price- and quality-sensitive travelers), vacationers (who travel to Mediterranean areas, mainly in small groups), and homebodies (domestic travelers with more needs).

The possibilities and effects of involving the elderly in the demand side of tourism sector (i.e., as tourists) has also been extensively studied (Morgan, Pritchard, and Sedgley 2015, Milman 1998). According to these studies, the results obviously show that, whereas regular and active participation in leisure-time activities does significantly contribute to seniors' level of well-being, involvement in tourism as travelers – except in the case of those who are socially deprived – does not do so, at least not to a significant extent.

Summary

By the beginning of the 20th century, being retired was still equal to a complete retreat from the labor market, and the positive and enjoyable connotations of this stage of life (e.g., *seaside, sunshine, relaxation, golfing, traveling without time pressures, fishing, education*, etc.) were yet further away (Coughlin 2017). Nowadays, with the aging of societies, the social and economic importance of pensions becomes greater than ever before. These days, there is not only the question of whether we perceive our final stage of life as a stigma or a reward, but the quality of this period also becomes unprecedentedly important as one of the most important components of senior well-being.

According to Filep (2012), in the future, despite all the well-observed mistakes in research, the issue of the well-being of tourism participants and their modeling work will continue.

There are several studies in the area of measuring objective and subjective well-being, and particularly ones concerning tourism. In summary, it can be said that travel can improve the well-being of travelers, though the positive effects can be felt only for a shorter period of time after returning, but, for regular travelers, the waiting period before traveling has a positive impact as well.

Tourism plays an increasing role in the case of the senior segment: they travel more and further than before and search for new, special, active experiences; however, health problems can create limitations. There are several pieces of research analyzing the impact of travel on the well-being of seniors, but there is a lack of analysis studying how participation in the tourism labor market can affect the well-being of seniors. As mentioned earlier, the elderly who have reached retirement age play an important role with the increasing amount of leisure time they have to spend. Many of them return to the labor market, and some are willing to work voluntarily; however, further research is needed to see how they are employed, why it is important from the point of view of tourism experiences (e.g., story telling), and how this kind of employment affects their well-being.

As for further future research directions, it would be interesting to involve the findings of certain behavioral economics-related studies in tourism-focused well-being research, in order to take a closer look not only at the well-being and benefits of employment of seniors, but also at the barriers they face. Applying the ideas of predictable, though irrational, decision-making and the concept of learned helplessness in the case of senior employment and well-being could probably reveal further useful insights.

Note

1 http://ec.europa.eu/eurostat/statistics-explained/index.php/Marriage_and_divorce_statistics and https://www.cdc.gov/nchs/pressroom/02news/div_mar_cohab.htm (downloaded: 1 December 2018).

This research has been supported by the European Union and Hungary and co-financed by the European Social Fund through the Project EFOP-3.6.2-16-2017-00017, titled "Sustainable, intelligent and inclusive regional and city models".

References

Albu, A., Chaşovschi, C., Müristaja, H., Tooman, H., and Patiar, S. (2015). *Handbook Senior Tourism.* Available at: www.cubitus-project.eu/index.php/download/category/13senior

Anderack, K. L., and Nyaupane, G. P. (2010). Exploring the nature of tourism and quality of life perceptions among residents. *Journal of Travel Research*, 50 (3), pp. 248–260.

Ateca-Amestoy, V., Serrano-del-Rosal, R., and Vera-Toscano, E. (2008). The leisure experience. *The Journal of Socio-Economics*, 37 (1), pp. 64–78.

Barska, A., and Šnihur, J. (2017). Senior as a challenge for innovative enterprises. *Procedia Engineering*, 182, pp. 58–65.

Bender, K. A. (2012). An analysis of well-being in retirement: The role of pensions, health, and "voluntariness" of retirement. *The Journal of Socio-Economics*, (41), pp. 424–433.

Betts Adams, K., Leibbrandt, S., and Moon, H. (2011). A critical review of the literature on social and leisure activity and well-being in later life. *Ageing & Society* (31), pp. 683–712.

Bloom, D. E., Canning, D., and Fink, G. (2008). Population Ageing and Economic Growth. Working Paper Series. Cambridge, MA: Program on the Global Demography of Aging.

Bruni, L., and Porta, P. L. (Eds.) (2007). *Handbook on the Economics of Happiness*. Cheltenham, UK: Edward Elgar Publishing.

Budruk, M., and Phillips, R. (2011). *Quality of Life Community Indicators for Parks Recreation and Tourism Management*. Social Indicators Research Series, 43. Amsterdam: Springer.

Chen, S. C., and Shoemaker, S. (2014). Age and cohort effects: The American senior tourism market. *Annals of Tourism Research*, 48 (2014), pp. 58–75.

Corvo, P. (2011). The pursuit of happiness and the globalized tourist. *Social Indicators Research*, 102, pp. 93–97.

Coughlin, J. F. (2017). *The Longevity Economy: Unlocking the World's Fastest-Growing, Most Misunderstood Market*. New York: Hachette.

Coyle, C. P., Lesnik-Emas, S., and Kinney, W. B. (1994). Predicting life satisfaction among adults with spinal cord injuries. *Rehabilitation Psychology*, 39 (2), pp. 95–112.

Csíkszentmihályi M., and Hunter, J. (2003). Happiness in everyday life. The uses of experience sampling. *Journal of Happiness Studies*, 4, pp. 185–199.

Csíkszentmihályi, M., and Lefevre, J. (1989). Optimal experience in work and leisure. *Journal of Personality & Social Psychology*, 56 (5), pp. 815–822.

De Bloom, J., Kompier, M. A. J., Geurts, S. A. E., De Weerth, C., Taris, T., and Sonnentag, S. (2009). Do we recover from vacation? Meta-analysis of vacation effects on health and well-being. *Journal of Occupational Health*, 51 (1), pp. 13–25.

Demunter, C. (2012). Ageing and tourism in the European Union. In: A. Albu, C. Chaşovschi, H. Müristaja, H. Tooman, and S. Patiar, S. (Eds.), *Handbook Senior Tourism*. Available at: www.cubitus-project.eu/index.php/download/category/13senior

Pilar Diaz-López, M. del, Aguilar-Parra, J. M., López-Liria, R., Rocamora-Pérez, P., Vargas-Muñoz, M. E., Padilla-Góngora, D. (2017). Skills for successful ageing in the elderly. Education, well-being and health. *Procedia – Social & Behavioral Sciences*, 237, pp. 986–991.

Diener, E. (1984). Subjective well-being. *Psychological Bulletin*, 95 (3), pp. 542–575.

Diener, E., and Seligman, E. P. (2002). Very happy people. *Psychological Science*, 13 (1), pp. 81–84.

Diener, E., and Suh, E. (1997). Measuring quality of life: Economic, social, and subjective indicators. *Social Indicators Research*, 40, pp. 189–216.

Dolan, P., Peasgood, T., and White, M. (2008). Do we really know what makes us happy? A review of the economic literature on the factors associated with subjective well-being. *Journal of Economic Psychology*, (29), pp. 94–122.

Dolnicar, S., Yanamandram, V., and Cliff, K. (2012). The contribution of vacations to quality of life. *Annals of Tourism Research*, 39 (1), pp. 59–83.

Donovan, N., Halpern, D., and Sargeant, R. (2002). Life Satisfaction? The State of Knowledge and Implications for Government. http://tidsverkstaden.se/filarkiv/file/Life%20satisfaction.pdf

Easterlin, R. (2001). Income and happiness: Towards a unified theory. *The Economic Journal*, 111, pp. 465–484.

Easterlin, R. (2006). Life cycle happiness and its sources – Intersections of psychology, economics and demography. *Journal of Economic Psychology*, 27, pp. 463–482.

Erikson, E. H. (1950). *Childhood and Society*. New York: W.W. Norton.

Euromonitor International (Euromonitor). (2017). *Megatrend Analysis: Putting the Consumer at the Heart of Business*, ed. S. Boumphrey and Z. Brehmer. Euromonitor.

Eurostat. (2015). *People in the EU: Who Are We and How Do We Live?* Eurostat Statistical Books, 2015 ed. Luxembourg: Eurostat.

Farkas, P. (2011). Nyugdíjkorhatár, demográfia, foglalkoztatás. *Demográfia*, 54 (4), pp. 270–282.

Filep, S. (2012). Positive psychology and tourism. In: M. Uysal, R. Perdue, and J. Sirgy (Eds.), *Handbook of Tourism and Quality of Life Research*. Heidelberg: Springer. pp. 31–50.

Fox, K. R. (1999). The influence of physical activity on mental well-being. *Public Health Nutrition*, 2 (3a), pp. 411–418.

Gilbert, D., and Abdullah, J. (2004). Holidaytaking and the sense of well-being. *Annals of Tourism Research*, 31 (1), pp. 103–121.

Goldman, D. P., Chen, C., Zissimopoulos, J., and Rowe, J. W. (2018). Measuring how countries adapt to societal aging. *Proceedings of the National Academy of Sciences of the United States of America*, 115 (3), pp. 435–437.

Green, L. S., and Oades, L. G., and Grant A. M. (2006). Cognitive-behavioral, solution-focused life coaching: Enhancing goal striving, well-being, and hope. *The Journal of Positive Psychology*, 1 (3), pp. 142–149.

Halleröd, B., and Seldén, D. (2013). The multi-dimensional characteristics of well-being: How different aspects of well-being interact and do not interact with each other. *Social Indicators Research*, 113, pp. 807–825.

Hawkley, L. C., and Cacioppo, J. T. (2013). Loneliness matters: A theoretical and empirical review of consequences and mechanisms. *Annals of Behavioral Medicine*, 40 (2), pp. 1–14.

Haworth, J., and Evans, S. (1995). Challenge, skill and positive subjective states in the daily life of a sample of YTS students. *Journal of Occupational and Organizational Psychology*, 68 (2), pp. 109–121.

Haworth, J. T. (2010). Life, work, leisure, and enjoyment: The role of social institutions. Working paper. 28 p. Available at: www.well-being-esrc.com/downloads/LifeWorkLeisure&Enjoyment.pdf

Helliwell, J. (2003). How's life? Combining individual and national variables to explain subjective well-being. *Economic Modelling*, 20, pp. 301–360.

Helliwell, J. F., and Putnam, R. D. (2004). The social context of well-being. *Philosophical Transactions of the Royal Society of London*, 359, pp. 1435–1446.

HelpAge International (HelpAge). (2013). *Global Age Watch Index 2013 – Purpose, Methodology and Results*. London: HelpAge.

Huang Y.-C., and Petrick, J. F. (2010). Generation Y's travel behaviours: A comparison with Baby Boomers and Generation X. In: G. Moscardo (Ed.), *Tourism and Generation Y*. Wallingford, UK: CAB International, pp. 27–37.

Iso-Ahola, S. E., and Mannell, R. C. (2004). Leisure and health. In: J. T. Haworth and A. J. Veal (Eds.), *Work and Leisure*. London: Routledge, pp. 184–199.

Iwasaki, Y., Mannell, R. C., Smale, B. J. A., and Butcher, J. (2005). Contributions of leisure participation in predicting stress coping and health among police and emergency response services workers. *Health Psychology*, 10, pp. 79–99.

Jeffres, L., and Dobos, J. (1993). Perceptions of leisure opportunities and the quality of life in a metropolitan area. *Journal of Leisure Research*, 25, pp. 203–217.

Kahneman, D., and Krueger, A. B. (2006). Developments in the measurement of subjective well-being. *Journal of Economic Perspective*, (20) 1, pp. 3–24.

Katsumata, Y. M. (2000). The impact of population decline and population aging in Japan from the perspectives of social and labor policy. UN Expert Group Meeting on Policy Responses to Population Ageing and Population Decline, New York, October 16–18.

Kemp, S., Burt, C. D. B., and Furneaux, L. (2008). A test of the peak-end rule with extended autobiographical events. *Memory & Cognition*, 36 (1), pp. 132–138.

Kiss, K. (2015). A szubjektív életminőség sajátosságai a Balkánon és Törökországban. Doktori értekezés. Szent István Egyetem Enyedi György Regionális Tudományok Doktori Iskola. Gödöllő, Hungary.

Kjell, O. N. E. (2011). Sustainable well-being: A potential synergy between sustainability and well-being research. *Review of General Psychology*, 15 (3), pp. 255–266.

Knight, K. W., Rosa, E. A., and Schor, J. B. (2013). Could working less reduce pressures on the environment? A cross-national panel analysis of OECD countries, 1970–2007. *Global Environmental Change*, 23 (4), pp. 691–700.

Központi Statisztikai Hivatal (KSH). (2012). Magyarország társadalmi atlasza. Budapest.

Logan, J. R., Ward, R., and Spitze, G. (1992). As old as you feel: Age identity in middle and later life. *Social Forces* 71 (2), pp. 451–467.

London, M., Crandall, R., and Seals, G. W. (1977). The contribution of job and leisure satisfaction to quality of life. *Journal of Applied Psychology*, 62 (3), pp. 328–334.

Lounsbury, J. W., and Hoopes, L. L. (1986). A vacation from work: Changes in work and nonwork outcomes. *Journal of Applied Psychology*, 71 (3), pp. 392–401.

Mactavish, J. B., Mackay, K. J., Iwasaki, Y., and Betteridge, D. (2007). Family caregivers of individuals with intellectual disability: Perspectives on life quality and the role of vacations. *Journal of Leisure Research*, 39 (1). Available at: www.questia.com/library/journal/1G1-159390972/family-caregivers-of-individuals-with-intellectual

McCabe, S., Joldersma, T., and Li, C. (2010). Understanding the benefits of social tourism: Linking participation to subjective well being and quality of life. *International Journal of Tourism Research*, 12, pp. 761–773.

Michalkó, G., Kiss, K., and Kovács, B. (2008). A szürke párduc útra kel – Az időskorúak utazásainak szerepe szubjektív jólétük tükrében. In: Á. Grábics (Ed.), *Aktív időskor*. Budapest: Központi Statisztikai Hivatal – Szociális és Munkaügyi Minisztérium, pp. 80–98.

Michalkó, G., Kiss, K., and Kovács, B. (2009). Boldogító utazás: a turizmus hatása a magyar lakosság szubjektív életminőségére. *Tér és Társadalom*, 23 (1), pp. 1–17.

Michalkó, G., Rátz, T., and Irimiás, A. (2010). Egy magyarországi fürdőváros lakosságának életminősége: az orosházi eset. *Turizmus Bulletin*, 14 (4), pp. 61–68.

Milman, A. (1998). The impact of tourism and travel experience on senior travelers' psychological well-being. *Journal of Travel Research*, 37 (2), pp. 166–170.

Moreno-Galbis, E., and Sopraseuth, T. (2014). Job polarization in aging economies. *Labour Economics*, (27), pp. 44–55.

Morgan, N., Pritchard, A., and Sedgley, D. (2015). Social tourism and well-being in later life. *Annals of Tourism Research*, 52, pp. 1–15.

Nawijn, J. (2010). Happiness through vacationing: Just a temporary boost or long-term benefits? *Journal of Happiness Studies*, 12, pp. 651–665.

Nawijn, J., Marchand, M. A., Veenhoven, R., and Vingerhoets, A. D. J. (2010). Vacationers happier, but most not happier after a holiday. *Applied Research in Quality of Life*, 5 (1), pp. 35–47.

Neal, J. D. (2000). *The Effects of Different Aspects of Tourism Services on Travelers' Quality of Life: Model Validation, Refinement, and Extension*. Blacksburg, VA: Virginia Polytechnic Institute and State University.

Neal, J. D., and Sirgy, M. J. (2004). Measuring the effect of tourism services on travelers' quality of life: Further validation. *Social Indicators Research*, 69 (3), pp. 243–277.

Neal, J. D., Sirgy, M.J., and Uysal, M. (1999). The role of satisfaction with leisure travel/tourism services and experience in satisfaction with leisure life and overall life. *Journal of Business Research*, 44, pp. 153–163.

Neal, J. D., Uysal, M, and Sirgy, M. J. (2007). The effect of tourism services on travelers' quality of life. *Journal of Travel Research*, 46, pp. 153–163.

New Economics Foundation. (2014). *The Happy Planet Index: 2012 Report – A Global Index of Sustainable Well-Being*. London: New Economics Foundation.

Organization for Economic Co-operation and Development (OECD). (2017). *Preventing Ageing Unequally – Action Plan*. Paris: OECD

Nosraty, L., Jylhä, M., Raittila, T., and Lumme-Sandt, K. (2015). Perceptions by the oldest old of successful aging, Vitality 90+ study. *Journal of Aging Studies*, 32 (2015), pp. 50–58.

Pachana, N. A. (Ed.) (2017). *Encyclopedia of Geropsychology*. Brisbane, QLD: Springer.

Pine, B. J., and Gilmore, J. H. (1999). *The Experience Economy: Work is Theater & Every Business a Stage*. Boston, MA: Harvard Business School Press.

Ponomarenko, V. (2016). Cumulative disadvantages of non-employment and non-standard work for career patterns and subjective well-being in retirement. *Advances in Life Course Research*, (30), pp. 133–148.

Puczkó, L, and Rátz, T. (1998). *A turizmus hatásai*. Budapest-Székesfehérvár: Aula-Kodolányi.

Puczkó L., and Smith, M. K. (2011). Tourism-specific quality of life index: The Budapest model. In: M. Budruk and R. Philips (Eds.), *Quality-of-Life Community Indicators for Parks, Recreation and Tourism Management*. Social Indicators Research Series 43. Dordrecht: Springer, pp. 163–184.

Richards, G. (1999). Vacations and the quality of life. *Journal of Business Research*, 44 (3), pp. 189–198.

Ryan, R. M., and Deci, E. L. (2001). On happiness and human potentials: A review of research on hedonic and eudaimonic well-being. *Annual Review of Psychology*, 52 (1), pp. 141–166.

Sen, A. (1993). Capability and well-being. In: D. M. Hausman (Ed.), *The Philosophy of Economics*. New York: Cambridge University Press, pp. 270–293. http://digamo.free.fr/hausman8.pdf#page=276

Silverstein, M., and Parker, M. G. (2002). Leisure activities and quality of life among the oldest old in Sweden. *Research on Aging*, 24 (5), pp. 528–547.

Sirgy, M. J. (2001). *Handbook of Quality-of-Life Research: An Ethical Marketing Perspective*. Dordrecht, Netherlands: Kluwer.

Sirgy, M. J., and Cornwell, T. (2001). Further validation of the Sirgy et al.'s measure of community quality of life. *Social Indicators Research*, 56 (2), pp. 125–143.

Sirgy, M. J., Kruger, P. S., Lee, D.-J. B., and Yu, G (2010). How does a travel trip affect tourists' life satisfaction? *Journal of Travel Research*, 20 (5), pp. 1–15.

Smith, M. K., and Diekmann, A. (2017). Tourism and wellbeing. *Annals of Tourism Research*, 66, pp. 1–13.

Souca, M. L. (2010). Accessible tourism – the ignored opportunity. Annals of Faculty of Economics from University of Oradea. 1154–1157. In: A. Albu, C. Chaşovschi, H. Müristaja, H. Tooman, and S. Patiar (Eds.), *Handbook Senior Tourism*. Available at: www.cubitus-project.eu/index.php/download/category/13senior

Sőrés, A. (2013). Az egészségturizmus hatása az életminőségre Hajdúszoboszlón. Doktori (PhD) értekezés. Debreceni Egyetem, Ihrig Károly Gazdálkodás- és Szervezéstudományok Doktori Iskola.

Spiers, A., and Walker, G. J. (2009). The effects of ethnicity and leisure satisfaction on happiness, peacefulness, and quality of life. *Leisure Sciences*, 31 (1), pp. 84–99.

Strauss-Blasche, G., Ekmekcioglu, C., and Marktl, W. (2000). Does vacation enable recuperation? Changes in well-being associated with time away from work. *Occupational Medicine*, 50 (3), pp. 167–172.

Sulyok, T. (2011). Az időskori tanulás lehetőségei – Időseink a munka világában: a munkanélküliség, a nyugdíj melletti munkavégzés és az idősoktatás lehetőségei. Lecture at Zsigmond Király Főiskola, Budapest.

Tempest, S., Barnatt, C., and Coupland, C. (2002). Grey advantage – New strategies for the old. *Long Range Planning*, (35), pp. 475–492.

Tiago, P. M. B. M. T., De Almeida Couto, P. J., Borges Tiago, F. G., and Costa Dias Faria, S. M. (2016). Baby boomers turning grey: European profiles. *Tourism Management*, (54), pp. 13–22.

Economist Intelligence Unit. (2005). The Economist Intelligence Unit's quality-of-life index. London: Economist Intelligence Unit. Available at : www.economist.com/media/pdf/QUALITY_OF_LIFE.pdf.

United Nations (UN). (2015). *World Population Ageing Report*. New York: UN.

United Nations (UN). (2017). *World Population Prospects – Key Findings & Advance Tables*, 2017 revision. New York: UN.

Uysal, M., Perdue, R., and Sirgy, J. (Eds.) (2012). *Handbook of Tourism and Quality of Life Research*. Heidelberg: Springer.

Veenhoven, R. (1984). *Conditions of Happiness*. Dordrecht, Netherlands: Kluwer Academic.

Veenhoven, R. (1993). Happiness in nations. Subjective appreciation of life in 56 nations 1946–1992. Available at: www2.eur.nl/fsw/research/veenhoven/Pub1990s/93b-part1.pdf

Villamagna, A., and Giesecke, C. (2014). Adapting human well-being frameworks for ecosystem service assessments across diverse landscapes. *Ecology & Society* 19 (1), pp. 1–18.

Waterman, A. S. (1993). Two conceptions of happiness: Contrasts of personal expressiveness (eudaimonia) and hedonic enjoyment. *Journal of Personality and Social Psychology*, 64 (4), pp. 678–691.

Waterman, A. S. (2008). Reconsidering happiness: A eudaimonist's perspective. *The Journal of Positive Psychology*, 3 (4), pp. 234–252.

Westman, M., and Eden, D. (1997). Effects of a respite from work on burnout: Vacation relief and fade-out. *Journal of Applied Psychology*, 82 (4), pp. 516–527.

Westman, M., and Etzion, D. (2001). The impact of vacation and job stress on burnout and absenteeism. *Psychology & Health*, 16 (5), pp. 595–606.

Wong, M. M., and Csíkszentmihályi, M. (1991). Motivation and academic achievement: The effects of personality traits and the duality of experience. *Journal of Personality*, 59 (3), pp. 539–574.

World Health Organization (WHO). (2015). *World Report on Ageing and Health*. Luxembourg: WHO.

Yang, K., and Victor, C. (2011). Age and loneliness in 25 European nations. *Ageing & Society*, 31 (8), pp. 1368–1388.

York, M., and Wiseman, T. (2012). Gardening as an occupation: a critical review. *British Journal of Occupational Therapy*, 75 (2), pp. 76–84.

18

SOCIAL PSYCHOLOGICAL EFFECTS OF TOURISM

Evaluation of the tourist–local people interaction within the context of Allport's intergroup contact theory

Sedat Çelik

Introduction

There is no complete and definitive explanation or description of what social psychology is. The reason for this is that social psychology is still an emerging science discipline (Kayaoğlu, 2011). There is also a distinction arising between the perspectives of psychologists and sociologists. As a subdivision of psychology, social psychology includes scientific studies that demonstrate how individuals think, feel and influence each other (Bordens & Horowitz, 2002). From a sociological point of view, social psychology is defined as "the discipline that studies the human behavior influenced, controlled and limited by the social environment". In fact, both perspectives focus on social behavior. Nowadays, these perspectives have been replaced by the situation suggesting that "the individual is in the society, and the society is in the individual" (G. Gurvich, cited in Göksu, 2007: 17). Social psychology is the behavioral science of the individual or individuals within a society. It also tries to understand an individual's emotions, thoughts, beliefs and attitudes affected by the social environment (Kağıtçıbaşı, 2014: 22). Social psychology, in broad terms, means the scientific examination of how people's thoughts, emotions and behaviors are affected by the real or imaginary existence of other people (Aronson, Wilson & Akert. 2012: 31).

Tourism is defined as "the temporary movement of people to destinations outside their permanent residence and destination, the activities they carry out during their stay in these destinations and the facilities created to meet the needs of the people" (Mathieson & Wall, 1982: 1). According to the definition that evaluates tourism as a sector, tourism can be defined as outputs, activities and processes that emerge from tourism, tourism suppliers, local institutions, local people and environmental relations (Goeldner and Ritchie, 2009: 6). Franklin emphasized that tourism could be combined with everything, and described it as "what tourists do" (Franklin, 2003: 28). The things that tourists do, which Franklin refers to very briefly, have positive and negative environmental, economic, sociocultural and social psychological effects on societies (Rátz, 2000). For this reason, tourism is very important for the development of countries, strengthening infrastructure, enhancing agricultural and commercial activities, providing employment opportunities, increasing the number of foreign investments, bringing new technologies into the country, producing local products and ensuring sociocultural co-existence (Golzardi, Sarvaramini, Sadatasilan, & Sarvaramini, 2012).

In tourism, an interaction occurs when local people encounter tourists (Rızaoğlu, 2012). Social psychology's attempt to explain the relationships within the society and groups and between individuals shows that the interaction arising from the relationship between tourists and local people can also be approached from a social psychological point of view. Indeed, it is seen that many studies (Crompton, 1979; Dann, 1981; Pearce, 1982; Ap, 1992; Gomez-Jacinto, San Martin-Garcia & Bertiche-Haud'Huyze, 1999; Maruyama & Woosman, 2015), from the past to the present day, have dealt with tourism from a psychological and sociological perspective. The studies (Snaith & Haley, 1999; Upchurch & Teivane, 2000; Tayfun, 2002; Gursoy, Kim & Uysal, 2004; Mansuroğlu, 2006; Alaeddinoğlu, 2007; Golzardi et al., 2012) conducted on the interaction of tourists with local people mainly focused on local people's perspective on tourism and tourists. The reactions of tourists towards local people have not been studied as much as the reactions of local people towards tourists (Pearce, 1982). Although there are a limited number of studies revealing the role of tourism, which especially enables interaction between different societies, in changing the attitudes (stereotypes and prejudices) of people living in the destination country towards people coming from other countries, tourism is gradually increasing (Amir, 1969; Pearce, 1980; Milman, Reichel & Pizam, 1990; Anastasopoulos, 1992; Sirakaya-Turk, Nyaupane & Uysal, 2014). This study, where we addressed the interaction between local people and tourists within the context of "intergroup contact theory" which was developed by Allport, one of the founders of social psychology, as a solution to changing attitudes, will bring a different perspective. At this point, it is considered that it will contribute to future studies on social psychology and tourism.

Interaction between tourists and local people

Interaction between tourists and local people is defined as a social relationship that occurs randomly in certain areas (Reisinger & Turner, 2003). This social relationship emerges while (a) a tourist is buying a product; (b) tourists and local people are using the same place, area or facility; or (c) tourists and local people are exchanging information or ideas (Dilek, 2016: 110). Lickorish and Jenkins (1997: 16) emphasized that the most important part of the holiday experience was the interaction between local people and tourists. Behaviors between tourists and local people can range from sincere to aggressive behavior. The intensity, form, quality, size, direction and place of interaction can have an effect on the communication between tourists and local people. Whether or not the expectations of tourists are met also has a role in this context (Rızaoğlu, 2012: 273).

As it is understood that tourism cannot develop without the support of local people, there have been more and more studies focusing on the relationship between tourists and local people, on top of the economic benefits of tourism since the mid-1970s (Lickorish and Jenkins, 1997: 77). According to Butler's (1980) model, which reveals the relationship between local people and tourism, whereas local people are uninterested in places where the tourists are few and the destination has been newly opened to tourism, they start to get more interested as the number of tourists increases, and their attitudes change in the negative direction as the number of tourists goes above the capacity of the destination (Brida, Osti & Barquet, 2010: 593; Akis, Peristianis & Warner, 1996). Similarly, with the irridex model, Doxey suggested that tourism destinations go through some stages, namely "euphoria", "apathy", "annoyance" and "antagonism" (Akis et al., 1996; Gürbüz, 2002; Duran & Özkul, 2012). Doxey suggested that, at the primary stage, tourism makes local people happy thanks to the economic benefits it brings, but, as the disadvantages of tourism become evident, locals' feelings go as far as hostility towards tourists (Boğan & Sarışık, 2016). Another approach to explain the relationship between local people and tourism has been put forth by Ap and Crompton (1993). Ap and Crompton stated that the interaction between local people and tourists varies in four stages: In the *embracement stage*, local people accept tourism and tourists; in the *tolerance* stage, local people are indecisive about accepting tourists and tourism; in the *adjustment* stage, local people deliberately try to prevent tourists from visiting the destination or make no effort to have them visit; and finally, in the *withdrawal* stage, local people want to leave the regions where they face tourist influx or fight with tourists and show reactions to tourists. In addition, Ap (1992) evaluated the relationship between tourists and local people within the framework of social change theory. In this context, it was suggested that tourism was adopted and supported by local people if its benefits were greater than its costs, and that they opposed tourism when it did more harm than good. We can say that this approach supports the development cycle in Butler's and Doxey's models, suggesting that local people support tourism while they gain economic benefits from it, in the first two stages, and lose interest as the harm caused by tourism increases in the other two stages.

The relationship between local people and tourists can be evaluated in two categories, namely the effects of tourism on local people and the effects of tourism on tourists. However, most of the studies (Waitt, 2003; Gursoy et al., 2004; Wang, Pfister & Morais, 2006; Pham & Kayat, 2011; Golzadri et al., 2012; Lopez, Virto, Manzano & Miranda, 2018) refer to the effects of tourism on local people (Pearce, 1982). Recently, there has been an increase in the number of studies (Amir, 1969; Pearce, 1980; Milman et al., 1990; Anastasopoulos, 1992; Sirakaya-Turk et al., 2014; Günlü et al., 2015; Nyaupane, Teye & Paris, 2016; Çelik, 2017a; Joo et al., 2018; Chen & Rahman, 2018) focusing on the effects of tourism on tourists (especially attitude changes).

Allport's intergroup contact theory

The intergroup contact theory, developed after the Second World War by Allport in 1954, one of the founders of behavioral social psychology in the field of social psychology, has been included in studies intensively because of its theoretical and political importance (Allport, 1979; Pettigrew, 1998: 66; Dörnyei & Csizér, 2005; Pettigrew & Tropp, 2006; Joyce, 2017). Allport stated in his theory that intergroup contact was a very effective way of reducing prejudices among different ethnic and religious groups or other opposing groups. In this context, the term "intergroup contact" refers to the relationship and interaction between two or more groups (Allport, 1979). According to this theory, hostility among groups is caused by the unfamiliarity and distance between these groups, and that hostility can be reduced by intergroup contact (Allport, 1979; Bordens & Horowitz, 2002; Yılmaz & Taşçı, 2015; Maruyama & Woosnam, 2015). However, each interaction has the potential to be positive, negative or neutral. At this point, in order for the contact between groups to be positive, he argued that there must be four optimal conditions, such as equal status of the groups, having intergroup cooperation, having common goals and being supported by the authority.

The well-known social psychologist Muzafer Sherif (1966), cited by Pettigrew and Tropp (2006), stated that, when there was no cooperation but rather competition, prejudice, discrimination and hostility increased. The optimal conditions stated in the previous paragraph are important for the interaction to be positive, but they are not necessary. In addition, some of the studies revealed that some cases, such as *having a common language, voluntariness* and *economic prosperity among the groups* (Wagner & Machleit, 1986, cited by Pettigrew, 1998), *absence of hostility* (Ruesch, 2011), *having social norms on equality* (Aronson et al., 2012) and *exhibiting care and empathy for one another* (Pettigrew & Tropp, 2008), are important for the intergroup contact to be effective in the positive direction.

Evaluation of the change in attitudes in tourists–local people interaction within intergroup contact theory

It is known that, as a result of different societies contacting each other, prejudices and tensions can be reduced, and intergroup interaction can be developed (Jaspars & Hewsone, 1982). Tourism is an experience that teaches people and opens their minds to the fact that the world is not a single life model, and there are other lives as well (Wintersteiner & Wohlmuther, 2014). This experience is an important way of establishing intergroup contact, intercultural interaction and communication (Gamper, 1981: 432). Therefore, tourism is effective in reducing prejudices, conflicts and tensions. Tourists traveling to foreign destinations may have good experiences with local communities, establish positive interactions and forge permanent friendships. On top of that, tourism contributes to world peace by enabling interaction among different nations and developing mutual understanding among people (Tomljenovic, 2010: 17; Pratt & Liu, 2015). The Global Code of Ethics for Tourism also addresses tourism and peace and emphasizes the importance of tourism in establishing peace and friendship among different people and lifestyles (UNWTO, 2018).

Allport's intergroup contact theory has an important role in explaining the interaction of local people with tourists who have different socio-economic and cultural characteristics in the field of tourism. However, it is not possible to arrange and organize how and when the contact will be realized in the tourism sector (Stangor, 2009). In almost every public space, tourists–local people interaction is possible, and contact can be made while purchasing products or services or during short meetings or information exchange (Yilmaz & Taşçı, 2015). Prejudices may be reduced thanks to these contacts. At this point, however, there are many questions. For example, do all tourism activities reduce prejudices? In particular, in communities that have survived colonization, would contact between the local people and tourists coming from the country that previously colonized them have a positive effect? Does inequality between local people and tourists cause a problem? As not every tourist is satisfied with everything, how does this dissatisfaction influence the contact (Pernecky, 2015)?

It is not possible to provide all the conditions (equal status of groups, having intergroup cooperation, having common goals, being supported by the authority) suggested by Allport (1979) in tourism. At this point, the factors that may be effective in reducing prejudices against tourists as a result of tourists–local population contact are listed below (Tomljenovic, 2010):

- A tourist's length of stay in a destination
- Amount of events/activities
- A tourist's travel motivation/purpose for coming
- A tourist's holiday satisfaction
- The quality, familiarity, cultural distance and language of the destination
- Intensity/power and direction of attitude before holiday
- Tourists' personality traits (intolerant, racist, ethnocentric, etc.).

Many factors can influence the interaction between local people and tourists, such as staying at a destination for a long or short term, temporariness, having equal status, having superficial or intensive contact, being natural, commercial, sincere, formal, competitive, responsive or unclear (Pizam, Uriely & Reichel, 2000; Reisinger & Turner, 2003). In addition to this, the traits (personality, tolerance, interest, generosity, etc.) that a tourist has (Çelik, 2017b) and the attitude of the local people towards the tourist (being respectful and understanding, etc.) influence the contact's being positive or negative.

As the *amount of outgroup contact* increases, group members have the opportunity to get to know one another, and this often leads to positive attitudes (Maruyama & Woosnam, 2015). González and his colleagues revealed a negative relationship between the amount of contact and prejudice (González, Verkuyten, Weesie & Poppe, 2008). In other words, they found that prejudices decreased as the amount of contact increased. From this point of view, it can be seen that tourists' length of stay in a destination and the number of overnight stays are effective in reducing prejudices. Besides, it has been revealed that social status is also effective in the interaction of local people and tourists (Triandis & Vassiliou, 1967). Negative attitudes (hatred, contempt, exclusion, etc.) may develop when people with low and high status encounter each other (Amir, 1969).

As stated in the contact theory, contact between tourists and local people may not always be positive; on the contrary, it can sometimes cause conflict of social values. For example, tourists come to Tahiti to see beautiful women. In a male-dominated society, a conflict of traditional values can emerge with the growing importance of women (Reisinger & Turner, 2003). The arrival of non-Muslims in Muslim countries can cause the deterioration of local, religious and cultural values regarding women's clothing, alcohol and sexuality issues. In this case, it is inevitable that tourists will be isolated and discriminated against by the local people. From another point of view, tourists can be victims of harassment during interaction between tourists and local people. Likewise, linguistic, spatial, security and health problems can arise in the relations between tourists and local people (Pearce, 1982). On the other hand, in underdeveloped countries, contact between tourists and local people may be negative, because rich tourists visiting underdeveloped countries mostly tend to dislike and disrespect the local people (Reisinger & Turner, 2003).

The intergroup contact theory is included in tourism studies mainly to show whether the attitudes of tourists change in a positive direction as a result of interactions with local people. There are many studies examining the effect of tourism on changing prejudices and stereotypes among societies (Amir & Ben-Ari, 1983; Milman et al., 1990; Pizam, Jafari, & Milman, 1991; Anastasopoulos, 1992; Maruyama & Woosnam, 2015). Some are briefly explained below.

Sirakaya-Turk et al. (2014) studied whether prejudices about Turkish people changed between before and after the tour in a group of 317 German tourists who came to Antalya. As a result of the research, it was revealed that prejudices towards Turkish people were even more negative after the tour. Dissatisfaction with the tourist experience and the tour guide, the all-inclusive tour concept and the shopping experience were found to be effective in the change of attitudes in a negative direction.

Grothe (1970) found in his study that American tourists started to hold different attitudes towards Russia. According to this, whereas there was a small positive change in their attitudes towards Russians, it was revealed that there were negative changes in attitudes towards the Russian government and the system.

Welds and Dukes (1985) stated that changes occurred in a positive direction in the attitudes of students participating in a travel program in the semester holiday, including cultural events, home visits and face-to-face interactions.

In a survey conducted with 263 Japanese students who visited Canada, Weiler (1989) identified significant changes in several attitudes held the students towards the local people. However, there was no change in attitudes towards Canada as a destination.

In their study in which 388 tourists working in Israel participated, Pizam et al. (2000) aimed to discover the influence of their contact with local people on satisfaction and attitude change.

The results of the study showed that their satisfaction with contact with local people changed their attitudes towards the local people positively. There was also a positive change in attitudes towards the state of Israel.

Amir and Ben-Ari (1983) conducted a study with 662 Israeli visitors and tried to reveal the changes in their attitudes towards Egyptians before and after the tour. According to the results of the survey, there was a negative change in the general attitudes of the Israelis towards Egyptians. However, their political attitudes did not change. In the Egyptians' opinion about Israel, there was negative change in intellectual competence matters and positive change in personal–social matters. No correlation was found between travel satisfaction and other variables.

Anastasopoulos (1992) studied whether the attitudes of Greeks visiting Turkey changed towards Turks and the Turkish government's policies after travel. In the study, conducted with a total of 97 tourists and a control group of 82 people, it was seen that Greek tourists' attitudes towards Turks often changed in the negative direction. As there was no change in the attitudes of the control group before and after, it can be said that the reason why their attitudes were even more negative was their travel in Turkey. However, it was also seen that there were positive changes in some attitudes (Anastapoulous, 1992). In addition, the attitudes that were positive before the travel did not become negative. The negative attitudes became even more negative.

In a study carried out with 82 Israelis who travelled to Egypt, Milman et al. (1990) revealed that tourism experiences had no effect on most of the attitudes towards Egypt and Egyptians. There was change in only 6 out of 33 attitude expressions due to tourism experience. Only one of these expressions changed in the positive direction. Attitudes towards Egypt were quite positive; only four expressions were negative, below the average.

In the study conducted by Pizam et al. (1991) on 24 American student tourists visiting Russia, it was seen that the participants' attitudes towards Russia were generally positive before travel. The overall satisfaction of the participants was high, and this prevented the participants from being negatively affected. Most of the negative attitudes towards Russia did not change. There was change in only five expressions. Only two out of five expressions were positive, and three of them changed in a negative direction.

Maoz (2010) interviewed 33 Israelis visiting Egypt and 29 Egyptians visiting Israel. According to the results of the interviews, there was no change in the attitudes of 69.3% of Israeli participants, and the attitudes of 26% changed in the positive direction. It was revealed that 60% of Egyptian tourists had great changes in their thoughts after the contact. At first, the Egyptians' attitudes toward Israelis were stronger and stronger, and it was seen that, after the contact, there were more positive changes in the attitudes of the Egyptians.

Gomez-Jacinto et al. (1999) tried to identify the factors that effected the attitude change by improving Fisher and Price's (1991) model. Gomez-Jacinto et al. (1999) tested the model with 164 French and Italian tourists. Only psychosocial motivation influenced intercultural interaction. In addition to tourist motivation, the prejudices of tourists towards Spanish people were influenced by holiday satisfaction, the amount of activities, intercultural interaction and quality of service. Holiday satisfaction was very effective in the positive change of attitudes towards Spanish people. In the change of attitude, tourism experiences are influential as well as the attitudes of people before they travel.

Conclusion and suggestions

In the study, the relationship between Allport's intergroup contact theory and tourism was examined in the context of tourism and social psychology in general. Although the optimal conditions suggested by Allport are not very effective in the tourism sector, the assumption that, where the groups are in contact with each other, relations will be more positive is acceptable in the tourism sector. In most of the studies presented in the literature, it was seen that there were positive changes in the attitudes of people participating in a tourism activity. However, each contact may not ensure a positive change. In this case, it is necessary to reveal the reasons for this. As Tomljenovic (2010) stated, many elements can be effective in changing the attitudes of tourists, such as the length of tourists' stay in the destination, the amount of events/activities, the holiday motivation of the tourist/purpose of the visit, holiday satisfaction of tourists, quality, familiarity, cultural distance and language of the destination, the intensity/power and direction of the attitude before the holiday, and tourists' personality traits (tolerance, ethnocentricity, etc.).

Therefore, it has been determined that the effects of tourism on societies are not only economic and sociocultural. The contribution of the tourism in eliminating prejudices and establishing national and international peace should be realized by governments and related institutions and organizations. Among the reasons for the occurrence of conflict in many countries today, there are the prejudices of societies and the lack of interaction that is caused by these prejudices. In this respect, seeing and using tourism as a means of peace will help to reduce prejudices, increase interaction and ensure peace.

Therefore, destination managers, local people, business managers and all other people who are in contact with tourists need to take steps to provide quality products and services to please tourists. Some important recommendations are given below for tourism-related institutions and organizations to provide quality services and to ensure more interaction between tourists and local people:

- Organize fairs, festivals, music and traditional dance events where tourists can spend time in the places they visit,
- Extend tour programs to longer periods,
- Increase the quality of service in tourism facilities and the quality of life in destinations,
- Destinations should give priority to tourist masses close to their own cultures,
- Raise awareness in local people about the effects of tourism.

This study has examined the relationship between tourism and prejudice in the context of Allport's intergroup contact theory in relation to social psychology and tourism. In future studies, the relationship between other theories of social psychology and tourism can be examined. By using quantitative and qualitative research methods, the social psychological effects of tourism can be determined. The results can be shared with sector representatives and local authorities to raise awareness on the subject.

References

Akis, S., Peristianis, N., & Warner, J. (1996). Residents' attitudes to tourism development: the case of Cyprus. *Tourism Management*, 17(7), 481–494.

Alaeddinoğlu, F. (2007). Van halkının turisti ve turizmi algılama şekli. *Coğrafi Bilimler Dergisi*, 5(1), 1–16.

Allport, G. W. (1979). *The Nature of Prejudice*. New York:: Perseus Book Publishing.

Amir, Y. (1969). Contact hypothesis in ethnic relations. *Psychological Bulletin*, 71(5), 319.

Amir, Y., & Ben-Ari, R. (1983). Cognitive cultural learning, intergroup contact and change in ethnic attitudes and relations. International Conference on Group Processes and Intergroup Conflict, Israel.

Anastasopoulos, P. G. (1992). Tourism and attitude change: Greek tourists visiting Turkey. *Annals of Tourism Research*, 19(4), 629–642.

Ap, J. (1992). Residents' perceptions on tourism impacts. *Annals of Tourism Research*, 19(4), 665–690.

Ap, J., & Crompton, J. L. (1993). Residents' strategies for responding to tourism impacts. *Journal of Travel Research*, 32(1), 47–50.

Aronson, E., Wilson, T. D., & Akert, R. M. (2012). *Sosyal psikoloji* (O. Gündüz, Çev.). Kaknüs Yayınları.

Boğan, E., & Sarışık, M. (2016). Yerel halkın turizm faaliyetlerine yönelik görüş ve algılamalarının belirlenmesi üzerine Alanya'da bir araştırma. *Kastamonu Üniversitesi iktisadi ve idari bilimler fakültesi dergisi*, (12), 325–342.

Bordens, K. S., & Horowitz, I. A. (2002). *Social Psychology* (2nd ed.). London: Lawrence Erlbaum.

Brida, J. G., Osti, L., & Barquet, A. (2010). Segmenting resident perceptions towards tourism a cluster analysis with a multinomial logit model of a mountain community. *International Journal of Tourism Research*, 12(5), 591–602.

Butler, R.W. (1980). The concept of a tourist area cycle of evolution: Implications for management of resources. *Canadian Geographer*, 24(1), 5–12.

Chen, H., & Rahman, I. (2018). Cultural tourism: An analysis of engagement, cultural contact, memorable tourism experience and destination loyalty, *Tourism Management*, 26, 153–163.

Crompton, J. L. (1979). Motivations for pleasure vacation. *Annals of Tourism Research*, 6(4), 408–424.

Çelik, S. (2017a). Does tourists perception of social distance towards the southeast people change thanks to tourism? I. International Congress on Social Sciences, Malaga, 584.

Çelik, S. (2017b). Turistlerin tolerans düzeyleri ve algıladıkları destinasyon memnuniyeti arasındaki ilişki, I. International Congress on Social Sciences, Malaga, 591–592.

Dann, G. M. (1981). Tourist motivation an appraisal. *Annals of Tourism Research*, 8(2), 187–219.

Dilek, S. E. (2016). Turist yerli etkileşimleri. In E. Duran & C. Aslan (Eds.) *Turizmin sosyal psikolojisi* (pp. 109–117). İstanbul: Paradigma.

Dörnyei, Z., & Csizér, K. (2005). The effects of intercultural contact and tourism on language attitudes and language learning motivation. *Journal of Language & Social Psychology*, 24(4), 327–357.

Duran, E., & Özkul, E. (2012). Residents' attitudes toward tourism development: A structural model via Akcakoca sample. *International Journal of Human Sciences*, 9(2), 500–520.

Fisher, R. J., & Price, L. L. (1991). International pleasure travel motivation and post vacation cultural attitude change. *Journal of Leisure Research*, 23, 193–208.

Franklin, A. (2003). *Tourism: An Introduction*. London: Sage.

Gamper, J. A. (1981). Tourism in Austria: A case study of the influence of tourism on ethnic relations. *Annals of Tourism Research*, 8(3), 432–446.

Goeldner, C. R., & Ritchie, J. R. B. (2009). *Tourism: Principles, Practices, Philosophy* (17th ed.). Hoboken, NJ: John Wiley.

Golzardi, F., Sarvaramini, S., Sadatasilan, K., & Sarvaramini, M. (2012). Residents' attitudes towards tourism development: A case study of Niasar, Iran. *Research Journal of Applied Sciences, Engineering & Technology*, 4(8), 863–868.

González, K. V., Verkuyten, M., Weesie, J., & Poppe, E. (2008). Prejudice towards Muslims in the Netherlands: Testing integrated threat theory. *British Journal of Social Psychology*, 47(4), 667–685.

Gomez-Jacinto, L., San Martin-Garcia, J., & Bertiche-Haud'Huyze, C. (1999). A model of tourism experience and attitude change. *Annals of Tourism Research*, 26(4), 1024–1027.

Göksu, T. (2007). *Sosyal psikoloji*. Ankara: Seçkin Yayıncılık.

Grothe, J. (1970). Attitude change of American tourists in the Soviet Union. Doctoral thesis, George Washington University.

Günlü, E., Özgen, H. K. Ş., Dilek, S. E., Kaygalak, S., Türksoy, S., & Lale, C. (2015), Turkish visitors in Armenia: Any changes in attitudes and perceptions? *Journal of Tourism & Hospitality Management*, 3(1), 29–43.

Gürbüz, A. (2002). Turizmin sosyal çevreye etkisi üzerine bir araştırma. *Teknoloji dergisi*, 5 (1–2), 49–59.

Gursoy, D., Kim, K., & Uysal, M. (2004). Perceived impacts of festivals and special events by organizers: An extension and validation. *Tourism Management*, 25(2), 171–181.

Jaspars, J., & Hewsone, M. (1982). Cross-cultural interaction, social attribution and inter-group relations. In S. Bochner (Ed.), *Cultures in Contact* (pp. 127–156). Oxford: Pergamon.

Joo, D., Tasci, A. D. A., Woosnam, K. M., Maruyama, N. U., Hollas, C. R., & Aleshinloye, K. D. (2018). Residents' attitude towards domestic tourists explained by contact, emotional solidarity and social distance. *Tourism Management*, 64, 245–257.

Joyce, N. (2017). *Intergroup Contact Theory. The International Encyclopedia of Intercultural Communication*. Wiley.

Kağıtçıbaşı, Ç. (2014). *Yeni insan ve insanlar: Sosyal psikolojiye giriş*. İstanbul: Evrim yayınları.

Kayaoğlu, A. (2011). Sosyal psikoloji nedir? In S. Ünlü, *Sosyal Pikoloji-I*, Anadolu Üniversitesi Yayını No: 2291, 2–19.

Lickorish, L. J., & Jenkins, C. L. (1997). *An Introduction to Tourism*. London: Routledge.

Lopez, M. F. B., Virto, R. N., Manzano, J. A., & Miranda, G. M. (2018). Residents' attitude as determinant of tourism sustainability: The case of Trujillo, *Journal of Hospitality & Tourism Management*, 35, 36–45.

Mansuroğlu, S. (2006). Turizm gelişmelerine yerel halkın yaklaşımlarının belirlenmesi: Akseki/Antalya örneği. *Akdeniz Üniversitesi Ziraat Fakültesi Dergisi*, 19(1), 35–46.

Maoz, D. (2010). Warming up peace: Encounter between Egyptian hosts and Israeli guests in Sinai. In O. Moufakkir & I. Kelly (Eds.), *Tourism, Progress and Peace* (pp. 65–82), Wallingford: UK: CABI.

Maruyama, N., & Woosnam, K. M. (2015). Residents' ethnic attitudes and support for ethnic neighborhood tourism: The case of a Brazilian town in Japan. *Tourism Management*, 50, 225–237.

Mathieson, A., & Wall, G. (1982). *Tourism, Economic, Physical and Social Impacts*. London: Longman.

Milman, A., Reichel, A., & Pizam, A. (1990). The impact of tourism on ethnic attitudes: The Israeli–Egyptian case. *Journal of Travel Research*, 29(2), 45–49.

Nyaupane, G. P., Teye, V., & Paris, C. (2016). Tourism and attitude change: The case of study abroad students. *Tourism Travel & Research Association: Advancing Tourism Research Globally*, 64, 221–227.

Pearce, P. L. (1980). A favorability–satisfaction model of tourists' evaluations. *Journal of Travel Research*, 19(1), 13–17.

Pearce, P. L. (1982). Tourists and their hosts: Some social and psychological effects of inter-cultural contact. In S. Bochner (Ed.), *Cultures in Contact* (pp. 199–221). Oxford: Pergamon.

Pernecky, T. (2015). Tourism, prejudice and societal conflict. In M. Lueck, J. Velvin, C. Eilzer & B. Eisenstein (Eds.), *The Social Side of Tourism: The Interface between Tourism, Society, and the Environment* (pp. 11–38). Frankfurt, Germany: Peter Lang Verlag.

Pettigrew, T. F. (1998). Intergroup contact theory. *Annual Review of Psychology*, 49(1), 65–85.

Pettigrew, T. F., & Tropp, L. R. (2006). A meta-analytic test of intergroup contact theory. *Journal of Personality & Social Psychology*, 90(5), 751.

Pettigrew, T. F., & Tropp, L. R. (2008). How does intergroup contact reduce prejudice? Meta-analytic tests of three mediators. *European Journal of Social Psychology*, 38(6), 922–934.

Pham, L. H., & Kayat, K. (2011). Residents' perceptions of tourism impact and their support for tourism development: The case study of Cuc Phuong National Park, Ninh Binh province, Vietnam. *European Journal of Tourism Research*, 4(2), 123–146.

Pizam, A., Jafari, J., & Milman, A. (1991). Influence of tourism on attitudes: US students visiting USSR. *Tourism Management*, 12(1), 47–54.

Pizam, A., Uriely, N., & Reichel, A. (2000). The intensity of tourist–host social relationship and its effects on satisfaction and change of attitudes: The case of working tourists in Israel. *Tourism Management*, 21(4), 395–406.

Pratt, S., & Liu, A. (2015). Does tourism really lead to peace? A global view. *International Journal of Tourism Research*, 18(1), 82–90.

Rátz, T. (2000). *The Socio-Cultural Impacts of Tourism Case of Lake Balaton*. Prague: Research Support Scheme.

Reisinger, Y., & Turner, L. W. (2003). *Cross-Cultural Behaviour in Tourism: Concepts and Analysis*. Oxford: Butterworth-Heinemann/Elsevier.

Rızaoğlu, B. (2012). *Turizm davranışı* (3rd ed.). Ankara: Detay.

Ruesch, M. (2011). A peaceful net? Intergroup contact and communicative conflict resolution of the Israel–Palestine conflict on Facebook. In A. Ternès (Ed.), *Probing the Boundaries* (pp. 13–31). Oxford: Inter-Disciplinary Press.

Sherif, M. (1966). *In Common Predicament*. Boston, MA: Houghton Mifflin

Sirakaya-Turk, E., Nyaupane, G., & Uysal, M. (2014). Guests and hosts revisited: Prejudicial attitudes of guests toward the host population. *Journal of Travel Research*, 53(3), 336–352.

Snaith, T., & Haley, A. (1999). Residents' opinions of tourism development in the historic city of York, England. *Tourism Management*, 20(5), 595–603.

Stangor, C. (2009). The study of stereotyping, prejudice, and discrimination within social psychology: A quick history of theory and research. In T. D. Nelson (Ed.), *Handbook of Prejudice, Stereotyping, and Discrimination* (pp. 1–22). New York: Psychology Press.

Tayfun, A., (2002). Turist yerli halk etkileşimi üzerine bir araştırma. *G.Ü. Ticaret ve Turizm Eğitim Fakültesi Dergisi*, 1, 1–12.

Tomljenovic, R. (2010). Tourism and intercultural understanding or contact hypothesis revisited. In O. Moufakkir & I. Kelly (Eds.), *Tourism, Progress and Peace* (pp. 17–34). Wallingford: UK: CABI.

Triandis, H. C., & Vassiliou, V. (1967). *A Comparative Analysis of Subjective Culture* (No. 43). Urbana: University of Illinois.

UNWTO. (2018). Global Code of Ethics for Tourism Ethics and Social Responsibility. Available at: http://ethics.unwto.org/en/content/global-code-ethics-tourism

Upchurch, R. S., & Teivane, U. (2000). Resident perceptions of tourism development in Riga, Latvia. *Tourism Management*, 21(5), 499–507.

Waitt, G. (2003). Social impacts of the Sydney Olympics. *Annals of Tourism Research*, 30(1), 194–215.

Wang, Y., Pfister, E. R., & Morais, B. D. (2006). Residents' attitudes toward tourism development: A case study of Washington, NC. In *Proceedings of the Northeastern Recreation Research Symposium*, pp. 411–418.

Weiler, B. (1989). The effects of international travel on tourist: Seeing and clearing methodological road-blocks, *Geojournal*, 19(3), 303–307.

Welds, K., & Dukes, R. (1985). Dimensions of personal change, coping styles, and self-actualization in a shipboard university. *Annals of Tourism Research*, 12(1), 113–119.

Wintersteiner, W., & Wohlmuther, C. (2014). Peace sensitive tourism: How tourism can contribute to peace. In C. Wohlmuther & W. Wintersteiner (Eds.), *International Handbook on Tourism and Peace* (pp. 31–61). Klagenfurt/Celovec, Austria: Drava.

Yilmaz, S. S., & Taşçı, A. D. (2015). Circumstantial impact of contact on social distance. *Journal of Tourism & Cultural Change*, 13(2), 115–131.

19

SOCIOCULTURAL IMPACTS OF TOURISM DEVELOPMENT ON HERITAGE SITES

Orhan Akova and Ozan Atsiz

Introduction

Tourism has grown rapidly, creating more investment and more jobs around the world. Now, more than a billion tourists travel to an international destination each year. One of the main motivations of this movement is the desire to explore cultural identities and cultural heritage sites. Cultural heritage sites are valued tourism assets that motivate travelers and distinguish destinations from others. It is important for these cultural heritage attractions to be protected and preserved as they are, because the tourist movement may spoil them. According to UNWTO (1998), tourism is evaluated as the *activities of persons travelling to and staying in places outside their usual environment for not more than one consecutive year for leisure, business and other purposes.* Also, it has been stated that tourism is a subset of travel. This movement is temporary, and tourists return to their normal place of work and residence. During their travelling and staying period, tourists expect their needs such as accommodation, food and beverages, facilities and so on to be catered for. These needs are satisfied by international or local tourism businesses. Together with their stay in the tourist destination region, this situation necessarily creates an interaction between local residents and tourists. The outcome of this relationship can be positive, such as opportunities for meeting interesting people, learning more about other nations, and improving language skills and quality of life, or can be negative, such as congestion, noise, drug abuse and lack of mutual confidence among people (Ratz, 2000).

Research has mostly been conducted into the sociocultural effects of tourism applied to various destinations. Findings obtained from these studies show that they differ between destinations. It is difficult to determine or measure the sociocultural impact of tourism as tourism can impact social and cultural changes directly or indirectly. Also, as stated in the tourism literature, the lack of a commonly used methodology prevents these impacts being clearly determined and measured. But these studies partly reveal the effects of tourism. This chapter will try to review the sociocultural effects of tourism using the perspective of previous studies conducted on heritage sites

Heritage sites and heritage tourism

Heritage sites are the most important attractions for tourists interested in experiencing authenticity, foreign cultures and their elements. Travelers visit heritage sites because of their unique, valued heritage, and these sites help them to know their self and boost their self-esteem and self-respect (World Bank, 1999; Li, 2003). Therefore, it can be concluded that cultural and heritage attractions have great potential to improve respect among differ-ent nations and can effectively promote destinations. Furthermore, they can offer favorable potential for local tourism improvement (van der Merwe & Rogerson, 2013). These heritage attractions can be promoted not only to local tourists but also to international (long-haul) tourists (Ivanovic & Saayman, 2013). Therefore, in the process of creating policy concerning tourism, heritage opportunities must be utilized locally and globally (Rogerson & van der Merwe, 2016). That means tourism policies should cover the cultural heritage opportunities both locally and globally

Heritage tourism is regarded as the most important niche market and more popular than other types of tourism (Chen & Chen, 2012; David & van der Merwe , 2016). Furthermore, it provides protection for the heritage attractions that sustain the local economy because of the collective responsibility that tourists feel for these elements (Nuryanti, 1996). Heritage tourism is a difficult concept to define (Li, Wu & Cai, 2008). There is little consensus on the definition of heritage tourism (Balcar & Pearce 1996, p. 203; Goh, 2010) Many definitions exist (Goh, 2010): nostalgia, romanticism, aesthetic pleasure and a sense of belongingness (Ashworth & Goodall, 1990), past images of history (Hewison, 1987), nostalgia and expe-rience of cultural landscapes (Zeppel & Hall 1992), landscapes, natural history, buildings, artifacts and cultural traditions (Prentice, 1993; Carter & Horneman, 2001), history, culture, wildlife and landscape (Sharpley, 1993), activities of rural tourism (Lane, 1994), sociocultural assets (Fyall & Garrod, 1998), and ethnicity, nationalism and global identity (Hitchcock & King, 2003). Heritage tourism can be defined as tourists' visits to a particular destination to experience the past, history, culture, traditions, arts and crafts, music, dance, aesthetics, sociocultural assets, ethnicity, authenticity and the objects or things that are related to herit-age. Heritage tourism can be classified into three groups. These are as follows (Jun, Nicholls & Vogt, 2004):

- Natural:
    - Landforms
    - Rural scenery
    - Flora and fauna

- Cultural:
    - Festivals
    - Arts/crafts
    - Traditional practices/products

- Built:
    - Historical buildings
    - Monuments
    - Industrial sites.

These categories, natural, cultural and built heritage, are so important for now and the future. Hence, heritage must be protected by stakeholders who have a role in the destination, such as local residents and tourist and destination managers. These categories have been extended by various authors (Perera, 2015). However, those generally accepted are listed as above. Besides, in the Nebraska Heritage Tourism Plan (2011), five clear principles have been put forward for good, sustainable heritage tourism. These are as follows:

- Collaborate
- Find the fit between community and tourism
- Make sites and programs come alive
- Focus on quality and authenticity
- Preserve and protect irreplaceable resources.

In heritage sites, local residents first expect to increase their income and to improve the community through tourism. Also, local residents expect investments, economic benefits which last a long time and infrastructure improvements to improve (Marschall, 2012). Local residents use their heritage elements of traditional rituals, dance, music and crafts in tourism and benefit from some economic gains (Günlü, Pırnar & Yağcı, 2009). However, when local residents benefit from the tourism industry, they actually interact with tourists, and an encounter happens with them first. This situation creates mutual influence, because tourists encounter a culture that they are unused to, and local residents interact with people that they do not know. Multiple studies have been conducted to measure and observe the impacts of these encounters (Bello, Neil, Lovelock & Xu, 2017; Eusébio & Carneiro, 2012; Marković & Klarić, 2015). But a few studies have investigated the impact on heritage sites (Okech, 2010; Rasoolimanesh, Roldán, Jaafar & Ramayah, 2017; Jimura, 2011; Nicholas, Thapa & Ko., 2009).

As heritage is the backbone of a tourist destination for local, regional and national development and identity owing to its cultural, environment and economic resources, it must be protected and developed sustainably. Therefore, it must be handled with an integrated approach among stakeholders (Bujdosó et al., 2015). This will provide economic benefits for the destination as well as local residents. This benefits local residents by protecting their heritage sites and sustains their heritage, which is tangible and intangible. This is so important because tourists desire to see authenticity in the destination and travel for it (Nicolaides, 2014).

Sociocultural impact of tourism

Apart from the economic and environmental impacts of tourism, there is also the sociocultural impact that causes positive or negative consequences in terms of social and cultural changes (Gjerald, 2005). The sociocultural impact of tourism has been defined by Pizam and Milman (1986, p. 29) as "the ways in which tourism is contributing to changes in value systems, individual behavior, family relationships, collective lifestyles, moral conduct, creative expressions, traditional ceremonies and community organization."

As stated above, tourism is a temporary relationship between local residents and tourists. Therefore, during a stay, some sociocultural impacts are revealed as a result of this interaction in the host society, including changes in value systems, individual behavior, family relationships, collective lifestyles, traditional ceremonies or community organization (Milman & Pizam, 1988). Also, the impacts that result from tourism are extremely important for tourism planning. The social impact of tourism is particularly important in order to acquire information from local communities (Ap, 1990).

Studies conducted on the sociocultural impacts of tourism have gradually increased. These can be classified into four main groups: host–guest interaction and relationship, sociocultural impacts of tourism in general, sociocultural impacts as perceived by local residents, and response to the impacts of tourism and adjustment strategies (Gjerald, 2005).

There are three main contexts for encounters between tourist and host: where the tourist is buying some good or is offered a service by the host, where they meet in any other place in a destination, and when they come face to face for the purpose of sharing information and ideas (de Kadt, 1979). Reisinger (2009) implied that social contact between tourists and hosts occurs usually at any tourist attractions and when tourists purchase goods or services from hosts. These contexts impact the results of the interaction taking place between tourists and host (Eusébio & Carneiro, 2012). Changes derived from this interaction in the host society's quality of life are revealed by two major factors, which are the tourist–host relationship and the development of the tourism industry (Ratz, 2000).

Encounters between different cultures in international tourism areas likely happen in terms of cross-cultural encounters, because a tourist who wonders about different cultures travels for this purpose and has contact with people who belong to those cultures (Chiemi, 2003). Besides, tourism, by definition, brings people together for a limited time in any destination in terms of the main characteristics of tourism, which are named the spatial and time aspects (Fennell, 2006). These characteristics provide an occurrence of the tourist–host interaction (Reisinger & Turner, 2003).

A number of features of the tourist–host relationship are characterized by various authors. These features differ in studies conducted in different destinations. They are listed below (UNESCO, 1975; Reisinger, 2009; Ronay, 2011; Jafari, 1986; de Kadt, 1979; Milman & Pizam, 1988):

- There is a transitory relationship, a lack of time and space, an inequality, and spontaneous encounters that occur between tourist and host society.
- As tourists generally stay in any destination for a short time, the relationship between them is not important. That means that there is no opportunity to improve their relationship.
- Before the development of tourism, the relationship was based on traditional hospitality in some destination. In the next phase of this development, this spontaneous hospitality turns into a commercial one, and those values are commercialized over time.
- Tourist–host interaction obviously leads to mistrust, exploitative behavior and deception. This, hence, impacts the host society substantially in terms of the sociocultural aspect.

One of the most important sociocultural impacts of tourism which is handled in tourism studies is regarded as the "demonstration effect"; it concerns visible differences between tourist and host and creates detrimental impacts on the socioculture of the host society (Mason, 2003). It usually occurs where interactions between tourist and host are relatively transitory, with a short-lived stay. Mathieson and Wall (1987) define the demonstration effect as people trying to imitate "the behaviors and spending patterns of others." On the other side, Xenos (1989) evaluates it as people copying their betters. In the light of this information, in tourism studies, it is defined as the host society copying tourists' behavior. In such a case, the hosts' behaviors change. But it is difficult to understand the demonstration effect in terms of how, when and why it occurred. Also, it must be noted that tourists can copy the host community's behavior patterns (Fisher, 2004). This concept is reinforced by Reisinger (2009) referring to local residents adapting the styles and manners of visiting tourists. Furthermore, the decision-making process of the demonstration effect has three basic propositions needed for it to exist. These are suggested to be (Fisher, 2004):

1   The behavior of tourists and hosts is initially different.
2   Behavioral patterns are transferred from one group to the other.
3   The imitators maintain the demonstrated behavior.

Apart from these effects, tourism can provide some improvements and changes in the quality of life, social structure and social organization of the local society (Ratz, 2000). Host communities are also affected by the tourism industry itself, as stated above. The tourism industry is believed to create the opportunity for new employment in the destination (Vroom, 1979; Kozak, Kozak & Kozak, 2017). However, because of the employment characteristic of tourism, the jobs are seasonal, lower-skilled or unskilled, the positions are temporary, and payments are lower and have no stability (Jolliffe & Farnsworth, 2003; Centre for Economics and Business Research, 2014; Barrett, 1987). The development of tourism can contribute to the destination's economy in terms of revenue, but this situation can impact or change utterly occupations in the destination or traditional work patterns such as those in agriculture. This adaptive process can be difficult for local society (Jayaprakashnarayana & Raghu, 2016). For instance, the existing agriculture in Kemer, located in Turkey, lost its workforce to tourism as a result of tourism development (Aykaç, 2009). Other important impacts of tourism development can be listed as follows (Marković & Klarić, 2015; Tsartas, 2004; Khadaroo & Seetanah, 2008; Milman & Pizam, 1988):

- Tourism creates some changes in the size of the host population and its demographic structure.
- Tourism provides mobility for women and young adults.
- Tourism development results in infrastructure development in the destination.
- Finally, tourism development can impact positively by improving the quality of life of local people.

All studies on tourism's sociocultural impacts should include all stakeholders and relevant parties concerned with the positive and negative effects of tourism from a sociocultural point of view. Therefore, taking into account the perceptions and attitudes of local people, the local population should benefit as much as possible from the positive effects, and the negative effects should be reduced.

A few models have been put forward about reactions of local residents' interactions with tourists. One of the most prominent and well known is known as Doxey's irridex or "irritation index" (Reisinger, 2009). According to this theory, a temporal sequence takes place in local communities with regard to tourists. It involves euphoria, apathy, irritation and finally antagonism. At the first level, there is an informal relationship and a sense of excitement and anticipation between them. Then, at the second level, tourists are seen as a source of income, and contacts between them become more formal. At the third level, the local community begins to be annoyed by the industry itself. At this level, visitors continue to increase, and investments continue to be made. Eventually, irritations are displayed, verbally and physically (Murphy & Murphy, 2004; Canavan, 2014).

Another model is Butler's (1980) tourist area life-cycle model. There is a relationship between Doxey's irridex and Butler's (1980) tourist area life-cycle model. This model identifies a few phases (exploration, involvement, development, consolidation, stagnation and decline or rejuvenation) in the evolution of tourism at any destination. Doxey's irridex and Butler's (1980) tourist area life-cycle model are evaluated under the extrinsic dimension with regard to theoretical and empirical aspects (Faulkner & Tideswell, 1997).

A continuum has been put forward by Ap and Crompton (1993) who reported four main strategies, which comprised embracement, tolerance, adjustment and withdrawal. Tourism creates positive and negative impacts, and, therefore, five strategies to cope with these results have been identified: resistance, retreatism, boundary maintenance, revitalization and adoption (Doğan, 1989). Also, the most significant contribution to this field is social exchange theory. Ap (1992) stated that this theory is the best and most relevant to measure the sociocultural impacts of tourism. It was first introduced by Emerson (1962). Ap (1992) applied it to tourism, where it explains impacts in the host community from tourism in terms of costs and benefits.

It has been stated in the Nebraska Heritage Tourism Plan (2011) that tourism protects cultural heritage values and development. Tourism policies should protect and develop cultural heritage values. Applying these policies, awareness is created, and local communities and tourists are informed by authorities. Thus, both are educated regarding cultural heritage values (Bello et al., 2017). When tourists visit a destination, they communicate with local people. Local people who have businesses are particularly obligated to learn their language. This situation encourages local people to learn a foreign language and creates new professions (Jack & Phipps, 2012; UNWTO, 2010). Besides, tourism provides gender mainstreaming between people and creates some improvements in women's rights. In particular, women participate in the division of labor and gain economic potential (UNWTO, 2010). Also, tourism increases not only economic awareness for women but also social and political terms changing traditional gender roles (Hemingway, 2004). Furthermore, tourism encourages the emergence of new social institutions. This happens especially in less-developed destinations (Milne & Ateljevic, 2001). Additionally, tourism improves recreational benefits (parks, playgrounds, sports fields, bike lanes, etc.) in a destination and presents leisure opportunities not only for tourists, but also for local residents (Cioban & Slusariuc, 2014).

On the other hand, tourism development changes the demographic structure of society, the age of the population and population location (UNWTO, 2012). In the destination, tourists are seen as wealthy people and are served by local people. However, not all local people participate in tourism. This creates a social imbalance between local people and changes the lifestyles of local people (Ronay, 2011). Tourism also creates cultural degeneration (Güzel, 2013), cultural diffusion, which refers to cultural elements between tourists and local people, cultural change (Reisinger, 2009) and cultural commercialization (Coronado, 2014). Furthermore, it causes an increased crime rate (Okech, 2010), hostility to foreigners (Reisinger, 2009), overcrowding (Gill & Williams, 1994) and language deterioration and corruption (Lytras & Papageorgiou, 2015).

Studies of sociocultural impacts of tourism development on heritage sites

Heritage sites have been evaluated as of great importance for tourism by academics, government and industry (Okech, 2010). Tourism based on the use of heritage sites has been increasing in developing countries and is taken into consideration by destination stakeholders. In general, some governments use these sites to decrease alleviation and create new jobs in these countries (Lapeyre, 2011). This is so important for a country which wishes to decrease statistics related to these situations. As tourism generates employment, large-scale revenues, exchange earnings and so on, the economic benefit is obvious and inevitable. Also, tourism stimulates the improvement and conservation of cultural heritage areas (Bello et al., 2017). Therefore, measuring the sociocultural impacts of tourism is crucial for these destinations. However, limited studies have directly studied heritage destinations.

A study by Okech (2010) was concerned with the sociocultural impacts of tourism from the communities' perspective in two heritage sites, Lamu (Kenya) and Zanzibar Islands. In this study, surveys, participant observation, existing literature and short informal interviews were used in a mixed methodological approach. A total of 220 sample sets and a survey were applied to adult family residents. The main results gained from the study were as follows (Okech, 2010):

- The majority of the participants (85%) had dwelt on the islands for more than 15 years (Lamu), and 45% of them were employed full time in tourism businesses, 30% part time, and the rest were running their own establishments. Hence, attitudes to tourism were positive, and nearly 70% of them favored the presence of tourists in the destination.
- On the two islands, the residents did not think that tourism deteriorated the image of the islands, with results of 6% in Lamu and 5% in Zanzibar. In other words, there was no difference between them.
- Social benefits included positive outputs toward local tourism and traditional lifestyles.
- Residents who dwelt on both Lamu and Zanzibar (18%) wanted to increase the number of tourists. However, 14% in Lamu and 15% in Zanzibar preferred not to increase it.
- On both islands, residents had a significant level of control over destination management, and residents in Lamu (73%) and residents in Zanzibar (64%) were aware that these destinations are World Heritage Sites.
- Participation in tourism varied between residents. Some of them implied that the government should encourage participation in tourism facilities. Others stated that it should be dependent on the government.
- Residents had a great deal of knowledge about their ecosystems.
- Residents thought that costs of living increased as a result of tourism.
- Residents were worried about negative impacts of tourism as a result of development. They thought that an increase in crime and vandalism, feeling less safe, degradation of their culture and heritage and traffic problems had been revealed.
- A measurement related to tourism management concluded that men (90%) dominated committees and groups.
- It was stated that local residents were perceived to improve some changes, such as cost of land, employment opportunities, cultural identity, standard of living, conservation of old buildings, littering and cultural facilities.
- It was concluded that an increase in cost of living, noise, crime and congestion were perceived to have been revealed by local residents.

In summary, the research by Okech (2010) suggested positive and negative sociocultural impacts from tourism. These impacts were revealed over time, and benefits were perceived by local residents. At this point, it can be said that there is support for Doxey's idea. Also, it is known generally that tourism benefits women in areas such as entrepreneurship and employment. However, in this study, women were not dominant in tourism management committees and groups. Therefore, it can be said that there is a gender difference in heritage sites. But it varies between destinations. In general, residents of heritage sites are aware of their culture and ecosystems and they resist some changes to their value systems.

In a study carried out to explore impacts of tourism in cultural and heritage sites by Gnanapala and Sandaruwani (2016), data were collected in semi-structured interviews, focused group discussions, documents and participant observation, and secondary data were obtained from online media. It was carried out in the Sacred City of Anuradhapura (1982), the Ancient City of Polonnaruwa (1982), the Golden Temple of Dambulla (1991), the Ancient City of Sigiriya (1982), the Sacred City of Kandy (1988) and the Old Town of Galle and its fortifications (1988). Findings obtained from the research process concluded that there were positive and negative impacts of tourism in terms of general impacts. Positive impacts are considered as income generation, employment generation, development of cottage and supportive industries, support for regional development such as road networks, water, electricity, safety and security, and so on. Negative impacts are listed such as over-concentration on tourism, conflicts of interests, unauthorized constructions and modifications, inappropriate behavior of tourists, misinterpretations through guiding, and poor site management and site facility management. In this study, the authors evaluated the general impacts of tourism and while the economic benefits were found to be positive, the sociocultural impacts of tourism were found to be negative. These effects are likewise revealed in the study by Nkwanyana (2012).

Ongkhluap (2012) measured the perceptions of the host community in terms of tourism impacts on the Ayutthaya World Heritage Site. The evaluation in this study concerned economic and sociocultural values. It was concluded that the community desired to develop heritage conservation via tourism, such as the enhancement of a good community image and the enhancement of the conservation of historical buildings and archaeological remains, and the study confirmed that tourism improves community members' quality of life. They stated that tourism should be managed and improved. Rasoolimanesh et al. (2017) investigated residents' perceptions of tourism development comparing differences between rural and urban World Heritage Sites. The study was carried out in two areas, rural Lenggong and urban George Town World Heritage Sites in Malaysia. The results of the study considered the positive and negative impacts of tourism associated with economic gain, community involvement, environmental attitude and community attachment. Positive impacts resulted in economic benefit, and locals perceived that tourism increased their standard of living. Among the negative impacts, one indicator of sociocultural impacts related to an increasing rate of crime due to tourism was revealed. They did not think tourism caused an increase in the rate of crime.

A study carried out in Mardin, located in Turkey, put forward perceived impacts of tourism development at cultural heritage sites. According to the results of the study, economic benefit, environmental problems and preservation of the heritage site are the effects of tourism development (Gündüz & Erdem, 2010). Akova (2006) conducted a study to determine residents' perceptions of and attitudes to tourism impacts on two different dates, in 2001 and 2003, in a newly developing cultural heritage destination in Cumalıkızık, Turkey. In the study, economic benefits, social cost, cultural enhancement and damage to the environment were determined as impact factors. In the results of the study, the factor of social cost perception varied between the two dates. In 2001, it was seen that those who do not work in tourism, those with a high average age, those who are native to Cumalıkızı, those who do not have contact with tourists, those with a low education level and males negatively perceived the social cost of tourism. In 2003, there were no significant differences between the social factors and the education-level variables. However, in 2003, there were significant differences between the social factors during the period of living in the region. Those who had a high average age in 2003 and who lived longer in the region, those who had no contact with tourists and those who did not work in tourism businesses were perceived as negative about all factors related to the social cost of tourism. Also, the factor of cultural enhancement perception varied between the two dates. It was revealed that, in 2001, those who had a higher level of education, those who had contact with tourists, and those who worked in tourism businesses positively perceived one or more of the factors of cultural enhancement. In 2003, those who had a higher average age, those who had a higher education level, those who worked in tourism businesses, and those who had contact with tourists perceived cultural enhancement positively. In 2003, there were differences in perceptions compared with 2001. In 2003, there was no significant difference in the perception of cultural enhancement factors among locals, but there was a significant difference between those with higher age averages and cultural enhancement factors. In this study, it was revealed that the perception of the social cost and cultural enhancement effects of tourism varies depending on the development level and demographic factors, and the perception of demographic factors may be affected by the level of development of the destination at the time.

Among these studies, only the study conducted by Okech (2010) directly examined the sociocultural impacts of tourism. In the literature, authors analyzed the general impacts of tourism at heritage sites, such as a mixture of cultural, economic and enviromental impacts. These are studies measured indirectly perceived impacts or interaction of tourist and local host encounters.

Conclusions

This chapter aims to reveal the sociocultural impacts of tourism development in heritage sites. Tourism is an important industry in the world and creates many economic benefits for countries and regions, and communities also benefit from tourism. On the other hand, the movement of people from one place to another creates some positive and some negative impacts for those concerned. These effects need to be managed for the sustainability of destinations. The sociocultural impacts of tourism are widely researched by academicians within the scope of the overall effects of tourism. But there are limited studies that focus on the sociocultural impacts of tourism. The sociocultural impact of tourism has been defined by Pizam and Milman (1986, p. 29) as "the ways in which tourism is contributing to changes in value systems, individual behavior, family relationships, collective lifestyles, moral conduct, creative expressions, traditional ceremonies and community organization." The sociocultural impacts of tourism cover these changes in a destination.

Sociocultural impacts are revealed as a result of interaction in the host society and include changes in value systems, individual behavior, family relationships, collective lifestyles, traditional ceremonies and community organization. Tourist–host interaction obviously can lead to mistrust, exploitative behavior and deception. This, hence, impacts substantially on the host society from a sociocultural point of view. Changes derived from this interaction in the host society's quality of life are revealed by two major factors, which are the tourist–host relationship and the development of the tourism industry. Tourism can provide some improvements and changes in quality of life, social structure and social organization of local society, family relationships and lifestyles, improve education in the region, develop a tolerant environment, aid progress in women's rights, improve leisure time activities and recreational benefits, develop awareness of historical and cultural values, lead to foreign language learning, create new professions and cause the emergence of new social institutions. On the other hand, it causes changes in the size of the host population and its demographic structure and lifestyles, increases imbalances between social classes, creates cultural diffusion, cultural pollution, cultural degeneration and cultural change, can increase foreign hostility and crime rates, and can cause cultural commercialization, overcrowding, deterioration in local traditions, language deterioration and destruction of traditional sectors.

Development of tourism can contribute to destination economies in terms of revenue, but this situation can utterly change occupations in the destination or traditional work patterns, such as in agriculture. This adaptive process can be difficult for the local society, and this change can also affect the sociocultural structure of the local community.

One of the most important sociocultural impacts of tourism handled in tourism studies is regarded as the "demonstration effect," which is interested in visible differences between tourist and host and creates detrimental impacts on the socioculture of the host society.

Heritage is an important part of a destination culture and attracts tourists with its unique cultural values. As the local heritage become part of a destination, undesired consequences may threaten heritage sites' sustainability, and, because of pressure on cultural resources and deterioration in the destination, residents may not support tourism development. Heritage site residents use their heritage elements, traditional rituals, dances, music and crafts in tourism and benefit from some economic gains (Günlü et al., 2009). However, when local residents benefit from the tourism industry, they actually interact with tourists, and an encounter happens first between them. This situation creates mutual influence, because tourists encounter an unfamiliar culture, and local residents interact with people that they do not know. Multiple studies have been conducted to measure and observe these encounter impacts. According to studies conducted in heritage sites, the negative sociocultural effects of tourism development are overconcentration on tourism, conflicts of interests, increase in cost of land, unauthorized construction and modifications, inappropriate behavior of tourists, misinterpretations through guiding, poor site management and site facility management, an increase in crime and vandalism, feeling less safe, degradation of culture and heritage, and traffic problems, and increases in cost of living, noise and congestion. On the other hand, the positive effects of tourism development are the desire to develop heritage conservation via tourism, such as the enhancement of a good community image, the enhancement of the conservation of historical buildings and archaeological remains, improvement in quality of life, income generation, employment generation, development of cottage and supportive industries, support for regional development such as road networks, water, electricity, safety and security, and so on, cultural identity, standard of living, littering and cultural facilities. Also, it can be emphasized that the sociocultural impacts of tourism vary depending on the development level and demographic factors, and the perception of demographic factors may be affected by the level of development of the destination at the time. These studies conducted in heritage sites show that tourism development improves and conserves cultural heritage areas and their infrastructure and develops quality of life at the destination. On the other hand, degradation of the culture and heritage and traffic problems, poor management, increases in cost of living, noise, crime and congestion are the main negative affects which local residents perceive from tourism development.

As a result, the sociocultural effects of tourism development in heritage sites are similar to those obtained from studies conducted in other areas. However, those living in these cultural heritage sites perceive that tourism development will protect the cultural heritage, preserve old structures and raise living standards. Cultural areas are of great importance in terms of human history. However, tourism activities that develop in cultural heritage sites cause both positive and negative effects. For this reason, it is necessary to protect cultural heritage sites and preserve them for future generations. The protection of cultural heritage and the achievement of the sociocultural and economic development of people living in cultural heritage areas depend on the adoption of sustainable tourism. Within the scope of sustainable tourism activities, it is possible to reduce the adverse effects of tourism on heritage sites. New business areas, employment opportunities, restoration of old buildings, and infrastructure and superstructure renewal in the heritage sites thanks to tourism development may change the public's point of view about tourism development for a certain period in a positive way. But, when the negative effects arise, residents' attitudes will become negative. For this reason, tourism development needs to be developed in line with sustainable tourism principles. For this, it is important for all stakeholders to participate in the tourism planning process to be carried out on tourism development. Also, the sociocultural effects of tourism development in heritage sites need to be studied more widely to develop an understanding of sustainable tourism in heritage sites.

References

Akova, O. (2006). Yerel halkın turizmin etkilerini algılamalarına ve tutumlarına yönelik bir araştırma. *Akademik İncelemeler Dergisi*, 1 (2), 1–34.

Ap, J. (1990). Residents' perceptions research on the social impacts of tourism. *Annals of Tourism Research*, 17 (4), 610–616.

Ap, J. (1992). Residents' perceptions on tourism impacts. *Annals of Tourism Research*, 19 (4), 665–690.

Ap, J., & Crompton, J. L. (1993). Residents' strategies for responding to tourism impacts. *Journal of Travel Research*, 32 (1), 47–50.

Ashworth, G., & Goodall, B. (1990). Tourist images: Marketing considerations, in B. Goodall, & G. Ashworth (Eds.), *Marketing in the Tourism Industry*, pp. 213–233. London: Routledge.

Aykaç, A. (2009). *Yeni işler, Yeni İşçiler: Turizm Sektöründe Emek*. İstanbul: İletişim Yayınları.

Balcar, M., & Pearce, G. (1996). Heritage tourism on the west coast of New Zealand. *Tourism Management*, 17 (1), 203–212.

Barrett, R. (1987). Tourism employment in Montana: quality versus quantity? *Western Wildlands*, 13 (2), 18–21.

Bello, F., Neil, C., Lovelock, B., & Xu, F. (2017). Local residents' perceptions of socio-cultural impacts of tourism in Mangochi, Malawi. *Advances in Hospitality & Tourism Research*, 5 (1), 1–22.

Bujdosó, Z. D., Tőzsér, A., Kovács, G., Major-Kathi, V., Uakhitova, G., Katona, P., et al. (2015). Basis of heritagization and cultural tourism development. *Procedia-Social & Behavioral Sciences*, 188, 307–315.

Butler, R. W. (1980). The concept of a tourist area cycle of evolution: Implications for management of resources. *Canadian Geographer/Le Géographe canadien*, 24 (1), 5–12.

Canavan, B. (2014). Beyond Doxey, beyond Butler: Building upon insights in small island tourism research to extend tourism theory. British Academy of Management Conference. Belfast, NI.

Carter, R., & Horneman, L. (2001). Is there a market for heritage tourism? *Bulletin of Australian Institute for Marine Archaeology*, 25, 61–68.

Centre for Economics and Business Research. (2014). *Understanding the Travel and Tourism Labour Market*. London: Association of British Travel Agents.

Chen, C. F., & Chen, P. C. (2012). Exploring tourists' stated preferences for heritage tourism services—The Case of Tainan City, Taiwan. *Tourism Economics*, 18 (2), 457–464.

Chiemi, Y. (2003). *Tourist Encounters with Other Tourists*. Queensland: James Cook University.

Cioban, G. L., & Slusariuc, G. C. (2014). The effect of leisure time on touristic resources and on the quality of life. *Ecoforum Journal*, 3 (1). www.ecoforumjournal.ro/index.php/eco/article/view/91

Coronado, G. (2014). Selling culture? Between commoditisation and cultural control in indigenous alternative tourism. *Pasos. Revista de Turismo y Patrimonio Cultural*, 12 (1), 11–28.

David, C., & van der Merwe, C. D. (2016). Tourist guides' perceptions of cultural heritage tourism in South Africa. *Bulletin of Geography. Socio-economic Series*, 34, 117–130.

de Kadt, E. (1979). *Tourism—Passport to Development? Perspectives on the Social and Cultural Effects of Tourism in Developing Countries*. New York: Oxford University Press.

Doğan, H. Z. (1989). Forms of adjustment: Sociocultural impacts of tourism. *Annals of tourism research*, 16 (2), 216–236.

Emerson, R. M. (1962). Power-dependence relations. *Annals Review of Sociology*, 27 (1), 31–41.

Eusébio, C. A., & Carneiro, M. J. (2012). Determinants of tourist–host interactions: An analysis of the university student market. *Journal of Quality Assurance in Hospitality & Tourism*, 13 (2), 123–151.

Faulkner, B., & Tideswell, C. (1997). A framework for monitoring community impacts of tourism. *Journal of Sustainable Tourism*, 5 (1), 3–28.

Fennell, D. A. (2006). Evolution in tourism: The theory of reciprocal altruism and tourist–host interactions. *Current Issues in Tourism*, 9 (2), 105–124.

Fisher, D. (2004). The demonstration effect revisited. *Annals of Tourism Research*, 31 (2), 428–446.

Fyall, A., & Garrod, B. (1998) Heritage tourism: At what price? *Managing Leisure*, 3 (4), 213–228

Gill, A., & Williams, P. (1994). Managing growth in mountain tourism communities. *Tourism Management*, 15 (3), 212–220.

Goh, E. (2010). Understanding the heritage tourist market segment. *International Journal of Leisure & Tourism Marketing*, 1 (3), 257–270.

Gjerald, O. (2005). Sociocultural impacts of tourism: A case study from Norway. *Journal of Tourism & Cultural Change*, 3 (1,)36–58.

Gnanapala, W. A., & Sandaruwani, J. A. (2016). Impacts of tourism development in cultural and heritage sites: An empirical investigation. *International Journal of Economics & Business Administration*, 2 (6), 68–78.

Gündüz, E., & Erdem, R. (2010). The perceived impacts of tourism development at cultural heritage sites—Mardin sample. Urban Transformation: Controversies, Contrasts & Challenges, IPHS 14th Biennial Conference, Isanbul, pp. 1–9.

Günlü, E., Pırnar, İ., & Yağcı, K. (2009). Preserving cultural heritage and possible impacts on regional development: Case of Izmir. *International Journal of Emerging & Transition Economies*, 2 (2), 213–229.

Güzel, F. Ö. (2013). Tourism as a paradox creative sector from socio-cultural perspective: A sociological analysis on Dalyan destination. *Journal of Human Sciences*, 10 (1), 780–794.

Hemingway, S. (2004). The impact of tourism on the human rights of women in South East Asia. *International Journal of Human Rights*, 8 (3), 275–304.

Hewison, R. (1987). *The Heritage Industry: Britain in a Climate of Decline*. London: Methuen.

Hitchcock, M., & King, V. (2003). Discourses with the past: Tourism and heritage in South East Asia. *Indonesia & Malay World*, 31 (89), 2–15.

Ivanovic, M., & Saayman, M. (2013). South Africa calling cultural tourists. *African Journal for Physical Health Education, Recreation & Dance*, 19, 138–154.

Jack, G., & Phipps, A. (2012). Tourism. In J. Jackson (Ed.), *The Routledge Handbook of Language and Intercultural Communication* (pp. 537–551). Abingdon, UK: Routledge.

Jafari, J. (1986). A systemic view of sociocultural dimensions of tourism. In: *President's Commission on American Outdoors* (pp. 33–50). Washington, DC: United States Travel and Tourism Administration.

Jayaprakashnarayana, G., & Raghu, A. (2016). *Tourism Management Philosophies, Principles and Practices*. Hyderabad: Zenon Academic Publications.

Jimura, T. (2011). The impact of World Heritage Site designation on local communities—A case study of Ogimachi, Shirakawamura, Japan. *Tourism Management* , 32 (2), 288–296.

Jolliffe, L., & Farnsworth, R. (2003). Seasonality in tourism employment: Human resource challenges. *International Journal of Contemporary Hospitality Management*, 15 (6), 312–316.

Jun, S. H., Nicholls, S., & Vogt, C. (2004). Heeding the call for heritage tourism: More visitors want an 'experience'in their vacations–something a historical park can provide. *Parks & Recreation*, 39 (9), 38–49.

Khadaroo, J., & Seetanah, B. (2008). The role of transport infrastructure in international tourism development: A gravity model approach. *Tourism Management*, 29 (5), 831–840.

Kozak, N., Kozak, M., & Kozak, M. (2017). *Genel Turizm İlkeler Ve Kavramlar*. Ankara: Detay Yayıncılık.

Lane, B. (1994). Sustainable rural tourism strategies: A tool for development and conservation. *Journal of Sustainable Tourism*, 2 (1/2), 102–111.

Lapeyre, R. (2011). The Grootberg lodge partnership in Namibia: Towards poverty alleviation and empowerment for long-term sustainability? *Current Issues in Tourism*, 14 (3), 221–234.

Li, Y. (2003). Heritage tourism: The contradictions between conservation and change. *Tourism & Hospitality Research*, 4 (3), 247–261.

Li M., Wu B., & Cai, L. (2008). Tourism development of world heritage sites in China: A geographic perspective. *Tourism Management*, 29 (2), 308–319.

Lytras, P., & Papageorgiou, A. (2015). *Tourism That Hurts: The Invisible and Defamatory Side of Tourism*. Athens: Papazisis.

Marković, I., & Klarić, Z. (2015). Attitudes of local population of tourism impacts on destination sustainability—Case of Croatia. *Turizam*, 19 (3), 98–110.

Marschall, S. (2012). Sustainable heritage tourism: The Inanda Heritage Route and the 2010 FIFA World Cup. *Journal of Sustainable Tourism*, 20 (5), 721–736.

Mason, P. (2003). *Tourism Impacts, Planning and Management*. Oxford: Elsevier, Butterworth-Heinemann.

Mathieson, A., & Wall, G. (1987). *Tourism: Economic, Physical, and Social Impacts*. Harlow, UK: Longman.

Milman, A., & Pizam, A. (1988). Social impacts of tourism on central Florida. *Annals of Tourism Research*, 15 (2), 191–204.

Milne, S., & Ateljevic, I. (2001). Tourism, economic development and the global–local nexus: theory embracing complexity. *Tourism Geographies*, 3 (4), 369–393.

Murphy, P. E., & Murphy, A. E. (2004). *Strategic Management for Tourism Communities: Bridging the Gaps*. Clevedon, UK: Channel View Publications.

Nebraska Heritage Tourism Plan. (2011). *Nebraska Heritage Tourism Plan*. Retrieved April 4, 2018, from govdocs.nebraska.gov/epubs/H6000/B027-2011.pdf

Nicholas, L., Thapa, B., & Ko, Y. (2009). Residents' perspectives of a World Heritage Site: The Pitons Management Area, St. Lucia. *Annals of Tourism Research* , 36 (3), 390–412.

Nicolaides, A. (2014). Authenticity and the tourist's search for being. *African Journal of Hospitality, Tourism and Leisure*, 3 (1), 1–11.

Nkwanyana, M. S. (2012). *The Potential of Cultural Heritage Tourism as a Driver of Rural Development in the Zululand District Municipality*. Doctoral dissertation, University of Zululand.

Nuryanti, W. (1996). Heritage and postmodern tourism. *Annals of Tourism Research*, 23 (2), 249–260.

Okech, R. (2010). Socio-cultural impacts of tourism on World Heritage sites: Communities' perspective of Lamu (Kenya) and Zanzibar Islands. *Asia Pacific Journal of Tourism Research*, 15 (3), 339–351.

Ongkhluap, S. (2012). Tourism impacts on the Ayutthaya World Heritage Site: Measuring the perceptions of the host community. *Journal of International & Thai Tourism*, 8 (1), 31–55.

Perera, K. (2015). The role of museums in cultural and heritage tourism for sustainable economy in developing countries. Colombo: Regional Centre for Strategic Studies.

Pizam, A., & Milman, A. (1986). The social impacts of tourism. *Tourism Recreation Research*, 11 (1), 29–33.

Prentice, R. (1993). *Tourism and Heritage Attractions*. London: Routledge.

Rasoolimanesh, S. M., Roldán, J. L., Jaafar, M., & Ramayah, T. (2017). Factors influencing residents' perceptions toward tourism development: Differences across rural and urban world heritage sites. *Journal of Travel Research*, 56 (6), 760–775.

Ratz, T. (2000). Residents' perceptions of the socio-cultural impacts of tourism at Lake Balaton, Hungary. In G. Richards & D. Hall (Eds.), *Tourism and Sustainable Community Development* (pp. 36–47). London: Routledge.

Reisinger, Y. (2009). *International Tourism: Cultures and Behavior*. Hungary: Butterworth-Heinemann-Elsevier.

Reisinger, Y., & Turner, L. (2003). *Cross-Cultural Behavior in Tourism*. Oxford: Elsevier Butterworth Heinemann.

Rogerson, C. M., & van der Merwe, C. D. (2016). Heritage tourism in the Global South: Development impacts of the cradle of humankind world heritage site, South Africa. *Local Economy*, 31 (1–2), 234–248.

Ronay, S. (2011). *Turizm Bir Sistem Analizi*. Ankara: Detay Yayıncılık.

Sharpley, R. (1993) *Tourism and Leisure in the Countryside*. Huntington, UK: ELM Publications.

Tsartas, P. (2004). Tourism development in Greek insular and coastal areas: Sociocultural changes and crucial policy issues. In B. Bramwell, *Coastal Mass Tourism: Diversification and Sustainable Development in Southern Europe* (pp. 68–84). Clevedon, UK: Channel View Publications.

UNESCO. (1975). The effects of tourism on socio-cultural values. *Annals of Tourism Research*, 4 (2), 74–105.

UNWTO. (1998). *Community Methodology on Tourism Statistics*. Luxembourg: European Union.

UNWTO. (2010). *Global Report on Women in Tourism 2010*. New York: UNWTO.

UNWTO. (2012). *Demographic Change and Tourism*. New York: UNWTO.

Van der Merwe, C. D., & Rogerson, C. M. (2013). Industrial heritage tourism at the "big hole", Kimberley, South Africa. *African Journal for Physical Health Education, Recreation & Dance*, 2, 155–171.

Vroom, J. A. (1979). Employment opportunity through tourism. *The Tourist Review*, 34 (3), 10–11.

World Bank. (1999). *Sustainable Tourism and Cultural Heritage: A Review of Development Assistance and Its Potential to Promote Sustainability*. Washington, DC: World Bank.

Xenos, N. (1989). *Scarcity and Modernity*. London: Routledge.

Zeppel, H., & Hall, C. (1992). Arts and heritage tourism. In B. Weiler & C. Hall (Eds.), *Special Interest Tourism* (pp. 47–68). London: Belhaven.

20

SOCIOECONOMIC IMPACTS OF TOURISM ON THE LOCAL COMMUNITY

Nkhata Bay district, Malawi

Grace Kamanga and Eugenio Njoloma

Introduction

Tourism has been one of the fastest growing industries in the world and it has emerged as a powerful change agent in terms of its economic contributions to local communities. Yet, as Nunkoo and Ramkissoon (2007) note, the industry is riddled with considerable social, economic, and environmental challenges for local communities. In addition to causing environmental damage and shaping cultural attitudes, the industry tends to benefit business owners and a few individuals in the community while restricting the majority of the local people's access to the very resources they used to live on before tourism development (Wattanakuljarus & Coxhead, 2008). Moreover, "many states and local governments attempt to optimise economic benefits [of tourism] with little regard to the social and environmental cost associated with tourism expansion" (Allen, Long, Perdue, & Kieselbach, 1988: 16). This is exacerbated by the increased tendency among most tourists to seek higher-standard facilities and products, which makes it hard for most people in the local communities to cope (Tourism Concern, 2000).

To appreciate the impact of tourism on a local community, there is need to consider economic, social, and environmental factors, which constitute the triple bottom line approach commonly used in tourism sustainability studies (Andersson & Lundberg, 2013; Prayag, Hosany, Nunkoo, & Alders, 2013). This approach helps in establishing the extent to which local communities benefit from or are affected by various tourism developments. In doing so, however, it is critical to recognize differences in terms of socioeconomic well-being and tourism's effects on perceptions and attitudes between local communities in developed and developing countries. This is in cognizance of the fact that "the factors that influence residents' perceptions and attitudes towards tourism, as well as the nature and the extent of impact, are likely to be different between developed and developing regions" (Sirakaya, Teye, & Sönmez, 2002: 58).

This chapter provides a context of a local community in a developing country. In particular, it focuses on Nkhata Bay district in Malawi, as it is one of the three most visited lakeshore tourist destinations in the country. Although the Nkhata Bay Socioeconomic Profile (Malawi Government, 2018) indicates the growing potential of tourism in lifting the district's socioeconomic level, the destination exudes a murky socioeconomic profile in comparison with other lakeshore tourist destinations in the country. This is compounded by the absence of significant evidence in support of socioeconomic benefits of the tourism industry to the local community in the district. This chapter, thus, not only reveals the role of individual destinations in constructing the face of the tourism industry in Malawi, but, importantly, also serves to inform the industry's socioeconomic contribution on local communities.

The significance of local communities to the tourism industry does not require special emphasis. As Ap (1992) contends, they remain central in influencing the success or failure of the tourism industry. In particular, local communities can enhance the success of tourism when they participate in the planning, development, and operation of tourist products. But, in addition, their overall friendliness to tourists can help in propping up the industry. As such, any intentional or spontaneous attempt to marginalize their significance can possibly discourage the tourism industry. This becomes apparent when local communities oppose tourism or display hostile behaviours or attitudes towards tourists. As Knox (1982: 77) observes, "the tourist may have his [or her] vacation spoiled or enhanced by the resident. The resident may have his [or her] daily life enriched or degraded by the unending flow of tourists". It is, perhaps, for this reason that Fallon and Schofield (2006) maintain that tourists' favourable attraction depends on the friendliness, honesty, and hospitality of the residents. As such, the "balance of residents' perceptions of the costs and benefits of tourism is a major factor in tourist satisfaction and is, therefore, vital for the success of the tourism industry" (Andriotis & Vaughan, 2003: 172).

The assessment of a local community's perceptions and attitudes about the socioeconomic contributions of tourism is, thus, key to unlocking the enigma about the impact of tourism on a local community. This is particularly important because "it can facilitate policies which minimize the potential negative impacts of tourism development and maximize its benefits leading to community development and greater support for tourism" (Stylidis, Biran, Sit, & Szivas, 2014: 1). The assessment is aided by social exchange theory (SET), which posits that perceptions about the impacts of tourism are influenced by the extent to which the indigenous populations benefit from tourism (McGehee & Andereck, 2009). This forms the basis for the local community's support of or opposition to the initiative. As McGehee and Andereck (2009) contend, tourism is regarded as a necessary evil by those who directly benefit from it. Yet there are often fears that the more the residents become overly dependent on tourism, the more they develop negative associations with the industry (Williams & Lawson, 2001; Pizam, 1978).

This chapter is divided into five sections. The following section provides the empirical setting followed by a methodological approach. Then, a theoretical exploration of SET is made. Subsequently, the chapter explains factors that shape the perceptions and attitudes of local communities towards tourism. Thereafter, a discussion of the socioeconomic impacts of the tourism industry in Nkhata Bay is followed by a conclusion.

Empirical setting

Nkhata Bay is one of the 28 districts of Malawi on the shores of Lake Malawi, in the country's northern region. The district is endowed with vast and unique natural features which makes it one of the country's premier tourist destinations (Malawi Government, 2018). Tourist attractions in the area include, for example, Lake Malawi, culture and heritage, forest reserves and plantations, hot springs, and lodging and conference facilities (Malawi Government, 2017). According to the 2008 Housing and Population census, the total population for the district is 215,789 and is mostly rural (Malawi Government, 2009). As with many districts of Malawi, the majority of the population lives below the poverty line, with unemployment levels pegged at 38.7 percent (Malawi Government, 2009). The majority of people engage in fishing and farming (Malawi Government, 2009). Tourism activities are also widespread in the district, with an approximate investment of US$373,000 and average annual revenue of US$227,000 (Malawi Government, 2018). By Malawian standards, this is quite significant, and the apparent growth of the industry is important in promoting people's livelihoods by unlocking social and economic opportunities for the local communities. However, there has not been adequate investigation into how the local community in the district benefits from the industry.

Methodological approach

The research conducted was mainly exploratory and used a qualitative technique. The data collection methods used were a mixture of primary and secondary research, with key informant interviews with local authorities and focus group discussions with community residents. Primary research was pursued given the difficulty in obtaining documented perceptions and attitudes of the local community in Nkhata Bay towards tourism. The significance of this is that it enabled the extraction of relevant information directly, as opposed to relying on second-hand sources (Meredith, 1998). Secondary information was obtained through desk research and was deemed crucial in providing the necessary literature and theoretical basis for the study.

Theoretical exploration

SET remains an important framework in examining the impact of tourism (Nunkoo & Ramkissoon, 2010; Kayat, 2002). It is widely hailed as useful for reflecting behaviourist and utilitarian thinking and recognizes the rationality of human beings as well as their awareness and capacity to employ cost–benefit analyses in order to inform their choices and decisions in their relationships. According to this theory, people tend to incline positively towards actions from which they benefit and are negatively inclined towards actions which would cost them in one way or another (McGehee & Andereck, 2009). This forms the basis upon which local communities become more supportive of tourism developments when they sense possible benefits (Nunkoo & Gursoy, 2012; Nunkoo & Ramkissoon, 2011).

The applicability of this theory is underlined by the process of social exchange, which Homans (1961: 13) defines as "the exchange of activity, tangible or intangible, and more or less rewarding or costly, between at least two persons". According to Blau (1986: 93), social exchange "involves the principle that one person does another a favor, and while there is a general expectation of some future return, its exact nature is definitely not stipulated in advance". Nonetheless, the exchange process in the tourism industry is not only defined by the social aspects; economic and environmental factors must also not be ignored (Jurowski & Gursoy, 2004). However, this enquiry seeks to establish the social and economic impacts of tourism on a local community.

Accordingly, the actors in the exchange process include the tourism industry and the local community. Each actor aims at maximizing the benefits while minimizing the costs associated with the relations and interactions (Cook et al., 2005). As alluded to above, actors in the exchange process engage in an exchange when they sense positive outcomes of value to them and when the perceived cost are not more than the perceived benefits (Ap, 1992). Although Woosnam, McElroy, and Van Winkle (2009) argue that the SET inclines towards the economic aspects, thereby treating the relationship between tourist and residents as a function of money, it (the theory) remains relevant for its focus on and respect for relationship between actors.

Key in the social exchange process are power and trust between the actors (Cropanzano & Mitchell, 2005). Here, power is defined as the ability of one actor to influence the behaviour of another actor (Wrong, 1979). In this regard, the power ought to be understood as the "residents' ability to control the resources required for tourism development (such as labour, capital, culture, and natural resources) and to secure personal returns from having tourism in their community" (Kayat, 2002:175). For trust, Rousseau, Sitkin, Burt, and Camerer (1998) define it as a psychological state which comprises the willingness to accept vulnerability on the basis of expected benefits from the other actor. Nunkoo and Ramkissoon (2012) conceive trust as a powerful tool for reducing conflicts and promoting effective partnerships and collaboration in planning and development in the tourism industry.

In most cases, the local community tends to be oppressed, vulnerable, and less powerful. This, then, denies it the right and opportunity to influence the tourism planning process (Moscardo, 2011), thereby defying the principle of reciprocity that is expected in the social exchange process. Perhaps it is for this reason that Ap (1992: 683) suggests that, "when the form of relation involves an imbalance and is asymmetrical, the disadvantaged host actors' perceptions will be negative". The existence of power relations helps to "uncover the winners and losers in particular social arrangements and the processes by which such power plays operate" (Kincheloe & McLaren, 2000: 281). Thus, because some groups are privileged over others, SET suggests that power can help to determine an actor's ability to take advantage of the outcomes of tourism development. Hence, an actor's level of power possesses considerable influence in the social exchange process (Ap, 1992). Usually, the one with less power becomes negatively inclined towards the exchange relationship (Ap, 1992). In the existence of power disparity, the achievement of trust becomes elusive. As noted by Cook et al. (2005: 40), power inequalities create "fertile ground for distrust" and "commonly block the possibility of trust".

Factors that shape perceptions and attitudes of local communities towards tourism

The presence of tourism activities in an area becomes inevitably subjected to various forms of judgement by local communities. Thus, this forms the local communities' perceptions and attitudes towards the tourism industry. This section, therefore, suggests a number of factors that help to explain how local communities' perceptions of and attitudes to tourism are shaped. As Jurowski and Gursoy (2004) suggest, proximity to tourist attractions is one such factor. According to Pizam (1978), residents who do not live close to touristic places often hold the tourism industry in less favourable regard. Their disinclination or indifference to the significance of tourism can be attributed to the absence of direct benefits to them from the tourism industry. This view is also shared by Ap and Crompton (1993), who argue that residents who directly benefit from tourism embrace the industry more than those who do not. Having said this, however, there is no guarantee that local communities in close proximity to tourist places will always hail the significance of tourism to them. As Williams and Lawson (2001) contend, some local communities close to touristic places exhibit negative attitudes towards tourism. This happens because of their susceptibility to the negative impacts of tourism, such as direct interaction with tourists, as well as pressure on resource usage.

Another factor that shapes local communities' perceptions of and attitudes to tourism is economic dependency. In particular, local communities that depend economically on tourism see the industry through positive lenses more than communities that lack this experience (Andriotis & Vaughan, 2003). A local community's economic dependence on tourism includes, for example, the operation of large- or small-scale businesses or even employment in the tourism industry. As such, more positive impacts of tourism development on local communities are likely to encourage residents' support for tourism development (Ko & Stewart, 2002).

Gender, age, income, and employment include some of the demographic characteristics that are also recognized as important in influencing how residents perceive the significance of tourism. Although the absence of consensus on these demographic variables is acknowledged, it has been established that the younger generation tends to see more positives in tourism than older people. As McGehee and Andereck (2004) contend, the youthful generation can easily grasp employment and business opportunities offered by the tourism industry, which does not provide many similar opportunities to the older generation. Likewise, women and, generally, residents who exhibit femininity traits are less likely to support tourism development and perceive tourism impacts more negatively than those with masculinity traits (Nunkoo & Gursoy, 2012). This is attributed to the fact that masculinity emphasizes independence and competition and is, hence, agency-focused, whereas femininity emphasizes sensitivity and concern for others and is, hence, community-oriented (Spence & Helmreich, 1978). Further, those employed in tourism businesses perceive tourism positively and, hence, enjoy the economic impacts of tourism more than those not employed in tourism as they do not directly benefit from tourism.

Community attachment, as another factor, is defined as the "extent and pattern of social participation and integration into community life, and sentiment or effect toward the community" (McCool & Martin, 1994: 30). Community attachment is closely linked to length of residence in the community. Some studies have found a significant relationship between length of stay and tourism impacts from tourism development; however, there is inconsistence in the direction of the relationship across studies (Jurowski, Uysal, & Williams, 1997; McGehee & Andereck, 2004). The longer people stay in the community, the more they develop negative attitudes towards tourism because they can easily see the repercussions caused by tourism in their community over time, and vice versa.

Community involvement is also a very significant factor in the study of tourism impacts. Communities are the hosts of tourist destinations and they play a very important role in the success or failure of the tourism industry. Community involvement in tourism also includes community awareness, consultation, and empowerment (Hall, 1999). Community awareness can be linked to imparting knowledge of tourism to the residents. According to Moscardo (2005), residents' knowledge of tourism or understanding of tourism development is central to the sustainability of the tourism sector. As noted by Andereck, Valentine, Knopf, and Vogt (2005), some studies have found that local communities that are knowledgeable about tourism are most likely to acknowledge the benefits and costs of tourism development. Although Látková and Vogt (2012) do not see knowledge as significant in determining the positive and negative impacts of tourism on local communities, it cannot be denied that knowledge is power (Lake, 2007). As such, local communities that seem disgruntled with tourism activities are often those that lack knowledge of the industry.

Socioeconomic impacts of tourism on the local community in Nkhata Bay district

The enquiry to establish the significance of tourism to the local community in Nkhata Bay required consideration of the entire local community in the district. However, local communities that existed further from touristic places appeared less inclined to contribute to the study for lack of any significant knowledge or appreciation of tourism activities. Meaningful insights that resulted in five themes were, thus, obtained from a sample of communities that exist in close proximity to tourist centres. The emerging issues include infrastructural development, job creation/employment opportunities, business opportunities, corporate social responsibility (CSR) expectations, and changes in cultural attitudes.

Infrastructure development

Infrastructure comprises the fundamental facilities and systems useful for the normal operation and/or functioning of an area. For the tourism industry, these facilities and systems include public safety, transportation services, medical systems, financial systems, education systems, and other services involved in the population's, as well as in tourists', demand (Ritchie & Crouch, 2005). The significance of infrastructure to tourism is underpinned by its role in supporting tourism development (Jovanovic & Ilic, 2016). In particular, it possesses the potential to increase the efficiency of the production and distribution of tourism services (Jovanovic & Ilic, 2016). According to Panasiuk (2007), tourism infrastructure is shaped by four basic elements, namely accommodation facilities, food and beverage facilities, accompanying facilities, and communication facilities. Particular facilities and services associated with these elements include, for example, hotels, lodges, apartments, hostels, and campsites; restaurants, bars, and cafes; transport; information bureaus; and car-rental companies.

Until 1992, the tourism industry in Nkhata Bay lacked vibrancy (Malawi Government, 2017). The absence of necessary infrastructure to attract or sustain stays by tourists deprived the area of not just tourists, but also any socioeconomic benefits which the local community could have accrued from the industry. This aptly echoes Jovanovic and Ilic's (2016: 288) assertion that the presence of "natural beauties" at a destination is meaningless to tourism development in the absence of accommodation facilities and quality road infrastructure. But, since 1992, Nkhata Bay has experienced significant growth in tourism activities with the rise of better accommodation structures from 1993 onwards (Malawi Government, 2017). Table 20.1 and Figure 20.1 below show the number of facilities in the district and the steady occurrence of visitors' arrivals between 2008 and 2015, respectively.

These facilities not only serve to attract tourists to the area, but they also, importantly, lift the face of Nkhata Bay, which had previously lacked significant modern structures that not only aid in beautifying the place but also, importantly, contribute to development status being accorded to a previously marginalized locality. The construction of roads, particularly the highway that connects Mzuzu City and the district, has also proved to be a considerable enhancement of tourists' travel in the area. Similarly, the electrification of certain resorts in typically remote areas has resulted in many homes also accessing electricity easily. Given the economic deprivation of most Malawians, the presence of electricity in the area provided the impetus for extensive domestic electrification. Moreover, it has helped in facilitating the use of various forms of machinery that support the livelihoods of most people in rural settings. For example, one member of a community near Kande beach opined that,

> [H]ad it not been that there is Kande Beach here, this area could have been in darkness today. For all these years, not even government bothered to electrify this area. See how better this road to the beach is. But also, see how beautiful and strong the road to Nkhata Bay from Mzuzu is.
>
> *(Interview with community member, Kande, Nkhata Bay)*

It can, thus, be argued that the increasing level of infrastructural development makes the local community appreciate the benefits of the tourism industry.

Employment opportunities

The significance of tourism to employment cannot be overemphasized. But also, as Aynalem, Birhanu, and Tesefay (2016: 1) contend, "employees is a sine qua non of tourism industry".

Table 20.1 Distribution of tourism facilities, establishments, and monuments at tourist centres in Nkhata Bay

Location	Lodges	Resthouses	Restaurants	Conference facilities	Diving facilities	Travel and tour agents/safaris	Horse facilities	Cottages	Guesthouses	Monuments
Nkhata Bay and Chikale	9	11	4	4	1	4	0	0	2	(2)
Chintheche/Bandawe and Thipula	10	4	3	0	0	0	0	1	1	(1) & (2)
Kande, Mwaya, and Kachere	3	0	1	0	1	0	1	0	0	0
Usisya	1	2	1	0	0	0	0	0	0	0
Ruarwe	1	0	0	0	0	0	0	0	0	0

Notes: (1) Museum, (2) monument.

Source: Nkhata Bay, Tourism District Office, Malawi Government, 2017.

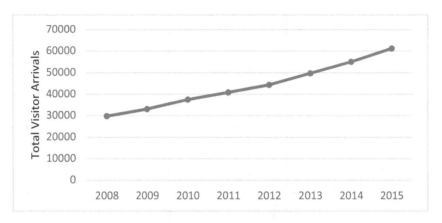

Figure 20.1   Total visitors to Nkhata Bay district, 2008–2015
Source: Nkhata Bay, Tourism District Office, Malawi Government, 2017.

The industry creates many employment opportunities in various areas including, for example, in accommodation and conferences, transportation, and attraction sites. Although unstable employment, low job status, long, antisocial working hours, and low pay are generally some of the constraints of employment in the tourism industry, thereby making it difficult to recruit suitable staff, the World Travel and Tourism Council (2017) indicates that the industry, directly and indirectly, provides more than 100 million and 200 million employment opportunities, respectively.

The growing number of facilities supporting the industry has enhanced employment opportunities for the local community in Nkhata Bay. This is in line with Jovanovic and Ilic's (2016) observation that the arrival of tourists enhances human resources' efficiency at the destination, as tourists require certain services for them to feel better during their stay at a particular tourist destination. According to Dayananda (2014), employment opportunities in the tourism industry can be created either directly or indirectly. In other words, direct employment includes job opportunities that are directly supported in the industry. In particular:

> employment by hotels, restaurants, travel agencies, tourism information offices, museums, protected areas such as national parks, palaces, religious sites, monuments, aircrafts, cruise lines, resorts or shopping outlets, souvenirs, photography, sightseeing tours, farmhouses, bed and breakfast, rural inns, and guest houses local transportation (state owned airlines and railways, private transport facilities), guides, cooks and scouts.
>
> *(Aynalem et al., 2016: 2)*

Indirect employment in the industry includes entities such as restaurant suppliers, construction companies that build and maintain tourist facilities, as well as necessary infrastructure, aircraft manufacturers, various handicrafts producers, marketing agencies, and accounting services, which are more or less dependent on the companies providing direct employment for their revenues (Aynalem et al., 2016).

The tourism industry in Nkhata Bay has indeed provided many people in the district with employment opportunities. Although jobs in senior positions such as management have not necessarily been occupied by people from the surrounding communities owing to the professional nature of the jobs, some community members have, nonetheless, benefited by being directly employed as front-desk officers, cooks, gardeners, guards, waiters, and waitresses. Informally, some, particularly women, provide cleaning services at the facilities and laundry services to overlanders and backpackers. In the absence of institutionalized tour guide services, young men in the district have seized the opportunity to informally operate as tour guides in exchange for money and other lucrative incentives from the tourists, who are usually perceived as wealthy. Indirectly, some people have been employed as curio vendors, and others work in gastronomy facilities such as restaurants, bars, and cafes which also serve tourists. The significance of people's involvement in tourism is that it affects a wider community, with those directly or indirectly in contact with tourism possessing obligations to their large, extended families back home.

Business opportunities

There is abundant evidence that points to the role of tourism in promoting business opportunities (see, for example, Nunkoo & Smith, 2013; Kim, Uysal, & Sirgy, 2013). This is also evident in Nkhata Bay district, where tourism has pushed some people into entrepreneurship. According to Kirzner (1997), entrepreneurship can be understood as the profitable activity of individuals based on knowledge and information gaps in the market. This is further extrapolated by Shane and Venkataraman (2000: 281), who see entrepreneurship as "how, by whom, and with what effects opportunities to create future goods and services are discovered, evaluated and exploited". In support of these perspectives, a manager at one resort at the main Nkhata Bay trading centre opined that, "the presence of tourism facilities in the district has facilitated entrepreneurial practices in many people in the district. People who did not have any economic activity can now find something to do through small businesses and employment" (interview with resort manager, Nkhata Bay).

As rightly observed during the study, for example, curio vending has become widespread in most touristic places. Although official government data recognize Nkhata Bay roadblock, Chintheche Inn turn-off at Malaza, and Kande along the Mzuzu–Nkhota-kota highway as the three main markets for tchotchkes (Malawi Government, 2017), the vending of souvenirs occurs almost everywhere with a significant concentration of tourists. Other small but steady businesses also include the supply of fish, fruits, and vegetables to restaurants. With the increased economic activities in those areas, local residents have opened mini-grocery shops where the money that is acquired through businesses and employment is spent. Given the significant levels of poverty in the district, tourism can be said to play an important role in providing people with some opportunities to generate income.

Corporate social responsibility expectations

CSR includes "the obligations of businessmen to pursue those policies, to make those decisions, or to follow those lines of action which are desirable in terms of the objectives and values of our society" (Bowen, 1953: 6). According to Johnson, Scholes, and Whittington (2008), CSR entails organizations' commitment to behave ethically and contribute to economic development while improving the quality of life of the workforce and their families, as well as the local community and society at large. The assumption here is that the tourism facility owners in Nkhata Bay possess the obligation to materially support the local community. However, the local community in Nkhata Bay possesses mixed experiences regarding the support the tourist centres render to communities. For example, a local community in Kande had hoped that, with the arrival of abundant numbers of tourists, the significant financial proceeds accrued by facility owners would be used in CSR initiatives. The main demand was for the construction of education centres in proximity to help lessen the distance school children have to travel to reach the existing schools. Although some tourists have turned philanthropists by supporting services such as early childhood development centres, it appears that, apart from providing business and employment opportunities, most facility owners have done little to support local communities materially.

This has also been observed by Bello, Banda, and Kamanga (2017: 16):

> Most of the establishments [are] not aware of CSR as an important aspect in operations, in its entirety. The major barriers to the adoption of CSR by hospitality establishments in Malawi [are] financial constraints and a lack of top management interest and awareness in CSR.

Given the absence of significant support from social services, the involvement of tourism establishments in CSR could have helped to alleviate some of the socioeconomic problems experienced by the local community in Nkhata Bay. But also, the presence of limited interaction between facility owners and the local community means that it would be difficult to make CSR demands of the facility owners.

Shifts in cultural attitudes

The local community, particularly that in close proximity to the tourist centres, reported some cultural 'shock' that is generated by tourists. This can be attributed to what Glensor and Peak (2004: 5) call "the tourist culture", which tends to lessen the tourists' sense of responsibility. According to Ryan (1993: 178), this results from tourists' search for "a familiar environment away from home in order to indulge in 'anti-social' or 'self-destructive' behaviour". In most cases, this manifests in situations where tourists engage in behaviours that contravene certain rules or laws of a particular society. For instance, sexual adventures by certain tourists encourage prostitution, a proscribed activity in certain societies (Newman, 2016). Others may engage in dealing illegal goods such as drugs (Lawson and Vines, 2014), particularly marijuana, whose users are often considered deviant in the traditional Malawian setting.

The shift in cultural attitudes has affected the younger generation more than the older one. In particular, it has affected young men most, who either serve as tour guides or seek to sinisterly benefit from the tourists. This has become apparent through the young men's deliberate assimilation of the foreign culture so as to help themselves identify with the tourists. For example, most young men either grow dreadlocks or leave their hair unkempt in portrayal of a different image from the traditionally submissive Malawian culture. This appearance is a strong announcement of their availability to the tourists and it has become a formidable symbol of identity to the tourists. As observed by one elderly woman whose life spans a number of generations,

> the lives of most young men have changed, not to the good but to the worst. They are openly smoking marijuana and they are freely moving about with white girlfriends while holding hands and, may be, kissing in public places. This is not what our culture permits.
>
> *(Interview with an elderly community member,*
> *Kande, Nkhata Bay)*

The significance of the tourists' impact on the cultural life of the local community has been aptly captured by Vanlangendonck and Leman (2007: 127), who argue that:

[T]ourists come and go but their collective identity of "touristhood" remains in the host culture, certainly in the so-called bulk destinations. The typical behaviour of tourists with typical tourist acts – to get a tan, to hunt for souvenirs, to visit tourist sanctuaries, to stroll in the streets, even "the tourist gaze" – makes them in the eyes of the inhabitants of host cultures a homogenous and particular "people", an ethnic group. In many cases, the locals have to share their territory for more than six months each year with their "new friends" and in some cases the sharing lasts for the whole year.

Although a number of young men have accrued material benefits such as electronic gadgets – for example, mobile phones – houses, cars, and cash, the impact of tourism seems to have negatively altered the cultural fabric of the local community in Nkhata Bay. To some extent, it has caused considerable dissatisfaction with tourism among some members of the community in Nkhata Bay.

Conclusion

The existence of the tourism industry in Nkhata Bay district has been an important generator of economic opportunities for most people in the area. However, their involvement in the industry appears to be on an ad hoc basis owing to their limited power to influence meaningful social exchange between the two actors. Given the lack of empowerment, it becomes difficult for people in Nkhata Bay to demand social and economic benefits. This, therefore, means that power to influence the relationship between the two actors is only concentrated on one side, which makes tourism development less meaningful to the local community in the district. Community empowerment can happen through attempts to ensure communities are involved in policy and decision-making, allowing them to have a voice on issues affecting their lives, in order to gain their support (Nunkoo & Gursoy, 2012). Raising awareness of and providing complete information on the costs and benefits of tourism would also help residents to make informed decisions related to tourism development. Residents should be placed at the van of the tourism development process (Choi & Sirakaya, 2005) because, much as they benefit from tourism, they are most affected by adverse consequences of the development of the tourism industry (Nunkoo & Ramkissoon, 2007).

References

Allen, L., Long, R., Perdue, R.R., & Kieselbach, S. 1988. The impact of tourism development on residents' perceptions of community life. *Journal of Travel Research*, 27, 16–21.

Andereck, K., Valentine, K., Knopf, R., & Vogt, C. 2005. Residents' perceptions of community tourism impacts. *Annals of Tourism Research*, 32, 1056–76.

Andersson, T.D., & Lundberg, E. 2013. Commensurability and sustainability: triple impact assessments of a tourism event. *Tourism Management*, 37, 99–109.

Andriotis, K., & Vaughan, R.D. 2003. Urban residents' attitudes toward tourism development: the case of Crete. *Journal of Travel Research*, 42(2), 172–85.

Ap, J. 1992. Residents' perceptions on tourism impacts. *Annals of Tourism Research*, 19, 665–90.

Ap, J., & Crompton, J. L. 1993. Residents' strategies for responding to tourism impacts. *Journal of Travel Research*, 32(1), 47.

Aynalem, S., Birhanu, K., & Tesefay, S. 2016. Employment opportunities and challenges in tourism and hospitality sectors. *Journal of Tourism & Hospitality*, 5, 257.

Bello, F.G., Banda, W.J.M., & Kamanga, G. 2017. Corporate social responsibility (CSR) practices in the hospitality industry in Malawi. *African Journal of Hospitality, Tourism & Leisure*, 6(3), 1–21.

Blau, P.M. (1986). *Exchange and Power in Social Life* (2nd ed.). New Brunswick, NJ: Transaction Books.

Bowen, H.R. 1953. *Social Responsibilities of the Businessman*. New York: Harper & Row.

Choi, H.S., & Sirakaya, E. 2005. Measuring residents' attitude toward sustainable tourism: development of sustainable tourism attitude scale. *Journal of Travel Research*, 43, 380–94.

Cook, K.S., Yamagishi, T., Cheshire, C., Cooper, R., Matsuda, M., & Mashima, R. (2005). Trust building via risk taking: a cross-societal experiment. *Social Psychology Quarterly*, 68(2), 121–42.

Cropanzano, R., & Mitchell, M.S. 2005. Social exchange theory: an interdisciplinary review. *Journal of Management*, 31(6), 874.

Dayananda, K. 2014. Tourism and employment: opportunities and challenges in Karnataka – special reference to Kodagu District. *IOSR Journal of Humanities and Social Science (IOSR-JHSS)*, 19, 11.

Fallon, P., & Schofield, P. 2006. The dynamics of destination attribute importance. *Journal of Business Research*, 59(6), 709–13.

Glensor, R., & Peak, K. 2004. Crimes against Tourists. Problem-Oriented Guides for Police, Problem-Specific Guides Series. US Department of Justice. Available at: https://cops.usdoj.gov/pdf/pop/e07042406.pdf (accessed 1 March 2018).

Hall, C.M. 1999. Rethinking collaboration and partnership: a public policy perspective. *Journal of Sustainable Tourism*, 7(3–4), 274–89.

Homans, G. 1961. *Social Behavior: Its Elementary Forms*. New York: Harcourt.

Johnson, G., Scholes, K. & Whittington, R. 2008. *Exploring Corporate Strategy*. Harlow, UK: Pearson Education.

Jovanovic, S., & Ilic, I. 2016. Infrastructure as important determinant of tourism development in the countries of Southeast Europe. *Ecoforum*, 5(1), 288–94.

Jurowski, C., and Gursoy, D. 2004. Distance effects on residents' attitudes toward tourism. *Annals of Tourism Research*, 31, 296–312.

Jurowski, C., Uysal, M., & Williams, R.D. 1997. A theoretical analysis of host community resident reactions to tourism. *Journal of Travel Research*, 36(2), 3–11.

Kayat, K. 2002. Power, social exchanges and tourism in Langkawi: rethinking resident perceptions. *International Journal of Tourism Research*, 4(3), 171–91.

Kim, K., Uysal, M., & Sirgy, M.J. 2013. How does tourism in a community impact the quality of life of community residents? *Tourism Management*, 36, 527–40.

Kincheloe, J.L., & McLaren, P. 2000. Rethinking critical theory and qualitative research. In *The Landscape of Qualitative Research*, ed. by N. Denzin & Y. Lincoln, pp. 279–314. Thousand Oaks, CA: Sage.

Kirzner, I.M. 1997. Entrepreneurial discovery and the competitive market process: an Austrian approach. *Journal of Economic Literature*. XXXV, 60–85.

Knox, J.M. 1982. Resident–visitor interaction: a review of the literature and general policy alternatives. In *The Impact of Tourism Development in the Pacific*, ed. By F. Rajotte, 76–107. Peterborough, ON: Environmental Resources Study Programme, Trent University.

Ko, D.W., & W.P. Stewart. 2002. A structural equation model of residents' attitudes for tourism development. *Tourism Management*, 23, 521–30.

Lake, R.W. 2007. Knowledge is power: power is knowledge. *Journal of Geography in Higher Education*, 15(1), 78–81.

Látková, P., & Vogt, C.A. 2012. Residents' attitudes toward existing and future tourism development in rural communities. *Journal of Travel Research*, 51(1), 50–67.

Lawson, K., & Vines, A. 2014. *Global Impacts of the Illegal Wildlife Trade: The Cost of Crime, Insecurity, and Institutional Erosion*. London: Chatham House, The Royal Institute of International Affairs.

Malawi Government. 2009. *Nkhata Bay District Assembly Socio-Economic Profile (2010–2012)*. Malawi: Nkhata Bay District Assembly.

Malawi Government. 2017. *Nkhata Bay District Tourism Review*. Malawi: Nkhata Bay District Council.

Malawi Government. 2018. *Nkhata Bay District Council Socioeconomic Profile*. Malawi: Nkhata Bay District Council.

McCool, S.F., & Martin, S.R., 1994. Community attachment and attitudes toward tourism development. *Journal of Travel Research*, 32(3), 29–34.

McGehee, N.G., & Andereck, K.L. 2004. Factors predicting rural residents' support of tourism. *Journal of Travel Research*, 43, 131–40.

McGehee, N.G., & Andereck, K. 2009. Volunteer tourism and the "voluntoured": the case of Tijuana, Mexico. *Journal of Sustainable Tourism*, 17(1), 39–51.

Meredith, J. 1998. Building operations management theory through case and field research, *Journal of Operations Management*, 16(4), 441–54.

Moscardo, G. 2005. Peripheral tourism development: challenges, issues and success factors. *Tourism Recreation Research*, 30(1), 27–43.

Moscardo, G. 2011. Exploring social representations of tourism planning: issues for governance. *Journal of Sustainable Tourism*, 19(4–5), 423–36.

Newman, R. 2016. New report says paying for sex in the UK should be made illegal and advises offence is extended to payments abroad. *The Independent*, 22 Feb. 2017. Available at: www.independent.co.uk/life-style/love-sex/sex-industry/sex-tourists-who-pay-for-prostitutes-abroad-should-face-prosecution-in-uk-a6888351.html (accessed 14 March 2018).

Nunkoo, R., & Gursoy, D. 2012. Residents' support for tourism: an identity perspective. *Annals of Tourism Research*, 39(1), 243–68.

Nunkoo, R., & Ramkissoon, H. 2007. Residents' perceptions of the socio-cultural impact of tourism in Mauritius. *Anatolia*, 18(1), 138–45.

Nunkoo, R., & Ramkissoon, H. 2010. Small island urban tourism: a residents' perspective. *Current Issues in Tourism*, 13(1), 37–60.

Nunkoo, R., & Ramkissoon, H. 2011. Developing a community support model for tourism. *Annals of Tourism Research*, 38(3), 964–88.

Nunkoo, R., & Ramkissoon, H. 2012. Power, trust, social exchange and community support. *Annals of Tourism Research*, 39(2), 997–1023.

Nunkoo, R., & Smith, S.L. 2013. Political economy of tourism: trust in government actors, political support, and their determinants. *Tourism Management*, 36, 120–32.

Panasiuk, A. 2007. Tourism infrastructure as a determinant of regional development. *Ekonomika ir vadyba: aktualijos ir perspektyvos*, 1(8), 212–15.

Pizam, A. 1978. Tourism's impacts: the social costs to the destination community as perceived by its residents. *Journal of Travel Research*, 20, 7–10.

Prayag, G., Hosany, S., Nunkoo, R., & Alders, T. 2013. London residents' support for the 2012 Olympic Games: the mediating effect of overall attitude. *Tourism Management*, 36, 629–40.

Ritchie, J.R.B., & Crouch, G.I. 2005. *The Competitive Destination: A Sustainable Tourism Perspective*. Wallingford, UK: CABI.

Rousseau, D.M., Sitkin, S.B., Burt, R.S., & Camerer, C. 1998. Not so different after all: a cross-discipline view of trust. *Academy of Management Review*, 23(3), 393–404.

Ryan, C. 1993. Crime, violence, terrorism, and tourism. An accident or intrinsic relationship? *Tourism Management*, 14(3), 173–83.

Shane, S., & Venkataraman, S. 2000. The promise of entrepreneurship as a field of research. *Academy of Management Review*, 25(1), 217–226.

Sirakaya, E., Teye, V., & Sönmez, S. 2002. Understanding residents' support for tourism development in the central region of Ghana. *Journal of Travel Research*, 41(1), 57–67.

Spence, J.T., & Helmreich, R.L. (1978). *Masculinity and Femininity: Their Psychological Dimensions, Correlates and Antecedents*. Austin, TX: University of Texas Press.

Stylidis, D., Biran, A., Sit, J., & Szivas, E.M. 2014. Residents' support for tourism development: the role of residents' place image and perceived tourism impacts. *Tourism Management*, 45, 260–74.

Tourism Concern. 2000. Fair trade in tourism. *Bulletin 2, Corporate Social Responsibility*, Autumn.

Vanlangendonck, M., & Leman, J. 2007. Tourism and cultural change: an empathic understanding approach. An introduction to tourism, anthropology and ethnicity. *Omertaa Journal for Applied Anthropology*, 126–30.

Wattanakuljarus, A., & Coxhead, I. 2008. Is tourism-based development good for the poor? A general equilibrium analysis for Thailand. *Journal of Policy Modeling*, 30(6), 929–55.

Williams, J., & Lawson, R. 2001. Community issues and resident opinions of tourism. *Annals of Tourism Research*, 28(2), 269–90.

Woosnam, K.M., McElroy, K.E., & Van Winkle, C.M. 2009. The role of personal values in determining tourist motivations: an application to the Winnipeg Fringe Theatre Festival, a cultural special event. *Journal of Hospitality Marketing & Management*, 18(5), 500–11.

World Travel and Tourism Council. 2017. Travel and Tourism Economic Impact 2017 World. Available at: www.wttc.org/-/media/files/reports/economic-impact-research/regions-2017/world2017.pdf (accessed 6 April 2018).

Wrong, D. 1979. *Power: Its Forms, Bases and Uses*. New York: Harper & Row.

PART IV

Environmental impacts of tourism

21

ENVIRONMENTAL IMPACTS OF TOURISM

Özge Kocabulut, Nisan Yozukmaz and Serkan Bertan

Introduction

All living species in the world continue to exist in mutual interaction in a certain setting formed by organic or inorganic matters. This setting, to which living species are bound with vital bonds, upon which they have an impact or by which they are affected, is called environment. In other words, from a home to a nest, all the settings where living species dwell are environments (Alım, 2006). Environment refers to the natural and artificial elements conditioning human life. Divided into such categories as physical, biological and social, the environment has continuously been under human influence since humans came to exist (Tuna, 2007). Demir and Çevirgen (2006) state that environment refers to the relationships between people; the mutual effects related to these relationships; the relationships and interaction between humans and other species such as plants and animals; and the relationships and interaction between humans and all the nonliving things such as air, water, underground treasures and climate.

The term, environment, is used to cover all factors of human behavior. All the aspects of environment, such as cultural, social, economic, political and natural, have a major impact on humans and the way they live and interact with each other. Since the second half of the 21st century, there have been many economic and technological developments in all industries which have led to the mass consumption of natural resources and ecological systems. These kinds of development have also caused some negative environmental alterations such as ozone depletion, acid rain, desertification and climate change (Holden, 2016).

Environment is divided into two segments, the physical and social environments. The physical environment means a living or nonliving setting in which living species dwell and perceive physically. The physical environment is also divided into two segments, the natural environment and artificial environment. Humans do not have any impact upon the formation of the natural environment, but they modify and change the artificial environment. As can be understood, humans are able to control nature (Yıldız, Sipahioğlu and Yıldız, 2000). In other words, human beings pollute sensitive ecosystems such as soil, water and air, which are physical components of the natural environment, without even realizing it. As a result of this, soil, water and air whose natural cycle is spoiled cannot function properly. Thus, environmental pollution occurs in the human environment and so affects living and nonliving environments. The quality of soil, water and air required for survival has become an important issue, and awareness of the environment has been modified in favor of the environment. Therefore, it is essential that natural resources are used, protected, preserved and planned in a sustainable way (Menteşe, 2017).

In this chapter, all dimensions of the relationship between the natural environment and tourism will be covered.

The relationship between environment and tourism

To be able to comprehend the relationship between tourism and the natural environment, first of all one should understand the complexity of tourism in all dimensions. Besides being an economic, sociological, managerial or mobility issue, it is a concept that exists with the components of the natural environment (Holden, 2016), which is the primary notion dealt with in this chapter.

Tourism is a multifaceted economic activity developing on the basis of natural and environmental resources. The tourism potential of a country can only be measured using its own social, historical, natural and cultural values (Tuna, 2007). As mentioned earlier, among all these, natural resources are of great importance for tourism in every way. A report published by the OECD (1980) states that environmental resources, which require particular attention, are grouped as wetlands (rivers, seas, coasts and water springs), natural spaces (soil, forests and air), architectural spaces (architectural buildings) and human spaces (human activities). When a tourism activity emerges and develops in a region, it either has an effect on these environmental resources or is built upon these resources. Thus, an environmentally friendly or environment-related tourism activity provides for both the sustainability of environmental resources and tourism in general. In this regard, the preservation and protection of environmental resources on which tourism is based require a high level of environmental awareness and sensitivity (Tuna, 2007).

Nature has beauty unique to one specific place, and every place has a specific climate, geographical and geological conditions and other unique features. Nevertheless, some places or areas have more advantages and are richer than other places in the sense that their natural resources are more plentiful, denser and have interesting characteristics. These kinds of feature make some places and regions more attractive for tourism. Natural tourism supplies comprise tourist needs related to nature, which can be listed as geomorphological landscape (landforms), flora and fauna, hydro mineral resources, wetlands, rivers, beaches, natural events and climate (Gündüz, 2004).

The environment is the natural and man-made physical setting around us. It has three functions, the first of which is the presentation of natural resources, the second is being the place where residues are dispatched, and the last is being an attraction involving natural beauties. Environmental pollution caused by technological developments since the 20th century, on the other hand, has definitely increased owing to the development of tourism and travel, according to Pınar (1993). In addition to the negative environmental effects of tourism, if tourism is considered not just with an environmental approach, but also from an economic perspective, it is obvious how important the protection of nature and the environment is.

To build a mutually beneficial relationship between tourism and environment, public intervention is needed for the management and planning of every component and for prioritizing the benefits of the tourism industry. For example, in a tourism and environment study led by the United Kingdom (English Tourist Board/Employment Department, 1991), the characteristics and dimensions of environmental problems caused by mass tourism in significant destinations were examined, and some principles for the solution of these problems were asserted. This study shows that there is a need to determine a fundamental resource for tourism activities. The problems specified as part of the study were listed as depreciation of the urban landscape, overcrowding and the problems related to social and cultural interactions between host community and visitors (Page, 2015).

According to Mathieson and Wall (1982), in a place which lacks an attractive environment, tourism is not even a matter for discussion. From basic attractions such as sea, sand and sun to historical places and buildings whose attractiveness is unquestionable, all the environmental aspects are the fundamentals of tourism. In this regard, the relationship between tourism and environment is a dependent relationship.

To be able to offer tourists or visitors the services they need, first of all, the infrastructure services required should be improved in a tourism destination. The infrastructure factor of tourism consists of roads, streets, harbors, airports, electricity, water and sewage systems. Besides these, superstructure systems are also needed. Tourism superstructure refers to the components directly related to visitor needs, such as reception centers, hotels, restaurants, car rental companies, tour operators and retailers. Improving the infrastructure and superstructure required in a destination determines the effects of tourism on the environment, too. But these effects can be minimized with good planning and regulation (Cook, Hsu and Marqua, 2014).

In recent years, there has been an increase in academic research on the effects of tourism on the environment. The positive impacts have been studied under such topics as the protection of tourism values, providing more recreational park areas, increasing recreational activities, raising environmental awareness and environmental value, enhancing destination image and protection, developing infrastructure and public activities and restoration or improvement of monuments and structures. On the other hand, the negative impacts are discussed under other topics such as the increase in environmental pollution, noise and traffic pollution, the harmful impacts of tourism activities on the natural resources and natural environment, destruction of resources, and damage towards cultural and historical ruins (Yoon, Gursoy and Chen, 2001; Ko and Stewart, 2002; Teye, Sönmez and Sırakaya, 2002; Kuvan and Akan, 2005; Pappas, 2008; Kozak, Akoğlan Kozak and Kozak, 2015).

Increasing numbers of tourists and fast growth in mass tourism put pressure on natural resources and the environment, including land, air, water and biodiversity. The needs of tourists and the services offered to them are always related to destination infrastructure and superstructure and so, accordingly, the natural environment. In this regard, whether the impacts of tourism on the environment would be positive or negative is directly parallel to the proper planning and management of environmental resources in a destination (Holden, 2016), because the quality of the environment, either natural or artificial, is essential to tourism. As the relationship between tourism and environment is mutually dependent and complex, attention should always be paid to the sustainability of environmental resources, especially at the time of decision-making about the planning and management of the infrastructure and superstructure of tourism destinations. Whereas bad decisions may lead to negative environmental impacts such as destroying environmental resources, good and proper decisions may create beneficial impacts on the environment and contribute to protecting and preserving the environment in a tourism destination. They can raise awareness of environmental issues and create financial support for sustainable usage of environmental and natural resources (Sunlu, 2003).

Tourism is an economic activity which has inevitable effects on the environment. Specifically in developing countries, sometimes highlighting and promoting the economic benefits of tourism may cause its harmful impacts on the environment to be ignored. But loss of environmental resources cannot be remunerated with economic resources. The demand for gaining revenue from an industry that is regarded as the fundamental means of living, such as tourism, leads to depletion and exhaustion based upon overuse of the limited resources on which this industry depends. Utilizing natural and cultural resources, tourism may also harm natural and cultural heritage. If activities in tourism destinations have negative impacts on the environment, this also influences other destinations offering tourism services. Increasing numbers of tourist movements towards the regions with natural attractions and cultural wealth may damage the environment. Thus, unless the region is protected with a good preservation policy, the long-term benefits of tourism are ignored, and the goal of short-term revenue is pursued; as a result of using natural resources in an irresponsible way, the natural environment and landscape of a destination are damaged, air, water and land are polluted, and, accordingly, public health deteriorates (Kaymaz, 2012). Mass tourism puts pressure on natural resources by increasing the consumption of scarce natural resources (Sunlu, 2003; Kaymaz, 2012). As natural resources are limited and scarce, all the actors in the tourism industry should have environmental sensitivity. Contrary to other economic industries, in the tourism industry, consumers have to go to the places where tourism products are produced. This characteristic of tourism affects touristic regions substantially. Every year, billions of people participate in tourism mobility and experience natural attractions in tourism destinations, and this intensity often leads to environmental damage in those destinations. Mass consumption of energy, food and other raw materials which are scarce in a destination causes environmental problems. Also, the seasonality of tourism leads to an increase in the intensity of interaction between tourism and the environment at certain periods. At popular tourism destinations, natural resources such as water resources, coastline, soil, landscape, flora and fauna and air may be harmed. Deforestation and loss of wetlands caused by land demand and mass housing caused by mass tourism, aesthetic pollution caused by housing built on coastlines, increasing amounts of waste and the pollution caused by dispatching these wastes into water resources are regarded as negative physical impacts of tourism on the environment (Kaymaz, 2012).

Negative effects of tourism emerge when the level of tourists' use is higher than the environment's ability to cope with the usage. Mass tourism threatens many natural resources in destinations. For example, tourism facilities often overuse water resources, which leads to water shortages, degradation of water supplies and production of great volumes of wastewater. Another example of the negative impacts of tourism is deforestation caused by fuel wood collection and land clearing. Also, emissions related to transportation, energy production and use which are increased by tourist mobility are the most important causes of acid rain, global warming and photochemical pollution. Lastly, in popular tourism destinations, waste disposal is a serious problem and may be a major despoiler of the natural environment, rivers, scenic areas and roadsides unless it is properly planned (Sunlu, 2003).

Current trends and issues in tourism and environment

In recent years, the environmental conscience has grown fast. Businesses now prefer environment-friendly technologies in order to both prove their environmental consciousness and meet consumer needs for environmental products. With the increase in consumer demand for eco-friendly products, marketing managers analyze their product range and make changes to meet the demand (Yücel and Ekmekçiler, 2008). In this sense, there is a significant need for tourism businesses to carry out marketing research on this issue and develop new marketing strategies and eco-friendly goods and services. In this part of the chapter, current goods and services in the field of eco-friendly tourism marketing will be discussed.

Ecolabelling

Ecolabelling is a system that gives awards for products acknowledged as less harmful towards the environment than other products on a voluntary basis. Whereas a certification system presents information about businesses offering special goods and services, the ecolabelling system gives information about special goods and services being presented (Yücel and Ekmekçiler, 2008). In its broadest sense, an ecolabel refers to the environment based on its content. For example, it can display the spatiotemporal situation of the natural or social environment or environmental management and performance measures. For this reason, the ecolabelling system comprises various environmental awards for certain goods and services within the concept of green tourism, nature tourism, sustainable tourism and ecotourism, membership programs for environmental performances, and documentation and accreditation schemes evaluated using specified environmental criteria (Buckley, 2002).

Within the scope of these applications, the fundamental purpose of ecolabelling is to provide simple, easy and comprehensible information for consumers in order to increase environmental awareness (Delmas and Grant, 2008), to help consumers choose products that are not harmful to the environment and to decrease the level of production of products which have negative impacts on the environment (Yücel and Ekmekçiler, 2008).

The importance of ecolabelling

The fundamental raw materials of the tourism industry are the natural, historical and cultural values of a country (Ünlüönen, Tayfun and Kılıçlar, 2007). Accordingly, the tourism industry is a system based more on the usage of natural and sociocultural resources than any other industry. It is inevitable that tourism uses these resources as inputs and, in a way, makes them scarce by its own nature. Managing these scarce resources with the aim of providing their long-term usage for coming generations brings the issue of sustainability. Developed for sustainability, the ecolabelling system both provides businesses with competitive advantage and mediates as an important environment policy for increasing the awareness of host communities, local governments and other parties (Akış, 1999).

In recent years, the importance of ecolabel goods and services has increased in the tourism industry, as in other industries (Buckley, 2002). Specifically, it is assumed that tourists seek more sustainable forms of tourism and they are ready to adopt more appropriate behavior in tourism environments owing to the fact that the demand and supply of ecolabel products have continued to grow. In short, the increase in the demand for ecolabel goods and services brings the acknowledgment of eco-friendly and green tourists' existence with it, because a greater environmental consciousness has caused tourists to react more to green messages and ecolabelling. For this reason, ecolabelling of tourism products is regarded as an efficient tool for transmitting the messages to a more conscience tourist group. For instance, the tourists who regard themselves as "good tourists" take advantage of ecolabel tourism products which give the opportunity of integrating tourists with the environment, instead of their colliding with local environments and cultures, by reacting to green messages of ecolabels (Font and Buckley, 2001). To sum up, ecolabels can help the tourism industry resolve critical environmental issues, accelerate the implementation of eco-productive resolutions and lead to efficient methods in the processes of monitoring and reporting environmental performances. Also, as well as helping tourism products to be sold, they can put emphasis on goods and services that are able to decrease the cost of businesses and usage of resources such as water and energy. They play a direct role in the bond between socio-economic problems and environmental protection. For instance, they provide income for host communities by encouraging tourists to use local products. Besides highlighting the importance of the environment to the tourism industry, they can contribute to the increase in environmental awareness of local communities (Yücel and Ekmekçiler, 2008).

Ecolabel applications in tourism

Tourism businesses perform eco-friendly activities in order to minimize negative impacts on the environment, to attract consumers with expectations, to create an image of eco-friendly business, to decrease costs and to demonstrate their sustainability because of the characteristics of the goods and services they offer. Among these activities, the most common is the ecolabelling system.

BLUE FLAG

The Blue Flag program, one of the ecolabelling activities, is carried out by the Foundation for Environmental Education (FEE), which is an international non-governmental organization. Initiated in 1985 in France, this program has become a global one. The program supports sustainable development in fresh water and marine ecosystems (Fışkın, Çakır and Özkan, 2016). With Blue Flag criteria, the program challenges local governments and beach facilities in the issues of bathing water quality, environmental management, and environmental education and life safety in order to reach higher standards. Today, Blue Flag has become a distinctive ecolabel bringing tourism and environmental industries together at local, regional and national levels (www.turizmdunyasi.com.tr, 2018). According to FEE's 2016 data, 50 member countries have 4,266 beaches labelled with Blue Flag.

GREEN KEY

The Green Key program is another international ecolabel aiming to contribute to sustainable tourism and prevent climate change by awarding initiatives for their efforts towards environmental protection. The implementation of the program started in 1994 in Denmark (www.turizmdunyasi.com.tr, 2018) and, with the support of FEE, has gained international status since 2002 (Fışkın *et al.*, 2016).

GREEN STAR

More specifically, within the scope of sustainable tourism, the Eco-Friendly Accommodation Facility Certificate (Green Star) has been given to hotel facilities which demand Green Star and have the qualifications required in order to protect and preserve the environment, develop environmental awareness, and promote and incentivize positive environmental contributions of tourism facilities (Tutar, 2015).

In sum, ecolabels differ by their geographical location, service type and their implementers. Although the main purpose of all these ecolabelling programs is sustainability, all of them consider changing conditions continuously. For this reason, tourism ecolabels have various classifications among themselves (Fışkın *et al.*, 2016). Some of the most commonly implemented ecolabels among 464 ecolabels involving the tourism industry are Beluga (Europe), BIO Hotels (Europe), EarthCheck (international), Carbon Neutral Certification (international), Green Seal (international), Green Key (international) and Nature's Best Ecotourism (Europe) (www.ecolabelindex.com, 2018).

Case study

An activity conducted in Hiiumaa Island in 1996 by the tourism industry can be shown as an ecolabelling example. Hiiumaa in Estonia is an island in the Baltic Sea and is famous for its rich, beautiful and untouched nature and warm, kind people. It was hard to formulate or implement strict rules or establish a surveillance bureau in Hiiumaa. But ecolabelling was based on the idea that an entrepreneur should self-regulate. In this instance, ecolabelling was regarded as an "information" sign rather than as an "award". Hiiumaa Green Label labels a destination or a food service run sustainably without affecting Hiiumaa's clean nature in its best way.

Destination and food service enterprises take responsibility for converting waste into compost or animal feed; sorting out recycling materials (waste paper) and dangerous waste (old batteries); minimizing waste production by avoiding useless plastic and small packages; using water economically and requesting guests to do so; using electricity economically and requesting guests to do so; using chemical cleaning materials in an eco-friendly way; appreciating local Hiiumaan and Estonian products; and being informative about nature and the attractions on the site (www.coastlearn.org, 2018).

Eco-friendly accommodation facilities

Understanding that to create eco-friendly tourism mobility, decision-makers and managers should initiate eco-friendly tourist activities, businesses have begun to adapt "green"-based management strategies (Kirk, 1998). Eco-friendly and green-based plans and strategies have gained importance for small and big enterprises since the 1990s (Revilla, Dodd and Hoover, 2001) and have quickly become key implementations in the policies of the accommodation industry as well. The green hotel concept, which has been used for qualifying hotels established via greenfield investments or modernization using green strategies, refers to the hotels offering quality service by using natural resources in a respectful way with their sustainable energy, water and waste management strategies. The Green Hotels Association defines green hotels as eco-friendly enterprises contributing to environmental protection and preservation by adapting implementations required to minimize wastes and save water and energy (Akdağ, Güler, Demirtaş, Dalgıç and Yeşilyurt, 2014; Lee, Hsu, Han and Kim, 2010).

The importance of eco-friendly applications in the hospitality sector

Maintaining operational activities in the tourism industry, which is one of the fastest-growing industries in the world, depends on the businesses' relationships and harmony with the social, cultural and environmental resources they use. Damaging these resources or jeopardizing their sustainability limits tourism activities (Akdağ *et al.*, 2014). For this reason, resource usage–consumption balance is an essential issue for the hospitality sector, which is an indispensable part of the tourism industry. The most important factors for eco-friendly management in the hospitality industry are generally discussed under the titles of water and energy usage, recycling, waste management and sensitivity to nature (Cooper, Fletcher, Fyall, Gilbert and Wanhill, 2008). Research conducted on these topics shows that 90 percent of a tourist's energy consumption is supplied by destination resources. According to another study, a tourist who stays at a hotel for two weeks consumes more than 100 kg of fossil fuel. On the other hand, if all facilities that can impact on the environment adapt positive strategies and are managed appropriately, they will not be remembered for their negative effects on environmental pollution and degradation (Güneş, 2011). Some research reveal that, when hotels implement eco-friendly activities, they gain advantages such as cost-saving, productivity, competitive advantage, new ranges of goods and services for changing consumer demand, a better business image, and consumer and shareholder satisfaction (Güler and Tufan, 2013). It can be deduced that tourists do not regard a hotel's eco-friendly strategies as an extra qualification, but as a requirement (Tutar, 2015).

Eco-friendly applications in accommodation facilities

All over the world, nature's warning has been heard in recent years, and some serious precautions have begun to be implemented. In this sense, the most important developments have been provided with eco-friendly applications in accommodation facilities.

ECO HOTELS RATING SYSTEM

As an example of green marketing campaigns run by the tourism industry, the eco hotels rating system can be shown. For the classification of eco-friendly hotels, a serious and comparable rating system has been developed by an organization named Eco Hotels of the World. According to this system, hotels can gain one to five stars for their applications in five different categories. By calculating the average number of stars gained for each of the categories, a number of green stars representing a hotel's sensitivity towards green and environmental matters is assigned. (www.ecohotelsoftheworld.com/, 2018). The hotels demanding green stars complete the application form in which they rate themselves from one to five in terms of their qualifications related to the categories of energy, water, waste disposal, eco-active and protection. After examining the application form, organization authorities contact the hotel manager, carry out necessary inspections and rate the hotel with an appropriate green star (Kızılırmak, 2011).

GREEN STAR ECO-FRIENDLY ACCOMMODATION FACILITY CERTIFICATE

Presented in 1975 in a seminar held by the American Marketing Association for the first time, the green marketing concept is a marketing strategy followed by hotels within the scope of environmental- and social-responsibility programs. Green Star, which is an ecolabel used by accommodation facilities, is an important part of this marketing strategy. It is worth studying and learning this strategy's importance in terms of sustainability and competitiveness as it is aimed at providing water and energy savings, minimizing waste and extending recycling (Tutar, 2015).

GENERAL MANAGEMENT SYSTEMS ISO (INTERNATIONAL ORGANIZATION FOR STANDARDIZATION) EMAS (EUROPEAN UNION ECO-MANAGEMENT AND AUDIT SCHEME)

ISO 14001 has international advantages but does not control detailed requirements. The details are built by hotel managements' commitment in a supportive way for continuous development (Tutar, 2015).

ECO-EFFICIENCY, LEED (LEADERSHIP IN ENERGY AND ENVIRONMENTAL DESIGN) AND BREEAM (BUILDING RESEARCH ESTABLISHMENT ENVIRONMENTAL ASSESSMENT METHOD)

International LEED and similar accreditations are focused more upon eco-efficiency, for example, leading energy consumption of a hotel building. This kind of accreditations offers brand recognition for guests (Tutar, 2015).

Within the frame of these applications, Environmentally Friendly Hotels presents some environmental regulations for hotels such as considering allergy-sensitive guests; utilizing alternative sources of energy; avoiding the use of harmful chemicals and cleaning materials in housekeeping and laundry departments as much as possible; utilizing alternative options for the protection and preservation of natural resources (such as using wastewater for watering gardens); offering guests local products and organic food; providing energy and water saving; managing conference and meeting halls with an environmental approach; preferring cotton or organic cotton products for towels, sheets and covers; increasing staff's and guests' awareness of environmental issues and highlighting environmental issues on the website to increase public awareness; participating in environmental actions; changing some products such as towels, sheets or pillows less frequently during the stay of same guests; including non-smoking rooms and a health club; and making extra, noteworthy efforts for environmental issues beyond the issues mentioned here (www. environmentallyfriendlyhotels.com, 2018).

Case study

Holiday Inn welcomes guests with a question on recycled paper asking for help for the environment, with an explanation on the paper and asking guests to dream about the damage caused by tons of bed linen washed unnecessarily and the chemicals used for washing them to water in all the hotels, all over the world, every day. Holiday Inn urges guests to act and help them stop this pollution. If a guest leaves this card on the bed, the linen will not be changed that day. Today, environmentalist tourists, whose numbers are increasing day by day and who demand eco-friendly accommodation, reveal their interest in issues such as waste disposal management and energy costs and modify their consumption habits in favor of the environment (Brown, 1996; Güneş, 2011). These kinds of action on Holiday Inn's part attract tourist groups who are environmentally sensitive. Thanks to these activities, costs are decreased, profits are increasing, and also awareness of hotel employees and guests towards the environment is created (Güneş, 2011).

Eco-gastronomy

It is widely acknowledged that economic, social and technological developments have caused major changes in tourism practices over the last 50 years, and these changes have been not only quantitative (increases in tourist numbers and tourism incomes, etc.), but also qualitative (tourist preferences, etc.) all over the world. For this reason, it is admitted that today's tourists like accommodation with regional culture and want to see all the elements of a culture, and, owing to these changes in tourists' demands, these tourists' environmental consciousness has caused the emergence of sustainable applications in the tourism industry (Durlu-Özkaya, Sünnetçioğlu and Can, 2013).

The scope, importance and components of eco-gastronomy

The purpose of eco-gastronomy research is to implement a way of gastronomy including conventional principles of sustainable development. Eco-gastronomy refers to producing eco-friendly food (Scarpato, 2002). It proves that if, along with eco-dining and environmental sustainability, consumer groups adhere to the most appropriate health standards, those groups can develop in their social and economic lives. With this regard, eco-gastronomy is also called sustainable gastronomy and interacts with all other components of a developing system. Thus, temporary visitors such as tourist groups should be considered as the members of the community whose regions they visit. Similarly, tourists should feel themselves as a part of this community. Eco-gastronomy would help that. Eco-gastronomy supports both the environment and the producers in terms of its contribution to the development of local agricultural activities, to the production and sales of local products, to the diversification of the quality of goods and services, to the process of local producers' being a part of the tourism industry, and to the protection and sustainability of local attractions and natural resources (Çalışkan and Yılmaz, 2016).

The components of sustainable gastronomy tourism are special restaurants, local foods, local food production systems, food festivals, special food events, natural shopping markets, natural and historical shopping centers, local culture, organic agriculture and organic products, local food production and traditional production (Durlu-Özkaya *et al.*, 2013).

Eco-gastronomy applications

These applications considered within the frame of sustainability, such as slow food, geographical indications and eco-villages, are among the important elements of eco-gastronomy.

SLOW FOOD

A group of political and cultural Italian activists prepared the Slow Food manifesto, which inspired the international Slow Food movement (Jones, Shears, Hillier, Comfort and Lowell, 2003). The Slow Food manifesto is focused more on the negative effects of fast living on our lives. According to this manifesto, standardization of tastes, threat to biodiversity, environmental depredation (because of agricultural industrialization), disappearance of small producers, disappearance of low-profit vegetables, fruit and grains and loss of cultural identity are negative impacts of globalization. Thus, this movement emphasizes that fast living feeding upon globalization disrupts all aspects of the traditional, especially the food system and consumption behavior (Sağır, 2017).

Slow Food is perhaps the only movement struggling for the fundamental right of everyone to have access to good, clean, fair food and combining food enjoyment and responsibility. The idea of quality developed for Slow Food involves the following three principles (www.slow food.com, 2018):

- The food must be good. This means that the food eaten by every person tastes good and gives pleasure in terms of reality and naturalness criteria implemented at a certain time, place and culture without feeling the need to modify its natural content.
- The food must be clean. Food should be produced in a sustainable way without causing any harm to the environment, animal welfare or human health. Each phase of the agricultural industry chain, including the production phase, should protect consumer and producer health, ecosystem and biodiversity.
- Food must be fair. Food producers should get a fair return for their operations conducted in humane conditions while their prestige, information and skills are protected.

To sum up, the Slow Food movement aims to protect and maintain traditional agricultural methods and techniques by preserving endangered traditional tastes, promoting right of taste and increasing awareness of food enjoyment with taste education (Petrini, 2001). This movement was initiated to decrease the homogenizing effect of fast food, protect food enjoyment and life, develop gastronomic culture, experience agricultural diversity and education and preserve endangered food (Pink, 2008). Also, thanks to this movement, international culinary arts and culture are protected, and biological diversity and local farming are promoted (Sağır, 2017).

GEOGRAPHICAL INDICATIONS

Geographical indications refer to industrial property rights defining a product originating from a region or representing a region, accredited to their geographical resources in terms of their qualities or their reputation. Geographical indications are the ones among distinctive indications who have a long history. Owing to their function as specifying products' origins, they emerge as the first form of brand and they are used for distinguishing important products in terms of their geographical origins. For a product to qualify as a geographical indication, it should bear some characteristics. These can be gathered under five points (Kan and Gülçubuk, 2015). First of all, an indication should specify a product. Geographical indications display the origin of a product and make a distinction between the product and others. Second, geographical indications refer to the products originating from a bordered location. Third, geographical indications are useful to distinguish some products from others. Fourth, products with geographical indications are differentiated from similar products by their unique characteristics, which may include differences of all kinds, from climatic components such as land, moisture and wind, to the materials used in their production by locals. Finally, this point is significant for the protection of cultural heritage and contributing to consumers' decision-making process by giving information about a product.

In conclusion, geographical indications help consumers learn more about many products and have trust in local and quality products, they are also used as legal and economic tools of cultural heritage production for rural development. Geographical indications create unique identities for some products by using a geographical origin and add economic value to local products (Durlu-Özkaya *et al.*, 2013).

SUSTAINABLE AGRICULTURE

For reasons such as soil degradation and environmental pollution that emerged during agricultural production, in many countries agriculture is evaluated with rural areas, and, accordingly, for economic purposes and sustainability of employment in rural areas, different application methods have developed in agriculture. These methods include systems supporting environment-oriented production with various rural activities. Eco-gastronomy practices such as sustainable agriculture essentially are aimed at increasing the environmental awareness of farmers and providing food safety. Protection of agricultural land is very important for the sustainability of food production (Pezikoğlu, 2012).

Sustainable agriculture is focused on enhancing rural living. In this way, people can get better food, organizations, external services, powerful structures and more options in their lives. In a report by the European Commission (2001), the purposes of sustainable agriculture and rural development are defined. In this report, economic, social and environmental issues are adopted as three parts of development synergy, and only by balancing these three components can the concept of sustainability be actualized. According to this idea, at the economic level, some criteria such as optimum usage of production factors, providing access to required equipment, a competitive agricultural industry and ensuring continuity for businesses are regarded as significant for efficiency (Pezikoğlu, 2012).

To sum up, sustainable agriculture is not just about the long-term protection of natural resources and guaranteeing their productivity but also about a balanced agricultural system in economic, social and ecological terms (Demiryürek, 2011). Also, sustainable agriculture is considered as the only option for human nutrition, respecting the Earth's carrying capacity and providing better life standards for farmers and consumers (Tencati and Zsolnai, 2012).

Case study

As a northern Aegean island in Turkey, Gokceada has similar characteristics to other Aegean islands. It is small and remote from the mainland. These two features also affect its gastronomic culture. Each food that is served has protected its essence and flavor. The introduction of Slow Food into Gokceada occurred when Carlo Petrini, the founder of the Slow Food movement, visited the island in 2006. Petrini asked for a Slow Food convivium to be established in Gokceada. In the same year, Dr. Rıdvan Yurtseven founded a Slow Food Convivium and thus Gokceada was recognized. Since the Slow Food movement was adopted, there have been many positive developments with regard to tourism in Gokceada. For example, there has been a visible increase in accommodation facilities and restaurants. In particular, food and beverage facilities serving local food and homemade meals have opened, and the number of guesthouses and boutique hotels has increased. With regard to income and employment, with the Earth market chain founded after the introduction of the Slow Food movement, local products have been highlighted, women living on the island have undertaken their sale, and thus the employment rate has increased. Also, the infrastructure and superstructure of the island have been developed. In terms of domestic and foreign visitors, there has been an increase not only in the number of foreign visitors, but also in the number of participants of meetings begun to be held within the scope of gastronomy tourism research (Bucak and Turan, 2016).

Eco-friendly applications in destination marketing

A lot of destinations have started competing with each other with the massification of tourism. For destinations which aim at attracting more tourists and earning more income than their competitors, providing sustainability is a must, because mass tourism movements also have economic, cultural, social and environmental impacts on destinations (Genç, Atay and Eryaman, 2014). For this reason, today, the importance of eco-friendly applications has increased in destination marketing.

The importance of eco-friendly applications in destination marketing

Eco-friendly applications in destination marketing are useful operations leading to economic, political and social changes and developments in urban operational environments. Today, these applications help cities or provinces increase their attractiveness and become a brand, and thus all the goods and services that a city offers become more desirable for target markets. Considering cities highlighted or promoted in tourism, it can be observed that some of these cities are preferred because of their cultural and historical heritage, some are chosen for their natural attractions such as sea, woods or mountains, and some of them are visited because of authentic handmade items or artifacts. Even though the reasons for choice or preference can differ, attraction factors in cities are supported and enhanced with environmentally friendly applications. Nowadays, a lot of destinations not only draw tourists from foreign countries by increasing the level of their attractiveness, but they also make efforts towards generating tourists' intentions to revisit and positive word-of-mouth recommendations (Giritlioğlu and Avcıkurt, 2010).

For this reason, eco-friendly applications and strategies are significant destination marketing components for tourists (Sohn and Park 1999).

Some examples of eco-friendly applications in destination marketing

Some applications such as Cittaslow, last chance tourism, Green Destination Platform and rural tourism considered within the scope of sustainability can be given as examples of eco-friendly applications in destination marketing.

CITTASLOW

The Cittaslow (Slow City) movement was initiated with the aim of increasing the quality of life in cities and of cities, with the idea of self-evaluation of cities to adopt a different development model in 1999. Cittaslow consists of the Italian word *citta*, meaning city, and an English word, slow (www.cittaslow.org, 2018).

The Cittaslow movement is an eco-friendly practice in which towns and cities can participate if they want to be on the world stage without losing their local identities and characteristics and unless they want to be one of the homogenized places created by globalization. Within the scope of the Cittaslow philosophy, cities consider in which aspects they are significant and special and develop strategies for protecting these characteristics; city residents and visitors experience the nature, colors, music and story of a city in harmony with an enjoyable pace; local crafts, tastes and arts are revitalized and shared with the following generations and visitors and guests; public health is promoted, and, with this aim, the levels of air, noise, light and electromagnetic pollution are controlled regularly and kept at an unthreatening level; precautions are taken for many issues such as garbage collection hours and disinfestation; local producers are supported, and sales centers or markets where they can sell their products are opened; alternative and renewable energy resources, which do not have negative effects on the environment and humans, are encouraged; and a city differentiates itself from thousands of similar cities in the world (Yücel and Karabağ, 2011). Although being a member of the Cittaslow network has not been purposefully used for destination marketing at all Cittaslow destinations, it is considered as a factor of sustainability and a factor increasing the life quality and standards of locals. In general, the priority of local administration is to protect the natural environment and the sustainability of natural resources, instead of increasing tourist numbers (Bekar, Yozukmaz, Sürücü and Gövce, 2015).

LAST CHANCE TOURISM

Last chance tourism offers people the chance to visit places under threat of extinction or disapperance before these places perish. This tourism type is encouraged by tour operators or tour guides in general. This trend is caused mostly by the increase in tourist numbers visiting polar areas and the Galapagos Islands, whose ecosystems are changing in a negative way (Lemelin, Dawson, Stewart, Maher and Lueck, 2010). With this tourism trend, public awareness would be raised to create consciousness of some places under threat. Also, people who live far away in places other than those that are faced with extinction can be informed about those places, and some places which are close to disappearing but have a chance of preservation can be taken under protection with public support (Burns and Bibbings, 2009). All over the world, the foremost example of a last chance tourism destination is the Great Barrier Reef in Australia, which hosts various marine species and is the biggest coral reef in the world. According to Great Barrier Reef research, for reasons such as increasing coral bleaching activities, sea level rise and decline in water quality, this process will end in ecosystem downfall by 2100 (Wolanski and De'ath, 2005).

In the literature, this tourism type is also called climate change tourism, extinction tourism, disappearance tourism, imperilment tourism and last chance to see tourism. Nevertheless, there are some common grounds to last chance tourism such as global warming. Some studies have drawn attention to global warming and its impacts on cultural and natural destinations (Lemelin *et al.*, 2010). Also, it is asserted that last chance tourism offers people a real and breathtaking experience because it gives visitors a chance to see disappearing wild nature and its features, such as landscapes and flora and fauna.

GREEN DESTINATIONS/GREEN SOLUTIONS PLATFORM

Turning activities conducted within the scope of sustainable tourism into a competitive advantage for businesses and destinations has caused solutions for environmental problems to increase and diversify. This also has led to the emergence of national or international, autonomous or semi-autonomous state institutions and organizations, which accredit, inspect and register tourism facilities and destinations as "sustainable" or "green". One of these organizations is the Green Destinations platform which has certified 887 destinations as sustainable or green. Considering destinations as tourism products of the tourism industry, it is known that activities, tourism businesses, image, accessibility and attractions should exist. For a destination to be evaluated as sustainable and green, these factors should be in accordance with the principle of sustainability in an integrated way (greendestinations.org, 2018).

In this sense, the Green Destinations platform presents a certification process based on 11 variables in total, such as wildlife, landscape, nature, secured space, clean air, culture and traditions, visitor reviews, security against crime, human rights, green economy and green policy regarding the aforementioned factors and it creates solutions for destinations to be more sustainable. By rating every variable, destinations can be certified as sustainable or green places (greendestinations.org, 2018).

Case study

Becoming a member of the Cittaslow network on November 28, 2009, Seferihisar broke new ground in Turkey. Entitled the first slow city (Cittaslow) in Turkey and the 121st in the world, Seferihisar town in İzmir continues to make efforts to fulfill the requirements of being a slow city with its municipality, residents and non-governmental organizations. One of the projects involved embellishing streets which used to have an ordinary town landscape, with satellite dishes hanging on the balconies, topsy-turvy electricity and phone cables and advertisement boards or signboards in various sizes. Other projects were bicycles running on solar power, new pedestrian paths, encouraging people to use bicycles or public transport, recycling at source and local markets or bazaars where only local farmers or producers could sell their products. Today it is widely known that foreign tourists in particular prefer to dine at restaurants with slow food certification. For this reason, in Seferihisar, slow food has become a common issue, and managers of restaurants have started to use natural products; also, many restaurants have received their certification after participating in slow food training or courses opened by the municipality. The heavy traffic in the town center has been reduced, and some activities and campaigns have been initiated for the protection of cultural and historical places.

Energy saving is supported and encouraged, and, with eco-friendly policies, an organic, hormone-free Seferihisar has been created (Yücel and Karabağ, 2011).

References

Akdağ, G., Güler. O., Demirtaş, O., Dalgıç, A., and Yeşilyurt, C. (2014) "Turizm ve Çevre İlişkisi: Türkiye'deki Yeşil Otellerin Gözünden Yeşil Otelcilik Uygulamalarının Getirileri". Türkiye Coğrafyacılar Derneği Uluslararası Kongresi, June 4–6, 2014, Muğla Sıtkı Koçman University.

Akış, S. (1999) Sürdürülebilir Turizm ve Türkiye. *Anatolia: Turizm Araştırmaları Dergisi, 10*(1), 36–46.

Alım, M. (2006) Avrupa Birliği Üyelik Sürecinde Türkiye'de Çevre ve İlköğretimde Çevre Eğitimi. *Kastamonu Eğitim Dergisi, 2* (14), 599–616.

Bekar, A., Yozukmaz, N., Sürücü, Ç., and Gövce, A. M. (2015) The concept of Cittaslow as a marketing tool for destination development: The case of Mugla, Turkey. *American International Journal of Social Science, 4*(3), 54–64.

Brown, M. (1996) Environmental policy in the hotel sector: "green" strategy or stratagem? *International Journal of Contemporary Hospitality Management, 8*(3), 18–23.

Bucak, T., and Turan, Ö. (2016) Bölge Turizmine Yeni Akımların Etkisi: Gökçeada Yavaş Yemek Örneği. *Journal of Yasar University, 11*(43), 211–219.

Buckley, R. (2002) Tourism ecolabels. *Annals of Tourism Research, 29*(1), 183–208.

Burns, P., and Bibbings, L. (2009) The end of tourism? Climate change and societal challenges. *Twenty-First Century Society, 4*(1), 31–51.

Cook, R. A., Hsu, C. H. C., and Marqua, J. J. (2014) *Tourism: The Business of Hospitality and Travel.* Harlow, UK: Pearson.

Cooper, C., Fletcher, J., Fyall, A., Gilbert, D., and Wanhill, S. (2008) *Tourism Principles and Practice.* Harlow, UK: Prentice Hall.

Çalışkan O., and Yılmaz, G. (2016) Gastronomy and tourism. In C. Avcıkurt, M.S. Dinu, N. Hacıoğlu, R. Efe, A. Soykan and N. Tetik (Eds.), *Global Issues and Trends in Tourism.* pp. 33–50. Sofia: St. Kliment Ohridski University Press.

Delmas, M. A., and Grant, L. E. (2008) *Eco-Labeling Strategies: The Eco-Premium Puzzle in the Wine Industry.* Chicago, IL: ISBER Publications.

Demir, C., and Çevirgen, A. (2006) *Turizm ve çevre yönetimi-sürdürülebilir gelişme yaklaşımı.* Ankara: Nobel Yayın Dağıtım.

Demiryürek, K. (2011) Organik tarım kavramı ve organik tarımın dünya ve Türkiye'deki durumu. *GOÜ, Ziraat Fakültesi Dergisi, 28*(1), 27–36.

Durlu-Özkaya, F., Sünnetçioğlu, S., and Can, A. (2013) Sürdürülebilir gastronomi turizmi hareketliliğinde coğrafi işaretlemenin rolü. *Journal of Tourism & Gastronomy Studies, 1*(1), 13–20.

English Tourist Board/Employment Department. (1991) *Heritage Sites Working Group: Report to the Tourism and Environment Task Force.* London: English Tourist Board/Employment Department Group.

European Commission. (2001) *A Framework for Indicators for the Economic and Social Dimensions of Sustainable Agriculture and Rural Development.* Brussels: European Commission Agriculture Directorate-General.

Fışkın, R., Çakır, E., and Özkan, E. D. (2016) Mavi Bayrak Uygulamasının Önemi, Ölçütleri Ve Ülkelere Göre Durum Analizi—The criteria and importance of Blue Flag implementation and the present situation analysis by countries. *Mehmet Akif Ersoy Üniversitesi Sosyal Bilimler Enstitüsü Dergisi, 8*(15), 224–247.

Font, X., and Buckley, R. (Eds.). (2001) *Tourism Ecolabelling: Certification and Promotion of Sustainable Management.* Wallingford, UK: CABI.

Genç, K., Atay, L., and Eryaman, M. Y. (2014) Sürdürülebilir destinasyon yaratma sürecinde örgütlenmenin önemi: Çanakkale turizmi üzerine bir araştırma. *Anatolia: Turizm Araştırmaları Dergisi, 25*(1), 49–61.

Giritlioğlu, İ., and Avcıkurt, C. (2010) Şehirlerin turistik bir ürün olarak pazarlanması, örnek şehirler ve Türkiye'deki şehirler üzerine öneriler (derlemeden oluşmuş bir uygulama). *Adıyaman Üniversitesi Sosyal Bilimler Enstitüsü Dergisi, 4*, 74–89.

Güler, O., and Tufan, E. (2013) Sürdürülebilir Bir Yatırım Örneği Olarak Yeşil Otelcilik. In A. Ş. Tekeltürk, and M. Boz (Eds.). *Turizmde Güncel Konu ve Eğilimler.* Ankara: Detay Yayıncılık.

Güneş, G. (2011) Konaklama sektöründe çevre dostu yönetimin önemi. *Karamanoğlu Mehmetbey Üniversitesi Sosyal Ve Ekonomik Araştırmalar Dergisi, 1*, 45–51.

Gündüz, F. (2004) Çevre ve Turizmin Sürdürülebilirliği. *Planlama, 1*, 58–66.

Holden, A. (2016) *Environment and Tourism* (3rd ed.). New York: Routledge.

Jones, P., Shears, P., Hillier, D., Comfort, D., and Lowell, J. (2003) Return to traditional values? A case study of Slow Food. *British Food Journal, 105*(4/5), 297–304.

Kan, M., and Gülçubuk, B. (2015) Kırsal ekonominin canlanmasında ve yerel sahiplenmede coğrafi işaretler. *Uludağ Üniversitesi Ziraat Fakültesi Dergisi, 22*(2), 57–66.

Kaymaz, M. (2012) Turizm Sektöründe Çevre Yönetimi: Marmaris'teki Konaklama İşletmeleri Örneği. Yayınlanmamış Yüksek Lisans Tezi. Muğla Üniversitesi, Fen Bilimleri Enstitüsü, Çevre Bilimleri Anabilim Dalı. Muğla.

Kızılırmak, İ. (2011) Dünyada Ve Türkiye'deki Turizm İşletmelerinde Çevre Korumaya Yönelik Uygulamalar: Amacı Ve Önemi. *Sosyal Bilimler Dergisi, 2*, 1–12.

Kirk, D. (1998) Attitudes to environmental management held by a group of hotel managers in Edinburgh. *International Journal of Hospitality Management, 17*(1), 33–47.

Ko, D. W., and Stewart, W. P. (2002) A structural equation model of residents' attitudes for tourism development. *Tourism Management, 23*, 521–530.

Kozak, N., Akoğlan Kozak, M., and Kozak, M. (2015) *Genel Turizm*. Ankara: Detay Yayıncılık.

Kuvan, Y., and Akan, P. (2005) Residents' attitudes toward general and forest-related impacts of tourism: The case of Belek, Antalya. *Tourism Management, 26*, 691–706.

Lee, J. S., Hsu, L. T., Han, H., and Kim, Y. (2010) Understanding how consumers view green hotels: How a hotel's green image can influence behavioural intentions. *Journal of Sustainable Tourism, 18*, 901–904.

Lemelin, H., Dawson, J., Stewart, E. J., Maher, P., and Lueck, M. (2010) Last-chance tourism: The boom, doom, and gloom of visiting vanishing destinations. *Current Issues in Tourism, 13*(5), 477–493.

Mathieson, A., and Wall, G. (1982) *Tourism: Economic, Physical and Social Impacts*. Harlow, UK: Longman.

Menteşe, S. (2017) Çevresel Sürdürülebilirlik Açısından Toprak, Su ve Hava Kirliliği: Teorik Bir İnceleme. *Uluslararası Sosyal Araştırmalar Dergisi, 10*(53), 381–389.

Organisation for Economic Co-operation and Development (OECD). (1980) *Technical Change and Economic Policy*. Paris: OECD.

Page, S. J. (2015). *Tourism Management*. New York: Routledge.

Pappas, N. V. (2008) City of Rhodes: Residents' attitudes toward tourism impacts and development. *Anatolia: An International Journal of Tourism & Hospitality Research, 13*(1), 51–70.

Petrini, C. (2001) *Slow Food: The Case for Taste*. New York, Columbia.

Pezikoğlu, F. (2012) Sürdürülebilir tarım ve kırsal kalkınma kavramı içinde tarım-turizm-kırsal alan ilişkisi ve sonuçları. *Karamanoğlu Mehmetbey Üniversitesi Sosyal Ve Ekonomik Araştırmalar Dergisi, 1*, 83–92.

Pırnar, İ. (1993) Turizmin Doğal Çevreye Etkileri ve Çevrenin Korunması. *Anatolia Turizm Araştırmaları Dergisi*, (Mayıs-Haziran), 15–17.

Pink, S. (2008) Sense and sustainability: The case of the Slow City movement. *Local Environment, 13*(2), 95–106.

Revilla, G., Dodd, H. T., and Hoover, C. L. (2001) Environmental tactics used by hotel companies in Mexico. *International Journal of Hospitality & Tourism Administration, 3*, 111–127.

Sağır, G. (2017) Küreselleşmeden Geleneksele Dönüşte Slow Food ve Cittaslow Hareketi. *The Journal of Social Science, 1*(2), 50–59

Scarpato, R. (2002) Sustainable gastronomy as a tourist product. In A. Hjalager and G. Richards (Eds.), *Tourism and Gastronomy* (pp. 146–166). London and New York: Routledge.

Sohn, H. S.. and Park, C. (1999) International visitors' satisfaction with Pusan city and its implications for city marketing. *Asia Pacific Journal of Tourism Research, 4*(1), 71–76.

Sunlu, U. (2003) Environmental impacts of tourism. In D. Camarda and L. Grassini (Eds.), *Local Resources and Global Trades: Environments and Agriculture in the Mediterranean Region* (pp. 263–270). Bari: CIHEAM.

Tencati, A., and Zsolnai, L. (2012) Collaborative enterprise and sustainability: The case of slow food. *Journal of Business Ethics, 110*(3), 345–354.

Teye, V., Sönmez, S. F., and Sırakaya, E. (2002) Residents' attitudes toward tourism development. *Annals of Tourism Research, 29*(3), 668–688.

Tuna, M. (2007) *Turizm, Çevre ve Toplum (Marmaris Örneği)*. Ankara: Detay Yayıncılık.

Tutar, F. K. (2015) Yeşil Ekonomi, Yeşil Turizm: Türkiye'de Turizm Sektöründe Yeni Trend Yeşillenen Oteller Projesi'. *Akademik Sosyal Araştırmalar Dergisi, 3*(13), 328–352.

Ünlüönen, K., Tayfun, A., and Kılıçlar, A. (2007) *Turizm Ekonomisi*. Ankara: Nobel.

Wolanski, E., and De'ath, G. (2005) Predicting the impact of present and future human land-use on the Great Barrier Reef. *Estuarine, Coastal and Shelf Science, 64*(2–3), 504–508.

Yıldız, K., Sipahioğlu, Ş., and Yıldız, M. (2000) *Çevre bilimi*. Ankara: Gündüz Eğitim ve Yayıncılık.

Yoon, Y., Gursoy, D., and Chen, J. S. (2001) Validating a tourism development theory with structural equation modelling. *Tourism Management*, *22*, 363–372.

Yücel, M., and Ekmekçiler, Ü. S. (2008) Çevre Dostu Ürün Kavramına Bütünsel Yaklaşım; Temiz Üretim Sistemi, Eko-Etiket, Yeşil Pazarlama. *Elektronik Sosyal Bilimler Dergisi*, 7(26), 320–333.

Yücel, F., and Karabağ, O. (2011) Şehirlerin Turistik Ürün Olarak Pazarlanmasında Cıttaslow (Sakin Şehir) Hareketi, 3. Uluslararası Balkanlarda Sosyal Bilimler Kongresi.

Online references

www.ecolabelindex.com/news/ Ecolabel Index (retrieved April 1, 2018).

www.coastlearn.org/tr/tourism/tools-cp-ecolabelling.htm (retrieved April 27, 2018).

www.environmentallyfriendlyhotels.com/ (retrieved April 27, 2018).

www.slowfood.com/about-us/slowfood.com (retrieved April 28, 2018).

http://greendestinations.org/ (retrieved May 6, 2018).

www.ecohotelsoftheworld.com/ (retrieved May 6, 2018).

www.turizmdunyasi.com.tr/arsiv/yazi/118-mavi-bayrak-yesil-anahtar-yesil-yildiz (retrieved May 6, 2018).

www.cittaslow.org/content/association (retrieved May 10, 2018).

22

TOURISM AND THE ENVIRONMENT

Mahmoud M. Hewedi and Reem Bahaa ElMasry

Introduction

Tourism is an increasing human activity in both developed and developing countries and is based on environmental resources, whether natural or man-made. Tourism is the largest service industry export and plays an important role in the international economy. In recent decades, tourism has witnessed remarkable changes, including emerging new destinations with different images and vacation styles and the inclusion of new technology into its business.

Sustainability, environmental tourism, ecotourism and its derivatives, resorts, protected areas, and other phrases and terms have emerged and been introduced to tourism in recent decades after the increased awareness and call for a sustainable world and green globe. Approaching that requires the different stakeholders, including scientists, practitioners, and authorities, to work together in order to maintain the balance between the results of vacationers' activities, the environment, and its ecosystem. Globally, the tourism industry has witnessed tremendous research projects, technical developments, and new regulations that assure its progress towards a sustainable and green globe

Globally, tourist influxes have grown from 25 million in 1950 to 278 million in 1980, 674 million in 2000, and 1,235 million in 2016. Similarly, international tourism grosses earned by destinations worldwide have surged from US$2 billion in 1950 to US$104 billion in 1980, US$495 billion in 2000, and US$1,220 billion in 2016. In 2017, numbers of international vacationers grew and reached 1.3 billion, and the figure is likely to touch 1.5 billion by 2020, generating US$2,000 billion. UNWTO's message highlights the need to turn these numbers into benefits for all folks and all communities. "Leaving no one behind" is the target for true sustainability, which must also decouple growth from supply use and place climate change response at the core of the tourism sector's schedule. Apollo (2018) reported that, worldwide, tourism represents 7% of the world's exports in goods and services, having increased one percentage point from 6% in 2015, and has developed quicker than world trade for the past five years. According to Tourism Towards 2030, it is expected that the number of arrivals of international vacationers worldwide will grow by an average of 3.3% a year over the period 2010–2030. It is expected that the speed of growth will steadily decrease over time, reducing from 3.8% at the beginning of the period to 2.9% towards 2030 (UNWTO, 2017).

Many new tourist destinations have emerged in addition to the popular ones of Europe and North America. Such destinations have undergone uninterrupted growth over time, despite occasional shocks, demonstrating the sector's strength and resilience (Dimitriou, in press).

Background

Tourism is a multidisciplinary industry that stems from the abundance of quality attractions, whether natural or man-made. Based on such attractions, other qualities of a tourism destination are developed to complement the tourism picture and make the destination ready to invite and receive tourists who will have a pleasant and unforgettable experience and leave the destination delighted or at least satisfied, with lots of documented memories, thus marketing the tourism destination on their own, without any interference or pressure from the destination itself. It is a smokeless industry (see, for example, Yan, 2014), with lots of benefits, and, at the same time, costs can be reduced or minimized through development based on sound planning, taking into consideration the carrying capacity and nature of the tourism destination

However, tourism is not an innocent activity and it adversely affects the environment (Edington and Edington, 1986); the following phrase was quoted by Bishop and should be given close consideration: "Tourism is not only the goose that lays golden eggs . . . it also fouls its own nest" (Bishop, 1988, quoting from Kamal Kumar Shrestha and cited in Mcconnell, 1991). Similarly, Green, Hunter and Moore (1990) concluded that tourism has dual effects. On the one hand, it has positive effects through generating funds that can be used to renovate buildings and develop the infrastructure. On the other hand, it adversely affects natural resources due to the limited attention paid.

Tourism has for years been accused of being a major cause of environmental damage, despite the fact that it has great potential economically and socioculturally; however, it is the worldwide economy growth driving force (Schmied et al., 2001). The latter added that tourists' diversified activities create pressure on the environment, threaten its natural foundations and lead to higher emissions of greenhouse gases, resulting in higher air pollution with negative consequences for biodiversity.

The contribution of tourism and the travel industry to the international economy is powerful and great. However, they significantly overuse and consume resources, such as energy, water, materials, and products, and generate tremendous amounts of waste leading to a significant impact on the environment and ecosystem (Davies and Cahill, 2000; Gössling, 2002, 2015; Gössling and Hall, 2006; Michailidou, Vlachokostas, and Moussiopoulos, 2015; Michailidou, Vlachokostas, Moussiopoulos, and Maleka, 2016).

De Freitas, Martín, and Román (2017) pointed out that tourism over the past six decades has witnessed and experienced continued growth and diversification to become one of the major economic sectors worldwide. It has revealed remarkable change, innovation, and development. More convenient transportation and technological advancements, emerging speedy progress in information technology coupled with growing prosperity, increased unrestricted income and time that is more discretionary have increased the demand for travel abroad (Goeldner, 2012; Holden, 2006). Geneletti and Dawa (2009) indicated that, over these years, the prospects of increased foreign revenue, higher levels of income and employment, as well as greater public sector revenues, have been attractive forces catalyzing governments to develop new destinations. Tourism is a fund-raising engine and positively supports the lives of locals (Eagles, McCool, and Haynes, 2002; Uddhammar, 2006). Uddhammar (2006) added that it plays a significance role in introducing the nation's heritage and culture.

Travel and tourism form an environmentally dependent activity. At the same time, however, tourists' activities may threaten or damage the environment, potentially destroying the primary attractions of any destinations. Therefore, understanding the nature and bases of tourism's environmental impacts and the means of minimizing them and working to mitigate or prevent damage when possible are of fundamental importance to the planning, management and development of long-term travel and tourism (Ikiara and Okech, 2002).

Tourism and environment

Tourism and environment are two faces of one coin and affect each other interchangeably, where an increase in tourism is certainly accompanied by escalation in environmental effects, resulting in reducing the quality of tourists' experiences unless it is properly managed (Gössling and Buckley, 2016; Chin, Moore, Wallington, and Dowling, 2000; Farrel and Marion, 2002; Lim and McAleer, 2005). The quality of the environment, both natural and man-made, is crucial to tourism and is a foremost element in the choice of a destination; however, the relationship between tourism and the environment and its impacts is complex (Gray, Canessa, Rollins, Keller, and Dearden, 2010; Green et al., 1990; Kim, Borges, and Chone, 2006; Lewis, 2006; Mieczkowski, 1995; Njole, 2011; Nyaupane and Poudel, 2011). Such impacts vary and could be direct, indirect, and even of a cumulative nature, where the visible effects take a long time to appear (Holden, 2006; Kreag, 2001; Mieczkowski, 1995). The human environment and the natural environment are interwoven, and both are affected by human activity (Mason, 2008).

The impacts of tourism on the environment have been studied extensively, and there are quite a lot of publications in different journals that cover different aspects, with particular focus on the intersects of tourism and environmental conservation and the environmental approaches that could inspire the development of sustainable tourism in protected areas (e.g., Balmford et al., 2009; Belsoy, Korir, and Yego, 2012; Imran, Alam, and Beaumont, 2014).

Many others have studied the different aspects of tourism, environment, and protected areas – for example, Badola et al. (2018), Dedeke (2017), Imran et al. (2014), Schweinsberg, Darcy, and Cheng (2017), and Zachrisson, Sandell, Fredman, and Eckerberg (2006). Gray et al. (2010), Kim et al. (2006), Lewis (2006), Njole (2011), and Nyaupane and Poudel (2011) pointed out that the relationship between tourism, stakeholders, and policymakers and their attitudes towards and perception of environmental issues and protected areas are crucial, complex, and dynamic. Therefore, it is vital to understand such a relationship because it significantly affects the accomplishment or devastation of the sustainable tourism process (Kim et al., 2006; Lewis, 2006). However, it should be kept in mind that compatibility and confrontation between tourism and the environment have been the subject of argument, and it is undoubtable that the tourism industry has a massively threatening ecological impact on the world's protected areas, but that argument experiences shifts where the environment is recognized as a valuable asset for ecotourism (Goodwin, 1996; McCool, 1995).

In their study entitled "Impact of Tourism on the Environment of a Destination," Šimková and Kasal (2012) reported that tourism is a source of adverse-influence externalities leading to an increase in the rate of pollution and aesthetic damages, and overall it has negative effects on the quality of life of citizens. They concluded that it is necessary to develop sustainable tourism and undertakings to avoid the undesirable effects of tourism. They highly recommend that monitoring and assessment play a crucial role in diminishing the negative impact of tourism and assure that both practices are very powerful and much cheaper compared with the requirements necessary to remove the negative impact and ensure recovery.

Semenova (2013) studied the impact of Pyynikki outdoor recreation on different resources, including quality of air and water, natural and geological resources, vegetation and wildlife, as well as the man-made environment. The results clearly revealed that, because the impact of tourism may be quite similar to any other industry, reaching full sustainability is not realistic. The author found that negative impacts include the considerable amount of carbon dioxide (CO_2) emissions into the air that represents the most serious and harmful impact, and the same author attributed that to the number of cars circling daily in the area and, additionally, the littering and damage to soil. Impacts of a positive nature were raising mindfulness about nature protection, increasing visitors' welfare, and gathering funding that is used for preservation and protection. The literature confirmed the crucial role of the environment in encouraging the growth of different tourist activities (Latimer, 1985), and, on the other hand, Day and Cai (2012) clearly indicated that the environment is exposed to pressure as a result of most tourism activities.

Holden (2009) studied the influence of the relationship between tourism and environment on the market ethics. He concluded that its role is not limited to changing the relationship between society and the environment, but it has global impacts where it contributes to increasing emissions of greenhouse gases (GHGs) owing to the growing numbers of tourists traveling using aviation. Negative impacts of tourism extend to destroy living species of flora and fauna and impede the health of eco-systems (Holden, 2009), and this leads the ethical debate to focus strongly on tourism repositioning the relationship between tourism and nature.

The nature of the environmental impact of tourism is complex (Holden, 2006). Such impacts vary and could be direct, indirect, or even of a cumulative nature, where the visible effects take a long time to appear (Holden, 2009; Mieczkowski, 1995; Kreag, 2001).

Ap and Crompton (1998), Belk and Costa (1995), Jamison (1999), Mathieson and Wall (1982), Tosun (2002), and others researchers have completed studies that investigate the effects of tourism on the environment, economy, society, culture, and political environment. These studies revealed that tourism leads to both negative and positive impacts, as noted in macro marketing studies. Additionally, Tosun (2002) indicated that sociocultural dissimilarities, economic benefits, and the gaps in buying power between the host community and vacationers result in conflict.

Further, Schwab (2017) revealed that the impact of services created for tourists, such as airports, transportation routes, and resorts or golf courses surrounding the visited area, can result in severe impacts on the environment and ecosystems that once flourished there. For every natural resource that exists, there are multiple impacts created by tourism. Environmental damage and changes because of tourism and the use of natural resources have long-term consequences that scientists and tourism operators alike are starting to observe and understand (Schwab, 2017).

Tourism sites are often located in attractive zones, and vacationers want easy access to the natural beauty they came to see. Lowry (2017) depicted that, as a result, hotels or resorts are created on or at the edge of delicate, fragile, or small natural zones; accordingly, buildings obviously change the aesthetic landscape and the flora, fauna, and soil on which they are built.

Air quality in popular tourism destinations can suffer from two main tourist acts: reduction in the number of trees and their air-cleaning properties, and a variety of pollutants from various modes of transportation (Rodrigue, Comtois, and Slack, 2017). When pollutants fill the air and rain falls, this acid rain can cause damage to soil and plant growth and can negatively influence agriculture and, thus, the food supply in an area. Finally, poor air quality can lead to a gray fog or haze in an area, affecting the views and natural beauty of a destination.

Holden (2009) and Lowry (2017) revealed that the impacts of tourism on the environment are many and unstoppable. Tourism affects flora, fauna, air, and water quality and quantity.

Understanding how tourism affects these natural resources, and what tourism operators can do to mitigate the impact, is an essential step to conserving the beautiful natural areas tourists want to visit (Lowry, 2017).

Positive and negative impacts of tourism on the environment

Positive and negative outcomes in areas where tourism activities take place have been investigated by many scholars (Day and Cai, 2012; Duffy, 2001; Belsoy and Korir, 2013; Zhong, Deng, Song, and Ding, 2011). Several authors pointed out that tourism is an intensive job generator (Belsoy et al., 2012; Michailidou et al., 2015) and economy enhancer and supporter (Belsoy et al., 2012; Zhong et al., 2011) that promotes protecting natural areas, limits the movement of locals, and improves their sociocultural level. On the other hand, they added that the negative impacts of tourism are remarkable and not limited to: massive consumption of natural resources, including ground (space), water, and energy; destruction of landscapes; escalation of the production of waste; change in ecosystems; the introduction of exotic types of animal and plant; damage to local traditions; the proliferation of prostitution; the spread of drugs; more forest fires; and increases in the price of goods and services (Zhong et al., 2011; Belsoy et al., 2012) .

Beladi, Chao, Hazari, and Laffargue (2009) concluded that, despite the fact that an increase in tourism leads to gains in terms of trade, such enlargement may also encourage more production of needed services leading to environmental damage, and therefore there is crucial need for rigid regulations in order to protect the environment. The negative impacts extended to include exhaustion of different natural assets – that is, water and local resources – land degradation, air pollution, increases in waste and sewage, and degradation of ecosystems.

The positive impacts of tourism on the environment are undeniable. There are several factors that, when implemented, lead to bridging the "knowledge action–impact gaps" and remarkable change towards positive impacts of tourism on the environment and protected areas (Bartos and Cihar, 2011; Imran et al., 2014; Sirivongs and Tsuchiya, 2012; Stern, 2000; Thøgersen and Schrader, 2012). These factors include, but are not limited to, understanding ecological dimensions, accessibility of resources and availability of information and knowledge, the teamwork concept and the participation of the beneficiaries in planning and management, and knowledge sharing. These factors among others will prevent the creation of the clashes and problems that frequently surface from attitudinal and personal factors linked to awareness and knowledge (Bartos and Cihar, 2011). Sirivongs and Tsuchiya (2012), Stern (2000) and Thøgersen and Schrader (2012) argued that other related factors, such as partaking in governance organization and the presence and engagement of shareholders in tourism planning, enhance positive environmental orientations that promote income-generating and employment opportunities, and laws and regulations that favor the environment.

Tourism, climate change, and GHG emissions

Wong (2002) pointed out that tourist movement considerably contribute to changes in the environment where the amounts of GHG emissions increase leading to biodiversity loss, air, land, and water pollution, and damage to coastal and rural areas. Not only that, but it produces almost 1,302 million tonnes CO_2 from international tourist travel, including same-day visitors, which is equivalent to 5% of global CO_2 emissions, mostly from transport, that contributes to climate change (Peeters and Dubois, 2010). However, according to Scott, Peeters, and Gössling (2010), the total contribution of tourism activities to universal warming potential is valued at 5.2–12.5%

owing to the radiative effects of all GHGs. It is expected that GHG emissions from tourism will grow by 135% over the period from 2005 to 2035 (UNWTO, UNEP, and WMO, 2008) owing to the remarkable increase in the numbers of international arrivals, expected to reach1.8 million by 2030. Peeters and Dubois (2010) noted that the number of vacationers, number of trips of long-haul tourism, and numerous holidays for a shorter length of stay greatly affect the future growth of tourist-related CO_2 emissions. As a result, despite gains in efficiency, the increase in the number of international visitors hinders the significant worldwide efforts to restrict GHG emissions from different economic sectors, including tourism, that are seen as the most energy-intensive and problematic to decarbonize (Peeters, Gössling, and Becken, 2006).

GHG emissions from tourism are a complex mix, associated mainly with transport and accommodation and the diversified activities of tourists, such as leisure, festivals, shopping, conferences, and so on (see Michailidou et al., 2015), and UNWTO et al. (2008) reported that the contribution from transport by aviation approached not less than 40% of tourism's CO_2 emissions, followed by 32% from transport by cars, and 21% from accommodation (see Peeters et al., 2006). The level of GHGs produced by the three sectors is continuously increasing owing to the remarkable growth of the number of tourists worldwide (UNWTO, 2017). Bows, Anderson, and Peeters (2009) mentioned that the contribution of CO_2 emissions from tourism transportation to climate change is considerable in comparison with other sectors. In their study, Peeters and Dubois (2010) found that implementation of developed technology is not sufficient to achieve the targets for CO_2 emission reduction for sustainability, and avoiding unsafe climate change requires a drastic shift in tourist travel organization and arrangement in the future. The IPCC is hoping to reduce GHG emissions by 80% of their current level by 2050 (IPCC, 2007). Peeters et al. (2006) consider it an aspirational goal, and achieving it requires tough mitigation across economic sectors, including tourism. The Organisation for Economic Co-operation and Development and United Nations Environment Programme (OECD and UNEP, 2011) and Scott et al. (2010) reported that the various approaches developed to reduce the increase in GHG emissions from worldwide tourism, including legal, economic, and technological ones, were found to be mostly unsuccessful.

The energy consumption in accommodation is used for space heating and air conditioning, which accounts for nearly 52%, followed by cooking and heating water (Beccali, La Gennusa, Coco, and Rizzo, 2009). Researchers found that the amount of energy in millions of joules (MJ) per guest per night varies substantially among hotels in different countries. For instance, whereas it is 32–112 MJ in Italy (Beccali et al., 2009), 32–110 MJ in New Zealand (Trung and Kumar, 2005), and 119 MJ in Germany (Gössling, 2015), it is 65–457 MJ in Vietnam (Trung and Kumar, 2005). Although Katircioglu, Feridun, and Kilinc (2014) depicted that inbound tourism raises energy demands and, therefore, increases CO_2 emissions that affect global climate change, earlier, Wunder (2000) described ecotourism as a necessary and desirable solution that delivers economic motivations in a form of nature safeguarding. Dwyer, Forsyth, Spurr, and Hoque (2010) analyzed travel patterns and concluded that the burning of fossil fuels –petroleum, natural gas, and coal – directly accounted for the major part of tourism CO_2 emissions.

Tools used to assess the environmental impacts are namely: ecological footprint analysis (Hunter and Shaw, 2007), environmental impact assessment (Geneletti and Dawa, 2009), life cycle assessment (LCA; De Camillis, Petti, and Raggi, 2008), and environmental indicators (Michailidou et al., 2015). They are dissimilar in their characteristics, particularly in the objective and the precision of the assessment process. De Camillis et al. (2010) claimed that LCA is the most appropriate tool to assess the environmental impacts of tourism. It is a crucial tool and gained scientific acceptance because it holistically evaluates environmental impacts from dissimilar angles and norms (see, for instance, Castellani and Sala, 2012, and De Camillis et al., 2010).

It is worth mentioning that LCA was first used in the tourism industry by Sisman in 1993 to assess the environmental impact of a package holiday in the Seychelles offered by British Airways Holidays. Five years later, UK CEED (1998) reported its use for a similar purpose, to assess a holiday package in St. Lucia undertaken by the same airline. Since then, it has been used for a variety of purposes in the hotel industry, where it has been applied in the USA (Chambers, 2004) to trace the direct and indirect supply chain environmental effects of the hotel service sector, in Italy (De Camillis et al., 2008), in Portugal (Konig, Schmidberger, and De Cristoraro, 2007), and in Poole, UK (Filimonau, Dickinson, Robbins, and Huijbregts, 2011).

LCA had been used to assess the impact of tourism on climate change (Filimonau, Dickinson, Robbins, and Huijbregts, 2011), to study package holidays in Taiwan (Kuo, Lin, Chen, and Chen, 2012), to study all-inclusive holiday package tours from the UK to Portugal (Filimonau, Dickinson, Robbins, and Reddy, 2013), and to explore energy use and CO_2 emissions in three Taiwanese islands (Penghu, Kinmen and Green islands; Kuo et al., 2012). Additionally, El Hanandeh (2013) used LCA to measure the global warming potential of Hajj (the pilgrimage to Mecca). Michailidou et al. (2016) found that LCA could play an essential part in reducing complication in strategic planning of tourism, specifically in local-to-regional areas of intense tourism.

Gössling and Buckley (2016) investigated persuasive communication using carbon labeling in tourism, and their results indicated that its arrangements are facing theoretical and practical shortcomings. The results of the same study also indicated that carbon labeling is not currently effective, although tourists care about their climate change impacts. However, the same authors added that there are promising chances of carbon labels being developed further and used successfully.

Tourism and the protected areas

A protected area is defined as "an area of land and/or sea especially dedicated to the protection and maintenance of biological diversity and of natural and associated cultural resources, managed through legal or other effective means" (IUCN, 1994).

Globally, tourism in natural areas is in massive demand, and the last two decades of the 20th century have witnessed an increase in the number of visitors (Hadwen, Arthington, Boon, Taylor, and Fellows, 2011). It is characterized by seasonality and occurs in narrow windows of time (Baum and Lundtorp, 2001; Grindley, 2005; Hadwen, Hill, and Pickering, 2008). It has been reported that, globally, the number of protected areas has reached more than 108,000 parks/protected zones in different developed and developing countries, covering a total of 13.5 million square kilometers – an area the size China and India combined. Protected areas are suitable and attractive places for the growth of tourism as they have natural diversity, valued assets, and exceptional potential for open-air activities. However, limiting all activities in national parks makes it problematic to maintain them and does not create social activities (Scott, Gössling, Hall, and Peeters, 2016). This represents a challenge for the managers of protected areas to ensure that, while visitors have opportunities to partake in wanted activities, they are aware of and retain the values. Linking to this context of natural assets, Schweinsberg et al. (2017) claimed that botanical gardens worldwide have been considered the epitome of a nation's cultural attainment.

Goodwin (1996) asserted that protected areas gain benefits from ecotourism through fundraising to manage and safeguard natural habitats and species, empowering indigenous society to gain economically from the protected areas, and proposing means to raise people's awareness of the significance of protection. Tourism produces gains including financial and economic benefits that enable, support, and motivate communities to conserve and protect the environment and tourist destinations (Coad, Campbell, Miles, and Humphries, 2008; Zhong et al., 2011). In general, protected areas are increasingly seen as a tool for the development of peripheral areas. Research in the Swedish mountain region suggests, however, that tourism does not have such great potential (Heberlein, Fredman, and Vuorio, 2002; Lundmark, 2005) and may still function as a door-opener to local societies by providing funding opportunities which might ease the progression of designating protected areas.

The values and benefits of the protected areas, either direct or indirect, through use or non-use, are multiple and even huge, including enhancing the economy and quality of life and protecting the natural and cultural heritage (see Lordkipanidze, Krozer, Kadiman, Crul, and Brezet, 2008). In this regard, for example, Rustagi and Garcia (2005) stated that the protected areas have direct and indirect values and benefits that greatly support the survival of human life and nature. Such benefits include preservation of the gene pool, environmental services, scientific investigation and education, eco-tourism and leisure, and people's traditional and spiritual mores. In the meantime, Adams (2004) and Sellars (2009) pointed out that protected zones have been sites of dispute over nature safeguarding, the livelihoods of rural citizens, and tourism expansion at least since the founding of the first national parks in the United States.

Communities perceive the ecosystem goods and services as ecological values of a protected area, and such values are measured and monitored through indicators, such as, species abundance, ecosystem integrity, and ecosystem resiliency (Prato and Fagre, 2005). Earlier, the IUCN (2006) identified the ecological services of protected areas as follows: recreation, tourism, water supply, habitat for fish and wildlife, conservation of biodiversity, and purification of air and water.

Regarding the inclusion of locals, Zachrisson et al. (2006) found that nature conservation witnessed a shift in its paradigm to include indigenous citizens in the management affairs of protected zones, and this apparently led to the increase of tourism's role in accomplishing economic growth in peripheral areas. They argued that, in such cases, locals might profoundly accept the protected areas, depending on appropriateness and process factors, but concluded that it is not enough on its own. Lack of involvement of local people in tourism development, management, and perceived benefits, limiting their rights to resources, and displacement in protected areas lead to negative attitudes towards the environment and conservation and, consequently, result in biodiversity loss (Imran et al., 2014).

Ecotourism

Ecotourism appeared in the late 1970s; it was meant as a type of nature-based tourism and considered to be an agent to protect natural sites and locations in specific countries. It specifically emphasizes environmental and ecological sustainability and thereby plays an important part in green development, particularly in less-developed countries. The concepts of ecotourism and sustainable tourism are used interchangeably (Dedeke, 2017), and researchers have intensively investigated the different aspect of ecotourism. Some emphasized its outlines, definitions, and principles, whereas others focused on its benefits as creator of jobs and economic growth (Fennell, 1999; Honey, 1999; Michailidou et al., 2015; Viljoen, 2011).

Ecotourism is a subdivision of sustainable tourism. However, there is no single definition of ecotourism. UNWTO (2002) defines sustainable tourism as "Tourism which leads to management of all resources in such a way that economic, social and aesthetic needs can be fulfilled while maintaining cultural integrity, essential ecological processes, biological diversity and life support systems." According to the International Ecotourism Society (TIES), ecotourism covers all trips to natural zones that protect the environment, supporting the prosperity of local people at the same time. Ceballos-Lascurain (1996) describes ecotourism as "traveling to relatively undisturbed or uncontaminated natural areas with the specific objectives of studying, admiring and enjoying the scenery and its wild plants and animals, as well as any existing cultural manifestations (both past and present) found in these areas" (see Abu Hanifah and Webb, 2015).

The establishment of TIES in 1990 led to greater support for the international ecotourism regime. This was followed by the 1992 United Nations Rio Earth Summit (Rio Declaration on Environment and Development), where all 178 countries agreed environmental initiatives including Agenda 21, which is a wide-ranging plan of action to be taken universally, nationally and locally. In 1992, the Convention on Biological Diversity (UN, 1992) contained guidance on ecotourism for decision-makers, where its three focal objectives were the protection of biological diversity, the sustainable use of the components of biological diversity, and the fair and unbiased allocation of the benefits arising out of utilization of genetic resources. The UN had declared 2002 as the International Year of Ecotourism (IYE). However, critics argue that the UN declaration of 2002 as the IYE has generated debate because of, as already noted, the rising awareness that the ecotourism industry is not as benign as initially believed (TWN, 2002; also see Abu Hanifah and Webb, 2015).

However, Simon (1999) argues that, although global bodies such as UNEP and the World Travel and Tourism Council are moving to provide a unified set of guidelines, their application will remain challenging owing to a lack of systematic measurement and enforcement.

Ecotourism supports the generation of jobs for the unqualified workforce in rural societies and creates plentiful export opportunities in inaccessible locations to guarantee a green economy (see Michailidou et al., 2015). In a similar vein, Viljoen (2011) pointed out that ecotourism is an appropriate tourism type to support economic growth in unindustrialized countries with a capital shortage and natural resource abundance.

Visiting natural beauty destinations has been intensively attractive to tourists in many countries worldwide (Kepe, 2001; Newsome, Moore, and Dowling, 2002; Yu, Hendrickson, and Castillo, 1997; Goodwin, Kent, Parker, and Walpole, 1998). This brand of visit or tourism style gained popularity under varying names, including "ecotourism," "green tourism," "agri-tourism," and so on. The concept of ecotourism was dominantly adopted and highly rated among other economic growth approaches by many less-developed countries, leading to enhancing hard currency earnings through attracting visitors from wealthier to poorer countries (De Los Monteros, 2002; Goodwin et al., 1998; Kepe, 2001; Roe, Leader-Williams, and Dalal-Clyton, 1997; Yu et al., 1997). Ceballos-Lascurain (1996) pointed out that rural areas are the focus of ecotourism owing to the robust link between ecotourism and biodiversity protection, and the formal and informal means and practices for protecting biodiversity and ecotourism themselves enhance and inspire biodiversity protection. Ecotourism operators were found useful, in some ways, for the safeguarding of species and habitats in the area (De Los Monteros, 2002). However, the same author noted that a limited number of other studies attempted to depict ecological ecotourism, and positive examples of ecotourism are still uncommon.

De Los Monteros (2002) reported that ecotourism in Mexico is perceived as an opportunity for safeguarding and improvement, and the administration is energetically encouraging tourism in protected natural zones. He affirmed that achieving this necessitated conducting ecotourism activities according to the domestic definition, ethics, and expectations of ecotourism. However, Cater (1993) and King and Stewart (1996) believed that there is no difference between ecotourism and conventional tourism, unless the first is wisely accomplished, managed, and controlled. Uncontrolled and badly managed conventional tourism, as well as large numbers of vacationers, pose a significant threat to numerous natural zones. These factors also build pressure on resources, leading to land damage, rising pollution, increases in discharges into the waterways, natural habitat damage, increased stress on scarce species, and heightened susceptibility to forest fires. Additionally, they create competitiveness between resources and, particularly, water and locals (UNWTO, UNEP, and WMO, 2008). Therefore, Font and Harris (2004) pointed out that it is crucial to implement effective tourism management tactics that incorporate tourism alongside safeguarding management priorities and enforce limits on the scale and types of tourism permitted.

References

Abu Hanifah, N., and Webb, A.-B. (2015). Ecotourism and biopiracy: A legal perspective on the sustainability of tourism destination in Malaysia. In A. Saufi, I. R. Andilolo, N. Othman, and A. A. Lew (Eds). *Balancing Development and Sustainability in Tourism: Proceedings of the Tourism Outlook Conference 2015*, pp. 9–19. Singapore: Springer Science+Business Media Singapore 2017

Adams, W. M., (2004). *Against Extinction*. London: Earthscan.

Ap, J., & Crompton, J. L. (1998). Developing and testing a tourism impact scale. *Journal of Travel Research*, *37*(2), 120–130.

Apollo, M. (2018). Ethics in tourism as a key to development, prosperity and well-being of all stakeholders. 3rd International Congress on Ethics and Tourism, Krakow, April 27–28, 2017.

Badola, R., Hussain, S. A., Dobriyal, P., Manral, U., Barthwal, S., Rastogi, A., and Gill, A. K. (2018). Institutional arrangements for managing tourism in the Indian Himalayan protected areas. *Tourism Management*, *66*, 1–12.

Balmford, A., Beresford, J., Green, J., Naidoo, R., Walpole, M., and Manica, A. (2009). A global perspective on trends in nature-based tourism. *PLoS biology*, *7*(6), e1000144.

Bartos, L., & Cihar, M. (2011). Socio environmental attitudes amongst the inhabitants of border mountain regions close to the former iron curtain: The situation in the Czech Republic. *Journal of Environmental Protection*, *2*(05), 609–619.

Baum, T., & Lundtorp, S. (2001). Seasonality in tourism: An introduction. In T. Baum and S. Lundtorp (Eds.), *Seasonality in Tourism*, pp. 1–5. Oxford, UK: Elsevier Science.

Beccali, M., La Gennusa, M., Coco, L. L., & Rizzo, G. (2009). An empirical approach for ranking environmental and energy saving measures in the hotel sector. *Renewable Energy*, *34*(1), 82–90.

Beladi, H., Chao, C. C., Hazari, B. R., and Laffargue, J. P. (2009). Tourism and the environment. *Resource & Energy Economics*, *31*(1), 39–49.

Belk, R. W., and Costa, J. A. (1995). International tourism: An assessment and overview. *Journal of Macromarketing*, *15*(2), 33–49.

Belsoy, J., and Korir, J. (2013). Tourism environmental impacts – A theoretical introduction to tourism. *Journal of Environment and Earth Science*, *2*(10), ISSN 2224–3216 (Paper) ISSN 2225-0948 (online), www.iiste.org

Belsoy, J., Korir, J., and Yego, J. (2012). Environmental impacts of tourism in protected areas. *Journal of Environment & Earth Science*, 2 10), 64–73.

Bows, A., Anderson, K., and Peeters, P. (2009). Air transport, climate change and tourism. *Tourism & Hospitality Planning & Development*, *6*(1), 7–20.

Castellani, V., and Sala, S. (2012). Ecological footprint and life cycle assessment in the sustainability assessment of tourism activities. *Ecological Indicators*, *16*, 135–147.

Cater, E. (1993). Ecotourism in the third world: Problems for sustainable tourism development. *Tourism Management*, *14*(2), 85–90.

Ceballos-Lascurain, H. (1996). *Tourism, Ecotourism, and Protected Areas: The State of Nature-Based Tourism around the World and Guidelines for its Development*. Gland, Switzerland: IUCN.

Chambers, T. (2004). Environmental Assessment of a "Mass Tourism" Package Holiday and a "Responsible Tourism" Package Holiday, Using Life Cycle Assessment and Ecological Footprint Analysis, MSc thesis, University of East Anglia, Norwich, UK.

Chin, C. L., Moore, S. A., Wallington, T. J., and Dowling, R. K. (2000). Ecotourism in Bako National Park, Borneo: Visitors' perspectives on environmental impacts and their management. *Journal of Sustainable Tourism*, *8*(1), 20–35.

Coad, L., Campbell, A., Miles, L., and Humphries, K. (2008). The costs and benefits of protected areas for local livelihoods: A review of the current literature. UNEP World Conservation Monitoring Centre, Cambridge, UK.

Davies, T., and Cahill, S. (2000). Environmental implications of the tourism industry. Washington, DC: Resources for the Future.

Day, J., and Cai, L. (2012). Environmental and energy-related challenges to sustainable tourism in the United States and China. *International Journal of Sustainable Development & World Ecology, 19*(5), 379–388.

De Camillis, C., Petti, L., and Raggi, A. (2008). LCA: A key-tool for sustainable tourism? In *Proceedings of the 8th International Conference on EcoBalance*, pp. 485–488, Tokyo, Japan, December 10–12, 2008.

De Camillis, C., Raggi, A., and Petti, L. (2010). Tourism LCA: State-of-the-art and perspectives. *The International Journal of Life Cycle Assessment, 15*(2), 148–155.

Dedeke, A. N. (2017). Creating sustainable tourism ventures in protected areas: An actor-network theory analysis. *Tourism Management, 61*, 161–172.

de Freitas, J. B., Martín, J. C., and Román, C. (2017). Service quality evaluation in the perception of the wine tourist with fuzzy logic and ideal solutions. *PASOS. Revista de Turismo y Patrimonio Cultural, 15*(2), 341–358.

De Los Monteros, R. L. E. (2002). Evaluating ecotourism in natural protected areas of La Paz Bay, Baja California Sur, Mexico: Ecotourism or nature-based tourism? *Biodiversity & Conservation, 11*(9), 1539–1550.

Dimitriou, D. J. (in press). Comparative evaluation of airports productivity toward tourism development. *Cogent Business & Management*, 1464378.

Duffy, R. (2001). *A Trip Too Far: Ecotourism, Politics and Exploitation*. London: Earthscan.

Dwyer, L., Forsyth, P., Spurr, R., and Hoque, S. (2010). Estimating the carbon footprint of Australian tourism. *Journal of Sustainable Tourism, 18*(3), 355–376.

Eagles, P. F. J., McCool, S. F., and Haynes C. D. (2002). *Sustainable Tourism in Protected Areas: Guidelines for Planning and Management*. Best Practice Protected Area Guidelines Series No. 8. Adrian Phillips (Series Ed.). Gland, Switzerland: IUCN and WCPA.

Edington, J. M., and Edington, M. A. (1986). *Ecology, Recreation and Tourism*. Cambridge: Cambridge University Press Archive.

El Hanandeh, A. (2013). Quantifying the carbon footprint of religious tourism: the case of Hajj. *Journal of Cleaner Production, 52*, 53–60.

Farrell, T. A., and Marion, J. L. (2002). The protected area visitor impact management (PAVIM) framework: A simplified process for making management decisions. *Journal of Sustainable Tourism, 10*(1), 31–51.

Fennell, D. (1999). *Ecotourism: An Introduction*. London: Routledge.

Filimonau, V., Dickinson, J. E., Robbins, D., and Reddy, M. V. (2011). A critical review of methods for tourism climate change appraisal: Life cycle assessment as a new approach. *Journal of Sustainable Tourism, 19*(3), 301–324.

Filimonau, V., Dickinson, J., Robbins, D., and Huijbregts, M. A. (2011). Reviewing the carbon footprint analysis of hotels: Life Cycle Energy Analysis (LCEA) as a holistic method for carbon impact appraisal of tourist accommodation. *Journal of Cleaner Production, 19*(17–18), 1917–1930.

Filimonau, V., Dickinson, J., Robbins, D., and Reddy, M. V. (2013). The role of "indirect" greenhouse gas emissions in tourism: Assessing the hidden carbon impacts from a holiday package tour. *Transportation Research Part A: Policy & Practice, 54*, 78–91.

Font, X., and Harris, C. (2004). Rethinking standards from green to sustainable. *Annals of Tourism Research, 31*(4), 986–1007.

Geneletti, D., and Dawa, D. (2009). Environmental impact assessment of mountain tourism in developing regions: A study in Ladakh, Indian Himalaya. *Environmental Impact Assessment Review, 29*(4), 229–242.

Goeldner, C. R. B. (2012). *Tourism, Principles, Practices, Philosophies*. Hoboken, NJ: John Wiley.

Goodwin, H. (1996). In pursuit of ecotourism. *Biodiversity & Conservation, 5*(3), 277–291.

Goodwin, H., Kent, I., Parker, K., and Walpole, M. (1998). *Tourism, Conservation and Sustainable Development: Case Studies from Asia and Africa*. Wildlife and Development Series No. 11. London: International Institute for Environment and Development.

Gössling, S. (2002). Global environmental consequences of tourism. *Global Environmental Change, 12*(4), 283–302.

Gössling, S. (2015). New performance indicators for water management in tourism. *Tourism Management, 46*, 233–244.

Gössling, S., and Buckley, R. (2016). Carbon labels in tourism: persuasive communication? *Journal of Cleaner Production, 111*, 358–369.

Gössling, S., and Hall, C. M. (Eds.). (2006). *Tourism and Global Environmental Change: Ecological, Social, Economic and Political Interrelationships* (Vol. 4). Abingdon, UK: Routledge.

Gray, D. L., Canessa, R., Rollins, R., Keller, C. P., and Dearden, P. (2010). Incorporating recreational users into marine protected area planning: A study of recreational boating in British Columbia, Canada. *Environmental Management, 46*(2), 167–180.

Green, H., Hunter, C., and Moore, B. (1990). Assessing the environmental impact of tourism development: Use of the Delphi technique. *Tourism Management, 11*(2), 111–120.

Grindley, M. E. (2005). Visitor characteristics in Mount Elgon National Park. Cited in Hadwen, W., Arthington, A. H., Boon, P.I., Taylor, B., Christine, S., and Fellows, C.S. (2011). Do climatic or institutional factors drive seasonal patterns of tourism visitation to protected areas across diverse climate zones in Eastern Australia? *Tourism Geographies, 13*(2), 187–208.

Hadwen, W. L., Arthington, A. H., Boon, P. I., Taylor, B., and Fellows, C. S. (2011). Do climatic or institutional factors drive seasonal patterns of tourism visitation to protected areas across diverse climate zones in eastern Australia? *Tourism Geographies, 13*(2), 187–208.

Hadwen, W. L., Hill, W., and Pickering, C. M. (2008). Linking visitor impact research to visitor impact monitoring in protected areas. *JournaL of ecoTourism, 7*(1), 87–93.

Heberlein, T. A., Fredman, P., and Vuorio, T. (2002). Current tourism patterns in the Swedish mountain region. *Mountain Research & Development, 22*(2), 142–149.

Holden, A. (2006). *Tourism Studies and the Social Sciences*. New York: Routledge.

Holden, A. (2009). The environment–tourism nexus: Influence of market ethics. *Annals of Tourism Research, 36*(3), 373–389.

Honey, M. (1999). *Ecotourism and Sustainable Development: Who Owns Paradise?* Washington, DC: Island Press.

Hunter, C., and Shaw, J. (2007). The ecological footprint as a key indicator of sustainable tourism. *Tourism Management, 28*(1), 46–57.

Ikiara, M., and Okech, C. (2002). *Impact of Tourism on Environment in Kenya: Status and Policy* (No. 19). Kenya Institute for Public Policy Research and Analysis.

Imran, S., Alam, K., and Beaumont, N. (2014). Environmental orientations and environmental behaviour: Perceptions of protected area tourism stakeholders. *Tourism Management, 40*, 290–299.

International Union for Conservation of Nature (IUCN). (1994). Annual Report – the World Conservation Union. Gland, Switzerland: IUCN.

International Union for Conservation of Nature (IUCN). (2006). Cited in Ramos, A. D., and Jimenez, P. S. (Eds). (2008). *Tourism Development: Economic Management and Strategy*. New York: Nova Science Publishers.

IPCC. (2007). *IPCC Climate Change 2007. The Physical Science Basis*, S. Solomon, D. Qin, M. Manning, M. Marquis, K. Averyt, M. M. B. Tignor, H. L. Miller, and Z. Chen (Eds.). Contribution of Working Group I to the Fourth Assessment Report of the Intergovernmental Panel on Climate Change. Cambridge: Cambridge University Press.

Jamison, D. J. (1999). Masks without meaning: Notes on the processes of production, consumption, and exchange in the context of first world-third world tourism. *Journal of Macromarketing, 19*(1), 8–19

Katircioglu, S. T., Feridun, M., and Kilinc, C. (2014). Estimating tourism-induced energy consumption and CO_2 emissions: The case of Cyprus. *Renewable & Sustainable Energy Reviews, 29*, 634–640.

Kepe, T. (2001). Tourism, protected areas and development in South Africa: Views of visitors to Mkambati Nature Reserve. *South African Journal of Wildlife Research, 31*(3–4), 155–159.

Kim, H., Borges, M. C., and Chon, J. (2006). Impacts of environmental values on tourism motivation: The case of FICA, Brazil. *Tourism Management, 27*(5), 957–967.

King, D. A., and Stewart, W. P. (1996). Ecotourism and commodification: Protecting people and places. *Biodiversity & Conservation, 5*(3), 293–305.

Kreag, G. (2001). *The Impacts of Tourism*. Minnesota: Minnesota Sea Grant.

Kuo, N. W., Lin, C. Y., Chen, P. H., and Chen, Y. W. (2012). An inventory of the energy use and carbon dioxide emissions from island tourism based on a life cycle assessment approach. *Environmental Progress & Sustainable Energy, 31*(3), 459–465.

Latimer, H. (Ed.). (1985). The impact of tourism and recreation on the environment. A miscellany of readings. Selected papers from a seminar at the University of Bradford, June 27–July 7, Occasional Paper, University of Bradford.

Lewis, A. (2006). Stakeholder informed tourism education: Voices from the Caribbean. *Journal of Hospitality, Leisure, Sport & Tourism Education, 5*(2), 14–24.

Lim, C., and McAleer, M. (2005). Ecologically sustainable tourism management. *Environmental Modelling & Software, 20*(11), 1431–1438

Lordkipanidze, M., Krozer, Y., Kadiman, T. Crul, M., and Brezet, H. (2008). Innovations for tourism in national parks. In A. D. Ramos and P. S. Jimenz (Eds.), *Tourism Development: Economics, Management and Strategy*, pp. 1–45. New York: Nova Science Publishers.

Lowry, L. (2017). Butler's tourism area life cycle and its expansion to the creative economy. In *The SAGE International Encyclopedia of Travel and Tourism*, pp. 2–9. Thousand Oaks, CA: Sage.

Lundmark, L. (2005). Economic restructuring into tourism in the Swedish mountain range. *Scandinavian Journal of Hospitality & Tourism, 5*(1), 23–45.

Mason, P. (2008). *Tourism, Impacts, Planning and Management*. Abingdon, UK: Routledge.

Mathieson, A., and Wall, G. (1982). *Tourism, Economic, Physical and Social Impacts*. Harlow, UK: Longman

McConnell, R. M. (1991). Solving environmental problems caused by adventure travel in developing countries: The Everest Environmental Expedition. *Mountain Research & Development, 11*(4), 359–366.

McCool, S. F. (1995). Linking tourism, the environment, and concepts of sustainability: Setting the stages. In S. F. McCool and A. E. Watson (Eds.), Linking Tourism, the Environment, and Concepts of Sustainability. Technical Report INT-GTR-323. Department of Agriculture, Forest Service – Intermountain Research, Ogden, UT.

Michailidou, A. V., Vlachokostas, C., and Moussiopoulos, N. (2015). A methodology to assess the overall environmental pressure attributed to tourism areas: A combined approach for typical all-sized hotels in Chalkidiki, Greece. *Ecological Indicators, 50*, 108–119.

Michailidou, A. V., Vlachokostas, C., Moussiopoulos, N., and Maleka, D. (2016). Life cycle thinking used for assessing the environmental impacts of tourism activity for a Greek tourism destination. *Journal of Cleaner Production, 111*, 499–510.

Mieczkowski, Z. (1995). *Environmental Issues of Tourism and Recreation*. Lanham, MD: University Press of America.

Newsome, D., Moore, S. A., and Dowling, R. K. (2002). *Natural Area Tourism: Ecology, Impacts and Management*. Clevedon, UK: Channel View Publications.

Njole, M. (2011). Tourism for sustainable local livelihoods and nature conservation: A case of Lake Manyara National Park. Wageningen University and Research Centre MSc MLE, Leisure, Tourism and Environment.

Nyaupane, G. P., and Poudel, S. (2011). Linkages among biodiversity, livelihood, and tourism. *Annals of Tourism Research, 38*(4), 1344–1366.

Organisation for Economic Co-operation and Development (OECD) and United Nations Environmental Programme (UNEP). (2011). *Sustainable Tourism Development and Climate Change: Issues and Policies*. Paris: OECD.

Peeters, P., and Dubois, G. (2010). Tourism travel under climate change mitigation constraints. *Journal of Transport Geography, 18*(3), 447–457.

Peeters, P., Gössling, S., and Becken, S. (2006). Innovation towards tourism sustainability: Climate change and aviation. *International Journal of Innovation & Sustainable Development, 1*(3), 184–200.

Prato, T., and Fagre, D. B. (2005). *National Parks and Protected Areas: Approaches for Balancing Social, Economic, and Ecological Values*. Hoboken, NJ: Wiley-Blackwell.

Rodrigue, J.-P.,. Comtois, C., and Slack, B. (2017). *The Geography of Transport Systems*, 4th ed. Abingdon, UK: Routledge.

Roe, D., Leader-Williams, N., and Dalal-Clyton, B. (1997). *Take Only Photographs, Leave Only Footprints: The Environmental Impacts of wildlife tourism*. Wildlife and Development Series No. 10. London: International Institute for Environment and Development.

Rustagi, D., and Garcia, J. (2005). Protected Areas in Pandemonium: Will optimisation of different values lead to sustainability, pp. 1–33. Center for Development Research. University of Bonn.

Schmied, M., Buchert, M., Hochfeld, C., and Schmitt, B. (2001). Environment and Tourism – Summary – From problem analysis to recommendations for action. Summary Ecological Research Plan of the German Federal Ministry for the Environment, Nature Conservation and Nuclear Safety R&D project 200 87 112.

Schwab, K. (2017). *The SAGE International Encyclopedia of Travel and Tourism*. Thousand Oaks, CA: Sage.

Schweinsberg, S., Darcy, S., and Cheng, M. (2017). The agenda setting power of news media in framing the future role of tourism in protected areas. *Tourism Management, 62*, 241–252.

Scott, D., Gössling, S., Hall, C. M., and Peeters, P. (2016). Can tourism be part of the decarbonized global economy? The costs and risks of alternate carbon reduction policy pathways. *Journal of Sustainable Tourism, 24*(1), 52–72.

Scott, D., Peeters, P., and Gössling, S. (2010). Can tourism deliver its "aspirational" greenhouse gas emission reduction targets? *Journal of Sustainable Tourism, 18*(3), 393–408

Sellars, R. W. (2009). *Preserving Nature in the National Parks: A History*, 2nd ed. New Haven, CT: Yale University Press.

Semenova, O. (2013). Environmental Impacts of Tourism Case: Pyynikki Outdoor Recreation Area. Bachelor's thesis, April, Tampere University of Applied Sciences.

Šimková, E., and Kasal, J. (2012). Impact of tourism on the environment of a destination. *People, 23*, 27.

Simon, F. (1999). Regulating ecotourism: Legal frameworks and market guidelines. Bulletin, Yale F&ES, p. 197.

Sirivongs, K., and Tsuchiya, T. (2012). Relationship between local residents' perceptions, attitudes and participation towards national protected areas: A case study of Phou Khao Khouay National Protected Area, central Lao PDR. *Forest Policy & Economics, 21*, 92–100.

Sisman, K. (1993). A Life-Cycle Analysis of a Holiday Destination: Seychelles. UK CEED, Cambridge UK. British Airways Environment Report 41:94.

Stern, P. C. (2000). Toward a coherent theory of environmentally significant behavior. *Journal of Social Issues, 56*(3), 407–424.

Third World Network (TWN). (2002). *International Year of Reviewing Ecotourism*. Penang, Malaysia: TWN.

Thøgersen, J., and Schrader, U. (2012). From knowledge to action – New paths towards sustainable consumption. *Journal of Consumer Policy, 35*(1), 1–5.

Tosun, C. (2002). Host perceptions of impacts: A comparative tourism study. *Annals of Tourism Research, 29*(1), 231–253.

Trung, D. N., and Kumar, S. (2005). Resource use and waste management in Vietnam hotel industry. *Journal of Cleaner Production, 13*, 109–116.

Uddhammar, E. (2006). Development, conservation and tourism: Conflict or symbiosis? *Review of International Political Economy, 13*(4), 656–678.

UK Centre for Economic and Environmental Development (UK CEED). (1998). An Assessment of the Environmental Impacts of Tourism in St. Lucia. British Airways Environment Report No. 5/98. Cambridge: UK CEED.

United Nations (UN). (1992). Convention on Biological Diversity. Rio de Janeiro: UN.

UN World Tourism Organization (UNWTO). (2002). *Tourism 2020 Vision: Global Forecasts and Profiles of Market Segments*, Vol. 7. Madrid: UNWTO.

UN World Tourism Organization (UNWTO). (2017). *Discussion Paper on the International Year of Sustainable Tourism for Development 2017*, p. 84. Madrid: UNWTO.

UN World Tourism Organization (UNWTO), United Nations Environment Programme (UNEP), and World Meteorological Organization (WMO). (2008) *Climate Change and Tourism: Responding to Global Challenges*. Paris and Madrid: UNWTO & UNEP.

Viljoen, W. (2011). Aid for trade and the green economy in Africa. *Bridges Trade BioRes Review, 5*(3). International Centre for Trade and Sustainable Development, Switzerland.

Wong, P. P. (2002). Tourism as a global driving force for environmental change. In I. Douglas (Ed.), *Causes and Consequences of Global Environmental Change (Encyclopedia of Global Environmental Change*, vol. 3, pp. 609–623. Chichester, UK: John Wiley.

Wunder, S. (2000). Ecotourism and economic incentives – an empirical approach. *Ecological Economics, 32*(3), 465–479.

Yan, L. (2014). Residents' attitudes toward tourism impacts in Zhouzhuang canal town. Master of Tourism, Mid-Sweden University.

Yu, D. W., Hendrickson, T., and Castillo, A. (1997). Ecotourism and conservation in Amazonian Peru: Short-term and long-term challenges. *Environmental Conservation, 24*(2), 130–138.

Zachrisson, A., Sandell, K., Fredman, P., and Eckerberg, K. (2006). Tourism and protected areas: Motives, actors and processes. *International Journal of Biodiversity Science & Management, 2*(4), 350–358.

Zhong, L., Deng, J., Song, Z., and Ding, P. (2011). Research on environmental impacts of tourism in China: Progress and prospect. *Journal of Environmental Management, 92*(11), 2972–2983.

23

ENVIRONMENTAL IMPACT OF THE UGLY FACE OF TOURISM

Pollution and management perspectives

Solmaz L. Azarmi, Roozbeh Vaziri, Ayman Kole,
Akeem A. Oladipo and Ahmet Bülend Göksel

Introduction

Tourism is one of the most significant socio-economic phenomena of the twentieth century and creates remarkable economic advantages for tourist destinations. The tourism industry, as a global and intricate industry, has powerful relations with politics, society, culture and the environment.

Nowadays, the tourism industry plays a major economic role in developing countries (Zaei & Zaei, 2013). As noted, owing to the increasing demand for tourism services and goods, this industry has seen much growth and is continuing to expand (Faulkner & Tideswell, 1997). Furthermore, this growth in the tourism industry is expected to create new jobs, thus contributing extensively to improving the quality and quantity of human life on a regional and national scale by means of economic benefit (Sirakaya, Teye & Sönmez, 2002).

Tourism is the second largest industry in Okavango, after the diamond industry, and as a result an increase in GDP was sighted in relation to tourism expansion (Mbaiwa, 2003). Because of foreign exchange, the quality of life of locals in those touristic destinations increased, and this was noted as a highly positive aspect of tourism. On the other hand, as the tourism industry began to develop, the negative aspects of the tourism industry gradually started to appear and, unfortunately, leave their mark on the environment (Mbaiwa, 2003).

In 1994, Hall stated that the natural environment is the main tourist attraction for travelers in Australia (Hall, 1994/forthcoming). That is, the majority of tourists were primarily interested in visiting natural environments or national parks (Blamey, 1995). Indeed, the breathtaking views and landscapes found in Australia have always been a favorite destination of tourists, together with the climate, which is mostly compatible with beach weather. For instance, the Nambung Natural Park of South Australia offers a unique landscape of weathered limestone pillars protruding out of the desert-like surroundings. The Undara Volcanic National Park, which offers a series of astounding tunnel formations and caves, serves as a noteworthy tourist attraction in Queensland. However, since 1970, environmental issues have emerged as pivotal topics concerning the tourism sector (Fennel, 1999).

In recent years, the rapid progress of the tourism industry has increasingly placed pressure on the environment. Unfortunately, this has led to destruction of biodiversity and has enabled the deterioration of pristine landscape, as well as altering the features of nature. There is a strong mutual relationship between tourism and quality of environment. To minimize the negative impacts of tourism, appropriate eco-friendly plans should be implemented by policymakers to achieve sustainable tourism, which is also known as eco-tourism (Mowforth & Munt, 2003). In 1993, eco-tourism was described by the Ecotourism Society as a responsible trip which protects natural areas and maintains the health of local individuals.

The Australian government has invested in infrastructure such as airports, roads and hotels in areas deemed tourist destinations in order to increase accessibility for tourists and promote a more comfortable and attractive stay. As expected, these changes have positive impacts on the quality of life of the locals. However, on the other hand, it can change the balance of nature and become harmful where the environment is concerned. As a result of this negative impact, any development in the tourism industry needs proper planning to ensure that the environment is not subject to severe damage during these important advances (Mbaiwa, 2003).

Therefore, it must be acknowledged that the development of the tourism industry should progress with the notion of preserving the environment rather than harming it. Indeed, excessive construction work in the name of the expanding tourism sector directly affects the quality of water and the flow of rivers, leading to the degradation of pastures and forests (Abdoreza & Somayyeh, 2010).

According to Aref, Redzuan, Emby and Gill (2009), who investigated the development of the tourism industry in Shiraz (Iran), these changes have the potential to damage the environment in the targeted touristic places. The negative effects stemming from the lack of environmental care during the growth of the tourism industry can have direct and indirect impacts on the quality of life of millions of people (Rabbany, Afrin, Rahman, Islam & Hoque, 2013).

In 1996, Ceballos-Lascurain classified the effects of tourism on the ecosystem such as soil, water, vegetation, minerals and landscape aesthetics. In addition, the impacts of coastal tourism activities have been comprehensively investigated for different ecosystems (GFANC, 1997). Among the literature, authors investigated the harmful effects of tourism on the ecosystem, such as natural resources, wildlife and biodiversity, causing soil erosion, ruining coral reefs, as well as generating solid waste and different types of pollution (Genot, 1997; Wong, 2002). As a matter of fact, the rise in marine pollution is the result of waste from the tourism and industrial sectors. Furthermore, the natural productivity and continuity of biological life in the sea rely largely on the amount of oxygen and water temperature. Therefore, marine pollution limits survival and destroys reproduction in the marine environment.

The majority of investigators stated that growth of the unconstrained economic benefits of tourism weakens the fundamentals of sustainable development and threatens the environment (Howes, 2013; Mowforth & Munt, 2015; Wells et al., 2016). For example, transport vehicles that are in constant use for the transportation of tourists are actually spreading airborne pollutants at an excessive level. On the other hand, liquid substances must be biodegradable and should be selected among environmentally friendly products. Further, extra care must be taken to minimize these substances' contact with soil.

Butler (1980) declared that policymakers are concerned about the harmful effects of the tourism sector on the environment. Furthermore, tourism generates environmental pollution such as congestion, noise and littering. Many tourist facilities have sewage problems owing to the lack of infrastructure, and, as a result, the infrastructure remains quite insufficient in terms of collection and disposal of garbage in designated touristic areas. Additionally, the constant emptying of solid and liquid wastes into the sea or areas used by tourism facilities is causing the seas and the environment to become polluted.

In 2016, despite the Guinness Mount Cameroon Race being a most important sporting event, Abam noted the negative impacts on the environment and how accurate planning was urgently needed to conserve ecology. Therefore, it must be acknowledged that environmental degradation such as the pollution of lakes and beaches has been generated by tourism activities in many destinations (Mill & Morrison, 2006).

Furthermore, waste production is also an impact of developing tourism which destroys ecology and the natural beauty of the landscape. Of course, huge amounts of garbage are generated by associated tourism facilities such as attractions, hotels and airlines. Moreover, an important issue for policymakers in coastal areas is the illegal disposal of solid waste, cargo debris and sewage by trade ships, which creates beach pollution.

Based on the UNEP4 survey, there are three significant impacts of tourism on the environment, which are pollution, depletion of natural resources and physical effects. Natural resources are under threat from the development of the tourism industry through the wasting of water and local resources. The UNEP reported that the consumption of water by tourists is around twice as much as the regular use by local people. Also, the extensive use of water for swimming pools and garden maintenance in hotels is a vital factor in relation to the tourism industry and water usage (UNEP, 2014). In another study, the authors illustrated that the ratio of tourism water use is increasing dramatically in some countries such as Cyprus, where it constitutes 40% of the total national water use (Gössling et al., 2012).

The contribution of tourism to environmental issues such as pollution and degradation of natural resources in the national parks of the USA has been discussed extensively (Rabbany et al., 2013). Tourism is responsible for adverse environmental impacts on local resources such as raw material, food and energy. According to a report by the UNEP in 2011, the biodiversity of coastal areas such as coral reefs and mountainous areas is damaged by the tourism sector. In 2014, investigators determined that tourists trekking in Nepal consume 5 kg of wood per day, which causes deforestation (UNEP, 2014). Furthermore, different kinds of pollution, such as air and noise pollution, wastewater and solid waste are associated with tourism activities. In Cape Cod (USA), individuals believe the tourism industry is responsible for their increasing noise, water and air pollution problem (Pizam, 1978). In a specific investigation, authors showed that 62% of local citizens in Hawaii requested their government to reserve an environment for tourist activities and also suggested that officials punish tourists who litter (Liu & Var, 1986).

Ghaderi (2004) stated that prosperous tourism development should involve appropriate planning to eliminate environmental problems. In 2000, Holden classified tourism-related pollution as air, water and aesthetic pollution (Holden, 2000). From research by a majority of scholars, the various types of pollution, such as sewage, solid waste, noise, air and visual, air emissions and littering, are created by tourist activities, resulting in deforestation, land degradation, loss of natural habitat and flora and fauna loss (e.g., UNEP, 2015; Kavallinis & Pizam, 1994).

Environmental impact of pollution

Air pollution

As tourism involves traveling, normally by motorcar, ship, train, bus or airplane, the contribution of each to air pollution is very clear. Of course, tourism transports such as vehicles, ferries and aircrafts emit waste and pollution into the environment, and therefore influence nature adversely. It must be noted that air pollution has a dangerous, direct effect on human life and health. It is the main cause of different kinds of cancer and asthma in children

(Nafstad et al., 2003; Lee, Wong & Lau, 2006; Vineis et al., 2006). Based on investigations, most tourism-related air pollution such as CO_2 emissions is generated by tour vehicles (Andereck, 1993).

According to Hunter and Shaw (2006), air pollution is the main cause of acid rain, which has a negative impact on the soil, water and underground water quality. In addition, air pollution has a significant role in climate change. According to the U.S. Environmental Protection Agency (U.S. EPA, 1998, December, Table A-1), automobiles emit more carbon monoxide than other vehicles. In 1997, automobiles emitted around 26 million tonnes, cruise ships 1.7 million tonnes, and aircraft 1 million tonnes of carbon monoxide into the environment. The development of the tourism industry runs parallel with the increasing number of tourists subsequently transported by road, rail and air. As provided by the International Civil Aviation Organization (ICAO) report in 2001, just a single flight across the Atlantic emits half of the carbon monoxide produced by other vehicles. A total of 60% of air transport is related to the tourism industry. Moreover, according to the ICAO report, the number of international air travelers was given as 88 million in 1972 and had increased to 344 million in 1994.

Paramati, Shahbaz and Alam (2017) surveyed the impact of tourism on CO_2 emissions as a negative effect on the environment of eastern and western European Union (EU) countries. It must be kept in mind that proper management and sustainable tourism policies could reduce CO_2 emissions.

In recent years, authors have utilized a panel framework to consider the effect of tourism on CO_2 in the EU (Lee & Brahmasrene, 2013). In summer, the amount of air pollution and solid waste increased in the Grand Canyon National Park by 2,000 tour vehicles in the canyon corridor (Sidles, 1997).

In the literature, several investigators have stated that tourism consumes a large amount of fossil fuel, and this theoretically results in CO_2 emissions into the ecosystem (Becken & Simmons, 2002; Gössling, 2002). In New Zealand, for instance, the tourism sector generates 1,400–1,600 kilotonnes of CO_2 emissions (Becken & Patterson, 2006). Williams, Noland and Toumi (2003) surveyed the role of tourism in relation to the greenhouse gas (GHG) emissions of British Columbia in Canada. Their study illustrated that 65% of Columbia's energy was utilized by the tourism sector, which produced high values of GHG. In another survey, the authors stated that tourism transport in EU countries emitted 916 million tonnes of CO_2 into the ecosystem (Peeters, Szimba & Duijnisveld, 2007). Furthermore, Kuo and Chan (2009) evaluated that each tourist consumes 1,606 MJ of energy, and 109,034 g of CO_2 is generated per trip to an island in Taiwan named Penghu. Air transport contributes 80% of CO_2 emissions and a high value of GHG intensity in Switzerland (Perch-Nielsen, Sesartic & Stucki, 2010). Between 1990 and 2012, there was a comprehensive investigation into the impacts of tourism activities on the environment which showed an increase of CO_2 emissions from 1,468.08 tonnes to 11,568.17 tones in Heilongjiang Province, China (Tang, Shang, Shi, Liu & Bi, 2014).

Another study states that the development of tourism operates as a catalyst for the growth of CO_2 emissions, which could affect climate change in Cyprus (Katircioglu, Feridun & Kilinc, 2014).

The UNWTO (2008) has undertaken an analysis of the impact of tourism on carbon emissions based on 2005 data. It also provides a breakdown of tourism carbon emissions. One result showed that domestic tourism was actually a larger contributor to GHG emissions than international tourism (although the data stem from 2005 and so may be subject to change over time). For both domestic and international tourism, aviation transport and accommodation account for a significant part of the emission process, whereas land transport is the largest contributor for domestic tourism.

Air emissions have a direct relation to the quality of fuel used, but, unfortunately, most ships and cruise ships use cheap fuel, which is 1,000 times dirtier than the fuel normally used for cars. Moreover, dangerous pollutants produced by ships could increase cancer risks more to 100 in 1 million. According to Klein (2003), each cruise ship reportedly produces 58% of GHGs and 95% of sulphur on the Vancouver coast. Based on one study in the Santa Barbara region, ships emitted 37% of nitrogen oxide, and this amount of pollution increased to 61% by 2015 (Copeland, 2008). Recently, some cruise ships have used solid waste instead of liquid fuel, which could be more dangerous for air pollution because of dioxins and other dangerous particles found therein (Carnival Corporation, 2007; RCI, 2009; Klein, 2003). Unfortunately, today, no one pays attention to the laws of deterrence on a local or international scale, regardless (Acidrain, 2008; Friedrich, Heinen, Kamakaté & Kodjak, 2007).

Based on the European Parliament Committee on Transport and Tourism report, the cost of air pollution by ships per person is €0.2413 per kilometer. For example, one voyage from Croatia to Venice is around 1,600 km. The total number of cruise ship passengers is given as 694,104 per year, and so the total air pollution cost is €266.5 million (TRT, 2007: 12, Table 8).

In addition, Rath and Gupta (2017) investigated the impacts of physical and environmental pollution generated by Indian tourism on different natural resources. In their study, they stated that the motors of tour buses ran continually in order to keep the air-conditioning in operation for the comfort of the tourists, even while the tourists were away from the bus in the Ajanta and Ellora caves. In a scientific survey, authors reported that the tourism industry contributes 60% of USA air travel and thus is the main cause of air pollution (Rabbany et al., 2013).

It is clear that the energy used in the tourism facilities produces air pollution which creates acid rain and contributes greatly to global warming. In addition, the CFCs and halons used in the hotel sector all contribute to ozone depletion (Middleton, 1998).

Water and sewage pollution

Activities or functions largely tailored for tourism, including accommodation, restaurants, swimming pools, cruises, mountain camps and various transportation vehicles, produce ineffective disposal of waste which, in turn, produces water pollution because of inadequate sewage systems and the use of herbicides in hotel gardens (Holden, 2008).

Authors have stated that the growth of tourist numbers led to proliferation of wastewater from tourism facilities such as resorts and hotels, and the discharge of wastewater into the sea causes destructive impacts on groundwater, aquatic animals and water resources.

Moreover, Middleton discovered that the different parts of hotels, such as laundries, swimming pools, golf courses and guest rooms, generate excessive water pollution by means of discharge of sewage and untreated waste water (Middleton, 1998).

The discharge of sewage into the seas by recreational boats degrades the water quality and thereby causes the spread of dangerous diseases such as typhoid fever, infectious hepatitis and dysentery (Seabloom, Plews & Cox, 1989).

As pointed out, many tourism facilities produce wastewater that contaminates the marine environment, lakes and streams. The majority of people believe that tourism brings about environmental damage and greatly increases the pollution problem (Lankford & Howard, 1994). Reports have stated that cruise ships generate around 70,000 tonnes of waste in the Caribbean region every year (UNEP, 1997). Moreover, the findings show that the degradation of water and the death of marine animals are caused by solid waste and littering (UNEP, 1997).

Therefore, activities designed for the tourism sector such as boating create water pollution in rivers, lakes and seas. Dixon, Hamilton, Pagiola and Segnestam (2001) illustrated that the solid waste generated by tourists in the Caribbean is twice the volume of the waste generated by local people. In addition, resorts and hotels in the Caribbean produce 75% of wastewater. In Jamaica, the statistics show that the disposal of waste and sewage into the sea decreases if the number of tourists is reduced (Sweeting, Bruner & Rosenfeld, 1998).

Also noteworthy, Crompton stated that hotels and resorts play a significant role in contaminating coastal waters (Crompton, 1999). However, the fact that underdeveloped countries implement very weak waste management programs, which in turn cause tremendous damage to the environment, must not be overlooked (Andereck, 1995).

As stated previously, accommodation and recreation facilities play a considerable role in terms of generating wastewater and sewage pollution, which damage flora and fauna, seas and coral reefs. In the coastal states of India, water pollution changes salinity and transparency, and siltation results, thus threatening the ecosystem (Rath & Gupta, 2017).

As the tourism industry develops, a huge increase in construction and infrastructure is noted, and hotels and countless other tourism facilities cause an increase in sewage pollution, and this has direct and indirect effects on the underground water quality, which generates vast problems concerning both human and animal life.

For example, in the coastal states of India such as Karnataka, Kerala, Maharashtra, Goa and Tamil Nadu, sewage pollution causes significant damage in relation to coral reefs. Furthermore, water polluted by tourist activities causes algae to grow, which act as a filter and lead to coral death (Davies & Cahill, 2000).

Noise pollution

Based on National Environmental Quality Standards, the maximum level for noise should be 85 dB, and anything above this limit is categorized as noise pollution. According to several studies in the low season, the noise value is normal and sometimes below the standard. However, during the high season, such as in June and July, the average noise value is very high, thus illustrating that noise pollution occurs in the months of active tourism.

Equally important, noise pollution causes many health problems, including sleep disturbance, which is actually one of the biggest health issues (Shujahi & Hussain, 2016).

Researchers confirm that, because of tourist transportation vehicles such as trains and aircraft, the local population is significantly disturbed by noise pollution in areas deemed tourist destinations (Holden, 2008). In addition, more research concludes that activities stemming from tourism such as discos, nightclubs, festivals and concerts also produce high noise pollution, which severely annoys the local people.

More research has found that the main sources of noise pollution in the national parks of America are snowmobiles and aircraft-borne tours that disturb the residents as well as other tourists (Butcher, 1997). Kirkwood (2011) further confirms that the pleasant environments of the national parks in USA are being harmed by noise pollution created by cars, buses and jet skis. Therefore, it is clear that the vast number of tourists contribute greatly to high levels of noise pollution by the excessive use of airplanes and other recreational vehicles in the service of the tourism sector. As can be deduced, this results in distress for local inhabitants and proves to be very harmful to nature (Rabbany et al., 2013).

Solid waste and littering

Besides the pollution of water by sewage, land, marine waters and coastal areas are contaminated with solid waste stemming from tourism facilities such as marinas, resorts and hotels.

Of course, tourist attractions, together with their large population of visitors, have the potential to generate solid waste which inevitably results in the contamination of roadsides, lakes and rivers (Azarmi, Oladipo, Vaziri & Alipour, 2018). Furthermore, it cannot be denied that trekking tourists produce huge amounts of solid waste such as garbage or oxygen cylinders in the Himalayan mountain areas (Rath & Gupta, 2017).

In fact, touristic regions such as beaches, mountains, lakes, rivers and other natural environments are potential target areas for waste, thus proving once again that disposal of material left over from the tourism sector is a grave problem. Unfortunately, these pristine environments end up becoming dumping grounds for garbage disposal because it is so difficult to install effective disposal facilities, and very few garbage collections are planned and carried out.

Also, huge amounts of waste are produced by tourism facilities such as hotels, restaurants, bars and so on, based on several factors. For example, in hotels, the volume of waste is related to size and type. According to Shanklin (1993), the average amount of waste generated per room in one month is 132.7 lbs at the Hilton in Walt Disney World Village. Also, the average amount of waste generated for one room is reportedly 40 lbs per month (Shanklin, Petrillose & Pettay, 1991).

Moreover, each tourist produces 5.5 kg of waste per day, which, during the low season, contributes to waste generation given as 66.7% for big hotels, 19.4% for medium hotels and 2.6% for small hotels in North Cyprus (Azarmi, Alipour & Oladipo, 2017).

Davies and Cahill (2000) reported that recreational boats and cruises generate an abundance of solid waste that results in catastrophic effects. Furthermore, investigators discovered that plant material and aquatic animals are being threatened by solid waste (Bash, Berman & Bolton, 2001).

Scholars declared that the devastating impacts of solid waste on beaches have been created by overpopulated tourist destinations and improper solid waste management (Davies & Cahill, 2000; Dibajnia, Soltanpour, Vafai, Jazayeri Shoushtari & Kebriaee, 2012).

In 2012, Belsoy stated that the great number of tourists generates massive solid waste and littering in tourism destinations and natural attractions, which pollute the roadsides, forests and rivers. In his study, the author also illustrated the degradation of water, loss of marine animals' life and contamination of mountain areas caused by solid waste.

Solid wastes include solid, liquid and semisolid materials and consist of approximately 75–85% inorganic waste and 15–25% organic waste. General waste produced by various tourism sectors is the same as household waste, which includes paper, vegetables, metal, plastic, food waste, and so on.

Two different reports were presented by the U.S. EPA in 2008 (2008a, 2008b). The first report recorded that the amount of waste generated during a cruise per person is around 0.3–0.8 kg, and, in the second report, the amount was given as 3.5–2.6 kg per person.

According to Nowlan and Kwan's (2001) research, each day 50 tonnes of solid waste are poured into international waters, with the cruise share given at around 24%.

Even though there are some rules, such as the "polluter pays" principle, to control and protect the environment, it must be admitted that this system is not very effective (CRO EPA, 2007). Although it is not easy to figure out how much waste a recreational boat could generate, it is calculated that every traveler daily produces 2 lbs of dry waste and 1.5 lbs of food waste (U.S. Coast Guard, 1998).

According to the rules implemented by the U.S. Coastguard, a fine of US$500,000 is imposed on any company that dumps plastic waste within 200 miles of the coast (Expensive Rubbish Disposal for Cruise Line, 1993). As a result, cruise ships started using new methods for their garbage disposal, such as waste incineration in accordance with the International Maritime

Organization policy. It has been found that there has been a decrease in the waste dropped by cruise ships over the past decade, and this decrease is around 50% (U.S. Coast Guard, 1998). The cruise industry is still trying to achieve the target of zero discharge of waste.

It is estimated that cruise ships in the Caribbean annually produce 70,000 tonnes of waste. It must be noted that solid waste and drainage can reduce the physical appearance of water and contaminate beaches (UNEP, 1997).

Aesthetic pollution

In some tourism destinations, tourism facilities such as hotels, billboards, resorts, parks, discos and shopping malls degrade the visual quality of the natural environment, and this is called aesthetic pollution. In addition, solid waste from hotels deteriorates the landscape and results in visual pollution (Middleton, 1998).

In 2002, Perdue described landscape pollution which includes all road signs, advertisements at the side of highways, street lights, information signs, billboards and buildings – basically anything that is unnatural in a natural setting (Perdue, 2002).

Furthermore, Mirjalili stated that the aesthetics of the environment are degraded by the poor development of tourism facilities in Caspian Sea coastal zones (Mirjalili, 2010), and Karimi emphasized that irregular development of tourism facilities such as villas, hotels and resorts has destroyed several coastal areas (Karimi, 2008). Meanwhile, the trend of constructing luxury hotels only serves to increase aesthetic pollution. It is not impossible to amalgamate hotel infrastructures with pleasant specifications necessary for the natural environment.

Strategies to minimize negative impacts of tourism on environment

Although tourists are always interested in visiting pristine natural environments such as forests, mountains, lakes, rivers, waterfalls and sea areas, their activities adversely affect the ecosystem. In fact, the natural environment should be protected by the government as the main authority of a tourism destination, but there is an inadequate commitment by administrations to accomplish their duties.

Yet the various types of tourism activity such as rafting, camping, horse riding and caving have different environmental hazards (Kuss & Graefe, 1985; Filion, Foley, Jacquemot & Munasinghe, 1994). As far as caving is concerned, artificial entrances opened in a cave for the pleasure and comfort of tourists brings about climate change in relation to airflow within the cave, and this in turn causes rock fall and thawing in different sections. However, the issue can be normalized somewhat if airlocks are built to preserve the temperature of the formations. In addition, electric lighting placed at intervals in the cave can promote the unwanted growth of algae and other plants. Roads above cave areas designed for tourists' travel also have an impact on the cave below, as various gases, toxic chemicals and oils from vehicles seep through openings as pollutants that will inevitably harm the cave. The environmental hazards of horse riding can be explained as soil erosion, weed spreading and disturbance of animals and plant life due to excessive trampling. Rafting and camping activities destroy forest and wildlife owing to poor sanitation that flows into the waters and the increased dumping of waste. In the literature, some authors have stated that the inappropriate and irresponsible behavior of visitors creates adverse impacts on the environment, which illustrates the need for environmental education for tourists (Briassoulis, 2002; Reopanichkul, 2009; Ramdas and Mohamed, 2014). Based on several investigations, there is a close relationship between water pollution and visitors' irresponsible behavior, incompetent and unsustainable tourism development and ineffective waste management (Briassoulis, 2002; Reopanichkul, 2009).

To help alleviate environmental pollution, countries' tourism policymakers should establish sustainable tourism infrastructures to reduce solid waste, sewage and noise, aesthetic and air pollution by exchanging ideas and experiences comprehensively.

Additionally, the foundation of tourism development is sustainability, which aims to preserve natural resources and the environment. To achieve substantiality, awareness on the part of visitors, local people, tourism companies and governmental institutions should be increased rapidly.

Based on several reports, waste reduction and pollution prevention strategies are implemented by the tourism sector to prevent degradation of the environment (WTO, 1995; UNEP, 1998).

Various types of managerial strategy such as codes of practice have been utilized by governmental institutions and NGOs and can restrict irregular tourist activities in the natural areas of different countries (Department of Conservation and Natural Resources Victoria, 1995; Tasmanian High Country Riders Association, 1992; Hawes, 1992).

In 1971, scholars demonstrated that ambiguous regulations for environmental protection have many drawbacks in countries because of expensive implementation, ineffectual impacts and difficult execution (Baumol & Oates, 1971).

Unfortunately, non-environmentally friendly projects have been supported by governments because of their political and financial interests in the tourism sector, and these projects have proved to have harmful effects on natural surroundings. Because of these concerns, environmental issues such as acquiring habitat and preserving nature become more important for scholars than constructing tourist attractions. In 2001, researchers proposed that dominant groups such as environmental NGOs should express their concerns about proper regulation to the government (Tuohino & Hynönen, 2001).

With regard to the preservation of the environment, it is imperative that planners encourage tourists to mitigate their harmful effects concerning natural values. In addition, tourism facilities and services should be well managed to create an environmentally friendly tourism sector. Brown, Turner, Hameed and Bateman (1997) looked at the development of tourism in environmental attraction areas of Nepal and the Maldives in relation to terrestrial wildlife, coral reefs and tropical beaches. According to their study, solid waste disposal and deforestation are significant examples of the impacts of tourism on the environment. Therefore, in order to overcome degradation of the environment, the governments of the Maldives and Nepal are utilizing dispersal techniques.

More forceful insistence must be placed on sustainable development and rational use of resources to control the negative results of tourism expansion, because the need for sound management of tourism resources is widespread. Therefore, it is considered vital that firms and governments play an active role in future tourism development (Koncul, 2007).

Additionally, government regulators should pass restrictive environmental rules to protect nature and to give more weight to other projects such as the eco-tourism industry, which could prove to be an advantageous alternative. Furthermore, governments should award economic incentives to motivate eco-tourism companies in order to reduce tourism demand and enhance environment-related work (Tuohino & Hynonen 2001). In addition, scholars propose the model of monopolistic competition, thus expressing that the uniqueness of a product could bring in more profits.

To mitigate the environmental pollution of the tourism industry, scholars have proposed that countries' education systems should comprise environmental training for local people to behave in an environmentally responsible way (Martinangeli, 2013). In 1990, Hungerford and Volk stated that there is a strong relationship between knowledge and attitude. Based on reasoned action theory and wilderness theory, greater environmental knowledge on the part of visitors and local people could change their harmful tourism activities and reduce tourism-related environmental pollution (Yzer, 2008; Taff et al., 2010). In 2008, Daudi announced that environmental knowledge intensifies the concerns of local people, tourists and tourism-related agencies about the destruction of the environment. Authors have stated that visitors who are aware of pollution protect natural resources and hinder the degradation of the environment (Harun, Hock & Othman, 2011; Lee, Jan & Yang, 2013).

Conclusion

This chapter has reviewed the literature concerning environmental pollution generated by the tourism sector, which degrades natural resources and harms the health of local people. The different types of environmental pollution have been discussed, and several applied strategies for mitigating the devastating impacts of tourism activities have been surveyed. To overcome the environmental pollution created by the tourism sector, four fundamental stages should be implemented properly, which are planning, management, education/awareness and pro-environmental regulation.

The current study proposes that governments as mainly responsible for the tourism industry and tourism-related NGOs should establish sustainable tourism plans to decrease the destructive effects of the tourism industry on natural resources. Furthermore, the natural resources of tourist attractions should be analyzed to enable proper planning for tourism development which prevents environmental deterioration.

In addition, the policymakers of the tourism industry should disseminate environmental knowledge among visitors and tourism organizations to increase tourists' awareness of the adverse effects of their activities. To protect natural areas, government organizations should allocate a proper budget to assist national park authorities and regulate firm rules to make special allowance for conservation activities by visitors. Moreover, the revenue from parking or entrance fees to natural areas should be allotted to be spent on solid waste management.

Environmentally friendly tourism development encourages tourism facilities such as hotels to modify their sewage systems, use green energy and utilize non-polluting construction materials. Moreover, the main intention of the above-mentioned model, if implemented, is to protect eco-tourism sites by suggesting special incentives such as paying a premium for a new experience and pristine environment. However, there is a general intention to preserve the environment and increase financial benefits for eco-tourism companies. Based on the economic interests of policymakers, the mismanagement of the tourism industry leads to weakening of environmentally friendly companies, which without a doubt harms the ecosystem. Current tourism produces large revenues, which could be invested in the protection of natural resources such as national parks, rivers, seas and jungles. Furthermore, the waste management stemming from tourism needs reviewing and enhancing in order to promote understanding in people, which could lead to the rehabilitation of ruined ecosystems.

References

Abam, E. N. (2016). The negative environmental effect of the Guinness Mount Cameroon Race: A case study of Buea Subdivision, *Arabian Journal Business & Management Review*, 6, 279.

Abdoreza, F., & Somayyeh, A. (2010). The relationship between tourism and environment. *Iranian Journal of Tourism & Hospitality*, 1 (1), 37–48.

Andereck, K. L. (1993). The impacts of tourism on natural resources. *Parks & Recreation*, 28 (6), 26–32.

Andereck, K. L. (1995). Environmental consequences of tourism: A review of recent research. In S. F. McCool & A. E. Watson (Eds.), *Linking Tourism, the Environment, and Sustainability – Topical Volume of Compiled Papers from a Special Session of the Annual Meeting of the National Recreation and Park Association*. Minneapolis, MN: Gen. Tech.

Aref, F., Redzuan, M., Emby, Z., & Gill, S. (2009). Barriers of tourism industry through community capacity building. *International Review of Business Research Papers*, 5 (4), 399–408.

Azarmi, S. L., Alipour, H., & Oladipo, A. A. (2017). Using artificial neural network and desirability function to predict waste generation rates in small and large hotels during peak and lean seasons. *Conference Proceedings, 7th Advances in Hospitality & Tourism Marketing & Management (AHTMM) Conference*, pp. 539–547.

Azarmi, S L., Oladipo, A. A., Vaziri, R., & Alipour, H. (2018). Comparative modelling and artificial neural network inspired prediction of waste generation rates of hospitality industry: The case of North Cyprus. *Sustainability*, 10 (9), 2965.

Bash, J., Berman, C. H., & Bolton, S. (2001). *Effects of Turbidity and Suspended Solids on Salmonids*. Seattle, WA: Center for Streamside Studies, University of Washington.

Baumol, W. J., & Oates, W. E. (1971). The use of standards and prices for protection of the environment. *The Swedish Journal of Economics*, 73 (1), 42–54.

Becken, S., & Patterson, M. (2006). Measuring national carbon dioxide emotion from tourism as a key step towards achieving sustainable tourism. *Journal of Sustainable Tourism*, 14 (4), 223–238.

Becken, S., & Simmons, D. (2002). Energy consumption patterns of tourist attractions and activities in New Zealand. *Tourism Management*, 23, 343–354.

Belsoy, J. (2012). Environmental impacts of tourism in protected areas. *Journal of Environment & Earth Science*, 2 (10).

Blamey, R. (1995). *The Nature of Ecotourism*. Occasional Paper No. 21. Canberra: Bureau of Tourism Research.

Briassoulis, H. (2002). Sustainable tourism and the question of the commons. *Annals of Tourism Research*, 29 (4), 1065–1085.

Brown, K., Turner, R. K., Hameed, H., & Bateman, I. (1997). Environmental carrying capacity and tourism development in the Maldives and Nepal. *Environmental Conservation*, 24 (4), 316–325.

Bruner, A. G., Sweeting, J. E. N., & Rosenfeld, A. B. (1998). *The Green Host Effect: An Integrated Approach to Sustainable Tourism and Resort Development*. Conservation International Policy paper. Washington, DC: Conservation International. Available from: https://pdfs.semanticscholar.org/8341/8abf681ab49 6f53295be29819bd9ef82e5be.pdf

Butcher, R. D. (1997). Part 18: Threat after threat. In *Exploring Our National Historic Parks and Sites*, pp. 473–500. Boulder, CO: Roberts Rinehart.

Butler, R. W. (1980). The concept of tourist area cycle of evolution: Implications for management of resources. *Canadian Geographer*, 24, 5–12.

Carnival Corporation. (2007). *Environmental Management Report Fiscal Year 2007* [online]. Miami: Carnival Corporation. Available from: www.fs.fed.us/sustainableoperations/documents/fy2007-environmental-footprint.pdf

Ceballos-Lascurain, H. (1996). *Tourism, Ecotourism, and Protected Areas*. Gland, Switzerland: IUCN.

Copeland, C. (2008). *CRS Report for Congress – Cruise Ship Pollution* [online]. Congressional Research, No. RL32450. Available from: www.ncseonline.org/NLE/CRSreports/08Aug/RL32450.pdf

Croatian Environmental Protection Agency (CRO EPA). (2007). *Republic of Croatia State of Environment Report*. Zagreb: CRO EPA and Ministry of Environmental Protection, Physical Planning and Construction.

Crompton, J. L. (1999). The economic impact of sports tournaments and events. *Parks & Recreation*, 34, 142–150.

Daudi, S. S. (2008). Environmental literacy: A system of best-fit for promoting environmental awareness in low literate communities. *Applied Environmental Education & Communication*, 7 (3), 76–82.

Davies, T., & Cahill, S. (2000). *Environmental Implications of the Tourism Industry*. Discussion Paper. Washington, DC: Resources for the Future.

Department of Conservation and Natural Resources Victoria. (1995). *4WD Touring Code*. Melbourne: Department of Conservation and Natural Resources Victoria.

Dibajnia, M., Soltanpour, M., Vafai, F., Jazayeri Shoushtari, S. M. H., & Kebriaee, A. (2012). A shoreline management plan for Iranian coastlines. *Ocean & Coastal Management*, 63, 1–15.

Dixon F. J., Hamilton K., Pagiola S., & Segnestam L. (2001). *Tourism and the Environment in the Caribbean: An Economic Framework*. Environmental Economic. Series. Washington, DC: World Bank.

Ecotourism Society. (1993). *Ecotourism: A Guide for Planners and Managers*. North Bennington, VT: Ecotourism Society.

Expensive Rubbish Disposal for Cruise Line. (1993). *Marine Pollution Bulletin*, 26 (6), 295.

Faulkner, B., & Tideswell, C. (1997). A framework for monitoring community impacts of tourism. *Journal of Sustainable Tourism*, 5, 3–28.

Fennel, D. A. (1999). *Ecotourism, an Introduction*, 2nd ed. London and New York: Routledge.

Filion, F. L., Foley J. P., Jacquemot, A. J., & Munasinghe, M. (1994). The economics of global ecotourism. In M. Munasinghe (Ed.), *Protected Area Economics and Policy: Linking Conservation and Sustainable Development*, pp. 235–252. Washington, DC: World Bank.

Friedrich, A., Heinen, F., Kamakaté, F., & Kodjak, D. (2007). *Air Pollution and Greenhouse Gas Emissions from Oceangoing Ships: Impacts, Mitigation Options and Opportunities for Managing Growth* [online]. Washington, DC: International Council on Clean Transportation. Available from: www.theicct.org/sites/default/files/publications/oceangoing_ships_2007.pdf

Genot, H. (1997). Tourism. In D. Brune, D. V. Chapman, M. D. Gwynne & J. M. Pacyna (Eds.), *The Global Environment: Science, Technology and Management* (vol. 1, pp. 64–75). Weinheim, Germany: VCH Verlagsgesellschaft.

German Federal Agency for Nature Conservation (GFANC; Ed.). (1997). *Biodiversity and Tourism*. Berlin: Springer.

Ghaderi, E. (2004). A look at the national tourism development program. The Islamic Republic of Iran (with an emphasis on regional strategies and developing human resources). *The House & Strategy*, 44, 52–63

Gössling, S. (2002). Human–environmental relations with tourism. *Annals of Tourism Research*, 29 (4), 539–556.

Gössling, S., Peeters, P., Hall, M. C., Ceron, J. P., Dubois, G., Lehmann, L. V. et al. (2012). Tourism and water use: Supply, demand and security. An international review. *Tourism Management*, 33 (1), 1–15.

Hall, C.M. (1994/forthcoming). Ecotourism in Australia, New Zealand and the South Pacific: Appropriate tourism or a new form of ecological imperialism? Forthcoming chapter in E. A. Cater & G. A. Lowman (Eds.), *Ecotourism – A Sustainable Option*. London: John Wiley/Royal Geographical Society.

Harun, R., Hock, L. K., & Othman, F. (2011). Environmental knowledge and attitude among students in Sabah. *World Applied Sciences Journal*, 14, 83–87.

Hawes, M. (1992). *Draft Walking Track Management Strategy for the Tasmanian Wilderness World Heritage Area*. Hobart: Department of Parks, Wildlife and Heritage.

Holden, A. (2000). *Environment and Tourism*. London and New York: Routledge.

Holden, A. (2008). *Environment and Tourism*. Abingdon, UK: Routledge.

Howes, M. (2013). *Politics and the Environment: Risk and the Role of Government and Industry*. Abingdon, UK: Routledge.

Hungerford, H., & Volk, T. (1990). Changing Learner Behaviour through Environmental Education. *The Journal of Environmental Education*, 21 (3), 8–21.

Hunter, C., & Shaw, J. (2006). Applying ecological footprint to ecotourism scenarios. *Environmental Conservation*, 32 (4), 294–304.

International Civil Aviation Organization (ICAO). (2001). Resolution A33-7: Consolidated Statement of Continuing Policies and Practices Related to Environmental Protection, Provisional ed. Resolution Adopted at the 33rd Session of the Assembly. Montreal, Canada: ICAO.

Karimi, T. (2008). Geographical and environmental effects of coastal tourism and sustainable development. Abhar Education and Training Administration – Geographical Education Group [online]. Available from: http://kubk.blogfa.com/post-15.aspx

Katircioglu, S., Feridun, M., & Kilinc, C. (2014). Estimating tourism-induced energy consumption and CO_2 emissions: The case of Cyprus. *Renewable & Sustainable Energy Reviews*, 29, 634–640.

Kavallinis, I., & Pizam, A. (1994). The environmental impacts of tourism – Whose responsibility is it anyway? The case study of Mykonos. *Journal of Travel Research*, 33 (2), 26–32.

Kirkwood, S. (2011). Clearing skies? National Parks Conservation Association. National Parks Conservation Association & Protecting Our National Parks for Future Generations. Web. 02 April.

Klein, R. A. (2003). *Cruising – Out of Control: The Cruise Industry, The Environment, Workers, and the Maritimes*. Halifax, NS: Canadian Centre for Policy Alternatives.

Koncul, N. (2007). Environmental issues and tourism. *Ekonomska misao i praksa*, 16 (2), 157–165.

Kuo, N.-W., & Chan, H. (2009). Quantifying energy use, carbon dioxide emission, and other environmental loads from island tourism based on a life cycle assessment approach. *Journal of Cleaner Production*, 17 (15), 1324–1330.

Kuss, F. R., & Graefe, A. R. (1985). Effects of recreation trampling on natural area vegetation. *Journal of Leisure Research*, 17, 165–183.

Lankford, S. V., & Howard, D. R. (1994). Developing a tourism impact attitude scale. *Annals of Tourism Research*, 21, 121–139.

Lee, S. L., Wong, W. H. S., & Lau, Y. L. (2006). Association between air pollution and asthma admission among children in Hong Kong. *Clinical and Experimental Allergy*, 36, 1138–1146.

Lee, T. H., Jan, F., & Yang, C. (2013). Environmentally responsible behavior of nature-based tourists: A review. *International Journal of Development & Sustainability*, 2 (1), 1–16.

Lee, W. J., & Brahmasrene, T. (2013). Investigating the influence of tourism on economic growth and carbon emissions: Evidence from panel analysis of the European Union. *Tourism Management*, 38, 69–76.

Liu, J. C., & Var, T. (1986). Resident attitudes toward tourism impacts in Hawaii. *Annals of Tourism Research*, 13, 193–214.

Martinangeli, A., & Zoli, M. (2013). *Exploring Environmentally Significant Behaviors in a Multidimensional Perspective*. Working Papers in Economics 561, 0–26.

Mbaiwa, E. (2003). The socio-economic and environmental impacts of tourism development on the Okavango Delta, north-western Botswana. *Journal of Arid Environments*, 54, 447–467.

Middleton, V. (1998). *Sustainable Tourism: A Marketing Perspective*. Oxford: Butterworth-Heinemann.

Mill, R. C., & Morrison, A. M. (2006). *The Tourism System*. Dubuque, IA: Kendall/Hunt.

Mirjalili, J. (2010). The effects of tourism industry in the rural areas of Mazandaran province: The history and tourism in exhaustive perspective [online]. Available from: http://mirjalilismj.blogfa.com/

Mowforth, M., & Munt, I. (2003). *Tourism and Sustainability: Development and New Tourism in Third World*, 2nd ed. London: Routledge.

Mowforth, M.. & Munt, I. (2015). *Tourism and Sustainability: Development, Globalisation and New Tourism in the Third World*. London: Routledge.

Nafstad, P., Håheim, L. L., Oftedal, B., Gram, F., Holme, I., Hjermann, I., et al. (2003). Lung cancer and air pollution: A 27 year follow up of 16,209 Norwegian men. *Thorax*, 58, 1071–1076.

Nowlan, L. & Kwan, I. (2001). *Cruise Control – Regulating Cruise Ship Pollution in the Pacific Coast of Canada*. Vancouver: West Coast Environmental Law.

Paramati, S. R., Shahbaz, M., & Alam M. S. (2017). Does tourism degrade environmental quality? A comparative study of Eastern and Western European Union. *Transportation Research Part D*, 50, 1–13.

Peeters, P., Szimba, E., & Duijnisveld, M. (2007). Major environmental impacts of European tourist transport. *Journal of Transport Geography*, 15, 83–93.

Perch-Nielsen, S., Sesartic, A., Stucki, M. (2010). The greenhouse gas intensity of the tourism sector: The case of Switzerland. *Environmental Science & Policy*, 13(2), 131–140

Perdue, R. R. (2002). Perishability, yield management, and cross-product elasticity: A case study of deep discount season passed in Colorado ski industry. *Journal of Travel Research*, 41, 15–22.

Pizam, A. (1978). Tourism impacts: The social costs to the destination community as perceived by its residents. *Journal of Travel Research*, 16, 8–12.

Rabbany M. G., Afrin, Sh., Rahman, A., Islam, F., & Hoque, F. (2013). Environmental effects of tourism. *American Journal of Environment, Energy & Power Research*, 1 (7), 117–130.

Ramdas, M., & Mohamed, B. (2014). Impacts of tourism on environmental attributes, environmental literacy and willingness to pay: A conceptual and theoretical review. *Procedia - Social & Behavioral Sciences*, 144, 378–391.

Rath, N., & Gupta, R. (2017). Environmental impact of tourism. *Ijariie*, 2 (3), 50–53.

Royal Caribbean International (RCI). (2009). *Royal Caribbean and the Environment, Waste Stream Operational Controls Chart* [online]. Available from: www.royalcaribbean.com/ourCompany/environment/rcAndEnvironment.doc

Reopanichkul, P. (2009). *The effects of tourism on water quality and coral reef communities*. PhD thesis, University of the Sunshine Coast, Australia.

Seabloom, R. W., Plews, G., & Cox, F. (1989). *The Effect of Sewage Discharges from Pleasure Craft on Puget Sound Waters and Shellfish Quality*. Olympia: Washington State Department of Health.

Shanklin, C. W., Petrillose, M. J., & Pettay, A. (1991). Solid waste management in selected hotel chains and individual properties. *Hospitality Research Journal: The Professional Journal of the Council on Hotel, Restaurant, & Institutional Education*, 15 (1), 59–74.

Shanklin, C. W. (1993). Ecology age: Implications for the hospitality and tourism industry. *Hospitality Research Journal: The Professional Journal of the Council on Hotel, Restaurant, & Institutional Education*, 17 (1), 219–229.

Shujahi, A., & Hussain, A. (2016). *Economic and Environmental Costs of Tourism: Evidence from District Abbottabad.* Islamabad: Department of Environmental Economics Pakistan Institute of Development Economics.

Sidles, D. (1997). *Changing the Way People Use Parks. Natural Resource Year in Review, Planning and Preservation.* Washington, DC: National Park Service.

Sirakaya, E., Teye, V., & Sönmez, S. (2002). Understanding residents' support for tourism development in the central region of Ghana. *Journal of Travel Research*, 41 (1), 57–67.

Swedish NGO Secretariat on Acid Rain (Acidrain). (2008). Agreement by IMO to curb shipping emissions [online]. *Acid News*, (2), 3–4. Available from: www.airclim.org/acidnews/2008/AN2-08.php#IMO_MEPC

Taff, M. A. M., Aziz, A., Nor, R., Raja, S., Rasyid, N. M., & Yasim, M. M. (2010). Residential outdoor education and environmental attitudes: An examination in a Malaysian university, *Journal of Outdoor Recreation, Education, & Leadership*, 2 (3), 198–216.

Tang, Z., Shang, J., Shi, C. B., Liu, Z., & Bi, K. X. (2014). Decoupling indicators of CO_2 emissions from the tourism industry in China: 1990–2012. *Ecological Indicators*, 46, 390–397.

Tasmanian High Country Riders Association. (1992). *Horseriding in the High Country – A Code of Practice for Riding in Tasmanian Highland Areas.* Hobart: Tasmanian High Country Riders Association.

Trasporti e Territorio Srl (TRT). (2007). *External Costs of Maritime Transport. European Union. Directorate General Internal Policies of the Union.* Brussels: European Parliament's Committee on Transport and Tourism.

Tuohino, A., & Hynönen, A. (2001). Ecotourism – imagery and reality. Reflections on concepts and practices in Finnish rural tourism. *2nd International Conference on New Directions in Managing Rural Tourism and Leisure – Local Impacts, Global Trends*, Ayshire, Scotland, September 5–8.

UNEP. (1997). *Coastal Tourism in the Wider Caribbean Region Impacts and Best Management Practices.* Kingston, Jamaica: UNEP.

UNEP. (1998). *How the Hotel and Tourism Can Protect the Ozone Layer.* Paris: UNEP.

UNEP. (2011). Tourism: Investing in energy and resource efficiency. In *UNEP Green Economy Report.* Paris: UNEP.

UNEP. (2014). *Tourism's Three Main Impact Areas* [online]. Available from: www.unep.org/resource efficiency/Business/SectoralActivities/Tourism/TheTourismandEnvironmentProgramme/Facts andFiguresaboutTourism/ImpactsofTourism/EnvironmentalImpacts/TourismsThreeMain ImpactAreas/tabid/78776/Default.aspx (accessed July 2014).

UNEP. (2015). *Impacts of Tourism.* Available from: www.unep.org/resourceefficiency/Business/ SectoralActivities/Tourism/FactsandFiguresaboutTourism/ImpactsofTourism/tabid/78774/Default. aspx (accessed February 15, 2015).

UNWTO. (2008). *Climate Change & Tourism: Responding to Global Challenges.* Madrid: UNWTO.

U.S. Coast Guard. (1998). *Pollution Incidents In and Around U.S. Waters 1997.* U.S. Coast Guard

United States Environmental Protection Agency (U.S. EPA). (1998). *National Air Pollutant Emission Trends Update: 1970–1997* (EPA 454/E-98-007). Washington, DC: U.S. EPA.

United States Environmental Protection Agency (U.S. EPA). (2008a). *Cruise Ship Discharge Assessment Report.* US EPA Oceans and Coastal Protection Division, EPA 842-R-07-005. Washington, DC: U.S. EPA.

United States Environmental Protection Agency (U.S. EPA). (2008b). *Report on the Environment* [online]. Available from: https://cfpub.epa.gov/roe/documents/EPAROE_FINAL_2008.PDF (accessed May 2008).

Vineis, P., Hoek, G., Krzyzanowski, M., Vigna-Taglianti, F., Veglia, F., Airoldi, L., et al., (2006). Air pollution and risk of lung cancer in a prospective study in Europe. *International Journal of Cancer*, 119, 169–174.

Wells, E. C., Zarger, R. K., Whiteford, L. M., Mihelcic, J. R., Koenig, E. S., Cairns, M. R., et al. (2016). The impacts of tourism development on perceptions and practices of sustainable wastewater management on the Placencia Peninsula, Belize. *Journal of Cleaner Production*, 111, 430–441.

Williams, V., Noland, R. B., & Toumi, R. (2003). Air transport cruise altitude restrictions to minimize contrail formation. *Climate Policy*, 3 (3), 207–219.

Wong, P. P. (2002). Tourism as a global driving force for environmental change. In I. Douglas (Ed.), *Causes and Consequences of Global Environmental Change (Encyclopedia of Global Environmental Change,* vol. 3, pp. 609–23. Chichester, UK: John Wiley.

World Tourism Organization (WTO). (1995). *What Tourism Managers Need to Know: A Practical Guide to the Development and Use of Indicators of Sustainable Tourism.* Madrid: WTO.

Yzer, M. (2008). The Integrative Model of Behavioural Prediction as a Tool for Designing Health Messages. In P. Swanepoel & H. Hoeken (Eds.), *Adapting Health Communication to Cultural Needs: Optimizing Documents in South-African Health Communication on HIV and AIDS,* pp. 49–70. Amsterdam: John Benjamins.

Zaei, M., & Zaei, E. (2013). The impacts of tourism industry on host community. *European Journal of Tourism Hospitality & Research,* 1 (2), 12–21.

24

SENSITIZATION OF TOURISTS ABOUT CLIMATE CHANGE AND ITS ASSOCIATED IMPACTS ON THE TOURISM SECTOR

The case of Mauritius

Adjnu Damar Ladkoo

Introduction

Climate change is a global phenomenon which is affecting developed, developing and even under-developed countries. Research from scientists has revealed that among the most affected places will be islands. As such, this chapter focuses on Mauritius, a small island developing state (SIDS) in the Indian Ocean and a vulnerable one. For Briguglio (2003), vulnerability may be defined as 'proneness to harm or damage originating from external forces', and this condition is often associated with SIDS because these tend to be inherently very exposed to factors outside their control. Undeniably, Mauritius is very likely to have to face the harsh consequences of climate change. Mauritius is well known as having a blooming tourism sector which contributes massively to the economy of the island. It is, therefore, imperative that all stakeholders in the tourism industry know and understand the changes that will have to be brought about as a means of mitigating and adapting to the impacts of climate change. Unfortunately, it is not only external factors which are the causes of climate change, but, in many cases, it has been noted that even the tourism industry is contributing towards climate change. As such, the tourism industry will have to be both reactive and proactive so as to be able to contribute to alleviating this alarming situation which is putting not only the industry, but also the country's survival, at stake.

The aim of this chapter is, therefore, to understand how some of the primary stakeholders of the tourism industry – tourists – have been made aware about climate change and its associated consequences. This permitted the study to attempt to evaluate the diverse methods of sensitization adopted in the tourist industry to make people knowledgeable about climate change and its associated impacts. The context of the study was Mauritius, and, during the search for local literature pertaining to sensitization of tourists, it was noted that minimal research had been conducted about such much-needed topics. While, on the one hand, the Mauritian government is working towards sustainability, on the other hand, unfortunately, some tourism organizations do not seem to be aware of the implications of such governmental endeavors in their key areas such as management and marketing. Thus, understanding about this global as well as local issue will help tourists to choose and consume in a more responsible manner.

Significance of chapter

As per Pandve (2007), motivation for voluntary mitigation is mostly dependent on perceived susceptibility to threats and severity of climate change or climate variability impacts, whereas adaptation is largely dependent on the availability of information relevant to climate change. In both cases, whether mitigation or adaptation, the need to sensitize people is evident. Sensitization is a vital response strategy for both adapting to climate change and mitigating its harsh effects. Understanding how the latter, which is equal to a lifesaving strategy, is being used and with what means will surely aid in reducing the vulnerability level of Mauritius as regards climate change and its impacts on the Mauritian tourism sector, because, as per Ekpoh and Ekpoh (2011), an informed public will make wiser and more accurate decisions and respond to climate change issues.

Research methodology

In line with the above, this exploratory topic required a methodology which allowed freedom to merge ideas, comments, strategies, and solutions. Interestingly, a qualitative methodology suited the need and was used. As climate change is a topic which is impacting on several dimensions of the society, it became important to go beyond numbers and focus more on words, feelings, and emotions connected to it. This research, therefore, not only focused on available records, reports, and documents, but also on personal observations made by the author. The data collected made it possible to determine how tourists were made aware about climate change and its associated impacts on the tourism sector. Among several other stakeholders, tourists are the focus of the chapter because, as per Gössling, Scott, Hall, Ceron, and Dubois (2012), tourists have the largest adaptive capacity of elements within the tourism system. Sensitizing tourists might eventually lead to faster remedial situations.

Impacts of climate change on the tourism sector

The travel and tourism industry is an important economic activity in most countries around the world; as well as its direct economic impact, the industry has significant indirect and induced impacts (World Travel and Tourism Council, 2018). This is equally the case for Mauritius, where, according to the Ministry of Tourism Mauritius (2018), today, tourism is one of the fastest growing socio-economic sectors and is fueling economic growth and creating jobs and business opportunities in the country. Alarmingly, for Uyarra et al. (2005), climate change may affect important environmental components of holiday destinations, which might have repercussions for tourism-dependent economies. Indeed, if one compares a tourist destination as it was 10 or 20 years ago with how it is now, the differences will unfortunately be huge, because climate change has had such huge impacts on the rich biodiversity of mountains, sea, lands, and architecture, among others. As per Viner (2006), it has been known anecdotally for some time that tourism is controlled by climate, in terms of the climate of the source and destination countries of these tourists. For Amelung and Viner (2006, cited in Viner, 2006), there is increasing evidence to suggest that climate change will start to impact upon the suitability of tourist destinations, either through the direct impacts of climate change or by altering the tourists' perceptions.

A paper by Agnew and Viner (2001) highlighting the potential impacts of climate change on international tourism stated that the most serious impacts will result from the effects of sea-level rise on small island states. Even if several organizations are portraying a positive picture about the growing tourism industry in Mauritius, needless to say, Mauritius is still on the list of such vulnerable islands. Agnew and Viner (2001) further added that other impacts likely to affect tourism include coral bleaching, outbreaks of fire, changed migration patterns of animals and birds, flooding, the spread of vector-borne diseases, and shorter skiing seasons, and, without appropriate adaptive measures, climate change could produce a shift in the comparative attractiveness of tourist destinations around the globe. Undoubtedly, one of the adaptive measures involves sensitization of the stakeholders of the tourism sector; tourists being one of the most important stakeholders to be sensitized.

Tourist sensitization measures

Sustainable development calls for wise management of natural, built, and sociocultural resources in destination areas (Briassoulis, 2002). Hotels are visibly adopting such practices so as to increase the lifespan of the tourism industry, but are tourists aided in making greener choices and purchases, and are hotels offering sufficient options in terms of green holiday packages? Answering the above questions will help in judging how sensitization about climate change is brought about. Many times, whenever sensitization about other emerging issues was carried out, it was noted that the so-called customers or respondents did not know why there had to be a change in their actions, who would benefit from it, or what would be the long-term effects. As per the European Climate Adaptation Platform (n.d.), large climate change awareness-raising campaigns are often a mixture of mitigation, energy efficiency, and sustainability measures, rather than adaptation measures; for example, as per Climate Adapt (2015), the aim of awareness-raising campaigns often differs between contexts but generally includes increasing concern, informing the target audience, creating a positive image, and attempting to change behavior. Hence, this chapter will be exploring the different means of sensitization that could be used to give tourists valuable understanding of how their changed behaviors – be the changes minor or drastic – would impact on several other indirect components of tourism and, eventually, the country.

The foundation is education

As per Hill, Wallner, and Furtado (2010), stakeholders could capitalize on the new opportunities thrown up by climate change to create a competitive advantage. However, for them to sensitize tourists correctly, the stakeholders should themselves be very aware of the implications of climate change. In the educational sector, teachers can play an important role in educating students about climate change, related issues, and solutions, and this is possible only when teachers themselves have the necessary level of awareness. Therefore, this necessitates the introduction of climate change programs into education reforms (Ekpoh and Ekpoh, 2011). As per unfccc.int (n.d.), climate change, as a subject per se, has not yet been included in the curricula of the formal education system in Mauritius as it is a new, developing science; incorporation of topics related to climate change in the curricula of primary and secondary education will provide future generations with sufficient scientific understanding of global climate change for them to take an intelligent and informed interest in the nation's climate change policies. Hence, it is imperative that the foundations be made strong so as to have sustainable, genuine, and responsible sensitization. Yet neither the country nor the industries are in a position to wait, because climate change has already done so much harm and it is vital to react and alleviate those damaging consequences. In the context of tourism and hospitality, the 'teachers' of tourists are none other than the people marketing the hotels or destinations. It is, therefore, vital for such marketers to be well versed with climate change and its impacts on the tourism sector so that they are able to extend this knowledge to tourists.

Use of technology

For unfccc.int (n.d.), newspapers, radio, TV, videotapes, posters, pamphlets, brochures, and factsheets are some of the popular and easy methods of communication that are being used to target the largest audience. However, in today's era, technology must be adopted in any business endeavor. As such, technological advancements can be incorporated so as to reach a larger community of tourists and at a faster pace. In today's era, social media marketing definitely does not go unnoticed. Facebook, WhatsApp, Twitter, Pinterest, LinkedIn, and Instagram are some of the most used social media platforms in Mauritius as well as abroad. Hence, whenever Mauritius is being promoted abroad, in forums or on the internet, it is vital to give tourists an aperçu of what is expected from them in terms of responsible actions that would help preserve the beauty of Mauritius and how this can help in saving the tourism industry which is fading as a result of climate change. In the new adverts projected, it would be important to portray both positive reinforcement and negative reinforcement. For the former, the benefits of responsible consumerism in the tourism sector can be shown, whereas, in the latter, the harsh consequences of bad consumerism can be showcased. Interestingly, as per Diedrichs (2017), more than eight in ten hotels say the issue of climate change impacts their decisions to make operational improvements and investments, according to Green Lodging Trends Report 2017. The latter further added that hotel guests are not only giving more feedback on hotel sustainability practices but are keen to make a positive environmental impact during their stay. So, if tourists are keen to be part of hotels' sustainability programs through use of technology, this has to be further promoted and encouraged. The rise of smart hotels can aid in reducing climate change and minimizing its impacts by, for example, using sensors that will alert tourists whenever they are using too much energy for specific hotel-related tasks, and, in some cases, there can be auto-adjustment of the devices. All is possible with technology using virtual platforms, but without neglecting proactive, face-to-face, and on-the-spot sensitization of tourists about climate change.

NGOs, universities, and hotels

As per unfccc.int (n.d.), the Mauritius Council of Social Services, an umbrella organization that brings together more than a hundred NGOs, recently organized workshops on environmental education for its members, with the purpose of creating a pool of trainers in environmental education. When, on one side, the help of NGOs can be sought and, on the other side, there are not only the trainers of the NGOs but also academics researching about climate change and the tourism sector, these can be valuable in delivering lectures and training sessions adapted for hotels and all their employees. The government can intervene by subsidizing such training sessions for the benefit of the industry and, eventually, for the island. Moreover, hotels which are keen to promote sustainable tourism development so as to mitigate and reduce the impacts of climate change can work in collaboration with either local or international universities in order to find better solutions to this alarming issue. Memorandums of understanding can be signed with groups of hotels and universities whereby the hotels might fund courses to be run about climate change, its impacts, mitigation, and adaptation strategies, and the universities's task will be to design and offer the courses. Many of the above measures can be considered to actually strengthen the foundations of understanding about climate change. Strategies devised can be both short term and long term. As per the University of Malta (2018), Scholarships in Climate Action are being offered as part of the Government of Malta's commitment under the Climate Finance Package to provide support for capacity building in developing states. Also, the Islands & Small States Institute promotes research and training on economic, social, cultural, ecological, and geographical aspects of islands and small states. It also offers postgraduate courses on islands and small states studies (University of Malta, 2018). Collaboration among the above organizations, as well as research and training, can help in identifying appropriate ways to sensitize tourists. As such, even the University of Mauritius and the University of Technology Mauritius have programs designed in relation to climate change and sustainable development so that the students of such courses can ultimately impart knowledge about climate change, which can be an important means of sensitizing tourists.

The community's role and power

In Mauritius, there seems to be minimal understanding about the scorching issue of climate change. Efforts must be made as early as possible to create awareness about climate change, although it sounds difficult to change human behavior. If the impacts of climate change such as visibly higher frequency of flash floods, thunder, and lightning strikes are highlighted to the population and tourists, the community can thus, at least under the pretense of not having to face such calamities, start to react and take the trouble to understand climate change. In fact, as per Peters (2015), for most people, climate change still seems like a fairly abstract problem – something that is happening far away, to polar bears or remote Pacific Islanders, or something that will not really happen until the distant future. Thus, if the community is rightly informed and educated about climate change, this would be helpful in converting the tourism industry into a better one where less waste and carbon dioxide would be emitted. Such conscious people would react to the slightest harm caused by climate change as a result of several factors emanating from the tourism sector. Whenever tourists would attempt to go against or manipulate existing laws and regulations protecting the island's touristic features, the society would react. For example, new movements can emerge such as that of 'clean tourism' – that is, tourism that does not pollute and sustainably helps the survival of all other living entities. As per Lytton (2013), more than 600,000 people have joined GetUp!, which is Action for Australia's movement to make democracy participatory, which is one of its biggest campaigns that bids to protect the Great Barrier Reef. As such, educating the community to make it powerful has a great role to play in alleviating, preventing, and bringing about sensitization to the impacts of climate change.

Celebrating the sensitization measures

Hotels, travel agencies, and other tourism organizations should focus at least one of their strategic visions on minimizing the impacts of climate change. The usual story on climate is based around apocalyptic doom, and, although the facts might justify that, it makes people stop listening (Peters, 2015). Thus, fun, enjoyment, and games can be considered by way of celebration. As such, hotels and airports can use the 'one-day celebration' concept – for instance, by each month celebrating the 'go-green' concept or the 'zero tolerance to pollution' concept or the 'be minimalist to save Mother Earth concept'. There can be a better outcome if participatory tourism is used, as tourists might feel that they truly have an important role to play in saving the island and the globe from impacts of climate change.

Emergence of alternative forms of tourism

It is of the utmost importance to move away from a sun, sand, and sea promotional tagline, as Mauritius can offer more than that. The focus can be on green tourism, dark tourism, heritage tourism, and sports tourism, among others. However, knowingly or unknowingly, sometimes there is usage of guilt-inducing messages in adverts or organizational purchase conditions, which can disastrously affect tourism firms. Many times, the motivation and ideas for promoting eco or green tourism are so fierce that consideration is not given to the possible high costs of such products/services, as well as the inconveniences connected to use of the latter compared with regular products/services. As such, instead of pointing out to the tourists that they are not being part of sustainable tourism development so as to minimize impacts of climate change, the organizations themselves can be the first to set the example so as to have tourists following them and doing the same actions. As example, an airline might have a carbon offset option set as a default, so people have to actively uncheck it if they do not want to use it, or a restaurant might always choose a vegetarian menu as specialty of the day (Peters, 2015). Likewise, hotels, travel agencies, and airports can stop marketing Mauritius for its sand, sun, and sea and focus on other interesting forms of tourism. Escalating pressures caused by climate change give today's tourism stakeholders a blurred picture about the future of coastal tourism in Mauritius. As per coastlearn.org (n.d.), most holidaymakers choose the sea (63%), and other main types of destination are the mountains (25%), cities (25%), and the countryside (23%). Coastal tourism, which focuses on a combination of the sea environment and surrounding lands, is today at risk owing to the harsh impacts of climate change on the rich biodiversity of the sea and its environs. Sand erosion, bleaching of corals, and migration of sea creatures are some of the visible impacts of rising temperatures as a result of climate change. Therefore, why not develop the inland tourism sector, which has so far been seemingly undervalued?

Until recently, there was not much focus on mountains or hill destinations, countryside or cities. Some evidence of inland tourism development noted around the world and to an extent in Mauritius are: (1) the emergence of shopping malls with connected hotels, (2) the rise of 'domaines' with logging facilities, (3) agro-tourism growth, (4) expansion of wine routes, (5) promotion of trail events in mountains, (6) control of coastal zone development, (7) driving up of coastal hotel prices, (8) banning of operation licenses to new coastal hotels, and others. As such, the right balance is needed between inland and coastal tourism development in order to maintain the beauty of the Mauritian tourism and hospitality sector. Tourists should be encouraged to focus on other activities which are not on the coast.

However, the question still remains as to how to develop inland tourism for it to survive into the future, because this can either directly or indirectly create huge internal competition in Mauritius between supporters of coastal tourism development and promoters of inland tourism development. Considering the above, it implies that the micro marketing environment has to be supportive towards both so as not to have opposing forces where eventually the effect will be null or that only one of the stakeholders wins this so-called battle of tourism development. Moreover, if inland tourism is developed, it should not reach a point where, after few years, only harm and destruction of nature and its surroundings are noted. There should be consideration given to sustainable inland tourism development. Consequently, the choice of holiday spots by tourists within the island is a crucial contribution to alleviating the impacts of climate change and to prevent it from happening further.

The value of personal selling and visual merchandising

Understanding consumer travel patterns will help companies create offerings to satisfy changing consumer demands driven by a changing climate (Suarez, 2011). However, usage of one or more promotional tactics can be truly helpful for this task. As such, personal selling can be used which, as per the Economic Times (2018), is also known as face-to-face selling, in which one person who is the salesman tries to convince the customer to buy a product, and it is a promotional method in which the salesperson uses his or her skills and abilities in an attempt to make a sale. However, personal selling is also advanced by the seizing of opportunities provided by technology and new means of face-to-face contact, such as use of virtual platforms, are considered. Salespeople make use of telepresence or video conferencing through Skype, Google Duo or WhatsApp to connect faster with potential or existing customers. As such, during the booking of hotels or air tickets, virtual communication including visuals and videos can aid in making tourists understand clearly about the green stances taken by these establishments. According to the World Tourism Organization and United Nations Environment Programme (2008, cited in Hower, 2017), tourism is responsible for about 5% of global greenhouse gas emissions. The above would, thus, enable them to realize how they will be contributing to alleviating the harsh impacts of tourism on the planet. This would also help build more ethical feelings about organizations in the tourism and hospitality sector and increase credibility of the latter, as many organizations seemingly avoid informing their customers about changes in the business environment as a result of climate change. Talking with salespeople would help tourists redefine their views and actions towards the destination they will be visiting, and, from the managerial perspective, it would be easier for the organizations concerned to modify their daily business tasks such as in regards to energy consumption. As per Hower (2017), 20% comes from the accommodation sector, which involves heating, air-conditioning, and maintaining bars, restaurants, and pools, but, of course, this varies according to the location and size of the accommodation, as well as the type of establishment – hotels having greater energy consumption than camping sites. Therefore, as per Wigder (2016), an honest dialogue may be the best way to attract tourists to the reef, while at the same time starting to unwind the prevailing narrative that the best vacation destinations have to be picture perfect.

Visual merchandising refers to anything that can be seen by the customer inside and outside a store, including displays, decorations, signs, and the layout of the space (learn.org, n.d.). As such, this technique can be wisely used for promoting and encouraging the purchase of green or eco-friendly products or services that would cause minimal or no harm to the planet through climate change. However, as per the Kangan Institute (2018), visual merchandising must be consistent across all platforms, including in-store displays, websites, and any other third-party websites and advertisements. Visual merchandising can have a positive impact on the brand equity of tourism organizations by encouraging customers to readily accept and adopt amended products and services that would be aiding in combatting the impacts of climate change.

Both visual merchandising and personal selling can be combined so as to let customers better connect with the product or service offered by the tourism organizations. Many times, salespeople make use of story-telling to support their endeavors in marketing something; this tallies with Hudson (2018), who stated that a display may lack a worded sign or an educational sign, and that is perfectly fine; as long as there is still a story, the sign can speak for itself.

Vacation home rentals and self-service apartments

Vacation home rental is a new concept in the tourism and hospitality sector and it has been viewed as helping to mitigate the impacts of climate change caused by this industry. As per the

International Tourism Partnership (2016, cited in Damar Ladkoo, 2016), continuing to build and buy new hotels, power plants, and aeroplanes means we would be locked in carbon dioxide increase for the next 30–100 years, and to stop this and see carbon dioxide emissions actually decline, we need to fundamentally alter our behaviors, or we will see a 6° increase in global temperature by the end of the century. As such, as per Damar Ladkoo (2016), using existing accommodation facilities such as those of vacation home rentals would not only aid in reducing the adverse impact of climate change, but will also help the survival of hotels. The latter can work in close collaboration with home owners who are willing to rent their properties for vacation whereby services proposed within hotels can be transferred to vacation homes as well. Encouraging tourists to vary their choices of places to stay can indirectly help lessen the extent to which tourism activities can be one of the causes of climate change.

Government intervention

There may be several sensitization measures, but there exist some that require support from the government. The government can bring forward new measures such as organization of national-level sensitization campaigns, which are not necessarily directly connected to climate change, but rather to patriotism. As per Tranter and Lester (2017), some scholars advocate mobilizing support for environmental issues by harnessing the notion of environmental patriotism, and taking action to reduce the impact of global warming has also been cast as a patriotic cause. If people want to ensure their country's survival, then patriotism can help by making them realize that they have a key role in adopting new behaviors and practices so as to minimize the impacts of and adapt to climate change. This might eventually make Mauritians become the torchbearers for such noble actions, and tourists will have no other choice than to adopt such new behaviors and cultures of being environmental friendly.

Moreover, as per the Organization for Economic Co-operation and Development (OECD, 2018), aligning energy prices with the costs of climate change and air pollution is a core element of cost-effective policy, and vast improvements are urgently needed. Even if some hotels are working towards green practices, use of renewable energy, and use of technology such that there is minimal use of resources and are finding new solutions for the waste that is polluting the planet, other hotels, unfortunately, seem to be still operating in their usual way, whereby there is minimal concern about climate change. As such, the government can redefine energy taxation and encourage hotels to use less energy as it will impact on the amount of tax that they will have to pay. Equally, taxation can be positively adopted by using it as a reward strategy for minimal energy usage. Hotels that have good energy solutions and are doing minimal harm to the planet and climate can be given tax holidays. Moreover, grants can be given to encourage hotels to understand their current energy usage so that they can then work on measures to save energy. As per Wild Singapore (n.d.), there have been concerns that an energy audit could be expensive, but various government grants are now available to help defray the cost; whereby Energy Smart Label winner, the Regent, said its complete energy audit cost S$28,000, and it paid less with the help of various government grants. The concept of energy smart hotels should be able to emerge with such endeavors from the government.

In-depth sensitization for keeping the island alive

It is people who make a country, and not the reverse. Undoubtedly, climate change is altering the layout and the setting of a society and eventually that of a country. As per McKirdy (2018, n.p.), the World Bank CEO Kristalina Georgieva stated in a report that, 'every day, climate change becomes a more urgent economic, social, and existential threat to countries and their people'. She further adds that, 'Increasingly, we are seeing climate change become an engine of migration, forcing individuals, families and even whole communities to seek more viable and less vulnerable places to live'. If such things truly start to happen in Mauritius, then the country will soon cease to exist. Without the people, there will be no life in organizations, and gradually all will vanish. If one was to imagine that other countries would be willing to welcome people from SIDS because they are prone to climate change impacts, it would be good. But one has to accept that such is not the case. From the above, it is also understood that migration will not only be towards other countries but might also involve internal migration such as movement of people from coastal areas to uplands, towns, and cities. This influx of people could have drastic economic as well as social impacts, because management of resources will be even more difficult. The government will have to proactively identify solutions for housing, infrastructure, employment, inland hotels, and tourist attractions. Sensitization campaigns should not, therefore, only focus on the most evident harms done by climate change, but also on its indirect impacts on the tourism sector. Tourists will have to understand clearly and value the importance of responsible tourism consumption so as to avoid bringing about such unimaginable scenarios.

Conclusion

In many cases, it has been noted that the success of the tourism industry is directly related to climate. Changes in the latter are significantly altering demand and purchase patterns. As per Solimar International (n.d.), whether it is changing weather patterns, melting glaciers, expanding deserts, or rising sea levels, the impacts on tourism, people, and the places where they live are hard to ignore, and where the tourism sector can be considered a contributor to climate change, it can also help with mitigation efforts through travel philanthropy, carbon offsetting programs, and other sustainability initiatives. As per the World Tourism Organization and United Nations Environment Programme (2008, cited in Suarez, 2011), tourism will likely move towards higher latitudes and altitudes, where negative climate change impacts will not be as drastic, and, if that happens, the competitive position of vacation spots will change, leaving some areas to decline as others become more popular. Hence, it is of the utmost necessity to sensitize all stakeholders, especially tourists, who are among the primary or main stakeholders, about climate change so as to permit vulnerable islands such as Mauritius to keep their tourism industry alive and to undeniably allow tourists to continue to benefit from the beauty of such amazing destinations. As rightly stated by Suarez (2011), the stakes are particularly high for coastal and island destinations, which are more vulnerable to rising sea levels, hurricanes, severe storms, flooding, water shortages, and beach erosion, and many of these regions – especially in developing countries – have a low capacity to adapt to the changing climate. As per Briguglio (2003), there are a number of SIDS – Singapore, Malta, and Cyprus are prime examples-that are economically vulnerable but have managed to generate high income per capita. Mauritius is also not far behind these countries because, as per BBC News (2018), once dependent on sugar exports, the island has built up a strong outsourcing and financial services sector and an important tourism industry and now boasts one of Africa's highest per capita incomes. For Briguglio (1995), it is possible for SIDS to build up their own resilience to improve their ability to cope with vulnerability. Indeed, because Mauritius has so far had a thriving tourism industry contributing massively to the foreign direct investment of the island; to say that it is a SIDS and will not have the ability to cope with climate change impacts would not be fair. With the right effort from all stakeholders, miracles can happen, and the right way to proceed will be through valuable sensitization of tourists. To ensure that a holistic approach is adopted, future research can focus on understanding the sensitization of other tourism stakeholders regarding climate change through both quantitative and qualitative research methodologies. Such knowledge will aid Mauritius to truly portray its potential and ability to cope with the challenges associated with climate change. For the European Climate Adaptation Platform (n.d.), there are various forms of media through which the message can be communicated – for example, through television, internet, and newspapers. In addition, several tools have been developed to increase decision makers' awareness (see, for example, the online tools on the UKCIP website, www.ukcip.org. uk/) and public awareness (see for example 'Keep it Cool', 'Ludo', and 'Clim-ATIC' board games). As such, sensitization should adopt a holistic approach by not solely focusing on one method, but on several simultaneously, to circulate a unified message about climate change across all platforms. Be it through individual tourist's behavioral changes and actions or those of groups, the contribution they will be making to keep Mauritius a mesmerizing country will always be valuable and worthwhile.

References

Agnew, M. D., & Viner, D. (2001). Potential impacts of climate change on international tourism. *Tourism & Hospitality Research, 3*(1), 37–60.

BBC News. 2018. *Mauritius Country Profile*. [Online] Available at: www.bbc.com/news/world-africa-13882233 (accessed March 17, 2018).

Briassoulis, H. (2002). Sustainable tourism and the question of the commons. *Annals of Tourism Research, 29*(4), 1065–1085.

Briguglio, L. (1995). Small island developing states and their economic vulnerabilities. *World Development, 23*(9), 1615–1632.

Briguglio, L. (2003, September). The vulnerability index and small island developing states: A review of conceptual and methodological issues. In *AIMS Regional Preparatory Meeting on the Ten Year Review of the Barbados Programme of Action: Praia, Cape Verde*. UNESCO.

coastlearn.org. (n.d.). *Sustainable Tourism*. [online] Available at: www.coastlearn.org/tourism/introduction.html (accessed March 5, 2018).

Climate Adapt. (2015). *Awareness Campaigns for Behavioural Change (2015)*. [Online] Available at: https://climate-adapt.eea.europa.eu/metadata/adaptation-options/awareness-campaigns-for-behavioural-change (accessed March 12, 2018).

Diedrichs, G. (2017). *Hotels Responding to Climate Change*. [Online] Available at: www.smartmeetings.com/news/102372/hotels-responding-climate-change (accessed March 12, 2018).

Economic Times. (2018). *Definition of Personal Selling*. [Online] Available at: https://economictimes.indiatimes.com/definition/personal-selling (accessed March 16, 2018).

Ekpoh, U. I., & Ekpoh, I. J. (2011). Assessing the level of climate change awareness among secondary school teachers in Calabar Municipality, Nigeria: Implication for management effectiveness. *International Journal of Humanities & Social Science, 1*(3), 106–110.

European Climate Adaptation Platform. (n.d.). *Awareness Campaigns for Behavioural Change (2015)*. [Online] Available at: http://climate-adapt.eea.europa.eu/metadata/adaptation-options/awareness-campaigns-for-behavioural-change (accessed March 12, 2018).

Gössling, S., Scott, D., Hall, C. M., Ceron, J. P., & Dubois, G. (2012). Consumer behaviour and demand response of tourists to climate change. *Annals of Tourism Research, 39*(1), 36–58.

Hill, M., Wallner, A., & Furtado, J. (2010). Reducing vulnerability to climate change in the Swiss Alps: A study of adaptive planning. *Climate Policy, 10*(1), 70–86.

Hower, M. (2017). *The Dirt on Tourism and Climate Change*. [Online] Available at: www.greenbiz.com/article/tourism-and-climate-complicated-relationship (accessed March 14, 2018).

Hudson, M. (2018). *5 Most Important Elements of Visual Merchandising*. [Online] Available at: www.thebalance.com/the-5-most-important-elements-of-visual-merchandising-2890501 (accessed March 15, 2018).

International Tourism Partnership. (2016). *We Turn Responsible Ambition and Good Ideas into Positive Action*. [Online] Available at: http://tourismpartnership.org/news/climate-change-and-the-hotel-industry (accessed March 16, 2018).

Kangan Institute. (2018). *Importance of Visual Merchandising*. [Online] Available at: www.kangan.edu.au/students/blog/importance-visual-of-visual-merchandising (accessed March 23, 2018).

Ladkoo, A. D. (2016). Vacation home rental concept and its connection to climate change – A literature review. *Theoretical Economics Letters*, *6*(05), 889.

learn.org. (n.d.). *What Is Visual Merchandising?* [Online] Available at: https://learn.org/articles/What_is_Visual_Merchandising.html (accessed March 14, 2018).

Lytton, C. (2013). *Top 10: Climate Change Campaigns*. [Online] Available at: www.theguardian.com/global-development-professionals-network/2013/nov/15/top-10-climate-change-campaigns (accessed March 15, 2018).

Ministry of Tourism Mauritius. (2018). *Tourism Sector*. [Online] Available at: http://tourism.govmu.org/English/Tourism%20sector/Pages/Tourism-Sector.aspx (accessed March 7, 2018).

McKirdy, E. (2018). *Climate Change Could Create 143 Million Migrants, World Bank Says*. [Online] Available at: https://edition.cnn.com/2018/03/20/world/world-bank-climate-migrants-report-intl/index.html (accessed March 15, 2018).

OECD. (2018). *Governments Should Make Better Use of Energy Taxation to Address Climate Change*. [Online] Available at: www.oecd.org/environment/governments-should-make-better-use-of-energy-taxation-to-address-climate-change.htm (accessed April 3, 2018).

Pandve, H. (2007). Global warming: Need to sensitize general population. *Indian Journal of Occupational & Environmental Medicine*, *11*, 86–87.

Peters, A. (2015). *5 Ways to Convince People to Actually Do Something about Climate Change*. [Online] Available at: www.fastcompany.com/3049540/5-ways-to-convince-people-to-actually-do-something-about-climate-change (accessed April 21, 2018).

Solimar International. (n.d.). *Climate Change & Tourism*. [Online] Available at: www.solimarinternational.com/tourism-development/climate-change-tourism (accessed April 2, 2018).

Suarez, C. (2011). *How the Tourism Industry Can Prepare for Climate Change*. [Online] Available at: www.greenbiz.com/blog/2011/08/08/how-tourism-industry-can-prepare-climate-change (accessed March 2, 2018).

Tranter, B., & Lester, L. (2017). Climate patriots? Concern over climate change and other environmental issues in Australia. *Public Understanding of Science*, *26*(6), 738–752.

Unfccc.int. (n.d.). *Education, Training and Public Awareness*. [Online] Available at: http://unfccc.int/resource/docs/natc/maunc1/chap5/chapter5.htm (accessed February 6, 2018).

University of Malta. (2018). *Scholarships in Climate Action*. [Online] Available at: www.um.edu.mt/newspoint/noticeboard/opportunities/2018/05/scholarshipsinclimateaction (accessed March 15, 2018).

Uyarra, M. C., Cote, I. M., Gill, J. A., Tinch, R. R., Viner, D., & Watkinson, A. R. (2005). Island-specific preferences of tourists for environmental features: Implications of climate change for tourism-dependent states. *Environmental Conservation*, *32*(1), 11–19.

Viner, D. (2006). Impacts of climate change on tourism. In P. J. Buckley, S. R. Dye, & J. M. Baxter (Eds.), *Marine Climate Change Impacts Annual Report Card 2006* (online summary reports). Lowestoft, UK: MCCIP. www.mccip.org.uk

Wigder, D. (2016). *For the Tourism Industry, There's No Vacation from Climate Change*. [Online] Available at: www.greenbiz.com/article/tourism-industry-theres-no-vacation-climate-change (accessed March 8, 2018).

Wild Singapore. (n.d.). *New Green Label for Energy Smart Hotels*. [Online] Available at: www.wildsingapore.com/news/20070708/070803-2.htm (accessed April 3, 2018).

World Tourism Organization and United Nations Environment Programme. (2008). *Climate Change and Tourism Report – Responding to Global Challenges*. [Online] Available at: http://sdt.unwto.org/sites/all/files/docpdf/climate2008.pdf (accessed March 16, 2018).

World Travel and Tourism Council. (2018). *Travel & Tourism Economic Impact 2017 Mauritius*. [Online] Available at: www.wttc.org/-/media/files/reports/economic-impact-research/countries-2017/mauritius2017.pdf (accessed March 7, 2018).

25

SUSTAINABLE TOURISM AS A CATALYST FOR POSITIVE ENVIRONMENTAL CHANGE

The case of LUX* Resorts & Hotels

Vishnee Sowamber and Haywantee Rumi Ramkissoon

Introduction

Positive environmental impacts from tourism are often understated in small island developing states. Sustainable tourism development is an opportunity to enhance quality of life, economic development and environmental quality (Nunkoo & Ramkissoon, 2011, 2016; Sowamber, Ramkissoon, & Mavondo, 2017). Over the last few decades, tourism has become one of the fastest growing sectors, with the increase in globalization and disposable incomes (Al-Badi & Al-Sawaei, 2017). It is estimated by the World Travel and Tourism Council (WTTC) that the direct contribution of this industry represents 9.8% of the world's GDP. Statistics show there were 1.235 billion international arrivals in 2016 and US$1.260 trillion earned from international tourism in 2015 (WTO, 2016), contributing to a rise in income of locals (Kotler, Bowen, & Makens, 2014).

Sustainable tourism can be an important catalyst to achieve the sustainable development goals (SDGs) and the Paris Climate Change Agreement, as there are various stakeholders connected to this industry at a point in time. Emmanuel Macron, president of France, launched the international climate summit "One Planet" in Paris on December 12, 2017, which was followed by the Global Pact for the Environment, inviting several countries to respond to climate change (One Planet Summit, 2017). Researchers and practitioners have called for more research documenting human activities and increased greenhouse gas (GHG) emissions (Magaril, Abrzhina, & Belyaeva, 2014). Global warming has caused the Earth's average surface temperature to rise by 1.1° Celsius since the late 19th century (NASA, 2017). The heat-trapping nature of GHGs has been demonstrated through scientific measures (NASA, 2017). Evidence suggests that climate change is the impact of global warming. Its consequences for humanity and Planet Earth are imminent (EPA, 2013).

Tourism can act as a catalyst to maximize positive environmental change to reduce global warming through reduction and reporting of carbon emissions (Ricaurte, 2016). Operators who manage their business in a responsible manner have the opportunity to maximize positive environmental impacts and meet customers' expectations (Martin & Ruiz, 2007; Deloitte, 2008; Mandhachitara & Poolthong, 2011; Rahbar & Abdul Wahid, 2011). The essential components of an environmental management system include initiatives and activities which reduce negative and maximize positive tourism impacts (Siti-Nabiha et al., 2014). Some examples are the maintenance of beaches at resorts and surrounding areas. Through sustainable tourism management, it is ensured that resources are utilized efficiently and value is created for all stakeholders involved (Ramkissoon & Uysal, 2014, 2018; Tyrrell, Paris, & Biaett, 2013), including the guests' experience and enhancement of the local community's quality of life (Ramkissoon, Mavondo, & Uysal, 2018; Rukuižienė, 2014). Tourism has the capacity to create harmony in diversity. It brings everyone together on a common mission for a better future with a mindset of oneness and solidarity.

The potential for positive environmental change may be exponential. Tourism and culture are inextricably linked (Ramkissoon, 2015; Ramkissoon, Uysal, & Brown, 2011), and this sector can be a catalyst for inclusive business and sustainable development (WTO, 2012), maximizing the positive change stakeholders can bring about. With a shift towards "greening" of the tourism sector, operators not only help protect the environment but, at the same time, benefit from savings derived from sound environmental management systems (UNEP, 2011). They can also improve their brand reputation (Aragon-Correa, Martin-Tapia, & de la Torre-Ruiz, 2015; Chomvilailuk & Butcher, 2010).

The needs and wants for travel and tourism continue to grow. With the heated debate on over-tourism (Cainelli, Mazzanti, & Zoboli, 2011; Segarra-Õna, Peiró-Signes, Verma, & Miret- Pastor, 2012), it would be intelligent to use this sector as a tool for positive environmental change through multi-stakeholder dialogues and involvement (Kim & Han, 2010; Molina-Azorín, Tarí, Pereira-Moliner, López-Gamero, & Pertusa-Ortega, 2015). Adopting environmentally friendly strategies and practices can lead to better business performance (Siti-Nabiha et al., 2014). It helps ensure employees' job satisfaction and customer satisfaction (de Leaniz & Rodriguez, 2015). Hence there is increased competitive advantage and financial benefits (Kim & Han, 2010; Kang, Lee, & Huh, 2010).

This chapter aims at exploring how a tourism operator has implemented a robust environmental initiative to align with the Paris Climate Change Agreement and local environmental policies for reduction in carbon emissions. To achieve this goal, the researchers use a case study approach of a major Mauritian hotel group, LUX* Resorts & Hotels, comprising 10 hotels within the destinations of Mauritius, Réunion Island, Maldives Island, China and Turkey. The chapter examines how the hotel group has implemented "Tread Lightly by LUX*" for environmental protection in its destinations and in other countries in Africa and Asia. It shows how it connects multi-stakeholders to achieve the set objectives of energy efficiency, carbon emissions reduction, carbon offsetting, water management, waste management and protection of biodiversity (Ramkissoon, 2014; Ramkissoon et al., 2018). The challenges and opportunities in achieving successful implementation of the Tread Lightly initiative are discussed. This chapter further brings insights to both practitioners and academics on how to view tourism as a tool for positive environmental change, with scope for future research in the field.

Literature review

Climate change and sustainable tourism

Climate change is defined as a change in state of the climate. The latter can be identified through the mean of its properties, and this change persists for a while (Palutikof, van der Linden, & Hanson, 2007). Scientific facts evidence the link between global warming and climate change.

It is stated that the year 2016 was the warmest year on record, and the oceans have absorbed this increased heat (Levitus et al., 2009), with a decrease in the amount of spring snow in the northern hemisphere (Derksen & Brown, 2012). In the last century, a rise in the global sea level of about 8 inches has been observed (Church & White, 2006). The thickness and extent of the arctic sea ice has declined (Kwok & Rothrock, 2009). Based on all these facts, the Paris Climate Change Agreement has set as its objective to reduce GHG emissions in order to counteract these impacts.

Various countries have tourism as a significant source of foreign exchange earnings. Tourism is estimated to represent 30% of exports in services globally (WTO, 2016). The benefits are not limited to socio-economic development but also bring environmental benefits through multi-stakeholder inclusiveness. The travel and tourism sector is expected to generate 150,139,000 jobs directly, which is an increase of 2.2% per year, over the next 10 years (WTTC, 2018). For every 11 tourists, one full time job is created in first world economies (WTO, 2016). With its unique profile of multi-stakeholder participation, the hospitality sector can act as a catalyst in mitigating negative tourism impacts, meeting this sustainability objective.

Hotels are becoming more and more environmentally friendly and introducing environmental management systems at the core of their operations (Kolodinsky, Madden, Zisk, & Henkel, 2010). Operators are considering environmental criteria, compliance and standards in order to align with legal requirements and reduce operations costs. This include the concepts of green building, light interior designs and lean management systems (Berezan, Millar, & Raab, 2014; Mishra, 2016). Tour operators have taken the initiative to include sustainable tourism management at the core of their strategy and are requesting hotels with which they have a contract to have an accredited sustainability certification which is recognized by the Global Sustainable Tourism Council (GSTC). Some of these sustainability certifications include Green Globe, Travelife and EarthCheck (GSTC, 2016). Half of the criteria of these certifications include environmental management. Hence, hotels are implementing environmental initiatives to meet those criteria. Sustainable tourism development is no longer an uncommon trend and is actually very well known among the tourism operators and stakeholders involved (Millar, Mayer & Baloglu, 2012; Sirakaya-Turk, Baloglu & Ramkissoon, 2016). Hotel managers go beyond providing quality services to guests; they ensure that these services include environmentally friendly practices such as energy, water and waste reduction (Kasim, Gursoy, Okumus, & Wong, 2014; Karimi, 2014). These are often the demands and desires of the guests and stakeholders (Altinay & Hussain, 2005). One of the key initiatives to reduce GHG emissions includes having a carbon reduction plan in the corporate and operations strategy. Adaptation or mitigation initiatives accompanied by recognized standards such as ISO 14,001 (Chan & Wong, 2006; Chan, 2009) are being implemented in several hotels. It is noted among tourism operators that, to be successful, there must be good planning and management in line with sustainable principles and with aim to protect the local natural heritage and reduce pollution (Choi & Sirakaya, 2006; Jenkins & Schröder, 2013; Jovicic, 2014). Resorts which are implementing sustainable practices are attracting more customers and their willingness to pay (Kang, Stein, Heo, & Lee, 2012) and, hence, improving hospitality organizations' financial performance.

Carbon management strategies in tourism

For the reduction of GHG emissions, carbon emissions need to be managed through carbon reduction strategies, such as energy efficiency measures, waste reduction (Ramkissoon & Smith, 2014) and transport emissions reduction. Carbon neutrality is now being adopted to address climate change and environmental concerns (Main, 2007). Some hotels are going towards a carbon neutral strategy, which involves mitigating carbon emissions-related impacts, carbon reduction and carbon offsetting initiatives (Gössling, 2009). This can be achieved through stakeholder inclusiveness and participation. Environmental responsibility can be achieved by influencing consumers' behavior. Their decision-making patterns on choice of destination and hotel can be aligned with sustainable tourism (Sirakaya-Turk et al., 2016). It is observed that environmental compliance can help enhance product quality and be an added value for consumers (García-Pozo, Sánchez-Ollero, & Marchante-Mera, 2013). The informed, sophisticated traveler looks for ways to reduce their impacts through carbon offsetting (Higgins, 2006). This is being used by hotels to further fine tune the carbon reduction strategy through implementation of corporate GHG reduction targets, reducing energy consumption and also enhancing their brand reputation (Sowamber et al., 2017). Carbon neutrality is a strategic advantage for many hotels as they demonstrate sustainable tourism management; this represents a qualifying asset of their business. The steps involved in carbon neutrality include first calculating the carbon footprint. This figure is set as the baseline for comparison with the set targets. Travelers are encouraged to offset their emissions by making voluntary contributions. The fund, which is derived from voluntary contributions, is used to purchase carbon offsets to compensate for emissions produced. The hotels also implement carbon reduction initiatives in parallel, such as energy efficiency, for carbon footprint reduction. Examples include implementation of renewable energy projects (Sowamber et al., 2017). The offsets help to fund projects that do not make use of fossil fuels to produce energy or projects that help in reforestation and reduction of transportation emissions (Conlin, 2007).

Some websites, such as https://sustainabletravel.org/ or www.terrapass.com, also provide the opportunity for travelers to calculate the footprint which they need to offset. In 2012, Hilton Worldwide launched a carbon offset program for events and meetings. This is aligned with its initiative "Lightstay", which involves reduction of energy, waste, emissions and water (Hilton Worldwide, n.d.). The carbon credits are expected to fund renewable energy projects. In 2011, a unified method to measure and report carbon emissions, the Hotel Carbon Measurement Initiative, was introduced by the International Tourism Partnership and the WTTC. This standard was reviewed by KPMG and the World Resources Institute prior to its launch. The various hotels in this working group were: Accor, Beijing Tourism Group, Orient-Express Hotels Ltd., Pan Pacific Hotel Group, Premier Inn – Whitbread Group, Starwood Hotels & Resorts Worldwide, Inc., Shangri-La Hotels and Resorts, The Red Carnation Hotel Collection, TUI AG, Wyndham Worldwide and many other hotels. It is observed that the tourism industry implements environmental initiatives for brand image and economic sustainability (Chan &Wong, 2006). Many hotels make use of this methodology to report on their GHG emissions.

The Association of British Travel Agents (ABTA) has a carbon reduction program called "Reduce My Footprint". This initiative offers a platform for travelers to be informed on how they can reduce their carbon footprint. The initiative "Make Your Holidays Greener" is another program launched by ABTA to invite holidaymakers and hoteliers to participate in activities to reduce carbon footprints. Virgin hotels provide guests with the opportunity to offset their carbon footprint through its initiative "Green Your Stay". The guests contribute US$1 per night, and this fund is used to purchase offsets which support a carbon-offsetting project somewhere else in the world and neutralize the emissions produced during the guests' stay. Radisson Blu hotel brand launched its program, "Blu Planet", which involves carbon-free meetings to reduce its footprint through multi-stakeholder participation. The hotel sector has optimized linking the tourism experience and the product to offsetting contribution (Gössling & Schumacher, 2010). The active involvement of guests is very important for businesses in the accommodation sector

(Han & Yoon, 2015). Customers at the same time find it an interesting way to address global warming compromising their holidays (Higgins, 2006). However, it is also clear that, in parallel, hotels are investing in technologies and projects to reduce their emissions and they are not relying only on carbon offsetting, as mentioned in the previous section.

Stakeholder engagement

Tourism has the potential to attract customers who are interested in sustainable management practices and make a positive environmental change (Dolnicar, 2015). The environment is a key capital for tourism development, and, hence, preserving the natural capital remains an important objective. To best achieve set objectives, stakeholder engagement is essential in sustainable tourism development (Byrd, 2007). Freeman (1984: 46) defines stakeholder as "any group or individual who can affect or is affected by the achievement of the organisation objectives". Maintaining a healthy relationship with stakeholders helps achieve mutual benefits (Polonsky & Scott, 2005). There is also informed participation through collaboration among stakeholders (Byrd, Cárdenas, & Greenwood, 2008). Uncertainties can better be faced when there is a strong cooperation with stakeholders, and there is also a reduced chance of opposition. It is important to engage stakeholders in the tourism development process; stakeholder engagement increases the level of trust and commitment and also enhances the quality of life (Morgan & Hunt, 1994; Nunkoo & Ramkissoon, 2012). By integrating stakeholders in the implementation of initiatives, a firm's performance on same can be enhanced (Rodgers & Gago, 2004). For example, Walmart has implemented initiatives such as the zero-waste targets through stakeholder engagement and participation (Higgins, Marguc, & Scholer, 2009). Unilever has, through stakeholder engagement, influenced positive change through sensitization on sustainability values (Polman & Bhattacharya, 2016). Another example includes Marks & Spencer, which has been able to implement a zero-carbon store through stakeholder engagement and participation. The stakeholders included architects, designers, contractors, employees and the local residents (Wilson & Beard, 2014). Firms are now collaborating with NGOs in order to work on common interests towards achieving positive change (Albareda & Waddock, 2016).

Tread Lightly – a catalyst for positive environmental change: a case of LUX* Resorts & Hotels

This section elaborates on the implementation of the Tread Lightly initiative at LUX* Resorts & Hotels. The key objective is to show how tourism can be a catalyst for positive environmental change and how exponential positive impacts can be achieved through multi-stakeholder involvement and participation (WTO, 2012; Dolnicar, 2015).

LUX* Resorts & Hotels is a rapidly growing Mauritian hotel group with its headquarters in Mauritius. It was founded as Naiade Resorts in 1987 and rebranded as LUX* in 2011. Since then, the hotel group has diversified its business strategy and is going more and more towards management contracts. However, the group still has some LUX*-owned assets in its portfolio. The group operates in Mauritius, the Maldives, Réunion Island, Turkey and China. The 5-star hotels are LUX* South Ari Atol Maldives, LUX* Belle Mare Mauritius, LUX* Grand Gaube Mauritius, LUX* Le Morne Mauritius, LUX* St Gilles Ile de la Réunion, LUX* Tea Horse Road Lijiang and LUX* Tea Horse Road Benzilan. The hotel has future openings planned in United Arab Emirates, the Maldives, China, Italy and Vietnam. LUX* also manages properties which fall under the Produced by LUX* portfolio, namely Tamassa hotel and Merville Beach hotel in Mauritius and Hotel Le Recif in Réunion. LUX* is the first hotel group in Mauritius forming part of the Sustainability Index of the Stock Exchange of Mauritius. The group has around 2,900 shareholders and 3,255 team members, with various nationalities around the globe.

The rapid growth of the hotel group implies sustainable management of resources within the destinations where hotels achieve better performance (Siti-Nabiha et al., 2014). This can at the same time help reduce costs (UNEP, 2011). Sustainable tourism management is also required by the destinations' authorities. For example, in the Maldives, there is a government policy relating to climate change and carbon neutrality, the National Strategy for Sustainable Development. In Mauritius, the Paris Climate Change Agreement has been ratified, and there are national commitments towards climate change. Réunion, being part of France and, hence, the European Union, has climate change objectives in its country strategy, the Green Energy Revolution – Reunion Island. Yunnan Province in China has also adopted the Paris Agreement and is working towards a clean air objective. China has been making bold decisions recently to tackle climate change. Tour operators, travel agents and airlines represent around 70% of LUX*'s business sources. They cover mainly the European markets, with some Asian markets. These business sources require sustainable tourism management from hoteliers and also recognized sustainability certification (Millar & Baloglu, 2011). Based on its sustainable development strategy and aligning itself to local and international environmental certification objectives of GHG emissions reductions and stakeholders' expectations, LUX* introduced its environmental initiative, Tread Lightly by LUX*, in 2011.

Tread lightly by LUX* has as its objective to reduce the hotel group's emissions through reduction projects and carbon offsetting (Sowamber et al., 2017) and achieve carbon neutrality through multi-stakeholder participation, aligning with Main (2007). "Though the implementation has been very challenging and with almost no investment, it has now blossomed into a project which brings revenue for projects' implementation and also multi-stakeholder collaboration", commented Paul Jones, CEO of LUX* Resorts & Hotels (private communication; see also Lux Resorts, 2017). It creates a platform to encourage guests' participation through voluntary contribution of €1 per night stay so that they can neutralize the carbon emissions produced during their visit, consistent with literature (e.g., Gössling, 2009; Higgins, 2006).

> From the one euro, 67.5% are used to fund emissions reduction projects while 32.5% are used to offset emissions by buying carbon credits in accredited offsetting projects. The 67.5% fund measures to reduce consumption on resources which are directly related to GHG emissions. Measures imply implementation of new technologies, operational efficiency, trainings and sensitization on efficient resource consumption.
>
> *(Paul Jones, LUX* CEO)*

Some examples include the implementation of low energy lighting; an energy management system, especially for heating, ventilation and air-conditioning; renewable energy project; and the LUX* Experience App to reduce paper used for in-room communications, in line with the study by Berezan, Raab, Yoo and Love (2013).

LUX* keeps a focus on having low transportation of goods to the destination. For example, in Mauritius, wine, which was imported from France, is now being imported from South Africa to reduce transportation emissions. LUX* mostly uses locally sourced ingredients (e.g., use of organic essential oils in the spa, fresh fruit and vegetables from local producers) in its attempt to support local businesses. Some of other projects involve protection of biodiversity through support of whale shark projects and preservation of endemic species. Frequent energy audits are carried out in the hotels by external auditors who produce an energy audit report accompanied by key recommendations on best practices. Recycling and composting are encouraged.

The group has reduced the use of plastic bottles and uses water in glass bottles, which can be recycled. Other projects in the pipeline include green building for new hotel projects and more solar projects.

With regards to the 32.5% of carbon offsetting (Gössling & Shumacher, 2010), the fund supports projects which are within or near the regions where LUX* operates. These include seven projects which hold the Gold Verified Carbon Standard. This means that the projects involve carbon clean technologies such as solar projects, reforestation, wind turbines and other renewable energy projects, and the projects support local community development at the same time (Conlin, 2007). The Tread Lightly initiative is also accompanied by carbon footprint calculation for the group and reporting on these figures and the funds. During the financial year 2016–2017, the emissions were reduced by 53% from the 2013–2014 financial year, the year in which the target was set. These figures are reported in LUX*'s integrated annual report which is aligned with the Global Reporting Initiative international standards. The objective set was to reduce emissions by 10% by the year 2020. The reduction has been mainly due to the reduction in energy consumption by 22% and the other mentioned measures taken to reduce emissions (Lux Resorts, 2017).

The impact of Tread Lightly by LUX* is very significant, not only for the hotel group but for all stakeholders involved, as also evidenced by some recent studies (e.g. Han & Yoon, 2015). It is worth communicating about this great tourism catalyst for positive environmental change. It not only maximizes positive environmental impacts but also brings together various stakeholders for a common purpose. It enhances trust (Bramwell & Lane, 2011; Nunkoo & Ramkissoon, 2012; Ramkissoon, 2016; Ramkissoon & Hristov, 2018) among shareholders, investors, tour operators and local authorities. The group is being approached by financiers such as GoSolar and Jabil Energy to invest 100% in energy reduction projects through profit-sharing schemes. LUX*'s sustainable environmental management practices may be of interest to destinations' managers and hoteliers, with important practical outcomes.

Implications

This Tread Lightly by LUX* case study gives insights into how sustainable environmental practices can be a catalyst for positive environmental change through stakeholder inclusiveness. It shows how this sector implements strategies to respond to climate change and carbon reduction by aligning corporate strategy to make contributions towards a common purpose through multi-stakeholder participation. Taking into consideration this information, policymakers, accreditation bodies, governance bodies, auditors and destination managers can optimize the tourism sector to maximize positive environmental impacts. The sector can help in the achievement of global and local sustainability objectives such as the SDGs and the Paris Climate Change Agreement for carbon reduction. NASA (2017) observed that the average surface temperature of the planet rose by 1.1° Celsius since the late 19th century, and the scientific measures have demonstrated that it is mainly owing to the greenhouse effect. The year 2016 was the warmest year on record, and this extra heat is being absorbed by oceans (Levitus et al., 2009). The tourism industry, with its unique potential of being exposed to multi-stakeholders, can help achieve objectives of carbon reduction as they go towards "greening" this sector through environmental systems that also bring savings (UNEP, 2011). Hoteliers are linking carbon offsetting with tourism experiences and products (Gössling & Schumacher, 2010).They are also implementing initiatives which are aligned with international standards such as ISO 14,001 (Chan & Wong, 2006; Chan, 2009). Other initiatives include green building, light interior designs and lean management systems (Berezan et al., 2016).

The tourism sector is very motivated to implement environmental management systems as they are able to enhance brand reputations (Sowamber et al., 2017). There is strong correlation between environmental management and profitability (Gómez-Haro, Ferrón-Vílchez, de la Torre-Ruiz, & Delgado-Ceballos, 2015). It also brings competitive advantages (Chi & Gursoy, 2009; Leonidou, Leonidou, Fotiadis, & Zeriti, 2013; Testa, Gusmerotti, Corsini, Passetti, & Iraldo, 2015). On the other hand, guests are keen to find ways to reduce their travel impacts through carbon offsetting (Higgins, 2006). Sustainable tourism is the goal of many tourism operators and stakeholders (Millar & Baloglu, 2011). It is, hence, wise to optimize the tourism sector for positive environmental change through multi-stakeholder inclusiveness. A very interesting aspect is that there are financing opportunities that can be tapped into. Investors are willing to accompany an organization in its quest for energy reduction and carbon reduction with 100% of the project being financed and working on a savings-sharing scheme.

Challenges and opportunities

Key challenges include the costs involved and doubts regarding the returns from implementing a sound environmental management system accompanied by projects and initiatives to meet the set objectives (Kumar, 2005). Hence, many hoteliers are reluctant to budget for this area of their business. This arises owing to lack of internal knowledge and skills and resource persons who are incentivized to achieve targets. There are also the issues of lack of professional advice and resistance to change. These barriers prevent hotels adopting environmental management systems and managing their social and environmental capitals (Garay & Font, 2012). Whenever economic conditions are unfavorable, the budget for sustainability projects is reviewed or stopped so that the money can go to other areas such as sales, marketing and branding-related projects. Hotels' managers and their teams are often reluctant to collaborate in the communication and implementation of environmental policies and projects as these often involve a change in long-established routines. They are also not convinced about the objectives of the environmental initiatives (Chan, Hon, Chan, & Okumus, 2014). From a management perspective, the involvement of employees implies extra workloads for them. For example, room attendants have to do waste segregation and control linens if guests do choose not to change them to reduce water and energy consumption. The structure in terms of human resources to manage sustainability key performance indicators (KPIs) in hotels is often informal and not incentivized. Hence, there is no direct control by management over the achievement of the KPIs. Another challenge is that some guests are not happy to compromise on comfort and luxury (Baker, Davis, & Weaver, 2014). On the other hand, there are a lot of advantages in collaborating for positive environmental change. The very products that hotels are marketing include the environment and the destination's landscape and features, and it makes sense that an unspoilt environment is an important element of a tourist destination. There is a strong correlation between environmental management and profitability (Gómez-Haro et al., 2015). Environmental strategies bring employee motivation (Renwick, Redman, & Maguire, 2013) and also increase customer satisfaction, (Berezan et al., 2014), and they give a competitive advantage over direct competitors, hence attracting more investment, including funding for sustainability projects (Chi & Gursoy, 2009; Leonidou et al., 2013; Testa, Gusmerotti et al., 2015; Testa, Boiral, & Iraldo, 2015). It is important to have the support and participation of local residents for sustainable tourism development (Lee, 2013).

This chapter sheds light on practical implications that policymakers and destination managers can optimize to respond to climate change and, more specifically, achieve carbon reduction, which is a global and national challenge. It is also worth noting that investors and guests are willing to support energy reduction and carbon reduction projects. The present information seeks to promote further research in the field with suggestions on how various stakeholders in the tourism and hospitality industry can seek to address climate change, working towards a common purpose of positive environmental change.

References

Al-Badi, A., & Al-Sawaei, S. (2017). Utilizing social media to encourage domestic tourism in Oman. *International Journal of Business & Management*, 12(4), 84–94.

Albareda, L., & Waddock, S. (2016). Networked CSR governance: A whole network approach to metagovernance. *Business & Society*, 57(4), 636–675.

Altinay, M., & Hussain, K. (2005). Sustainable tourism development: A case study of North Cyprus. *International Journal of Contemporary Hospitality Management*, 17, 272–280.

Aragon-Correa, J.A., Martin-Tapia, I., & de la Torre-Ruiz, J. (2015). Sustainability issues and hospitality and tourism firms' strategies: Analytical review and future directions. *International Journal of Contemporary Hospitality Management*, 27(3), 498–522.

Baker, M.A., Davis, E.A., & Weaver, P.A. (2014). Eco-friendly attitudes, barriers to participation, and differences in behavior at green hotels. *Cornell Hospitality Quarterly*, 55(1), 89–99.

Berezan, O., Raab, C., Yoo, M.. & Love, C. (2013). Sustainable hotel practices and nationality: The impact on guest satisfaction and guest intention to return. *International Journal of Hospitality Management*, 34, 227–233.

Berezan, O., Millar, M., & Raab, C. (2014). Sustainable hotel practices and guest satisfaction levels. *International Journal of Hospitality & Tourism Administration*, 15, 1–18.

Bramwell, B., & Lane, B. (2011). Critical research on the governance of tourism and sustainability. *Journal of Sustainable Tourism*, 19(4–5), 411–421.

Byrd, E. (2007). Stakeholders in sustainable tourism development and their roles: Applying stakeholder theory to sustainable tourism development. *Tourism Review*, 62(2), 6–13.

Byrd E.T., Cárdenas, D.A., & Greenwood, J. (2008). Factors of stakeholder understanding of sustainable tourism. *Hospitality & Tourism Research*, 8(3), 192–204.

Cainelli, G., Mazzanti, M., & Zoboli, R. (2011). Environmentally oriented innovative strategies and firm performance in services: Micro-evidence from Italy. *International Review of Applied Economics*, 25(1), 61–85.

Chan, E., & Wong, S. (2006). Motivations for ISO14001 in the hotel industry. *Tourism Management*, 27(3), 481–492.

Chan, E.S.W., Hon, A.H.Y., Chan, W., & Okumus, F. (2014). What drives employees' intentions to implement green practices in hotels? The role of knowledge, awareness, concern and ecological behavior. *International Journal of Hospitality Management*, 20, 20–28.

Chan, W.W. (2009). Environmental measures for hotels' environmental management systems: ISO 14001. *International Journal of Contemporary Hospitality Management*, 21(5), 542–560.

Chi, C.G., & Gursoy, D. (2009). Employee satisfaction, customer satisfaction, and financial performance: An empirical examination. *International Journal of Hospitality Management*, 28(2), 245–253.

Choi, H.C., & Sirakaya, E. (2006). Sustainability indicators for managing community tourism. *Tourism Management*, 27(6), 1274–1289.

Chomvilailuk, R., & Butcher, K. (2010). Enhancing brand preference through corporate social responsibility initiatives in the Thai banking sector. *Asia Pacific Journal of Marketing & Logistics*, 22(3), 397–418.

Church, J.A., & White, N.J. (2006). A 20th century acceleration in global sea level rise. *Geophysical Research Letters*, 33, L01602, doi:10.1029/2005GL024826

Conlin, J. (2007). Going green, one spring break at a time. *New York Times*, February 25.

de Leaniz, P.M.G., & Rodriguez, I.R.D.B. (2015). Exploring the antecedents of hotel customer loyalty: A social identity perspective. *Journal of Hospitality Marketing & Management*, 24(1), 1–23.

Deloitte Consumer Survey. (2008, June 5). Business travelers are starting to demand green lodging.

Derksen, C., & Brown, R. (2012). Spring snow cover extent reductions in the 2008–2012 period exceeding climate model projections. *Geophysical Research Letters*, 39. https://doi.org/10.1029/2012GL053387

Dolnicar, S. (2015). Environmentally sustainable tourists? In M. Hall, S. Gössling, & D. Scott (Eds), *The Routledge Handbook of Tourism and Sustainability*. New York: Routledge, pp. 140–150.

EPA. (2013). Future Climate Change. Available at: www.epa.gov/climatechange/science/future.html (August).

Freeman, R.E. (1984). *Strategic Management: A Stakeholder Approach*. Boston, MA: Pittman.

Garay, L., & Font, X. (2012). Doing good to do well? Corporate social responsibility reasons, practices and impacts in small and medium accommodation enterprises. *International Journal of Hospitality Management*, 31(2), 329–337.

García-Pozo, A., Sánchez-Ollero, J.-L., & Marchante-Mera, A. (2013). Environmental sustainability measures and their impact on hotel room pricing in Andalusia (southern Spain). *Environmental Engineering & Management Journal*, 12(10), 1971–1978.

Gómez-Haro, S., Ferrón-Vílchez, V., de la Torre-Ruiz, J.M., & Delgado-Ceballos, J. (2015). What motivates hotel managers to become ecopreneurs: A case study on the Spanish tourism sector. In P. Kyrö (Ed.), *Handbook of Entrepreneurship and Sustainable Development Research*, Cheltenham, UK: Edward Elgar, pp. 258–274.

Gössling, S. (2009). Carbon neutral destinations: a conceptual analysis. *Journal of Sustainable Tourism*, 17(1), 17–37.

Gössling, S., & Schumacher, K.P. (2010). Implementing carbon neutral destination policies: Issues from the Seychelles. *Journal of Sustainable Tourism*, 18(3), 377–391.

Han, H., & Yoon, H.J. (2015). Hotel customers' environmentally responsible behavioral intention: Impact of key constructs on decision in green consumerism. *International Journal of Hospitality Management*, 45, 22–33.

Higgins, E.T., Marguc, J., & Scholer, A.A. (2009). Working under adversity: How opposing versus coping affects value. Unpublished manuscript, Columbia University.

Higgins, M. (2006). Raising the ante on eco-tourism. *New York Times*, December 10.

Hilton Worldwide. (n.d.). [Online]. http://newsroom.hilton.com/index.cfm/news/hilton-world wide-introduces-carbon-offset-program-for-events-and-meetings-in-southeast-asia https://www. environmentalleader.com/2012/06/marriott-hilton-hyatt-among-23-hotels-launching-carbon-measurement-standard/ (accessed May 13, 2018).

Jenkins, I., & Schröder, R. (2013). *Sustainability in Tourism*. Berlin: Springer Gabler.

Jovicic, D. (2014). Key issues in the implementation of sustainable tourism. *Current Issues in Tourism*, 17(4), 297–302.

Kang, K.H., Lee, S., & Huh, C. (2010). Impacts of positive and negative corporate social responsibility activities on company performance in the hospitality industry. *International Journal of Hospitality Management*, 29(1), 72–82.

Kang, K.H., Stein, L., Heo, C.Y., & Lee, S. (2012). Consumers' willingness to pay for green initiatives of the hotel industry. *International Journal of Hospitality Management*, 31(2), 564–572.

Karimi, E. (2014). Relationship between green operations practices and operational performance of hotels in the coastal region, Kenya. Unpublished MBA project, University of Nairobi, Nairobi, Kenya.

Kasim, A., Gursoy, D., Okumus, F., & Wong, A. (2014). The importance of water management in hotels: A framework for sustainability through innovation, *Journal of Sustainable Tourism*, 22(7), 1090–1107.

Kim, Y., & Han, H. (2010). Intention to pay conventional hotel prices at a green hotel – A modification of the theory of planned behavior. *Journal of Sustainable Tourism*, 18, 997–1014.

Kolodinsky, R., Madden, T., Zisk, D., and Henkel, E. (2010). Attitudes about corporate social responsibility: Business student predictors. *Journal of Business Ethics*, 91(2), 67–81.

Kotler, P., Bowen, J.T., & Makens, J. (2014). *Marketing for Hospitality and Tourism*. Harlow, UK: Pearson Education.

Kumar, S. (2005). Resource use and waste management in Vietnam hotel industry. *Journal of Cleaner Production*, 13(2), 109–116.

Kwok, R., & Rothrock, D.A. (2009). Decline in Arctic sea ice thickness from submarine and ICESAT records: 1958–2008. *Geophysical Research Letters*, 36, paper no. L15501.

Lee, H.T. (2013). Influence analysis of community resident support for sustainable tourism development. *Tourism Management*, 34, 37–46.

Leonidou, L.C., Leonidou, C.N., Fotiadis, T.A., & Zeriti, A. (2013). Resources and capabilities as drivers of hotel environmental marketing strategy: Implications for competitive advantage and performance. *Tourism Management*, 35(April), 94–110.

Levitus, S., Antonov, J.I., Boyer, T.P., Locarnini, R.A., Garcia, H.E., & Mishonov, A.V. (2009). Global ocean heat content 1955–2008 in light of recently revealed instrumentation problems, *Geophysical Research Letters*, 36, L07608, doi: 10.1029/2008GL037155

Lux Resorts. (2017). Annual Report 2017. Available at: www.luxresorts.com/media/3356674/annual report2017.pdf

Magaril, E, Abrzhina, L., & Belyaeva, M. (2014). Environmental damage from the combustion of fuels: Challenges and methods of economic assessment. *WIT Transactions on Ecology and the Environment*, 190, 1105–1115.

Main, E. (2007). Shifting into neutral. In *The Green Guide*. Available at: www.thegreenguide.com/doc/119/neutral

Mandhachitara, R., & Poolthong, Y. (2011). A model of customer loyalty and corporate social responsibility. *Journal of Services Marketing*, 25(2), 122–133.

Martin, L., & Ruiz, S. (2007). "I need you too!" Corporate identity attractiveness for consumers and the role of social responsibility. *Journal of Business Ethics*, 71(3), 245–260.

Millar, M., & Baloglu, S. (2011). Hotel guests' preferences for green guest room attributes. *Cornell Hospitality Quarterly*, 52(3), 302–311.

Millar, M., Mayer, K.J., & Baloglu, S. (2012). Importance of green hotel attributes to business and leisure travelers. *Journal of Hospitality Marketing & Management*, 21, 395–413.

Mishra, P.P. (2016). How green are our hotels? Evidence from Thailand. *Environment & Urbanization Asia*, 7, 132–148.

Molina-Azorín, J.F., Tarí, J.J., Pereira-Moliner, J., López-Gamero, M.D., & Pertusa-Ortega, E.M. (2015) The effects of quality and environmental management on competitive advantage: A mixed methods study in the hotel industry. *Tourism Management*, 50(October), 41–54.

Morgan, R.M., & Hunt, S.D. (1994). The commitment-trust theory of relationship marketing. *Journal of Marketing*, 58, 20–38.

National Aeronautics and Space Administration (NASA). (2017, Jan. 18). Goddard Institute for Space Studies. Data show warmest year on record globally [online]. Available at: www.giss.nasa.gov/research/news/20170118/ (accessed May 13, 2018).

Nunkoo R., & Ramkissoon H. (2012). Power, trust social exchange and community support. *Annals of Tourism Research*, 39(2), 997–1023.

Nunkoo, R., & Ramkissoon, H. (2011). Developing a community support model for tourism. *Annals of Tourism Research*, 38(3), 964–988.

Nunkoo, R., & Ramkissoon, H. (2016). Stakeholders' views of enclave tourism: A grounded theory approach. *Journal of Hospitality & Tourism Research*, doi: 10.1177

Palutikof, J., van der Linden, P., & Hanson, C. (Eds). (2007). *Fourth Assessment Report of the Intergovernmental Panel on Climate Change*. Cambridge: Cambridge University Press, pp. 687–716.

One Planet Summit. (2017). Paris 2017 Climate Finance Day. Dec 12. Available at: www.climatefinance day.com/one-planet-summit/ (accessed May 13, 2018).

Polman, P., & Bhattacharya, C.B. (2016). Engaging employees to create a sustainable business. *Stanford Social Innovation Review*, 34–39. Available at: https://ssir.org/articles/entry/engaging employees_to_create_a_sustainable_business

Polonsky, M.J., & Scott, D. (2005). An empirical examination of the stakeholder strategy matrix. *European Journal of Marketing*, 39, 1199–1215.

Rahbar, E., & Abdul Wahid, N. (2011). Investigation of green marketing tools' effect on consumers' purchase behavior. *Business Strategy Series*, 12(2), 73–83.

Ramkissoon, H. (2014). Understanding household water saving behaviours to inform policy: Evidence from Australia. International Conference on Water, Informatics, Sustainability & Environment. Gatineau, Canada.

Ramkissoon, H. (2015). Authenticity, satisfaction, and place attachment: A conceptual framework for cultural tourism in African island economies. *Development Southern Africa*, 32(3), 292–302.

Ramkissoon, H. (2016). Place satisfaction, place attachment and quality of life: Development of a conceptual framework for island destinations. In P. Modica & M. Uysal (Eds.), *Sustainable Island Tourism: Competitiveness and Quality of Life*. Wallingford, UK: CABI, pp. 106–116.

Ramkissoon, H., & Hristov, D. (2018). Tourism Institutions and Agencies, In C. Cooper, S. Volo, B. Gartner, and N. Scott (Eds.), *The SAGE Handbook of Tourism Management: Theories, Concepts and Disciplinary Approaches to Tourism*. Lond: Sage publications, pp. 485–501.

Ramkissoon, H., Mavondo, F., & Uysal, M. (2018). Social involvement and park citizenship as moderators for quality-of-life in a national park. *Journal of Sustainable Tourism*, 26(3), 341–361.

Ramkissoon, H., & Smith, L.D.G. (2014). Evaluating the effectiveness of Wipe for Wildlife and its campaign elements. Technical report. Melbourne, Australia.

Ramkissoon, H., & Uysal, M.S. (2014). Authenticity as a value co-creator of tourism experiences. In N.K. Prebensen, J.S. Chen, & M. Uysal (Eds), *Creating Experience Value in Tourism*. Wallingford, UK: CABI, pp. 113–124.

Ramkissoon, H., & Uysal, M.S. (2018). Authenticity as a value co-creator of tourism experiences. In N.K. Prebensen, J.S. Chen, & M. Uysal (Eds), *Creating Experience Value in Tourism*, 3rd ed. Wallingford, UK: CABI, pp. 98–109.

Ramkissoon, H., Uysal, M., & Brown, K. (2011). Relationship between destination image and behavioral intentions of tourists to consume cultural attractions. *Journal of Hospitality Marketing & Management*, 20(5), 575–595.

Renwick, D.W., Redman, T., & Maguire, S. (2013). Green human resource management: A review and research agenda. *International Journal of Management Reviews*, 15(1), 1–14.

Ricaurte, E. (2016). Hotel sustainability benchmarking index 2016: Energy, water, and carbon. *Cornell Hospitality Report*, 16(16), 3–13.

Rodgers, W., & Gago, S. (2004). Stakeholder influence on corporate strategies over time. *Journal of Business Ethics*, 52, 349–363.

Rukuižienė, R. (2014). Sustainable tourism development implications to local economy. *Regional Formation & Development Studies*, 3(14), 170–177.

Segarra-Õna, M., Peiró-Signes, Á., Verma, R., & Miret-Pastor, L. (2012). Does environmental certification help the economic performance of hotels? Evidence from the Spanish hotel industry. *Cornell Hospitality Quarterly*, 53(3), 242–256.

Sirakaya-Turk, E., Baloglu, S., & Ramkissoon, H. (2016). Values, sustainability and destination choice of North Americans. The BEST EN Think Tank XVI, Eberswalde, Germany, July 12–15.

Siti-Nabiha, A.K., George, R.A., Wahid, N., Amran, A., Mahadi, R., & Abustan, I. (2014). The development of a green practice index for the Malaysian hotel industry. *Issues in Social & Environmental Accounting*, 8(1), 23–47.

Sowamber, V., Ramkissoon, H., & Mavondo, F. (2017). Impact of sustainability practices on hospitality consumers' behaviors and attitudes. The case of LUX* Resorts & Hotels. In D. Gursoy (Ed.), *Routledge Handbook of Hospitality Marketing*. New York: Routledge, p. 388.

Testa, F., Boiral, O., & Iraldo, F. (2015). Internalization of environmental practices and institutional complexity: can stakeholders' pressures encourage greenwashing? *Journal of Business Ethics*, 147(2), 287–307.

Testa, F., Gusmerotti, N.M., Corsini, F., Passetti, E., & Iraldo, F. (2015). Factors affecting environmental management by small and micro firms: The importance of entrepreneurs' attitudes and environmental investment. *Corporate Social Responsibilities and Environmental Management*, 23(6), doi: 10.1002/csr.1382

The Global Sustainable Tourism Council (GSTC). (2016). GSTC Industry Criteria for Hotels. Available at: www.gstcouncil.org/gstc-criteria/gstc-industry-criteria-for-hotels/ (accessed December 11, 2016).

Wilson, J.P., & Beard, C.M. (2014). Constructing a sustainable learning organization: Marks and Spencer's first plan a learning store. *The Learning Organization*, 21(2), 98–112.

Tyrrell, T., Paris, C.M., & Biaett, V. (2013). A quantified triple bottom line for tourism: Experimental results. *Journal of Travel Research*, 52(3), 279–293.

United Nations Environment Programme (UNEP). (2011). *Towards a Green Economy: Pathways to Sustainable Development and Poverty Eradication*. Nairobi: UNEP.

World Tourism Organization (WTO). (2012). World Tourism Day 2012. Tourism – Linking Cultures. Available at: http://wtd.unwto.org/en/content/about-theme-tourism-linking-cultures (accessed February 25, 2019).

World Tourism Organization (WTO). (2016). *Tourism Highlights 2016 Edition*. Madrid: UNWTO.

World Travel and Tourism Council (WTTC). (2018). Travel and Tourism Economic Impact 2018. Available at: www.wttc.org/-/media/files/reports/economic-impact-research/regions-2018/world 2018.pdf (accessed March 1, 2019).

PART V

Political impacts of tourism

26

POLITICAL IMPACTS OF TOURISM

Richard Butler and Wantanee Suntikul

Introduction

It has long been generally accepted that tourism brings about change and thus has impacts and effects on the localities and communities in which it takes place (Mathieson and Wall 1982). The conventional treatment of such impacts has been to categorise them into three groups, economic, environmental and social, but such a division both is too simple and misses a number of other areas in which tourism has impacts. One such area is that of politics and the bringing about of political change. These changes are often bidirectional rather than unidirectional; that is, tourism brings about changes in the political realm but also responds to, and is itself changed by, political factors. This relationship between tourism and governance and politics has been relatively neglected compared with research conducted in the three main areas of impact studies noted above (Butler and Suntikul 2010, 2017). This chapter develops a framework to place such impacts and changes in a theoretical context, particularly in relation to the other impacts of tourism. It examines what changes in political systems and approaches have been influenced and caused by tourism, using examples from specific countries and regions, including Cuba, Egypt, Canada, China, the United States and the United Kingdom. Changes include those in personnel, in international relations, in development policy, in border-crossing procedures and in treaty agreements, and occur in both origin and destination countries. The chapter demonstrates how complex the relationship between the political realm and tourism is, the interplay between the different forms of tourism, and the likely impacts upon politics, politicians and the international scene.

Impacts of tourism

The effects of tourism and tourists on economies, communities and natural environments have been studied for more than a century, initially with a focus on the economic benefits of tourism, particularly at the regional and local levels, followed by an interest in the effects on natural environments, including flora and fauna, and most recently in the effects of tourism on residents of tourist destinations. The interrelationships between these three areas of interest were perhaps best expressed in the seminal work by Mathieson and Wall (1982), and more recently by the same authors again (Wall and Mathieson 2006). As they and others (e.g. Hall and Lew 2009; Holden 2008; Weaver and Lawton 2014) have noted, much of the specific research effort has gone into single-sector examinations of impacts, thus missing many related but less direct effects of tourism on destinations and the links between the various sectors. The adoption of a more integrated approach to impact assessment, partly brought about by the acceptance in principle, if less so in practice, of sustainable development, and more specifically in this case, sustainable tourism, has seen an improvement in the understanding of the complexity of tourism and its effects. Sustainable development was proposed and promoted as a holistic concept (WCED 1987), incorporating all elements and attempting to coordinate development to meet multiple goals and interests. Traditionally, proponents of sustainable tourism (and to a considerable extent of sustainable development itself) have tended to portray areas of concern as being linked in a "triple bottom line", involving the three traditional areas of impact, economics, environmental and sociocultural.

As has been argued elsewhere (Butler 2013), the triple-bottom-line approach excludes direct consideration of a fourth factor, politics, which, in reality, influences, and even controls, many of the other sectors. However much proponents of particular actions and controls aiming at securing a more sustainable form of tourism may push their case and even achieve support for particular steps to be taken with respect to tourism development, unless such steps meet with political approval, they are unlikely to be implemented. This situation can be seen in the many sustainable tourism plans which have not been fully implemented and thus have not achieved their goal of sustainable tourism (Dodds and Butler 2010).

The effects of tourism on the political realm come about in a number of ways, some direct, others indirect and even unnoticed by many observers. Figure 26.1 illustrates the most common way in which tourism-induced changes at the political level are generated. Discontent with the status quo with respect to tourism may stem from the impacts, both positive and negative, experienced in the three general areas. As a result of these impacts, those desiring change call for a response from policymakers and those in charge of development, infrastructure and services. Such demands may be positive or negative, or for changes in any or all of the various aspects of tourism, such as the type, rate, timing and location of tourism. Some calls may be for increases in services and facilities and improvements in infrastructure in order to attract more tourism to a destination, or in response to crowding and overuse of existing facilities. Other calls may be to reduce or restrict current numbers of tourists or further growth on the grounds of congestion, pollution, damage to flora and fauna, denial of local access to resources and increases in problems such as crime and loss of amenity. In both situations, if the calls for political response and action result in changes being implemented, these are direct political impacts of tourism, in that the effects have come about because of real or perceived impacts in other areas.

The caveat of "perceived" impacts is necessary because it is clear (Wall and Mathieson 1982) that not all impacts claimed to have been caused by tourism are in fact the result of tourism, either alone or even in conjunction with other developments. As well, some impacts in one location that have been attributed to tourism in that location may be the result of either tourism or other activities elsewhere, and thus potential local remedial actions may be inappropriate or ineffective. Although levels of crime may rise as tourist numbers rise in a destination, it is rarely tourists who are responsible for such actions; in reality, tourists are more likely to be the victims of crime than the perpetrators. However, the rise in numbers of tourists may attract additional criminals as the visitors represent a relatively easy target for illegal activity. It is necessary, therefore, to differentiate, in some situations at least, between the impacts of tourism and the impacts of tourists, and many residents of tourist destinations are quite capable of separating the two (Brougham and Butler 1981), even if such a distinction is often not made.

The political dimension of tourism has implications for all three of the conventional facets of the "triple bottom line" with differing areas of concern depending on the political level examined (see Table 26.1).

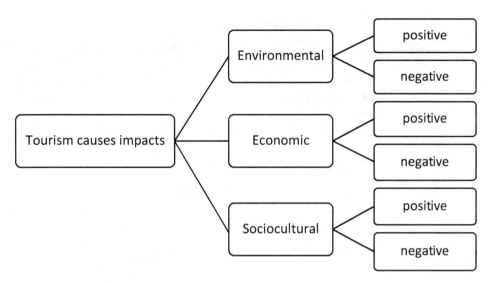

Figure 26.1 Tourism and impacts (resulting in action at different political levels)

Table 26.1 Areas of concern in political impacts of tourism at different political levels

Level	Area of concern		
	Economic	*Sociocultural*	*Environmental*
Local	Jobs, income	Congestion	Pollution
Regional	Economic development	Infrastructure	Habitats
National	Visitor numbers	Redistribution of benefits	National parks
International	Balance of payments	Heritage	Sustainability

The realisation of the importance of the role of politics and governance in tourism has come relatively late, and the effects of politics (Butler and Suntikul 2010, 2017; Elliott 1997; Hall 1994), including changes in ideologies, in alliances, in attitudes towards development in general as well as tourism, and in the opening and closing of borders, have not been investigated as fully as they might have been. (Rather surprisingly, given Hall's expertise and record in the area of linking politics and tourism (Amore and Hall 2016), the political impacts of tourism are not specifically identified or discussed even in Hall and Lew's (2009) book on tourism impacts.) Part of this broad neglect has undoubtedly been caused by a failure on the part of researchers in other fields to appreciate fully the dimensions and significance of tourism, both domestically and internationally, resulting, therefore, in their ignoring its likely effects on policy at a governmental level. Such influences are both real and, in some cases, profound and can have international repercussions, whereas in other cases they represent changes at a very local level reflecting the responses of residents in destinations to tourism and tourists (Doxey 1975). Such concerns can be seen most recently in the growth of the concept of "overtourism" and protests over the levels of tourism in places such as Barcelona and Venice, and in many concerns over the impacts of tourism development and the numbers of visitors on communities, their infrastructure and their environments (WTTC 2018). Thus, the acknowledged impacts relating to the triple bottom line noted above can readily translate into calls for political action to mitigate and prevent such impacts, which, if implemented, represent one form of the political impact of tourism.

Political impacts of tourism

To definitively be a political impact of tourism, the taking of an action must be the result of the effect of tourism, either directly or indirectly. This may be the creation of, or the cancellation of, a policy – for example, to institute or to cancel a tax on tourists, as implemented by the regional government of Calvia (Spain), which took both actions in the 1980s (Dodds 2007). It may also be the election of a candidate on the basis of their position and proposed actions with regard to tourism, or the rejection of an elected representative on similar grounds (Martin 2006). In such cases, the influence of tourism is clear and unambiguous. In other cases, the effect or impact of tourism may be less obvious and be a part of a wider political platform, such as regional development, where policies favouring tourism may be introduced after successful lobbying by the tourism industry, as in New Jersey for the legalisation of gambling in Atlantic City. Alternatively, negative attitudes towards tourists and tourism-related development for a variety of reasons, such as overcrowding and congestion, pollution or loss of amenity and access to resources, may result in the establishment of policies restricting or preventing further growth of tourism or selected elements (e.g. in Bermuda, with limits on the number of cruise ships allowed in the port of Hamilton at any one time). Other impacts may be much less visible and only be reflected in more generalised efforts to support or oppose tourism development as part of efforts such as urban renewal, disaster regeneration or wider international trade arrangements. Tourism is sometimes hailed as a panacea for many ills, not all economic, as in, for example, the ongoing argument that tourism is a "force for peace" (D'Amore 1988) and about whether the development of tourism between hitherto unfriendly countries, such as South and North Korea, could bring about a lasting peace and even reunion (Shin 2010).

The nature of the subjects affected by tourism vary by level of political control (Table 26.2), as do the degree of importance of tourism in decision-making and the resulting actions taken in response to pressure from affected parties.

The picture becomes more confused when one attempts to allocate responsibility for particular political actions and to determine how much, if any, influence tourism had in such developments. One such case is Vietnam in the aftermath of the Vietnam War and the establishment of the Doi Moi or "Open Door" policy of its government. This policy has proved extremely beneficial economically to Vietnam, and tourism has been a major factor in the country's subsequent economic growth. It would be naïve and certainly inaccurate to argue that this policy was adopted because of the potential for tourism growth, but, equally, it is unlikely that tourism was not considered when that policy and subsequent changes in legislation, including visa and access arrangements for foreign visitors, were made (Suntikul, Butler and Airey 2010). The subsequent growth in tourism was followed over the years by the loosening of restrictions on investment and ownership by foreign agents, changes in the operation and management of the national airline, and changes in the presentation of artefacts and features relating to the aforementioned war (Laderman 2013). In a reciprocal fashion, the rise in popularity of Vietnam as

Table 26.2 Nature of political action in tourism at different governmental levels

Level	Subject of effect	Level of importance	Effects
Local	Individuals, elections, local issues	High	Policies, short-term, dynamic, vulnerability
Regional	Economic development	Medium	Redistribution, image
National	Image, expenditure	Mostly minor	Policy, major issues only
International	Cross-border issues	Mostly minor	Treaties, visas, trade

a vacation destination, particularly among Americans, reflects a change in political attitudes towards a country once viewed, admittedly not by the entire US population, as a bitter enemy, and is an indication of the ability of tourism to both reflect and to change political attitudes (Lema and Agrusa 2013). Thus, although tourism may not have been proven to be a force for peace in the sense of ending conflicts, it may be a force for reducing post-conflict hostility and aiding the development of positive attitudes between residents of formerly warring countries. The numbers of present-day visitors to Germany and Japan by their former enemies in World War II is indicative of a change in attitudes among those tourists, and one may argue that, in that sense at least, a part of the change in attitudes has been influenced by the effect of tourism (Eades and Cooper 2013).

In some cases, despite the apparent wish of residents of one country to visit another, government political action may prevent such traffic. The US government's policies with respect to American citizens visiting Cuba are one such example. Since the institution of communism there and the Cuban Missile Crisis of the mid 1960s, the US has imposed a trade embargo on Cuba, including a ban on tourism between the two countries (Hinch 2006). Despite this, citizens of other Western countries, even strong allies of the US such as Canada and the UK, have visited Cuba in increasing numbers. They have been welcomed by the Cuban government, which has changed its policies on private enterprise, travel and investment in order to take advantage of this growing market. The liberalisation of its former policies is undoubtedly at least in part because of the potential economic benefits of tourism to the Cuban economy and, indirectly, the maintenance of its existing government (Hinch and Acharya 2017). More recently, the decision of North Korea to participate in the 2018 Winter Olympics, which has become both a sporting and a tourism event, appears to have been influenced by a desire to use sport and tourism, and the resulting media coverage, to begin a process of positive engagement with its opponents. The use of tourism and recreation developments in political negotiations – for example, a ski resort in North Korea built by capital from South Korea (Shin 2010) – is not a new tactic of the North Koreans, and this, along with the fact that limited numbers of foreign tourists have been allowed access to North Korea, may also indicate an attempt to influence its image and policies in the West.

One area in which tourism and the political realm interact with increasing frequency is that of indigenous rights and development. Stewart and Draper (2010) comments on the effect of a one-person demonstration against tourism when the cruise ship *Hanseatic* visited the Inuit settlement of Pond Inlet. The demonstration was in opposition to the European Union ban on seal skin imports (most of the passengers on the ship being from European countries), and, as a result, the ship did not return to Pond Inlet on subsequent voyages. In other areas, Inuit and other indigenous peoples have reacted to bans on seal skin products by keeping tourists away from indigenous hunting activities and in some cases rejecting "Greenpeace" tourists because of their negative views on traditional activities (Hinch 1998). Stewart also points out (2010, p. 72) that, when the Nunavut Land Claims Agreement was signed in 1993, resulting in major changes in governance in the Canadian Arctic, including the establishment in 1999 of the territory of Nunavut, the complexity of managing tourism in that area was recognised, and a specific proviso included "a provision to re-examine the Travel and Tourism Act" because it did not reflect Inuit rights or the responsibilities of Inuit organisations in the area. A similar situation arose in British Columbia in the lead-up to the Winter Olympic Games hosted by Vancouver in 2010. Williams and Gill (2017) describe how the local indigenous peoples in the Whistler area, the Squamish and Lil'wat First Nations, were able to obtain local political power and involvement in the planning and development of the Olympic facilities and related infrastructure. Their success built upon earlier land claim agreements in the province relating mostly to forestry, mining and fishing, and, as Williams and Gill (2017, p. 75) note, "this has encouraged a growing number of aboriginal communities to leverage their emerging rights for tourism purposes". Their actions in using newly acquired legal rights to gain agreements related to the Olympics enabled the First Nations to become "embedded in future governance decision-making" (Williams and Gill 2017, p. 86), illustrating that large-scale tourism developments can result in legal and political changes being enabled.

Perhaps the most vivid example of the effect of perceived impacts of tourism on politics is that of the Indian Gaming Regulatory Act (IGRA) of 1988 in the United States. For many years, most Indian reservations in the United States had been dogged by poverty and lack of economic opportunity, which had prevented the achievement of sovereignty (Ferber and Chon 1994). Legal decisions in the 1980s allowed Indian bands to operate high-stakes gaming on reservations free of state regulation (Long 1995). These decisions opened the door for many bands to establish casino operations on their reservations, which resulted in the establishment of the IGRA and National Gaming Commission, which allowed the federal government to regulate such operations. Carmichael and Jones (2007, p. 99) note that, "Gaming provides a tool for restoring sovereignty for Native American Nations . . . [and] . . . a route to economic development". Thus, gaming on Indian lands and the tourism that resulted from its legalisation have had profound political impacts throughout the United States (Stansfield 1996) and also in Canada, which saw a similar process occur. The desire to use gaming to revitalise the declining New Jersey resort of Atlantic City, finally achieved in 1976, had similar effects throughout the United States, breaking the self-imposed monopoly on legal gaming held by Nevada (Stansfield 1978). Thus, clearly in the case of gambling, the steps taken to legalise the operation of gambling were directly in order to achieve the economic benefits of tourism associated with the activity, and these have resulted in massive economic and political changes throughout the whole of North America.

International examples of tourism impacts

The example of "Brexit", the UK departure from the European Union, is an interesting one and illustrates the relatively little attention given to tourism or its impact on major political agreements and policy formulation on such occasions, a point made recently by a chief executive of the Association of British Travel Agents (Wright 2018). Although one may have thought that, given the economic and social importance of tourism within the European context, tourism might have featured regularly in discussions over future arrangements post-Brexit, this does not appear to have happened. The only minor impact of any tourism-related issue has been a discussion over a decision to have post-Brexit UK passports produced by a French company. Although the UK has never been a signatory to the Schengen agreement on travel, European nationals have become familiar with visa-less travel throughout Europe, and there does not appear to have been any consideration given to the likely reaction of tourists in the post-Brexit era to the possibility of needing visas or additional documentation to passports for travel between the UK and European Union countries, in either direction. There are similar issues with respect to air travel and regulations relating to landing rights and airline ownership, and, although these have been raised, they are generally discussed only in the context of economic impact on the companies concerned and the possibility of relocating head offices and bases of operation, rather than any impact on travellers and their vacations.

Some examples of deliberate political responses to tourism aimed specifically at the international markets can be seen clearly in the cases of Egypt and Tunisia. Both of these countries have been negatively affected by terrorism, with catastrophic effects on their tourism industries (Alfonso-Rodriguez 2017; Tomazos 2017). Given the reliance of these countries on the income, foreign exchange and employment generated by tourism, it is not surprising that both countries have taken political actions aimed at improving security, particularly for tourists in tourist destinations; changing regulations on investment; creating new tourism advertisements; and modifying national tourism organisations. The economic dimension of tourism has clearly had an impact and resulted in political changes in these countries aimed at restoring the numbers of international tourists, improving the image of the country and increasing the level of security (Steiner 2007).

Similarly, as Henderson (2015) notes, economic development and destination competitiveness have been reflected in public policy formulation. In Myanmar, although the potential tourist market led to significant changes in policy, including changed visa requirements, improved infrastructure related to tourism, and massive investment in restoring and recreating temples and other historic features (Suntikul and Rogers 2017), the possibility of a sharp fall in tourist numbers resulting from the mistreatment of the Rohingya populations does not appear to have had any political impact. For a number of years, NGOs made Myanmar the subject of attempted boycotts of the country by tourists because of the government's record on human rights. These were relatively unsuccessful, the government and tourists paid little attention to such protests, and the government began a policy of increasing tourism investment and development (Mercer 2017). Tourism was seen as a source of considerable foreign income, and this led to changes in the military leaders' attitudes towards opening the country to visitors. Myanmar, therefore, represents an intriguing case, where the desire to gain greater tourism revenues generated policy changes, but the possibility of losing this income did not result in any subsequent overt policy change. Whether it was felt that, once started, tourism would continue regardless of such negative publicity (given the lack of success of earlier boycotts) because of the attractions of the country, or whether political and religious forces outweighed any consideration of tourism, regardless of the reaction of potential visitors, is not clear.

The Chinese example

In Asia, the rapid increase in tourism over the last three decades in particular has led several countries to actively pursue further tourism development as a political as well as an economic tool, in ways that exemplify the interrelationship between flows of people, economic development and diplomatic and political mechanisms. Sofield (2017) illustrates clearly how China has changed its policies towards visitors greatly in order to make the industry one of the pillars of the economy. The PRC government's incremental loosening of restrictions on its own citizens' international travel since the 1970s was instrumental in setting in motion the trajectory that has led China to become one of the world's major tourism source markets, such that China can be seen to be one of the leading countries globally in both inbound tourists and its own citizens' participation in international tourism.

Tourism development and policy play a pivotal role in the Chinese government's "Belt and Road" initiative, aimed at increasing China's influence and connectivity across the globe, but they are also being used strategically within China's more immediate geographical sphere of influence. The history of the diplomatic relations between the PRC and Taiwan has been paralleled by the very intentional use, by both countries, of the modulation of tourist flows as an instrument to signal and influence the tone of cross-strait political relations at a given time (Hsiao 2015; Kastner 2011). The influence of tourism-related contact between citizens of the two nations has a complex dynamic, in that the interactions that happen in the context of tourism can be as likely to highlight the differences in values and cultural norms as they are to engender better understanding between the two nations and their people.

In a similar vein, the regulation of inbound and outgoing tourism between the Chinese mainland and the erstwhile colonies – now "special administrative regions" – of Hong Kong and Macao has been used as a political instrument in the ongoing experiment of integrating these territories back into the Chinese nation while preserving elements of their political exceptionalism (Suntikul 2017). Particularly in the case of Hong Kong, tensions between the political agendas of the Beijing government and Hong Kong localist sentiments have been manifested at a person-to-person level in friction between locals and mainland Chinese visitors in the context of tourism (Commerce and Economic Development Bureau 2013; LaFraniere 2012). The internal politics of China have also had an impact on the country's outbound tourism patterns. President Xi Jinping's crackdown on corruption at all levels of government in China has led to a reluctance on the part of political officials to be seen as engaging in profligate spending on travel, among other things. This is reflected perhaps most directly in a marked drop in tourism revenues in Macao, the economy of which is largely dependent on the gambling industry, which in turn has been a notorious channel for the laundering of ill-gotten funds from the Chinese mainland (Monaghan 2014).

Discussion

A fundamental question is whether changes in policies and other political actions that affect tourism are the result of the impacts of tourism or are unrelated. In some cases, changes in policies are deliberate attempts to increase the volume and value of tourism to specific destinations, ranging from the local urban level to the national level. In such cases, they represent the *potential political impact of tourism* in that they have come about because of the anticipated effect on, and of, tourism in that political unit. Where changes in policies have been implemented to immediately restrict or control specific aspects of tourism – the unacceptable behaviour of tourists, for example (Horne, 2016) – such actions can be viewed as *direct political impacts of tourism*. There are many examples that fall between these two categories and represent both the actual effects of tourism on policymakers and what is perceived to be the likely future effects on the same individuals. Thus, prohibiting certain forms of tourism may be to preserve sensitive or important natural environments such as wildlife habitats, both in order to respond to local and sometimes international pressure for such conservation actions, and also in order to correct an unacceptable situation, regardless of public or interest-group attention. The establishment of national parks is one area which illustrates the complexity of such interventions. Many countries have established national parks on the basis of the importance of protecting important or significant features, including landscapes, flora and fauna, cultural and natural heritage and even for political reasons (e.g. the establishment of national parks in the extreme north of Canada in the 1960s to confirm sovereignty rights). In many cases, it is clear, both from resulting increases in tourist numbers and from policy statements, that the establishment of such parks reflects a desire to see an increase in visitation (especially by foreign tourists), as well as any obligation to protect the associated feature(s). Such decisions can cause conflict between different agencies of the national governments concerned – for example, when agencies charged with preservation are concerned with limiting numbers of visitors because of resulting visitor impacts, whereas agencies charged with economic development desire increased tourism for the resulting employment and visitor expenditures. In some cases, this contradiction is embodied in the legislation involved, as is the case in Canada, where the basic reasons for the establishment of national parks include benefit, education and enjoyment, as well as economic return, and many of the early Canadian parks were clearly established with developing tourism as a fundamental purpose (Lothian 1977, cited in Butler and Boyd 2000). Altering such policies in response to changes in tourism reflects a direct impact of tourism on policy, whether the impetus comes from the recognition of one or more specific problems, or is in response to stakeholder input and pressure.

In some cases, stakeholder pressure can result not only in policy implementation, as in the case of the imposition of the "green tax" by the regional government of Calvia, on the Balearic Island of Majorca, but also in changes in direct political representation through impacts upon election results. Such situations are rarely well recorded, but two specific examples have been documented. Martin, McGuire and Allen (1998) record the impact of local residents' attitudes towards tourism and tourism development being expressed in local election results in South Carolina. They note that tourism development and, subsequently, tourism numbers had grown considerably in the community of Hilton Head, and there had been many expressions of discontent with the rate of growth of tourism and its accompanying impacts. As a direct result, a new mayor was elected on what he assumed was a "no more tourism platform" (Martin 2006, p. 237) and, during his tenure, campaigned against tourism development. Many residents, despite their concerns over the impacts of tourism, were also concerned that a decline in tourism resulting from a perceived negative attitude of residents towards tourism would cause economic damage to the community. In the subsequent election, the mayor was defeated and replaced by a building contractor who was subsequently re-elected twice. Martin's study revealed clearly that the negative impacts of tourism had led to the election of the "anti-tourist" mayor in 1993, and that fear of a decline in tourism had resulted in his defeat and the election three times of a proponent of managed growth of tourism. At the local level, at least, tourism is capable of bringing about direct political change in governance.

Dodds (2007) notes the institution and then the ultimate reversal of the Calvian tax following a subsequent regional election when the governing party, which had instituted the tax, was removed from power following an intensive lobbying campaign by local hoteliers and others who felt unfairly treated by that legislation. The bed night tax was not collected from all visitors, as higher levels of government refused to allow collection at airports and ports of arrival. This meant that it was not collected from tourists such as those staying in private houses and second homes, whereas it was applied to those staying in registered accommodation such as hotels, thus increasing costs and sometimes prices in those establishments. Such direct actions are perhaps rare because it is only in specific cases that tourism assumes a key level of significance and importance over other issues in elections. Despite local expressions of concern over the issues of "overtourism" in urban centres such as Venice, where turnstiles were erected to control tourist entry (Kington 2018), and Barcelona, it is unlikely that national or even regional governments will institute policies to reduce overall tourism, but, at the local level, pressure may be high enough to result in action (Fan, Xie and Wang 2016). Local policies relating to Airbnb is one example, with several cities (Barcelona, Valencia, Dubrovnik) contemplating action (Keeley 2018) against the increasing trend of renting out rooms via the Internet because of the pressure this places on residential rental properties in general and related problems such as affordable housing and homelessness in the cities involved. Palma, Majorca, is the latest example of local politicians reacting to pressure from residents over the impacts of tourism, with the mayor announcing that, in July 2018, there would be a ban on the rental of local residences to tourists, as only 645 of 11,000 rentals in the town have the appropriate licence (BBC News 2018). It is possible that such is the pressure being exerted in some centres by Internet rentals that action may be taken at national levels, especially when the potential taxation benefits (not normally obtained by governments, as such properties are usually not declared for income purposes) are perceived at the national level. However, recent media reports state that the city of Paris is intending to sue Airbnb for lost revenue because of the use of unregistered property owners not paying the appropriate city taxes (Sage 2018). Support is likely to be found for such policies from bodies such as hotel associations, which normally oppose taxation on tourism, because they experience a loss of business while this new competitor remains untaxed. Equally, however, local opposition to development may be overruled by higher levels of government, more concerned with economic issues, including revenue and job creation, as noted by Hall and Lew (2009) in the case of golf course development in Scotland by the Trump Organization, initially rejected at the local level but approved after intervention by the first minister and the governing party in the devolved Scottish parliament at Holyrood.

Conclusions

Much of the reaction to tourism has developed relatively recently as tourist numbers have reached what are seen as excessive levels in some destinations. A century ago, most current tourist destinations were seeking more tourism and more tourists and urging governments to stimulate growth by improving facilities and infrastructure and promoting their locations to potential markets. As noted earlier, concerns over what were perceived as the negative affects or costs of tourism did not become well researched until a few decades ago, and much research was based on single studies at one point in time, sometimes with inappropriate methodologies, and produced results of various levels of reliability. Many responses to such findings were "knee-jerk" reactions, often inappropriate and/or ineffective in dealing with the problems discovered or claimed. As increasing attention has been paid to tourism, not least because of its now vast size and economic significance, so the research has improved, and one would hope that decisions made as a result are more appropriate and effective. In some areas, however, familiar mistakes seem to occur regularly. Events, particularly mega events such as the Olympics, almost always have inaccurate and overblown forecasts of benefits, which allow political elements to gain credibility for supposed national, regional and local beneficial results on the announcement of gaining such events, whereas little is heard of the actual effects of the events some years afterwards (Weidenfeld, Butler and Williams 2016). In some cases, the effects or non-effects of such events are apparent even during and immediately after the events (Aldrigui 2017), as the Brazilian Olympics demonstrated, and the involvement of political corruption in such events can be seen both in Brazil and in the football world cup organisation by FIFA. The lure of political prestige and financial rewards from such events is clearly another example of the political impacts of specific tourist (and sporting) events.

Thus, it is clear that tourism has political impacts in a variety of ways and in different areas, economic particularly, but also in environmental and socio-cultural realms, resulting in political change such as policy adoption and abandonment, election results and international agreements. It is perhaps unfortunate that, in many cases, the political impacts come about as a result of mistakes or miscalculations by decision-makers or their failures to fully understand the dimension, impacts and social importance of many aspects of tourism.

References

Aldrigui, M. (2017) Tourism on the Fringe of Politics Brazil, in R.W. Butler and W. Suntikul (Eds), *Tourism and Political Change*, 2nd ed., pp. 200–213. Oxford: Goodfellow.

Alfonso-Rodriguez, J.A. (2017) Evaluating the dynamics and impact of terrorist attacks on tourism and economic growth. *Journal of Policy Research in Tourism, Leisure & Events*, 9 (1), 56–81.

Amore, A., and Hall, C.M. (2016) From governance to meta-governance in tourism? Re-incorporating politics, interests and values in the analysis of tourism governance. *Tourism Recreation Research*, 41 (2), 109–122.

BBC News. (2018) Spain's Palma to ban holiday rentals after residents' complaints. Available at: www.bbc.co.uk/news/world-europe-43878007 (accessed April 23 2018).

Brougham, J.E., and Butler, R.W. (1981) A segmentation analysis of resident attitudes to the social impacts of tourism. *Annals of Tourism Research*, 8 (4), 569–590.

Butler, R.W. (2013) Sustainable tourism – the undefinable and unachievable pursued by the unrealistic? *Tourism Recreation Research*, 38 (1), 221–226.

Butler, R.W., and Boyd, S.W. (2000) *Tourism and National Parks Issues and Implications*. Chichester, UK: John Wiley.

Butler, R.W., and Suntikul, W. (2010) *Tourism and Political Change*. Oxford: Goodfellow.

Butler, R.W., and Suntikul, W. (2017) *Tourism and Political Change*, 2nd ed. Oxford: Goodfellow.

Carmichael, B.A., and Jones, J.L. (2007) Indigenous owned casionos and perceived local community impacts: Mohegan Sun in South East Connecticut, USA, in R.W. Butler and T. Hinch (Eds), *Tourism and Indigenous Peoples Issues and Implications*, pp. 95–109. New York: Butterworth Heinemann.

Commerce and Economic Development Bureau. (2013) *Assessment Report on Hong Kong's Capacity to Receive Tourists*. Available at: www.legco.gov.hk/yr13-14/english/panels/edev/papers/edevcb1-765-e. pdf (accessed 12 September 2015).

D'Amore, L. (1988) Tourism: A vital force for peace. *Annals of Tourism Research*, 15 (2), 269–270.

Dodds, R. (2007) Sustainable tourism and policy implementation: lessons from the case of Calvia, Spain. *Current Issues in Tourism*, 10 (4), 296–322.

Dodds, R., and Butler, R.W. (2010) Barriers to implementing sustainable tourism policy in mass tourism destinations. *Tourismos*, 5 (1), 35–52.

Doxey, G.V. (1975) A causation theory of visitor–resident irritants: methodology and research inferences, in *Sixth Annual Conference Proceedings of the Travel Research Association*, pp. 195–198. San Diego, CA: Travel Research Association.

Eades, J., and Cooper, M. (2013) Soldiers, victims and neon lights: the American presence in post-war Japanese tourism, in R. Butler and W. Suntikul (Eds), *Contemporary Geographies of Leisure, Tourism and Mobility: Tourism and War*, pp. 205–218. London: Routledge.

Elliott, J. (1997) *Tourism: Politics and Public Sector Management*. New York: Routledge.

Fan, Y., Xie, Y., and Wang, Z. (2016) The role of power in decision making by tourist destinations: a critical discourse analysis of news on Shangjiushan Village, China. *Tourism Tribune*, 31 (1), 28–36.

Ferber, S.R., and Chon, K.S. (1994) Indian gaming: issues and prospects. *Gaming Research & Review Journal*, 1 (2), 55–65.

Hall, C.M. (1994) *Tourism and Politics: Policy, Power and Place*. Chichester, UK: John Wiley.

Hall, C.M., and Lew, A.A. (2009) *Understanding and Managing Tourism Impacts: An Integrated Approach*. London: Routledge.

Henderson, J.C. (2015) The new dynamics of tourism in South East Asia: economic development, political change and destination competitiveness. *Tourism Recreation Research*, 40 (3), 379–390.

Hinch, T. (1998) Tourists and indigenous hosts: diverging views on their relationship with nature. *Current Issues in Tourism*, 1 (1), 120–124.

Hinch, T. (2006) Tourism as an instrument of foreign policy: the US trade embargo on Cuba, in R.W. Butler and W. Suntikul (Eds), *Tourism and Political Change*, pp. 97–107. Oxford: Goodfellow.

Hinch, T., and Acharya, B.P. (2017) The politics of tourism in Cuba, in R.W. Butler and W. Suntikul (Eds), *Tourism and Political Change*, 2nd ed., pp. 138–152. Oxford: Goodfellow.

Holden, A. (2008) *Environment and Tourism*. London: Routledge.

Horne, M. (2016) Cathedral bans tourists from funerals after selfies taken, *The Times*, p. 22, 10 August.

Hsiao, A. (2015) China not sharply cutting tourist numbers: official. *Taipei Times*. Available at: www. taipeitimes.com/News/taiwan/archives/2015/10/14/2003630027 (accessed 12 August 2015).

Kastner, J. (2011) Crash course in political risk for Taiwan's tourism. *Asia Times*. Available at: www.atimes. com/atimes/China_Business/ME19Cb01.html (accessed 5 August 2015).

Keeley, G. (2018) Adios Airbnb: Valencia bans rentals. *The Times*, p. 35, 10 May.

Kington, T. (2018) Sorry we're full: Venice to start turning tourists away. *The Times*, p. 31, 26 April.

Laderman, S. (2013) From the Vietnam War to the "war on terror": tourism and the martial fascination, in R.W. Butler and W. Suntikul (Eds), *Tourism and War*, pp. 26–35. London: Routledge.

LaFraniere, S. (2012) Mainland Chinese flock to Hong Kong to give birth. *New York Times*. Available at: http://nytimes.com/2012/02/23/world/asia/mainland-chinese-flock-to-hong-kong-to-have-babies. html (accessed 5 August 2015).

Lema, J., and Agrusa, J. (2013) Revisiting the war landscape of Vietnam and tourism, in R.W. Butler and W. Suntikul (Eds), *Tourism and War*, pp. 245–253. London: Routledge.

Long, P.T. (1995) Casino gambling in the United States – 1994 status and implications. *Tourism Management*, 16 (3), 189–197.

Lothian, W.F. (1977) *A History of Canada's National Parks.* Ottawa: Parks Canada.

Martin, B. (2006) The TALC model and politics, in R.W. Butler (Ed.), *The Tourism Area Life Cycle, Volume 1, Applications and Modifications*, pp. 237–249. Clevedon, UK: Channel View Publications.

Martin, B., McGuire, F.A., and Allen, L.A. (1998) Retirees' attitudes towards tourism: implications for sustainable development. *Tourism Analysis*, 3, 43–51.

Mathieson, A., and Wall, G. (1982) *Tourism: Economic, Physical and Social Impacts.* Harlow, UK: Longman.

Mercer, D. (2017) Marketing Myanmar: the religion/tourism nexus in a fragile polity, in R.W. Butler and W. Suntikul (Eds), *Tourism and Religion Issues and Implications*, pp. 161–181. Clevedon, UK: Channel View Publications.

Monaghan, A. (2014) China's gambling capital Macau is world's fourth-richest territory. *The Guardian.* Available at: www.theguardian.com/world/2014/jul/02/macau-china-gambling-capital-fourth-richest-in world-per-capita (accessed 16 August 2015).

Sage, A. (2018) Paris council sues Airbnb for €43m a day. *The Times*, p. 33, 13 April.

Shin, Y. (2010) How stable is peace linked to tourism? The case of Mt Geumgand Tourism Development Project on the Korean peninsula, in O. Moufakkir and I. Kelly (Eds), *Tourism, Progress and Peace*, pp. 199–211. Wallingford, UK: CABI.

Sofield, T. (2017) China: government policy and tourism development, in R.W. Butler and W. Sunntikul (Eds), *Tourism and Political Change*, 2nd ed., pp. 38–54. Oxford: Goodfellow.

Stansfield, C. (1978) Atlantic City and the resort cycle: background to the legalisation of gambling. *Annals of Tourism Research*, 5 (2), 238–251.

Stansfield, C. (1996) Reservations and gambling: Native Americans and the diffusion of legalised gambling, in R.W. Butler and T. Hinch (Eds), *Tourism and Indigenous Peoples*, pp. 129–149. London: International Thompson Business Press.

Steiner, C. (2007) Political instability, transnational tourist companies and destination recovery in the Middle East after 9/11. *Tourism & Hospitality Planning & Development*, 4 (3), 169–190.

Stewart, E.J., and Draper, D. (2010) Political change and tourism in Arctic Canada, in R.W. Butler and W. Suntikul (Eds), *Tourism and Political Change*, pp. 68–81. Oxford: Goodfellow.

Suntikul, W. (2017) Political changes and tourism in the 'Other Chinas', in R.W. Butler and W. Suntikul (Eds), *Tourism and Political Change*, 2nd ed., pp. 55–71. Oxford: Goodfellow.

Suntikul, W., Butler, R.W., and Airey, D. (2010) Implications of political change on national park operations: Doi Moi and tourism to Vietnam's national parks. *Journal of EcoTourism*, 10 (3), 201–218.

Suntikul, W., and Rogers, P. (2017) Myanmar: opening for tourism, in R.W. Butler and W. Suntikul (Eds), *Tourism and Political Change*, 2nd ed., pp. 123–137. Oxford: Goodfellow.

Tomazos, K. (2017) Egypt's tourism industry and the Arab Spring, in R.W. Butler and W. Suntikul (Eds), *Tourism and Political Change*, 2nd ed., pp. 214–229. Oxford: Goodfellow.

Wall, G., and Mathieson, A. (2006) *Tourism: Change, Impacts and Opportunities.* New York: Prentice Hall.

Weaver, D.B., and Lawton, L.J. (2014) *Tourism Management.* Brisbane: Wiley.

Weidenfeld, A., Butler, R.W., and Williams, A.M. (2016) *Visitor Attractions and Events: Locations and Linkages.* London: Routledge.

Williams, P.W., and Gill, A.M. (2017) Towards decolonisation: indigenising resort governance in Canada, in R.W. Butler and W. Suntikul (Eds), *Tourism and Political Change*, 2nd ed., pp. 75–89. Oxford: Goodfellow.

World Commission on Environment and Development (WCED). (1987) *Our Common Future.* Oxford: Oxford University Press.

Wright, O. (2018) Travel chief warns lack of clarity is harming tourism. *The Times*, p. 7, 20 March.

World Travel and Tourism Council (WTTC). (2018) *Coping with Success: Managing Overcrowding in Tourism Destinations.* London: McKinsey and WTTC.

27

TOURISM PERFORMANCES, GOVERNMENT EFFECTIVENESS AND LOCAL GROWTH

The Italian cultural heritage perspective

Dante Di Matteo

Introduction

Tourism represents one of the largest and growing economic sectors worldwide. The World Travel & Tourism Council (WTTC) estimates that the travel industry is able to support about 292 billion jobs, generating about 10.2% of global GDP. The tourism industry, despite occasional shocks, is a sector exhibiting uninterrupted growth, and an increasingly broader number of destinations worldwide have turned tourism into a key driver for boosting social and economic progress by encouraging investment in infrastructure, creating jobs and enterprises and generating consistent revenues for national and local economies (UNWTO, 2017). Estimates from the World Tourism Barometer (UNWTO, 2018) reveal that, in 2017, international tourist arrivals grew by higher percentages (+7%) than the previous 7 years (when the growth rate was between +4% and +5%), reaching about 1.322 billion visitors worldwide. In this scenario, Europe – led by the Mediterranean countries – is confirmed to be the most attractive destination with 671.1 million tourists, of which 266.8 million arrivals relate to southern and Mediterranean Europe. Italy still continues to pose a significant role in Mediterranean Europe and it remains one of the leading countries in terms of international tourist arrivals. The Italian destination is still the third most visited country in Europe, after France and Spain, and it is part of the top ten countries worldwide both for tourist arrivals and for tourist receipts.

In particular, data from a WTTC report (2017) indicate that, in 2016, Italy hosted about 52.7 million tourist overnight stays. The total contribution of the tourism industry to Italian GDP accounted for US$207.6 billion, representing 11.1% of national GDP, and these results are in line (with a slightly higher percentage) with the world average. This has resulted in 2.876 thousand jobs related to the tourism sector, accounting for 12.6% of total employment in 2016. As for government expenditures on travel and tourism services directly linked to visitors, such as cultural or recreational services (museums or national parks), the Italian government accounts for US$1.6 billion, and, regarding capital investments made by all industries directly involved in travel and tourism (concerning, for example, accommodation facilities, passenger transport equipment, restaurants and all other types of leisure facility), total Italian spending accounted for US$10.6 billion in 2016, which is still lower than the pre-crisis values of 2009 (when capital investments accounted for more than US$20 billion).

Within this framework, the UNESCO committee has from the start recognized the strong linkage between tourism and the areas coming under the protection of UNESCO. In 2002, in the first practical manual for managing UNESCO sites, Pedersen stated that World Heritage Sites (WHSs) – including cultural and natural areas carefully selected in the multilateral agreement involving 175 countries – represent major attractions from a touristic perspective. Anyway, managing a WHS implies benefits and drawbacks: if, for example, it is undoubted that tourism offers well-established advantages from an economic development perspective at local and national levels (visitors fees, concessions, funds, financial contributions, promoting cultural values and supporting regional and local handicrafts), it is also true that an "uncontrolled tourism development can have major negative impacts on these jewels of humanity's heritage" (Pedersen, 2002, p. 5). In these regards, in the first manual for managing UNESCO WHSs, several managerial and practical implications have been reported. For instance, one of the main issues related to tourism activities in WHSs concerns the growth of accommodation capacity: increasing tourism and attracting more tourists to a destination could represent an economic benefit for surrounding communities (Hawkins, Chang, & Warnes, 2009) and – at the same time – a problem of carrying capacity for the host community. In this view, the decision to concentrate or disperse tourism around an attraction placed under UNESCO protection reflects government policy goals and management objectives: depending on the key goal of a local host community (increase revenues or maintain and restore environmental/cultural assets), the strategy could lead towards an expansion of accommodation capacity or towards a more conservative policy. The appropriate equilibrium is achieved when the policy meets the expectations of local communities in terms of economic development or restoration of natural resources.

Notwithstanding that reinforcing accommodation capacity represents an effective driver for engaging more tourist flows to destinations involved into UNESCO protection programmes (Santa-Cruz & López-Guzmán, 2017; Hassan, Jailani, & Rahim, 2014; Huang, Tsaur, & Yang, 2012; Yang, Lin, & Han, 2010; Wager, 1995), especially for what concerns non-OECD members (Culiuc, 2014), it is also claimed that this determinant could represent a boomerang effect for mature destinations (Park & Almeida Santos, 2017; Cuccia, Guccio, & Rizzo, 2015), which in most cases correspond to countries with advanced economies. In these cases, what is often recognized as an instrument for boosting local economies may represent a reason causing a downturn in the tourism and travel industry. With this in mind, government effectiveness in addressing policies at national and local levels represents a key variable for determining the success or depression of the leisure industry. This study, weighted at provincial scale, analyses the effectiveness of the major tourism determinants for understanding to what extent cultural resources are able to generates positive impacts on economic growth in Italy. By considering all provinces involved in UNESCO protection programmes, it appears quite evident that accommodation overcapacity generates negative impacts on growth, suggesting that spreading government funding towards the surrounding communities would represent the best way to rebalance cultural heritage tourism and gain the maximum economic profitability from cultural endowments.

Effects of cultural heritage on growth: the theoretical framework

International literature concerning heritage tourism encompasses several studies exploring the impact of WHSs on national and local economic development. The debate around WHSs as place markers for enhancing tourism, economies and benefits of local communities has been addressed from multiple measuring points. A global critical review concerning the period 2009–2014, conducted by Leask (2015), has highlighted that studies about impacts of visitors' attraction as whole part of the management represent a key area for managing WHSs, also indicating that quantitative methods have increased for evaluating tourism experiences. A large variety of works have focused on the capability to enlarge tourism flows towards a UNESCO site after its inclusion on the World Heritage List (WHL), meaning that the status of "protection" represents an attractor and works as a stimulus to engage more international tourism flows. In this case, the majority of academicians used overnight stays as the dependent variable of multiple regression models or similar, in order to predict to what extent a heritage site could be favoured from inclusion on the WHL, in terms of enhanced tourism flows towards the area concerned. Other studies – to a lesser extent – have focused on the impact of heritage tourism flows on the economic growth of the host area, taking into account several WHSs worldwide as case studies.

Among the main findings, the literature generally agrees in arguing that the enhancement of tourism flows and the reinforcement of the structural characteristics of supply within WHSs (accommodation capacity, quality of transport towards the interested area, cleanliness of urban spaces, etc.) are able to produce positive impacts on local growth; in this kind of estimation, variables such as "GDP" or "per capita GDP" are usually used as dependent variables in order to predict in what measure an area interested in UNESCO protection programmes could benefit from the effects deriving from the inclusion on the WHL. Other kinds of study have tried to assess values of perceived authenticity, residents' engagement, community participation, local interaction, use values or preservation values, tourists' willingness to pay for visiting a protected area, motivation, knowledge and power about residents' perception and many other measurement items. What is particularly evident from key findings of such studies is that there is no absolute certainty that a common policy can guarantee the same results in different geographical areas: whereas, for instance, in some local communities the recognition of WHS represents a valid determinant for enhancing foreign tourism flows towards the area, in other communities it could have a deterrent effect on tourists' and/or residents' perception about the site concerned.

Among the main studies regarding the effects of UNESCO certification on tourism flows, a worldwide estimation conducted by Su and Lin (2014) reveals that the status of WHSs is able to generate between 300,000 and 800,000 visitors to a country; in particular, the more cultural sites listed (more than 21), the higher the possibility of increasing flows to the country concerned. Furthermore, WHS endowment is also likely to affect the travelling choices of domestic tourists: a spatial interaction model – weighted on a regional scale – applied to Italian regions shows a negative direct effect on neighbouring destinations, meaning that regions that want to increase their domestic tourism flows are strongly urged to negotiate new WHS designations within their geographical perimeters, in order to compete with others (Patuelli, Mussoni, & Candela, 2013). Consistent with these findings, but at a provincial level, Borowiecki and Castiglione (2012) confirm that WHSs are also able to increase international tourism flows to Italy, where museum attendance is the main driver for explaining foreign interest in Italian cultural heritage. By looking at some site-based studies, Caust and Vecco (2017, pp. 4, 8) have even defined as "dramatic" and "uncontrolled" the increase in tourist numbers in three cultural sites in Asian countries (Angkor Wat in Cambodia, Hoi An in Vietnam, and Luang Prabang in the Lao People's Democratic Republic), highlighting the need for sustainability measures to avoid negative impacts on the sites' practices and resources. Something similar has occurred in Val di Noto (Sicily, Italy), where a significant increase in tourist numbers has been registered since UNESCO certification; in this case, the blast of tourism flows gave rise to a significant proliferation of beds and accommodation structures, while the problem of seasonality remains noticeable (Cuccia, 2012). Improvements in infrastructures and services made by local government have also resulted in a massive growth in domestic and overseas tourism flows in the case of Lijiang (China), where the WHS endowment also generated an increase in earnings of about 20% in the period 1996–2005 (Su & Teo, 2008). The results are different in the case of Mount Fuji in

Japan (Jones, Yang, & Yamamoto, 2017), where the authors found that, after the inscription on the WHL of the highest Japanese peak, the number of climbers increased, but to a lesser extent compared with other contexts.

As for the economic impacts deriving from UNESCO certification, Arezki, Cherif and Piotrowski (2009) evaluated the effects of WHS status on economic growth from a worldwide perspective and they found that, generally, the ascription of sites on the WHL does have a positive impact on the GDP per capita of countries involved in UNESCO protection programmes. The economic value of a WHS has also been estimated through many other measurement items: for instance, the willingness-to-pay determinant was regarded as influential for engaging visitors in the cases of Changdeok Palace in Korea (Kim, Wong, & Cho, 2007) and Chitwan National Park in Nepal (Pandit, Dhakal, & Polyakov, 2015), where the entry fee was well below the perceived value of the site expressed by visitors, meaning that an increase in the entry fee in some WHSs could predict exactly the maximum revenue level for the site concerned, whenever tourists are well provided with certain characteristics and services. Having been used differently than in other studies, the determinant of "perceived authenticity" is revealed to be a good predictor of the economic value of the sites of Hwaseong and Namhansanseong in Korea (Kim, Oh, Lee, & Lee, 2018), showing that higher values of authenticity perceived by tourists correspond to higher expected results in terms of economic benefits for the host community.

Satisfactory achievements for WHSs are also determined by the level of attachment and participation of hosting local communities. From the residents' perspective, the constructs of *positive perceptions, opportunity, awareness* and *knowledge* are found to be influences on resident participation in the site of George Town in Malaysia (Rasoolimanesh, Jaafar, Ahmad, & Barghi, 2017), and *positive perceptions* are particularly significant to strengthen the sense of belonging of young residents in the heritage site of Lenggong Valley in northern Malaysia (Jaafar, Noor, & Rasoolimanesh, 2015); similarly, *community commitment, environmental attitude* and *effectiveness of place marketing communications* are able to enhance residents' engagement in place promotion in the heritage site of the Amalfi Coast in Italy (Vollero, Conte, Bottoni, & Siano, 2018); as for the Chinese Summer Palace heritage site in Beijing (Rasoolimanesh, Jaafar, & Barghi, 2017), positive perceptions – deriving from latent constructs of *perceived power, knowledge* and *economic gain* – are revealed to be significant for supporting local tourism development. These latter findings are consistent with Su and Wall (2015), who, in the same case of the Summer Palace, found that *perception, motivation* and *satisfaction* are significant loading factors not only for residents, but also for domestic tourists, proven also for the WHS of Cuenca in the Spanish region of Castilla-La Mancha (Vargas Vargas, Jiménez, Santamaría, & Navarro, 2009).

Last but not least, necessary for understanding the economic impacts of tourism on local development are the potential conflicts which can occur between cultural heritage endowment and local development policies (Xu, Liu, Qian, & Wang, 2017; Zhang, Fyall, & Zheng, 2015), with particular emphasis on environmental concerns (Hawkins et al., 2009) and carrying capacity of the host communities (Kirkpatrick, 2001).

Italian heritage-based tourism: the World Heritage Sites' endowment

The first ascription to the WHL in Italy dates back to 1979 and concerns the site of Valle Camonica in the Lombardy province of Brescia. In the 1980s, five major Italian cities and their most representative heritage sites – Milan, Rome, Florence, Pisa and Venice – were included on the list. The busiest period regarding the recognition of Italian WHSs was the 1990s, when 25 sites, including some historical centres (Siena, Naples, Urbino) and a series of areas characterized by high landscaping and architectural values (Sassi of Matera, the residences of the Royal House of Savoy in

Piedmont, the 18th-century Royal Palace at Caserta, and so on), were added to the WHL. The first decade of the 21st century saw the inscription of 13 sites, and in the second decade another 9 sites have been included on the list. In total, the endowment of Italian WHSs accounted for 53 active sites in 2018, of which 48 are cultural sites (90%), and only 5 are natural sites (10%). It often happens that one WHS encompasses more than one point of interest, and, on such a basis, Lazio, Piedmont, Lombardy, Veneto and Campania are the regions with higher densities of cultural heritage points of interest. Figure 27.1 shows the Italian distribution of WHSs per province.

From Figure 27.1, it is evident that the majority of WHSs are located in the northern Italian provinces, and lower densities are noticeable in central and southern Italy, with a substantial

Figure 27.1 Spatial distribution of World Heritage Sites among Italian provinces, 2018

absence of WHSs on the central Adriatic side (Marche, Abruzzo and Molise). In some cases, we observe the contemporary presence of cultural and natural sites in the same province (Varese, Trento, Verona, Vicenza, Udine, Viterbo, Foggia, Potenza and Matera), and, in the case of islands, Sicily shows a balanced distribution of WHSs among the provinces, whereas Sardinia only accounts for the province of Cagliari with the archeological site of Su Nuraxi.

The Italian scenario of WHSs is constantly evolving: starting from 2006, there are still another 40 sites included on the Tentative List, many of which are characterized by strong historical, archeological and morphological relevance (e.g. Romanesque cathedrals in Puglia, the Lower Palaeolithic Palaeosurfaces at Isernia, Lake Maggiore and Lake D'Orta lakelands, etc).

Estimation modelling and results

Most studies concerning heritage sites have tried to assess in what measures WHS certification is able to boost tourism flows towards the area concerned. Relatively few studies have focused on the impact of WHS endowment on economic growth, and, in the case of mature destinations such as Italy, where tourism flows towards the majority of destinations are semi-standardized, such a kind of analysis is missing. For these reasons, this chapter is proposing a generalized estimating equations (GEE) population averaged model (Liang & Zeger, 1986) based on longitudinal data involving the 58 Italian provinces with WHS endowment for the period 2004–2011, and this will lead to evaluation of the extent to which territories gain economic benefits from UNESCO certification. The general model is as follows (Weaver, 2009):

$$g\left(E\left[\frac{Y_{ij}}{x_{ij}}\right]\right) = x'_{ij}\beta \tag{1}$$

where x_{ij} is a vector of p covariates, β represents a set of p interested regression parameters, g is the link identity function, and Y_{ij} is the j-product ($j = 1, .., J$) for each i-subject ($i = 1, .., N$). The $J \times J$ covariance matrix for Y can be write as:

$$V_i = \emptyset A_i^{1/2} R(a) A_i^{1/2} \tag{2}$$

Where $\emptyset$ is a dispersion parameter related to the generalized linear model, A is a diagonal matrix of variance functions, and $R(a)$ is the correlation matrix of Y, which is set under the independence criteria and assumes the following structure:

$$R(a) = \begin{pmatrix} 1 & \cdots & 0 \\ \vdots & \ddots & \vdots \\ 0 & \cdots & 1 \end{pmatrix} \tag{3}$$

The output of this model is the equivalent of a linear regression model, but ignores the panel structure of the data; for this reason, a robust check is provided by also computing the random-effects generalized least squares (GLS) model, in order to ensure discrete reliability of the results. The absence of correlation between independent variables – the basis of random-effects models – is ensured thorough the control of the Pearson correlations matrix, in which all independents are well below the 0.5 cut-off value; the choice of random-effects instead of fixed-effects comes after Hausman and Breusch–Pagan Lagrangian multiplier (LM) tests.

As for the variables of the model, the panel data comprise the *provincial GDP* as dependent variable; the first main independent variable consists of *government effectiveness* provided by Nifo and Vecchione's database (2014), a synthetic indicator explaining the endowment of social and economic structures in Italian provinces and governmental capacity related to health, waste and urban environmental policies. The other main independent variable is the provincial *accommodation density* per 10,000 inhabitants, which is given by $(Beds_{jt}/Pop_{jt} \times Sur_j) \times 10,000$, where $Beds_{jt}$ indicates the available bed places in j-province at t-time, Pop_{jt} is the resident population in j-province at t-time, and Sur_j indicates the j-province territorial surface in square kilometres; this is also known as the index of composed accommodation capacity and measures the tourist density of a territory adjusted for territorial extension. The control for tourism flows towards the provinces concerned is given by including in the model the variables related to *overnight stays*, tested both for year-round and for non-seasonal months, and the *tourism coverage indicator*, which is given by $(OVNs_{jt} + Pop_{jt})/Sur_j$, where $OVNs_{jt}$ indicates the number of overnight stays in j-province at t-time. This last gives a measure of the weight of tourism overnight stays on a territory by taking into account the size of the resident population. All variables are expressed thorough their natural logarithm, except for *government effectiveness* and *accommodation density*. The descriptive statistics of the variables are summarized in Table 27.1.

The estimation has been conducted by including in the sample all the provinces in which there is at least one point of interest belonging to a WHS (excluding the province of Barletta-Andria-Trani, which was instituted in 2009, and all those provinces – for example, L'Aquila – whose WHSs were included on the list after 2011). "Non-seasonal" means tourist overnight stays outside the months of June, July, August and September; such a choice helps understanding of whether the results are affected by the seasonality typical of the summer months. The results of GEE and GLS estimations are shown in Table 27.2.

Table 27.1 Descriptive statistics of variables

Name	Description	Source	Mean	Std. dev.	Min	Max
GDP_{nl}	Natural logarithm of *provincial gross domestic product*	Eurostat, Istat	23.28	0.8392	21.68	25.77
GE	*Government effectiveness* indicator	Nifo & Vecchione (2014) database, https://siepi.org/institutional-quality-index-dataset-disponibile/	0.381	0.1506	0	0.770
AD	*Accommodation density* indicator	Eurostat, Istat; then own calculation	0.335	0.3500	0.021	1.945
$OVNs\text{-}y_{nl}$	Natural logarithm of *year-round overnight stays*	Eurostat, Istat	14.58	1.2863	11.52	17.37
$OVNs\text{-}n_{nl}$	Natural logarithm of *non-seasonal months overnight stays*	Eurostat, Istat	13.69	1.2394	11.03	16.67
$TC\text{-}y_{nl}$	Natural logarithm of *tourism coverage indicator* for year-round overnight stays	Eurostat, Istat; then own calculation	6.98	1.0162	4.67	9.58
$TC\text{-}n_{nl}$	Natural logarithm of *tourism coverage indicator* for non-seasonal months overnight stays	Eurostat, Istat; than own calculation	6.34	0.9547	4.52	8.88

Table 27.2 Effects of government effectiveness and tourism performances on growth in WHSs' provinces

Dependent variable: GDP_{nl}

	Year-round		Non-seasonal months	
	GEE	GLS random-effects	GEE	GLS random-effects
Regressors	(i)	(ii)	(iii)	(iv)
GE	1.177***	0.393***	0.720***	0.384***
	(0.1304)	[0.0496]	(0.1215)	[0.0515]
AD	−1.715***	−0.174***	−1.270***	−0.181***
	(0.0566)	[0.0610]	(0.0473)	[0.0646]
OVNs-y_{nl}	0.258***	−0.000		
	(0.0250)	[0.0711]		
TC-y_{nl}	0.424***	0.242**		
	(0.0353)	[0.1015]		
OVNs-n_{nl}			0.365***	−0.094
			(0.0216)	[0.0720]
TC-n_{nl}			0.316***	0.391***
			(0.0294)	[0.1301]
Constant	16.68***	21.50***	16.41***	22.00***
	(0.2179)	[0.5571]	(0.1867)	[0.4963]
Wald χ^2	1921.34	107.47	2413.39	104.48
(Prob > χ^2)	(0.000)	(0.000)	(0.000)	(0.000)
R^2-between		0.526		0.503
Breusch–Pagan LM test		1444.50		1437.97
(Prob > LM)		(0.000)		(0.000)
Sigma$_u$		0.376		0.342
Sigma$_e$		0.041		0.040
rho		0.988		0.986
theta		0.961		0.958
Groups control	No	Yes	No	Yes
Provinces	58	58	58	58
Observations	464	464	464	464

Notes: Standard errors for GEEs are given in round brackets; robust standard errors for GLSs are given in square brackets; *** denotes statistical significance at p<0.01, ** denotes statistical significance at p<0.05.

The general goodness of fit of (i) and (iii) is given by good values of Wald χ^2, while, in case of robust check through (ii) and (iv) models, as well as Wald χ^2, also parameters related to R^2-between, sigma$_u$, sigma$_e$, rho and theta show an excellent fit of the data to the proposed models. Good values for the Lagrange multiplier ratio test confirm that the random-effects model is regarded as preferable in this analysis. In particular, as for (ii) and (iv), R^2-between shows that the variance explained by the models is more than 50%, suggesting that these predictors could be useful for addressing policies.

Findings and policy implications

All four models confirm the early general assumption of the chapter; that is to say, an increase in *government effectiveness* would probably produce positive impacts on provincial growth. In particular, not checking for provinces in GEE models, (i) shows an impact of +1.177 on provincial

GDP, and the same, but to a lesser extent, occurs when referring to non-seasonal estimation (iii), where the coefficient shows a positive impact of +0.720. By contrast, controlling for groups of provinces in GLSs random-effects models, it is observed that the coefficients maintain a positive direction, and they are basically identical both for year-round model (ii), with positive impact of +0.393, and for non-seasonal estimation (iv), where the impact on growth is +0.384. These first findings imply that provincial improvements in social and economic structure, as well as governmental capability with regard to territorial policies, are likely to produce benefits not only in high-density tourist seasons, but also throughout the year. The harmonization of central government and local administrations' policies with private sector investments in heritage management is needed to achieve tangible results in local growth, and this is consistent with Janssen, Luiten, Renes and Stegmeijer (2017).

With regard to *accommodation density*, it is not surprising to see that overcapacity in the tourism accommodation supply could represent a negative factor for growth in UNESCO-led provinces. From the (i) and (iii) GEE models, it is evident that an increase in *accommodation density* would generate negative impacts on growth, both for year-round (−1.715) and for non-seasonal estimations (−1.270). Such a negative value is confirmed by the control for provinces in GLSs random-effects models, where the year-round and non-seasonal values account for, respectively, −0.174 (ii) and −0.181 (iv), still maintaining a negative direction in sign. The problem of accommodation overcapacity is more probably to be found in mature destinations rather than emerging destinations, where, contrariwise, several studies have demonstrated how an increase in accommodation capacity is able to boost tourism growth and produce benefits for local communities. The negative sign for *accommodation density* in this analysis is consistent with early general guidelines of the UNESCO Committee and many other studies (Park & Almeida Santos, 2017; Cuccia et al., 2015; Hawkins et al., 2009; Kirkpatrick, 2001), meaning that uncontrolled tourism growth represents a threat to the integrity and sustainability of the site concerned, also damaging the related potential economic profitability. In terms of policy implications, government strategies should be more oriented to rebalancing the already existent tourism accommodation supply instead of promoting and funding additional and supplementary tourism structures in provinces involved in UNESCO protection programmes. From a spatial perspective, this would lead to a gain in economic benefits not only for major centres where WHSs are located – in which tourism flows and revenues from tourism are already robust – but also for the surrounding communities which, in such a way, could benefit from positive shadow effects from major centres.

For what concerns *overnight stays*, although positive in GEE estimations of (i) and (iii) models, with coefficients of +0.258 and +0.365, the non-significance in GLS random-effects models (ii) and (iv) is the logical consequence of the negative sign of *accommodation density*. In other terms, this means that policies aimed at attracting more tourists towards UNESCO destinations does not represent the priority in Italian provinces, for the above-mentioned reasons regarding saturation issues with mature destinations, and such unidirectional attracting policies in some cases could even result in de-listing discussions after experiences with tensions and excessive 'museumification' of World Heritage centres (Ashworth & Tunbridge, 2017).

Rather, the positive sign of *tourism coverage indicator* in all four estimations reveals that what is really need to maximize economic benefits for provinces involved in UNESCO protection programmes is a better-balanced territorial distribution of tourism flows. Furthermore, if the related coefficients in the four models are observed, it appears quite clear that the *tourism coverage indicator* represents a good predictor of provincial GDP, and the almost equal extent of coefficients in all the estimations indicates that this parameter is not affected by seasonality. In particular, as for GEEs, the *tourism coverage indicator* shows a positive impact of +0.424 for year-round estimation (i) and a slightly lower, but positive, coefficient of +0.316 for non-seasonal estimation (iii); when considering the control for provinces in GLS random-effects models, we observe a positive coefficient of +0.242 for year-round (ii), and this value is even higher in the case of non-seasonal months (iv), with a coefficient of +0.391. In terms of provincial policies, these values indicate that a general improvement in the distribution of tourism flows in the territory, with opportune measures for decentralization of flows from major centres to surrounding communities, would probably be reflected in a generalized increase of 0.3% of provincial GDP for those territories involved in UNESCO programmes. On the basis of provincial GDP data from provinces involved in this analysis, efforts to redistribute tourism flows into surrounding communities would mean – numerically – an increase in earnings from tourism of about €6 billion on average per province.

Conclusions

This study was proposed to understand what the major determinants for enhancing economic growth of territories involved in UNESCO protection programmes are. The Italian framework of WHSs is very complex and particular: with an approximately regular distribution of more than 50 WHSs throughout the peninsula, best practice examples and appropriate management implications are needed. The Italian context of cultural heritage can undoubtedly be ascribed to the class of destinations that are at the maturity stage of their life cycle. In these latter cases, irregular growth due to tourism congestion may occur, and the self-sustaining growth achieved by positive synergies among the various components of the tourism offer could represent an opportunity to overcome the carrying capacity threshold (Cole, 2012). From the supply-side perspective, when considering destinations with robust, well-established tourism flows towards a WHS, this could mean that policies aimed at redistributing flows are suggested rather than investment or funding for attracting more people towards the destinations concerned. Contrariwise, from the demand-side perspective, the findings of this work are also strongly consistent with the "platinum status" theory of Kozac and Martin (2012), who argue that, to avoid the risk of losing popularity and competitiveness, typical of mature destinations, tourism managers are called upon to work on tourists' loyalty, by developing strategies able to convert a "gold tourist" into a "platinum tourist", so as to make tourists engaged beyond major heritage place markers.

Definitively, spreading tourism throughout the territory and encouraging a broader coverage of the flows represent recommended practices for maximizing the economic benefits of mature destinations involving WHSs, in parallel with increased government effectiveness and a restrained accommodation density.

References

Arezki, R., Cherif, R., & Piotrowski, J. (2009). Tourism Specialization and Economic Development: Evidence from the UNESCO World Heritage List. IMF Working Paper, 09/176, 1–24.

Ashworth, G. J., & Tunbridge, E. (2017). Multiple approaches to heritage in urban regeneration: the case of City Gate, Valletta. *Journal of Urban Design*, 22(4), 494–501.

Borowiecki, K. J., & Castiglione, C. (2012). Cultural Participation and Tourism Flows. An Empirical Investigation of Italian Provinces. Discussion Papers on Business and Economics, 21, 1–14.

Caust, J., & Vecco, M. (2017). Is UNESCO World Heritage recognition a blessing or burden? Evidence from developing Asian countries. *Journal of Cultural Heritage*, 27, 1–9.

Cole, S. (2012). Synergy and congestion in the tourist destination life cycle. *Tourism Management*, 33, 1128–1140.

Cuccia, T. (2012). Is it worth being inscribed in the World Heritage List? A case study of "The Baroque Cities in Val di Noto" (Sicily). *Rivista Italiana di Economia Demografia e Statistica*, 66(2), 169–190.

Cuccia, T., Guccio, C., & Rizzo, I. (2015). The effects of UNESCO World Heritage List inscription on tourism destinations performance in Italian regions. *Economic Modelling, 53*, 494–508.

Culiuc, A. (2014). Determinants of International Tourism. IMF Working Paper, 14/82, 4–43.

Hassan, Z. A., Jailani, M. A. K., & Rahim, F. A. (2014). Assessing the situational analysis of heritage tourism industry in Melaka. *Procedia Social & Behavioral Sciences, 130*, 28–36.

Hawkins, D. E., Chang, B., & Warnes, K. (2009). A comparison of the National Geographic Stewardship Scorecard Ratings by experts and stakeholders for selected World Heritage destinations. *Journal of Sustainable Tourism, 17*(1), 71–90.

Huang, C.-H., Tsaur, J.-R., & Yang, C.-H. (2012). Does World Heritage list really induce more tourists? Evidence from Macau. *Tourism Management, 33*, 1450–1457.

Janssen, J., Luiten, E., Renes, H., & Stegmeijer, E. (2017). Heritage as sector, factor and vector: conceptualizing the shifting relationship between heritage management and spatial planning. *European Planning Studies, 25*(9), 1654–1672.

Jaafar, M., Noor, S. M., & Rasoolimanesh, S. M. (2015). Perception of young local residents toward sustainable conservation programmes: a case study of the Lenggong World Cultural Heritage Site. *Tourism Management, 48*, 154–163.

Jones, T. E., Yang, Y., & Yamamoto, K. (2017), Assessing the recreational value of world heritage site inscription: a longitudinal travel cost analysis of Mount Fuji climbers. *Tourism Management, 60*, 67–68.

Kim, H., Oh, C.-O., Lee, S., & Lee, S. (2018). Assessing the economic values of World Heritage Sites and the effects of perceived authenticity on their values. *International Journal of Tourism Research, 20*, 126–136.

Kim, S. S., Wong, K. K. F., & Cho, M. (2007). Assessing the economic value of a world heritage site and willingness-to-pay determinants: a case of Changdeok Palace. *Tourism Management, 28*, 317–322.

Kirkpatrick, J. B. (2001). Ecotourism, local and indigenous people, and the conservation of the Tasmanian Wilderness World Heritage Area. *Journal of the Royal Society of New Zealand, 31*(4), 819–829.

Kozac, M., & Martin, D. (2012). Tourism life cycle and sustainability analysis: profit-focused strategies for mature destinations. *Tourism Management, 33*, 188–194.

Leask, A. (2015). Visitor attraction management: a critical review of research 2009–2014. *Tourism Management, 57*, 334–361.

Liang, K.-Y., & Zeger, S. L. (1986). Longitudinal data analysis using generalized linear model. *Biometrika, 73*(1), 13–22.

Nifo, A., & Vecchione, G. (2014). Do institutions play a role in skilled migration? The case of Italy. *Regional Studies, 48*(10), 1628–1649.

Pandit, R., Dhakal, M., & Polyakov, M. (2015). Valuing access to protected areas in Nepal: the case of Chitwan National Park. *Tourism Management, 50*, 1–12.

Park, S., & Almeida Santos, C. (2017). From translocal to transnational: WHS articulations. *Annals of Tourism Research, 64*, 102–113.

Patuelli, R., Mussoni, M., & Candela, G. (2013). The effects of World Heritage Sites on domestic tourism: a spatial interaction model for Italy. *Journal of Geographical System, 15*, 369–402.

Pedersen, A. (2002). *Managing Tourism at World Heritage Sites: a Practical Manual for World Heritage Site Managers.* Paris: UNESCO World Heritage Center.

Rasoolimanesh, S. M., Jaafar, M., Ahmad, A. G., & Barghi, R. (2017). Community participation in World Heritage Site conservation and tourism development. *Tourism Management, 58*, 142–153.

Rasoolimanesh, S. M., Jaafar, M., & Barghi, R. (2017). Effects of motivation, knowledge and perceived power on residents' perceptions: application of Weber's theory in World Heritage Site destinations. *International Journal of Tourism Research, 19*, 68–79.

Santa-Cruz F. G., & López-Guzmán, T. (2017). Culture, tourism and World Heritage Sites. *Tourism Management Perspectives, 24*, 111–116.

Su, X., & Teo, P. (2008). Tourism politics in Lijiang, China: an analysis of state and local interactions in tourism development. *Tourism Geographies, 10*(2), 150–168.

Su, Y.-W., & Lin, H.-L. (2014). Analysis of international tourist arrivals worldwide: the role of world heritage sites. *Tourism Management, 40*, 46–58.

Su, M. M., & Wall, J. (2015). Exploring the shared use of World Heritage Sites: residents and domestic tourists' use and perceptions of the Summer Palace in Beijing. *International Journal of Tourism Research, 17*, 591–601.

UNWTO. (2017). *Tourism Highlights, 2017 Edition.* Madrid: UNWTO.

UNWTO. (2018). *World Tourism Barometer, 16.* Advance release, January 2018.

Vargas Vargas, M., Jiménez, J. M., Santamaría, M. L. M., & Navarro, J. L. A. (2009). Measurement of cultural motivations in World Heritage Cities: an analysis using fimix-pls algorithm. *Statistica Applicata, 21*(2), 153–165.

Vollero, A., Conte, F., Bottoni, G., & Siano, A. (2018). The influence of community factors on the engagement of residents in place promotion: empirical evidence from an Italian heritage site. *International Journal of Tourism Research, 20*, 88–99.

Wager, J. (1995). Developing a strategy for the Angkor World Heritage Site. *Tourism Management, 16*(7), 515–523.

Weaver, M. A. (2009). *Introduction to Analysis Methods for Longitudinal/Clustered Data, Part 3: Generalized Estimating Equations.* Family Health International. Presentation at Goa, India, September 2009.

WTTC. (2017). *Travel and Tourism. Economic Impact 2017. Italy.* London: WTTC.

Xu, S., Liu, Y., Qian, Y., & Wang, Q. (2017). The significance of the West Lake pattern and its heuristic implications for creating China's heritage tourism economics. *Tourism Management, 58*, 286–292.

Yang, C.-H., Lin, H.-L., & Han, C.-C. (2010). Analysis of international tourist arrivals in China: the role of World Heritage Sites. *Tourism Management, 31*, 827–837.

Zhang, C., Fyall, A., & Zheng, Y. (2015). Heritage and tourism conflict within World Heritage Sites in China: a longitudinal study. *Current Issues in Tourism, 18*(2), 110–136.

28

IMPACTS OF CORRUPTION ON TOURISM

A stop-and-go period for Brazilian tourism

Roseane Barcellos Marques, Carlos Alberto Alves,
and Elizabeth Kyoko Wada

Introduction

Developing tourism in Brazil is historically a challenge for public and private institutions. The country has cultural, social, and environmental/natural attractions that support its insertion into international tourist routes, but the limitations, peculiar to a country with its level of economic development, impose a trade-off between the tourism sector and other economic sectors. Between 2002 and 2017, with the 2014 World Cup and 2016 Summer Olympics, Brazilian tourism reached national and international relevance owing to the volume of investments in infrastructure and tourist flow in the events' host cities. However, infrastructure financing raised an old Brazilian dilemma: corruption. This is because the infrastructure necessary for the events in Brazil was basically financed with public resources, either directly through federal public constructions in partnership with state governments, or by subsidizing credit to the private sector for the construction of other tourism-specific services.

Tourist activity, as an economic activity, offers products and services to satisfy the needs of those visiting a receiving nucleus, including: transportation, accommodation, travel agencies, and leisure activities. Development of these products and services alters the routine of the resident population in the receiving nucleus (Körössy, 2008), causing impacts (Ruschmann, 1997) that can be positive or negative (Partidário and Jesus, 2003). Among the positive impacts of tourism, there is the potential to generate jobs, expand infrastructure, and boost the local economy; among the negative impacts are speculative pressures, disorderly occupation of spaces, practices incompatible with the use of land, conflicts with consolidated traditional values, and increases in the price of consumption patterns (Hawkins, Shafer, and Rovelstad, 1980; Pearce, 1981, 2012; Boullón, 1985; OMT, 2003; Almeida, 2009). These impacts are part of the process of tourism development and are sometimes an argument in its favor, sometimes effects that limit its growth.

This chapter highlights the possible positive economic impacts of the economic development promoted by investment in infrastructures that meet the needs of tourists and respond to the demands of the host population. Therefore, it assumes that tourism development offers positive results to the hosts, as well as to visitors. This study analyzed the relation between visitors and hosts within the period of two mega-events, the World Cup (2014) and the Summer Olympics (2016), which took place in Brazil. Brazil is a country with 27 federative units and

5,570 cities, 12 of which hosted the World Cup (Belo Horizonte, Brasília, Cuiabá, Curitiba, Fortaleza, Manaus, Natal, Porto Alegre, Recife, Rio de Janeiro, Salvador, and São Paulo). Distributing the games between 12 cities is justified, with regard to tourism development, by their potential to stimulate national and international interest in visiting Brazil. In 2016, six cities (Rio de Janeiro, Belo Horizonte, Brasília, Manaus, Salvador, and São Paulo) that hosted the World Cup also hosted the Olympic Games, which kept these destinations on the Brazilian tourism route and used the spaces built for the earlier event.

There were considerable public and private investments in infrastructure to promote the events, and they were expected to leave a legacy for tourism development with the juxtaposition between tourism structural constraints and the infrastructure of events. Dilemmas emerged with denunciations of corruption in the actions of public, private, and public–private institutions. Investigations at the time confirmed practices of passive and active corruption that resulted in the conviction of some of those involved. The events corroborated the stop-and-go perspective of Brazilian tourism development and encouraged this study.

However, this study presents the impacts of public investments within the relationship established between them and the private sector, which caused behaviors contrary to the principle of morality in the scope of public administration (Brasil, 1988). These behaviors, beyond administrative improbity, paved the way for the outbreak of corruption allegations. Therefore, this chapter discusses the impacts of corruption on Brazilian tourism, revealing its stop-and-go behavior – that is, a history of brief periods of growth and stagnation, consistent with the historical evolution of Brazilian economic data.

The data used to meet the objectives were surveyed by searching content related to corruption, infrastructure, mega-events, Cup/2014, Olympics/2016, tourism, and economy, in digital and printed news that presented current data. Reports from institutions such as the Brazilian Institute of Geography and Statistics (IBGE), the National Bank, the Brazilian Public Prosecutor's Office, the Brazilian Department of Sports, the Ministry of Justice and Public Security, the Federal Constitution of 1988, and other information from federal entities were analyzed, owing to the institutional/legal nature of the research. The data corroborated the examples given by the conceptual findings, following the conceptual characteristic of the chapter.

Finally, the contents of the chapter are divided into three parts. The context of tourism studies is presented in the first part, with the goal of clarifying approaches regarding infrastructure and the multiplier effect of tourism investments with Keynesian bias. The strong presence of public investments and the corruption deflagrated by the official supervision, investigation, control, and criminalization bodies in Brazil have given rise to discussions about the formation of the Brazilian state and the institutionalization of public policies regarding corruption. These contents are the explanatory basis for the empirical relationship between tourism, mega-events, and corruption, in which the objective is to clarify that corruption minimized the positive impacts expected from investments in infrastructure, in economic activities, especially in tourism, and consequently in the Brazilian economy. The expectation regarding the investments' multiplier effect, in an environment of high uncertainty, was replaced by a climate of instability and political, economic, and social insecurity.

Tourism

The discussion about tourism permeates several fields of knowledge, either because of its multidisciplinary character or because of its influence on people's lifestyles. People's migratory needs originated in the ancient civilizations, which maintained this behavior for survival, searching for food, better living arrangements, maintenance of power, or longing for glory and power.

The development of different and fast types of transport over time has allowed this elementary behavior of human nature to enable the development of knowledge, both cultural and educational. People's mobility throughout the world's vast territorial extent has broadened information repertoires about the way other cultures built their history to this day. It is in this current scenario that tourism gets mixed up with its motivations and its fragmentation, which have become better known than the original concept.

In 1942, the United Nations (UN) clarified that tourism is displacement outside the location of residence for a period longer than 24 hours and shorter than 60 days, motivated by non-economic reasons, a concept that was changed, in 1991, by the UN World Tourism Organization (UNWTO), to activities carried out by persons during a trip and stay in a place other than their natural habitat for a consecutive period not exceeding 24 months, for the purpose of leisure, business, and others (Sancho and Rodriguez Corner, 2001, pp. 35–49). In Brazil, among other definitions, tourism is an elaborate and complex process of deciding what to visit, where, how, and at what price. This process is influenced by a series of factors that define the destination, the length of stay, the way of traveling, and the type of accommodation (Paiva, 1989; M. C. Beni, 2006; Lohmann and Panosso Neto, 2008; Panosso Neto, 2010). The term tourist is derived from this conceptual discussion, as the person who practices tourism in activities that surpass 24 hours of stay, and the term excursionist, as the person who stays for a period of less than a day. Both are visitors and demand infrastructure from the places they visit.

There is a conceptual inconsistency regarding the scientific framework of the economic sciences that creates a gap between the economy and the social character of tourism. Economic sciences, as well as the concept of tourism, are inserted into the field of social sciences, and so they can be characterized as complex phenomena. This complexity hinders a single conceptual perspective, although there is a set of definitions rooted in their studies. The conceptual discussion that centralizes tourism in sociological discussions can be found in the book by Dann and Liebman Parrinello (2009), the content of which offers a review of European sociological studies on tourism, whereas contents with an administrative nature can be analyzed in Jamal and Robinson (2009) in North American bases, as observed from a comparative perspective by Sampaio (2013).

The definition of tourism as an economic activity stems from its specificity regarding the offer of products and services that are produced with the objective of satisfying the needs of tourists. Among them there is transportation, accommodation, travel agencies, leisure activities, and others. In this economic perspective, the tourism sector presents concepts such as supply, demand, and tourism products, which can have positive and negative impacts.

The impacts are constituted by a set of interventions and transformations resulting from tourist development in the receiving nuclei (Körössy, 2008) – that is, a result of the process of interaction between the tourists, the communities, and the receiving means (Ruschmann, 1997). These results can be seen as negative or positive (Partidário and Jesus, 2003). The positive impacts category discusses tourism in terms of job creation, local development, infrastructure construction, and local economy dynamism. Classified as negative impacts are speculative pressures, disorderly occupation of space, practices incompatible with land use, conflicts with consolidated traditional values, and increases in the price of consumption patterns (Hawkins et al., 1980; Pearce, 1981, 2012; Boullón, 1985; OMT, 2003; Almeida, 2009).

Analysis dimensions show a fragmentation of the impacts (M. Beni, 2006), such as the economic impacts of the generation of direct and indirect jobs, enabled by the degree of skilled workforce needed for this absorption; the psychological impacts found in the valorization of culture and the cultural identity of the community, which finds it difficult to maintain its initial characteristics with excessive exposure; and, finally, the social impacts related to behavioral and relationship changes from the interaction between the host community and the tourists.

The theoretical discussion about the impacts of tourist activity reaches socio-anthropological and economic contents. The former show the negative effects on the native population (Körössy, 2008), and the latter focuses on the sector's economic potential, with contributions to social welfare due to the remuneration for services (M. Beni, 2006).

Within the discussion about the applicability of impact studies is the context of sustainable tourism, with meaning rooted in the socio-anthropological scope, that worries about social disintegration, loss of cultural identity of indigenous communities, prostitution, and changes in ecosystem equilibrium. On the other hand, the economic approach brings the context of development and planning of tourism activities, with emphasis on the quality of life (of peoples and nations) that must be achieved with social progress. The conflicts within the word *development* are widely present in national and international literature. Research in this area can clarify these issues and make it possible to optimize the use of resources, which would culminate in minimizing the negative impacts and maximizing the positive ones (Partidário and Jesus, 2003; M. Beni, 2006; Körössy, 2008; Dann and Liebman Parrinello, 2009; Pearce, 2012).

This chapter demonstrates the potential for positive economic impacts on the well-being of the Brazilian population through the tourism sector from the legacy of the infrastructure built for the World Cup (2014) and the Summer Olympics (2016). In this way, the starting point of this study is the idealization of the multiplier effect of investments in gross fixed capital formation that would encourage tourism by the capillarity of the intensification of international and national tourist flow in the first instance, and the economic benefits as to the degree of development of the country as a long-term legacy.

The structural analysis of tourism (M. C. Beni, 2006), which presents the tourism system, was created from general systems theory (von Bertalanffy, 2008; Churchman, 2015; Dekkers, 2017) and contains the sets of environmental relations, structural organization, and operational market actions. The set of environmental relations contains the ecological, economic, social, and cultural subsystems. The superstructure consists of a legal management element for management and control of the system. It investigates factors such as strategic tourism planning, macroeconomic indicators, and formalization and supervision of tourism operators. In relation to the infrastructure subsystem, the main element is the study of conditions of accessibility to the tourist destination areas and services, covering the following sectors: basic sanitation, power and communications, support services, road and transportation system, and urban territorial organization (Table 28.1).

Table 28.1 Activities, items, and public and private sphere

Activities	Items	Sphere
Facilitation	Tickets, stay, internal trips, and visitors outings	Public
Infrastructure development	Highways, ports, airports, road works, public services, sanitation, power, water, sewage, social equipment, among others	Public
Transportation and communication	Land, air, sea, and river transportation, telecommunications services	Public
Education and training	Formation of resources for the sector at different levels	Public and private
Services (for tourists)	Lodging, carriers, restaurants and the like, fun and entertainment, travel agencies, rental companies, among others	Private

In Brazil, these activities are coordinated by their respective spheres, but the political-administrative arrangements with the private sector have changed over time – for example, activities that interfere with the public sector, such as education, which is also offered by the private sector. However, it should be noted that "tourism is an activity that requires prominent intervention from the State's, due to what it represents in its fundamental characteristics" (Beni, 2006, p. 100)

Infrastructure has a general and specific character because it cannot be attributed to a sector, with specific focus on the public good characteristics of its items. The construction of an airport will meet both the needs of Brazilian citizens and demands from tourism. In this way, general infrastructure is characterized, in the Tourism System (SISTUR), by investments that will be used by all other sectors of the economy, including tourism. However, the investment in specific infrastructure results in economic activities focused on structural investments in strictly tourist sites.

The complexity and diversity of elements that compose tourism are argued and inserted in subject matters that demand discussion and detail in their studies. Tourism is inserted in the heart of societies and, therefore, is under the aegis of social theories. Social theories are essentially complex (Curvello and Scroferneker, 2006; Neves and Neves, 2006; Morin, 2007; Pablo Gonnet, 2015). However, all forms of systematization of social environments are complex, and the creation of systems is an attempt to reduce this complexity.

The analytical perspective on the concept of systems, especially a tourism system, assumes that the organization of the constituent elements of the tourist experience comprises parts that are integrated in a whole, those being the elements that orbit the tourist structure and the whole, the experience itself. This is a strictly economic discussion, as it refers to the way in which contributive investments in the development of tourism place it as a sector of economic activity that can germinate other economic sectors, as well as boost them, and, above all, induce the specific activities of the sector, through the multiplier effect of tourism investments (Carvalho and Vasconcellos, 2006; Cooper, Fletcher, Fyall, Gilbert, and Wanhill, 2007; Stabler, Papatheodorou and Sinclair, 2010).

The "tourism multiplier" phenomenon is the result of the chain of successive effects of tourist spending. These effects can only be described by economic models that can contain the set of impacts that they produce in the economy from the different transformations, directly or indirectly, or induced, in terms of value creation, creation of jobs, or generation of foreign currency, among others (Ball, Ibañez and Picardi de Sastre, 2003; Fernández and Ruff, 2017).

Analyzing the literature on the multiplier effect of tourism reveals at least two aspects. The first, of a qualitative nature, observes the effect of the outlay of tourists (tourist spending) that generates a multiplier effect in tourism products in a microeconomic perspective of the tourism sector, and the second, quantitative, aspect, through the calculation of the multiplier effect investment in a macroeconomic approach.

The exemplification of the first analytical format suggests a reflection on the circulation of tourist spending – for example, if a person has R$100.00 and spends R$80.00 on a lodging. This lodging is also a consumer and acquires laundry services from another company. The amount outlaid by the all guests of this lodging will be distributed by the other service providers that contribute to the economic activity of the establishment that received the R$80.00, the laundry will pay for the supplies used to clean the clothes, and so on. In addition, other services purchased by tourists, such as transportation, restaurants, art, and others, will impact the tourism sector, which will influence the local economy. This phenomenon characterizes the multiplier effect of tourism.

This ability to germinate investments in the economy is discussed in the light of Keynesian theory (Stabler et al., 2010), regarding the second aspect of the investment multiplier effect. That is, investment is placed as an inducer of economic growth. Contrary to the neoclassical theory, represented by Say's Law, Keynes separates aggregate demand into investment (I) and consumption (C); thus, the products offered in the economy can satisfy different needs of the demanders, and, therefore, the demands determine the supply. The investment generates, thus, its own savings through the multiplier (Tobin, 1986; Giambiagi and Amadeo, 1990; Keynes, 1996; Araujo, 1998; Amado, 2000).

The theoretical perspective of the relationship between savings and investment is an old discussion between neoclassical economists and Keynesian economists. Whereas the former are concerned with the conditions of supply, in full employment economies, the latter focus on the conditions of demand in economies with idle capacity (Giambiagi and Amadeo, 1990). Considering that suppliers and applicants are sine qua non in market relations, the pertinent point of reflection seems to be the stage of economic activity of the society under analysis. The axioms of this concept assume that consumption tends to grow with rising incomes. There is a tendency to save when consumption is less than the total value of income. The savings generated by non–consumption will be transformed into financial assets that can be invested productively. It is concluded, then, that part of the earned income tends to be transformed into investment.

From the Keynesian perspective, income is generated by the degree of consumption, or by the degree of spending in an economy whose conceptual foundation is the concept of effective demand; in this way, both spending and investment are relevant to economic growth. It is important to add to this analytical perspective one of the economic principles of the savings and investment relationship: The resources saved that are transformed into investments are considered a reduction in spending now for generating expenditure in the future. "Policies to stimulate consumption would be advisable for shorter periods, but sustaining growth would entail containing this consumption to increase the country's saving coefficient." This is because "Keynes envisioned a world in which the main constraint on growth was insufficient demand" (Giambiagi and Amadeo, 1990, p. 2). The stage of economic growth, to a certain extent, creates a trade-off between consumption and investment. The Keynesian multiplier can be calculated as follows:

Keynesian identity regarding income:

$$Y = DA = C + I$$

Where

$$C = A + cY$$

We have:

$$Y = A + cY + I$$

One can infer that:

$$Y - cY = Y(1 - c) = A + I, \text{ where, } Y = (A+ I)\ 1/(1-c)$$

As:

$$C + S = Y \text{ e } Y - C = S$$

Resulting in:

$$S = I$$

Where: Y = income or product; A = autonomous expenditure in production (in the equation it is a constant); C = consumption; I = investment; S = savings; AD = aggregate demand; c = marginal propensity to consume; $1/(1 - c)$ = Keynesian multiplier.

In this way, tourism is a sector capable of inducing economic growth by generating demand in other sectors, and the tourism multiplier effect presents its performance quantitatively (Stabler et al., 2010; Fernández and Ruff, 2017) and impacts on the level of economic activity in the country.

The analysis proposed in this chapter does not present a quantitative discussion. The model is presented to illustrate the conceptual discussion. However, for a broader understanding of the applicability of the Keynesian model to tourism data, it is necessary to understand the statistical and mathematical specificities pertinent to the conceptual discussion in the respective areas of knowledge. What is expected to be demonstrated here is that the infrastructure relevant to tourism development is built by investments made to satisfy the host population and will meet the needs of tourists by improving the services provided. These constructions, in Brazil, come mainly from public investments. Historically, in Brazil, infrastructure investments, influenced by the Keynesian approach, came from public resources, which explains, to a certain extent, why the periods of Brazilian economic growth were preceded by, or juxtaposed with, periods of public investment (Betty, 1975; Mello, 1997; Kon, 1999; Bresser-Pereira, 2017b).

What this study intends to demonstrate is that public investments for the World Cup and the Summer Olympics in Brazil were part of a new round of investments aimed at promoting economic development, this time considering the development of one of the sectors with the greatest capillarity in the Brazilian economy, even if it was not previously valued, and even if this was not the main objective of attracting these events to the country. However, in practice, studies on the sector pointed in that direction by investigating and confirming the tourism impacts on the country's economic performance.

Considering the Keynesian perspective, which states that expenditures generate income and that present investments tend to generate future income and expenditure, and if the tourism sector is considered to be driven by expenditure, then the volume of public resources allocated to infrastructure for the mega-events, even if they were not on the radar of the agents who made the decision to invest, would stimulate the host population spending, domestic tourist spending, and international demand, which would boost the development of the sector and the economy as a whole. The variable that remained outside the model was corruption. The phenomenon of corruption, which is also historical, has entered the model and, by entering, it has not only impacted the internal dynamics of the national economy, but also affected the international demand, and since then Brazilian society has coexisted with this unhealed scar.

Brazil and corruption

The construction of a nation-state is the reflection of the collective thinking of a society. The state enables individuals to live under the aegis of their thinking and, in this way, it transforms the collective thinking about how one should live into a real act of how people live, which characterizes it as an "objective spirit" (Hegel, 1968). "If the State is the objective spirit, then only as a member does the individual have objectivity, truth and morality" (Hegel, 1968, § 258, p. 217).

Hegel's historical-philosophical discussion presents the conception of a modern state with form and content. This is because the individual's understanding of their insertion in the world of meanings, the "becoming," is one of the pillars of the formation of this content of the state. The form consists of the construction of a state bureaucracy, that is, the construction of a collective body of individuals present in the state and capable of materializing its fundamental principles.

The guarantee of rights by the state comes from the legitimate condition of exercising the force or monopoly of violence. This kind of power granted to the state reduces its subjects to obedience, even if the use of force is necessary. This is a characteristic of the state, which alone holds the monopoly of legal coercion. Submission to the force of the state promotes, as stated by contractualism (Quirino and Sadek, 2003; Weffort, 2006, 2008), the civilizatory stage of society. The civilizatory stage is a transformation of man in his "natural state" into a citizen with rights and duties, in the Hegelian approach. The natural state is the struggle of man against man, "the werewolf of man himself" (Hobbes, 1974); the social contract that shapes the state aims to guarantee the freedom of all, by partially giving up individual freedom; man seeks the equality of freedom between men through the state.

The division of state power into three branches, executive, legislative, and judicial (Quirino and Sadek, 2003; Aron and Bath, 2008), is explained by the central argument that, in order to avoid an absolute state, a balance is needed for the decisions made by rulers. The government is the instrument that personalizes and represents the state, that is, that performs the functions of the state. In this way, the division of powers is summarily important to avoid the concentration of power.

However, the division of powers contributes to the functional balance between the functions exercised by the state. The executive administers and executes laws, the legislature legislates, and the judiciary arbitrates conflicts between the other powers, between society and the executive, between the public authorities, and between individuals. There is a balance of functions and, therefore, a functional distribution, but there is also a spatial distribution in federal regimes. The modus operandi of the spatial division is organized at the federal level by the president of the Republic, who represents the executive branch, and there is the federal legislature and the federal judiciary. At the state level, there is the state governor, who represents the state executive, the state legislature, and the state judiciary. The power of the state, in this way, is divided functionally and spatially, revealing the complexity of this institution called the state.

Kant's "perpetual peace" seeks to clarify that respect for the laws instituted by the state, through its members, leads to peace for all. The state offers the conditions for men to be free if they act rationally by respecting the laws, which, for Kant, are the product of human reason: "A state is not patrimony. It is a society of men over which no one but itself has the right to rule or to dispose" (Kant, 1989, p. 5). From this perspective, the state is a product of human reason, and its rationality is present in the creation of laws that will regulate the conduct of individuals and will give them freedom if they respect the laws they create.

Conversely, the legal definition adds to the debate about the state its character as a body of legal production. It is this body that produces the legal order that governs the society, the economy and the political institutions that integrate it. In a circular manner, the state is still a product of the laws that configure its characteristics, being the result of a legal order. This conception of the state as a legal product of its own laws reduces it to a mode of production and subordination to laws and to the legal order. This order is constituted by elements capable of regulating human conduct, and, when it is regulating human conduct, legal norms, subject to a legal order, establish its format (Kelsen, 2009). The state, as a "legal order," has the task of ensuring collective security. In the face of these norms, all citizens have the obligation to respect the rules, norms, and laws to which they are subjugated. If each person respects the format established as correct, everyone will be protected by the state in collective security.

For contractualists, as in Locke, Hobbes, and Rousseau, in the studies of political philosophy and, more recently, in the studies of political science, the state is considered the most important political institution, before all others, with the preponderance of the sovereignty that characterizes it as state and the legitimate coercion which it monopolizes. In this sense, the contract is signed by all, although there is in the constitution of the state, through the social contract, the predominance of those who will organize the process with means to engender the dominant characteristic (Souza and Mattos, 2007).

Marx, discussing and opposing the Hegelian definition, argues that conflicts in the "realm of necessity" have not been solved in the "realm of rationality." On the contrary, this passage privileged the bourgeoisie which, in this historical process, created class differences and intensified conflicts arising from these differences. This formed the state that Marx will interpret as the "executive committee of the ruling classes" (Bobbio, Bovero and Versiani, 2000; Weffort, 2006, 2008).

In Marx, the state is not a product of human reason, but the very reason that stands sovereign in the conduct of individuals. It is the setting of human thinking, capable of perpetuating domination among the social classes, owners of the means of production (capitalists), and the labor force (proletarians). The sociological conception of the state in Marx and Engels is explained by a historical process that generated the class struggle, oppressors and oppressed, under the aegis of the state. In this sense, Marx demonstrates that the state is not the "principle of universality and rationality" present in Hegel's definition, much less the product of a social contract, the definition of contractualists, but a historical construction, a result of social relationships, inherent in the capitalist production mode and centered on economic factors, which can only be explained from a historical perspective.

The social, economic, and political context at the time of (Weber, 2004, 2008) was different from that of Marx, which allowed him to see the relationship between state and capitalism in a more concrete and, at the same time, more complex manner. By witnessing, historically, the formation of the states around the world and the complex form in which each society conceived it and was influenced by it, he attributed the source of all the sociological explanations regarding the state to social action. It is the social action of men, guided by the behavior of other men, that contains not only the sociological analysis, but also an explanation for it, deriving from how men relate in society. However, it is a social action whenever the action is guided by the behavior of another. The historical-theoretical trajectory which the definition of state underwent allows us to consider that there is no single definition, but a definition that is shaped and formed from the historical experiences of each society.

In the contemporary scenario, the state consists of the nation-state as an institutional-legal and sovereign system that monopolizes legitimate violence (Bresser-Pereira, 1995, 2017b). This institutionalization guarantees civil, political, and social rights and has the prerogative of promoting economic growth by increasing productivity, assigning the coordination of economic activities to the market, and providing social protection.

The nation-state is a central concept in Bresser-Pereira's thesis because the author places it as the "main political-territorial unit" of modern societies. It is this political-territorial unity that promotes the convergence of the actions of the nation-state in pursuit of the objectives of "state," namely: to meet the demands of society pursuing objectives that will consolidate its industrialization. Integration through this political-capitalist unity is the way to increase productivity, inherent in the industrial process, which is the pillar of support for nation-states.

The nation-state, conceived as the principle of this economic development, pursues its goal of productivity as the path to accumulate capital that triggers other historical mechanisms of the concept. However, the nation-state is a political institution composed of three essential elements: the modern state, the nation, and the territory. In this sense, public administration holds legitimate sovereignty, as it has the prerogative to formulate public policies and, at the same time, it is a rationally defined social system because it is the result of a historical process. Bobbio et al. (2000, p. 10) state that, "Government is the set of people who exert the political power and that determine the political orientation of a society."

Finally, the state is like an entity "incarnated" in political representations, the government is like a conductor that commands the orchestra of the actions of the state, and the public administration materializes these actions.

It is this context of power relations between the government and the governed, in the conception of the sovereign state formed by three powers, the executive, the legislature, and the judiciary, sole holder of legal coercion and constituted by a group of people who exercise political power, called government, with technical instruction to materialize the political orientation of a society, that the concept of the capable state is contained, one that is capable of protecting itself and its citizens and creating spaces for republican rights.

The capable state (strong and republican) in Bresser-Pereira (1995, 2017a) is a state that enforces its laws and, therefore, is legitimate. What this means is that this state has political and administrative conditions and legitimacy with civil society to enforce its laws, even in a state, such as Brazil, which is characterized by producing "laws that do not take." The fact is that these laws are applied to their objectives and seek to solve problems raised by social and political actors in the conception phase of state action, or public policy (Evans, Rueschemeyer, and Skocpol, 1985).

After analyzing Brazil and classifying it as "a fragmented presidential party-system," Mainwaring (1993) clarifies that this is one of the possible combinations in presidentialism, as a "subgroup of presidential systems." In this way, the author points out that, in Brazil, political party coalitions have affected the governability of presidents throughout Brazil's history, before and after the period of the military dictatorship (1964–1985). Thus, coalitions have not only become necessary procedures for the governability of the president, but also interfere with the progress of state actions, or public policies, when there is no approval or when there are delays in voting on these actions.

When discussing democracy in Brazil under the aegis of presidentialism, party coalitions, and the decision-making process, Limongi (2006) highlights the matter of governability of the president regarding issues such as federalism, power of governors, and the diversity and heterogeneity of Brazilian society, but particularly discusses the party coalition at the parliamentary level.

The institutional foundations that structure the relations between the executive and legislative branches have undergone fundamental changes regarding governability from the 1946 Democratic Constitution to the Constitution that promulgated re-democratization in 1988. Mainwaring (1993) argues that the 1988 text gave the executive a level of autonomy in relation to the legislative.

The term presented by Limongi (2006) as a "Progressive Executive and a Conservative Congress" seeks to explain the divergence between the issues raised by the executive to approve matters pertaining to its government program, which are sometimes rejected by the legislative. This is because, in addition to the commitment made by the executive to the voters, the president needs to argue, negotiate, and convince his allied base as to the necessity of the actions contained in the folders sent for approval at the congress, to achieve this and fulfill campaign promises.

The dichotomy between progressive president and conservative congress, according to the author, is inherent in the institutional design of the Brazilian political system, in which the power of the majority, of the legislature, is put to the test by the power of the minority, the executive, by the veto power which the executive maintains in relation to the legislature when deciding which topics will be placed on the agenda.

For that, it is necessary that the political actions of the executive be supported by knowledge and intelligence regarding the characteristics of each member of congress and of each party that makes up the legislature. This knowledge is the database with which the executive will work, but, to "anticipate the reactions," it must interpret how each actor, consonant or not with their party, acts in this arena. This act of the executive would contribute to improving its performance, and thus its governability, because it would put it in a position to respect the ideologies and aspirations pertinent and relevant to the legislature.

The capable state, then, is characterized by a state able to understand the characteristics of the actors and the way they act in the political system, concomitantly with understanding the driving force of the politicians, who crystallize the demands of society in each actor and in each political action.

However, this state demonstrates capacity when it constructs institutions that may reprimand practices that go against the purpose of capitalist development. By building an institution capable of defending its citizens in the various situations contrary to the feeling of belonging to a republican nation-state, this state reveals some capacity.

In Brazil, the 1988 Federal Constitution (CF-88), which establishes the format of the Brazilian state and its public administration, is in force. Regarding public administration, the Constitution establishes the characteristics of its formation and ensures the criteria for possible misconduct in the performance of its functions (Brasil, 1988).

It is this discussion about the formation of the state, particularly the formation of the Brazilian state, that contains the prerogatives on how the 1988 Federal Constitution was enacted in Brazil, a constitution that was supposed to be the most "democratic" of all constitutions instituted in Brazil and laid the foundations of the law-based Brazilian democratic state, based on the foundations of sovereignty, citizenship, dignity of persons, social values of work and free initiative, and political pluralism. In relation to political pluralism, it is emphasized that, "All power emanates from the people, who exercise it through elected representatives or directly, under the terms of this Constitution" (CF-88). For this purpose, it constituted the "powers of the Union, independent and harmonious among themselves, the Legislative, the Executive and the Judiciary."

The Federative Republic of Brazil aims to build a free, fair, and supportive society, guarantee national development, eradicate poverty and marginalization and reduce social and regional inequalities, and promote good for all, without prejudice of origin, race, sex, color, age, and any other forms of discrimination (CF-88). In relation to the "Organization of States," the Constitution establishes that the direct and indirect public administration of any of the "Powers of the Union, of the States, of the Federal District and of the Municipalities shall obey the principles of legality, impersonality, morality, publicity and efficiency" (CF-88).

Observing Hegel's "objective spirit," where there is the idea that only as members of a state do individuals have objectivity, truth, and morality, and also considering Kant's thought about laws as a product of human reason instituted by the state, created by its members, who offer the conditions for man to be free, the CF-88 is based on historical principles and the theoretical repertoire regarding the formation of the state. Morality has gained space in the Brazilian constitutions since 1930, under the name "administrative morality," with the conception that a person who embodies the presence of the state must act with a high degree of legality and clearness, because the performance is not by itself or for itself, but for the community.

The presence of the term morality has two analytical approaches. If, on the one hand, reinforcing it suggests its relevance to the public administration, on the other, an excess of it makes its use in daily practices imprecise. This imprecision is reported in history books about Brazil and in daily reports that show misappropriation of monetary resources, derived from deviations of character, by public representatives of different levels. Thus, to the same extent that the rules are created, there is a need to create regulatory acts for deviations from the rule, in relation to the law, to be investigated, criminalized, and sentenced. Absence of administrative morality is analyzed as "administrative improbity," consisting of any form of compromise of the principles that inform the public administration (Costa, 2005).

Damage to administrative morality is express grounds for the annulment of injurious acts to the public patrimony through popular action, in defense of morality for the exercise of electoral office, in a complementary law that establishes ineligibility to protect the administrative probity which is also guarded in the crimes of responsibility attributable to the president of the Republic. In the same sense, acts of administrative improbity may lead to the annulment of political rights, loss of public office, unavailability of assets, and obligation of reimbursement to the Treasury, according to the law that regulates the sanctions applicable to acts of administrative improbity. Parliamentary decorum is in turn an elementary requirement for the exercise of political mandate, subject to loss in the event of a procedure incompatible with it, which includes the perception of undue advantages. The appointment of Minister of the Union Court of Auditors requires moral suitability and an unblemished reputation comparable with the moral element indispensable for access to the positions of Minister of the Federal Supreme Court and Minister of the Superior Court of Justice. Among the fundamental values placed as guidelines in the Constitution is the dignity of people, and the essential purpose of the Republic is to build a fair society, with the guarantee of inviolability of honor and expression of citizenship, a basic element of the democratic rule of law (Tácito, 1999).

The deviations, or misrepresentations, committed by agents internal or external to the public administration are denominated corruption. The act of corrupting, or offering something to someone to obtain, in return, an advantage or benefit is characterized as corruption. The term was constituted and revealed in the political sphere and violates the principle of morality instituted as a cornerstone of the activities of public administration, but it can occur in all human relations. In social relations, whether motivated by living in society or by economic factors, the act of influencing others to commit some deviation of character or function to receive benefits as a counterpart is a form of corruption. When these isolated acts become a characteristic of social dynamics, systemic corruption is established, corresponding to acts of corruption normally perpetrated by citizens. Corruption is malignant in all dimensions, but its insertion into social relations occurs for different and complex reasons and silently, which makes its identification and assessment difficult and time-consuming.

The political-philosophical meaning that explains the formation of the state clarifies that corruption is inherent to humans, and that it "is the most difficult of all tasks; moreover, a perfect solution is impossible: from such a twisted wood, from which man is made, nothing of straight can be done" (Kant, 1784, p.11). In this sense, human beings are conditioned to act under the prism of "perfection" when a superior being induces them to walk a "straight line." Living in society, under the tutelage of the state, conditions citizens in this direction. The challenge is to lead the actions of those who hold the legitimate power to govern this state in the same direction. In this way, corruption is a historical characteristic inherent to the human condition, and, when becoming citizens, humans perceives themselves as more dignified beings, who seek to act according to what is established as correct by society, but they become alienated from society by corrupting their primitive needs (of human nature) to follow the needs of society (Rousseau, 2011; Oliveira, 2015)

Religions associate corruption with a tendency to sin, that is, the hearts of humans tend to deviations that lead them to walk along paths to human decency, just as they lead them to walk on paths contrary to this dignity (St. Augustine). "Beings may be imperfect because they are born defective or because they act voluntarily in a distorted manner" by committing a moral evil or, in theological language, a sin. And, in defining original sin, he explains what corruption is: "*Corrupção* is a word in the Portuguese language that translates *corruptus*, from Latin. *Corruptus* is the one who has a corrupted heart," and adds that, "man is born with a corrupted heart because he, being a creature, is imperfect, and being imperfect, tends to moral evil." (St. Augustine, cited in Cabral, 2009)

However, whether in the philosophical, political, or religious context, corruption is a historical manifestation of the human condition that leads man to act in the opposite direction to what was established as correct by the social group of which he is a party, with rights, duties, and obligations. As a characteristic of the human being, corruption is present in different human activities. The expression of corruption in the world has reached international debates and has promoted the involvement of entities such as the United Nations and its sectoral departments (United Nations, 2003, 2004, 2015).

The history of American economy, for example, portrays corrupt elements such as those of developing economies, such as basic cleaning services, construction, and bribes received by civil servants, which led governments to adopt severe anti-corruption measures (Glaeser and Goldin, 2006). This perception of corruption as inserted in different instances of society is relevant because it makes each country, once aware of it, initiate the process of adjustments and the creation of public measures that can ameliorate or solve its harmful effects on life under the guidance of the politic body.

Independent institutions such as Transparency International, a global movement seeking a "world free of corruption," created the Corruption Perceptions Index, revealing that systemic corruption and social inequality are mutually reinforcing, leading to lack of confidence of the people in political institutions. In 2016, 69% of the 176 countries surveyed obtained results that inserted them in the area classified as highly corrupt, on a scale from 0 (perceived as highly corrupt) to 10 (perceived as highly intact). They have concluded, to date, that there is no country free of corruption, even sharing aspects such as open government, independent judicial systems, and civil liberties, even countries that are among the five most respected have some degree of corruption (Transparency International, 2017). Public trust associated with corruption causes ruptures, because either the public is convinced that no person in that society is engaged in any honest activity or that the institutions set up to verify corruption in the public body are not efficient, or the people feel a sense of impunity. Transparency regarding activities in the political system is coordinated by a constitution and a charter. Corruption is conceptual and historical, and public trust is a residue of the degree of understanding about the suitability of the people who are members of a society, the political system instituted by this society, and the institutions of control and supervision of these actions and relations. In this way, it is necessary to distinguish between perception of corruption and its verification, because the feeling of systemic corruption is usually associated with external information that induces collective thought, and not with the monitoring of the actions performed by the inspection and control organs instituted and the respective collection so that these bodies exercise, with suitability, their functions.

Actions and discussions under the economic context in microeconomic and macroeconomic studies have been incorporated and discussed to describe aspects of modern life considered to be appalling, such as: violent video games that corrupt the morals of young people, corruption of politics, and decline of civic virtue and public administration, which places non-circumscribed corruption in the field of monetary, social, and political costs/benefits. Economy researchers have started studying the "economics of corruption," because some aspects of the concept of corruption are susceptible to economic analysis, such as payments to agents (public and private) where economic agents are induced by bribes or other forms of induction to ignore the interests of the institutions for which they work to favor private/particular interests. In this case, research in the field of economics is focused on revealing the gains made by corruption in the exchange arrangements between ordinary people, business enterprises, and public officials (Rose Ackerman, 2006).

In the Brazilian public administration, corruption is one of the manifestations of administrative improbity, and the difference between the different manifestations is whether they are conditioned as a crime. Whereas corruption is constituted in the criminal sphere as corruption and governed, therefore, by the penal code, the second administrative improbity is embedded in the civil, not criminal, sphere and is governed by the Federal Constitution as a deviation from administrative morality (Tácito, 1999; Costa, 2005; Machado, 2015)

In the Penal Code of Brazil, instituted by Decree-Law number 2.848 of 1940, there is the definition of passive and active corruption in relation to crimes committed in the condition of administrative improbity (see Table 28.2).

The designations of corruption typified in the scope of public administration, in this chapter, justify the construction of the corpus of research constituted by the volume of public resources invested in infrastructure that represented old demands of the Brazilian population that also contributed to meeting the needs of the visitors and tourists on the occasions under analysis. During operational activities, the reports of active and passive corruption took over the news, circulating in the national and international media. These reports and investigations, pressed by strong popular demand, shook the foundations of the formation of the state which, in the end, demonstrated all the historical fragilities of its colonial roots, covered by laws that, as usual, reached the status of "laws that do not take."

The morality of texts and discourses was transformed into input to legal debates in various instances. The "old" or "new" policy that was in effect for so many years in the processes and

Table 28.2 Active and passive corruption

Passive corruption	Art. 317: Requesting or receiving, for oneself or for another, directly or indirectly, even if out of office or before taking over it, but because of it, improper advantage, or accepting promises of such an advantage:
	Penalty: confinement, from two (2) to twelve (12) years, and a fine.*
	1st §: The penalty is increased by one-third if, because of the advantage or promise, the official employee delays or ceases to practice any act of office or practices inflicting official duty.
	2nd §: If the employee practices, fails to practice or delays an official act, in a violation of official duty, yielding at the request or influence of others:
	Penalty: detention, from three months to one year, or fine.
Active corruption	Art. 333: Offering or promising an undue advantage to a public official, to determine them to practice, omit or delay official acts:
	Penalty: confinement, from two (2) to twelve (12) years, and a fine.**
	Sole paragraph: The penalty is increased by one-third if, because of the advantage or promise, the official employee delays or ceases to practice any act of office or practices inflicting official duty.

Notes: * Law no. 10.763, from 12.11.2003; ** Law no. 10.763, from 12.11.2003.

Source: The authors, adapted from the Penal Code of Brazil, 1940.

limitations of social and economic classes was placed under suspicion. And so the aspirations for Brazil's economic and social development, with cultural exchange and the spread of the Brazilian green heritage that was expected to be the memories each one would take from the 2014 World Cup and 2016 Olympics, disappeared in the great " smoke" formed by the scandals that erupted in the public and private sphere involving politicians. The contributions of the mega-events were perceived in many facets of Brazilian society. Owing to the allegations of corruption, the Brazilian population began claiming the rights, duties, and obligations of public and private agencies, through frequent and large protests, which was not characteristic.

Thus, as each society has created states through collective thinking, it also constructs their idea of justice, of moral and ethical conduct, which causes every distorted act of this moral conception to find, contrary to facts, its agent. The definition of corruption is centered on the deviance of conduct from what was instituted as correct, as accepted, as worthy, as cleared by the society en masse. However, there are no adjectives for corruption; what exist are essences and forms that come together and fragment into the most diverse aspects of human life.

Tourism, mega-events, and corruption

In Brazil, tourism has always been an economic promise, as well as an opportunity to solve social dilemmas, as it is present in places where natural beauty coexists with high levels of need, where incomes border poverty and penury. In this way, attracting tourists to different Brazilian states is a way of turning this promise into concrete acts and testing the capacity of this economic activity to solve social problems. In other words, tourism development in Brazil is embedded in the promotion of social welfare by reaching populations that live farthest from the great centers that generate wealth, among which are the capital cities of Rio de Janeiro, São Paulo, and Belo Horizonte. Faced with this premise, the 2014 World Cup and the 2016 Olympics emerged as flags of worldwide visibility for Brazil, as it is a country with extensive territories filled with wonders capable of enchanting visitors. "Brazil is one of the most important economies in the world. The continental proportion, population size, abundance of natural resources, agricultural productivity and the performance of some industries offer unquestionable evidence of its importance for the global economy" (Haider, Kotler, Rein, and Gertner, 2006, p. 103).

Regarding Brazilian social and economic characteristics, it should be noted that the Brazilian state has a population estimated at 207,660,929 inhabitants, distributed across 27 federal units and a federal district, fragmented into 5,570 cities in a territory of 8,515,759,090 km², and with about 13.4 million people (6.45% of the total population) below the poverty line, that is, living on less than US$1.90 per day, the figure established by the World Bank to classify extreme poverty (IBGE, 2017).

States and cities in Brazil receive budgets from the federal government in the distribution of state participation funds (FPE) and city participation funds (FPM). These funds consist of a constitutional transfer of financial resources from the union to the states and cities, according to data from the General Accounting Office (TCU), 2017, which are administered autonomously by these entities. The budget revenue of the federal, state, and city governments is used to pay off commitments and to fulfill the demands of the population. The population has peculiar characteristics because of colonization, especially by the Portuguese, that define the image of the Brazilian people (Ribeiro, 1995), the Brazilian roots (Freyre, 2003; Holanda, 2015; Marques, 2015), and its economic formation (Furtado, 2006; Prado Júnior, 2011). The years have passed, but history is crystallized in the foundations of the edifice, which means that the human relations of a society have their roots, which will always be present, even if they are metamorphosed in the present and future generations, as well as in political, cultural, and economic transformations.

This information is presented to explain the reasons why a country with a passion for soccer had its reasons to distribute the stadiums that received the World Cup matches across 12 host cities. The goal here is not to justify, but to minimize the usual discourse about this subject. Although the expenditure on each construction is questionable, the multiplier effect of the investment and the legacy expected from hosting events of this magnitude are, at least, contents that enrich this reflection.

In the current context, the Brazilian economy is among the ten largest in the world, as presented in Table 28.3. Although internal and external factors contributed to a recession in Brazil, which went from a growth of 7.5% in 2010 to almost three years of decline (from 2014 to 2016), it is still among the 10 largest economies of the world. In 2017, the GDP signaled a resumption of economic growth (IBGE/Banco Central, 2018).

Analyzing the data of the gross domestic product (GDP) and of the GDP per capita, at current prices, in dollars, it is possible to perceive that these values suffered different variations when the variation of one year is analyzed in relation to the previous year. In relation to GDP, the country's annual production effort remained valued at billions of dollars in the period from 2000 to 2005, with the variation of the current year in relation to the previous year showing negative results at the beginning of 2000–2001, but in spiraling growth until 2005. In 2006, the economy presented current values of GDP in trillions of dollars, but the result in terms of growth between 2005 and 2006 presented a decrease of 33.3% and 24.1%, respectively. As a result, variations between years are irregular, with increases and reductions that demonstrate the economic instability that the country experiences to this day. Analyzing especially the years 2014 and 2016, in terms of variation in relation to the previous years, 2013 and 2015, respectively, the behavior of GDP continued to fall from 2013 to 2014 and showed poor growth from 2015 to 2016. This last period deserves attention because, even though the result is unimpressive

Table 28.3 Gross domestic product (GDP)

Period	GDP Δ %	GDP in millions of US$	Population in thousands	GDP per capita	
				Δ %	US$[1/]
2000	. . .	655,707	173,447	. . .	3,780.44
2001	−14.7	559,563	175,895	−15.9	3,181.24
2002	−9.2	508,101	178,288	−10.4	2,849.89
2003	10.1	559,465	180,627	8.7	3,097.34
2004	19.6	669,340	182,913	18.1	3,659.33
2005	33.3	892,033	185,144	31.7	4,818.04
2006	24.1	1,107,131	187,322	22.7	5,910.32
2007	26.2	1,396,797	189,445	24.7	7,373.11
2008	21.2	1,693,147	191,514	19.9	8,840.87
2009	−1.2	1,672,625	193,528	−2.2	8,642.80
2010	32.1	2,209,751	195,488	30.8	11,303.76
2011	18.3	2,614,482	197,394	17.2	13,245.01
2012	−5.8	2,463,549	199,245	−6.6	12,364.44
2013	0.2	2,468,456	201,041	−0.7	12,278.36
2014	−0.6	2,454,846	202,783	−1.4	12,105.79
2015	−26.8	1,796,168	204,470	−27.4	8,784.51
2016	0.1	1,797,234	206,102	−0.7	8,720.12
2017	14.4	2,055,184	207,679	13.5	9,895.96

Source: The authors, adapted from IBGE/Banco Central (2018).

in 2016, with a growth of 0.1%, the productive effort was significant, as the economy had shown a reduction of −26.8% from 2014 to 2015, which means a recovery, even if it did not reach the absolute values of 2014.

The behavior of GDP per capita – GDP value divided by the country's population – in the same year shows growth in absolute terms until 2009. In terms of variations, at current prices of the year in force in relation to the previous year, this begins the period with negative results. Even oscillating between growth and reduction between the years reveals an improvement in per capita until 2009. Then, the variation presented a negative result, -2.2, resumed growth in 2010 and 2011, and again there were negative variations between 2012 and 2016. In absolute terms, there is a prospect of socio-economic improvement, as the results went from US$2,849.89 to US$8,720.12, but growth rates between the years do not show a steady growth behavior. This economic behavior, alternating between brief periods of growth and reduction, signals the stop-and-go characteristic of the Brazilian economy.

It must be noted that the memory of a population whose economy has, historically, remained in a developmental stage also refers to short periods. After all, what does a historical series mean for a collective thinking whose history is constantly changing. In this way, analyzing the growth of the present year in relation to the previous year is a way to approximate the current data to the dominant collective thinking, that is, the perception that life was not so simple for Brazilians in recent years, even with two events of the magnitude of the 2014 World Cup and the 2016 Olympics.

Although the economic results indicate a complex panorama of the Brazilian economy, to be chosen to host the two mega-events (2014 FIFA World Cup and 2016 Olympic Games) was a huge achievement. This victory led to resumed investments in infrastructure, long demanded by the population, and created expectation of positive impacts that these investments would germinate in the economy, which created a Brazilian "euphoria." The mega-events brought in public and private investments and strategic planning to manage them and promote the image of Brazil internationally. Regarding Brazil's image, there was considerable expenditure in the years prior to the mega-events to promote the country's image abroad and intensify the Brazil brand (Haider et al., 2006).

The Brazilian "euphoria" in relation to the mega-events was justified by the expansion of investments in infrastructure, as they would allow large-scale public gatherings and increase the number of visitors to the host cities, having a positive socio-economic impact on the country (Gursoy, Milito, and Nunkoo, 2017, p. 2). The increase in flow of people, Brazilian and foreign, into the host cities, promoted by the mega-events (Wada, Amikura and Vilkas, 2018) also contributed to leveraging national tourism. In this sense, considering the capacity of tourism to promote socio-economic progress through job creation, new businesses, generation of revenue, and strengthening infrastructure development (UNWTO, 2016), the positive expectations were warranted; it was not simply a "euphoria" regarding entertainment and leisure, but a feeling that Brazil had conquered its moment in history.

The mega-events – the 2014 World Cup and 2016 Olympic Games – demanded and received public and private investments of great proportions in the 12 cities chosen to host the Cup games (Belo Horizonte, Brasília, Cuiabá, Curitiba, Fortaleza, Manaus, Natal, Porto Alegre, Recife, Rio de Janeiro, Salvador and São Paulo), 6 of which (Rio de Janeiro, Belo Horizonte, Brasília, Manaus, Salvador and São Paulo) also hosted activities for the 2016 Olympics. However, the numbers of these investments in relation to the economy did not reach expectations, and, regarding tourism, they did not have the expected positive impacts. The events happened and shone, illuminating the world with the light emanating from each Brazilian. However, the historical aspects of this society were revealed, such as corruption and the bad deeds of public administration, and the whole party was set in a cloud of corruption allegations that began punctually, but, given their breadth in public administration activities and in questionable relationships between the private sector and the public sector, including relations with FIFA, reached systemic status. This corruption determined the course of the history of these mega-events in Brazil.

The investigation into the accusations was incorporated into the investigation called "Lava Jato," triggered by a union between the Brazilian Public Prosecutor's Office, the Federal Police, and the Supreme Federal Court; the numbers involved in 2018 were: 193 corruption-instituted allegations, 100 accused persons, and seven criminal actions (Ministério Publico Federal, 2018). Presenting the issue of corruption that has taken proportions in monetary values and number of people involved, in the corruption scheme deflagrated by Operation Lava Jato in Brazil highlights one of the legacies of the mega-events, and it contradicts the expectations created previously when the events were in the embryonic stage. To illustrate, the cities that hosted the World Cup in Brazil, the construction of the stadiums (infrastructure), and the actors mentioned in the investigations of corruption were highlighted (Table 28.4).

However, to build the necessary infrastructure for the mega-events, sampling the 12 stadiums/arenas showed that all were involved in passive and/or active corruption schemes. Public investment exceeded the planned figures (Ministério do Esporte, 2013) in almost all stadiums. Only Arena Castelão, in Fortaleza, managed to remain within the initially budgeted amount, but the complaints indicated that there was a cartel formation by the companies responsible for building the stadiums. It is possible to understand the gap between the planned values and the actual amounts in civil construction; however, in this case, the investigations discovered corruption schemes, and some people were convicted. Thus, all stages were paved or renewed under corruption schemes that alternated between active and passive, as internal actors in the public administration organized the bidding format for the construction of the mega-events' infrastructure, and the allegations led to the identification of schemes between external institutions and public administration actors.

The corruption that deflagrated at the time of the construction of the infrastructure to host the World Cup in Brazil hampered Brazil's image, benefited private interests with the use of public power, and maximized the inefficiency of the results obtained from infrastructure investment (Morris, 1991; Kaufmann and Vicente, 2005; Senior, 2006; Locatelli, Mariani, Sainati, and Greco, 2016). In short, the uncertainty about the 2014 World Cup was due to the delays in the construction needed to host the games, and the popular protests and demonstrations demanding transparency and mobilizing against the mega-events were analyzed as phenomena that negatively impacted the expected results of the 2014 World Cup and 2016 Olympics regarding tourism performance, nationally and internationally. These results impacted the economic expectation and minimized the multiplier effect of the investment.

The participation of Brazilian tourism in the world did not change significantly in percentage terms in the years 2014 and 2016 (UNWTO, 2017; Ministério do Turismo, 2018). The number of tourists that landed in Brazil between 2014 and 2016 went from the historical 5% to about 6%, but this volume, although reduced considering the magnitude of the events, did not significantly affect the participation of Brazilian tourism in the world, which maintained a historical participation of 0.5%. This chapter seeks to demonstrate that these mega-events affected the Brazilian economy, but these effects were not translated into positive aspects that could influence a new characterization of events and tourism in Brazilian economic activity, and it did not change the historical trajectory of the perception of Brazil in the world. What was expected to be "the turn of Brazil in the world" changed into a certainty that, from colonization, we

Table 28.4 Corruption allegations

Host city/stadium	Cost, R$	Allegations
São Paulo/Arena Corinthians	Initial cost: 820 million Final cost: 1080 billion +31.7%	Federal deputy accused of receiving bribes
Rio de Janeiro/ Maracanã	Initial cost: 600 million Final cost: 1.2 billion +100%	Former governor and president of the State Audit Court accused of receiving bribes
Brasília/Arena Mané Garrincha	Initial cost: 745.3 million Final cost: 1.6 billion +88.2%	Former governors accused of receiving bribes. A cartel determined that the work would be done by the construction company Andrade Gutierrez
Belo Horizonte/ Arena Mineirão	Initial cost: 426.1 million Final cost: 695 million +63.1%	Agreement between contractors would give the work to Andrade Gutierrez, but the plan was not implemented
Salvador/Arena Fonte Nova	Initial cost: 591.7 million Final cost: 689.4 million +16.5%	A cartel determined that the work would be done by the construction company Odebrecht
Recife/Arena Pernambuco	Initial cost: 529.5 million Final cost: 532.6 million +0.6%	A cartel determined that the work would be done by the construction company Odebrecht
Fortaleza/Arena Castelão	Initial cost: 623 million Final cost: 518 million −15.2%	A cartel determined that the work would be done by the construction company Queiroz Galvão
Manaus/Arena Amazônia	Initial cost: 515 million Final cost: 660.5 million +28.2%	Bribe payment to former governors of Amazonas
Natal/Arena das Dunas	Initial cost: 350 million Final cost: 417 million +14.2%	Senator accused of receiving bribes to facilitate loans
Cuiabá/Arena Pantanal	Initial cost: 454.2 million Final cost: 646 million +25.5%	Former governor of Mato Grosso accused of receiving bribes
Porto Alegre/ Arena Beira-Rio	Initial cost: 130 million Final cost: 366 million +181.5%	A cartel determined that the work would be done by the construction company Andrade Gutierrez, involved in the investigations concerning other stadiums
Curitiba/Arena da Baixada	Initial cost: 184 million Final cost: 354 million +92.4%	Conviction for bribe payment

Source: The authors, adapted from Ministério do Esporte (2013) and national media in 2018

inherited "the current shape of our culture; the rest was plastic matter, which subjected poorly or well to this form" (Holanda, 2015).

The literature about mega-events explains they have positive impacts, but also negative externalities and social costs, where corruption and lack of transparency are probably among the most documented practices (Gursoy et al., 2017). The Brazilian case was no different; corruption was triggered, and there are countless lawsuits in the Lava Jato operation. However, the 2014 FIFA World Cup and the 2016 Olympic Games proved capable of boosting tourism in

Brazil. Regardless of the content of the news and the numbers released, the fact is that Brazil has achieved expressiveness in national and international media and has been the subject of debates, studies, discussions, and academic motivations around the world.

Conclusion

The conclusion of this chapter reveals three characteristics regarding the "impacts of corruption in Brazilian tourism," inserted in three analytical dimensions: the economic dimension, with a conceptual analysis regarding the multiplier effect of investment; the institutional/legal dimension, presenting the theoretical context of the construction of the Brazilian nation-state along with the criminalization of corruption; and, finally, the socio-economic dimension of tourism, discussing the impacts of corruption from the perspective of tourism growth in the mega-events of the 2014 World Cup and the 2016 Olympics.

In the economic dimension, the analyzed data did not present significant values that demonstrated an economic boost resulting from the mega-events. The numbers analyzed in the light of contemporaneity and from a historical perspective did not reveal a growth consistent with the conceptual indication, nor did the events alter the participation of Brazilian tourism in the world context. This result makes it impossible to verify the multiplier effect of the economic investment in tourism owing to its macroeconomic character. In this sense, specific studies with an empirical approach to microeconomic data could verify the changes and results of the relations established between the economic agents involved, for example in the hotel sector and in the bars and restaurants sector, activities that boosted the national economy.

The institutional/legal dimension, presented for understanding the formation of the rights, duties, and obligations of Brazilian society by the Federal Constitution of 1988, was the highlight in this chapter because, in presenting the criminal classification of corruption, it elucidated the meaning of the misconduct committed by members of the public administration, passive corruption, and, in relations established with institutions from the private sector, active corruption. The investigation, control, and criminalization bodies demonstrated a certain degree of effectiveness in investigating the accusations, advancing in the analysis of the facts found, and, where appropriate, convicting those involved.

Regarding the socio-economic dimension of tourism, the acts of corruption disseminated intensely by digital and printed media that imputed an image of systemic corruption in Brazil deconstructed the image of the "Brazil" brand in the world propagated before the mega-events. The expectation of receiving a large volume of tourists with the potential to return more often to Brazil and of boosting Brazilian tourism was not met. The figures show a growth in tourist flow, but less than the worst forecasts, because, in relation to world tourism, the numbers did not move from the historical mark of 0.5%. The most optimistic view about this legacy is the perception that at least Brazilians could get to know and experience the multicultural effervescence of foreign visitors in the 12 host cities, cultural memories that were crystallized in the memories of the World Cup and the Olympics.

It is possible to conclude that there will always be a positive aspect to be addressed and discussed in relation to the literature on the impacts of tourism. However, this study found that the Brazilian economy in the period analyzed was really stop-and-go, with periods of growth and retraction. The same was not found for the numbers on tourism, which remained practically constant. The stop-and-go movement of tourism numbers was expected by researchers and professionals of this economic activity that, once again, stood on the fringes of conceptually forecasted benefits.

References

Almeida, M. V. (2009) 'Matriz de Avaliação do Potencial Turístico de Localidades Receptoras,' *Revista Turismo em Análise*, 20(3), pp. 541–563.

Amado, A. (2000) 'Limites monetários ao crescimento: Keynes e a não-neutralidade da moeda,' *Ensaios FEE*, pp. 408–409. Available at: http://revistas.fee.tche.br/index.php/ensaios/article/view File/1960/2339%5Cnhttp://revistas.fee.tche.br/index.php/ensaios/article/viewArticle/1960.

Araujo, J. T. (1998) 'Modelos de crescimento de inspiração keynesiana: uma apreciação,' *Estudos Econômicos*, 28(1), pp. 5–32.

Aron, R., and Bath, S. (2008) *As etapas do pensamento sociológico*. São Paulo: Martins Fontes.

Ball, F., Ibañez, J., and Picardi de Sastre, M. S. (2003) *Multipliacador Turístico*. San Juan Bosco. Available at: www.aaep.org.ar/anales/works/works2003/Ball_Ibanez_Picardi.pdf (accessed April 16, 2018).

Beni, M. (2006) *Política e planejamento de turismo no Brasil*. Aleph. Available at: http://livraria.folha.com. br/livros/lazer-e-entretenimento/politica-planejamento-turismo-brasil-mario-1095302.html (accessed April 16, 2018).

Beni, M. C. (2006) *Análise estrutural do turismo*. 11th ed. Editora Senac São Paulo. Available at: https://www. livrariacultura.com.br/p/livros/viagem/atividade-economica/analise-estrutural-do-turismo-116256 (accessed April 16, 2018).

von Bertalanffy, L. (2008) *Teoria geral dos sistemas: fundamentos, desenvolvimento e aplicações*. Vozes. Available at: www.estantevirtual.com.br/livros/ludwig-von-bertalanffy/teoria-geral-dos-sistemas/341571820 (accessed February 22, 2018).

Betty, M. (1975) *Planejamento no Brasil*. São Paulo: Perspectiva. Available at: www.estantevirtual.com.br/ apoenacultural/betty-mindlin-lafer-planejamento-no-brasil-999826473 (accessed April 20, 2018).

Bobbio, N., Bovero, M., and Versiani, D. B. (2000) *Teoria geral da política : a filosofia política e as lições dos clássicos*. Campus. Available at: www.livrariacultura.com.br/p/livros/ciencias-sociais/ciencias-politicas/ teoria-geral-da-politica-3035820 (accessed April 23, 2018).

Boullón, R. C. (1985) *Planificación del espacio turístico*. Editorial Trillas.

Brasil (1988) 'Constituição da República Federativa do Brasil,' *Texto constitucional originalmente publicado no Diário Oficial da União de 5 de outubro de 1988.*, 2016, p. 496. doi: 10.1007/s13398-014-0173-7.2.

Bresser-Pereira, L. C. (1995) 'É o Estado capaz de se autorreformar ?' pp. 11–20. Available at: www. bresserpereira.org.br/papers/2011/11.36.Estado_capaz_autoreformar.pdf (accessed April 23, 2018).

Bresser-Pereira, L. C. (2017a) 'Estado, Estado-Nação e formas de intermediação política,' *Lua Nova: Revista de Cultura e Política*, (100), pp. 155–185.

Bresser-Pereira, L. C. (2017b) *The Political Construction of Brazil: Society, Economy, and State since Independence*. Boulder, CO: Lynne Rienner.

Cabral, A. M. (2009) *Jonas Rezende: o poeta da fé*. 1st ed. Rio de Janeiro: Mauad X. Available at: https:// books.google.com.br/books?id=3qwQBAAAQBAJ&pg=PT109&lpg=PT109&dq=Santo+Agostinho+ corrupção+coração&source=bl&ots=g_J8qDhgNp&sig=1JivRwd0Hb4f6Tz_ThhIhMoLRb4&hl=pt-BR&sa=X&ved=0ahUKEwiCuYap-t3aAhVJGJAKHUaDCtM4ChDoAQhOMAY#v=onepage (accessed April 28, 2018).

Carvalho, L. C. P. de, and Vasconcellos, M. A. S. de (2006) *Introdução à economia do turismo*. Saraiva.

Churchman, C. W. (2015) *Introdução à Teoria dos Sistemas*. Rio de Janeiro: Vozes. Available at: www. amazon.com.br/Introdução-à-Teoria-dos-Sistemas/dp/8532651313/ref=sr_1_1?ie=UTF8&qid=1519 261794&sr=8-1&keywords=teoria+dos+sistemas+churchman (accessed February 21, 2018).

Cooper, C., Fletcher, J., Fyall, A., Gilbert, D., and Wanhill, S. (2007) *Turismo princípios e práticas*. Bookman. Available at: www.livrariacultura.com.br/p/livros/viagem/atividade-economica/turismo-principios-e-praticas-2178105?id_link=13574&gclid=CjwKCAjwk9HWBRApEiwA6mKWaZVGm1PFLxLuL Xe8xOimcjV2_DSHXfjsr-_QpneupU1P2_jFKX74ahoC9ZwQAvD_BwE (accessed April 16, 2018).

Costa, H. P. (2005) 'Corrupção e improbidade administrativa,' *Revista do Ministério Público - Alagoas*, 15.

Curvello, J. J. a, and Scroferneker, C. M. a (2006) 'A comunicação e as organizações como sistemas complexos: uma análise a partir das perspectivas de Niklas Luhmann e Edgar Morin,' *E-Compos, Brasília*, 11, pp. 1–16.

Dann, G., and Liebman Parrinello, G. (2009) *The Sociology of Tourism : European Origins and Development*. Bingley, UK: Emerald.

Dekkers, R. (2017) *Applied Systems Theory*. Springer. Available at: https://books.google.com.br/books?id =CavNDgAAQBAJ&pg=PA10&lpg=PA10&dq=applied+system+theory&source=bl&ots=7Y5_gDRP1 R&sig=fTRWH1PDV87Vgd7BIqXZ3IIpkwI&hl=pt-BR&sa=X&ved=0ahUKEwi_hOXisbjZAhUJIp AKHZbtAi4Q6AEIXzAF#v=onepage&q=applied system theory&f=false (accessed February 21, 2018).

Evans, P. B., Rueschemeyer, D., and Skocpol,T. (1985) 'Bringing the state back in', in *Bringing the State Back*, p. 406. doi: 10.1017/CBO9780511628283

Fernández, R. A., and Ruff, T. E. (2017) 'Estimacion del multiplicador keynesiano del turismo internacional em Argentina,' *Estudios y Perspectivas en Turismo Volumen*, 26, pp. 248–266. Available at: www. scielo.org.ar/pdf/eypt/v26n2/v26n2a02.pdf (accessed April 16, 2018).

Freyre, G. (2003) *Casa-grande e senzala : formação da família brasileira sob o regime da economia patriarcal*. Global Editora. Available at: www.livrariacultura.com.br/p/livros/historia/historia-do-brasil/casa-grande-e-senzala-722208 (accessed October 24, 2017).

Furtado, C. (2006) *Formação econômica do Brasil*. Companhia das Letras. Available at: www.companhiad asletras.com.br/detalhe.php?codigo=12386 (accessed October 24, 2017).

Giambiagi, F., and Amadeo, E. (1990) 'Taxa de poupança e politica econômica: notas sobre as possibilidades de crescimento numa economia com restrições,' *Revista de Economia Política* , 10(1), pp. 75–90. Available at: www.rep.org.br/pdf/37-4.pdf (accessed April 18, 2018).

Glaeser, E. L., and Goldin, C. D. (2006) *Corruption and Reform : Lessons from America's Economic History*. Chicago, IL: University of Chicago Press. doi: 10.1017/CBO9781107415324.004.

Gursoy, D., Milito, M. C., and Nunkoo, R. (2017) 'Residents' support for a mega-event: The case of the 2014 FIFA World Cup, Natal, Brazil,' *Journal of Destination Marketing & Management*, 6(4), pp. 344–352.

Haider, D. H., Kotler, P., Rein, I., and Gertner, D. (2006) *Marketing de Lugar - Como conquistar crescimento de longo prazo na América Latina e no Caribe*. Brazil: Pearson Prentice Hall. Available at: http:// livraria.folha.com.br/livros/marketing/marketing-lugares-donald-h-haider-1245028.html?tracking_ number=773&gclid=CjwKCAjwq_vWBRACEiwAEReprDNHR2VcQLrl_os0xng1wamCcD_76s7 QkBqJkAgWzHRs3hhAoDS49RoCFqAQAvD_BwE (accessed April 24, 2018).

Hawkins, D. E., Shafer, E. L., and Rovelstad, J. M. (1980) *Tourism Planning and Development Issues*. Washington, CD: George Washington University. Available at: http://demo.libsys.my/cgi-bin/koha/ opac-detail.pl?biblionumber=17810&shelfbrowse_itemnumber=29649 (accessed April 22, 2018).

Hegel, G. W. F. (1968) *Princípios Da Filosofia Do Direito*. São Paulo: Guimaraes. Available at: www. estantevirtual.com.br/maciellivros/g-w-f-hegel-principios-da-filosofia-do-direito-1125859116 (accessed April 23, 2018).

Hobbes, T. (1974) *Leviatã*. São Paulo: Abril Cultural. Available at: www.estantevirtual.com.br/sebolim abarreto/thomas-hobbes-de-malmesbury-leviata-1110003675 (accessed April 23, 2018).

Holanda, S. B. de (2015) *As raízes do Brasil*. Available at: www.companhiadasletras.com.br/detalhe. php?codigo=13938 (accessed October 24, 2017).

IBGE. (2017) 'Ministério do Planejamento, Orçamento e Gestão. Instituto Brasileiro de Geografia e Estatística. Estimativas da população residente no Brasil e Unidades da Federação com data de referência em 1º de julho de 2017,' pp. 1–118.

IBGE/Banco Central. (2018) 'PIB Banco Central 2000 a 2018.' Banco Central do Brasil. Produto Interno Bruto e taxas médias de crescimento. Available at: www.bcb.gov.br/acessoinformacao/legado? url=https:%2F%2Fwww.bcb.gov.br%2Fpec%2FIndeco%2FPort%2Findeco.asp

Jamal, T., and Robinson, M. (Eds.). (2009) *The SAGE handbook of tourism studies*. London: Sage.

Kant, I. (1784) *Universal Com Um Propósito Cosmopolita*. Covilhão: Lusofia Press. Available at: www.lusoso fia.net/textos/kant_ideia_de_uma_historia_universal.pdf (accessed April 28, 2018).

Kant, I. (1989) *A paz perpétua*. São Paulo: L&PM. Available at: www.estantevirtual.com.br/balaiodigital/ immanuel-kant-a-paz-perpetua-1115879480 (accessed April 23, 2018).

Kaufmann, D., and Vicente, P. C. (2005) 'Legal corruption.' Available at: www.worldbank.org/wbi/ governance/pubs/legalcorporate (accessed April 28, 2018).

Kelsen, H. (2009) *Teoria pura do Direito*. São Paulo: Martins Fontes. Available at: www.livrariacultura.com.br/p/ livros/direito/teoria-pura-do-direito-5086788?id_link=13574&gclid=CjwKCAjwiPbWBRBtEiwAJ akcpHGV0GdP6-OqZXh-yaUSM1wR3ET1oxkwg-_Kh_IvOwvwFB9D74faORoCH3QQAvD_ BwE (accessed April 23, 2018).

Keynes, J. M. (1996) 'A teoria geral do emprego, do juro e da moeda,' *Editora Nova Cultural*, pp. 1–23.

Kon, A. (1999) *Planejamento no Brasil II*. São Paulo: Perspectiva. Available at: www.estantevirtual.com.br/ largodacarioca/anita-kon-planejamento-no-brasil-ii-629975353 (accessed April 20, 2018).

Körössy, N. (2008) 'Do "turismo predatório" ao "turismo sustentável": uma revisão sobre a origem e a consolidação do discurso da sustentabilidade na atividade turística,' *Caderno Virtual de Turismo*, 8(2), pp. 56–68.

Limongi, F. (2006) 'A democracia no Brasil: presidencialismo, coalizão partidária e processo decisório,' *Novos Estudos - CEBRAP*. Centro Brasileiro de Análise e Planejamento, (76), pp. 17–41.

Locatelli, G., Mariani, G., Sainati, T., and Greco, M. (2016) 'Corruption in public projects and megaprojects: There is an elephant in the room!' doi: 10.1016/j.ijproman.2016.09.010.

Lohmann, G., and Panosso Neto, A. (2008) *Teoria do turismo*. São Paulo: Aleph. Available at: www.edit oraaleph.com.br/informativo/teoriaturismo/cadastro_Teoria do Turismo.doc

Machado, M. R. (2015) 'Crime E/Ou Improbidade? Notas Sobre a Performance Do Sistema,' *Revista Brasileira de Ciências Criminais*, 112, pp. 189–211.

Mainwaring, S. (1993) 'Democracia Presidencialista multipartidária: o caso do Brasil,' *Lua Nova: Revista de Cultura e Política*. CEDEC (28–29), pp. 21–74.

Marques, R. B. (2015) *Trabalho escravo contemporaneo e Estado capaz no Brasil*. Fundação Getúlio Vargas SP.

Mello, J. M. C. (1997) *O Capitalismo Tardio*. São Paulo: Brasiliense. Available at: www.estantevirtual. com.br/livrariadidatica/joao-manuel-cardoso-de-mello-o-capitalismo-tardio-6-edicao-1093657152 (accessed April 20, 2018).

Ministério do Esporte. (2013) 'Matriz de Responsabilidades Consolidada,' pp. 10–13.

Ministério Publico Federal. (2018) 'A Lava Jato em números - STF,' pp. 1–4.

Morin, E. (2007) *As duas globalizações: complexidade e comunicação uma pedagogia do presente*. 3rd ed. EDIPUCRS. Available at: www.travessa.com.br/as-duas-globalizacoes-complexidade-e-comunicacao-uma-pedago gia-do-presente/artigo/8c798056-8666-405c-aaea-57f64dba6fb4 (accessed April 16, 2018).

Morris, S. D. (1991) *Corruption and Politics in Contemporary Mexico*. Tuscaloosa, AL: University of Alabama Press.

Ministério do Turismo. (2018) *Anuário estatístico de turismo – 2017*. Available at: file:///C:/Users/fast analia/ Downloads/Anuario_Estatistico_Turismo_2017.pdf

Neves, C. E. B., and Neves, F. M. (2006) 'O que há de complexo no mundo complexo? Niklas Luhmann e a Teoria dos Sistemas Sociais,' *Sociologias*, (15), pp. 182–207.

Oliveira, R. R. (2015) 'J.J. Rousseau e o drama da historia humana,' *Revista de Filosofia* , 42(132), pp. 25–60.

OMT. (2003) *Guia de Desenvolvimento do Turismo Sustentável, Organização Mundial de Turismo*. Bookman. Available at: www.wook.pt/livro/guia-de-desenvolvimento-do-turismo-sustentavel-organizacao- mundial-de-turismo/53354 (accessed April 16, 2018).

Pablo Gonnet, J. (2015) 'Durkheim, Luhmann y la delimitación del problema del orden social,' *Revista Mexicana de Ciencias Políticas y Sociales*, 60(225), pp. 285–310.

Paiva, M. das G. (1989) 'Possibilidades e riscos do crescimento do turismo no nordeste,' *Revista de Administração Pública*, 23(1), pp. 64–70.

Panosso Neto, A. (2010) *O que é turismo*. 1st ed. São Paulo: Editora Brasiliense. Available at: www.livraria cultura.com.br/p/livros/viagem/o-que-e-turismo-22299923 (accessed April 16, 2018).

Partidário, M. R., and Jesus, J. (2003) *Fundamentos de Avaliação de Impacte Ambiental, Universidade Aberta*. Available at: www.bertrand.pt/livro/fundamentos-de-avaliacao-de-impacte-ambiental-maria-do-ros ario-partidario/188114 (accessed April 16, 2018).

Pearce, D. G. (1981) *Tourist Development*. Harlow, UK: Longman.

Pearce, D. G. (2012) *Frameworks for tourism research*. Wallingford, UK: CABI.

Prado Júnior, C. (2011) *Formação do Brasil contemporâneo : colônia*. Companhia das Letras. Available at: www.livrariacultura.com.br/p/livros/historia/historia-do-brasil/formacao-do-brasil-contempora neo-22999815 (accessed 24 April 2018).

Quirino, C. N. G., and Sadek, M. T. A. (2003) *O pensamento político clássico : Maquiavel, Hobbes, Locke, Montesquieu, Rousseau*. São Paulo: Martins Fontes.

Ribeiro, D. (1995) 'O povo brasileiro,' *São Paulo: Companhia das Letras*, p. 467. Available at: http://cole gioarco.net/o povo brasileiro parte 1.doc

Rose Ackerman, S. (2006) *International Handbook on the Economics of Corruption*. Cheltenham, UK: Edward Elgar.

Rousseau, J.-J. (2011) *Do Contrato Social*. São Paulo: Penguin Companhia das Letras. Available at: www. livrariacultura.com.br/p/livros/filosofia/do-contrato-social-22491057 (accessed April 28, 2018).

Ruschmann, D. van de M. (1997) *Turismo e planejamento sustentável: a proteção do meio ambiente*. Papirus Editora. Available at: https://books.google.com.br/books/about/Turismo_e_planejamento_sustentável. html?hl=pt-BR&id=kvK5ujzbZdIC&redir_esc=y (accessed April 16, 2018).

Sampaio, S. (2013) 'Estudar o turismo hoje: para uma revisão crítica dos estudos de turismo,' *Etnografica*, 17(1), pp. 167–182.

Sancho, A., and Rodriguez Corner, D. M. (2001) *Introdução ao turismo*. Roca. Available at: https://books. google.com.br/books/about/Introdução_ao_turismo.html?id=EpbphLuS1LIC&redir_esc=y (accessed April 16, 2018).

Senior, I. (2006) *Corruption – The World's Big C: Cases, Causes, Consequences, Cures.* London: Institute of Economic Affairs, in association with Profile Books.

Souza, J., and Mattos, P. (2007) *Teoria crítica no século XXI.* Available at: www.annablume.com.br/loja/product_info.php?products_id=969&osCsid=fepbaq56u55j4rgpmkd398isr2 (accessed April 23, 2018).

Stabler, M., Papatheodorou, A., and Sinclair, M. T. (2010) *The Economics of Tourism.* Abingdon, UK: Routledge.

Tácito, C. (1999) 'Moralidade Administrativa,' *Revista de Direito Administrativo*, 218, pp. 1–10.

Tobin, J. (1986) 'O futuro da economia keynesiana,' *Pesquisa e Planejamento Economico*, 16(2), pp. 237–250.

Transparency International. (2017) *Corruption Perceptions Index 2017.* Available at: www.transparency.org/news/feature/corruption_perceptions_index_2017#research (accessed April 28, 2018).

United Nations. (2003) *UN Guide for Anti-Corruption Policies.* New York: United Nations. Available at: www.unodc.org/corruption.html (accessed April 28, 2018).

United Nations. (2004) *United Nations Handbook on Practical Anti-Corruption Measures for Prosecutors and Investigators.* Vienna: United Nations. Available at: www.unodc.org/pdf/crime/corruption/Handbook.pdf (accessed April 28, 2018).

United Nations. (2015) *National Anti-Corruption Strategies: A Practical Guide for Development and Implementation.* New York: United Nations. Available at: www.unodc.org/documents/corruption/Publications/2015/National_Anti-Corruption_Strategies_-_A_Practical_Guide_for_Development_and_Implementation_E.pdf (accessed April 28, 2018).

UNWTO. (2016) *UNWTO Tourism Highlights*, 2016 ed., p. 140. doi: 10.18111/9789284418145.

UNWTO. (2017) *Annual Report 2016 World Tourism Organization.* doi: 10.18111/9789284418725.

Wada, E., Amikura, L., and Vilkas, A. (2018) 'A falácia da hospitalidade : quem cuida do anfitrião em megaeventos esportivos?' *Pasos Revista de Turismo y Patrimonio Cultural*, 16(1), pp. 135–146.

Weber, M. (2004) *Economia e sociedade : fundamentos da sociologia compreensiva.* University of Brasília. Available at: http://livraria.folha.com.br/livros/sociologia/economia-sociedade-fundamentos-sociologia-compreensiva-1088469.html (accessed April 23, 2018).

Weber, M. (2008) 'Escritos políticos'. WMF São Paulo: Martins Fontes. Available at: www.wmfmartinsfontes.com.br/produto/1331-escritos-politicos (accessed April 23, 2018).

Weffort, F. C. (2006) *Os clássicos da política : Burke, Kant, Hegel, Tocqueville, Stuart Mill, Marx.* Ática. Available at: www.livrariacultura.com.br/p/livros/ciencias-sociais/ciencias-politicas/classicos-da-politica-os-v2-1833165 (accessed April 23, 2018).

Weffort, F. C. (2008) *Os clássicos da política.* Ática.

PART VI

Technology and tourism impacts

29

SMART TOURISM ECOSYSTEM IMPACTS

Beykan Çizel and Edina Ajanovic

Introduction

Developments in the sphere of information and communication technologies (ICT) have always had the power to induce changes in both the tourism demand and supply sides, all with the aim to facilitate the satisfaction of constantly increasing travelling needs. The latest transformation in the industry can be seen with the introduction of smart technologies, which have changed the way some tourist segments understand and participate in tourism activities. On the other hand, tourism, in all its complexity, serves as an inspiration for further development in smart technology application as tourist movements, interaction between tourists, locals and natural and cultural heritage at destinations, governance of tourist regions, as well as a complex network of business relations occurring in the tourism and hospitality industry represent a suitable context to implement the latest technological achievements. Indeed, companies that directly or indirectly offer services related to the tourism sector have throughout history tried to follow ICT developments. Stakeholders in this sector were among the first to adopt these developments, creating corporate web pages, upgrading these into more user-friendly and responsive ones, engaging and managing customers' relations through various social media channels, as well as adopting automation and Internet-based technologies for successful management of operational and marketing activities and strategic management. This was the case with airlines, hotels, online travel agencies, meta-search engines and many other entities that were evolving and adopting their business activities to suit to the challenges that e-tourism development introduced. The e-tourism concept was adopted widely in all segments of tourism destinations and industry (Buhalis, 2003). Technology was mostly being used in innovations with a significant impact of development on the tourism industry (Hjalager, 2010).

The latest ICT developments led to the introduction of smart technology and smart places, which have been recognized as a cause for a paradigm shift within the tourism industry (Buhalis, 2015). This chapter has the aim of providing a theoretical view of the effects that smart technologies have had on tourism, as well as of how smart tourism is shaping tourist experiences and the supply side of the industry. In the first part of the chapter, definitions of smart city and smart tourism systems/destinations will be reviewed, and common principles among these will be derived. In addition, the main technological pillars of smart urban and touristic areas will be briefly presented. The second part will be devoted to how technology has shaped the tourist experience and what the potential is of smart technology uses in this context. Next, new approaches to marketing in the scope of smart tourism destinations will be presented, as well as how the smart technology paradigm may affect companies on the tourism supply side as well as challenges at destinations. Finally, this chapter will finish with some concluding implications as well challenges that different stakeholders are facing when dealing with smart technologies and transition towards smarter systems.

Smart cities and smart tourism systems/destinations

There are a large number of research papers that provide comprehensive and commonly cited definitions of smart cities, their main requirements and goals (Harrison et al., 2010; Caragliu, Del Bo, and Nijkamp, 2011; Thite, 2011; Dameri, 2013; Piro, Cianci, Grieco, Boggia, and Camarda, 2014; Albino, Berardi, and Dangelico, 2015). In its essence, a smart city is a creative area that nurtures the creative culture and economy by investing in quality of life. This emphasis on creativity will open up the possibility to generate and attract the most knowledgeable and creative workers to live and continue their activities in the smart city area (Thite, 2011). In this way, through their creative potential, smart cities are able to achieve a competitive advantage over their rivals by constantly nurturing the flow of creative people and practices inside their boundaries. One of the main goals of smart cities is sustainability or advocation of economic growth that will be based on wise management of natural resources. According to Caragliu et al. (2011), this may be through investment in human capital, adequate level of governance and infrastructure that will support the dissemination of valuable information. Human capital, infrastructure/infostructure and information are seen as the three main pillars on which the smartness of these cities should be based (Komninos, Pallot, and Schaffers, 2013). However, there is a necessity for intelligent governance consisting of clearly defined subjects with the ability and allowance to create rules and policies (Dameri, 2013) that will lead to the accomplishment of the smart city's sustainable vision. Synergy between various actors inside the city (both creative human capital attracted to the city and residents who live in these areas) in order to enhance the quality of life can be established through use of modern information and communication technologies (Meijer and Bolívar, 2015). What is common to all the smart city definitions is that they emphasize the use of modern ICT and systems that should be embedded into the city's physical infrastructure, together with social and business infrastructures, in order to leverage the collective intelligence of the city (Harrison et al., 2010).

After analyzing various definitions of smart cities that are commonly mentioned in the tourism research papers on this topic, it may be concluded that the main goal of smart urban areas is to enhance the quality of life of their citizens by following these main principles: creativity, sustainability and synergy among the city's stakeholders through intelligent governance and pervasive use of latest ICT (Figure 29.1).

As a follow-up to the smart city development, both theoretical and practical research interest in smart tourism has emerged (Buhalis and Amaranggana, 2014). In order to fulfill the goal of more efficient and sustainable urban development, the smart city assumes that citizens should be directly involved in the process of co-creation of products and services in the relevant area (Bakıcı, Almirall, and Wareham, 2013). However, besides the effect that the potential introduction of smart technology may have on the everyday life of the people who live in cities, the effects of visitors coming from outside the borders of these cities are still present as locals will continue their interaction with them. In touristic destinations, tourists get to interact with each other and the natural and cultural heritage at the destination, as well as with locals. Inside smart

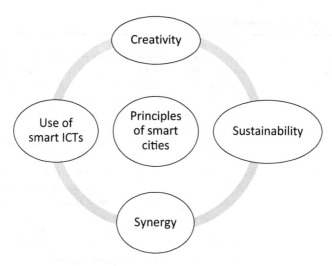

Figure 29.1 Main principles of smart cities

cities, this interaction is a source of inspiration for innovation in delivering products and services that will be useful for both parties. Therefore, it is necessary to collect, store and analyze the data coming from tourist visits to smart cities, or, as Guo, Liu and Chai (2014) stated, "informatization" of tourism should take place in smart cities. After data collection, smart cities should work on deriving meaningful predictions for the potential use of city resources in the tourism context. This is one of the main reasons why the "smart" topic in the tourism context has become one of the most popular and interesting ones. From the literature on smart tourism applications, it can be seen that there is a clear link between smart cities and smart tourism systems or smart destinations. Some of the most common definitions of smart tourism are presented in Table 29.1).

Corresponding to the main goal of smart cities to enhance their citizens' quality of life, the primary focus of smart tourism systems is to enhance the touristic experiences of visitors to these cities. In order to fulfill this goal, investment in human and social capital (Lamsfus and Alzua-Sorzabal, 2013), as well as synergy between various stakeholders at destinations (Buhalis and Amaranggana, 2014), is necessary for the sustainable development of tourist areas and delivery of an enhanced experience for both visitors and local people. Another strong link between smart cities and smart tourism systems/destinations lies in their firm statements about the importance of state-of-art ICT. Zhang et al.'s (2012) definition put greater emphasis on the technological aspects of smart tourism destinations as platforms where the use of the latest ICT, such as AI, cloud computing and the IoT is vital for the collection and management of information. After comparison of the definitions of smart cities and tourism, it can be concluded that four main principles of smart cities – creativity, sustainability, synergy between stakeholders through intelligent governance and pervasive use of ICT – can be transferred to the context of smart tourism systems or smart destinations. These principles should be followed to collect, create and exchange information in order to manage and deliver intelligent products and services leading to enriched real-time tourist experiences.

Considering that smart ICT is considered both the principle and the tool in governing smart cities, the main concepts about smart technology used in these aspects will be explained in the following.

Table 29.1 Review of smart tourism definitions

Authors	Definitions of smart tourism
Gretzel, Werthner, Koo and Lamsfus (2015, p. 560)	A smart tourism system takes advantage of smart technology to create, manage and deliver intelligent touristic services/experiences, characterized by intensive information sharing and value co-creation
Lamsfus and Alzua-Sorzabal (2013, p. 19)	A smart tourism destination is one in which investments in human and social capital, traditional transport and modern ICT communication infrastructure meet the social, cultural, economic, leisure and personal needs of visitors
Lopez de Avila (2015)	A smart destination is an innovative tourist destination, built on an infrastructure of state-of-the-art technology guaranteeing the sustainable development of tourist areas, accessible to everyone, which facilitates visitors' interaction with and integration into their surroundings, increases the quality of the experience at the destination, and improves residents' quality of life
Buhalis and Amaranggana (2014)	A smart tourism destination requires stakeholders to be dynamically interconnected through technological platforms in order to collect, create and exchange information that can be used to enrich tourism experiences in real time
Zhang, Li and Liu (2012)	Smart tourism is defined as an ICT-integrated tourism platform that integrates tourism sources and ICT, such as artificial intelligence (AI), cloud computing and the Internet of Things (IoT), to provide explicit information and satisfactory services to tourists based on the development of innovative mobile communication technologies
Buhalis (2015)	A smart tourism destination successfully implements smartness which is fostered by open innovation, supported by investments in human and social capital, and sustained by participatory governance in order to develop the collective competitiveness of tourism destinations and to enhance social, economic and environmental prosperity for all stakeholders
Perfetto, Vargas-Sánchez and Presenza (2016, p. 252)	The main aim of smart tourism is to develop information and communication infrastructure and capabilities so that it can improve management/governance, facilitate service/product innovation, enhance the tourist experience, as well as improve competitiveness of tourism companies and destinations

Technological basis of smart cities and destinations

Studies that were interested in defining some aspects of "smart" in modern tourism literature usually refer to the work of Gretzel, Sigala, Xiang and Koo (2015), who presented it as a buzz word about sensors, big data, open data and new ways of connectivity and exchange of information. Basic knowledge on some of these smart technologies will be provided in the following.

Smart technology

According to Debnath, Chin, Haque and Yuen (2014), smart technology refers to self-operative and corrective systems that require little or no human intervention, consisting of sensors and command and control units allowing them to sense, process, control and communicate (p. 48). Levels of smartness of technology may vary, and so not every smart device can reach the highest level of autonomy. This was put forward by Derzko (2007), who identified six levels of smartness for technology (see Figure 29.2):

1 Adapting or modifying behavior according to the environment
2 Sensing in terms of ability of technology to provide awareness of things
3 Inferring or drawing conclusions based on observations
4 Learning from previous experiences
5 Anticipating what to do next
6 Self-organizing.

Smart objects have the ability to: be identifiable (anything identifies itself), to communicate (anything communicates) and to interact (anything interacts) among themselves, building networks of interconnected objects, or with end-users or other entities in the network (Miorandi, Sicari, De Pellegrini and Chlamtac, 2012). Understanding the basics of smart objects is important as they are vital for conceptualization of the IoT concept that is inevitable in a smart city and/or tourism context.

Internet of Things

The IoT is a comprehensive term implying the existence of a wide variety of "things" and "objects" with embedded identification, sensing and/or actuation capabilities which allow them to interact and cooperate with other objects towards a common goal (Atzori, Iera and Morabito, 2010; Miorandi et al., 2012). Among these "things" in the context of tourism literature, we can read about radio-frequency identification tags, sensors, kiosks, mobile personal phones and other similar devices, cameras, medical devices, the Web, as well as other similar data-acquisition systems, including social networks (Harrison et al., 2010). In order to assure the success of IoT systems, it is necessary to develop Internet technologies that will evolve from just connecting end-users to the Internet into a technology that will allow interconnection between two physical objects as well as these objects and humans. As a result, a global network of interconnecting

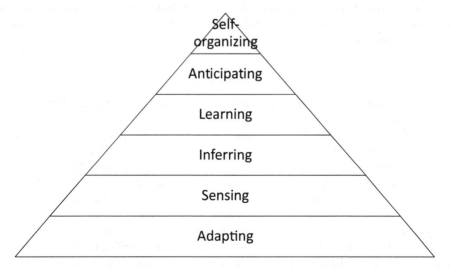

Figure 29.2 "Smartness" levels of technology

objects will be established. At the same time, it is also important to use the set of supporting technologies necessary to establish this network, and the set of services and applications that have the ability to balance physical and virtual dimensions, creating new business markets and opportunities (Atzori et al., 2010).

According to Chui, Löffler and Roberts (2010), use of IoT in the context of smart tourism systems can be seen in: (1) information on and analysis of tourist locations and behavioral patterns so that presence-based advertising and payments can be implemented and 2) automation and control in terms of numbers of visitors, the carrying capacity of heritage sites, and so on (Wang, Li and Li, 2013).

Cloud technology

When introduced in the IT industry, cloud computing was seen as the technology that has the potential to revolutionize the way in which the Internet and information systems operate (Sharif, 2010). The US National Institute of Standards and Technology provided the most comprehensive definition of cloud computing, describing it as "a model for enabling ubiquitous, convenient, on-demand network access to shared pool of configurable computing resources (e.g. networks, servers, storage, applications and services) that can be rapidly provisioned and released with minimal management effort or service provider interaction" (Mell and Grance, 2011, p. 2). Cloud computing is also being transformed into a model where users access services based on their requirements, regardless of where the services are hosted or how they are delivered, meaning that it can be considered as a traditional utility such as water, electricity, gas or similar (Buyya, Yeo, Venugopal, Broberg and Brandic, 2009). The goal of this new computing world is to develop software that can be easily reached through the Internet by millions of consumers. This leads to a decrease in installment costs, which are usually high with desktop-based software, and users are obliged to pay just for accessing these services. Cloud computing services can provide seamless, convenient and quality-stable technology support for the user (Buyya et al., 2009), with these services being provided in three forms: infrastructure as a service, platform as a service and software as a service (Miller and Veiga, 2009; Sultan, 2010). The reason why cloud computing was being considered an important aspect of smart tourism systems is that it represents the realm or dimension where data collected with smart devices and objects can be stored and used as the basis for future prediction analysis and decision-making activities.

Artificial intelligence

The analysis of this interconnected information stored in the clouds must yield new insights that drive decisions and actions towards improvement of systems' process outcomes, organization and industry value chains. In smart tourism areas, use of intelligent IoTs, data warehouses and cloud computing will lead to the collection of data that will contribute to the generation of rich, real-time intelligence about tourists' needs and responses to them. In their review on tourism recommendation systems, Borras, Moreno and Valls (2014) listed the studies where these systems were using some of the AI techniques such as: *intelligent autonomous agents* that can analyze the user's behavior, learn about their profile and derive proactive recommendations; automatic *planning* and scheduling recommendations in a certain period of time; *optimization* in terms of offering a detailed timetable of the visit according to the opening hours of the site; *clustering* or classifying tourists with similar characteristics; inferring the preferences of the users through *approximate reasoning* methodologies; deducing users' preferences through *reasoning procedures*; and representation and reasoning of tourism domain knowledge through *ontologies* (Borras et al., 2014, pp. 7370–7371).

After a review of the most common definitions and basic technological concepts used in the context of smart areas, the main characteristics of smart tourism ecosystems (STEs) will be described, as through this concept tourism researchers in this field were trying to capture all of this technological knowledge and provide explanations and understanding of its use in complex tourism systems.

Main characteristics of smart tourism ecosystems

In the current tourism literature, one of the most comprehensive approaches to explaining the smart tourism destination (STD) is the one that sees it as an ecosystem (Gretzel, Werthner et al., 2015; Perfetto et al., 2016). When conceptualizing STEs, Gretzel, Wethner et al (2015) proposed a shift from a tourism business-centric ecosystem to one that includes a variety of "species." Besides tourists on the demand side and tourism suppliers, which were always seen as elements of tourism systems, local consumers, tourism intermediaries (travel agencies and tour operators), companies providing supporting services (banking, insurance, telecommunications), social media platforms and media (Facebook, TripAdvisor, Airbnb), government agencies and NGOs, tourist and residential infrastructure (pools, park, museums) are all considered as "species" inside the STE (Gretzel, Wethner et al., 2015, p. 560). These tourism ecosystems may be considered as smart business networks, the main characteristic of which is their openness, as new elements can easily enter the system and contribute to its success. At the same time, information is easily accessible and shared among the various elements of the system.

Perfetto et al. (2016) proposed a conceptual model of a smart industrial tourism business ecosystem (SITBE) by combining knowledge from complexity theory, business ecosystems and smart tourism. This model was mainly proposed for the purposes of the industrial system. However, as it can be used for any tourist ecosystem, the authors named it the Smart Tourism Business Ecosystem (p. 258). This model can be examined at different levels, such as:

- *Local level*, which includes core businesses or, in the case of tourism, suppliers and other business-oriented actors that connect through smart technology in order to create new and enhanced services
- *Intermediary level*, which will use related elements inside the business ecosystem such as stakeholders, markets, competition, and government agencies. On this extended enterprise level, according to Perfetto et al. (2016), customers, second-layer suppliers and standard-setting bodies, trade associations, unions, universities and other research bodies are found. All these players should form a coalition in order to provide a platform for protecting and preserving tourist resources through encouraging participation among different stakeholders and enabling interaction and co-creation in order to achieve a "common interest."
- The third level is the *global level*, with emphasis on external elements influencing the ecosystem: international competition and international markets.

In their study on conceptualizing the core components of smartness and how these are connected to co-create value in smart tourism destinations, Boes, Buhalis and Inversini (2016) used the service-dominant logic that posits the collaboration among different actors towards value creation (Vargo and Lusch, 2008). The results of this study suggest that the mere integration of technology infrastructure within a tourism destination, which is considered hard smartness (Harrison et al., 2010), will not be sufficient for a tourism destination to become a smart one. Besides the apparent presence of technology, Boes et al. (2016) derived four additional soft smartness components that should be present at the destination: innovation, social capital, human capital and leadership. Therefore, it can be concluded that a destination that is simply technologically well equipped will not achieve smartness in its functioning; it is necessary to incorporate tourists, governments and suppliers in its functioning. Tourists and locals should share their interactions and impressions about the destination, service providers should work together and share information in order to be able to deliver enhanced experiences, and governments should be in charge of the organization and management of dynamics inside the virtual ecosystems.

Hunter, Chung, Gretzel and Koo (2015) put forward the notion of the soft power of smart tourism, which is based on encouragement rather than the use of force, with the source of power being in possession of critical capabilities or resources. The emergence of e-tourism has emphasized the soft power of international tourism as now, through virtual reality and augmented reality, destinations have the opportunity to promote their sociocultural and natural heritage and customs. In addition, use of the latest ICT systems allows for increased interactivity and communication among different stakeholders who can work together towards building a stronger destination image. At the same time, this information is available to visitors, locals, government institutions and other partners, which may bring enhanced smart destination experiences.

In the scope of the STE concept, special emphasis is placed on the fact that tourism consumers also posses resources vital for the successful management of STDs. Smart tourists can organize themselves and interact between each other and local citizens in order to create new products and values for mutual financial and experiential benefits (examples are user-sharing platforms such as Uber or Airbnb). Resources that they produce and exchange in this context are data, which have a significant quality in the construction of a successful STD eco-system. Therefore, it can be useful to have a deeper understanding of how tourism experiences are changed with the use of technology, the level of that technological use, as well as the willingness of tourists to use smart devices during travel.

Towards smart tourism experiences

The relationship between technology and tourism experiences was assessed in the study by Neuhofer, Buhalis and Ladkin (2014), who adopted a holistic approach towards discovering the types of technology used in experiences and how its intensity determines these experiences. In addition, they provided an explanation of what constitutes technology-enhanced tourism experiences and what their levels are. In order to address this issue, the authors used the technology-enhanced tourism experiences framework proposed by Neuhofer and Buhalis (2012), which combines conventional tourism experiences, multiple ICTs and experience co-creation to produce as its outcome the technology-exchanged experience in all stages of the tourism consumption process.

Technologies that are mainly used by tourists range from interactive websites, ordering systems and mobile platforms, to diverse social media channels (Facebook and Twitter) and mobile applications that can have a supplementary role in supporting the tourism experience, or they can be an integral part of the experience in becoming the experience itself. This study claimed the existence of several types of technology-enhanced experience by linking different levels of technology use (low technology, technology use and technology core) with intensification of co-creation. There are four types of traditional tourism experience, with low levels of technology use and co-creation. Experiences in which technology plays a more important role may be derived as follows:

Technology-enhanced co-creation experience: this occurs at company–consumer level, where technology is used to enhance the quality of its core service with the data obtained in the interaction with the customer.

Technology-enhanced multiplier co-creation experience: this is the case where not only are customers included in the co-creation process, but, through social network technology, other stakeholders are involved in this process as well.

Co-created technology experience: this is where technology is the core element of the experience, whereas co-creation is provided through personalization and interaction with the company.

Technology-empowered multiplier experience: this experience type requires technology as the core part of the experience throughout the whole tourist consumption process while allowing for a multiplier level of co-creation. This type of experience may be considered as the one that should be delivered at smart tourism destinations.

Neuhofer et al. (2014) derived the tourist experience hierarchy which depicts four levels of experiences in terms of technology and respective increase in co-creation: conventional, technology-assisted, technology-enhanced and technology-empowered experiences. Understanding the different types of tourist experience as well as the effects of technology in these experiences will be useful for evaluating the current position of companies aiming at providing services to tourists and, at the same time, providing insights into how they can achieve competitive advantage. In the vision of future use of IoT systems, users will be provided with always-responsive situated services, composed in real time to respond to the specific tourist need and accounting for the context (Miorandi et al., 2012). As a result, this will lead to technology-empowered experiences representing the result of successful optimization efforts in providing tourists with their desired services.

One of the most researched concepts in recent ICT-related tourism research regarding tourist consumption and experience in the smart tourism context is about the use of customers' mobile devices. Mobile phones are considered as "catalysts" and "travel buddies" that are able to enhance tourists' experience (Lalicic and Weismayer, 2016). Especially as these mobile devices evolve and become smart, the research interest in their effect on the tourism consumption process is increasing. Smartphones are nowadays the most popular and accessible sensor devices, with various functions that can be useful for potential travelers. These can be used at all stages of tourism consumption for different purposes, such as: logistical, or searching for locations of interest during a trip; relational through use of social media; informational or exploring touristic opportunities available at a destination; and entertainment through playing games or watching video content (Campbell and Kwak, 2011). Wang, Xiang and Fesenmaier (2014) have provided a similar categorization in the tourism context: facilitation, communication, information search and entertainment. The same authors provided a description of the main changes that the use of smartphones has brought into everyday life such as: increased communication with family and friends through text messaging and online social networking, support in filling free time, more information searches, and users becoming more "tech-savvy" as they explore and learn about new apps and technology and give up using laptops and desktop computers for small tasks (Wang, Xiang and Fesenmaier, 2016).

Considering the changes that smartphones have brought into people's everyday life, it is understandable why they have become one of the inevitable mobile devices that they use while traveling. Use of smartphones during travel should be observed through complex interactions between contextual factors, cognitive beliefs, previous experiences and everyday use, which all have great potential to transform tourist experiences (Wang et al., 2014). Passion about use of smartphones while traveling was studied by Lalic and Weismayer (2016), who found that the perceived socialness of these devices significantly affects passionate behaviour and affective outcomes. Passionate use of smartphones and all the changes it has brought in everyday use have the potential to bring value in all stages of travel consumption:

1   fast and easy search engine opportunities in the travel anticipation and planning phase,
2   use at destination where desired locations can be easily found or capturing moments at destination through video or photos that can be shared in real time through online social networks,
3   easy retrieval of desired content in returning-from-travel phase, and
4   memorizing preferences in recollecting and new travel anticipation phase.

One of the biggest effects of smartphones is the fact that there is no need for advanced planning, and changes of plans are facilitated (Fotis, Buhalis and Rossides, 2011; Wang et al., 2014).

Besides their wide use and all the benefits that smartphones have brought to tourism-related activities, there are still arguments that mobile phone use can alter tourist experiences in that it may actually cause disengagement and disembodied experiences (Gretzel, 2010). As a consequence, tourists may lose the sense of place and miss having a more concrete, one-to-one interaction with other tourists and locals. Concerns about the use of smartphones while on holiday were also found in Dickinson, Hibbert and Filimonau's (2016) study conducted in the context of campsites. Here, the authors pointed out that tourists and visitors like to disconnect while on holiday owing to the desire to get away from their everyday routine and usual business interaction through mobile apps.

New marketing approach in smart tourism

Considering tourists' wide use of digital technologies throughout the whole tourism consumption process, as well the potential of these technologies to shape the tourist experience, there was a necessity to introduce a new marketing approach for the smart tourism context. This approach was presented in the conceptual work of Buhalis and Foerste (2015), which brought together a range of social media, context-aware and mobile marketing strategies and combined them to create a comprehensive "SoCoMo" marketing framework. More profound information in the SoCoMo marketing context comes from users, product suppliers, as well as big data collected from a wide range of sensors inside one smart tourism destination. SoCoMo is short for "social context mobile," which comprises context-based marketing, social media and mobile devices. Contextual information gains importance owing to the IoT technology that allows collection of big data from a wide range of sensors in real time and has the power to affect the tourist experience while on site. It combines different aspects of social, location and proximity as well as mobile marketing to bring about opportunities for co-creation through the interrelation of personal information and content and dynamic interaction with the users' context.

The benefits of this marketing concept are numerous as tourism companies and destinations can now work together with customers on the co-creation of tourism products and services.

SoCoMo marketing strategies are ideal for tourists because they are usually unfamiliar with the local environment and conditions and they are open to any recommendations regarding service suppliers, as long as they are going to be delivered with the enhanced tourism product and experience. Marketers can help travelers cope with unexpected situations in the destination, such as bad weather, heavy traffic or even accidents and emergencies by providing them with suggestions for alternative routes, activities and sights. This information will be value-added and will allow tourists to make better-informed and more spontaneous travel-related decisions while at a destination. When they realize the benefits of this information and its role in the creation of a memorable tourist experience, the desire for more SoCoMo applications in the future will be established.

How smart destinations, hotels and attractions can be

In their work, Della Corte, D'Andrea, Savastano and Zamparelli (2017) were evaluating how smart the cities in the scope of their research were by examining the connection between six destination components that the authors adopted and six dimensions of smartness proposed by Cohen (2014). On one side in the methodological framework there were six As of a destination: attractions, access, amenities, assemblage, accommodation and anciliary services; on the other side, there were Cohen's (2014) six dimensions that compose the smart city wheel: smart economy, smart government, smart people, smart living, smart environment and smart mobility. After analyzing each of the four case destinations, Della Corte et al. (2017) proposed a matrix in which these cities could be placed, based on whether they were scoring high or low on systemic organization and the experiential approach variables. Accordingly there are four types of city:

Untrue smart cities: those that declare they are smart but score low in both experiential and systematic approach;

Time-honored cities: those where the main emphasis is on use of technology but they neglect the experiental components of innovation;

Anarchical smart cities: these are the opposite of the time-honored ones as they are innovative in marketing terms but lack a systematic approach;

Avant-garde smart cities: those that are innovative in both experiential and systematical terms.

Conceptual work on smart tourism was extended from the destination level to the level of a single sector inside the tourism industry. This was the case with the hospitality sector, as Buhalis and Leung (2018) proposed a framework for smart hospitality that should include three layers: network, cloud-data and AI layers. The network layer assumes investment in infra- and infostructures that will allow connection between systems of a hotel's business partners as well as sensors that should collect important data from the hotel's environment. An intelligent hospitality network should be based on the collection and transmission of data that will promote sustainable practices throughout the hotel, be used as an important element in the co-creation process, as well as establish a flow of data among hotel and business partners that will minimize human error. The cloud-data layer should represent a virtual place where big data coming from internal sources (reservations, guest records, cost analysis, and internal statistics) and the external context (external macro-environment, such as economic, political and environmental data, as well as nearby event profiles) can be stored in order to be used for future comprehensive business analysis. Big data collected in the cloud will be essential for an effective decision-making process as well as in the creation of different prediction scenarios towards the optimization of business activities in hospitality. These intelligent analyses, predictions and decision-support activities will be conducted in the third, AI, layer.

It is believed that the future of hotels in smart destinations will lie in their ability to adapt their business operations to modern ICT developments and establish new marketing approaches and visions so that they can become fully effective elements and important "species" inside STEs. The structure should be compatible with the open structure of smart business networks and compatible with other elements of the STE, which may represent their direct or indirect partners, customers and local as well as governmental institutions that are to define the rules and manage the dynamics inside this system.

Following the propositions for the use of the main smart tourism technologies, as well as service-demand logic model, Wang, Li, Zhen and Zhang (2016) investigated smart tourism attractions as being ones that feature co-creation processes, well-connected and well-informed services, diverse and personalized products, better value for money and time, social and technological engagement, efficient communication and management together with multiple smart tourism devices (Wang, Li et al., 2016, p. 311). They also derived 28 items grouped into eight categories that are considered important aspects of the smart tourist attraction: "smart information systems," "intelligent tourism management," "smart sightseeing," "e-commerce system," "smart safety," "intelligent traffic," "smart forecast" and "virtual tourist attraction" (Wang, Li et al., 2016, p. 317).

The above three frameworks derived in the context of smart tourism destinations, hotels and touristic attractions can be used in future empirical studies that are intended to address the level of "smartness" of different stakeholders inside smart tourism systems.

Conclusion

The strength of smart tourism lies in its soft power and soft smartness components and not just in its use of highly sophisticated technologies. A soft smartness approach will focus on human capital from the tourist-centric perspective where smart tourist attractions should offer the right smart devices and services that best fit the needs and preferences of visitors (Wang, Li et al., 2016). Only by understanding visitors' needs and preferences and including them as part of the smart touristic attraction will it be allowed to reach its full smart potential. In order to benefit most from smartphone usage, tourism and hotel marketers should work on defining tailor-made travel-related applications that will suit the needs of potential customers and, at the same time, have the possibility to induce the affective feelings derived from mobile device use. However, prior to putting emphasis on developing smartphone-compatible applications, it is necessary to understand the preferences of potential visitors and whether they are interested in using their smartphones while on holiday, and at what level. Therefore, smart planning on what devices could be the best choice for the technology-enhanced travel experience will be of vital importance. In this context, a constructivist approach to research into the tourist experience, evolving through advances in mobile and connected technology and the destination's and tourists' ability or willingness to use such technology, is needed (Hunter et al., 2015).

It is necessary for all the stakeholders at a destination to raise awareness of the extension of the Internet or Web into the physical dimension as covered by IoT. It will be of great importance to understand the vision and opportunity that IoT brings in terms of enlightening the linkage between digital and physical entities through appropriate ICT, allowing the emergence of new applications and services (Miorandi et al., 2012). Following the work of Della Corte et al. (2017) on how one smart city can become a successful smart destination, it is necessary to establish a systematic approach to structuring the tourist offer as well as an experiential approach in terms of building a strong and positive brand image. It will start the circle of increased positive image that will lead to a better quality of life for both local residents and tourists, in an atmosphere that fosters the collaboration of different stakeholders in co-creation of value that will again affect the urban image of the city and close the circle of this effect.

As can be concluded from the current tourism literature, SoCoMo marketing is considered an innovative and powerful approach in the co-creation of tourist experiences (Buhalis and Foerste, 2015). Use of mobile context-based social network applications will bring about a revolution in understanding and collaboration among tourism organizations in terms of how they will conceptualize their marketing strategies, communicate them and actualize their activities. This is where the importance of big data comes into play, and greater understanding of what benefits aggregated data may bring is crucial. In this context, tourism companies should invest in technologies and interaction with their customers through social media channels that will collect data from both internal and external environments that will help in profiling consumers within a particular context. Mining big data can create a comprehensive picture of the consumer context, and current and previous data can be compared so that better predictions of consumers' behavior can be made and work can be done on creating contextualized products and services that will suit the anticipated customers' needs. Aggregation of data that can be useful for definition of customized services can be done at both single-company and destination levels.

However, there are many challenges that are being faced in the attempts to shift towards a smart tourism paradigm and apply it to its full potential. Some of these challenges are related to use of IoT, cloud computing, AI, and so on. As intelligent systems capture information about their environment and users, this information can be highly personal, which implies the emergence of ethical issues on privacy protection (Michael, Fusco, and Michael, 2008). In addition, there are many challenges that cloud technology has to face, such as questions of security, lack of measurement standards for cloud-provided services, interoperability of cloud services with legacy systems, and resistance of employees to learn and use cloud-based software (Miller and Viega, 2009). These issues and challenges are transferred into the context of smart tourism destinations as well (Gretzel, Werthner et al., 2015). In addition, one challenge is to set up a tourism destination system based on self-organization and interaction (Perfetto et al., 2016), which may be problematical because of the complexity of the systems and difficulty of establishing a system where there will be no need for external control.

One of the challenges in attempts to conceptualize smart tourism systems is the fact that there are a significant number of travel-related companies, such as hotels, airlines, travel agencies and other stakeholders, that do not meet some of the minimum technological requirements of the modern age. Correspondingly, the shift towards SoCoMo marketing will represent a hard-to-achieve challenge if some crucial changes in their future business visions are not made. In order for the idea of smart cities and smart tourism to become more than a utopian view of how the future urban and touristic areas should look, it is necessary to raise awareness among various stakeholders at destinations of the benefits that technological development may bring. It will be important to understand the new travel experiences which are induced, enhanced or empowered by the use of technology. Better understanding of technology-enhanced tourism experiences may help tourism companies to evaluate their current position in the market and provide them with a good opportunity to gain competitive advantage. Therefore, more empirical research should be done so that the vision of future smart tourist destinations and systems can be concretized and provide firm guidelines for a revolutionary business shift among those SMEs that are still not investing enough in their technological infrastructure.

References

Albino, V., Berardi, U., & Dangelico, R.M. (2015). Smart cities: Definitions, dimensions, performance, and initiatives. *Journal of Urban Technology*, 22 (1): 3–21.

Atzori, L., Iera, A., & Morabito, G. (2010). The internet of things: A survey. *Computer Networks*, 54 (15): 2787–2805.

Bakici, T., Almirall, E., & Wareham, J. (2013). A smart city initiative: The case of Barcelona. *Journal of Knowledge Economy*, 4 (2): 135–48.

Boes, K., Buhalis, D., & Inversini, A. (2016). Smart tourism destinations: Ecosystems for tourism destination competitiveness. *International Journal of Tourism Cities*, 2 (2): 108–124.

Borras, J., Moreno, A., & Valls, A. (2014). Intelligent tourism recommender systems: A survey. *Expert Systems with Applications*, 41: 7370–7389.

Buhalis, D. (2003). *eTourism: Information Technology for Strategic Tourism Management*. London: Pearson (Financial Times/Prentice Hall).

Buhalis, D., & Amaranggana, A. (2014). Smart tourism destinations. In Z. Xiang & I. Tussyadiah (Eds.), *Information and Communication Technologies in Tourism* (pp. 553–564). Cham, Switzerland: Springer.

Buhalis, D. (2015). Working Definitions of Smartness and Smart Tourism Destination. http://buhalis. blogspot.co.uk/2014/12/working-definitions-of-smartness-and.html (accessed May 2, 2018).

Buhalis, D., & Foerste, M. (2015). SoCoMo marketing for travel and tourism: Empowering co-cration of value. *Journal of Destination Marketing & Management*, 4: 151–161.

Buhalis, D., & Leung, R. (2018). Smart hospitality – Interconnectivity and interoperability towards an ecosystem. *International Journal of Hospitality Management*, 71: 41–50.

Buyya, R., Yeo, C.S, Venugopal S., Broberg J., & Brandic I. (2009). Cloud computing and emerging IT platforms: Vision, hype, and reality for delivering computing as the 5th utility. *Future Generation Computer Systems*, 25: 599–616.

Campbell, S.W., & Kwak, N. (2011). Mobile communication and civil Society: Linking patterns and places of use to engagement with others in public. *Human Communication Research*, 37: 207–222.

Caragliu, A., Del Bo, C. & Nijkamp, P. (2011). Smart cities in Europe. *Journal of Urban Technology*, 18 (2): 65–82.

Chui, M., Löffler, M., & Roberts, R. (2010). The internet of things. *McKinsey Quarterly*, 2: 1–9.

Cohen, B. (2014). The Smartest Cities in the World 2015: Methodology. www.fastcompany.com/ 3038818/the-smartest-cities-in-the-world-2015-methodology (accessed May 2, 2018).

Dameri, R.P. (2013). Searching for smart city definition: A comprehensive proposal. *International Journal of Computers & Technology*, 11 (5): 2544–2551.

Debnath, A.K., Chin, H.C., Haque, M.M., & Yuen, B. (2014). A methodological framework for benchmarking smart transport cities. *Cities*, 37: 47–56.

Della Corte, V., D'Andrea, C., Savastano, I., & Zamparelli, P. (2017). Smart cities and destination management: Impacts and opportunities for tourism competitiveness. *European Journal of Tourism Research*, 17: 7–27.

Derzko, W. (2007). Smart Technologies. Presentation at Ontario Centers of Excellence Discovery 07 To NEXT, Toronto, Ontario, May 1. http://archives.ocediscovery.com/2007/presentations/ Session3WalterDrezkoFINAL.pdf (accessed May 2, 2018)

Dickinson, J.E., Hibbert, J.F., & Filimonau, V. (2016). Mobile technology and the tourist experience: (Dis)connection at the campsite. *Tourism Management*, 57: 193–201.

Fotis, J., Buhalis, D., & Rossides, N. (2011). Social media impact on holiday travel planning: The case of the Russian and the FSU markets. *International Journal of Online Marketing*, 1 (4): 1–19.

Gretzel, U. (2010). Travel in the network: Redirected gazes, ubiquitous connections and new frontiers. In M. Levina & G. Kien (Eds.), *Post-Global Network and Everyday Life* (pp. 41–58). New York: Peter Lang.

Gretzel, U., Werthner, H., Koo, C., & Lamsfus, C. (2015).Conceptual foundations for understanding smart tourism ecosystems. *Computers in Human Behaviour*, 50: 558–563.

Gretzel, U., Sigala, M., Xiang, Z., & Koo, C. (2015). Smart tourism: Foundations and developments. *Electronic Markets*, 25 (3): 179–188.

Guo, Y., Liu, H., & Chai, Y. (2014). The embedding convergence of smart cities and tourism internet of things in China: An advanced perspective. *Advances in Hospitality & Tourism Research (AHTR)*, 2 (1): 54–69.

Harrison, C., Eckman, B., Hamilton, R., Hartswick, P., Kalagnanam, J., Paraszczak, J., et al. (2010). Foundations for smarter cities. *IBM Journal of Research & Development*, 54 (4): 1–16.

Hjalager, A.-M. (2010). A review of innovation research in tourism. *Tourism Management*, 31 (1): 1–12.

Hunter, W.C., Chung, N., Gretzel, U., & Koo, C. (2015). Constructivist research in smart tourism. *Asia Pacific Journal of Information Systems*, 25 (1): 106–120.

Komninos, N., Pallot, M., & Schaffers, H. (2013). Open innovation towards smarter cities. In *OPEN INNOVATION Yearbook* (pp. 34–41). Luxembourg Publications Office of the European Union.

Lalicic, L., & Weismayer, C. (2016). Being passionate about the mobile while travelling. *Current Issues in Tourism*, 21 (8): 950–963.

Lamsfus, C., & Alzua-Sorzabal, A. (2013). Theoretical framework for a tourism internet of things: Smart destinations. *tourGUNE Journal of Tourism and Human Mobility*, 2: 15–21.

Lopez de Avila, A. (2015). Smart destinations: XXI century tourism. Presented at the *ENTER 2015 Conference on Information and Communication Technologies in Tourism*, Lugano, Switzerland, February 4–6.

Meijer, A., & Bolívar, M.P.R. (2015). Governing the smart city: A review of the literature on smart urban governance. *International Review of Administrative Sciences*, 82 (2): 392–408.

Mell, P., & Grance, T. (2011). The NIST definition of cloud computing. National Institute of Standards and Technology U.S. Department of Commerce Special Publication 800–145. https://nvlpubs.nist.gov/nistpubs/Legacy/SP/nistspecialpublication800-145.pdf (accessed May 2, 2018).

Michael, M.G., Fusco, S.J., & Michael, K. (2008). A research note on ethics in the emerging age of überveillance. *Computer Communications*, 31 (6): 1192–1199.

Miller, H.G., & Veiga J. (2009). Cloud computing: Will commodity services benefit users long term? *IT Professional*, 11 (7): 57–59.

Miorandi, D., Sicari, S., De Pellegrini, F., & Chlamtac, I. (2012). Internet of things: Vision, application and research challenges. *Ad Hoc Networks*, 10: 1497–1516.

Neuhofer, B., & Buhalis, D. (2012). Understanding and managing technology enabled enhanced tourist experiences. In *The 2nd Advances in Hospitality and Tourism Marketing & Management Conference*, Corfu, Greece, May 31–June 3.

Neuhofer, B., Buhalis, D., & Ladkin, A. (2014). A typology of technology-enhanced tourism experience. *International Journal of Tourism Research*, 16: 340–350.

Perfetto, M.C., Vargas-Sánchez, A., & Presenza, A. (2016). Managing a complex adaptive ecosystem: Towards a smart management of industrial heritage tourism. *Journal of Spatial & Organizational Dynamics*, 4 (3): 243–264.

Piro, G., Cianci, I., Grieco, L.A., Boggia, G., & Camarda, P. (2014). Information centric services in smart cities. *The Journal of Systems & Software*, 88: 169–88.

Sharif, A.M. (2010). It is written in the cloud: The hype and promise of cloud computing. *Journal of Enterprise Information Management*, 23 (2): 131–134.

Sultan, N. (2010). Cloud computing for education: A new dawn? *International Journal of Information Management*, 30, 109–116.

Thite, M. (2011). Smart cities: Implications of urban planning for human resource development. *Human Resource Development International*, 14 (5): 623–631.

Vargo, S.L., & Lusch, R.F. (2008). Service-dominant logic: Continuing the evolution. *Journal of the Academy of Marketing Science*, 36 (1): 1–10.

Wang, D., Li, X., & Li, Y. (2013). China's "smart tourism destination" initiative: A taste of the service-dominant logic. *Journal of Destination Marketing & Management*, 2: 59–61.

Wang, D., Xiang, Z., & Fesenmaier, D.R. (2014). Adapting to the mobile world: A model of smartphone use. *Annals of Tourism Research*, 48: 11–26.

Wang, D., Xiang, Z., & Fesenmaier, D.R. (2016). Smartphone use in everyday life and travel. *Journal of Travel Research*, 55 (1): 52–63.

Wang, X., Li, X., Zhen, F., & Zhang, J. (2016). How smart is your tourist attraction? Measuring tourist preferences of smart tourism attractions via a FCEM-AHP and IPA approach. *Tourism Management*, 54: 309–320.

Zhang, L., Li, N., & Liu, M. (2012). On the basic concept of smarter tourism and its theoretical system. *Tourism Tribune*, 27 (5): 66–73.

30

THE ONWARD MARCH OF TECHNOLOGY AND ITS IMPACT ON THE WORLD OF TOURISM

Sagar Singh

Introduction

Technology has been the single most important factor for driving up the volume of tourists internationally and within nations all over the world. From the stage coaches of the 18th century to the railway steam engines and steam ships, to diesel motors and the automotive internal combustion engine, to electric vehicles and cable cars in high mountain areas, technology has made accessible what was remote and a no-man's land for potential tourists. But how has this impacted the mindset of would-be tourists, so that world tourism has become the single most important phenomenon in making travel and the mobile world the most important variable in sustainable development? For, tourism (and travel) and development go hand in hand, so that Africa changed from being the Dark Continent to the most colonized one in a couple of centuries, all owing to travel and tourism, and this is now becoming the one factor that has the power to overcome the effects of droughts and famine, if tourism is sustainable and pro-poor. This chapter views the history of technology in travel and tourism, from the engine to artificial intelligence (AI) and how these are shaping how we view the world post-tourism, as all world-views are not the isolated or isolationist views that they were a few centuries ago, but developed with, after, and for tourism, the crucial single factor for influencing which has been technology. The impacts of tourism were, and are, the direct outcome of technology not only for travelling, but also for assessing and experiencing the world with and/or without tourism. This becomes even more clear when we look at countries that have been somewhat left out of the tourism trail and consequently suffer from being considered backward in the world march towards globalization.

A review of technological impacts and tourism

Although it is clear that technology has, by and large, brought those who were geographically far away closer, it is paradoxical that it has also made those who could have developed lasting relationships and hence become closer, more socially distant. But this is the negative impact of transport technology, not all technology. With the development of AI tools and robots, especially in the 21st century, people who felt alienated from their hosts (commercial establishments) have started feeling that they are being given what they had sought but did not get: the personal touch. The second paradox of technology and tourism is just this: AI technology, such as bots that assist in menu selection from far away and then recommend

418

choice restaurants, has ensured that people who once consulted other people (hosts – waiters, residents – or fellow tourists), and thus began sometimes short-lasting relationships that could turn into permanent ones through friendship or through relationship management by hosts of guests, are now becoming alienated by technology that breeds indifference. The most common complaint expressed on social media such as Facebook by people who miss the 'good old days' of tourism is that mobile phones and laptops have become so commonplace and ubiquitous that people, including tourists, are seen constantly bent over their phones, and do not engage in social things such as talking to others, conversing with hospitality staff or even conversing with fellow tourists, including the ones who are in their company. Thus, once again, technology has begun alienating people. Both these two types of alienation can be thought of as the alienation that technology capitalism brings in its wake. It would not be far-fetched to say that, though Marx did not envisage it, his theory of capitalism works even in this sphere (cf. McLellan 1975). The rest of this chapter is devoted to considering the ramifications of these two paradoxes, the place of technology in monetary capitalism, and the impacts of technology as a key ingredient in various capitalisms. Additionally, it will discuss how technology is likely to affect our world-views.

Transport technology and tourism

The explorers of yesteryear saw the world as a magical place, full of strange people, including marauding pirates, head-hunters and cannibal tribes that were a threat to civilized people. Constant and increasing tourism reduced that image to that of a tame world, where every sort of experience, including that of being in a 'dangerous' place, could be bought at a price. Thus the *shikari* (hunter, often a raja or a colonial Britisher) told accounts of his exploits in the jungles of India and Africa, right up to the 1960s, when such tales were received with favour and stirred envy and admiration. So, the character of ace flier James Bigglesworth of the UK's Royal Air Force, created by Captain W.E. Johns, began his journey, before entering the world wars, as a teenage shikari in India. Also, most histories of tourism involve teasing out the exotic just as much as tourists themselves seek the exotic or, at the very least, the anecdotal and hence 'juicy' (see, e.g., Walton 2005, Machin 2016). Thus, in the 2005 panorama of *Histories of Tourism* (Walton 2005), at least five chapters deal with history during or between the two world wars and their associated cultures. Although it is natural for a historian to see the world in this way, a majority of non-historians, excepting dark tourism scholars, would like to see the world minus this view, in which technology and its impacts on tourism sans war is an important omission. Thus, Machin (2016) gives a better insider's view of the development of tourism in Britain seen through the length of its history, from ancient times to the 19th century. Yet the greatest developments have taken place after the creation of the steam engine and the diesel locomotive on rails, through the invention not only of the private automotive or car, but also of macadamized roads facilitating fast passage from one city to another or to the countryside by land; and by far the greatest development, which saw both positive impacts and negative, was the development of air transport, which brought out-of-reach continents to the tourist's doorstep.

The net effects of these developments in transport were the same. Strangers who could have developed into friends – for that is what most tourists, deep down, want: to nurture relationships – remained strangers or even became more so. Human society has developed as a result of social intermixing and interbreeding. If humans are one species or even one race, it is owing to this intermixing, and that could not have come about without tourism. Thus tourism was built into society for thousands of years, not hundreds (see also Lomine 2005; Machin 2016). And it is here that we need to see how rapidly technology changed tourism and society in modern times, upsetting the apple cart of institutionalization of the social process that is tourism (cf. Singh 2003). It is important to recall here the definition of tourism as a social adaptive process given by Singh (2014: 49):

> Tourism and mobility is the human necessity to move across, and stay in, different geographical and/or ecological habitats in order to fulfil physical, social, societal, cultural, psychological, ecological, economic and linguistic needs and wants, and for general adaptation in order to survive and evolve as a race or species.

Thus, adaptation is at the heart of tourism and mobility. Yet, when technology brought strangers (of the sort who were perhaps seen once in 40 years in a remote place) in droves, it made the strange familiar, but in a negative way. Familiarity is said to breed contempt, but it does so where the behavioural process is negative in net effect: the colonial shikaris created some awe and some fear, for they were the rulers. When strangers who brought and bought nothing and meant nothing to the residents started constantly appearing and brought a culture of disrespect (for the tourists, mostly, residents in developing countries were poor, coloured people, for whom they had little respect), familiarity bred contempt. Often, for the poor residents, the tourists were rich but unsympathetic outsiders who flashed money but had none to give the 'real hosts'; tourists appeared to have 'loose morals' and displayed a contempt for local people and their traditional attire, being themselves so very often clad in scant clothes. Although tourism has been called a form of neo-colonialism (Kobasic 1996) and imperialism (Nash 1989), the fault lay not with the tourists or their behaviour: they behaved much as the former colonialists behaved, only 'worse' in that they read and understood local society less even than colonial people did. This did not mean that they did not want to respect local society: it was just too 'foreign' for them to adjust to in the few days they visited it. Thus, technology enabled quick tours to distant lands, and monetary constraints dictated a few days' stay at the most, in which they had little time to adjust and adapt to local culture; what little good could have come out of it was prevented by hotel staff and tour operators showing them glimpses of the land while creating the tourist 'environmental bubble' in such a way that it seemed exotic (precisely because it was alien). The tourists, further, had no stake in learning the local language or customs as their stay was predetermined and short, a result of the peculiar 'technology' of packaged tours. Thus, tourist cultures developed that were remarkably the same, especially when they were packaged (Steward 2005). Tourism is said to have brought about commodification of culture (Greenwood 1989), but is less said to be *itself a commodity*. The alienation was natural, as an essentially social process became a commodity, and the tourists were seen as the culprits (which they may well have been, but largely because an industry sold 'life' to them that way). Thus, what was an essential process of adaptation to different natural and human environs became just a matter of touch-and-go, largely as a result of fast transport to distant lands.

It would be pertinent to point out here what Lomine (2005) has remarked about tourist–host relationships in the past, which underscores the justification of terming residents 'hosts' and tourists as 'guests'. Lomine points out that the Oxford Latin Dictionary defines

> a person who travels around as a *peregrinator*. This substantively etymologically means a person who has gone through lands (*per* meaning through, *ager* meaning land), which suggests quite a long trip rather than a short, local, one-day excursion . . . *Peregrinator* . . . comes from the Latin word *peregrinare*, which has an ambiguous meaning: it means 'to go abroad, to travel' (Cicero, *Brutus* 13, 51) as well as 'to be a stranger'.
>
> *(Lomine 2005: 70–71)*

Lomine remarks on a second important Roman concept of *otium*, which means *productive* relaxation or leisure, and a third term, *hospitium*. The last word has a 'meaning . . . much stronger than hospitality as a kindness in welcoming guests and strangers' (Lomine 2005: 71). It refers to 'the permanent relationship existing between host and guest, the ties of hospitality' (*Oxford Latin Dictionary*, Glare 1968: 807). 'If in the city he is about to visit, there lives a person with whom he happens to be linked by *hospitium* (e.g. because his father had once put up or helped their father), an Augustan traveller is bound to stay at that place, where he will be received with honour' and can stay there for many weeks 'like a prince'. But, 'if ever this person (or someone recommended by them) visits him, he will be obliged to offer the same services' (Lomine 2005: 71–72). The same sort of relationship existed in India in the Himalayas for pilgrims (the example of Lal Baba; see Singh 2004) and exists in the rest of India (and in other countries) between distant relatives and fellow villagers who have someone living in the city. This shows that the basis of the relationship between tourist and host is social rather than that of trade, though the industry has inured travellers to a kind of hospitality where everything comes at a price. This is a result of technology putting a distance between host hospitality-givers and receiver-tourists: someone who just stepped off a jet plane and carries expensive cameras and bags cannot be related to by poor people who serve them. Thus, the jet plane and the car (technology) become symbols of the tourist and signs of alienation. Also, fast transport technology has increased the volumes of tourists in all tourist places of the world and has introduced tourists where there were none. As social relationships of genuine hospitality, as mentioned before, take time to develop, the sheer volume of tourism made possible by technology ensures that the relationships remain fleeting ones; in fact, the tourist him/herself becomes a commodity. This is no wonder, given the steep rise in international tourists alone (not to mention domestic tourism in various countries): up from just 25 million in 1950 to 1,322 million in 2017 (UNWTO 2018).

Recently, while environmentalists have been shouting themselves hoarse about the ill effects of automotives on greenhouse gas emissions and global warming, the USA has backed out of offering the compensation to developing countries (despite the adverse impact of such technology and tourism/travel on the poorest of the poor, who cannot protect themselves from ecological catastrophes resulting from climate change) that Barack Obama's government had promised. Similarly, Australia, under Prime Minister Abbott, had threatened to wash its hands of any deal to help developing countries counter the adverse impact of fossil fuel consumption through better, environment-friendly technology or monetary help. It is important to realize that the lobbies of the pro-fossil fuel industry, mainly the oil and petroleum lobby, have been supporting scientists who argue against the reality of the phenomenon of human-induced climate change, whereas the fact that oil and gasoline contribute to global warning has been known since 1912 (as a newspaper clipping shows; Alan Machin, Facebook communication, 2017).

As a result of growing human-created problems of traffic, efforts to make driving easier and more mechanical and developments in AI have created the self-driving car, which, however, is far from a success as yet. Besides, the social implications of such technology have not been suitable discussed (Hiltzik 2018), although at least 16 companies are in the race to create and sell such cars for huge profits. On March 18, 2018, in Tempe, Arizona, USA, a woman was killed by an Uber self-driving car, and five days later the 'driver-owner' of a self-driving Tesla Model X car on auto-pilot was killed in a crash in Northern California (Mountain View). In 2016, another Tesla car crash in Florida killed the owner when the driverless car hit a truck it could not 'see' (Hiltzik 2018). Such incidents have led to companies such as Uber stopping the experimental testing of such cars in some areas where it had started, such as Arizona, but the profits from such cars are huge, so that one can expect that testing of such cars will continue in the future. Although a lot could be written on how such technology will benefit tourists or tourism, it would be largely theoretical.

However, some points for and against such technology for tourism need to be made. First, the exploitation of tourists by cab drivers would be largely undermined by such a development. Second, if such technology becomes realistically implementable, a lot of traffic in developed countries would become safer, or, at least, its directions in terms of possible accidents would be known. Third, digital money would become more popular, and radio-taxis of the kind Uber and Lyft are promoting would be a great source of ease and comfort to weary travellers. Fourth, in developed countries such as the UK, where the routes can be accurately mapped by computers and geographical information systems, and where the lack of enough suitable signposts often irk travellers, such situations could be a boon for self-driving cars: where it has been shown that signs can provide disinformation to commuting cars, a lack of signs but accurate mapping could lead to success in the enterprise, helping tourists. Fifth, advances in human–machine interaction (such as voice commands) and developments in machine learning, including possible event-decided protocols, can ensure success for such ventures.

On the negative side, such cars can allow the exploitation of tourists by machines, if prepaid amounts are not used. Second, these cars could prove to be a hazard on the road, as recent events have shown. In developing countries such as India, they are nearly impossible to drive safely, owing to the haphazardness of the traffic and the flouting of traffic rules by a lot of people. Third, digital money fraud would become more common through the use of such cars, either by companies or by unscrupulous franchisees. Fourth, experience and testing to date have shown that such cars can be easily misguided by tampered road signs, leading to tourists getting lost. Fifth, as a result of the last, hijacking of cars (and tourists) would be easy. Sixth, accountability is a big and serious issue, especially as regards threat to human life due to accidents and insurance liability in individual cases. Seventh, all in all, this is disruptive technology, and many cab drivers would have to pay the price. Companies would earn a lot of income, while cab drivers would become unemployed, with massive losses including even, unfortunately, suicides as a result of joblessness. This leads us to the area of information and communication technology (ICT) and AI, and the tourism impacts. Although new methods of super-fast low carbon footprint transport, such as the hyper-loop technology of SpaceX, are being devised today, the technology has yet to find an opportunity in developing countries, or even in developed ones, given the logistic problem of space for tubes.

ICT, AI and tourism impacts

ICT has been used in many ways to promote, direct and help tourism. Although fly-by-wire technology and wireless technology in aeroplanes, as well as computerized reservation systems, are well known, new ways are being devised to help solve the problem of tourism and conservation through ICT. Even in India there is discussion about developing smart cities, to which ICT is central. However, in developing countries, the solutions to problems of conservation through ICT in areas either highly visited by tourists or prone to deep-seated problems that a delicate environment or ecology engenders are often not feasible. One reason for this impasse is the lack of ICT developers, most of whom migrate to the USA; a second reason is that ICT depends on computerized machines that, in turn, depend on electricity, which is often not available in remote areas. Yet new ways are being devised by technocrats even as this chapter is being written.

By far the greatest impact that technology has and will have is through AI, which is a special case of ICT. AI and robots have been making the news for the past five years, but especially in the last three years (Finley 2015; *Economic Times* 2016; Boztas 2017), with the commissioning of Connie, a concierge robot developed on IBM Watson software, in use at the Hilton at McLean, Virginia, USA, and Yumeko, a humanoid 'female' robot with long, dark hair in Henn-na Hotel, Japan, as well as Mario in Belgium, a robot that helps with checking into rooms and is said to 'speak' in 19 languages (Pacurar 2017). At the end of 2017, the 'female' robot Sophia made its debut in the sense of being the first non-human to become a citizen of Saudi Arabia. Non-robotic AI systems on their own are also making headlines, such as the IBM Watson-based Ivy from Go Moment that takes care of customers as soon as they check in, helping with room rating and supplying Wi-Fi passwords, rooms with a better view and dinner reservations, among other things; it is used in hotels in the Hilton chain and many others (Pacurar 2017). Although AI has only now earned respect, the foundations of AI go back to the development of artificial neural networks in 1943 and two years later, when Isaac Asimov coined the term 'robotics'; AI really developed with the Turing test, which British computer expert Alan Turing developed in 1950. Yet it was only in 1956 that John McCarthy coined the term 'artificial intelligence', going on to develop LISP programming language, the first for AI. AI is a method of making computers, computer-controlled robots and software 'think' in a manner similar to a human. This 'fact', however, is itself controversial, with opposite camps arguing that AI and robotic systems do not think like humans, but act rationally, and that too with 'limited rationality' (Russell & Norvig 2010: 1020–1025).

Although intelligence can be of many types, including linguistic intelligence, logical-mathematical intelligence, musical intelligence, spatial intelligence, bodily kinesthetic intelligence, intra-personal intelligence and interpersonal intelligence, not all forms are equally amenable to AI. Today, AI has developed in almost all these fields, but is limited where extra creativity is concerned, such as in the composition of music scores or painting or writing poetry, though robots and computer programs have been doing the first of these tasks as well for the past 20 years, with mixed results and equivocal acclaim. AI, like human intelligence, consists of reasoning, learning, problem-solving, perception and linguistic ability (Russell & Norvig 2010). In all of these ways, AI affects tourism and has an impact on tourism experiences.

In the past 30 years, AI and robotics have witnessed a spiralling of interest, with the creation of the intelligent chess-playing program Deep Blue, which defeated the then world champion, Garry Kasparov, in 1997, and, in 2000, when pet robots became commercially available, making it a first in would-be hospitality. Massachusetts Institute of Technology, USA, created Kismet, a robot with a face that can 'show' emotions in the same year, and Nomad was also created, a robot that explored remote regions of the Antarctic, in 2000. Major advances in all areas of AI include significant multi-agent planning, demonstrations of machine learning, data mining, case-based reasoning, (a limited amount of) natural language understanding and translation, and development of vision and virtual reality (Russell & Norvig 2010; Castro, Gelbukh, & Gonzalez 2013). Advances in scheduling, as well, by such organizations as National Aeronautics and Space Administration (NASA, USA), may therefore find applications in creating comforts and logistics for space tourism and hospitality. Besides this, AI is used in computer-based games that are popular all over the world, such as Xbox and the recent Pokémon. AI is also used in software such as TripAdvisor, which is used to help would-be tourists to choose recommended destinations, hotels, restaurants and places for excursions, though there has been some disenchantment with its method of only promoting businesses and disregarding the negative points mentioned by visitors, though it must be added that conflicts of interests exist on both sides of the debate.

AI and robotics have found substantial applications in hospitality other than in hotels. Although robots are being used all over the Western world, currently South East Asian countries such as South Korea (531) and Japan are ahead of European countries such as Sweden

(212) in the number of robots per 10,000 employees used by companies (*Arirang News* 2017). As international tourism to these countries is on the rise, as well as to developed countries (such as the UK, in the case that it leaves the EU; *BBC News* 2017), and as domestic tourism all over the world continues to surge, the use of AI and robots not only in taking up those tasks that are mundane (such as cleaning floors at airports), but also in areas where there is high employment turnover is important. The use of AI and robots is making the carrying-out of such tasks reliable and consistent for visitors, making sure that tourism and hospitality remain positive employers of less skilled people who supplement or complement robots and AI programs (Pacurar 2017; Singer 2016). So, their role is not working against humans, making many people jobless (as it is presumed), but working in tandem and in collaboration with people (Singer 2016). Thus, AI and robotics ensure a positive response to developments in hospitality, though the widest implications of their role, or their application, has not yet been thoroughly mapped (*Arirang News* 2017).

Futurists are warning that robots may take over many tasks from humans, creating joblessness. Whether this may be just a fear (Hintze 2017) or may be a developing reality is open to scrutiny. This could be true for hospitality firms, such as hotels, restaurants, and airlines and airports, and this, therefore, makes it worthwhile studying to find out the extent to which this may or may not be true. For instance, robots are very far from taking over tasks that require creativity and emotions, or emotional intelligence, such as those that require interpersonal skills (including waiting in restaurants). It can be hypothesized that humans can learn from machines and vice versa, and that this reciprocal learning is crucial for further development of AI and robotics in hospitality. A theoretical question is: How much can AI-dependent machines and computers learn from humans, and how much can humans learn from machines? The latter was found to be a viable goal of AI in recent work, such as when the Facebook AI Research (FAIR) team recently found two chatbots conversing with each other in a language that they appeared to have created on their own, which was less intelligible to humans (Wilson 2017). This gave rise to the notion that humans can make machines learn more by "talking" to them in a language that is easier for machines to understand (Wilson 2017). The focus of AI tools such as IBM's Watson is that they are pledged to 'augment, not replace, human intelligence', a view shared by Skyscanner, a tool used to choose airlines (Boztas 2017).

Moreover, AI is increasingly being used by applications (apps) to find the best restaurants for both tourists and those locals (excursionists) who prefer dining out (Finley 2015), with a new device called Luka, much like the apps Yelp and Siri that are used in metropolitan cities such as San Francisco and New York. These AI tools can sometimes be used by conversation-driven interfaces such as Microsoft's Cortana to help the tourist or diner in coming to a decision on what to eat where. Yu and Schwartz (2006) used AI for forecasting tourism demand, with such complex cybernetic tools as fuzzy time-series theory, grey theory, neural networks, genetic algorithms and expert systems. However, little development has taken place in channelling demand in restaurants and hotels through use of AI. Also, IBM's view means that, whether we call it human-assisted machine cognition or computer-augmented human cognition, AI does not mean fewer jobs for people (Woodie 2016; Boztas 2017).

Russell and Norvig (2013) pose a relevant question when they ask: Is AI's traditional focus on higher-level cognitive abilities (such as those used in tourism and hospitality) misplaced? In answer to this, some authors have claimed that perception and motor skills are the most important part of intelligence. It is also argued that 'higher level' capacities are necessarily parasitic, simple add-ons, and that most of evolution and the brain have been devoted to perception and motor skills. Also, AI has found tasks such as game playing and logical inference easier than perceiving and acting in the real world (Damasio 1994; Wilson 2010). This is because, in AI, the theory of intelligence creation is based on intelligent agents that use a precept to understand the environment and then act on it. According to Craik (1943), there are three key steps of a knowledge-based agent: (1) the stimulus must be translated into an internal representation; (2) the representation is manipulated by cognitive processes to derive new internal representations; and (3) these, in turn, are translated into action. However, the second of these steps has been found very difficult when the full environment is to be preconceived, and embodied AI approaches have continued to fail (to create an agent that thinks and reasons 'just like humans', without any external input), largely because the landscapes of possibilities (or domains) that they have to fill in or recreate are too vast (Rusell & Norvig 2010).

However, this does not mean that today, with AI, we cannot create agents that can invent on their own, as the FAIR team found out in 2017. The theoretical questions remain: How can we make machines learn from humans, and vice versa? Can robots and AI systems be made to perceive in such a way that they learn in the same way as humans, or near enough, to make a difference in hospitality and research? Moreover, as Wilson (2010) has argued, following Damasio (1994), 'high-level cognitive capacities are more intertwined with emotion than many had previously assumed' (Wilson 2010: vi). She quotes the author of *Descartes' Error*: 'Emotions and feelings may not be intruders in the bastion of reason at all: they may be enmeshed in its networks, for worse *and* for better' (Damasio 1994: xii; original emphasis). To make a crucial point for this research, Wilson says that, 'cognition and affect, mind and embodiment and the world, high-level expertise and infantile states . . . the attenuation, amplification and management of these affects have been a significant force in AI and cybernetic research from the beginning' (Wilson 2010: viii). This is supported by almost all the latest research on how we learn (Carey 2014), making affect or the emotions an important variable in human–machine and machine–human learning, especially because love and other emotions have been known to play a significant part in perception and tourism/hospitality (Goleman 1995; Merleau-Ponty 1965; Singh 2002). Also, the foremost way in which humans learn involves patterns and even, in the case of language, patterns of patterns (not just semantics and syntactic structures, as argued by John Searle: see Russell & Norvig 2010: 1034).

To this end, the interviewing of the female robot Sophia by journalists shows that robots are still far from being able to carry on intelligent conversations with humans for a long time. However, one of the leading developments in this field, which will have a lot of positive impact on robots and AI being used in tourism and hospitality firms or spaces, is the recognition of emotions in human voices with the help of IBM's Watson AI tool. This tool can differentiate between good humour and anger, irritation and peaceful emotions by analysing rise and fall in tones of the voice. As a lot of good hospitality is about learning about and responding to emotions among customers, this will have a very substantial impact on the use of AI in tourism and hospitality. The question remains: Will we be able to end the alienation of tourist from tourist (important for tourist satisfaction), tourist from host, and host from host (also important, in such relationships as hotel manager and bell-boy, or restaurant captain and waiter) with AI? Or will the end result be further alienation, leading to a fall in the number of tourists?

Conclusion

As management guru Peter Drucker said (and anthropologists agree), 'Technology is not about tools, it deals with how man works' (Drucker 1972: 7). Tourism is a form of social, cultural, intellectual and spiritual capitalism that intermeshes with monetary capitalism owing to workers being part of an industry that runs on money, and the tourist being a typical consumer, whether willing or not. As technology is an essential component of monetary capitalism, other forms of capitalism in tourism get isolated and disavowed, leading to alienation. Alienation of workers from their products is typical of monetary capitalism (Marx 1932), but in tourism we find alienation of the worker *as well as* the consumer from the commodity, and also alienation of the producer (i.e. the tourist is also the producer of the 'commodity' of tourism, while being a consumer of 'tourist products'). Technology plays a central role in tourism by driving up volumes of both international and domestic tourists across the world. The ecological catastrophes that tourism technology brought in its wake are often not clearly documented because it is usually difficult to separate the impacts of visitors or travellers in general (such as commuters, officials, migrants) from those of tourists. But, when tourism is seen in general as a variant of mobility that is essential for the adaptation of the human race to its geographical and ecological habitats, it is clear that it is largely technology that is to blame for the negative impacts, though it is also responsible for some positive ones. In any case, the technological impacts of tourism bring about social alienation: of residents from their land, of workers from the product of their labour, and of tourists from their hosts, who should or could have been their friends. Thus tourism technology acts as an impediment to those very relationships that tourism seeks to build, and, therefore, technology is not the prime mover of tourism. Prime mover theories seek to establish the social or triggering cause of a social phenomenon, whereas history reminds us that the Romans and ancient Indians, as well as the Chinese and all those who belonged to the 'Ancient World' had tourism, though they did not have the same technology. In fact, history tells us that only when we separate the impact of technology on tourism from its social aspects are we able to see the real hospitality relationships that are the building blocks of tourism; hence, technology has merely been a facilitator of modern tourism. The real tourism experience is best analysed by qualitative research into what tourists feel and enjoy, and how. Technology is at best an enhancer of tourism volume; at worst, an impediment to tourists' leisure experiences and a reason for alienation.

References

Arirang News. (2017) New era of robotics [video]. *Arirang News*, S. Korea, July 13.

BBC News. (2017) Weak pound sees surge in tourists visiting UK. Accessed 13 July 2017 at www.bbc. com/news/business-40592623?

Boztas, S. (2017) Automated holidays: how artificial intelligence is affecting the travel industry. Accessed 10 April 2017 at www.theguardian.com/sustainable-business/2017/feb/17/holidays-travel-automated-lastminute-expedia-skyscanner

Carey, B. (2014) *How We Learn*. London: Macmillan.

Castro, F., Gelbukh, A., & Gonzalez, M. (Eds). (2013) *Advances in Artificial Intelligence and Its Applications*, 12th ed. Berlin: Springer.

Craik, K.J. (1943) *The Nature of Explanation*. Cambridge: Cambridge University Press.

Damasio, A. (1994) *Descartes' Error: Emotion, Reason and the Human Brain*. New York: Putnam.

Drucker, P.F. (1972) *Technology, Management and Society*. London: Pan.

Economic Times. (2016) KFC launches first AI enabled outlet in Beijing. Accessed 10 April 2017 at http://economictimes.indiatimes.com/KFC-launches-first-AI-enabled-outlet-in-Beijing/article show/56182644.cms

Finley, K. (2015) App uses powerful AI to find perfect places for you to eat. Accessed on 15 April 2017 at www.wired.com/2015/02/luka

Glare, P.G.W. (1968). *Oxford Latin Dictionary*. Oxford: Clarendon Press.

Goleman, D. (1995) *Emotional Intelligence: Why It Can Matter More than IQ*. New York: Bantam.

Greenwood, D. (1989) Culture by the pound: an anthropological perspective on tourism as cultural commoditization. In V.L. Smith (Ed.), *Host and Guests: The Anthropology of Tourism*, 2nd ed. (pp. 171–185). Philadelphia: University of Pennsylvania Press.

Hiltzik, M. (2018) Self-driving car deaths raise the question: Is society ready for us to take our hands off the wheel? *Los Angeles Times*. Accessed 5 April 2018 at www.latimes.com/business/hiltzik/la-fi-hiltzik-self-drive-20180403-story.html

Hintze, A. (2017) Should we fear the rise of intelligent robots? Accessed 17 April 2017 at www.livescience. com/59802-should-we-fear-intelligent-robots.html?utm = notification

Kobasic, A. (1996) Level and dissemination about academic tourism findings. *Tourism* 44(7), 169–181.

Lomine, L. (2005) Tourism in Augustan society (44BC–AD 69). In J.K. Walton (Ed.), *Histories of Tourism* (pp. 71–87). Clevedon, UK: Channel View.

Machin, A. (2016) *The Beckoning Horizon: Making Sense of Tourism No. 1*. Halifax, UK: Westwood Start.

Marx, K. (1932) *Economic and Philosophic Manuscripts of 1844*. Moscow: Progress.

McLellan, D. (1975) *Marx*. Fontana Modern Masters series. Glasgow: Fontana.

Merleau-Ponty, M. (1965). *The Phenomenology of Perception*. London: Routledge.

Nash, D. (1989) Tourism as a form of imperialism. In V. Smith (Ed.), *Hosts and Guests: The Anthropology of Tourism*, 2nd ed. (pp. 31–47). Philadelphia: University of Pennsylvania.

Pacurar, A. (2017) Can artificial intelligence help the hotel industry? *Accessed* 22 July 2017 at www.cp executive.com/post/can-artificial-intelligence-help-the-hotel-industry

Russell, S., & Norvig, P. (2010) *Artificial Intelligence: A Modern Approach*, 3rd ed. New York: Prentice Hall.

Singer, R. (2016) Robots and artificial intelligence in the hotel industry. *ITB Berlin*. Accessed on 21 July 2017 at www.itb-kogress.de/media/itbk/itbl_dl_de/itbk_dl_de_itb kongress/itbk_archiv_2016/ itb_hospitality_day_3

Singh, S. (2002) Love, anthropology and tourism. *Annals of Tourism Research* 29(1), 261–264.

Singh, S. (2003) Travel and aspects of societal structure: a comparison of India and the United States. *Current Issues in Tourism* 6(3), 209–234.

Singh, S. (2004) Religion, heritage and travel: case references from the Indian Himalayas. *Current Issues in Tourism* 7(1), 44–65.

Singh, S. (2014) Anthropology, tourism and mobility: new directions for research. *The Eastern Anthropologist* 67(1–2), 39–60.

Steward, J. (2005) 'How and where to go': the role of travel journalism in Britain and the evolution of foreign tourism, 1840–1914. In J.K. Walton (Ed.), *Histories of Tourism* (pp. 39–54). Clevedon, UK: Channel View.

UN World Tourism Organization (UNWTO). (2018) 2017 International tourism results: the highest in seven years. Accessed 16 April 2018 at http://media.unwto.org/press-release/2018-01-15/ 2017-international-tourism-results-highest-seven-years

Walton, J.K. (Ed.). (2005) *Histories of Tourism*. Clevedon, UK: Channel View.

Wilson, E.A. (2010) *Affect and Artificial Intelligence*. Washington, DC: University of Washington Press.

Wilson, M. (2017) AI is inventing its own perfect languages. Should we let it? Accessed on 21 July 2017 at www.fastcodesign.com/90132632/ai-is-inventing-its-own-perfect-languages-should-we-let-it?

Woodie, A. (2016) Unleashing artificial intelligence with human-assisted machine learning. Accessed 10 July 2017 at www.datanami.com/2016/03/17/unleashing-artificial-intelligence-human-assisted-machine-learning

Yu, G., & Schwartz, Z. (2006) Forecasting short time-series tourism demand with artificial intelligence models. *Journal of Travel Research* 45, 194–203.

31

SMART TOURISM ECOSYSTEMS' IMPACTS ON TOURISM DESTINATIONS

Erdem Aktaş and Avşar Kurgun

Business ecosystems

Researchers often create new labels by putting old things in different formats. For example, the concept of "core competency" actually means things that an individual or an enterprise is good at. Another example of this is the concept of "cloud computing", which in the past has been referred to as "time sharing". One of the last examples of the desire to create new buzzwords for the business world is valid for the concept of "ecosystem", but the concept of ecosystem has a richer meaning than a typical business buzzword (Hwang, 2014).

Tansley was the first to use the term "ecosystem" (Trudgill, 2007, p. 518). He defined ecosystems as (Tansley, 1935, p. 299):

> [T]he systems so formed which, from the point of view of the ecologist, are the basic units of nature on the face of the earth. Our natural human prejudices force us to consider the organisms (in the sense of the biologist) as the most important parts of these systems, but certainly the inorganic "factors" are also parts – there could be no systems without them, and there is constant interchange of the most various kinds within each system, not only between the organisms but between the organic and the inorganic. These ecosystems, as we may call them, are of the most various kinds and sizes.

The ecosystem analogy is very useful in providing a model for loosely connected business networks. As with biological ecosystems, large, loosely connected networks of entities form business ecosystems (BEs). As with species in biological ecosystems, firms interact with each other in complex ways, and the health and performance of each firm are dependent on the health and performance of the whole. Firms and species are therefore simultaneously influenced by their internal complex capabilities and by the complex interactions with the rest of the ecosystem (Iansiti & Levien, 2002, p. 20).

BEs are inspired by the mechanisms of biological ecosystems, representing networks that try to preserve local specificities, tradition, and culture, and frequently benefit from (local) government incentives. A BE, also sometimes called a digital ecosystem, is similar to a cluster or industry district, although it is not limited to one sector but rather tends to cover the key sectors within the geographical region. In most aspects, BEs simply represent a renaming of the industrial district concept. Namely, differences are subtle and can perhaps be found only in a clearer emphasis on the involvement of a diversity of their actors – the living forces of a region – in addition to companies, and a more intense use of advanced ICT tools to support collaboration. The ICT support is "freeing" these BEs from the boundaries of a geographical region (Camarinha-Matos, Afsarmanesh, Galeano, & Molina, 2009, p. 50). This ICT support also affects the types and roles of stakeholders involved in the complex structure of ecosystems. In addition, this support also leads to an evolution of the border concept for ecosystems.

A BE, like its biological counterpart, gradually moves from a random collection of elements to a more structured community. Think of prairie grassland that is succeeded by stands of conifers, which in turn evolve into a more complex forest dominated by hardwoods. BEs condense out of the original swirl of capital, customer interest, and talent generated by a new innovation, just as successful species spring from the natural resources of sunlight, water, and soil nutrients (Moore, 1993, p. 76). Just like an ecosystem, the BE is a complex adaptive system which is composed of independent main bodies and has no central control. Every enterprise operates in the way of self-adaptation and demonstrates the characteristics of the system through self-organization (Liu & Chen, 2007, p. 1198).

Peltoniemi and Vuori defines a BE as a dynamic structure which consists of an interconnected population of organizations. These organizations can be small firms, large corporations, universities, research centers, public-sector organizations, and other parties, which influence the system (Peltoniemi & Vuori, 2004, p. 13). Peltoniemi and Vuori's definition is important for emphasizing the diversity of ecosystem stakeholders.

Another definition of a BE is a network of suppliers and customers around a core technology, who depend on each other for their success and survival (Hartigh & Asseldonk, 2004, p. 21). The essential characteristic that distinguishes the BE concept from sectors or supply networks is the explicit modeling of the mutual dependence of the actors: when one actor leaves the network, the value of the network for the other actors declines. When a new actor enters the network, the value of the network for all actors rises. Each member of a BE ultimately shares the fate of the network as a whole (Hartigh, Tol, & Visscher, 2006, p. 2).

An important aspect of modeling a BE is to identify and define the components, the relationships between them, and their placement in a specific environment (Galateanu & Avasilcai, 2013, p. 79). A business environment contains various opportunities and different levels of organizations such as industry associations, competitors, and policymakers. All of these organizations have a big impact on industry development, especially at the point of change (Rong, Liu & Shi, 2011, p. 172). The BE could be divided into three levels: policy-related organizations, including government agencies and quasi-government organizations; industry-related organizations such as industry alliances, associations, and supply networks; and firm-level organizations, such as suppliers, competitors, and customers (Rong, Hu, Hou, Ma, & Shi, 2013, p. 276). Internet technologies provide an unlimited opportunity to create links, both within and between these three levels.

Every BE develops in four distinct stages: birth, expansion, leadership, and self-renewal – or, if not self-renewal, death. In reality, of course, the evolutionary stages blur, and the managerial challenges of one stage often crop up in another. There are four stages in many companies over time, across businesses as diverse as retailing, entertainment, and pharmaceuticals. What remains the same from business to business is the process of co-evolution: the complex interplay between competitive and cooperative business strategies (Moore, 1993, p. 76).

Galateanu and Avasilcai (2014, p. 1101) define the BE roles as follows:

- Initiator: This category comprises the elements that have a greater impact on the whole BE. These elements will provide an impulse in establishing the continuous development of the BE and will play a significant role in the value creation process.
- Developer: This role can be assigned to those elements who provide innovation inside the BE, have major importance for BE differentiation, and contribute to value creation by developing new dynamic capabilities.
- Dominator: This is characteristic of those elements of the BE structure that strongly influence the development of growth directions and opportunities identified for the BE.
- Parasitic elements: These are the elements that co-exist with other participants in the BE but do not participate or contribute to value creation and other processes.

The dynamics of business networks have important operational implications for business practitioners. By recognizing their position within the ecosystem – niche player, dominator, or keystone – and pursing strategies appropriate to their role, firms can set realistic expectations for themselves and their investors. By understanding how innovations propagate through the network of firms in an ecosystem, innovative firms can better target their relationships. By understanding the dynamics of integration and niche formation, product architects can create their designs in anticipation of how these will fit into the ecosystem as a whole. Perhaps most importantly, all ecosystem members can better understand their operational challenges, and respond to and synergize with the collective behavior of their ecosystems (Iansiti & Levien, 2002, p. 55).

Smart tourism ecosystem

The term smart describes economic and social developments armed with technology that utilizes sensors, hardware, software, embedded systems, big data, and special connectivity (i.e. Internet of Things (IoT), radio frequency identification (RFID), quick response (QR) code, and near field communication (NFC); Al-Omari & Al-Marghirani, 2017, p. 76). Smartness takes advantage of the interconnectivity and interoperability of integrated technologies to reengineer processes and data in order to produce innovative services, products, and procedures towards maximizing value for all stakeholders (Buhalis, 2005, p. 8). In their research, Boes, Buhalis, and Inversini (2016, p. 117) underpinned the presence of hard smartness and identified four soft smartness components (innovation, social capital, human capital, and leadership) that are critical for developing smart places' ecosystems.

Gretzel, Werthner, Koo, and Lamsfus (2015, p. 561) express the smart tourism ecosystem (STE) model as shown in Figure 31.1.

In the STE portrayed in Figure 31.1, tourist consumers have resources and, because of their ability to tap into the digital ecosystem, can organize among themselves or mingle with the closely related residential consumer species and act like producers (a phenomenon often referred to as the sharing economy). Tourist and residential consumers produce data through social media activities or the use of location-based services and consume data produced by other species or the physical environment, often made palatable through mobile apps. Tourism suppliers or other business-focused species can connect through smart technology and create new service offerings. Data/information are the main food source for STE species, and effectively and efficiently turning it into enriched tourism experiences ensures longevity. Data aggregators are particularly supported by the digital ecosystem and process data to create resources of value to other species. Indeed, telecommunication companies and banking/payment support services

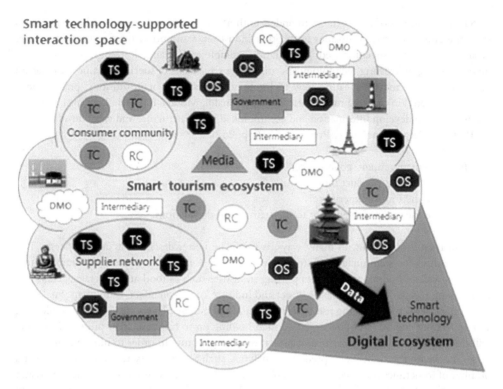

Figure 31.1 Smart tourism ecosystem model

Notes: TC = tourist consumer; RC = residential consumer; TS = tourism supplier; OS = other industry; DMO = destination marketing organization.

represent suppliers from other industries (OS) and are important predators in the STE, but also feed the system with critical information and offer opportunities for enhanced value creation; destination marketing organizations (DMOs) fulfil traditional information brokerage, marketing, and quality control functions, and intermediaries of all kinds facilitate transactions through innovative uses of data and devices (Gretzel et al., 2015, p. 561).

Smart tourism in cities based on the idea of intelligence and smartness is a novel idea which is being adopted by countries worldwide. The results are apparent in terms of the improvements in tourist experiences. However, there are certain implications such as concerns about the privacy of personal data generated by smart devices, owing to overindulgence in technology. If measures are taken to answer all these concerns, the smart tourism idea can bring huge benefits to its stakeholders as well as tourists (Kaur & Kaur, 2016, p. 361). The core function of the smart tourism system is collecting, processing, and exchanging tourism-relevant data within the ecosystem and then feeding it back into the system where it can be used to enhance and improve the functions already in place, or in the creation of new ones (Kauppila, 2016, p. 8). This situation necessitates the development of applications in order to ensure the safety of data belonging to tourists in parallel with smart cities. However, this development alone may not be enough. It is also important to raise awareness about the hazards that will arise when tourists share individual data. For this reason, data security should be considered as a two-way phenomenon. In this context, data requests for intelligent systems should be limited to open principles, and tourists should reach a certain level of awareness on this issue.

STEs are systems of actors (users intended both as customers and citizens, other companies from the same industry, companies from other industries, transport systems and infrastructure, local government, associations, etc.) integrating tangible and intangible resources at the same time: (1) using preexisting technology and institutions as means of successful value co-creation in the short run; and (2) creating new technology (innovation) or institutions (praxis, social rules, values, etc.) in the long run (Polese, Botti, Grimaldi, Monda, & Vesci, 2018, p. 11). Smart tourism aims to develop information and communication infrastructure and capabilities in order to (Perfetto, Vargas-Sánchez, & Presenza, 2016, p. 252):

- Improve management/governance;
- Facilitate service/product innovation;
- Enhance the tourist experience;
- Improve the competitiveness of tourism firms and destinations.

Tourism is an industry but, in many ways, it might be better described as an ecosystem. The players in this ecosystem include – but are not limited to – visitors, governments, tourism businesses, as well as a whole range of supporting industries such as food and beverage, retail, and transportation, which experience the direct and indirect knock-on effects of tourism. Fueled by increasing connectivity and the rise of smart technologies, these players are constantly collecting and generating copious amounts of data – each holding on to bits of a larger puzzle.. Not only will the players gain access to critical data that they may require in order to improve their processes, but, with the right use of predictive analytics, such a cohesive system can also uncover a number of sometimes unexpected, actionable insights that players can act on to generate greater value for their businesses and the ecosystem as a whole (Deloitte, 2016, p. 1). The huge amount of data that is mentioned has a critical value for the global productivity of the tourism industry. These large amounts of data, which will form the key input of the business models to be created in the tourism ecosystem, should be processed quickly and effectively. The outputs will be beneficial for all tourism ecosystem stakeholders, especially tourists and businesses.

An important phenomenon to consider within the context of such STEs is the convergence of information technologies, business models, and tourist experiences. This means new interaction paradigms and new forms of both symbiotic relationships and rivalries (e.g. in the case of Airbnb or Uber) emerge. Another significant element is the ever-greater ability to embed smart technology in the physical environment. Tourism is a geographically based activity that can take great advantage of such technological infrastructure (Werthner, Koo, Gretzel & Lamsfus 2015, p. 556). The new interaction paradigms are both responding to and influencing the differentiated tourist experiences. In this new dynamic environment, businesses that maintain classic business models can be predicted to face great difficulties in staying out of the ecosystem. On the other hand, for new entrepreneurs operating in the ecosystem with new paradigms and business models, continuous improvement and adaptation to this new dynamic environment may come into question.

Consequently, the tourism paradigm is transformed as types of infrastructure-oriented, knowledge-intensive, interoperable, and productive means for sustainable competitive advantage emerge. The first important factor is connectivity methods (e.g., searching, booking, paying, reviewing, and recommending). These methods enable smart city citizens and smart tourism tourists, from outbound tourists (i.e., those leaving their residence country) to inbound tourists (i.e., those arriving in a different country), to find better tourism products and services in a particular context. Second, relationships should be robust in turbulent environments for existing companies to sustain stable tourism business activities. Third, creativity from outsiders or among stakeholders generates disruptive products and services for tourism markets. Finally, productivity indicates an attempt to increase operational excellence in productions between smart city and tourism ecosystems (Koo, Park & Lee, 2017, p. 683).

Smart tourism technologies

The technological revolution experienced by the tourism industry in the last few years has conditioned the behavior of tourism demand, the marketing processes, and the design of the tourism supplied (Bernebau, Mazon, Giner & Baidal, 2016, p. 13). With their growing popularity, constantly improving functionality, and the resulting favorable experiences, smart tourism technologies play an increasingly important role in travel and tourism (Huang, Goo, Num & Yoo, 2017, p. 758). ICT make cities more accessible and enjoyable for both residents and visitors through interactive services interconnecting all local organizations to provide real-time services and use data centrally for better coordination (Buhalis & Amaranggana, 2014, p. 554).

With the support of big data, cloud services, sensors, and ambient ecosystems can collect data dynamically, and decision support systems can support business functions in order to maximize the value for all stakeholders and intelligence. This will enable all actors to develop the collective competitiveness of the entire hospitality ecosystem and co-create value for all stakeholders (Buhalis & Leung, 2018, p. 42). The creation of this value is related to the success of the ecosystem information cycle. At the end of the information cycle of large data that the ecosystem has, it needs to be transformed into knowledge. Information to be obtained should be disseminated to ecosystem stakeholders through feedback methods.

ICT in smart tourism has an instrumental role in driving institutional and structural market changes (Barile, Ciasullo, Troisi, & Sarno, 2017, p. 818). Recently, the adoption of ICT has changed the traditional viewpoint of tourism from conventional towards electronic tourism (e-tourism). Using smartphone-based services to provide smart tourism might be called smart tourism instead of e-tourism. Different technologies have been adopted to support using technology in tourism. For instance, IoT, RFID, QR codes, and NFC are examples of such technologies. In this work, the researchers have chosen QR codes for implementation (Al-Omari & Al-Marghirani, 2017, p. 76). However, it should be remembered that it is important to use these different technologies for holistic applications that will create benefit in the ecosystem. In addition, it is a prerequisite for these technologies to become widespread and for the emergence of new products using these technologies to achieve a sufficient level of basic technological infrastructure and facilities.

Enhancing smart hospitality requires either standardization of data communication or comprehensive interoperable infrastructures that enable automatic data interchange among systems (Buhalis & Leung, 2018, p. 43). The role of technology in tourism can be summarized in the following functions (Sigala, 2018, p.152), as:

- A way of "individual" expression: for example, tourism brands communicating and forming their image, tourists sharing experiences and information to self-construct their social image and identity;
- A decision support tool for firms (e.g., logistics and pricing tool) and tourists (price comparison tools, meta-search engines, recommender systems);
- A market intelligence source for collecting, storing, analyzing, sharing, visualizing, and interpreting big data (characterized by volume, variety, velocity, veracity and value);
- An e-learning tool, evolving education and knowledge management from an instruction-led and self-service paced learning mode to collaborative, constructivism, dialectic, and nowadays open connectivism learning models (e.g., Moocs);

- An automation tool, substituting labor and "predictable" – programmable – tasks (e.g., self-driven cars), but also augmenting labor by informing and optimizing decision-making processes and outputs;
- A game changer, enabling new business models (e.g., cyber-intermediaries, multi-sided markets, sharing economy) and new management practices (open innovation, crowdsourcing, crowdfunding, gamification);
- A transformer of tourism experiences – for example, virtual tours, technology-mediated or augmented tourism experiences;
- A co-creation platform (e.g., review websites, wiki-based tourism guides, peer-to-peer marketplaces) empowering and providing the space, functionality, and connectivity for all tourism actors to actively engage and participate in value co-creation.

Smart destination impacts

Bringing "smartness" into tourism destinations requires dynamically interconnecting stakeholders through different concepts of ICT with tourists (Bosnjak, Sladic, & Luburic, 2017, p. 93). Tourism service providers can develop and extract a multidimensional set of valuable data, known as big data, to create better insight into tourists, to improve services, and to provide related information to tourists (healthcare, safety, etc.). Tourists can use their smart devices to explore a destination and plan their travel based on data analytics (Rotchanakitumnuai, 2017, p. 4). It is essential for ICT infrastructure in smart tourism destinations to be concentrated on both the technological and tourist aspects simultaneously (Sedarati & Baktash, 2017, p. 3). The concentration of full-time tourist information access in terms of tourists, the development of ITC-based tourist goods and services, and the sharing of electronic data create benefits among the tourism ecosystem stakeholders.

The smart tourism experience is rich and efficient in meaning. Visitors are active, vigorous participants in the creation of smart tourism by not only consuming the service but also creating, annotating, or otherwise enhancing the information that constitutes the basis of the experiences – for instance, hashtagging or uploading pictures to social media, and so on. There are many ways to perform smartness as a tourism destination. Referring to the technological aspect, smartness is also shown by the implementation of tourism-related applications that can be used within smart cities' components (Dalli & Bri, 2017, p. 11).

Smart tourism practices have also changed the role of tourists as well as other stakeholders in the ecosystem. With the possibilities provided by smart tourism practices, tourists gradually gain prosumer qualities – for example, planning, announcing, and realizing many organizations that have a tourist value through social media. Alternatively, they provide opportunities for new tourist goods and services, as well as increasing the quality of tourist goods and services through data entry on the Internet. However, more importantly, they are playing a role in the design of tourist goods and services in the intelligent tourism ecosystem, where they have been using intelligent tourism applications extensively.

Stakeholders of intelligent tourism ecosystems will increasingly create more powerful stakeholder integration. This integration will generate a stream of information that is formatted based on Web 4.0 and smart applications. This stream will bring together a fast, flexible, and customized new production approach to the STE that can provide individualized tourist goods and services for all tourists.

The intensive use of that technological infrastructure should lead to the reinforcement of the consumer's perspective, enhancing the tourism experience of visitors in terms of its co-creation and customization, with visitors playing the double role of consumers and producers of data/information. The implementation of technological advances is the back-drop of a smart tourism destination, but this is just the tip of the iceberg. In fact, its marketing rationale and its implications for its governance are equally critical aspects. Without them, its technological dimension would not have any clear direction and would be unable to provide sustainable competitive advantages (Vargas-Sánchez, 2011, p. 181).

One of the significant impacts of STEs on smart cities will be related to the technology carrying capacity. Just as a smart tourism destination's carrying capacity is taken into consideration, this new case must be meticulously addressed, because it is inevitable that the technological infrastructure required by the STE puts an important burden on smart tourism destinations. Besides the multitude of intelligent systems, it is also important for the integration of applications for residents and tourists.

Technological carrying capacity can be overcome in two ways. First, insufficient hardness possibilities are provided (insufficient Internet speed and connection points, smart applications and device incompatibilities, inability to process big data collected by technological infrastructure, etc.). Second, actions such as policy and regulations regarding the use of smart applications in the smart tourism destination cannot respond to the features of applications (Uber applications, use of bitcoins, etc.).

A smart tourism destination should be able to include technological development and develop innovation activities, incorporating capacities, digital spaces, information processing, and tools for these activities, which enable the transfer of technology and knowledge sharing. ICT infrastructures such as cloud computing and the IoT can provide the infrastructure required for the development of a smart tourism destination (Liberato, Alen & Liberato, 2017, p. 8).

Wu, Chen, Wu, and Lytras (2018, p. 2) propose a hierarchical structure framework of smart city systems with levels of complexity ranging from low to high and interconnections and inter-active relationships in five dimensions: the IoT, cloud computing, big data, mobile network, and smart business. The IoT and cloud computing play an important role in gathering data in the intelligent tourism ecosystem. Big data refers to the information stored and processed in cloud computing to be distributed to STE stakeholders. It can be said that the mobile network has a two-way function. First, the mobile network allows tourists to enter data into the intel-ligent tourism ecosystem. The mobile network serves as a channel to provide tourism services, which are the output of STE, to tourists and businesses. Smart can be evaluated in terms of shaping the business models of stakeholders operating in the STE according to this structure. Such businesses should operate with intelligent tourism ecosystem, smart city, and intelligent service-based business models.

Smart tourism destination management has become more complex since current developments in technology have empowered the collective integration of resources for value co-creation by all actors within the smart tourism destination ecosystem. This unique combination of intercon-nected and interoperable technological systems and knowledgeable people enhances the potential for sustained competitive advantage in tourism destinations. To take full advantage of the cur-rent possibilities provided by smartness, destination managers have to integrate the entire range of smartness components and ensure interoperability and interconnectivity of both soft and hard smartness (Boes et al., 2016, p. 117).

The co-development of hard and soft smartness dimensions is important in the quality of smart cities. Hard smartness alone cannot provide the expected results when it develops too much. Hard smartness, representing basic technological infrastructure and practices, collects and distributes data in STEs. On the other hand, soft smartness refers to factors such as policies, regu-lations, and human capital for STEs. The success of the STE is possible with a successful collabo-ration of hard and soft smartness. Soft smartness should play a role as regulator and determinant in the construction of hard smartness. An integration problem determines which policies will be shaped by the technological infrastructure (created with hard smartness).

Bringing smartness into tourism destinations requires dynamically interconnecting stakeholders through a technological platform on which information relating to tourism activities can be exchanged instantly. This integrated platform has multiple touch points that can be accessed through a variety of end-user devices, which will support the creation and facilitation of real-time tourism experiences and improve the effectiveness of tourism resources management throughout the destination at both the micro and macro level. Smart tourism destinations take advantage of: (1) technology-embedded environments; (2) responsive processes at micro and macro levels; (3) end-user devices in multiple touch points; and (4) engaged stakeholders who use the platform dynamically as a neural system. The ultimate aim is to utilize the system to enhance the tourism experience and improve the effectiveness of resource management towards maximizing both destination competitiveness and consumer satisfaction while also demonstrating sustainability over an extended time frame (Buhalis & Amaranggana, 2014, p. 557).

In their smart cities' ecosystems model, Abella, Ortiz-de-Urbina-Criado, and De-Pablos-Heredero (2017, p. 51) divided ecosystems into three main actors: First, the city as the source of data; second, the citizens as final users (i.e., directly or indirectly) of the innovative services deployed; and finally, the agents as re-users of data. The indicators analyze three dimensions for the actors in this ecosystem, including economic, direct and indirect, and social. The economic impact could increase the positive incomes of the actor, or it could save costs of existing activities. The social indicators are divided into those related to engagement, experience, security, and trust.

It can be expected that, in the coming period, continuous progress in ICT will encourage increased communication and collaboration between tourists and destination stakeholders, contributing to the achievement of the goals of both sides: the realization of a high-quality tourist experience and successful business results for destination stakeholders. Bringing smartness into tourism destinations may also facilitate the process of integration between production and consumption and increasing linkages between suppliers and consumers (Jovicic, 2017, p. 4).

The smart economy in smart tourism destinations will continue to be influenced by increasing smart practices. With these effects, it will change and continue to face new challenges. In the near future, tourism businesses will need to tailor business models to smart tourism applications. Competition-sensitive data for these new models will have critical value. Who will own the data to be obtained is important: Private companies that set up technological systems? Alternatively, the government or the municipalities? As well as how to obtain the data, the contract will determine which data will be acquired, and by whom.

One of the important applications to support the smart economy in smart tourist destinations will be the monitoring of tourist attractions within the city and the statistical evaluation of intensity. This will be important in smart cities in terms of reducing tourist traffic as well as distributing it in ways that will increase economic mobility with different points of attraction.

Smart society will continue to be an important agent in solving the problems that are important for intelligent tourism and for catching the opportunities. Both residents and tourists will have a strong influence by playing important roles in this process. In smart cities, converting social life experiences into data and transferring them to the intelligent tourism system will create significant benefit. This development will mean that the technology embedded in the intelligent city system is buried and active in social life at the same time.

Smart governance will face many challenges when collecting data for the STE. Individuals should be informed about the purpose of the information collected to overcome these difficulties. In addition, the manner in which information is collected must be transparent, and it must be obtained from individuals. In addition, it is necessary to comply with national and international law.

The philosophy of smart systems should not be defined as surveillance of individuals and events. Instead, it should be formulated as data collection for collective benefit. In addition, users should be persuaded that the entire process is transparent, secure, and under the governance guarantee. The most important risk for an STE is a data security problem that will prevent users from entering data. If such a problem arises, users can react in two different ways. First, they may limit data entry. Only limited data can be shared through trusted smart applications. Later, they may prefer to use new practices that provide independence and privacy. In both cases, it is clear that significant losses will occur for the big data of STEs.

An important issue for smart governance is the use of smart chatbots (SCs). The use of SCs can provide higher levels of tourist satisfaction in both public services and tourism businesses. SCs ensure that tourists can reach information at anytime and anywhere, rather than at a static point. SCs can offer tourists faster, higher-quality, up-to-date, and cheaper information than tourism information officers. SCs can offer all these services at much lower cost and with greater efficiency.

Smart mobility will become even more effective with the development of autonomous public transport. In smart cities, it may be possible to optimize signals to detect traffic congestion and reduce bottlenecks. In addition to intelligent parking systems, intelligent traffic systems (such as using bicycles, hiking, public transport) that reward good behavior will be important.

Smart environments will evolve further with applications such as intelligent waste management, intelligent buildings, and intelligent lighting. Intelligent buildings partially covered with vegetation on the ground can create green walls and roofs. This will ensure that the building cools itself down to a certain extent, and the urban heat can be reduced. With intelligent lighting, more aesthetic and attractive streets can be created. Energy costs can be reduced. The result of low lighting failure will be lower material and labor costs. Street lamps will be able to use stress-relieving colors and help visitors enjoy their time. In addition, intelligent street lamps can identify the number of people at a certain distance and how much illumination they need.

The vertical development of intelligent cities due to condensation will increase the value of vertical transportation within buildings. It is important that the elevators are connected to the Internet, and user data are collected. It may be possible for users to use the elevator with mobile phone applications, not with keys. In addition, long-term elevator trips will have to be designed to contribute to the tourist experience. Comfortable and attractive touristy designs that will provide a social climate among passengers will gain importance.

Within smart living, applications that will enable the creation of visualizations that can help city leaders make decisions based on the database will gain importance. For example, intelligent applications that automatically detect security incidents through data analysis and generate warnings can be developed. A real-time monitoring-based approach may also provide a significant increase in response speed (health, judicial incidents, accidents, social events, etc.).

These developments in smart economy, smart society, smart governance, smart mobility, smart environment, and smart living will make micro models in smart cities. On the other hand, international organizations and technology companies will continue to develop macro smart models using the capabilities of Web 4.0. Smart cities will reinforce the links between micro and macro models in meso-intelligent models to be drawn among themselves. As a result, the STE will continue to evolve into a macro model that offers global tourism opportunities with the contribution of micro and meso smart models.

The most critical point in an STE is where we think it should evolve. Will we create Leonardo da Vinci's Vitruvian Man, who is constantly improving, creative, enhancing the tourist experience with big data, Web 4.0, and smart applications, and aiming for perfect harmony between all stakeholders of the system? Will we create the demon of Pierre Simon, Marquis de Laplace, using scattered and intimate data gathered in unethical ways to limit and direct the tourist experience?

References

Abella, A., Ortiz-de-Urbina-Criado, M., & De-Pablos-Heredero, C. (2017). A model for the analysis of data-driven innovation and value generation in smart cities' ecosystems. *Cities*, 64, 47–53.

Al-Omari, A.H., & Al-Marghirani, A.S. (2017). Smart tourism architectural model: Kingdom of Saudi Arabia: A Case Study. *International Journal of Advanced Computer Science and Applications*, 8(10), 76–81.

Barile, S., Ciasullo, M.V., Troisi, O., & Sarno, D. (2017). The role of technology and institutions in tourism service ecosystems: Findings from a case study. *The TQM Journal*, 29(6), 811–833.

Bernebau, M.A.C., Mazon, J.N., Giner, D., & Baidal, J.I. (2016). *Big data and smart tourism destinations: Challenges and opportunities from an industry perspective*. Retrieved from www.researchgate.net/profile/Marco_A_Celdran_Bernabeu/publication/310793861_Big_Data_and_Smart_Tourism_Destinations_Challenges_and_opportunities_from_an_industry_perspective/links/5836f2d108aec3fe331e1f16.pdf

Boes, K., Buhalis, D., & Inversini, A. (2016). Smart tourism destinations: Ecosystems for tourism destination competitiveness. *International Journal of Tourism Cities*, 2(2), 108–124.

Bosnjak, A., Sladic, G., & Luburic, N. (2017). Smart tourism destinations: Enhancing interconnection between stakeholders and tourist through information personalization and feedback system. *Seventh International Conference on Information Society and Technology ICIST 2017*, March 12–15, Kopaonik, Serbia.

Buhalis, D. (2005). *Smart tourism and the competitive destination of the future*. Retrieved from www2.unwto.org/sites/all/files/pdf/dimitrios_buhalis_smart_etourism_.pdf

Buhalis, D., & Amaranggana, A. (2014). Smart tourism destinations. In Z. Xiang & I. Tussyadiah (Eds.), *Communication Technologies in Tourism 2014: Proceedings of the International Conference in Dublin, Ireland, January 21–24, 2014* (pp. 553–564). New York: Springer.

Buhalis, D., & Leung, R. (2018). Smart hospitality: Interconnectivity and interoperability towards an ecosystem. *International Journal of Hospitality Management*, 71, 41–50.

Camarinha-Matos, L.M., Afsarmanesh, H., Galeano, N., & Molina, A. (2009). Collaborative networked organizations – Concepts and practice in manufacturing enterprises. *Computers & Industrial Engineering*, 57, 46–60.

Dalli, A., & Bri, S. (2017). Design of electronic ticket system for smart tourism. *Advances in Computing*, 7(1), 11–14.

Deloitte. (2016). *Smart tourism: The destination is always ahead*. Retrieved from www2.deloitte.com/content/dam/Deloitte/sg/Documents/public-sector/sg-ps-smart-tourism.pdf

Galateanu, E., & Avasilcai, S. (2013). Business ecosystems architecture. *Annals of the Oradea University: Fascicle Management & Technological Engineering*, 1, 79–84.

Galateanu, E., & Avasilcai, S. (2014). Business ecosystem's health revised. In V. Dermol, M. Smrkolj, & G. Dakovic (Eds.), *Human Capital without Borders: Knowledge and Learning for Quality of Life; Proceedings of the Management, Knowledge and Learning International Conference 2014* (pp. 1097–1104). Portoroz, Slovenia: ToKnowPress.

Gretzel, U., Werthner, H., Koo, C., & Lamsfus, C. (2015). Conceptual foundations for understanding smart tourism ecosystems. *Computers in Human Behavior*, 50, 558–563.

Hartigh, E., & Asseldonk, A. (2004). Business ecosystems: A research framework for investigating the relation between network structure, firm strategy, and the pattern of innovation diffusion. *European Chaos /Complexity in Organizations Network Conference*, October 22–23.

Hartigh, E., Tol, M., & Visscher, W. (2006). The health measurement of a business ecosystem. *European Chaos /Complexity in Organizations Network (ECCON) Conference*, October 20–21.

Huang, C.D., Goo, J., Num, K., & Yoo, C.W. (2017). Smart tourism technologies in travel planning: The role of exploration and exploitation. *Information & Management*, 54, 757–770.

Hwang, V.W. (2014, April 16). The next big business buzzword: Ecosystem? *Forbes*. Retrieved from www.forbes.com/sites/victorhwang/2014/04/16/the-next-big-business-buzzword-ecosystem/#63b6ee0a5456

Iansiti, M., & Levien, R. (2002). *The new operational dynamics of business ecosystems: Implications for policy, operations and technology strategy*. Retrieved from http://citeseerx.ist.psu.edu/viewdoc/download?doi=1 0.1.1.203.4002&rep=rep1&type=pdf

Jovicic, D.Z. (2017). From the traditional understanding of tourism destination to the smart tourism destination. *Current Issues in Tourism*, 20(16), 1–7.

Kauppila, S. (2016). *Smart tourism: Achieving sustainable development*. Unpublished bachelor's thesis, University of Jyvaskyla, Jyvaskyla, Finland.

Kaur, K., & Kaur, R. (2016). Internet of Things to promote tourism: An insight into smart tourism. *International Journal of Recent Trends in Engineering & Research (IJRTER)*, 2(4), 357–361.

Koo, C., Park, J., & Lee, J.N. (2017). Smart tourism: Traveler, business, and organizational perspectives. *Information & Management*, 54, 683–686.

Liberato, P., Alen, E., & Liberato, D. (2017). Smart tourism destination triggers consumer experience: The case of Porto. *European Journal of Management & Business Economics*, 27(1), 6–25.

Liu, L., & Chen, Y. (2007). Enterprise niche and e-business strategy. *International Conference on Research and Practical Issues of Enterprise Information Systems (CONFENIS 2007)*, October 14–16, Beijing, China.

Moore, J.F. (1993, May–June). Predators and prey: A new ecology of competition. *Harvard Business Review*. Retrieved from www.researchgate.net/profile/James_Moore29/publication/13172133_Predators_ and_Prey_A_New_Ecology_of_Competition/links/59a9ad2d0f7e9bdd114ac690/Predators-and-Prey-A-New-Ecology-of-Competition.pdf

Peltoniemi, M., & Vuori, E. (2004). *Business ecosystem as the new approach to complex adaptive business environments*. Retrieved from http://citeseerx.ist.psu.edu/viewdoc/download?doi=10.1.1.103.6584&rep=rep 1&type=pdf

Perfetto, M.C., Vargas-Sánchez, A., & Presenza, A. (2016). Managing a complex adaptive ecosystem: Towards a smart management of industrial heritage tourism. *Journal of Spatial & Organizational Dynamics*, 9(3), 243–264.

Polese, F., Botti, A., Grimaldi, M., Monda, A., & Vesci, M. (2018). Social innovation in smart tourism ecosystems: How technology and institutions shape sustainable value co-creation. *Sustainability*, 10, 1–24.

Rong, K., Hu, G., Hou, J., Ma, R., & Shi, Y. (2013). Business ecosystem extension: Facilitating the technology substitution. *International Journal of Technology Management*, 63(3/4), 268–294.

Rong, K., Liu, Z., & Shi, Y. (2011). Reshaping the business ecosystem in China: Case studies and implications. *Journal of Science & Technology Policy in China*, 2(2), 171–192.

Rotchanakitumnuai, S. (2017). Barriers to Bangkok as a smart destination with internet of things technology. *Thammasat Review*, 20(2), 1–17.

Sedarati, P., & Baktash, A. (2017). Adoption of smart glasses in smart tourism destination: A system thinking approach. *Tourism Travel and Research Association: Advancing Tourism Research Globally 2017 International Conference*, June 20–22, Quebec, Canada.

Sigala, M. (2018). New technologies in tourism: From multi-disciplinary to anti-disciplinary advances and trajectories. *Tourism Management Perspectives*, 25, 151–155.

Tansley, A.G. (1935). The use and abuse of vegetational concepts and terms. *Ecology*, 16(3), 284–307.

Trudgill, S. (2007). Classics in physical geography revisited: Tansley, A.G. 1935: The use and abuse of vegetational concepts and terms. *Progress in Physical Geography*, 31(5), 517–522.

Vargas-Sánchez, A. (2011). Exploring the concept of smart tourist destination. *Enlightening Tourism. A Pathmaking Journal*, 6(2), 178–196.

Werthner, H., Koo, C., Gretzel, U., & Lamsfus, C. (2015). Special issue on smart tourism systems: Convergence of information technologies, business models, and experiences. *Computers in Human Behavior*, 50, 556–557.

Wu, S.M., Chen, T., Wu, Y.J., & Lytras, M. (2018). Smart cities in Taiwan: A perspective on big data applications. *Sustainability*, 10, 1–14.

32

TOWARDS THE DIGITAL ERA

Adding value through ICT in the tourism industry

Fisun Yüksel

Introduction

Information and communications technology (ICT) is utilized in order to obtain cutting-edge advantages in different aspects of the tourism industry such as accommodation, transportation, and attractions. More and more enterprises around the world are adding value to their core product in the tourism industry using ICT. ICT contains a set of technologies facilitating smart products associated with digital and physical processes in the big data environment. This chapter aims to help comprehend how the industry is changing and adopting related technologies as a salient factor in survival on a global scale. Therefore, to embrace Industry 4.0 technologies in the future, service providers need to review how their operations work today, welcome the advantages the digital era offers them, and then make the necessary alterations accordingly. The results of the research will indicate the latest developments in interrelated fields in terms of activities and applications for practioners and scholars.

Former studies generally examined the function of Internet usage, particularly Web.2.0 and 3.0 practices, in tourism marketing. However, the latest revolution of Web 4.0, its relationship with digital marketing, and their interaction in the tourism industry have not been investigated so far. Therefore, this research wants to provide a better insight into how new ICT is related to Industry 4.0, and its effects on digital marketing will be highlighted. Moreover, the function of digital marketing between the supply and demand sides of the tourism industry will be investigated.

This research intends to provide a deeper comprehension of ICT in line with the strategic paradigm modification by digital marketing in the tourism industry. The research questions include the following:

- What does the merging of technology and marketing mean for the tourism industry?
- How will the digital era modify the holiday concept for the tourism supply side in the light of the latest phenomenon, Industry 4.0?
- How does the demand side of tourism, tourists, perceive this paradigm change?

The study compares digital marketing with traditional marketing in the competitive environment. The first part of the chapter presents the role of ICT and how it relates to Industry 4.0.

The second part explores the role of service provision, digital marketing, and how they are affected by the latest revolution to gain competitive advantage in the context of strategic thinking.

Literature review

Technology plays a key role in creating economic expansion by means of the travel and tourism industry. There are numerous studies being carried out in the field of tourism, assessing the impacts of ICT on the management of tourism enterprises. The study endeavours to investigate the conditions that gave rise to the evolution of the digital era and its impacts on the tourism industry from the point of view of strategic management and marketing. More specifically, the fourth revolution, Industry 4.0, within the big data concept forms the basis of recent developments in digital marketing at the conceptual and operational levels of tourism organizations. Therefore, the research aims to investigate the issue from the supply side's paradigm change and its implications for the demand side's applications in the day-to-day management of tourism enterprises.

The advancement of ICT has had a phenomenal effect in the tourism and hospitality industry. This tremendous impact reflects a changing paradigm or philosophy of the practice of day-to-day management for both the supply and demand sides of the industry. Globalization as a prominent trend has notably triggered a transition process in ICT through the invention of the Internet and developments in the transportation and communications industries. These developments have been reflected in such industries as travel, tourism, and hospitality by means of computer reservation and management systems

Big data

Big data refers to the huge amount of data that cannot be collected, stored, or processed by traditional devices such as computers within a given time frame. Big data includes more than analytical and process-based data. It also comprises videos, social networking conversations, medical scans, sensor networks, search indexes, environmental conditions, and so forth (Lee, Baghari, & Kao, 2014). Some questions to be answered include: how we can convert all this information into knowledge? Similarly, how do we unravel the flow of data? What does big data mean to enterprises (YouTube, 2017)? These issues form a real challenge to enterprises' management at a strategic level. Enterprises constantly produce and collect data through computers, smartphones, social media, and GPS in real time. Big data is also being generated by the expanding Internet of Things (IOT). In this sense, the connection between human and machine is expanding. Figure 32.1 illustrates why big data may be beneficial to organizations' day-to-day management.

Big data is invaluable to business enterprises for a number of reasons. First, it is useful and practical in helping to understand customer behaviour. Second, it assists prediction of how consumers will behave in the future. Finally, companies can allocate their resources more effectively as a result of information generated using big data (Lorenz, Küpper, Rüßman, Heideman, & Bause, 2016). In this respect, big data helps organizations pick out the relevant data in order to deal with efficiency and productivity issues. Similarly, business enterprises optimize their operations and business processes in line with big data. Therefore, it is clear that, for tourism organizations, it may be wise to consider big data for their future viability in the long run.

Table 32.1 illustrates the amount of data that is being produced in 1 minute by the Internet in the context of big data.

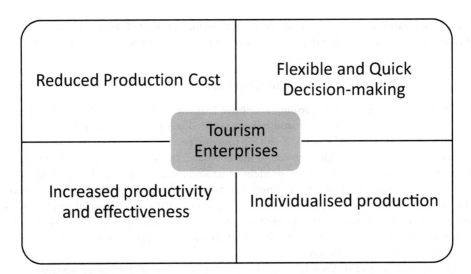

Figure 32.1 Core benefits of big data for tourism enterprises

Table 32.1 Amount of data collected by different sources on the Internet

Company	2011	2013	2015	2016	2017
Facebook, photos shared via Messenger	684,478	2,469,000	4,1666,667	216,302	
YouTube	48 hours	72 hours	300 hours	400 hours	4,146,600 videos
Twitter, tweets	100,000	277,000	347,222	9,678	456,000
Instagram	3,600 photos	216,000 photos	1,736,111 likes	2,430,555 likes	46,740 photos
Google, searches	2,000,000	4,000,000		69,500,000	3,607,080
Apple, application downloads	47,000	48,000	51,000		
Amazon		US$83,000	4,310 visitors	US$222,283	US$258,751.90 shopping

Source: Modified from DOMO, n.d.

Industry 4.0

Industrial revolution 4.0 seems to be one of the most commonly debated issues in the literature. Hermann, Penteck, and Otto (2016) state that it can be described as a reformation that unites industrial procurement, communications, and information technologies. Similiarly, Industry 4.0 is defined as "a shift towards a digital era" in manufacturing and marketing processes. China's rising power in the manufacturing industries forms a threat to the whole world, and notably to the USA and Europe (Erkollar & Oberer, 2016; Ersoy, 2016; Chen, Tsou, & Huang, 2009; Böhme, 2015; Yüksel, 2017). Europe, therefore, has decided to end this over-dependence on China by bringing production processes back to its own landscape. This progress has led to the emergence of "dark factories" (Böhme, 2015; Broadman, 2016; Lorenz et al., 2016).

According to the World Economic Forum (WEF, 2016), Industry 4.0 will completely transform service, energy, manufacturing, transportation, agriculture, and other related segments of the economy, which account for almost two-thirds of the global domestic product (GDP), within 10 years. Technological innovations in relation to digital technologies such as big data, cloud computing, smart factories, 3D printing, and robotics will substantially change how people work through new interactions between humans and machines. Klaus Schwab, founder and chairman of the WEF argued that, "Industry 4.0 will not only change what we do, but also who we are" (The Dualarity, n.d.). The labour force has already started to be replaced by robots and artificial intelligence as a result of this shift. The modification in the philosophy appears to be a radical transition in technical know-how, in terms of speed, flexibility, and productivity in manufacturing and marketing industries. Furthermore, physical and time distances no longer exist between humans and machines (De Ridder, 2016). It was estimated that, by 2020, it was highly likely that 14 billion appliances would be connected to one another as a result of the Internet of Things (IOT).

This phenomenon emerged in 2011 in Germany and is becoming more significant – it is more than a passing technical phase in the society we live in. About €140 billion will have been invested in the field of IOT in Europe by 2020 (Aegean Region Chamber of Commerce, 2015).

Table 32.2 shows the historical growth of the Industrial Revolution (Ersoy, 2016).

The core achievement of Industry 1.0 seems to be the invention of aircraft, automobiles, and the telegraph, together with steam machines and a sewing machine. Industry 3.0's innovations, on the other hand, started with the invention of the Internet, the emergence of mobile phones and GPS, together with desk-top computers and Boeing 747 aircrafts. Furthermore, Industry 3.0's inventions include smartphones, hybrid cars, and vehicles exceeding the speed of sound. Innovations in the Industrial Age 4.0 are predominantly computers becoming smarter than humans, autonomous aerial vehicles, the spread of autonomous cars, and the widespread use of the IOT (Khalil, 2000).

The structure of the 4.0 Industrial Revolution highlights basic principles, as follows (Chen, Calontone, & Chung, 1992; Barcik & Jakubiec, 2013; Flint, 2004):

- Technological structure based on digital network systems,
- More productive and flexible procurement, enriched competitiveness,
- Product life cycles offer smart, value creation chains,
- Collaboration and communication between people, machines, instruments, logistic systems and products,
- Product life cycles include product concept, refinement, production, utilization, renovation, and recycling of the yield. Besides, customer expectations are related to every phase of the services,
- Products are customized because of individual customer demands,
- Individual production and maintenance phases may lead to development of a new product,
- Supply chain network may alter the whole value chain,
- Rapid information system ensures raw material beforehand,
- Resources and energy are saved as a result of supervised production.

Table 32.2 Historical evolution of the industrial revolutions

Industry 1.0	1784, Doncaster, UK	Mechanical steam power
Industry 2.0	1870, Cincinnati, USA	Electrical energy
Industry 3.0	1969	Electronic and ICT systems
Industry 4.0	2011, Germany	Robotics and artificial intelligence

The next section discusses service innovation in tourism and traditional marketing versus digital marketing.

Service innovations in tourism industry

The importance of services has been growing at an increasing rate in economics over the last 40 years for many nations. This is owing to the fact that inventive technologies and changing business patterns have shifted service settings (Song, Song, & Di Benedetto, 2009). Computer reservation systems (CRSs), together with the discovery of the Internet, have had profound impacts on the nature of tourism throughout the world (Buhalis & Law, 2008).

Service innovation refers to introducing a novel item into people's lifestyle or restructuring foundations in terms of the timing and installation of associated and personal procedures regarding consumers (Sorescu, Frambach, Singh, Rangaswamy, & Bridges, 2011; Bilgihan & Nejad, 2015). In other words, innovation involves technological and non-technological outlooks (Barcet, 2010). Key ICT-related innovations in the tourism industry are as follows (Chen, Tsou and Huang; 2009; Gregory 2015; Ferreira, Alves, & Quicom 2014; British Museum, 2017; Bilgihan & Nejad, 2015; Morrison, Jing, O'Leary, & Cai, 2001):

- Mobile booking
- Mobile self-check-in
- Self-service check in kiosk
- Electronic luggage tags
- Smartphones as keys
- Smartphones as boarding passes
- Mobile optimization systems for hotels
- Virtual museums
- Service provision through robots at hotels.

Pine and Gilmore (1999) have proposed the term "experience economy" identifying the modified economic and social theories. Additionally, the nature of consumers has also altered as they seek out more experiences than ever. Similarly, Prahalad and Ramaswamy (2004) also argue that innovative technologies bring about attitude changes in consumers. Therefore, the term "consumer" is being replaced with "prosumer" in the experience economy.

The changing role of consumers in marketing has also deeply affected the tourism industry's structure. In that respect, tourists are more willing to perform active roles in experience formation (Andersson, 2007). Their role seems to be as co-creator rather than as subject. It should be noted that the latest developments in information and communications in applied sciences – in other words, ICT – intertwine tourist experiences (Lis, 2008). ICT enables tourists to have a hassle-free experience by simplifying every stage of the procedure (Buhalis & Law, 2008). There is a fast-growing trend among enterprises that are keen to strengthen their customer-centricity through a better comprehension of customer interactions, or "touchpoints", called "customer touchpoint management". Touchpoint management indicates that the target audience is more effectively reached through communication channels by affecting mental, sensory, and action priorities (Hirschman, 1984). Touchpoints are all of the interactions clients experience during their relationship lifecycle with an enterprise. Regardless of the instruments they utilize, the concept is significant, because customers build perceptions of an organization and brand based on their cumulative touchpoint experiences (Hekkert, 2006).

Conceptual framework of the research

This chapter proposes an interrelated conceptual framework, illustrated in Figures 32.2 and 32.3, to exemplify the relations and connections among the terms used within the given disciplines. Technology is the leading instrument reflecting the 4.0 revolution and transmitting the knowledge into experience through artificial intelligence and robots to the demand side of the tourism industry. Knowledge is processed as input in the tourism industry in the form of raw material.

More specifically, the supply side of the industry channels the knowledge through digital marketing to the demand side. In this context, it should be noted that Web 2.0, Web. 3.0, and Web 4.0 function as agents of digital marketing. As a result, the demand side converts the knowledge into action in the form of outcome as an experience by means of Web 2.0, Web 3.0, and Web 4.0 technologies. In other words, tourists or users transform the knowledge into outcome through a personalized experience as co-creator.

This holistic conceptual model proposes that how the combination of these three distinct disciplines works in interaction and harmony contributes to the formation of a new paradigm, the highest level of strategic thinking. In other words, the complementary nature of these disciplines triggers a form of new structure on an ideological base. The shift in ideology alters the technical know-how and gives rise to new business models within the industry. According to Schumpeter's (1947) "destructive creation", former concepts do not vanish when another concept is being formed or emerges; on the contrary, it emerges within the antecedents of three revolutions.

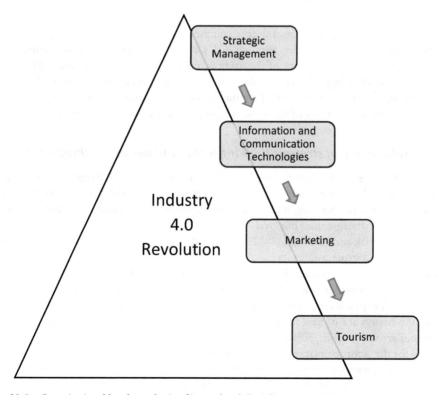

Figure 32.2   Organizational level: synthesis of interrelated disciplines comprising Industry 4.0

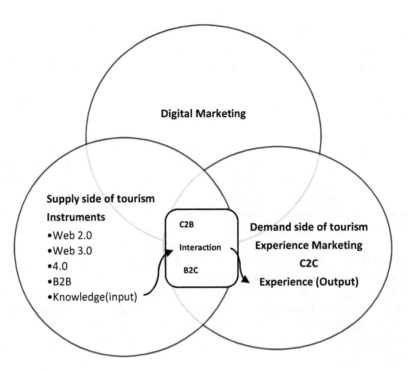

Figure 32.3 Operational level: application of 4.0 by digital marketing in tourism industry

The conceptual model provides a deeper comprehension of the newly emerging theoretical understanding of the 4.0 revolution through ICT's instruments in the digital marketing of tourism organizations. The framework of the study is intended to be a new mindset at the highest level of strategic thinking. Although traditional marketing concepts impact on ICT, this study has only focused on the impacts of ICT on the marketing discipline and, in line with this specification, how the new version of the marketing domain impacts on the tourism industry.

Adaptation of strategic thinking within Industrial Revolution 4.0

Strategic thinking is a procedure that describes the way or style in which organizations consider, examine, and evaluate the future for their institutions. Bryson and Bromiley (1993) suggest three levels of strategic thinking, which are context, process, and outcome. Okumuş (2001) has included another strategic thinking level – content, followed by context, process, and outcome. According to Torlak and Altunışık (2012), strategic thinking occurs at three levels of operations: events, trends, and structures.

This research framework has focused on the last strategic thinking level. The third level of strategic thinking corresponds to Schumpeter's (1947) destructive creation. Such a concept represents the deepest level of strategic thinking that redefines the structure of competition and sets out the emergence of new trends. Old versions of the concept exist within the new system and do not actually vanish. This way of thinking suggests that the rules of the game should be switched for the actors or players within the industry.

Industry 4.0 promotes Porter's "cost leadership" strategy for those enterprises that are seeking to be cost-effective operations (Porter, 1980). Therefore, this phenomenon is likely to be adopted by advocates of the production industry. Revolution Industry 4.0 is based on the

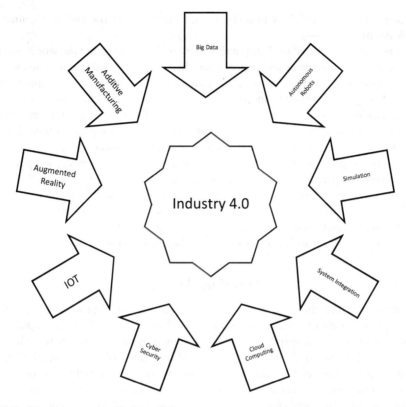

Figure 32.4   The components of Industry 4.0
Source: Modified from Platform Industry 4.0, 2016.

transition to cyber-physical systems in the age of communication between machines by equipping industrial production with high technology on a global scale (Porter, 1985). In this process, concepts of intelligent products and smart factories have emerged, and the idea of reducing the workforce has been introduced. The replacement of the labour force by artificial intelligence would probably lead to unemployment in society. And such progress is bound to encourage the development of different kinds of ability or talent within the big data environment.

New economy (digital economy) versus traditional economy: emergence of the digital era

New economy has become a popular catchphrase for many scholars. Organizations should have a sustainable competitive advantage in order to (a) survive, (b) make a profit, and (c) expand. Sustainable competitive advantage refers to the creation of "superior value advantageous" to consumers. Market orientation, or the target group's needs and demands, changes in external factors or their impacts on internal environment have called for strategic components (Tek & Özgül, 2004).

Today, radical changes have occurred in the field of marketing in the light of various phenomena. Although it has been interchangeably called Internet, e-commerce, or computerization of businesses, it means that business organizations communicate through intensive use of computer technology to create and use information. This concept differs between genuine and virtual businesses in the same economy, such as creating value for the customer, relating to customers and employees, how to do business, behaviour patterns, and management styles (Kotler & Armstrong, 2004).

In that respect, "connectedness" may well underline this concept and the words attached to it. This is largely because people and societies have become connected to one another, no matter how far apart they are. There are basically four areas that characterize and support the new economy: (1) Digitalization and connection to wired or wireless (mobile phone, m–commerce) communication networks (intranet, extranet, Internet). (2) Electronic mediators are being reactivated (e.g. Facebook, Amazon), whereas classic mediators are being deactivated. (3) Special production and customization – that is, customer-specific production and customer-specific marketing mix – together with marketing communications, logistics, service, and price, and so on. (4) Synthesis of operational personification and marketing personification is called customization in the literature; in other words, it means the convergence of different industries (Kotler, 2000). The new economy concept has brought about several e-related business management applications, such as e-finance, e-commerce, e-marketing, and so on, into the literature.

The next section discusses digital marketing and how it is connected to the new economy.

Digital marketing

Marketers have moved their attention away from the traditional promotion fields of TV, radio, and printed material towards electronic devices as a result of ICT developments. The real-time conversations enterprises have with consumers as they interact with websites, laptops, tablets, and mobile applications have changed the nature of marketing (Kotler, 2000). Marketing departments need to unite the imaginative side of the field with the technical aspects of data that are digital engineering and analytics. The rise of smartphones and related applications suggests that marketers need to improve digital skills to communicate with customers efficiently in order to keep up with recent changes. The two fields do not always go hand in hand. Employing inspired marketers to collaborate with technical staff may be an essential task for organizations (Kotler & Armstrong, 2004).

E-commerce applications are carried out in four ways: business to customer, business to business (B2B), consumer to business (C2B), and consumer to consumer (C2C). E-commerce is also significant for marketers as it deals with communication patterns between marketer and consumer and between consumer and consumer in social media usage (Ging, 2014).

B2C: Most B2C business involves selling books, music, hotel reservations, airline tickets, clothing products, CDs, flowers, and electronic devices. The common feature of selling products through this sort of e-commerce is that they are homogeneous and that information about the product can be determined specifically by consumers (Pride and Ferrel, 2003).

B2B: This form of e-commerce allows every department of the business to have instant access to another business in order to share information or to sell products. This can be said to be the biggest impact of Internet marketing on e-commerce from a business point of view (Engel, Blackwell, & Miniard, 1990).

C2B: This is an e-commerce method that includes business proposals that consumers make to businesses. In this form of e-commerce, consumers suggest a product, service, or information to a business that carries commercial value to them (Schiffman & Kanuk, 2007).

C2C: This consists of channels of communication and sharing that consumers themselves establish between them (Tek & Özgül, 2010).

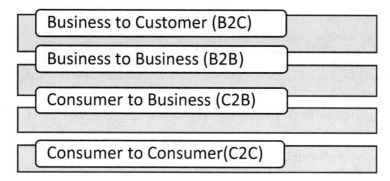

Figure 32.5 Forms of e-commerce

The current Industrial Revolution applications in tourism appear to be more like utilizing innovative technologies for digital marketing. For instance, an Amazon travel advisor employs chatbots in the daily operations of tourism companies such as booking a flight or making a reservation. It basically involves using a computer program by means of text messages and voice messages. It seems to be a new form of relationship between human and machine. People who do not want to download the application to their smartphone may alternatively download it via WhatsApp or Facebook Messenger (Flint, 2004).

Conclusion

The line of vision put forward in this study sheds more light on the latest progress of digital marketing and its impacts on the tourism field within interrelated fields. The holistic perspective provided in this research indicates a contribution to the theoretical background as well as to operational management. In line with the paradigm change, in the context of strategic management, actors on the supply side may need to consider redesigning the product in order to enrich it and to live up to the demand side's changing expectations within the highest level of strategic thinking.

As a result of this updated analysis, perhaps it would not be far-fetched to claim that some players may need to redefine their role in the supply change management of the industry not only to gain competitive advantage, but also to survive. Some may need to develop new skills or to adopt a new vision to get through this phenomenon smoothly. A significant limitation of the study lies in the absence of empirical data from academics and practioners. Therefore, it is suggested that future studies should involve an empirical data collection process. Nevertheless, the study appears to be one of the pioneers of related studies discussing Industry 4.0 in the big data environment and how the compatible fields collaborate in harmony to contribute to a formation of the latest invention.

The research suggests a holistic conceptual model of ICT applications in digital marketing in the tourism industry in order to look into the issue with a different philosophy. The remarks mentioned here can be of some interest to those who have to make decisions on the supply side of the tourism industry in order to design future holiday concepts in line with the latest industrial revolution. The latest developments of 4.0 pertain to the highest level of strategic thinking so as to promote a new mindset by means of ICT applications and digital marketing. Developing the right mindset is critical to gaining a cutting-edge advantage in the competitive environment.

References

Aegean Region Camber of Commerce. (2015) *Industry 4.0*. Report. Izmir, Turkey.

Andersson, T. D. (2007) The tourist in the experience economy. *Scandinavian Journal of Hospitality & Tourism* 7(1): 46–58.

Barcet, A. (2010) Innovation in services: a new paradigm and innovation model. In F. Galloj & F. Djellal (Eds), *The Handbook of Innovation and Services: A Multidisciplinary Perspective* (49–67). Cheltenham, UK: Edward Elgar.

Barcik, R., & Jakubiec, M. (2013) *Marketing Logistics University of Bielsko-Biala*. Faculty of Management and Computer Sciences, Poland.

Bilgihan, A., & Nejad, M. (2015) Innovation in hospitality and tourism industries. *Journal of Hospitality & Tourism Technology* 6(3). https://doi.org/10.1108/JHTT-08-2015-0033

Böhme, H. (2015) Industry 4.0 at the starting gate. Retrieved 6 June 2016 from www.dw.com/en/industry-4.0-at the starting Gates/a-18379432

British Museum. (2017) New virtual reality tour of the museum with Oculus. Retrived 1 March 2019 from https://blog.britishmuseum.org/new-virtual-reality-tour-with-oculus/

Broadman, T. (2016) Why Industry 4.0 is not just about industry? Retrieved 6 June 2016 from www.euroactiv.com/section/digital/opinion/why-industry-4.0-is not-just-about-industry/

Bryson, J., & Bromiley, P. (1993) Critical factors affecting the planning and implementation of major projects. *Strategic Management* 14(5), 319–337.

Buhalis, D., & Law, R. (2008) Progress in information technology and tourism management: 20 years on and 10 years after the Internet the state of e-tourism research. *Tourism Management* 29(4), 609–623.

Chen, I. J, Calontone R. J., & Chung, C. H (1992) The marketing–manufacturing interface and manufacturing flexibility. *Omega*, 20(4), 431–443.

Chen, J., Tsou, H., & Huang, Y. (2009) Service delivery innovation: antecedents and impact on firm performance. *Journal of Service Research* 12(1), 36–55.

De Ridder, B. (2016) Industry 4.0: threat or opportunity? Retrieved 7 June 2016 from http://digital2020.be/industry-4.0 threat-or-opportunity/

DOMO. (n.d.) Data never sleeps 4.0. Retrieved 12 April 2017 from www.domo.com/learn/data-never-sleeps-4-0

Dualarity, The. (n.d.) Retrieved 15 March 2017 from www.thedualarity.com/1187-2/

Engel, J. F., Blackwell, R. D., & Miniard, P. W. (1990) *Consumer Behaviour*, 6th ed. Orlando, FL: Dryden Press.

Erkollar, A., & Oberer, B. (2016) Industry 4.0: big data revolutions require smart technologies, 3. *Uluslararası Yönetim Bilişim Sistemleri Konferansı*, İzmir, Turkey.

Ersoy, A. (2016) On the way to Industry 4.0: digital enterprise. Retrieved 12 April 2017 from http://summit.itu.edu.tr/wp-content/uploads/2016/04/ali_riza_ersoy.pdf

Ferreira, F., Alves, A. P., & Quico, C. (2014) Location based transmedia storytelling: enhancing the tourism experience in Rodolfo, Baggio. In M. S. Alessandro & I. J. Pesonen (Eds), *Information and Communication Technologies in Tourism*, e-Proceedings of the ENTER 2014 PhD Workshop in Dublin, Ireland, 1(21).

Flint, D. J. (2004) Strategic marketing in global supply chain: four challenges. *Industrial Marketing Management* 33(1), 45–50.

Gregory, J. (2015) The special HotSOS: how mobile optimization systems increase hotel efficiency. *Insights*, 11(2). https://insights.samsung.com/2015/09/02/the-special-hotsos-how-mobile-optimization-systems-increase-hotel-efficiency/

Hekkert, P. (2006) Design aesthetics: principles of pleasure in product design. *Psychology Science* 48(2), 157–172.

Hermann, M., Penteck, T., & Otto, B. (2016) Design principles, for Industry 4.0 Scenarios. *49th Hawai International Conference on System Sciences* (HICESS), IEEE, 3928–3937.

Hirschman, E. C. (1984) Experience seeking: a subjectivist perspective of consumption. *Journal of Business Research* 12(1), 115–136.

Ging, J. (2014) Tourism marketing communications on a Chinese social media platform. *Information and Communication Technologies in Tourism 2014*. E-Proceedings of the Enter 2014 Phd Workshop, 1(21), Ireland.

Khalil, T. M. (2000) *Management of Technology: The Key to Competitiveness and Wealth Creation*. New Delhi: McGraw Hill.

Kotler, P. (2000) *Marketing Management Millenium Edition*. Upper Saddle River, NJ: Prentice Hall Business.

Kotler, P., & Armstrong, G. (2004) *Principles of Marketing*, 10th ed. Engle Wood Cliffs, NJ: Prentice Hall.

Lee, J., Baghari, J., & Kao, H. A. (2014) *Cyber Integrated Big Data Analytics Agent for Industry 4.0 Applications*, Conference on Expert Forum on Agent for Industry 4.0, (5).

Lis, P. T. (2008). Destination visual image and expectation of experiences. *Journal of Travel & Tourism Marketing*, 02(28), 129–144.

Lorenz, M., Küpper, D., Rüßmann, M., Heidemann, A., & Bause, A. (2016) Time to accelerate in the race towards Industry 4.0, big perspectives. Retrieved 6 June 2016 from https://fbkfinanzwirtschaft. wordpress.com/2016/06/16/time to-excelerate-in-the-race-toward-industry-4-0/

Morrison, A. M., Jing, S., O'Leary, J. T., & Cai, L. A. (2001) Predicting usage of the Internet for travel bookings: an exploratory study: *Information Technology & Tourism* (4), 15–30.

Okumuş, F. (2001) Towards a strategy implementation framework. *International Journal of Contemporary Hospitality Management* 13(7), 327–338.

Pine, J. B., & Gilmore, J. H. (1999) *The Experience Economy: Work is a Theatre and Every Business a Stage*. Cambridge, MA: Harvard Business School.

Platform Industry 4.0. (2016) Website. Retrieved 1 March 2019 from www.plattform-i40.de/I40/ Navigation/EN/Home/home.html, 12.04.2017

Porter, M. E. (1980) *Competitive Strategy*. New York: Free Press.

Porter, M. E. (1985) *Competitive Advantage: Creating and Sustaining Superior Performance*. New York: Free Press.

Prahalad, C. K., & Ramaswamy, V. (2004) Co-creation experiences: the next practice in value creation. *Journal of Interactive Marketing* 18(3): 5–14.

Pride, W. M., & Ferrel, O. C. (2003) *Marketing Concepts and Strategies*, 10th ed. Boston, MA: Houghton Mifflin.

Schiffman, L. G., & Kanuk, L. L. (2007) *Consumer Behaviour*, 9th ed. Harlow, UK: Pearson Prentice Hall.

Schumpeter, J. A. (1947) The creative response in economic history. *The Journal of Economic History* 7(2), 149–159.

Song, L. Z., Song, M., & Di Benedetto, C. A. (2009) A staged service innovation model. *Decision Sciences* 40(3), 571–599.

Sorescu, A., Frambach, R. T., Singh, J., Rangaswamy, A., & Bridges, C. (2011) Innovation in retail business models. *Journal of Retailing* 87, 3–16.

Tek, Ö., & Özgül, E. (2010) *Modern Pazarlama İlkeleri*, 3rd ed. İzmir: Birleşik Matbacılık.

Torlak, Ö., & Altunışık, R. (2012) *Pazarlama Stratejileri-Yönetsel Bir Yaklaşım*, İstanbul: Beta Publishing.

What is big data? www.youtube.com/watch.: Retrieved April 11, 2018.

World Economic Forum. (2016) Industrial Internet of Things: unleashing the potential of connected products and services. Retrieved 16 May 2016 from http://reports.weforum.org/industrial-intenet-of –things/

Yüksel, F. (2017) Industry 4.0 Digital Era: Is it a Milestone or an end? Euroefe, Aydın: Adnan Menderes University.

PART VII

Methods used to study tourism impacts

33

A CRITICAL REVIEW OF STATISTICAL TECHNIQUES AND APPLICATIONS USED TO STUDY TOURISM IMPACTS

Edward C. Bolden, III

Research on tourism impacts

This section will introduce the three distinct methodological approaches to research on tourism impact: qualitative, quantitative, and mixed methods. The ways in which each of these approaches has been implemented and published in recent tourism literature varies widely, and so this chapter provides an overview of how each of these is represented in the published research. Although a brief review of each of the three methods is included, a more in-depth look into quantitative analysis and statistical techniques most commonly used in the tourism impact literature follows. The breadth of tourism impact research presents a challenge when discussing how approaches have been applied to the field as a whole, but this chapter should serve as a helpful guide in presenting a representative sample of research methodologies addressing the potential impact of tourism.

To establish a scope for this chapter, the literature has been strictly limited to include research on how tourism impacts the host location on a cultural, social, environmental, and/or economic level. Studies included cover dates extending beyond 20 years to establish a foundation strictly pertaining to this definition of tourism impacts. Such research has looked at single events such as the FIFA World Cup (Lee & Taylor, 2005), the Olympic Games (Waitt, 2003), and the British Open (Gelan, 2003), and others have looked more broadly at tourism's impact on the host location. These broad tourism impact studies often look at tourism holistically as it impacts an aspect of life for residents (e.g., Alam & Paramati, 2016; Haley, Snaith, & Miller, 2005; Strickland-Munro, Allison, & Moore, 2010). Therefore, the techniques and applications covered here address a lot of potential impacts of tourism, with some being more challenging to measure than others.

Qualitative research

The impact tourism may have on residents is often difficult to generalize. How tourism impacts one resident may be quite different from how another member of the same community perceives visitors. The collection of rich, in-depth data from few subjects is considered qualitative research (Merriam & Tisdell, 2016). The focus of the qualitative research approach is on the quality of information provided (hence, "qualitative"), rather than sheer quantity of data that could be collected on a wider range of topics. The richness of the data and details collected via this method is the key strength of qualitative research, which allows for a true story to be told by residents as to how tourism impacts their lives. There are considered to be two main weakness of this approach: (1) potential concerns about reliability and generalization of the data collected, and (2) the extensive time commitment required to collect such data. The time necessary to conduct qualitative research appropriately is a substantial research investment, both in the collection and analysis of the data. Although the qualitative method promotes details and depth not possible in a quantitative approach, this is often with the risk of a much smaller sample size, and the conclusions that are drawn cannot necessarily reflect the broader sentiments of the host community.

The most common qualitative data collection techniques in tourism impact include observations, interviews, and focus groups. Local residents and hosts are frequently subjects of interviews with the purpose of collecting detailed information relevant to how tourism impacts them. Information relevant to all areas of impact can be collected via focus groups, and observations can validate host comments and tourist behaviors. Ethnographic approaches and case studies are also approaches within qualitative research, with case studies being one of the most common methods used, as researchers explore the permeability of tourism as it impacts many walks of life for residents. Ethnographic studies are seemingly underrepresented, as they would be able to identify cultural shifts and changes in customs as a result of increased tourism, but must be conducted over time.

There is great appeal to employing qualitative research in exploring tourism impacts because it enables researchers to explore behaviors, attitudes, and opinions that cannot be collected through closed-ended survey questions or an exploration of metrics. Researchers using these methods focus on information that underlies attitudes and behaviors through asking questions as simple as "why?" Often, qualitative data can serve to inform development of both quantitative data collection instruments and greater theories related to how tourism could be impacting the local people and environment. Within the tourism impact literature, qualitative research has its place, but it is often overshadowed when implemented as the sole research method; much more frequently qualitative methods are combined with a quantitative approach to establish a mixed methods design.

Quantitative research

Quantitative research involves the collection and subsequent analysis of statistical or numerical data, gathered via objective measurements (Dimitrov, 2009). Numerical data can be contrived from direct measurement of phenomena or observation, as well as surveys, polls, questionnaires, or structured interviews. The transformable, measurable data are then used to allow for comparisons and identification of patterns in the defined variables. Quantitative research typically involves a larger sample population (hence, quantity) and is widely considered to be more structured than qualitative methods. An exploration of statistical applications and techniques will be the main focus for much of this chapter, and so they will be discussed in more detail later in the chapter.

Most tourism impact research is quantitative in nature, where variables such as number of visitors, employment rate, and estimated economic impact of tourism are all numerical. Further, perceptions of tourism, attitudes toward impacts, and enthusiasm are quantified in ways that allow them to be measured and analyzed quantitatively. Quantitative methods offer an appeal that includes the ability to report reliable and valid information from a large sample, leading to more generalizable conclusions because the data are derived from objective measurements. Countered by qualitative research, the major weakness of this approach is that the amount of detail collected is lacking, often leaving unanswered the question of "why?"

Mixed methods research

The combination of both qualitative and quantitative components in one research study is considered a mixed methods design. The mixing of methods allows for the triangulation of information collected as a source of validation, at the same time maximizing the strengths of both approaches with the intention of minimizing weaknesses, whether perceived or actual (Creswell & Plano Clark, 2011). In this approach, the data sources supplement each other—the researcher is able to use the qualitative information to better describe or explain the quantitative data, while at the same time using the quantitative data to maximize the validity and reliability of the qualitative information. When the data are effectively able to complement each other, the sources are used to triangulate the data, and the mixed methods style is considered a well-rounded and sound approach.

Often seen in the tourism impact literature is the employment of a structured interview. Though often considered a qualitative research approach, the structured interview allows for data to be collected by an interviewer who asks questions as they appear on a questionnaire (Lindlof & Taylor, 2002). In the tourism impact research, the interviewer seeks to obtain complete, valid data from the participant that can then be used for later data analysis. The use of scales that are analyzed quantitatively later contributes to the structured interview being a mixed method data collection tool.

This combination of methodologies is particularly attractive in assessing tourism impact, where there is broad appeal to collecting quantitative data on economies or attitudes, but also incorporating the rich, deep qualitative information that can be collected. As an example, it is easy to find useful data on the impact of tourism in a certain location given economical contributions, visitor numbers, or locals' perceptions or attitudes toward the tourists. Incorporating information from qualitative sources allows the hosts to provide details not found in the numbers, including personal feelings of direct impact, what factors influence their attitudes or beliefs, or other sociocultural impacts they have experienced caused by tourists. Mixed methods approaches are widely utilized as they are able to overcome some weaknesses evident in each method independently.

Statistical techniques and applications

This section focuses on a review of the statistical techniques and applications present in the tourism impact literature. What is provided here is a brief summary of the technique and how it has been applied to measure tourism impact. This section is not intended to serve as a how-to guide for implementing the following techniques, but as a sample of prominent uses of statistics and methods that are commonly applied when assessing the impact of tourism. Many of the techniques require in-depth training and advanced knowledge to be implemented correctly. For more detailed information on any of these techniques, a list of further readings is provided. The overview of applications here will be presented within the context of measuring and assessing tourism impact.

Comparing groups

The measurement of tourism impact is often followed by an exploration of differences between different groups. For instance, does tourism more negatively impact people who have been residents longer than people who have not resided in the destination very long? The comparison of groups using statistical techniques ranges from simple to complex, from groups based on demographic characteristics (e.g., age, income level) to those based on levels of a trait (e.g., enthusiasm, attitudes). The distinctions between groups are often noted in hopes of determining differential impacts of tourism based on group membership.

The ways in which researchers compare groups is dependent upon two primary factors: (1) the types of variable to be included in the analysis, and (2) the number of groups that are to be compared. Variables divided into categories or grouping variables such as race/ethnicity and sex are distinct from variables that are continuous in nature, such as age or income. These two types of variable are compared in different ways, and the analysis that is most appropriate will be discussed here. The number of groups to be compared is the other consideration in which technique to employ. Because one method of comparing groups is much more common than the others, it will be the primary focus of this section.

Analysis of variance

The analysis of variance (ANOVA) constitutes a collection of procedures for testing variability among the means of two or more groups (Aron & Aron, 2003). Because of ANOVA's ability to meet many needs, it is the most frequently used analysis for comparing group means. An ANOVA is appropriate for comparison of two or more groups or for levels of an independent variable to be compared on one or more continuous dependent variables (Dimitrov, 2009). The number of possible groups to be compared using ANOVA is only limited by the sample size and complexity of the interpretation of the results. Using similar techniques, a researcher is able to compare groups on multiple dependent variables simultaneously (MANOVA), control for other variables in the analysis (ANCOVA), or account for repeated measures using the same general approach to analysis. A discussion of all of the possible analyses within the ANOVA family is outside the scope of this work, but several applications are highlighted here as they are presented in the tourism impact literature.

Although evidence of ANOVA variations is found in the literature, rarely do they exist as the sole analysis in published research. In most cases, especially those assessing the impact of tourism, these analyses are part of a larger research initiative that includes exploring interrelationships among variables or prediction of impact using regression techniques. Owing to this, identifying a representative sample of studies employing ANOVA methods was challenging. Consequently, the low frequency with which these analyses are reported reflects a preference toward more complex analyses.

The ways in which ANOVA can be used should not go overlooked. In his comparative tourism study, Tosun (2002) compared the attitudes toward tourism of individuals from three different locations using an ANOVA. Measuring tourism impact in a way that allows comparison of groups, even across studies, provides relevant information on how impact is perceived by different residents. In a more complex approach, Andereck, Valentine, Knopf, and Vogt (2005) tested relationships between multiple variables and what they identified as impact factors using multivariate analysis of variance (MANOVA). Given the variables they explored (and the relationship between the impact factors that served as their dependent variables), MANOVA was the appropriate approach to explore residents' attitudes toward tourism.

Overall, the ANOVA methods appear to be used less frequently than expected given attempts to detect differences in groups. This could be a product of evolving research questions. As ANOVA is conducted to analyze whether or not there are differences between groups, more advanced analyses such as regression can help depict differences in an alternate frame. Ultimately, the fact that ANOVA is not reported frequently does not mean research-ers are not interested in differentiating between groups; there are just a few different ways to detect such differences.

Other methods for comparing means

There are two other methods for comparing means that are rarely seen in the tourism impact literature: chi-squared tests and *t*-tests. Chi-squares tests are used in cases where both variables to be compared are categorical, leading to the exploration of frequencies in categories rather than scores on a dimension (Aron & Aron, 2003). An example of a chi-squared test could be if researchers explored level of perceived tourism impact (i.e., low vs. high) by employment status (i.e., full-time, part-time, unemployed). In that case, the analysis explores the frequencies within the groupings and applies the chi-squared statistic to test if the frequencies represent a pattern or association between variables outside what is expected. The chi-squared test is fundamental in nature but could serve to compare groups in some tourism impact cases.

The other analysis is a *t*-test. Similar to ANOVA, the *t*-test allows for the comparison of groups but is limited to two groups being compared on a single continuous dependent variable. As an example, a researcher may be interested in exploring tourism's impact on the economy comparing responses of tourists and residents. Residents and tourists may feel that tourism has a different effect, but using a *t*-test the researcher is limited to two groups (tourists and residents) on one dependent variable (tourism's impact). Owing to these limitations, there are minimal mentions of using a *t*-test in the tourism impact literature outside testing individual groups as a follow-up to an ANOVA or regression analysis.

Correlation and regression analyses

It is very common for researchers in tourism impact to explore relationships among variables. As one variable changes, the ways in which other variables change as well are important when measuring impact. Correlational analysis is the most basic way to explore relationships among variables, with the correlation coefficient as the statistical value that represents the degree of relatedness between two variables. The more two variables are related, the more one variable can be used to predict another through the process of regression. A regression analysis allows the researcher to explore multiple variables with the goal of determining which variable from a set most strongly predicts the variable of interest. The goal for this section is to provide a detailed description of correlational and regression analysis.

Correlational analysis

The extent to which two variables are related, or how changes in one variable are met with changes in another, is considered a correlational analysis (Dimitrov, 2009). The value that rep-resents the strength and direction of the relationship between two continuous variables is the correlation coefficient (Hinkle, Wiersma, & Jurs, 2003). The two most common correlation coefficients are Pearson's *r* and Spearman's rho (ρ); Pearson's *r* is most appropriate for two con-tinuous variables, whereas Spearman's rho should be used for ordered or ranked (i.e., ordinal) variables. Correlation coefficients assume values that range from −1 to +1, with negative values indicating the relationship between variables is inverse (i.e., as one variable increases, the other decreases). The higher the absolute value of the correlation coefficient, the stronger the rela-tionship between variables. The correlation coefficient value summarizes the direct relationship between two variables, which is necessary to establish before exploring more advanced concepts such as regression, factor analysis, or structural equation modeling (SEM).

Because correlation is a necessary and fundamental step to other analyses, correlation values are often reported in the tourism impact literature. Correlations must be established before any variable can be used to predict another, which is often the focal point of statistical analyses. As far as where correlations are reported in the literature, they can often be seen when exploring relationships among factors when developing instruments (e.g., Ap & Crompton, 1998; Lankford & Howard, 1994) or exploring respondent characteristics. Tosun (2002) explored many relationships within his work, including variables such as level of support for tourism, age, and number of children, using the correlation analyses to test those relationships. Similar to ANOVA as discussed above, correlational analyses are foundational building blocks upon which more advanced analyses are based. Therefore, it is not unusual to see fewer studies publishing correlation coefficients, but it remains an extremely important analysis nonetheless.

Regression

Researchers can apply the statistical relationships between variables with the goal of estimation, a process known as regression (Fox, 2016). Regression is applied widely in forecasting metrics and predicting outcomes given the interrelationships present among the variables of interest. Like most analyses, regressions can range from simple (i.e., including only one independent variable predicting the dependent variable) to complex, where there are two or more independent variables. Through applying simple linear regression techniques, the researcher is relying on the statistics to determine how much the independent variable can predict the dependent variable. As regressions become more complex, with additional independent variables, researchers can explore the interrelatedness among many variables as they contribute to predicting the dependent variable simultaneously. Conducting a multiple regression analysis allows for the exploration of unique contributions from each of the predictors as they relate to each other as well as the dependent variable.

The tourism impact literature is full of examples of a regression analysis. To note a few, Haley et al. (2005) tested the abilities of socioeconomic and demographic characteristics, economic reliance, and perceptions of tourism to predict residents' attitudes to tourism development, and Ivanov and Webster (2013) explored globalization as a predictor of a country's tourism contribution to economic growth while controlling for multiple variables using the regression analysis. The application of regression techniques ranges from the simple to the complex, using the interrelatedness among variables to help establish predictive ability. Predicting how residents will perceive tourism development and establishing what factors influence enthusiasm for tourists and how tourism impacts local culture, economy, and society are extremely useful applications of regression. In many cases, the prediction resulting from regression techniques is recommended for use in policy changes.

Factor analysis techniques

In factor analysis, the correlations between multiple variables are analyzed in order to best group the variables into a lesser number of underlying variables termed "factors" (Thompson, 2004). Through the exploration of relationships among variables, factor analysis allows the researcher to combine variables in a meaningful way, thus leading to the identification or generation of underlying factors that are fewer in number than the original number of variables. Factor analysis techniques are classified into two main categories: They can be either exploratory or confirmatory in nature, dependent upon the presence of any existing, hypothesized theory. Where there is no underlying theory that predicts how variables organize into factors, exploratory factor analysis (EFA) is used to explore the underlying structure of the interrelationships. Contrary to the exploratory analysis, confirmatory factor analysis (CFA) is used to test or validate how well the data fit the theorized model of inter-variable relationships.

Within the tourism impact literature, CFA is much more prominent than EFA. This is likely owing to the establishment of underlying theories which are tested, rather than a clear exploration of how variables are related. Exploratory analyses have been most commonly used in instrument development, where the developer is looking to validate the scale based on factors identified in the analysis. The strongest example of EFA is provided by Lankford and Howard (1994) as they developed the tourism impact attitude scale. This was EFA in its purest form, contrary to Ap and Crompton's (1998) tourism impact scale, which used a similar factor analysis technique but for the purposes of validating domains they identified through the instrument development process. Outside instrument development and validation, Haley et al. (2005) also implemented EFA to assess underlying dimensions of responses to tourism development issues. There, the researchers sought to clearly define common factors that arise when residents identify concerns with tourism. In each instance, EFA served the purpose of identifying items that were similar with the intention of identifying factors within their instruments.

To supplement the work employing EFA, CFA is often seen as a method of confirming measurement scale properties based on data collected. Within the tourism impact research, confirmatory analyses are often used to check the reliability and validity of indicators that are used as part of other analyses, such as structural equation models. As an example, Kim, Uysal, and Sirgy (2013) conducted a CFA to validate the factor structure before proceeding to test their structural equations. Likewise, Yolal, Gursoy, Uysal, Kim, and Karacaoglu (2016) used CFA to validate each component individually before testing their overall measurement model using SEM as well. In short, factor analysis techniques have a firm place in tourism impact research, but, like other analyses, rarely occur in isolation. Both exploratory and confirmatory factor analyses provide researchers with a powerful statistical technique to explore the relationships between variables in a way that becomes extremely useful when combined with other analyses.

Path analysis and structural equation modeling

Path analysis is an extension of multiple regression where the researcher analyzes the relationships between variables in a way that focuses on determining effect based on the interrelationships of the variables (Olobatuyi, 2006). Path analysis is presented here as it is an integral part of SEM. Path analysis is appealing because it allows the researcher to apply the relationships between multiple variables that then serve as predictors in one single path model. Researchers are able to formulate and test the impact multiple variables have on each other and on an outcome, which is not possible given just multiple regression techniques. Path and confirmatory factor analyses are similar in the way that they are tested, which is through assessing fit between the model and the data. Path analysis is rarely used independently, but serves as a component of SEM, the topic of the rest of this section.

Extending from multiple regression and factor analysis is SEM, which allows the researcher to explore relationships of unobserved, latent variables (Schumacker & Lomax, 2015). Combining the techniques of regression, path analysis, and confirmatory factor analysis helps to establish how the observed variables relate to underlying latent variables, and then how those latent variables can be interrelated. Technically, confirmatory factor and path analyses are classified under the umbrella of structural equation models (Kline, 2011); however, they are most commonly referred to by their more specific names for clarity. The ability for complex data structures to be modeled using SEM leads it to be an increasingly used tool across many areas of research, not just tourism impact.

SEM is able to account for many variables simultaneously, which is one of the strengths of this advanced technique. The hallmark of SEM is testing the extent to which the data align with the model, based on theory and formulated through the research hypothesis. Computer-based SEM programs allow for complex interrelationships to be calculated much more quickly, allowing the theory and accompanying analyses to become increasingly complex without the usual limitations of calculations. Although there are many advantages to using SEM, the major weakness is that sample size must increase with the complexity of the model, often leading to difficulty collecting enough data to reliably test the research hypothesis. SEM can also be criticized for being an underdeveloped technique, as the testing of complex relationships involves a substantial amount of estimation, without clear agreement on when a model and data align.

Researchers assessing tourism impact are particularly interested in SEM as a technique based on the large number of variables and exploring how they relate to each other. A great example is Yolal et al.'s (2016) use of SEM to explore the interrelationships between the sociocultural impacts of a festival and the subjective well-being of residents. Here, variables related to social benefits and social costs were hypothesized to contribute to a resident's feeling of well-being, with the hypotheses forming different aspects of the structural model. Kim et al. (2013) also explored residents' perceptions of tourism impact as it relates to residents' well-being and overall life satisfaction. These two studies provide great examples of how SEM can account for the interrelationships between many variables with the intention of drawing multiple conclusions simultaneously.

Advanced economic modeling and cost–benefit analysis

There has been rising interest in applying other techniques to help measure tourism impact. Because of tourism's direct impact on the host economy, several researchers have explored tourism impact through the use of economic modeling techniques or cost–benefit analysis. These approaches attempt to examine the relationship between tourist attractions and their quantifiable effects. Both approaches rely heavily on economic indicators (e.g., employment, gross domestic product, and socioeconomic changes), and it can be considered a strength that the values are quantifiable. However, this could also be considered a weakness, as reliability is strongly dependent upon the input of the models. Values that are incorrect bring about serious concerns with the model, leading the validity to be questioned. A short discussion of economic modeling and cost–benefit analysis follows.

Economic modeling

There have been many economic models applied with the intention of measuring tourism impact. Each of these models differs strongly in complexity, assumptions, and data collected, as well as the nature and precision of the results (Klijs, Heijman, Maris, & Bryon 2012). Two of the more prominent are input–output models and computable general equilibrium (CGE). Input–output analysis was more widely used through the 1990s, whereas CGE has become more popular during the past decade.

Input–output models allow the researcher to assess the impact of tourism at three levels—direct, indirect, and induced effects—through the use of a general equilibrium approach. These models provide a comprehensive view of the host economy while allowing the researcher flexibility in developing the model, providing detail when necessary (Fletcher, 1989). Flexibility to focus on areas of interest to the researcher has been one of the major draws to implementing input–output models, particularly as they assist in developing policy. These models also have the ability to account for interdependencies among economic sectors and are widely seen as an approach that is independent of public policy (Fletcher, 1989). Input–output models are declining in popularity, but have served a strong purpose in exploring tourism's impact on local economies (e.g., Horvath & Frechtling, 1999; Johnson & Moore, 1993).

Although the application of input–output models showed some promise, several key issues have been identified that led to developments of other approaches. Input–output models work with restrictive assumptions that do not apply to all economies and they work with narrow impacts that can be accounted for using CGE modeling (Dwyer, 2015). That is, there is a lot of interaction among variables that is not correctly accounted for in traditional models. The model is only as strong as the assumptions that can be met, and the researcher is limited in the ability to answer only certain questions regarding the economic system's impact from tourism (Briassoulis, 1991). Input–output analysis had been widely used because of its comprehensiveness and flexibility, but the major weaknesses, such as (a) the strictness of assumptions to be met and (b) the relationships explored in the analysis not including interactions, present methodological challenges to using the technique. Additionally, it cannot account for intangible impacts of tourism (e.g., Gelan, 2003) and is an expensive and time-consuming method, further contributing to the development of alternative techniques.

CGE models attempt to counter the limitations of input–output analysis by being composed of model equations that describe the economic impacts on households, government, businesses, and the greater global economy (Dwyer, 2015). These models are based on a set of input–output models, but are able to account for more variables and explore the impact of tourism more broadly. How tourism impacts the economy is a common application of these models across the world (e.g., Meng, 2014; Narayan, 2004). More recently, Li, Li, Song, Lundberg, and Shen (2017) employed CGE to determine how strongly the economy of New Zealand was impacted by the release of two major film series. A more detailed description of these models' work is outside the scope of this chapter; please see further readings for more information on this promising exploration of tourism impact.

Cost–benefit analysis

Cost–benefit analysis is best simplified as the identification of all income (i.e., benefits), less expenditures (i.e., costs), to determine the impact. As this translate to tourism impact, cost–benefit analysis is most often explored through the lens of hosting an event (e.g., Mules & Dwyer, 2005; Torre & Scarborough, 2017) or the expenses of tourism development and subsequent impact on the local economy (e.g., Hefner, Crotts, & Flowers, 2001). In all cases, host locations would employ a form of cost–benefit analysis to determine if their investment in infrastructure, attractions, and/or people would be justified based on the expected return brought about by tourists.

Cost–benefit analysis is appealing in tourism impact research because it seems rather simple up front: Identify the potential benefits to the economy through employment and/or tourist spending and subtract the amount of capital invested to determine the net benefit of the investment. However, the complexities of economies, limitations of resources, and actual impact make it challenging to identify true costs and benefits. Much like in the economic models, tourists bringing in money have direct, indirect, and induced impacts on the economy (Mules & Dwyer, 2005), which ripple out and make measuring with precision nearly impossible. The field of cost–benefit analysis is much more complex than can be discussed here, with concerns around the true valuation of benefits and costs, units of measurement, and market characteristics, and so the focus will shift to how cost–benefit analysis has been used to measure tourism impact.

First, Mules and Dwyer (2005) applied cost–benefit analysis techniques to assess the economic impact of sporting events. More broadly, public money is spent to bring attractive sporting events to locations that become tourist attractions for the purposes of this event. As the public is the financier of such events, cost–benefit analysis served its purpose in offering up a reasonable conclusion after identifying the potential costs and benefits of such events (Mules & Dwyer, 2005). Torre and Scarborough (2017) attempted to explore the use of cost–benefit analysis to assess cultural tourism's impact on the local economy through an art exhibit. They were met with difficulty in identifying the appropriate data necessary to estimate benefits appropriately and identified the constraints of cost–benefit analysis as a major limitation to its wider implementation in tourism impact research, but noted that cost–benefit analysis could be beneficial as a supplement to other econometric analyses (Torre & Scarborough, 2017). Each research independently notes the broader impacts and unmeasurable impacts not identified within the analysis, furthering the utility of cost–benefit analysis as a supplement to another method. Despite identifying those limitations, both articles also include a substantive discussion on cost–benefit analysis and would be useful for further exploration of the topic as it applies to tourism impact.

Summary of techniques in current research

Trends

The use of statistics in hospitality marketing research has become increasingly advanced over the past several years. The publication of summaries and articles reflecting tourism impacts depicted by descriptive statistics and simple analyses related to single events or tourism as a whole for a certain location will always serve to meet a need. However, advanced training, software, and application of approaches from other domains such as economics and quantitative sciences have made it easier to explore complex relationships and interactions among variables of interest. In many cases, measurement techniques and underlying theories have expanded in their sophistication, and the statistical analysis techniques have adapted to accommodate testing these theories. Given this shift to more complex questions and answers, multiple regression, factor analyses, and SEM are becoming more common in the exploration of tourism impact.

Notable approaches that have been employed in impact publications include economic modeling, cost–benefit analysis, and mixed method approaches, including structured interviews, which are popular within the tourism literature. These common approaches in other subject areas are becoming increasingly relevant research approaches to tourism impact and have been applied in a way to help contribute to knowledge of how tourism impacts, culturally, socially, environmentally, and economically. Several techniques used in tourism impact research are used frequently, such as multiple regression and SEM; however, there continue to be novel research applications and innovative approaches as the impact of tourism is being viewed with a broader lens in the more recent literature. Given the complexity and promise of each of the approaches, the most appropriate research method and statistical tool to be used should be considered based on the research question to be answered.

Across the hospitality and tourism domain, research in general has become increasingly complex; however, both qualitative and basic quantitative designs still serve researchers well when addressing critical research questions. Often, the most impactful applications are seen with the most basic statistics presented (e.g., World Travel & Tourism Council, 2017). Though the summary may reflect a trend of increasing complexity of statistical techniques, there are still the most basic approaches to form the foundation upon which researchers build increasingly detailed and multifaceted investigations to push the exploration of tourism impact forward.

Evaluation of techniques

This chapter was intended to display the diversity of methodologies and statistical analyses applied to measure tourism impacts in the published literature. This section sought to present several popular analyses as well as a few more rarely used techniques, and to summarize them through the lens of current research interests and publications. The increased application of advanced statistical techniques such as multiple regression and SEM, as well as the implementation of methods from economics and quantitative sciences, is evidenced here as more sophisticated theories have been developed, and the advances in technology help researchers collect and analyze the complex, interrelated data. Ultimately, these advancements in techniques and approaches have been able to meet the changing needs of researchers as they explore more variables, relationships, and effects in hopes of measuring tourism impact on people and the environment.

It is most important to note that these methods have been implemented with accuracy and integrity. Through the review of tourism impact articles, the researchers have made sound cases for implementing methodology and techniques appropriate to the data they have collected and the research questions they have attempted to answer. Evaluating tourism impact is challenging relative to several other areas of research within hospitality and tourism, but the researchers who undertake the questions of impact reliably and validly implement practical approaches given the data they collect. Though the research is intended to focus on a narrow aspect of tourism impact (i.e., impact on host from a cultural, social, environmental, and/or economic point of view), the methodology presented in the literature has been clearly defined, implemented diligently, and interpreted in a way that contributes to the strength of the field of tourism and hospitality research. Thus, this critical review serves only to reinforce the quality of research that has been done on tourism impact over the past several years.

Future directions and recommendations

The past 10–20 years have brought about greater advancement in methodologies and statistical applications within the realm of tourism impact, and in research within tourism and hospitality as a whole, as education and technology contribute to making analyses more available and make it possible to address increasingly complex research questions. The increase in complexity of research questions, methodologies, and analyses has been brought on by exposure to and training in these methods, promoting the research within the field as a whole. Through the exploration of tourism impact, researchers are increasingly able to develop multifaceted theories that depict multivariate relationships and to apply leading-edge techniques to answer their questions, a trend that is very likely to continue to push the field forward. Tourism is heavily impacted by forces such as politics, economics, and culture, and the impact tourism has on local environments, economies, and people is going to continue being an area of research interest. It is clear that current trends in tourism impact have become more complex, and that will undoubtedly continue to contribute to developing even more advanced techniques to evolve theory and provide more data from which to draw conclusions.

In the near future, the interconnectivity between individuals and assessment of impacts is expected to continue increasing, leading to an overwhelming amount of data available for analyzing the impact of tourism. Making connections between host locations, people, tourists, and researchers could provide a plethora of data around which more theories could be contrived, research questions could be developed, and hypotheses could be tested. Metrics and data that have never before been collected can become available and be analyzed in a relevant way, including, but not limited to, data from locations, social networking, and the consequential approach of social network analysis. Social network analysis could be an extremely powerful approach from a tourism impact perspective, if implemented correctly, and could become a promising area of future research for those in tourism as a whole.

The principal recommendation is for researchers interested in exploring tourism impact to continue to apply the techniques appropriate to their research, regardless of complexity. The result is that researchers ought to continue their investigations guided by theory rather than introducing unnecessary complexity. Though advanced statistical techniques have been published with greater frequency over the last several years, there is still a need for qualitative, mixed method, and basic approaches to data interpretation. Evaluating the impact of tourism can be an extremely convoluted task when not properly framed and when no limitations are set. The foundation upon which the advanced techniques are based relies on strong, testable hypotheses that are clear in theory and demonstrate the most basic relationships between variables. Only then can complex analyses such as multiple regression and SEM be utilized to address higher-order, advanced research questions.

Lastly, researchers exploring the impact of tourism should keep their focus on the consumer and general public in such a way that they are provided with useful interpretations and meaningful data. More convoluted analyses lead to greater need for explanations of variables and interpretations of the results that might not be meaningful to those who consume the research in everyday experience. Focusing on what the results mean, and what impact tourism has on people and places, is the ultimate goal of tourism impact research. Research is conducted to inform practice, so those in the tourism and public-service sectors should be able to apply impact results to contrive best practices from the research. Only through clear reporting and explanation of methodology and findings by those conducting the research can the results be communicated and deemed useful to those in practice.

Summary

This chapter intended to provide a brief background of the research types and common statistical approaches utilized in the tourism impact literature. A review of qualitative, quantitative, and mixed methods research was provided, along with context of how each has been applied to assess and evaluate the impact of tourism. Within the qualitative domain, interviews and case studies were discussed. The quantitative section focused on statistical techniques and applications ranging from a basic comparison of groups to multilevel regression and SEM. The quantitative section was followed by an overview of mixed methods approaches, focusing primarily on structural interviewing. The middle of the chapter provided more details on several quantitative analyses, accompanied by how they have been utilized in relevant tourism impact literature, which served as the focal point of the critical review. Lastly, several recommendations have been presented alongside an outlook on the future of tourism impact research from a methodological perspective.

Overall, the complexity of research and accompanying statistical analysis has expanded substantially in the past two decades within the tourism impact literature. The availability of data has spurred more elaborate theory development, resulting in more advanced statistical analyses. Each of these has evolved to provide together a more comprehensive examination of the impact of tourism on economies, people, and places. Researchers continue to apply statistical techniques to best meet the needs of the research, implementing and interpreting analyses with fidelity to contribute to meaningful literature. Though questions, methods, and analyses continue to become more advanced, researchers should continue appealing to the typical consumer and provide a useful interpretation that can be understood to inform tourism, hospitality, and public-service professionals.

References

Alam, M. S., & Paramati, S. R. (2016) The impact of tourism on income inequality in developing economies: Does Kutnets curve hypothesis exist? *Annals of Tourism Research* 61, 111–126.

Andereck, K. L., Valentine, K. M., Knopf, R. C., & Vogt, C. A. (2005) Residents' perceptions of community tourism impacts. *Annals of Tourism Research* 32, 1056–1076.

Ap, J., & Crompton, J. (1998) Developing and testing a tourism impact scale. *Journal of Travel Research* 37, 120–130.

Aron, A., & Aron, E. N. (2003) *Statistics for Psychology*, 3rd ed., Upper Saddle River, NJ: Prentice Hall.

Briassoulis, H. (1991) Methodological issues: Tourism input–output analysis. *Annals of Tourism Research* 18, 485–495.

Creswell, J. W., & Plano Clark, V. L. (2011) *Designing and Conducting Mixed Methods Research*, 2nd ed., Thousand Oaks, CA: Sage.

Dimitrov, D. M. (2009) *Quantitative Research in Education: Intermediate and Advanced Methods*, Oceanside, NY: Whittier Publications,.

Dwyer, L. (2015) Computable general equilibrium modelling: An important tool for tourism policy analysis. *Tourism & Hospitality Management* 21, 111–126.

Fletcher, J. E. (1989) Input–output analysis and tourism impact studies. *Annals of Tourism Research* 16, 514–529.

Fox, J. (2016) *Applied Regression Analysis & Generalized Linear Models*, 3rd ed., Thousand Oaks, CA: Sage.

Gelan, A. (2003) Local economic impacts: The British Open. *Annals of Tourism Research* 30, 406–425.

Haley, A. J., Snaith, T., & Miller, G. (2005) The social impacts of tourism: A case study of Bath, UK. *Annals of Tourism Research* 32, 647–668.

Hefner, F., Crotts, J. C., & Flowers, J. (2001) The cost–benefit model as applied to tourism development in the state of South Carolina, USA. *Tourism Economics* 7, 163–175.

Hinkle, D. E., Wiersma, W., & Jurs, S. G. (2003) *Applied Statistics for the Behavioral Sciences*, 5th ed., Belmont, CA: Cengage Learning.

Horvath, E., & Frechtling, D. C. (1999) Estimating the multiplier effects of tourism expenditures on a local economy through a regional input–output model. *Journal of Travel Research* 37, 324–332.

Ivanov, S., & Webster, C. (2013) Tourism's impact on growth: The role of globalization. *Annals of Tourism Research* 41, 231–236.

Johnson, R. L., & Moore, E. (1993). Tourism impact estimation. *Annals of Tourism Research* 20, 279–288.

Kim, K., Uysal, M., & Sirgy, M. J. (2013) How does tourism in a community impact the quality of life of community residents? *Tourism Management* 36, 527–540.

Klijs, J., Heijman, W., Maris, D. K., & Bryon, J. (2012) Criteria for comparing economic impact models of tourism. *Tourism Economics* 18, 1175–1202.

Kline, R. (2011) *Principles and Practice of Structural Equation Modeling*, 3rd ed., New York: Guilford.

Lankford, S.V., & Howard, D. R. (1994) Developing a tourism impact attitude scale. *Annals of Tourism Research* 21, 121–139.

Lee, C., & Taylor, T. (2005) Critical reflections on the economic impact assessment of a mega-event: The case of the 2002 FIFA World Cup. *Tourism Management* 26, 595–603.

Li, S., Li, H., Song, H., Lundberg, C., & Shen, S. (2017) The economic impact of on-screen tourism: The case of The Lord of the Rings and the Hobbit. *Tourism Management* 60, 177–187.

Lindlof, T. R., & Taylor, B. C. (2002) *Qualitative Communication Research Methods*, 2nd ed., Thousand Oaks, CA: Sage.

Meng, S. (2014) The role of inbound tourism in the Singaporean economy: A computable general equilibrium (CGE) assessment. *Journal of Travel & Tourism Marketing* 31, 1071–1089.

Merriam, S. B., & Tisdell, E. J. (2016) *Qualitative Research: A Guide to Design and Implementation*, 4th ed., San Francisco, CA: Jossey-Bass.

Mules, T., & Dwyer, L. (2005) Public sector support for sport tourism events: The role of cost–benefit analysis. *Sport in Society* 8, 338–355.

Narayan, P. K. (2004) Economic impact of tourism on Fiji's economy: Empirical evidence from the computable general equilibrium model. *Tourism Economics* 10, 419–433.

Olobatuyi, M. E. (2006) *A User's Guide to Path Analysis*, New York: University Press.

Schumacker, R. E., & Lomax, R. G. (2015) *A Beginner's Guide to Structural Equation Modeling*, 4th ed., New York: Routledge.

Strickland-Munro, J. K., Allison, H. E., & Moore, S. A. (2010) Using resilience concepts to investigate the impacts of protected area tourism on communities. *Annals of Tourism Research* 37, 499–519.

Thompson, B. (2004) *Exploratory and Confirmatory Factor Analysis: Understanding Concepts and Applications*, Washington, DC: American Psychological Association.

Torre, A., & Scarborough, H. (2017) Reconsidering the estimation of the economic impact of cultural tourism. *Tourism Management* 59, 621–629.

Tosun, C. (2002) Host perceptions of impacts: A comparative tourism study. *Annals of Tourism Research* 29, 231–253.

Waitt, G. (2003) Social impacts of the Sydney Olympics. *Annals of Tourism Research* 30, 194–215.

World Travel & Tourism Council. (2017) *Travel & Tourism Economic Impact 2017*, London: World Travel & Tourism Council.

Yolal, M., Gursoy, D., Uysal, M, Kim, H. L., & Karacaoglu, S. (2016) Impacts of festivals and events on residents' well-being. *Annals of Tourism Research* 61, 1–18.

Further reading

Briassoulis, H. (1991) Methodological issues: Tourism input–output analysis. *Annals of Tourism Research* 18, 485–495.

Creswell, J. W., & Plano Clark, V. L. (2011) *Designing and Conducting Mixed Methods Research*. 2nd ed., Thousand Oaks, CA: Sage.

Dimitrov, D. M. (2009) *Quantitative Research in Education: Intermediate and Advanced Methods*, Oceanside, NY: Whittier Publications.

Fox, J. (2016) *Applied Regression Analysis & Generalized Linear Models*, 3rd ed., Thousand Oaks, CA: Sage.

Hinkle, D. E., Wiersma, W., & Jurs, S. G. (2003) *Applied Statistics for the Behavioral Sciences*, 5th ed., Belmont, CA: Cengage Learning.

Kline, R. (2011) *Principles and Practice of Structural Equation Modeling*, 3rd ed., New York: Guilford.

Lindlof, T. R., & Taylor, B. C. (2002) *Qualitative Communication Research Methods*, 2nd ed., Thousand Oaks, CA: Sage.

Merriam, S. B., & Tisdell, E. J. (2016) *Qualitative Research: A Guide to Design and Implementation*, 4th ed., San Francisco, CA: Jossey-Bass.

Olobatuyi, M. E. (2006) *A User's Guide to Path Analysis*, New York: University Press.

Schumacker, R. E., & Lomax, R. G. (2015) *A Beginner's Guide to Structural Equation Modeling*, 4th ed., New York: Routledge.

Thompson, B. (2004) *Exploratory and Confirmatory Factor Analysis: Understanding Concepts and Applications*, Washington, DC: American Psychological Association.

34

A BAYESIAN MODELING APPROACH TO ASSESS THE MODERATING EFFECT OF GENDER AND NATIONALITY ON PERCEPTION OF RESIDENTS TOWARDS SUPPORT OF TOURISM DEVELOPMENT IN THE UNITED ARAB EMIRATES

Nada Al-Sabri, Avraam Papastathopoulos,
and Syed Zamberi Ahmad

Introduction

Tourism is a sector of hope that demonstrates resilience in the current global conditions and in the face of security threats. In 2016, tourist arrivals worldwide reached 1,235 million, compared with 25 million in 1950 (UNWTO, 2017). Tourism can bring about many social and cultural changes in the daily life of a community (Stylidis, Biran, Sit, & Szivas, 2014) that may influence residents' perceptions of the impacts of tourism (Brida, Osti, & Faccioli, 2011). Previous studies have suggested that residents' perceptions of the impacts of tourism can influence their support for tourism development (ST; Andereck, Valentine, Knopf, & Vogt, 2005; Látková & Vogt, 2012; Long & Kayat, 2011; Nunkoo & Gursoy, 2012). Residents who perceive the impacts of tourism positively are supportive of tourism development and are more willing to participate in tourism activities, whereas residents who perceive the impacts of tourism negatively are less supportive of tourism development (Sharpley, 2014; Stylidis et al., 2014). It is therefore important for tourism planners and officials to understand residents' perceptions of the impacts of tourism to gain their ST.

Over the past few decades, a rich body of literature has investigated the relationship between residents' perceptions of tourism impact and their ST (Andereck et al., 2005; Gursoy, Chi & Dyer, 2010; Látková & Vogt, 2012; Long & Kayat, 2011; Nunkoo & Gursoy 2012; Sharpley, 2014). The findings of these studies have revealed that residents' perceptions of the impacts of tourism influence their ST, and the level of support is likely to increase if their perceptions are positive and to decrease if their perceptions are negative (Hammad, Ahmad, & Papastathopoulos, 2017b; Sinclair-Maragh, 2017). Tourism studies examining residents' perceptions have identified demographic characteristics as factors that influence residents' perceptions of tourism (Andereck et al., 2005; Almeida-García, Peláez-Fernández, Balbuena-Vázquez, & Cortés-Macias, 2016; Lopez & Mercader, 2015; Sinclair-Maragh, 2017; Wang, 2013). The term "perception" is used to describe the individual attributes of an object and the demographic characteristics that can explain variations among residents in their perceptions of tourism. For example, residents' nationality can influence their perceptions of tourism development (Lopez & Mercader, 2015). Alhemoud and Armstrong (1996) noted that Kuwaiti national residents had different preferences regarding tourist attractions in Kuwait than English-speaking foreigners living in Kuwait. Furthermore, residents' gender can also explain their perceptions of tourism development (Wang, Bickle, & Harrill, 2010). Sinclair-Maragh (2017) argues that it has become a trend in Jamaica for females to take care of the financial needs of the family; therefore, tourism is viewed as an opportunity for entrepreneurial activities and to provide financial independence. According to Lundberg (2017), the ability to provide precise information about residents contributes to tourism planning processes. Understanding the factors that influence residents' perceptions of the impacts of tourism can provide valuable data for government officials and tourism stakeholders in terms of developing initiatives and policies that emphasize the positive impacts of tourism and eliminate or mitigate the negative impacts. As noted by Gursoy et al. (2010), the assessment of tourism impacts is likely to vary among individuals, which makes it almost impossible to receive endorsement from all residents. Therefore, there is a need to examine different demographic variables to achieve a better understanding of and insights into residents' perceptions of tourism (Khoshkam, Marzuki, & Al-Mulali, 2016). According to Prayag and Ryan (2012), nationality is one of the strongest demographic characteristics that influence residents' perceptions. Similarly, gender can be used to explain the relationship between residents' perceptions of the impacts of tourism and their ST (Sinclair-Maragh, 2017). To address the gap in previous studies, this study examines the moderating effect of gender and nationality on the relationship between residents' perceptions of the impacts of tourism and their ST. To that end, this study aims to answer two main research questions. First, what is the relationship between residents' perceptions of the impacts of tourism and their ST? Second, how do gender and nationality moderate this relationship? Aiming to answer these two questions, this study developed and tested a theoretical model that posited relationships between tourism impacts, in particular social and cultural impacts, and residents' ST.

The remainder of the chapter reviews the literature concerning the impacts of tourism, describes the conceptual development of the theoretical model and the methodology used for this study, presents the results and discussion, and concludes by presenting the theoretical contributions and managerial implications of the study.

The study area (UAE)

The United Arab Emirates (UAE) is one of the wealthiest countries in the world, with high income levels and a high standard of living for the residents. More than US$6.86 billion was allocated in 2017 for social development and benefits for UAE residents (MOF, 2018). Tourism is one of the main economies through which the government can achieve such a goal and is a key contributor to the UAE gross domestic product (GDP), with a direct contribution by the travel and tourism sector of more than AED68.5 billion (US$18.7 billion) in 2016. The UAE has experienced significant growth in the number of tourist arrivals, which nearly doubled in the last decade, increasing from 8 million in 2006 to 15.3 million in 2016; therefore, in recent years, the UAE has experienced greater numbers of visitors than its number of residents.

The UAE tourism source markets for tourist arrivals are highly diverse and include countries from all over the world. In 2017, the 15.8 million tourist arrivals in the UAE included visitors from India, Saudi Arabia, Oman, Pakistan, the UK, the USA, China, Germany, Iran, and Kuwait (UAE Tourism Report, 2017).

Similar to the diverse source markets for tourist arrivals in the UAE, UAE society is also considered diverse, as national residents represent less than 20% of the total number of residents. The UAE is home to more than 100 different nationalities, and many foreigners have lived and worked in the UAE for many years. Although the majority of the residents of the UAE arrived after the discovery of oil in the 1960s, several groups inhabited the land before the discovery and depended on the scarce resources available in the desert and coastal and mountain areas. These groups included the Bedouins, who lived in the desert and followed a nomadic lifestyle that allowed them to move often in the pursuit of resources such as food and water for themselves and their animals. Another group was the urban and coastal population, who depended mainly on the sea for economic opportunities such as fishing, pearling, and trade. The society also included inhabitants of agricultural lands, mountain dwellers, island inhabitants, and a group of Arabs who moved between the Arabian Gulf and the Persian shore of the Arabian Gulf.

During the 1960s, the UAE attracted many foreign inhabitants of a mixture of races, including of Arab origin, nationals of Iranian origin, Indians, and Africans who moved to the UAE before the discovery of oil (Ghubash, 1992). UAE society included two main classifications for residents before the discovery of oil: the influential and wealthy group, consisting of the royal family, merchants, and ship owners, and the group of common workers, such as pearl divers, ship repair laborers, farmers, and fishermen (Sarhan, 1995). After the discovery of oil and the formation of the UAE in 1971, the traditional economy changed, and more options became available for government investment, which provided UAE residents with one of the highest standards of living worldwide (Al-Mansoori, 2004). The income created from oil and massive infrastructure investments led to a massive influx of people who came to the UAE in search of work opportunities, better living conditions, and new experiences, which led to the emergence of new classifications within the worker group: skilled, semiskilled, and unskilled (Shaheem, 2014). The majority of the UAE workforce is nonnational, which has caused a gender division of more males than females. According to official UAE statistics, when the UAE total population reached 9,121,167 in 2016, 6,298,294 residents—or 69% of the total population—were male, and 2,822,873—or 31% of the total population—were female (FCSA, 2018). Despite the dominant percentage of males in the UAE, women enjoy the same constitutional rights as men (UAE Government, 2017a). In addition, the UAE government recently announced that the Council of Ministers had approved a gender equality law that is designed to guarantee equal pay for men and women in the UAE (*Gulf Business*, 2018). The UAE government is also attentive to the national residents, who receive benefits and advantages from the governments of the emirates, such as free housing, free public schools, citizenship rights, reductions in utility payments, pension programs, social benefits for the elderly, and scholarship and sponsorship programs that are unavailable to nonnational residents (Al Ahbabi, 2016; Shaheem, 2014). UAE government regulations are designed to protect the rights of residents to celebrate their cultures and religions, regardless of nationality or ethnicity. The UAE society is based on a tolerant, tribal Muslim culture that provides a welcoming environment for various cultures that have been brought to the UAE by nonnationals (Al-Shamsi, 2009) and for the millions of tourists who visit the UAE each year.

Literature review

Within the considerable literature related to residents' perceptions of the impacts of tourism, the theories most commonly used to explain the influence of various demographic aspects on residents' perceptions of tourism and their ST are social exchange theory (Ap, 1992; Dyer, Gursoy, Sharma, & Carter, 2007; Gursoy, Jurowski, & Uysal, 2002; Gursoy & Rutherford, 2004; Miyakuni, 2012; Spanou, 2016; Stylidis et al., 2014; Yu, 2011) and social identity theory (Kaewnuch, 2010; Palmer, Koenig-Lewis & Jones, 2013; Soontayatron, 2010; Vines, 2005). The current study utilizes social exchange theory and social identity theory as guides to enhance our understanding of residents' perceptions of tourism development. The fundamental basis of social exchange theory is that individuals are likely to engage in an exchange if they anticipate that the benefits received exceed the costs incurred (Maurer, 1977). Social identity theory suggests that individuals tend to classify themselves into in-groups and out-groups based on certain criteria (Haobin Ye, Qiu Zhang, Huawen Shen, & Goh, 2014). Therefore, utilizing both theories is considered suitable for building a theoretical framework to examine residents' perceptions of the impacts of tourism and then to analyze how residents' gender and nationality can influence the relationship between their perceptions and their ST.

Social exchange theory

Social exchange theory indicates that people are likely to participate in an exchange if they anticipate that the gains, or benefits, that they will receive will exceed the costs, or inconveniences, that might result from the exchange (Maurer, 1977). The basis of the theory in the context of the tourism literature is that residents are willing to endorse tourism development if they perceive that the positive impacts of tourism are greater than the negative impacts (Dyer et al., 2007). The theory became popular from the 1990s onward in tourism research, in particular when residents' perceptions of tourism were being investigated (Stewart, 2009). Jurowski, Uysal, and Williams (1997) utilized social exchange theory to develop a model that examined the relationship between residents' perceptions of economic, social, and environmental impacts and their ST. A study conducted in Washington, North Carolina, by Wang and Pfister (2008) reported that noneconomic value domains can influence residents' perceptions of tourism, as the residents expressed positive perceptions of tourism and recognized social benefits associated with tourism development even though they did not report direct economic gain from tourism. Researchers continue to build on extant studies that use social exchange theory; for example, Stylidis (2012) developed and tested a model that included three additional factors that can influence residents' perception: residence image, potential economic benefit, and community attachment. The findings reported by Stylidis (2012) confirmed the value of social exchange theory in explaining residents' perceptions of tourism. Based on the preceding discussion, the following hypotheses are proposed:

H1: There is a direct positive relationship between residents' perceived positive social impacts of tourism and their support for tourism development.

H2: There is a direct negative relationship between residents' perceived negative social impacts of tourism and their support for tourism development.

H3: There is a direct positive relationship between residents' perceived positive cultural impacts of tourism and their support for tourism development.

H4:   There is a direct, negative relationship between residents' perceived negative cultural impacts of tourism and their support for tourism development.

Social identity theory

The relationship between residents' perceptions of tourism impacts and their support for tourism can be further explained by social identity theory. The basic idea of social identity theory is that a social category such as nationality or political affiliation, into which an individual falls and in which the individual forms a sense of belonging, provides a definition of who the individual is in terms of the defining characteristics of that category (Hogg, Terry, & White, 1995). Thus, people of the same nationality or members of the same club often consider themselves one group. Social identity theory is based on the idea that individuals have a fundamental need to perceive their own group as superior to other groups (Maruyama & Woosnam, 2015). As noted by Shaheem (2014), social identity theory argues that people are motivated to maintain a positive self-image, as when individuals attribute favorable characteristics to their in-group members and negative characteristics to out-group members (Maruyama & Woosnam, 2015). For example, Soontayatron (2010) explained that migrant groups in Thailand, which are considered minority groups, often experience both negative stereotyping and attitudes from local residents, who are the majority. Soontayatron (2010) further explained that this negative perception can lead the migrant groups to adopt various responses to change their social identity and repair their self-esteem. Using social identity theory, this study focuses on gender and nationality as key variables for group differentiation to examine the moderating effect of those factors on the perceptions of the residents.

Gender

The gender of a resident has a significant influence in predicting the individual's perceptions of tourism development (Wang, 2013). However, findings in the literature regarding the influence of gender on the perceptions of residents have been contradictory. Although some studies found the influence of gender to be nonsignificant (Mensah, 2012; Rasoolimanesh, Jaafar, Kock, & Ramayah, 2015), other researchers argued that females are more likely than males to have positive perceptions of tourism because of the benefits they receive from tourism (Erul, 2014; Sinclair-Maragh, 2017; Wang & Pfister, 2008; Wang, 2013). Wang et al. (2010) observed that female residents of Shandong, China, evaluated tourism more positively but were more negative about the changes associated with it, whereas male residents had a more positive attitude towards the economic impacts of tourism. Thrane (2008) argued that male residents working in tourism earn on average 20% higher annual wages than female residents working in similar jobs. Although receiving economic benefits from tourism can influence residents' perceptions of tourism (Dyer et al., 2007), unfair treatment or unequal pay can lead to differences in perceptions. In addition, understanding the perceptions of residents in relation to their gender can help tourism marketers target male and female residents differently during the process of internal marketing (Wang, 2013). We therefore proposed the following hypotheses:

H1a: Gender has a moderating effect on the direct positive relationship between residents' perceived positive social impacts of tourism and their support for tourism development.

H2a: Gender has a moderating effect on the direct negative relationship between residents' perceived negative social impacts of tourism and their support for tourism development.

H3a: Gender has a moderating effect on the direct positive relationship between residents' perceived positive cultural impacts of tourism and their support for tourism development.

H4a: Gender has a moderating effect on the direct negative relationship between residents' perceived negative cultural impacts of tourism and their support for tourism development.

Nationality

Residents possess the legal documentation issued by a government that makes them citizens of that country. Nationality refers to possessing the legal documents issued by the government of a country. National residents have legal rights that are often not available to nonnational residents. Nationality is an important factor in tourism marketing research because it is measurable, substantial, and sizable; accessible in terms of being a segment that can be targeted and reached; and actionable, which means it can be targeted using marketing or advertising programs (Thrane & Farstad, 2012). Nationality is commonly used in tourism marketing research to examine tourists' spending habits while traveling (Thrane & Farstad, 2012), travel motivations (Jönsson & Devonish, 2008; Kozak, 2002; Peter & Anandkumar, 2014), and satisfaction with a destination (Kozak, 2001; Lee, Lee, & Wicks, 2004), and residents' perceptions of the impacts of tourism (Lopez &Mercader, 2015). According to Lopez and Mercader (2015), national and nonnational residents of Spain have different perceptions of tourism. Nonnational residents show more positive perceptions of the positive economic impacts of tourism, whereas national residents show more concern for the negative impacts of tourism. Jönsson and Devonish (2008) argued that it is difficult to rely solely on nationality in the case of destinations that are multicultural and comprise immigrants of various nationalities without understanding the context of a study. In examining the use of nationality in the context of the study area (the UAE), which is considered a multicultural destination, a study conducted by Bashir (2011) to compare differences in the consumption of dairy products among national and nonnational residents yielded confirmation of the usefulness of nationality as a means of market segmentation in the UAE. Hence, the following hypotheses are proposed:

H1b: Nationality has a moderating effect on the direct positive relationship between residents' perceived positive social impacts of tourism and their support for tourism development.

H2b: Nationality has a moderating effect on the direct negative relationship between residents' perceived negative social impacts of tourism and their support for tourism development.

H3b: Nationality has a moderating effect on the direct positive relationship between residents' perceived positive cultural impacts of tourism and their support for tourism development.

H4b: Nationality has a moderating effect on the direct negative relationship between residents' perceived negative cultural impacts of tourism and their support for tourism development.

The proposed model

To address the research hypotheses, the model proposed in Figure 34.1 suggests that there is a relationship between residents' perceptions of the impacts of tourism and their ST, and that gender and nationality moderate this relationship.

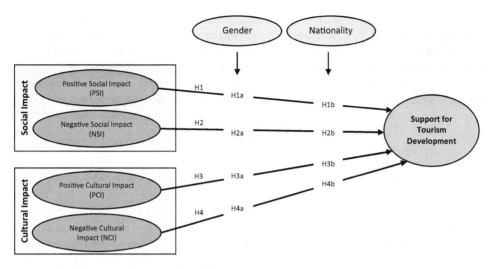

Figure 34.1 The proposed theoretical model

Research methodology

Data collection

This study used random sampling to select a group of residents living in the UAE who were 18 years or older, regardless of their nationality, to participate in the study. The questionnaire was initially written in English and then translated into Arabic, the official language of the UAE, using an authorized legal translation service to ensure the reliability of the translated version. Using professional bilingual translators is common in social science studies and has been found to be appropriate (Al-Shamsi, 2009). The data were collected using self-administered questionnaires. Two media were used, a hard copy and an online version, in both languages. Yun and Trumbo (2000) explained that using multimode survey techniques improves the representativeness of a sample without biasing the results. During the data collection, 1,000 questionnaires were distributed to potential respondents, and 726 questionnaires were returned. Of these, 53 were removed from the analysis owing to missing data, thus yielding a 67% response rate. A link to the online version was sent to respondents using email, smartphone applications, and social media. These 350 individuals received an invitation to complete an online questionnaire with a link provided in the email, application, or post. The response rate was 87%, as 306 online questionnaires were returned. The advantage of using both online and hard-copy questionnaires was that targeted responses were collected within 4 weeks, and 979 usable questionnaires were returned by various residents. A total of 46 nationalities residing in the UAE participated in the survey. The total of 979 responses used for data analysis included 608 nonnational residents and 371 national residents.

Measurement of variables

The demographic variables analyzed were gender, age, city of residence, level of education, length of residency, and nationality. Six age groups were included: 18–20, 21–30, 31–39, 40–49, and 50 or more years. The respondents selected from options regarding their gender and the city in which they resided, but they wrote in their nationalities. The five constructs assessed in this study are positive social impacts (PSIs), negative social impacts (NSIs), positive cultural impacts (PCIs), negative cultural impacts (NCIs), and ST. Each construct was measured using five questions. The respondents rated their responses using a 7-point, Likert-type scale (from 1 = strongly disagree to 7 = strongly agree) and were offered a "no" option if they did not wish to share a response. The questions were worded positively, and no reverse questions were included. The study used measurement scales that have been used in previous tourism impact studies (Gursoy & Rutherford, 2004; Ko & Stewart, 2002; Lin, 1999; Long & Kayat, 2011; Nunkoo & Ramkissoon, 2010), and the scales were refined and modified to assess the constructs proposed in the study. According to Stylidis (2012), universal measurement scales are rare; most studies that measure residents' perceptions of tourism impacts use different variables and scales, and disparate statements are sometimes used even in similar studies. A similar process of measurement selection and testing was used by Kim (2002), Stylidis (2012), and Yu (2011). The selection was based on several criteria: The items must be universally recognized at tourism destinations, yet must apply to the study area (Stylidis et al., 2014), such as traffic congestion and the physical appearance of a destination. Five items measured residents' perceptions of the PSIs of tourism, all of which were measured in previous studies (Faulkner & Tideswell, 1997; Gursoy et al., 2010; Ko & Stewart, 2002). Five items measured residents' perceptions of the NSIs of tourism, all of which were drawn from previous studies (Lin, 1999; Long & Kayat, 2011; Miyakuni, 2012; Yu, 2011). Five items measured residents' perceptions of the PCIs of tourism, all of which were drawn from past research (Andereck, Valentine, Vogt, & Knopf, 2007; Dyer et al., 2007; Faulkner & Tideswell, 1997; Gursoy et al., 2010; Jurowski, 1994; Ko & Stewart, 2002). Five items measured residents' perceptions of the NCIs of tourism, all of which appeared in research by Feng (2008), Kim, Uysal, and Sirgy (2013), Lin (1999), and Soontayatron (2010). The last section included items that measured residents' ST, all of which were adapted from previous studies (Kim, 2002; Stylidis, 2012; Yu, 2011; Miyakuni, 2012).

Data analysis

The covariance-based structural equation modeling approach

Structural equation modeling (SEM) is a commonly accepted tool, often used for research hypothesis testing in psychology and the social sciences (Lee, Song, & Tang, 2007). It has shown itself to be a powerful multivariate tool for testing, confirming, or comparing theories (Song & Lee, 2012), as it combines a structural model test, whereby multiple dependence relationships can be analyzed at the same time, with a test for the measurement model used—that is, confirmatory factor analysis (CFA; (Bagozzi & Yi, 2012). Therefore, researchers can use it for testing cause-and-effect relationships with latent variables (Hair, Black, Babin, Anderson, & Tatham, 2010).

Traditionally, SEM employs a covariance-based approach focusing on "fitting the covariance structure of the model to the sample covariance matrix of the observed data" (Lee & Song, 2014, p. 276). This statistical methodology uses a confirmatory (hypothesis-testing) approach to structural theory analysis bearing on certain phenomena (Byrne, 2001). Usually, this theory represents causal processes that produce observations for many variables (Bentler, 1988). The hypothesized model can then be statistically tested in a simultaneous analysis of the whole system of variables to determine how consistent it is with the data. If goodness-of-fit is sufficient, the model argues that the postulated relations among variables are plausible. However, if it is insufficient, the tenability of such relations is dismissed.

The Bayesian structural equation modeling approach

Muthén and Asparouhov (2012) introduced an approach to model specification and estimation in SEM based on Bayesian methods. Their Bayesian SEM concentrated on the long-standing issues with and limitations of conventional SEM. As a result, it offered major benefits for empirical applications. Their approach was a major step in the continuous development of Bayesian methods for SEM (Jedidi & Ansari, 2001; Lee, 2007; Palomo, Dunson, & Bollen, 2007; Scheines, Hoijtink, & Boomsma, 1999). Zyphur and Oswald (2013) named the swift expansion of this Bayesian approach across an increasing number of social science fields the "Bayesian revolution." As previously noted, SEM traditionally employs a covariance-based approach focusing on "fitting the covariance structure of the model to the sample covariance matrix of the observed data" (Lee & Song, 2014, p. 276). Nonetheless, the covariance-based approach does have certain shortfalls. Specifically, it is "unable to produce correct results for statistical inferences" (Lee & Song, 2014, p. 277) for some structures with complicated data. What is more, model assumptions and statistical properties of the estimates, and the goodness-of-fit test generated from these approaches, are "asymptotically true only" (Lee & Song, 2004, p. 653). The Bayesian approach can be used to overcome this problem (Assaf, Tsionas, & Oh, 2018).

The typical frequentist approach used by SEM obtains statistical inferences through estimating the probability of an event occurring according to a set or a series of samples. The precision of the estimates relies on the extent to which the samples explain and show the population at any given time. Consequently, in this approach, frequency provides the concept of probability. If the true values of the model parameters are fixed, the probability of an event occurring will be slightly different and will depend on the magnitude of the statistical error. As Arbuckle (2016) noted, the presumption lies in the fact that the true population values are seen as fixed but unknown, and the estimates for the given sample are seen as random but unknown. This discrepancy is considered a statistical problem in the interpretation of probability in a symmetric distribution (Woodside, 2013). However, those who employ the Bayesian technique consider the true value of model parameters to be unknown and random. Unknown values are believed to be distributed based on a probability distribution that shows what is known about the parameters before obtaining the data set. After obtaining the data set, the distribution is updated to reflect the new information by way of Bayes's theorem. This approach gives rise to a "posterior distribution" (Arbuckle, 2016; Bolstad & Curran, 2016). As the true values of the model parameters are unknown, the probability of events occurring will vary across the probability distribution. This situation is a *key difference between the frequentist and Bayesian approaches.* Universally, the Bayesian approach to data analysis is believed to be more flexible (Kanapathy, Khong, & Dekkers, 2014; Muthén & Asparouhov, 2012). Progress in computational algorithms based on Markov chain Monte Carlo (MCMC) sampling led to the increased use of Bayesian tools for statistical modeling. The MCMC algorithm is used in software programs such as WinBUGS (Lunn, Thomas, Best, & Spiegelhalter, 2000), in various packages in the R archive (R Development Core Team, 2016), and lately in Mplus (Muthén & Muthén, 2012) and AMOS (Arbuckle, 2016).

A significant assumption for covariance-based SEM is *multivariate normality* within the data distribution. However, many covariance-based SEM applications over the last two decades have been based on ordered-categorical data (e.g., Likert scales), in which case this assumption cannot hold true (Bulmer, 2012; Tucker, 1962). *Treating Likert rating scale data as ongoing outcomes* in CFA *violates the multivariate normality assumption* (Lubke & Muthén, 2004). The same authors argue that, in a multigroup context, such as the context of this study, an analysis of Likert data under the multivariate normality assumption may *alter the factor structure* in a different manner among groups. Although it has become common practice to treat these ordinal data as if they were constantly being scaled (Byrne, 2016), failure to manage the ordinal nature of data may lead to biased research findings (DiStefano, 2002). For this study, the normality of the data was examined using Kolmogorov–Smirnov and Shapiro–Wilk tests, which are preferred when examining skewness, kurtosis, or both because of their good power properties (Mendes & Pala, 2003). The data are not normally distributed, and, therefore, the need for a Bayesian SEM approach is evident (Table 34.3). One way to manage the ordinal nature of empirical data in SEM analysis is to use the Bayesian estimation approach, rather than the traditional frequentist methods—for example, maximum likelihood estimation.

Apart from considering the ordinal nature of data, *Bayesian estimation offers researchers two more benefits*:

- First, it offers additional, and more accurate, information on the estimated model parameters (i.e., information on the joint probability distribution of the parameters) in comparison with the traditional estimation procedures in covariance-based SEM. In addition, it permits researchers to use prior distribution information so as to estimate these parameter distributions, specifically posterior distributions (Song & Lee, 2012).
- Second, previous research has shown that Bayesian estimation results are more accurate and reliable in estimating SEMs when relatively small sample sizes are used (Lee & Song, 2004).

Although Bayesian statistics in empirical management research have been attracting growing attention recently (e.g., Jebb & Woo, 2015; Zyphur & Oswald, 2013), there seems to be rather limited insight into and understanding of this estimation approach. Moreover, its application in empirical tourism research is rare. For the purposes of this study, the authors analyzed data based on the Bayesian estimation procedure in AMOS 24. To analyze categorical data, this software uses the Bayesian approach as a default method (Byrne, 2016).

Results

Demographic profile of respondents

For this study, the data were collected from 979 participants, of whom 371 were national residents (37.9%) and 608 were nonnational residents (62.1%). Regarding gender, the majority of the respondents were males (542, or 55.4%), and the remaining 437 (44.6%) were females. The demographic profile of the respondents is presented in Table 34.1.

Measurement model

The Bayesian estimation of posterior values was initially used to examine the psychometric properties of all study measures (Table 34.3). Except for the means commonly provided by Bayesian estimation, all standardized factor loadings also had to be estimated. No items were dropped during the CFA process, given that all items of the latent constructs were statistically significant (p < 0.05) and greater than 0.5. This indicates that our constructs have convergent validity (Hair et al., 2010). Frequentist reliability and validity measures, such as composite reliability and Cronbach's, are based on multivariate normality. As a result, it is not possible for them to be calculated for ordinal variables (Van Poucke, Matthyssens, & Weeren, 2016).

The Fornell–Larcker criterion (Fornell & Larcker, 1981; Hair et al., 2010) was used to assess discriminant validity . Based on this approach, the square root of average variance extracted (AVE)

Table 34.1 Profile of respondents

Category		Frequency (N)	Percentage (%)
Gender	Male	542	55.4
	Female	437	44.6
Nationality	National	371	37.9
	Nonnational	608	62.1
Age	18–20	28	2.9
	21–30	250	25.5
	31–39	334	34.1
	40–49	236	24.1
	≥50	131	13.4
Education	High school or less	123	12.6
	Technical education	124	12.7
	Bachelor's degree	520	53.1
	Master's degree and above	212	21.7
Length of residency	Less than 5 years	193	19.7
	5 years or more but fewer than 10	138	14.1
	10 years or more but fewer than 20	191	19.5
	20 years or more	457	46.7
Residence	Abu Dhabi	408	41.7
	Dubai	438	44.7
	Other Emirates	133	13.6

Table 34.2 Correlation matrix and discriminant validity

	PCI	NSI	PSI	ST	NCI	Discriminant validity
PCI	**0.731***					Achieved
NSI	−0.259**	**0.738**				Achieved
PSI	0.648	−0.254	**0.722**			Achieved
ST	0.639	−0.340	0.646	**0.801**		Achieved
NCI	−0.368	0.705	−0.320	−0.382	**0.713**	Achieved

Notes: * Diagonal elements in bold denote the square root of average variance extracted; ** lower triangle denotes the posterior means of the correlations.

values is compared with the latent variable correlations. Moreover, the square root of each construct's AVE must be greater than its highest correlation with any other construct. The posterior distributions of the covariances and variables for all the model variables were calculated based on the Bayesian estimation procedure; any correlations were also computed from these. The correlations were lower than the square root of the AVEs. This proved discriminant validity (Table 34.2).

The Bayesian estimation procedure uses MCMC algorithms to repeatedly draw random samples from the posterior distribution of the model parameters (Muthén & Muthén, 2012). The posterior distributions by trace and autocorrelation plots (Muthén & Muthén, 2012) were monitored so as to assess convergence of the MCMC algorithm in distribution. The posterior parameter trace plots depict the sampled parameter values over time. Rapid convergence in distribution is indicated through quick up-and-down fluctuations and absence of long-term trends in the plot (Arbuckle, 2016; Kaplan & Depaoli, 2012). Autocorrelation plots also depict the extent of nonindependence of consecutive posterior draws in the MCMC chains (Kaplan & Depaoli, 2012; Muthén & Muthén, 2012). To allow the MCMC procedure to converge to the

Table 34.3 Key descriptive statistics, test of normality, and psychometric properties

Construct	Items	Test of normality K–S[a] test Statistic	AVE	S.D.	B	Sig.
Positive social impacts	**PSI1:** Tourism improves the quality of life of UAE residents	.229**	.521	1.258	.680	*
	PSI2: Tourism improves the positive image of the UAE	.267**		.962	.754	*
	PSI3: Tourism improves the quality of service in restaurants, shops, and hotels	.241**		.939	.739	*
	PSI4: Increased tourism provides more recreational opportunities for UAE residents	.245**		1.095	.731	*
	PSI5: Tourism development makes the residents more satisfied with their lives in the UAE	.211**		1.319	.703	*
Negative social impacts	**NSI1:** Tourism causes unpleasant overcrowding of public and leisure spaces in the UAE	.139**	.545	1.740	.671	*
	NSI2: Tourism causes security and crime problems	.142**		1.784	.781	*
	NSI3: An increase in the number of tourists in the UAE will lead to friction between residents and tourists	.149**		1.770	.693	*
	NSI4: Tourism contributes to social problems such as crime, drug use, prostitution, etc., in the UAE	.130**		1.822	.784	*
	NSI5: The UAE's recreational resources are overused by tourists	.145**		1.732	.756	*
Positive cultural impacts	**PCI1:** Tourism increases the availability of cultural, historical, and entertainment activities in the UAE	.260**	.535	1.087	.644	*
	PCI2: Meeting tourists from all over the world is definitely a life-enriching experience	.249**		1.212	.713	*
	PCI3: Tourism helps to preserve the cultural identity of the UAE	.199**		1.573	.674	*
	PCI4: Tourism stimulates cultural exchange in the UAE	.246**		1.203	.853	*
	PCI5: Tourism has increased residents' pride in the local culture of the UAE	.243**		1.313	.755	*
Negative cultural impacts	**NCI1:** Tourists' style of dress is considered inappropriate and not conservative enough for the UAE	.143**	.509	1.733	.703	*

	NCI2: The commercial demands of tourists cause changes in the style and forms of traditional arts and crafts in the UAE	.139**		1.599	.659	*
	NCI3: Current tourism activities that are available for tourists do not reflect the authentic culture of the UAE	.131**		1.676	.667	*
	NCI4: Tourism causes loss of traditional values and behavior patterns among UAE residents	.121**		1.769	.860	*
	NCI5: Tourism development causes disruption to religious practices among UAE residents	.149**		1.891	.656	*
Support for tourism development	**ST1:** I believe that further tourism development would positively affect my quality of life in the UAE	.188**	.642	1.371	.639	*
	ST2: I think that the UAE should attract more tourists	.217**		1.427	.831	*
	ST3: I support future tourism development in the UAE	.234**		1.213	.894	*
	ST4: I think that tourism is the best strategy for economic diversification for the UAE	.225**		1.326	.784	*
	ST5: I believe that the overall impact of tourism development in the UAE is positive	.248**		1.207	.836	*

Notes: ᵃ K–S = Kolmogorov–Smirnov test; ** denotes values significant at a = 0.01; * denotes significance at 0.05 level in the sense that the 95% Bayesian credibility interval does not cover zero (the numerical values represent posterior means of the standardized estimates).

true combined posterior distribution, AMOS draws burn-in samples. As soon as AMOS draws and discards the burn-in samples, it then draws additional samples to provide a clear overview of the combined posterior distribution. The default limit of this software is 100,000 MCMC samples. When AMOS reaches this limit, it starts the so-called thinning process. This involves keeping an equally spaced subset of samples, rather than all the samples. AMOS starts the MCMC sampling process by keeping all the samples up to the limit of 100,000. When it reaches that point, if the sampling process is not disrupted by the analysis of the data, it discards one-half of the samples by removing every alternate one. This way, the lag-1 dependence in the rest of the sequence is the same as the lag-2 dependence of the original, un-thinned sequence. AMOS continues the sampling process from that point, retaining one out of every two samples generated, until reaching the upper limit of 100,000 again, and so on. The thinning process works out the autocorrelation between successive samples. Therefore, a thinned sequence of 100,000 samples gives more information than an un-thinned sequence of the same length. In the case we studied, the results were based on 90,000 samples, collected following the thinning process.

Bayesian estimation provides the posterior predictive value as a general goodness-of-fit measure to assess model fit (Scheines et al., 1999). MCMC convergence of posterior parameters demonstrates that an adequate number of samples has been drawn from the posterior distribution so as to accurately estimate posterior parameter values (Arbuckle, 2016). In our model, the posterior predictive value was 0.52, indicating that the model has a very good fit (Gelman, Carlin, Stern, & Rubin, 2014). MCMC convergence is also assessed through the potential scale reduction (PSR) convergence criterion (Gelman et al., 2014; Gelman & Rubin, 1992). The PSR criterion is used to compare within- and between-chain variation of parameter estimates. When using a single MCMC chain, the PSR compares variation within and between the third and fourth quarters of the repetitions. Perfect convergence is represented by a PSR value of 1,000 (Kaplan & Depaoli, 2012; Muthén & Muthén, 2012). When the number of parameters is large, convergence of the MCMC sequence is obtained when the PSR is less than 1.100 for each parameter (Muthén & Muthén, 2012). The PSR value in our model was 1.0019, indicating that convergence had been obtained.

Structural model

According to the results of the structural model (Table 34.4), support was achieved for H1, demonstrating a strong positive relationship of perceived PSI on support for tourism (Mean: 0.394, Confidence interval: 0.318 to 0.478). The NSI were found to have a negative impact on support for tourism. Nonetheless, this effect was weak (Mean: −0.098, Confidence interval: −0.153 to −0.045), providing support for H2. Additionally, H3 was also supported, demonstrating that the impact of perceived PCI on support for tourism was strongly positive (Mean: 0.491, Confidence interval: 0.396 to 0.595). Moreover, our analysis showed support for a negative, yet weak, effect on support for tourism of NCI (Mean: −0.07, Confidence interval: −0.132 to −0.009), providing support for H4.

The moderating roles of gender and nationality

Multigroup analysis in SEM is quite useful, as it allows researchers to compare multiple samples across multiple population groups for any identified structural equation model (Byrne, 2016). In other words, it allows researchers to test whether different groups do indeed differ significantly through meeting the assumption that they are equal by examining their invariance. In our case, we used the gender and nationality of respondents as the grouping criteria.

Before arguing the significance of gender and nationality and assessing whether the suggested hypotheses differ, the baseline models were studied separately and then combined in a single model (configural model). The estimation of baseline models does not require between-group constraints (Marsh, 1994). Therefore, it is best initially to analyze the data separately for each group. When testing for invariance, equality constraints are placed on particular parameters. So it is necessary to analyze the data for all groups simultaneously to obtain the results (Bentler, 2006; Joreskog & Sorbom, 1993). Nonetheless, the pattern of fixed and free parameters is consistent with the baseline model specification for each group. As a result, the first type of invariance examined is configural. The configural invariance is achieved provided that the model structure is invariable for all groups. This is a critical model because, if the data do not support identical patterns of fixed and non-fixed parameters for all the groups, then it will also not support more restrictive models (Bollen, 1989). Given this, we examined the fit of the two baseline models. A posterior predictive value of 0.52 and a PSR value of 1.018 (50,000 samples) were obtained for *Group A* (i.e., male group), whereas a posterior predictive value of 0.53 and a PSR value of 1.0017 (67,000 samples) were obtained for *Group B* (i.e., female group). This demonstrated that convergence had succeeded in both models. The analyses performed for the combined model (Groups A and B) showed that the model meets the configural invariance criterion,

Table 34.4 Structural model results

Hypothesis	Path	Mean	S.E.	S.D.	C.S.	95% lower bound	95% upper bound	Min.	Max.	Supported/ not supported
H1	Positive social impact → support for tourism	0.394	0.002	0.041	1.002	0.318	0.478	0.260	0.573	Supported
H2	Negative social impact → support for tourism	−0.098	0.002	0.028	1.002	−0.153	−0.045	−0.197	0.006	Supported
H3	Positive cultural impact → support for tourism	0.491	0.003	0.051	1.002	0.396	0.595	0.316	0.674	Supported
H4	Negative cultural impact → support for tourism	−0.07	0.002	0.032	1.002	−0.132	−0.009	−0.181	0.036	Supported

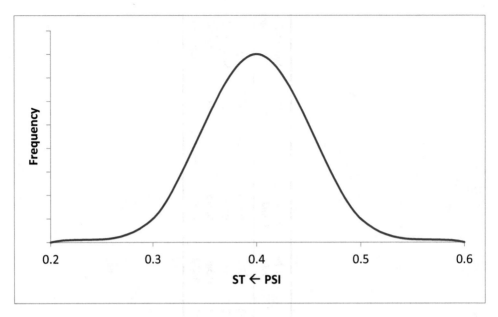

Figure 34.2   Posterior distribution from the effect of positive social impacts on support for tourism development

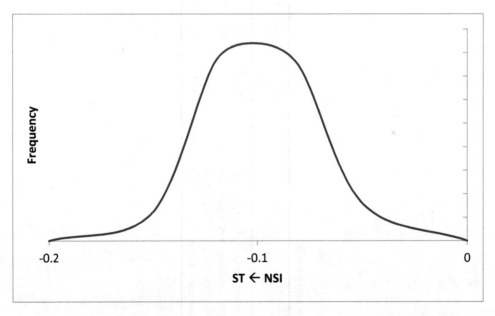

Figure 34.3   Posterior distribution from the effect of negative social impacts on support for tourism development

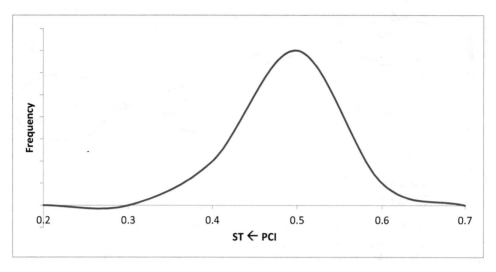

Figure 34.4 Posterior distribution from the effect of positive cultural impacts on support for tourism development

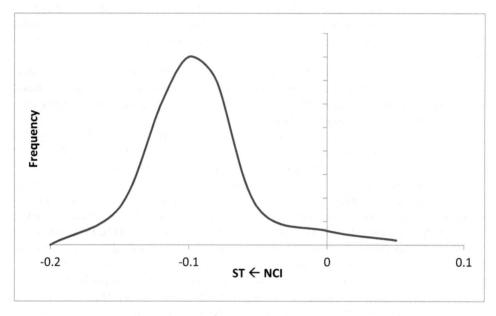

Figure 34.5 Posterior distribution from the effect of negative cultural impacts on support for tourism development

with a posterior predictive value of 0.53 and a PSR value of 1.016 (58,000 samples), allowing the multigroup analysis to continue. In terms of the Bayesian estimation procedure, the invariance hypotheses are ideally tested using Bayes's factors that compare the marginal likelihoods of the models with and without invariance constraints, and MCMC algorithms can be applied to evaluate different restricted versions of the model (Verhagen & Fox, 2013). The deviance information criterion (DIC) value (Spiegelhalter, Best, Carlin, & van der Linde, 2002) is applied

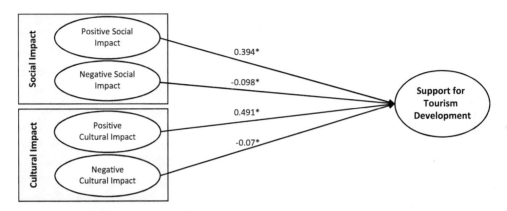

Figure 34.6 Results of the hypothesis testing and loadings of support for tourism development

Notes: The numerical values represent posterior means of the standardized estimates. * Indicates significance at the 0.05 level in the sense that the 95% Bayesian credibility interval does not cover zero.

to compare the fit models with and without invariance constraints. We tested the assumption of structural invariance by comparing the estimated DIC of the model with constrained structural paths and the invariant model. The models are not invariant if the estimated DIC of the invariant model is higher (Verhagen & Fox, 2013). Based on the results, the constrained model has a DIC value of 31,904.61, and the invariant model has a value of 32,061.96; therefore, the models differ.

Table 34.5 outlines the results of the Bayesian structural model with regard to the model-specific effects that need to be compared so as to examine the moderating role of gender. Based on the results, the effect of NSI on ST is not supported in the male group, and a negative relationship between these two constructs is supported in the female group (mean: −0.125; confidence interval: −0.225 to −0.033). Moreover, although, in the male group, NCI has a negative effect on ST (mean: −0.099; confidence interval: −0.180 to −0.019), this relationship is not verified in the female group. With regard to the moderating impact of gender on the effect of PSIs and PCIs on support for tourism, the effects were higher in the female group, with a mean of 0.437 (confidence interval: 0.319–0.567), compared with means of 0.399 (confidence interval: 0.297–0.501), 0.586 (confidence interval: 0.420–0.765), and 0.441 (confidence interval: 0.321–0.572), respectively (Table 34.6), demonstrating support for H1a, H2a, H3a, and H4a.

With regard to the moderating role of nationality, we also examined the fit of the two baseline models. A posterior predictive value of 0.51 and a PSR value of 1.016 (62,000 samples) were obtained for *Group C* (i.e., national group), whereas a posterior predictive value of 0.54 and a PSR value of 1.0019 (64,000 samples) were obtained for *Group D* (i.e., nonnational group). This demonstrated that convergence had succeeded in both models. The analyses performed for the combined model (Models c and d) showed that the model meets the configural invariance criterion, with a posterior predictive value of 0.52 and a PSR value of 1.018, allowing the multigroup analysis to continue. We tested the assumption of structural invariance by comparing the estimated DIC of the model with constrained structural paths and the invariant model. Based on the results, the constrained model has a DIC value of 31,546.79, whereas the invariant model has a value of 32.061.96; therefore, the models differ.

Table 34.7 presents the Bayesian structural model results regarding the model-specific effects that must be compared for the moderating role of nationality to be examined. According to the results, the effect of NCIs on ST is not verified for the two groups;

Table 34.5 Bayesian structural model results: baseline models using the gender grouping criterion

Path	Mean	S.E.	S.D.	C.S.	95% lower bound	95% upper bound	Min.	Max.
Group A (males)								
Positive social impact → support for tourism	0.399	0.002	0.053	1.001	0.297	0.501	0.193	0.618
Negative social impact → support for tourism	−0.012	0.002	0.04	1.002	−0.092	0.068	−0.164	0.15
Positive cultural impact → support for tourism	0.441	0.003	0.064	1.001	0.321	0.572	0.194	0.72
Negative cultural impact → support for tourism	−0.099	0.002	0.04	1.002	−0.180	−0.019	−0.267	0.04
Group B (females)								
Positive social impact → support for tourism	0.437	0.003	0.063	1.001	0.319	0.567	0.201	0.728
Negative social impact → support for tourism	−0.125	0.003	0.049	1.002	−0.225	−0.033	−0.37	0.051
Positive cultural impact → support for tourism	0.586	0.005	0.09	1.002	0.420	0.765	0.263	1.09
Negative cultural impact → support for tourism	−0.07	0.003	0.056	1.002	−0.184	0.041	−0.307	0.134

Table 34.6 The moderating role of gender

Hypotheses	Path	Mean		Moderating effect of gender
		Group A (males)	Group B (females)	
H1a	Positive social impact → support for tourism	0.399*	0.437*	Yes
H2a	Negative social impact → support for tourism	−0.012	−0.125*	Yes
H3a	Positive cultural impact → support for tourism	0.441*	0.586*	Yes
H4a	Negative cultural impact → support for tourism	−0.099*	−0.07	Yes

Note: * Indicates significance at the 0.05 level.

therefore, H4d is not supported. However, the results indicate a stronger impact of PSIs on ST among nonnationals (mean: 0.457; confidence interval: 0.349–0.577) than among nationals (mean: 0.380; confidence interval: 0.262–0.514). Moreover, the negative impact of NSIs on ST is verified only in the national group (mean: −0.122; confidence interval: −0.229 to −0.021). Finally, the positive impact of PCIs on ST is higher in the national group, with a mean of 0.593 (confidence interval: 0.436–0.765), than in the the nonnational group, with a mean of 0.382 (confidence interval: 0.249–0.523). Therefore, hypotheses H1b, H2b, and H3b are supported, whereas H4b is rejected (Table 34.8).

Discussion

Understanding the relationship between residents' perceptions of the impacts of tourism and their ST and what factors can influence this relationship is essential for tourism planning. Identifying the influence of each factor can assist tourism planners in their strategic and operational decision-making for tourism development (Sinclair-Maragh, 2017). The current study adds to the existing body of knowledge concerning residents' perceptions of the impacts of tourism. The purpose of this study was to examine the moderating effect of gender and nationality on the relationship between residents' perceptions of the impacts of tourism and their ST. This study used the Bayesian estimation approach to analyze data collected from 979 residents in the UAE. Social exchange theory and social identity theory are used as theoretical foundations for this study.

The findings showed that gender and nationality are significant moderators of the relationship between residents' perceptions of the impacts of tourism and their ST. Female residents were found to exhibit a stronger relationship between their perceptions of the PSIs and PCIs of tourism than male residents. Therefore, it can be concluded that the influence of gender on the relationship between residents' perceptions of the PSIs and PCIs of tourism and their ST is significantly higher for females than for males. This finding is in line with the findings of Sinclair-Maragh (2017), who examined residents' gender in relation to their ST in Jamaica and reported that female residents were generally more supportive of tourism development than males. In other words, female residents tend to perceive the PSIs and PCIs more positively than male residents. Regarding the relationship between residents' perceptions of the NSIs of tourism and their ST, the results show that this relationship is supported only for female residents. Regarding the relationship between residents' perceptions of the NCIs of tourism and their ST,

Table 34.7 Bayesian structural model results: baseline models using the nationality grouping criterion

Path	Mean	S.E.	S.D.	C.S.	95% lower bound	95% upper bound	Min.	Max.
Group C (nationals)								
Positive social impact → support for tourism	0.380	0.003	0.064	1.001	0.262	0.514	0.172	0.675
Negative social impact → support for tourism	−0.122	0.003	0.053	1.002	−0.229	−0.021	−0.371	0.061
Positive cultural impact → support for tourism	0.593	0.004	0.084	1.001	0.436	0.765	0.314	0.934
Negative cultural impact → support for tourism	−0.088	0.004	0.069	1.002	−0.224	0.049	−0.329	0.152
Group D (nonnationals)								
Positive social impact → support for tourism	0.457	0.004	0.059	1.002	0.349	0.577	0.251	0.763
Negative social impact → support for tourism	−0.045	0.002	0.036	1.001	−0.117	0.025	−0.187	0.081
Positive cultural impact → support for tourism	0.382	0.004	0.07	1.002	0.249	0.523	0.108	0.666
Negative cultural impact → support for tourism	−0.064	0.002	0.038	1.001	−0.140	0.010	−0.222	0.058

Table 34.8 The moderating role of nationality

Hypothesis	Path	Mean		Moderating effect of nationality
		Group C (nationals)	Group D (nonnationals)	
H1b	Positive social impact → support for tourism	0.380*	0.457*	Yes
H2b	Negative social impact → support for tourism	−0.122*	−0.045	Yes
H3b	Positive cultural impact → support for tourism	0.593*	0.382*	Yes
H4b	Negative cultural impact → support for tourism	−0.088	−0.064	No

Note: * Indicates significance at the 0.05 level.

the results show that this relationship is supported only for male residents. These findings contradict the findings of Almeida-García et al. (2016), who reported that gender showed no effect on any impacts of tourism in Spain.

With respect to the influence of nationality, the findings showed that nonnational residents reported greater positive perceptions of the PSIs of tourism than national residents. However, the relationship between residents' perceptions of the NSIs of tourism and their ST is supported only for national residents. In addition, the relationship between residents' perceptions of the PCIs of tourism and their ST is significantly higher for national residents than for nonnational residents.

The results suggest that nationality does not have a moderating effect on the relationship between residents' perceptions of the NCIs of tourism and their ST, and these findings suggest that neither the national nor the expatriate residents associate NCIs with tourism development. The findings of the current study are consistent with the findings of Gursoy and Rutherford (2004), who found no relationship between residents' perceptions of NCIs and their ST. However, the findings of the current study contradict findings from Benalmadena, Spain, as the research conducted by Almeida-García et al. (2016) found that national residents reported more negative perceptions of the NCIs of tourism than nonnational residents.

Theoretical contribution

From an academic perspective, the theoretical contribution of this study derives from examining the moderating effect of gender and nationality on residents' perceptions of the impacts of tourism. This study suggests that residents are a heterogeneous group that holds disparate perceptions of the impacts of tourism, and that their ST varies based on their perceptions. Residents were categorized based on their gender, as male and female residents, and based on their nationality, as national and nonnational residents. The findings demonstrate that gender and nationality moderate the relationship between residents' perceptions of tourism impacts and their ST. More specifically, gender moderates the relationship between PSIs and NSIs and PCIs and NCIs and residents' ST, and nationality moderates the relationship between PSIs and NSIs and NCIs and residents' ST.

This study focuses on examining residents' perceptions of the social and cultural impacts of tourism and their relationships with ST. Although the extant research examines similar classifications, the current study differentiates between the social and cultural impacts of tourism and provides constructs to examine residents' perceptions of each of them. The findings of this study contribute to the body of knowledge by revealing factors that moderate the relationship between residents' perceptions of the social and cultural impacts of tourism and their support for tourism development. The results corroborate the usefulness of social exchange theory and social identity theory in explaining residents' perceptions of the impacts of tourism.

Residents of 46 different nationalities participated in this study, which provided diverse views of the impacts of tourism from diverse groups of residents who live in a multicultural tourism destination in the Middle East. The findings corroborate the hypothesis that male and female residents have different perceptions of the impacts of tourism. The findings also suggest that nonnational residents share views that are different from those of national residents regarding their perceptions of tourism's impacts.

Managerial implications

The findings of this study are important for tourism officials in the UAE in both the local and federal government. Tourism planners at multicultural tourist destinations should plan tourism development strategies that consider the diversity of society and different groups of residents, given rapid changes to the populations of these types of destination and the unbalanced ratio of male and female residents. The male population is higher owing to the higher numbers of male immigrants seeking work and the increasing number of jobs available in construction, energy, and transportation. The goals are to emphasize the positive perceptions of residents and reduce or eliminate negative perceptions by addressing attributes that negatively or positively influence residents' perceptions in the social and cultural domains. The findings can be utilized to design marketing campaigns to be more appealing based on gender and nationality preferences.

Regarding the influence of gender on the perceptions of residents, the findings suggest that female residents are more concerned with the NSIs of tourism, and that male residents are more concerned with its NCIs. The government should consider more interactive programs and opportunities to teach UAE customs and traditions to children in schools and, for female residents, opportunities to practice local crafts and arts and prepare traditional food that they can demonstrate publicly at exhibitions and festivals. Allowing UAE residents to share their practices with tourists can provide an opportunity to preserve the practices of UAE society and will improve the perceptions of female residents regarding the social impacts of tourism. In addition, government officials should attract more national residents to work as tour operators and more female tour guides to work with families and with female travelers. This approach, which will allow cultural exchanges in an appropriate environment that will enable female residents to interact with tourists and, therefore, have an opportunity to be involved in tourism activities, will improve the outcome and benefits gained from tourism for residents in general, and female residents in particular.

Regarding the influence of nationality on the perceptions of residents, the findings suggest that only national residents showed concern regarding the NSIs of tourism. A possible explanation is that the national residents are Muslims, and the majority of them are conservative, whereas nonnational residents are from various countries, religions, and cultures. Therefore, the perceptions of the nonnational residents of the NSIs of tourism are considered nonsignificant. This finding can also be explained by the fact that the UAE has experienced rapid social and economic development in the past few years, which led to a large influx of immigrants who moved to the UAE and impacted the daily routine of national residents. Regarding the nonnational residents, especially those who moved to the UAE in recent years, after the population reached millions of residents, they did not experience this change and therefore did not observe the rapid changes in UAE society.

Although they belong to different groups, nationality did not moderate the relationship between residents' perceptions of NCIs resulting from tourism development and their ST. This finding can be explained by the fact that the UAE has been a multicultural destination for many years, and that the residents live there with respect, tolerance, and understanding. The results show that the perceived NCIs of tourism in the UAE appear to be outweighed by the perceptions of the PCIs of tourism. A possible explanation is that, although UAE residents recognize the NCIs of tourism, this realization does not decrease their ST. These findings can be explained by the government efforts to preserve the cultural identity of the UAE. For example, the government declared 2008 the year of national identity to promote and preserve the national identity of the UAE. In the same year, the UAE government declared that Arabic is the official language, to be used in all federal agencies and government establishments (*Gulf News*, 2008).

The study area provides further explanations of the findings. In recent years, the UAE government announced several initiatives to help preserve UAE culture and national identity. These initiatives include establishing the *Al Bayt Mitwahid* (Our Home Is United) Association, introducing a UAE national service law for national residents, and developing an identity program: the Emirates ID card (UAE Government, 2017b). These programs are designed to promote the national identity of the UAE and to emphasize the value and importance of unity. However, the government should continue initiatives and programs that focus on UAE heritage and culture, which will encourage the preservation of culture while attracting more tourists.

Government officials should review the training programs available for tour guides to ensure that they have official resources to provide tourists with accurate information. Such efforts will allow residents to interact with tourists and improve cultural exchanges, while providing authentic experiences for tourists. Focusing on developing cultural tourism in UAE will allow the destination to become more unique for tourists while enhancing UAE residents' positive perceptions of the social and cultural impacts of tourism.

Limitations and future research

Like any research, this study encompasses some limitations. It does not consider factors other than gender and nationality that may moderate the relationship between residents' perceptions of the social and cultural impacts of tourism and their ST. Future research should include other variables, such as culture or ethnicity. With respect to nationality, this study considered non-national residents as a homogeneous group, which might not be the case, because the data were collected from residents of 46 different nationalities. Therefore, future research should consider investigating the moderating role of nationality for specific nationality groups, such as Arabs, Asians, and others. This study uses a quantitative research method and, therefore, limits the findings to the predefined variables. Further research should consider a qualitative method to explore additional variables that influence the perceptions of residents.

Finally, this study uses cross-sectional data that represent the current perceptions of UAE residents, but the tourism industry is highly dynamic and is growing rapidly in the UAE. Therefore, longitudinal studies will be useful to monitor changes in residents' perceptions over time.

References

Al Ahbabi, N. M. N. M. (2016). *Towards leading effective secondary schools in Abu Dhabi, UAE: Stakeholders' perceptions*. Unpublished doctoral dissertation, University of Glasgow, UK.

Alhemoud, A. M., & Armstrong, E. G. (1996). Image of tourism attractions in Kuwait. *Journal of Travel Research*, *34*(4), 76–80.

Al-Mansoori, A. K. (2004). *The Distinctive Arab Heritage: A Study of Society, Culture and Sport in the United Arab Emirates*. Abu Dhabi: Emirates Heritage Club.

Almeida-García, F., Peláez-Fernández, M. Á., Balbuena-Vázquez, A., & Cortés-Macias, R. (2016). Residents' perceptions of tourism development in Benalmádena (Spain). *Tourism Management, 54*, 259–274.

Al-Shamsi, S. A. A. S. (2009). *Multiculturalism in the UAE perceptions of national identity and diversity*. Unpublished doctoral dissertation, University of Aberdeen, UK.

Andereck, K. L., Valentine, K. M., Knopf, R. C., & Vogt, C. A. (2005). Residents' perceptions of community tourism impacts. *Annals of Tourism Research, 32*(4), 1056–1076.

Andereck, K. L., Valentine, K. M., Vogt, C. A., & Knopf, R. C. (2007). A cross-cultural analysis of tourism and quality of life perceptions. *Journal of Sustainable Tourism, 15*(5), 483–502.

Ap, J. (1992). *Understanding host residents' perception of the impacts of tourism through social exchange theory*. Unpublished doctoral dissertation, Texas A&M University, College Station, TX.

Arbuckle, J. L. (2016). *AMOS 24 User's Guide*. IBM. Retrieved from www.pdfdrive.com/ibm-spss-amos-24-users-guide-e34473898.html

Assaf, A. G., Tsionas, M., & Oh, H. (2018). The time has come: Toward Bayesian SEM estimation in tourism research. *Tourism Management, 64*, 98–109.

Bagozzi, R. P., & Yi, Y. (2012). Specification, evaluation, and interpretation of structural equation models. *Journal of the Academy of Marketing Science, 40*(1), 8–34.

Bashir, K. A. (2011). Consumption of dairy products in the UAE: A comparison of nationals and expatriates. *Journal of the Saudi Society of Agricultural Sciences, 10*(2), 121–125.

Bentler, P. M. (1988). Causal modeling via structural equation systems. In J. R. Nesselroade & R. B. Cattell (Eds.), *Handbook of Multivariate Experimental Psychology* (pp. 317–335). Boston, MA: Springer US.

Bentler, P. M. (2006). *EQS 6 Structural Equations Program Manual. Multivariate Software*. Encino, CA: Multivariate Software, Inc. Retrieved from www.econ.upf.edu/~satorra/CourseSEMVienna2010/EQSManual.pdf

Bollen, K. A. (1989). *Structural Equations with Latent Variables* (1st ed.). Wiley Series in Probability and Mathematical Statistics. Applied Probability and Statistics Section. Hoboken, NJ: Wiley-Interscience.

Bolstad, W. M., & Curran, J. M. (2016). *Introduction to Bayesian Statistics* (3rd ed.). Hoboken, NJ: John Wiley.

Brida, J., Osti, L., & Faccioli, M. (2011). Residents' perception and attitudes towards tourism impacts: A case study of the small rural community of Folgaria (Trentino-Italy). *Benchmarking, 18*(3), 359–385.

Bulmer, M. G. (2012). *Principles of Statistics (Dover Books on Mathematics)* (revised ed.). New York: Dover.

Byrne, B. (2016). *Structural Equation Modeling with AMOS: Basic Concepts, Applications, and Programming* (3rd ed.). New York: Routledge.

Byrne, B. M. (2001). *Structural Equation Modeling with AMOS: Basic Concepts, Applications, and Programming*. Retrieved from http://ezproxy.usherbrooke.ca/login?url=http://search.ebscohost.com/login.aspx?direct=true%7B&%7Ddb=psyh%7B&%7DAN=2000-14005-000%7B&%7Dsite=ehost-live

DiStefano, C. (2002). The impact of categorization with confirmatory factor analysis. *Structural Equation Modeling: A Multidisciplinary Journal, 9*(3), 327–346.

Dyer, P., Gursoy, D., Sharma, B., & Carter, J. (2007). Structural modeling of resident perceptions of tourism and associated development on the Sunshine Coast, Australia. *Tourism Management, 28*(2), 409–422.

Erul, E. (2014). *Antalya residents' attitudes regarding the impacts of all-inclusive resorts in the Turkish coastal destination*. Doctoral dissertation, Texas A&M University, College Station, TX.

Faulkner, B., & Tideswell, C. (1997). A framework for monitoring community impacts of tourism. *Journal of Sustainable Tourism, 5*(1), 3–28.

FCSA. (2018). *The Federal Competitiveness and Statistics Authority, UAE*. Retrieved from http://fcsa.gov.ae/en-us/Pages/Statistics/UAE-Population-2016.aspx

Feng, X. (2008). *Economic and socio-cultural impacts of tourism development in Fenghuang county, China*. Doctoral dissertation, Washington State University, Pullman, WA.

Fornell, C., & Larcker, D. F. (1981). Evaluating structural equation models with unobservable variables and measurement error. *Source Journal of Marketing Research, 18*(1), 39–50.

Gelman, A., Carlin, J. B., Stern, H. S., & Rubin, D. B. (2014). *Bayesian Data Analysis* (3rd ed.). Texts in Statistical Science. Boca Raton, FL: Chapman & Hall/CRC.

Gelman, A., & Rubin, D. B. (1992). Inference from iterative simulation using multiple sequences. *Statistical Science, 7*(4), 457–472.

Ghubash, R. O. (1992). *Socio-cultural change and psychiatric disorder: An epidemiological study of women in the Emirate of Dubai (UAE)*. Unpublished doctoral dissertation, University of London, UK.

Gulf Business. (2018). UAE's Council of Ministers approves gender equality law. Retrieved from http://gulfbusiness.com/uaes-council-ministers-approves-gender-quality-law

Gulf News. (2008). UAE makes Arabic official language. Retrieved from http://gulfnews.com/news/uae/government/uae-makes-arabic-official-language-1.90822

Gursoy, D., Chi, C. G., & Dyer, P. (2010). Locals' attitudes toward mass and alternative tourism: The case of Sunshine Coast, Australia. *Journal of Travel Research, 49*(3), 381–394.

Gursoy, D., Jurowski, C., & Uysal, M. (2002). Resident attitudes: A structural modeling approach. *Annals of Tourism Research, 29*(1), 79–105.

Gursoy, D., & Rutherford, D. G. (2004). Host attitudes toward tourism: An improved structural model. *Annals of Tourism Research, 31*(3), 495–516.

Hammad, N., Ahmad, S. Z., & Papastathopoulos, A. (2017a). Evaluating perceptions of residents towards impacts of tourism development in Emirates of Abu Dhabi, United Arab Emirates. *Tourism Review, 72*(4), 448–461.

Hammad, N., Ahmad, S. Z., & Papastathopoulos, A. (2017b). Residents' perceptions of the impact of tourism in Abu Dhabi, United Arab Emirates. *International Journal of Culture, Tourism & Hospitality Research, 11*(4), 551–572.

Haobin Ye, B., Qiu Zhang, H., Huawen Shen, J., & Goh, C. (2014). Does social identity affect residents' attitude toward tourism development? An evidence from the relaxation of the Individual Visit Scheme. *International Journal of Contemporary Hospitality Management, 26*(6), 907–929.

Hogg, M. A., Terry, D. J., & White, K. M. (1995). A tale of two theories: A critical comparison of identity theory with social identity theory. *Social Psychology Quarterly, 58*(4), 255–269.

Jebb, A. T., & Woo, S. E. (2015). A Bayesian primer for the organizational sciences. *Organizational Research Methods, 18*(1), 92–132.

Jedidi, K., & Ansari, A. (2001). Bayesian structural equation models for multilevel data. In G. A. Marcoulides & R. E. Schumaker (Eds.), *New Developments and Techniques in Structural Equation Modeling* (pp. 129–157). Mahwah, NJ: Lawrence Erlbaum.

Jönsson, C., & Devonish, D. (2008). Does nationality, gender, and age affect travel motivation? A case of visitors to the Caribbean island of Barbados. *Journal of Travel & Tourism Marketing, 25*(3/4), 398–408.

Joreskog, K. G., & Sorbom, D. (1993). *LISREL 8: Structural Equation Modeling with the SIMPLIS Command Language*. Chicago, IL: Scientific Software International.

Jurowski, C. (1994). *The interplay of elements affecting host community resident attitudes toward tourism: A path analytic approach*. Unpublished doctoral dissertation, Virginia Polytechnic Institute and State University, Blacksburg, VA.

Jurowski, C., Uysal, M., & Williams, D. R. (1997). A theoretical analysis of host community resident reactions to tourism. *Journal of Travel Research, 36*(2), 3–11.

Kaewnuch, K. (2010). *The perceptions of members of the Karen and Hmong Hill tribes of the impacts upon their communities resulting from the development of tourism in Northern Thailand*. Doctoral dissertation, Bournemouth University, Bournemouth, UK.

Kanapathy, K., Khong, K. W., & Dekkers, R. (2014). New product development in an emerging economy: Analysing the role of supplier involvement practices by using Bayesian Markov chain Monte Carlo technique. *Journal of Applied Mathematics, 2014*, 1–12.

Kaplan, D., & Depaoli, S. (2012). Bayesian structural equation modeling. In R. H. Hoyle (Ed.), *Handbook of Structural Equation Modeling* (pp. 650–673). New York: Guilford Press.

Khoshkam, M., Marzuki, A., & Al-Mulali, U. (2016). Socio-demographic effects on Anzali wetland tourism development. *Tourism Management, 54*, 96–106.

Kim, K. (2002). *The effects of tourism impacts upon quality of life of residents in the community*. Doctoral dissertation, Virginia Polytechnic Institute and State University, Blacksburg, VA.

Kim, K., Uysal, M., & Sirgy, M. J. (2013). How does tourism in a community impact the quality of life of community residents? *Tourism Management, 36*(6), 527–540.

Ko, D. W., & Stewart, W. P. (2002). A structural equation model of residents' attitudes for tourism development. *Tourism Management, 23*(5), 521–530.

Kozak, M. (2001). Comparative assessment of tourist satisfaction with destinations across two nationalities. *Tourism Management, 22*(4), 391–401.

Kozak, M. (2002). Comparative analysis of tourist motivations by nationality and destinations. *Tourism Management, 23*(3), 221–232.

Látková, P., & Vogt, C. A. (2012). Residents' attitudes toward existing and future tourism development in rural communities. *Journal of Travel Research*, *51*(1), 50–67.

Lee, C. K., Lee, Y. K., & Wicks, B. E. (2004). Segmentation of festival motivation by nationality and satisfaction. *Tourism Management*, *25*(1), 61–70.

Lee, S.-Y. (2007). *Structural Equation Modeling: A Bayesian Approach* (1st ed.). Wiley Series in Probability and Statistics. Chichester, UK: John Wiley.

Lee, S.-Y., & Song, X.-Y. (2004). Evaluation of the Bayesian and maximum likelihood approaches in analyzing structural equation models with small sample sizes. *Multivariate Behavioral Research*, *39*(4), 653–686.

Lee, S.-Y., & Song, X.-Y. (2014). Bayesian structural equation model. *Wiley Interdisciplinary Reviews: Computational Statistics*, *6*(4), 276–287.

Lee, S.-Y., Song, X.-Y., & Tang, N.-S. (2007). Bayesian methods for analyzing structural equation models with covariates, interaction, and quadratic latent variables. *Structural Equation Modeling: A Multidisciplinary Journal*, *14*(3), 404–434.

Lin, L. C. (1999). *Analysis of resident perceptions and attitudes toward gambling development in Kansas City (Missouri)*. Unpublished doctoral dissertation, Kansas State University, Manhattan, KS.

Long, P. H., & Kayat, K. (2011). Residents' perceptions of tourism impact and their support for tourism development: The case study of Cuc Phuong National Park, Ninh Binh Province, Vietnam. *European Journal of Tourism Research*, *4*(2), 123–146.

Lopez, F., & Mercader, S. (2015). Perceived impact of tourism by the resident population in Torrevieja: National versus non-national residents. *European Journal of Tourism Research*, *10*, 120–126.

Lubke, G. H., & Muthén, B. O. (2004). Applying multigroup confirmatory factor models for continuous outcomes to Likert scale data complicates meaningful group comparisons. *Structural Equation Modeling: A Multidisciplinary Journal*, *11*(4), 514–534.

Lundberg, E. (2017). The importance of tourism impacts for different local resident groups: A case study of a Swedish seaside destination. *Journal of Destination Marketing & Management*, *6*(1), 46–55.

Lunn, D. J., Thomas, A., Best, N., & Spiegelhalter, D. (2000). WinBUGS—A Bayesian modelling framework: Concepts, structure, and extensibility. *Statistics & Computing*, *10*(4), 325–337.

Marsh, H. W. (1994). Confirmatory factor analysis models of factorial invariance: A multifaceted approach. *Structural Equation Modeling: A Multidisciplinary Journal*, *1*(1), 5–34.

Maruyama, N., & Woosnam, K. M. (2015). Residents' ethnic attitudes and support for ethnic neighborhood tourism: The case of a Brazilian town in Japan. *Tourism Management*, *50*, 225–237.

Maurer, R. C. (1977). *Resident attitudes toward rural industrialization: A southeastern Ohio regional study*. Unpublished doctoral dissertation, Ohio State University, Columbus, OH.

Mendes, M., & Pala, A. (2003). Type I error rate and power of three normality tests. *Information Technology Journal*, *2*(2), 135–139.

Mensah, C. (2012). Residents' perception of socio-economic impacts of tourism in Tafi Atome, Ghana. *Asian Social Science*, *8*(15), 274–287.

Miyakuni, K. (2012). *Residents' attitudes toward tourism—Focusing on ecocentric attitudes and perceptions of economic costs: The case of Iriomote Island, Japan*. Unpublished doctoral dissertation, Michigan State University, East Lansing, MI.

MOF. (2018). *UAE Ministry of Finance. Budget 2017*. Retrieved from www.mof.gov.ae/En/budget/fedralBudget/Pages/Budget2017.aspx

Muthén, B., & Asparouhov, T. (2012). Bayesian structural equation modeling: A more flexible representation of substantive theory. *Psychological Methods*, *17*(3), 313–335.

Muthén, L. K., & Muthén, B. O. (2012). *MPlus User's Guide: Statistical Analysis with Latent Variables*. Los Angeles, CA: Author. https://doi.org/10.1111/j.1600-0447.2011.01711.x

Nunkoo, R., & Gursoy, D. (2012). Residents' support for tourism: An identity perspective. *Annals of Tourism Research*, *39*(1), 243–268.

Nunkoo, R., & Ramkissoon, H. (2010). Small island urban tourism: A residents' perspective. *Current Issues in Tourism*, *13*(1), 37–60.

Palmer, A., Koenig-Lewis, N., & Jones, L. E. M. (2013). The effects of residents' social identity and involvement on their advocacy of incoming tourism. *Tourism Management*, *38*, 142–151.

Palomo, J., Dunson, D. B., & Bollen, K. (2007). Bayesian structural equation modeling. In Lee, S.-Y. (Ed.), *Handbook of Latent Variable and Related Models* (pp. 163–188). Amsterdam: Elsevier.

Peter, S., & Anandkumar, V. (2014). Dubai shopping festival: Tourists' nationality and travel motives. *International Journal of Event & Festival Management*, *5*(2), 116–131.

Prayag, G., & Ryan, C. (2012). Visitor interactions with hotel employees: The role of nationality. *International Journal of Culture, Tourism & Hospitality Research, 6*(2), 173–185.

Rasoolimanesh, S. M., Jaafar, M., Kock, N., & Ramayah, T. (2015). A revised framework of social exchange theory to investigate the factors influencing residents' perceptions. *Tourism Management Perspectives, 16*, 335–345.

R Development Core Team. (2016). *R: A Language and Environment for Statistical Computing.* Vienna, Austria: R Foundation for Statistical Computing.

Sarhan, H. A. S. (1995). *Drugs abuse in the United Arab Emirates.* Unpublished doctoral dissertation, University of Newcastle upon Tyne, UK.

Scheines, R., Hoijtink, H., & Boomsma, A. (1999). Bayesian estimation and testing of structural equation models. *Psychometrika, 64*(1), 37–52.

Shaheem, S. (2014). *Emirati students in the UK: Cultural identity transformation.* Unpublished doctoral dissertation, University of East London, UK.

Sharpley, R. (2014). Host perceptions of tourism: A review of the research. *Tourism Management, 42*(1), 37–49.

Sinclair-Maragh, G. (2017). Demographic analysis of residents' support for tourism development in Jamaica. *Journal of Destination Marketing & Management, 6*(1), 5–12.

Song, X.-Y., & Lee, S.-Y. (2012). *Basic and Advanced Bayesian Structural Equation Modeling. Basic and Advanced Bayesian Structural Equation Modeling: With Applications in the Medical and Behavioral Sciences.* Chichester, UK: John Wiley.

Soontayatron, S. (2010). *Socio-cultural changes in Thai beach resorts: A case study of Koh Samui Island, Thailand.* Doctoral dissertation, Bournemouth University, Bournemouth, UK.

Spanou, E. (2016). *A study of residents' attitudes towards the socio-cultural impacts of tourism in the Larnaca region, Republic of Cyprus.* Unpublished doctoral dissertation, Middlesex University, UK.

Spiegelhalter, D. J., Best, N. G., Carlin, B. P., & van der Linde, A. (2002). Bayesian measures of model complexity and fit. *Journal of the Royal Statistical Society: Series B (Statistical Methodology), 64*(4), 583–639.

Stewart, E. J. (2009). *Comparing resident attitudes toward tourism: Community-based cases from Arctic Canada.* Doctoral dissertation, University of Alberta, Calgary, Canada.

Stylidis, D. (2012). *Tourism and community life: Building a conceptual framework.* Unpublished doctoral dissertation, University of Surrey, UK.

Stylidis, D., Biran, A., Sit, J., & Szivas, E. M. (2014). Residents' support for tourism development: The role of residents' place image and perceived tourism impacts. *Tourism Management, 45*, 260–274.

Thrane, C. (2008). Earnings differentiation in the tourism industry: Gender, human capital and socio-demographic effects. *Tourism Management, 29*(3), 514–524.

Thrane, C., & Farstad, E. (2012). Nationality as a segmentation criterion in tourism research: The case of international tourists' expenditures while on trips in Norway. *Tourism Economics, 18*(1), 203–217.

Tucker, H. G. (1962). *An Introduction to Probability and Mathematical Statistics.* (R. P. Boas, Ed.). New York: Academic Press.

UAE Government. (2017a). *Gender Equality/ Women in the UAE.* Retrieved from https://government.ae/en/about-the-uae/leaving-no-one-behind/5genderequality

UAE Government. (2017b). *Initiatives to Preserve the National Identity of the UAE.* Retrieved from https://government.ae/en/information-and-services/social-affairs/preserving-the-emirati-national-identity/initiatives-to-preserve-the-national-identity-of-the-uae

UAE Tourism Report. (2017). Q1 2017. London: Business Monitor International.

UNWTO. (2017). *UNWTO World Tourism Barometer and Statistical Annex.* Retrieved from http://cf.cdn.unwto.org/sites/all/files/pdf/unwto_barom17_01_january_excerpt_.pdf

Van Poucke, E., Matthyssens, P., & Weeren, A. (2016). Enhancing cost savings through early involvement of purchasing professionals in sourcing projects: Bayesian estimation of a structural equation model. *Journal of Purchasing & Supply Management, 22*(4), 299–310.

Verhagen, A. J., & Fox, J. P. (2013). Bayesian tests of measurement invariance. *British Journal of Mathematical & Statistical Psychology, 66*(3), 383–401.

Vines, R. (2005). *Conflicts created by the social impacts of tourism.* Unpublished Master's dissertation, Royal Roads University, Victoria, British Columbia, Canada.

Wang, S. (2013). Predicting effects of demographics and moderating power of engagement on residents' perceptions of tourism development. *European Journal of Tourism Research, 6*(2), 170–182.

Wang, S., Bickle, M., & Harrill, R. (2010). Residents' attitudes toward tourism development in Shandong, China, *International Journal of Culture, Tourism & Hospitality Research, 4*(4), 327–339.

Wang, Y. S., & Pfister, R. E. (2008). Residents' attitudes toward tourism and perceived personal benefits in a rural community. *Journal of Travel Research, 47*(1), 84–93.

Woodside, A. G. (2013). Moving beyond multiple regression analysis to algorithms: Calling for adoption of a paradigm shift from symmetric to asymmetric thinking in data analysis and crafting theory. *Journal of Business Research, 66*(4), 463–472.

Yu, C. P. (2011). *Investigating resident attitudes toward tourism development: A community quality of life perspective.* Unpublished doctoral dissertation, Indiana University, Bloomington, IN.

Yun, G. W., & Trumbo, C. W. (2000). Comparative response to a survey executed by post, E-mail, & web form. *Journal of Computer-Mediated Communication, 6*(1), 1–26.

Zyphur, M. J., & Oswald, F. L. (2013). Bayesian probability and statistics in management research. *Journal of Management, 39*(1), 5–13.

35

A REVIEW OF THE APPLICATION OF SOCIAL EXCHANGE THEORY IN TOURISM RESEARCH

Dan Musinguzi

Introduction

The application of theories in research is an important undertaking that highlights how previous and current studies contribute to knowledge advancement in a given field of study. Nash (1979; as cited in Smith, Xiao, Nunkoo & Tukamushaba, 2013) argues that data-driven research does not provide an adequate understanding of tourism unless it is based on theory. This observation is in line with J. Ap's counsel (personal communication, 2009) that theory drives research, and methodology does not. Smith et al. (2013) commented that Smith and Lee's (2010) analysis of theory in top tourism journals showed an increasing use of the word "theory" and its application in tourism research. It should be noted that, "the use of theory permits the formation of testable hypotheses as well as provides a basis for recognizing potentially meaningful patterns and testing those hypotheses" (Smith et al., 2013, p. 877). There has been a growing "interest in assessing the state of tourism research and scholarship" (Xiao & Smith, 2008, p. 62).

Understanding theories and their application is crucial to advancing knowledge. Ap (1990) recommended that the "application of social exchange theory (SET) should at least be explored in future studies" (p. 614). Surprisingly, to date, no studies have explored the application of SET in tourism research. As a consequence, there is no current information on whether the "power of or between tourism actors" (the central tenet of SET) has been incorporated or acknowledged in tourism impacts research. This study bridges this knowledge gap.

Literature review

The realization that tourism is an engine for development has led to recognition of the need for research on tourism's impacts, and on residents' attitudes towards tourism. This topic is one of the extensively researched topics in the field of tourism. However, most of the early research on residents' attitudes toward tourism was atheoretical and could not explain why residents support and/or do not support tourism development in their communities (Ap, 1990; Kayat, 2002; Nunkoo, 2016). Ap (1990) commented that the atheoretical orientation of early studies indicated a field in the early stages of development and recommended that, "future studies should attempt to link the central concepts to some theory, without which a better knowledge and understanding of the problem may be inhibited" (p. 614), as the conceptual and theoretical understanding of a problem is necessary for the development of any research field.

In tourism impacts research, SET, which was briefly mentioned by Perdue, Long, and Allen (1990) and later advocated by Ap (1990, 1992), has been used to explain why residents develop positive and/or negative perceptions toward tourism in their communities (Ap, 1992; Nunkoo & Ramkissoon, 2011). Ap (1992) describes SET as "a general sociological theory concerned with understanding the exchange of resources between individuals and groups in an interaction situation" (p. 668). SET addresses the lack of theoretical grounding in tourism impact studies (Nunkoo, 2016; Ward & Berno, 2011). Other authors posit that SET has been used to predict and explain community attitudes toward tourists (Ward & Berno, 2011).

As humans, we engage in different forms of exchange daily, and this explains why SET has remained an important theory in the field of social interactions and social structures (Cook, Cheshire, Rice, & Nakagawa, 2013). Usually, social interactions exhibit forms of the power of those involved in the interactions, and in the tourism context this is classified as "power between tourism actors."

The central tenet of SET as it applies to tourism is the power between tourism actors. Tourism actors may include residents, investors, policy makers, government agencies, tourists, educational institutions, and other groups and individuals interested in tourism and its development in a community. Nunkoo and Ramkissoon (2011) note that residents are usually the relatively less powerful tourism actors/stakeholders. Ap (1992) argues that, "power, the central variable of exchange, provides the basis for determining the form of the exchange relation" (p. 678). Given the different levels of power among actors, the possible outcomes for any social exchanges between actors are either a "balanced mutual exchange," an "unbalanced exchange" (advantaged actor), an "unbalanced exchange" (disadvantaged actor), or a "balanced unrewarding exchange" (adapted from Cohen and Bradford, 1990, by Ap, 1992, p. 681). These different outcomes determine community residents' perceptions of tourism development. Residents who have more/enough power to influence development in local communities have positive perceptions and attitudes toward tourism, contrary to residents with less power (Nunkoo & Ramkissoon, 2011). Less powerful residents may be excluded from major decision-making processes related to tourism planning and development in their communities. In this context, less powerful residents become the recipients of decisions made by those with more power. When applying SET, researchers need to understand and acknowledge that power between tourism actors is the foundation for all social exchanges. Power influences trust between the actors involved in social exchanges (Nunkoo & Ramkissoon, 2012; Oberg & Svensson, 2010), and these concepts are equally important in the tourism context (Nunkoo, Ramkissoon, & Gursoy, 2012). For example, "when one actor has a power advantage over the other, he/she may ignore, coerce, or override the other, because of dependence upon the former. This creates tension and conflict, and hinders cordial and amicable relationships between the actors" (Ap, 1992, p. 677).

In the tourism context, power between tourism actors determines the benefits individual actors or groups of actors derive from tourism, or the costs they incur, and these benefits and costs in turn influence actors' reactions and attitudes toward tourism development. In addition, "power is derived from having and controlling resources that another actor needs and values. . . . An actor with power is one who has an array of valued resources available to exchange with the other actor" (Ap, 1992, p. 679). Another scholar defines power as "residents' ability to take advantage of the opportunities offered by tourism development" (Kayat, 2002, p. 179), and may include resources such as ownership of land, access to capital, knowledge level, and leadership position (Kayat, 2002, p. 179).

Earlier in this section, Ap (1992) was referenced as commenting that the inclusion of power in SET is important, because the level of power that exists between the tourism actors determines the nature of the outcome of the exchange. This explains why power has been considered a central tenet of SET and social exchanges between actors.

Musinguzi and Ap (2010) observed that most tourism impact studies have neglected to consider the power of and between tourism actors. These authors commented that studies using SET should consider the dimension of power between tourism actors. SET accounts for both the positive and negative impacts of tourism, given that this power influences the outcomes of exchanges, and the reactions of actors involved in the exchanges (Ap, 1992).

Cropanzano and Mitchell (2005) conducted an interdisciplinary review of SET and concluded that, "many important components of social exchange theory have been overlooked, or simply neglected" (p. 891). These authors further argue that:

> [D]espite the usefulness of the social exchange theory framework, we believe the difficulties facing social exchange theory are systemic: The core ideas that comprise social exchange theory have yet to be adequately articulated and integrated . . . many tests of social exchange theory leave out critical theoretical variables.
>
> *(p. 875)*

To be specific, Nunkoo (2016) indicated that power, one of the core constructs for social exchange relationships, has been left out. No studies have investigated why power is left out of tourism research on social exchange. "Power helps explain who gains and who loses from tourism development" (Kayat, 2002, p. 190), and, in the context of tourism development, power is of great interest and importance in the planning and decision making process (Nunkoo et al., 2012).

Purpose of the study

This study aims to fill the existing research gap by critically examining the application of SET in the tourism research that has been published in three leading tourism journals (such as *Annals of Tourism Research*, *Journal of Travel Research*, and *Tourism Management*) classified by McKercher, Law, and Lam (2006), Ryan (2005), and Jamal, Smith, and Watson (2008). Specifically, this study examines whether the dimension of power between tourism actors was incorporated into research that applied and/or mentioned SET. Given that these journals are regarded as leading journals in the field of tourism, it is important that we understand how SET has been applied in the tourism impacts research. Leading journals set research precedents in many fields, because they are expected to publish good quality research, and they are also among those most cited.

Significance of the study

This study conducted a critical examination of the application of SET, which has been largely neglected by most tourism studies. This research has, for the first time, revealed a disturbing trend that power between tourism actors has been neglected in most of the studies published in three leading tourism journals. The major cause for this trend has been identified as the fact that the majority of tourism impacts researchers did not cite or consult the works of Homans (1961), Emerson (1962), Blau (1964), and Levi-Strauss (1969), in which today's SET is rooted (Ap, 1990, 1992). What this study has exposed could be the tip of the iceberg of the possible omissions of central tenets of other theories in tourism research.

Therefore, this research proposes a new research agenda, calling for an extensive examination of the application of theories and models in tourism and hospitality research. This study does not discredit previous studies, but rather points out that power (the central tenet of SET) has largely been overlooked by most researchers studying residents' attitudes to tourism, and no justification for this omission has been provided in the literature. To address this omission, this study recommends that tourism researchers review the classical works of the pioneers of SET (Homans, 1961; Emerson, 1962; Blau, 1964; Levi-Strauss, 1969), and especially Ap (1992), who first proposed its application in tourism research.

Method

To conduct this study, the author identified and examined research articles that applied or mentioned SET and had been published in one of the, top-tier tourism journals, namely, *Annals of Tourism Research, Journal of Travel Research*, and *Tourism Management*. These journals have been classified as top-tier by Gursoy and Sandstrom (2016), Benckendorff and Zehrer (2013), McKercher et al. (2006), Ryan (2005), Jamal et al. (2008), and Pechlaner, Zehrer, Matzler, and Abfalter (2004). McKercher (2015) argues that, "the high tier journals actively encourage new ideas, studies that expand the body of knowledge and think pieces that challenge existing dogma" (p. 2). Similarly, Stringer, Sales-Pardo, and Amaral (2008) indicate that the leading journals are the first points of reference when people are looking for research information. Generally, research published in leading journals is considered and expected to be of high quality. These journals have relatively high impact factors, and their manuscript review processes are rigorous (Dolnicar & Chapple, 2015).

"Social exchange theory" and "social exchange" were the keywords used to identify the relevant articles for analysis in the target journals. The articles selected had to: (a) document the application of SET or mention this theory and (b) be full-length. Research notes, conference reports, and book reviews were not included in the analysis. The search yielded a total of fifty-three research articles. Twenty-six of the articles had been published in the *Annals of Tourism Research*, and eleven and sixteen of them were taken from the *Journal of Travel Research* and *Tourism Management*, respectively. Every article was analyzed, to assess whether it contained information about the power between tourism actors. Data gathered from every article were recorded in an Excel spreadsheet. Furthermore, given that SET has been developed from the works of Homans (1961), Emerson (1962), Blau (1964), and Levi-Strauss (1969), the author also recorded the number of research articles that cited or did not cite such earlier studies.

The author examined the articles to determine whether they cited the works of Perdue et al. (1990) and Ap (1992), because these researchers were the first to propose the application of SET in the tourism context. Finally, the articles were read carefully to ascertain whether the exclusion of power between tourism actors had been acknowledged as a study limitation, or whether the different authors had provided any justification for the exclusion. Other important details recorded in the Excel spreadsheet included article titles, authors' names, the journal's name, and the year of article publication. The data were analyzed using simple descriptive statistics, such as frequencies and percentages.

Results and discussion

This section briefly presents and discusses the major findings of the analysis of the fifty-three journal articles published in the three leading tourism journals—*Annals of Tourism Research, Journal of Travel Research*, and *Tourism Management*. The results summarized in Table 35.1 reveal

Table 35.1 Summary of the results

Criteria/ Journals	Had information on "power between actors"		Cited Homans (1961)		Cited Emerson (1962)		Cited Blau (1964)		Cited Levi-Strauss (1969)		Cited Perdue et al. (1990)			Cited Ap (1992)		
	Yes	No	Yes	No	Yes	No	Yes	No	Yes	No	Yes	No	N/a	Yes	No	N/a
ATR	46%	54%	23%	77%	27%	73%	23%	77%	4%	96%	61.5%	30.8%	7.7%	65.4%	23.1%	11.5%
JTR	18%	82%	0%	100%	18%	82%	9%	91%	0%	100%	73%	27%	n/a	82%	18%	n/a
TM	31%	69%	6%	94%	13%	87%	13%	87%	0%	100%	44%	56%	n/a	56%	44%	n/a
Average, %	31.7	68.3	9.7	90.3	19.3	80.6	15	85	1.3	98.7	59.5	37.9	2.6	67.8	28.4	3.8

Notes: ATR = Annals of Tourism Research; JTR = Journal of Travel Research; TM = Tourism Management. Total number of articles reviewed = 53 (ATR = 26; JTR = 11; TM = 16).

that most (an average of 68%) of the articles that applied or mentioned SET did not include any information about the power between tourism actors. Only an average of 32% of the articles contained information on the power between tourism actors (See Table 35.1).

The results further revealed that the largest percentage of research articles in each of the three journals (see Table 35.1) did not cite or reference the work of Homans (1961), Blau (1964), Levi-Strauss (1969), or Emerson (1962), yet these authors are considered key contributors to the SET (Cook et al., 2013). Most researchers who applied SET in an attempt to understand residents' perceptions of tourism impacts did not consider the seminal works on social exchange and power relations published before 1990. This could imply that there is a limited understanding of the power between tourism actors, as a tenet of SET. If tourism as a field of study is to move to the next level of theoretical development, theories and their tenets borrowed from other fields need to be applied appropriately.

On the other hand, most of the studies analyzed cited the works of Perdue et al. (1990) and Ap (1992). On average, 60% of the articles cited Perdue et al. (1990) and 68% cited Ap (1992; as illustrated in Table 35.1). Even though Ap (1992) discusses the power between tourism actors extensively in his seminal article in the *Annals of Tourism Research*, the majority of the authors who cited Ap (1992) did not discuss or mention the power between tourism actors. This trend could be attributed to the fact that most researchers relied on secondary sources (that neglected power) to cite Ap (1992), without reading the original paper. In Simkin and Roychowdhury's (2003) study titled "Read before you cite," 80% of the authors did not actually read the original papers and instead relied on secondary sources. Could a similar situation be occurring in tourism research? Researchers should embrace reading the original sources, because doing so helps them avoid misinterpretations or omissions that may be contained in second-hand materials/ articles. Also, when undertaking research, it should be noted that concentrating on recently published studies, while paying little attention to older studies, limits researchers' knowledge and understanding of a topic.

Analysis of the articles that applied or mentioned SET or social exchange revealed that the articles did not include information on power between tourism actors, and did not mention the absence of this information as a study limitation. Similarly, most authors did not allude to the fact that power between tourism actors should be taken into consideration when applying SET. This trend may indicate a major oversight among some scholars who are researching tourism impacts and residents' perceptions and attitudes toward tourism.

Some scholars have argued that tourism as a field lacks theoretical development (Echtner & Jamal, 1997; Tribe, 1997) and continues to borrow theories from other fields (Tribe, 2010). I argue that, to enable them to move beyond this state, scholars need to first understand how to apply the theories (and tenets) they have borrowed from other fields.

Limitations of the study and future research

No study is without some limitations (Patton, 2002), but study limitations are resources for research, because they highlight areas that need further investigation (Yang, Wang, & Su, 2006). A major limitation of this study is that it is focused entirely on research articles using SET published in the three most influential tourism journals—*Annals of Tourism Research*, *Tourism Management*, and *Journal of Travel Research*. Although McKercher et al. (2006) identified forty and thirty tourism and hospitality journals, respectively, a review of the application of SET in such a large number of journals was beyond the scope of this study. Future studies should take this research to the next level by exploring the application of SET in other tourism and tourism-related journals.

There are a number of non-journal outlets—such as dissertations/theses, books, book chapters, research notes, and conference proceedings—in which scholars/researchers have published some work on SET, but such outlets were not considered for this study. I suggest that future research should examine the application of SET in these non-journal outlets.

Another limitation of this research is that it did not employ sophisticated/advanced statistical analysis techniques, and relied instead on simple frequency counts and percentages to present and summarize key study findings. It is recommended that future research collect and analyze more data using advanced statistical techniques.

Nunkoo and Ramkissoon (2012) observed that "power" and "trust" are concepts central to social exchanges, and they found that there was a statistically significant relationship between them. However, they cautioned that their study should not be considered conclusive, and suggested that further research should be conducted on the use of these concepts as constructs of social exchange. This study echoes this call for further research on these concepts, as there is limited knowledge of how they have been treated in social exchange and tourism impacts research.

Conclusion

This review of fifty-three tourism impact studies published in three leading tourism journals has revealed that most scholars researching residents' perceptions of tourism impacts over the past two decades have consistently neglected the tenet of SET (i.e., the power between tourism actors). There has been no major theoretical advancement in the tourism impacts literature during this time. No study has attempted to extend or revise SET in the context of tourism. Most studies reviewed in this research have concentrated on applying SET, but incorrectly, in that they do not take into consideration the power between tourism actors. If research on residents' perceptions of tourism impacts is to be advanced to the next level of theoretical maturation, tourism impact researchers should revisit and understand the literature of social exchange. What this research has revealed about the incorrect application of SET could be the tip of the iceberg as regards the possible omission of the central tenets of other theories in tourism and tourism-related studies.

Implications of the study

The lack of proper application of SET in tourism research could be hindering theoretical advancements of research on tourism impacts. Given that the goal of tourism research is "to develop knowledge and to derive practical recommendations for tourism industry and policy makers" (Dolnicar & Chapple, 2015, p. 161), correct application of theories and models is necessary, if this goal is to be achieved.

Ap (1992) made a significant contribution to the literature of tourism impacts by proposing the SET, so as to:

> extend existing knowledge through developing a theoretical orientation toward understanding and predicting residents' perceptions of the impacts of tourism; and providing a basis for the identification and definition of the central concepts involved in measuring residents' perceptions of the impacts of tourism.
>
> *(p. 686)*

This research agenda will not be realized if tourism impact researchers continue to exclude the central tenet of SET. The author of this paper recommends that researchers should use the works of Ap (1992), Homans (1961), Blau (1964), Levi-Strauss (1969), and Emerson (1962) as a foundation for understanding the theoretical perspective of social exchanges.

Based on what has been observed in tourism impacts research published in the leading tourism journals, it may be inferred that most of the tourism impact studies that applied SET and were published in other tourism journals do not incorporate power between tourism actors as a central tenet of SET. Future research should confirm or discount this argument. The present study recommends further research on the application of theories and their tenets in tourism research.

Given that most researchers using SET paid little attention to the concept of power in social exchanges discussed by earlier authors, researchers need to understand that early studies are important for informing present research.

Journal editors and reviewers should pay more attention to how theories (for example, SET) or models are applied in the manuscripts submitted for publication. One important aspect to consider before accepting manuscripts for publication is whether the authors who used a particular theory or model attempted to incorporate its central tenet/s. Alternatively, plausible justifications for not doing so should be provided by manuscript authors.

This study represents just the first, preliminary step toward an investigation of the application of theories and models in tourism research.

References

Ap, J. (1990). Residents' perceptions research on the social impacts of tourism. *Annals of Tourism Research, 17*(4), 610–616.

Ap, J. (1992). Residents' perceptions on tourism impacts. *Annals of Tourism Research, 19*(4), 665–690.

Benckendorff, P., & Zehrer, A. (2013). A network analysis of tourism research. *Annals of Tourism Research, 43*, 121–149.

Blau, P. (1964). *Exchange and power in social life*. New York: John Wiley.

Cohen, A. R., & Bradford, D. L. (1990). *Influence without authority*. New York: John Wiley.

Cook, K. S., Sheshire, C., Rice, E. R. W., & Nakagawa, S. (2013). Social exchange theory. In J. Delamater & A. Ward (Eds.), *Handbook of social psychology* (pp. 61–88). Netherlands: Springer.

Cropanzano, R., & Mitchell, M. S. (2005). Social exchange theory: An interdisciplinary review. *Journal of Management, 31*(6), 874–900.

Dolnicar, S., & Chapple, A. (2015). The readability of articles in tourism journals. *Annals of Tourism Research, 25*, 161–179.

Echtner, C. M., & Jamal, T. B. (1997). The disciplinary dilemma of tourism studies. *Annals of Tourism Research, 24*(4), 868–883.

Emerson, R. (1962). Power-dependence relations. *American Sociological Review, 27*(1), 31–41.

Gursoy, D., & Sandstrom, J. K. (2016). An updated ranking of hospitality and tourism journals. *Journal of Hospitality & Tourism Research, 40*(1), 3–18.

Homans, G. C. (1961). *Social behavior in elementary forms*. New York: Harcourt, Brace & World.

Jamal, T., Smith, B., & Watson, E. (2008). Ranking, rating and scoring of tourism journals: Interdisciplinary challenges and innovations. *Tourism Management, 29*(1), 66–78.

Kayat, K. (2002). Power, social exchanges and tourism in Langkawi: Rethinking resident perceptions. *International Journal of Tourism Research, 4*(3), 171–191.

Levi-Strauss, C. (1969). *The elementary structures of kinship*. Boston, MA: Beacon Press.

McKercher, B. (2015). Why and where to publish. *Tourism Management, 15*, 306–308.

McKercher, B., Law, R., & Lam, T. (2006). Rating tourism and hospitality journals. *Tourism Management, 27*(6), 1235–1252.

Musinguzi, D., & Ap, J. (2010). Developing a revised and comprehensive monitoring framework of tourism impacts on local communities. Proceedings from: *The International Conference on Sustainable Tourism in Developing Countries*, Tanzania, pp. 37–49.

Nunkoo, R. (2016). Toward a more comprehensive use of social exchange theory to study residents' attitudes to tourism. *Procedia Economics & Finance, 39*, 588–596.

Nunkoo, R., & Ramkissoon, H. (2011). Developing a community support model for tourism. *Annals of Tourism Research, 38*(3), 964–988.

Nunkoo, R., & Ramkissoon, H. (2012). Power, trust, social exchange and community support. *Annals of Tourism Research, 39*(2), 997–1024.

Nunkoo, R., Ramkissoon, H., & Gursoy, D. (2012). Public trust in tourism institutions. *Annals of Tourism Research, 39*(3), 1538–1564.

Oberg, P., & Svensson, T. (2010). Does power drive our trust? Relations between labor market actors in Sweden. *Political Studies, 58*(1), 143–166.

Patton, M. Q. (2002). *Qualitative research and evaluation methods.* Thousand Oaks, CA: Sage.

Pechlaner, H., Zehrer, A., Matzler, K., & Abfalter, D. (2004). A ranking of international tourism and hospitality journals. *Journal of Travel Research, 42*(4), 328–332.

Perdue, R. R., Long. P. T., & Allen, L. (1990). Resident support for tourism development. *Annals of Tourism Research, 17*(4), 586–599.

Ryan, C. (2005). The ranking and rating of academics and journals in tourism research. *Tourism Management, 26*(5), 657–662.

Simkin, M. V., & Roychowdhury, V. P. (2003). Read before you cite. *Complex Systems, 14*, 269–274.

Smith, S., & Lee, H. (2010). A typology of "theory" in tourism. In D. Pearce & R. Butler (Eds.), *Tourism research: A 20–20 vision* (pp. 28–39). London: Goodfellow.

Smith, S. L. J., Xiao, H., Nunkoo, R., & Tukamushaba, E. K. (2013). Theory in hospitality, tourism, and leisure studies. *Journal of Hospitality Marketing & Management, 22*(8), 875–894.

Stringer, M., Sales-Pardo, M., & Amaral, L. (2008). Effectiveness of journal ranking schemes as a tool for locating information. *PLoS One, 3*(2), 1–8.

Tribe, J. (1997). The indiscipline of tourism. *Annals of Tourism Research, 24*(3), 638–657.

Tribe, J. (2010). Tribes, territories and networks in the tourism academy. *Annals of Tourism Research, 37*(1), 7–33.

Ward, C., & Berno, T. (2011). Beyond social exchange theory: Attitudes towards tourists. *Annals of Tourism Research, 38*(4), 1556–1569.

Xiao, H., & Smith, S. L. J. (2008). Knowledge impact: An appraisal of tourism scholarship. *Annals of Tourism Research, 35*(1), 62–83.

Yang, Z., Wang, X., & Su, C. (2006). A review of research methodologies in international business. *International Business Review, 159*(6), 601–617.

INDEX

507